Teaching Developmental Writing

Background Readings

Fourth Edition

Susan Naomi Bernstein

Bedford/St. Martin's   Boston ◆ New York

For Bedford/St. Martin's

Developmental Editor: Alicia Young
Production Supervisor: Lisa Chow
Marketing Manager: Christina Shea
Project Management: DeMasi Design and Publishing Services
Text Design: Claire Seng-Niemoeller
Cover Design: Marine Miller
Composition: Jeff Miller Book Design
Printing and Binding: RR Donnelley and Sons

President, Bedford/St. Martin's: Denise B. Wydra
Presidents, Macmillan Higher Education: Joan E. Feinberg and Tom Scotty
Editor in Chief: Karen S. Henry
Director of Marketing: Karen R. Soeltz
Production Director: Susan W. Brown
Associate Production Director: Elise S. Kaiser
Manager, Publishing Services: Andrea Cava

Library of Congress Control Number: 2012939218

For information, write: Bedford/St. Martin's, 75 Arlington Street, Boston, MA
02116   (617-399-4000)

ISBN: 978-0-312-60251-2

Acknowledgments

Preface

The fourth edition of *Teaching Developmental Writing: Background Readings* discusses questions that we ask in our everyday teaching lives. How can we design courses that truly meet our students' needs? How can we most effectively work with students whose cultural or linguistic or learning backgrounds may be different from our own? How should we approach assessment at both the classroom and the institutional levels, and, perhaps most significantly, how do these issues affect our day-to-day teaching? The selected readings in this book can help us address these questions and more, both as individual teachers/scholars[1] and as a community of professionals in basic writing, second language writing, developmental education, writing studies, rhetoric and composition, and related fields.

While the focus here is generally on basic writing, the questions just raised often remain relevant for first-year writing courses and for advanced composition—and for ourselves as teachers/scholars as we practice and theorize about our profession throughout our careers. If we conceive of basic writing as Mina Shaughnessy did, as an opportunity for "inexperienced writers" to gain more experience and practice with learning to write, then we can extend Shaughnessy's description to encompass writers across the spectrum of college writing courses and across the curriculum.[2] Students need to gain experience as they encounter each new writing challenge and rhetorical hurdle. As teachers/scholars, we also have the potential to learn and grow when we face new pedagogical questions. The purpose of *Teaching Developmental Writing: Background Readings* is to help foster that growth for our students and for ourselves.

The new editorial apparatus is divided into four separate parts and twelve different chapters. Introductions to each part present context for the chapters and offer perspectives on the issues to be discussed. Another new section, "Resources for Teaching and Research," provides ideas for creating classroom projects based on ideas or concepts from the readings. This section also allows room for professional reflection and action, offering ideas for contributing to the discussions taking place in our hallways, offices, staff meetings, and elsewhere in our institutions—as well as the virtual and face-to-face forums of our journals, conventions, listservs, and social networking sites. Each of these parts is explained in the Introduction on page vii to guide you as you chart your journey through this book.

This edition includes new and updated readings on adapting the writing process and teaching and learning in multimedia environments. There are new selections on second language writing, writing centers, and addressing racial, cultural, and linguistic differences. The readings' headnotes identify the most important features of the selection, and the Alternative Contents lists the selections according to more general subject headings, including transitions to college, diversity and democracy, practical pedagogy, and research and writing center and writing program administration.[3]

As developmental writing teachers, we may find that our questions and concerns fall both within and beyond the margins of mainstream rhetoric and composition theory and writing studies. The needs of our students and the complicated nature of our working conditions can require pragmatic and conceptual perspectives from a wide range of fields. How can we create a supportive working environment for students who may be under extreme economic and personal pressures that we can only begin to imagine? How can we be effective teachers if we spend our professional lives as "freeway fliers," rushing across town and across communities to our various classrooms? How can we reshape our classroom practices in the ever-shifting worlds of twenty-first-century multimedia?

Although *Teaching Developmental Writing: Background Readings* does not provide simple solutions to these dilemmas, the book does present a range of perspectives offered by experienced educators, and it emphasizes practical approaches to the everyday challenges of our classrooms and our institutions. Each article invites us to examine classroom practice and to take part in professional discussions about our students, our teaching, and ourselves.

Acknowledgments

To Bedford/St. Martin's—I would like to thank Denise Wydra, president; Joan Feinberg, former president; Charles Christensen, former president; and Karen Henry, editor in chief, for their commitment to providing teachers with the best possible tools for meeting the needs of their students. Thanks especially to my current editor, Alicia Young, who listened carefully, provided thoughtful editorial suggestions, and guided me toward greater clarity; and special appreciation to Sophia Snyder, Christina Georgiannis, Brian Donellen, Caitlin Quinn, Michelle Clark, Alexis Walker, and others who have nourished this work now and in the past, and who have provided unprecedented opportunities to foster scholarship in basic writing.

To the reviewers of *Teaching Developmental Writing*, who have offered thorough and inspiring insights for revision over the last decade: Sonya Armstrong, Northern Illinois University; Barbara Bird, Taylor University; Barbara Gleason, City College of New York–City University of New York; Valerie Kinloch, Ohio State University; Andrea Muldoon, University of Wisconsin–Stout; and Eric Paulson, Texas State University, for the third edition; and Mary Ann Gauthier, St. Joseph College; Guy Kellogg, Kapiolani Community College; Matthew Parfitt, Boston University; Alice Savage, North Harris Community College; and Karen Uehling, Boise State University, for the first two editions.

To Steve Cormany, basic writing teacher and advocate, dearest spouse, and dedicated writer, in appreciation of your love and support for my work through nearly three decades of challenges and celebrations.

To my first teachers, first students: my cousin Debbie Sternecky, my brothers Aaron Bernstein and David Bernstein, and the Corley, Cormany, Davis, Martin, and Starcher nieces and nephews; and to the educators who opened the way for an attentive lifelong love of learning—Angela, Carol, Craig, Janis, Jon, Nicholas, Suzanne, and in memory of Jay.

To my students in New York, Ohio, Texas, and Pennsylvania: Your writing and your lives move me beyond words, and remind me to represent the truth of your experiences with meticulous urgency.

To colleagues in Ohio, Pennsylvania, Texas, New York, in the Council of Basic Writing, and on Facebook, including Jonathan Alexander, Shannon Carter, Linda Cheskey, J. Elizabeth Clark, Jennifer Kwon Dobbs, Michelle Gibson, Barbara Gleason, Ann E. Green, Valerie F. Kinloch, Laura Paskell-Brown, Lynn Reid, Tegan Rein, Johanna Schmertz, Anthony Whitehurst, and so many more who listen patiently and respond with critical compassion. Particular thanks go to Amy Winans, Aaron Kerley, and Mick Parsons, extraordinary scholars and mindful educators; and to my colleagues from the now-closed Center for Access and Transition at the University of Cincinnati, especially Sonya Armstrong, Jen Lile, Eric Mast, Eric Paulson, Deborah Sanchez, and Africa Renee Smith. The Center may be gone, but the energy of its best days infuses these pages.

To my readers: May we keep our practices of teaching, learning, writing, collaborating, researching, deliberating and organizing for basic writing clearly in mind as we strive to create the future for our students and ourselves.

To the memory of Adam Vine (1977–2011), 2009 Tutor of the Year, empathic writing consultant and editor, and beloved friend: "Identify your passion, then find co-conspirators."

Susan Naomi Bernstein

Notes

1. I use the term *teachers/scholars* to suggest that as instructors of basic writing we simultaneously teach and study our own teaching. Such self-study provides opportunities to add to the scholarship of teaching and learning by creating innovations in our own pedagogies—and by implementing

these innovations in our classrooms and sharing what we have learned with our colleagues and other professional communities.

2. I am grateful to Barbara Gleason for this insight. See also Ward's introduction to her 1994 book, and the collection edited by McNenny.

3. Most of the articles include well-researched and up-to-date bibliographies. Other references to new and classic articles relevant to basic writing are available in many of the headnotes and endnotes accompanying the readings. For a comprehensive bibliography of basic writing research, see Glau and Duttagupta.

Works Cited

Cochran-Smith, Marilyn, and Susan Lytle. *Inside/Outside: Teacher Research and Knowledge*. New York: Teachers College P, 1993. Print.

Glau, Gregory R., and Chitrakeka Duttagupta, eds. *The Bedford Bibliography for Teachers of Basic Writing*, 3rd ed. Boston: Bedford, 2010. Print. The *Bibliography* also is available online at <http://bcs.bedfordstmartins.com/basicbib3e/>.

McNenny, Gerri. *Mainstreaming Basic Writers: Politics and Pedagogies of Access*. Mahwah: Erlbaum, 2001. Print.

Ward, Irene. *Literacy, Ideology, and Dialogue: Towards a Dialogic Pedagogy*. Albany: State U of New York P, 1994. Print.

Introduction

Things weren't all concise or refined, but enough of it got through to them, their own processes would start. I came to realize that in one term that is the most you can do. There are people who can give chunks of information, perhaps, but that was not what I was about. The learning process is something you can incite, literally incite, like a riot. And then, just possibly, hopefully, it goes home, or on.

—Audre Lorde on her first experiences of teaching
basic writing at City College of New York

Audre Lorde's well-chosen analogy for the learning process inspires this fourth edition of *Teaching Developmental Writing: Background Readings*. Her verb *incite* calls up its homophone, *insight,* because the learning process endures as both a call to action and a means of reflection—not the reflection of jotting down initial impressions, but what Paulo Freire called "authentic reflection," which conceives of "people in their relations with the world." As teachers, we gain insight through authentic reflection on our individual learning and the implications of our learning for the world beyond the classroom.[1]

One spring day in 2008, I had the opportunity to discover for myself the meaning of Lorde's analogy in a beginning basic writing class. Students were working on the skill of connecting reading comprehension to the writing process; their text was Martin Luther King Jr.'s "Beyond Vietnam: A Time to Break Silence" speech. In small groups, students interpreted a passage from King's speech and prepared presentations to explain to the rest of the class the passage and its possible connections to twenty-first-century events. During a presentation, someone discovered a student named Devin using the camcorder on his mobile phone to record the projects. I was intrigued. Generally I asked students to turn off or silence their mobile phones when they entered the classroom (everyone knew the frustration of a ringtone singing out when we needed quiet time for writing or the ensuing embarrassment if you turned out to be the owner of said phone).

However, Devin's use of his phone in this context did not seem to be a moment of either inattention or inappropriate multitasking. In fact, it made me wonder if using the camcorder widget could be a means of staying clearly focused on the work of the class. "Devin," I asked, "would you record the rest of the projects, please? I don't think I can record and take notes at the same time." "I can't, Ms. B," Devin said, "My group is presenting next." "Well, I'll do it," another student named Helen said. "I'll record. Just show me what to press and where to focus." Helen recorded the project that Devin and his group performed, as well as different angles of the classroom and the students. She also offered commentary as she recorded. Taking in Devin's drawing of two birds kissing over a contrasting drawing labeled "War Zone," Helen remarked, "That's symbolism. I like that." Her analysis of visual and verbal conceptions that engaged her attention continued throughout the presentation. Everyone else played to the camera.

That day was hardly the beginning of the students' or my Web 2.0 education, but it was a day when we experienced the ways in which new media could figure into the learning process. A lesson that initially called for twentieth-century materials and practices entered the world of twenty-first-century multimedia. For the students, this moment may have been unusual because I had spontaneously changed a classroom practice. Using the mobile phone as an instrument of learning instead of banishing it as a source of distraction was an entirely new proposition, for both the students and for me. I reflect often on this classroom moment, which for me remains an insight that transformed my thoughts on teaching and learning with multimedia especially as it relates to teaching basic writing. I became more mindful of my students' perspectives on and of the classroom and the ways in which their experiences of multimedia differed from mine.

Initially, I viewed the use of twenty-first-century multimedia in the classroom as a transition that often seemed like an add-on to other aspects of my teaching. But for most of the students in this class, there had been no transition: They grew up with the Internet and had long used their mobile phones for multiple purposes, not simply for making calls. The students taught me to envision multimedia as an engine for driving critical thinking, not merely as just another tool or technology for writing (as my dearly departed portable manual typewriter had been throughout college). At the same time that the students were teaching me how and why to use new technologies, I was endeavoring to teach the students how and why to use critical reading as a catalyst to analytic writing. In that moment of reciprocal teaching and learning, I understood more deeply Audre Lorde's analogy of how the learning process can be changed and incited and her hope that learning "goes home, or on," continuing after the course ends. And that story is just one of the many stories of insight and learning that readers will find in this edition of *Teaching Developmental Writing*.

Changing Times, Sustaining Practices

The previous edition of *Teaching Developmental Writing* was published in 2007, and five years later so much about basic writing has changed. By the end of the 2000s, I had taught in three open admissions programs at three different university systems; by 2011, all three of these open admissions programs were gone, including the class for beginning writers that I describe above. Another developmental education program, which was housed at the main campus of a university located in a small and struggling city in a Rust Belt state, was eliminated altogether. The branch campuses in the suburbs still offered Basic Writing, but public transportation to those suburbs remained unreliable, the campuses almost unreachable without a car. Inner-city residents who could not make the long commute to the suburbs were left with few options for postsecondary education.

Indeed, the meaning of postsecondary education itself has undergone drastic revision in the last half decade, spurred by state legislation and private philanthropic organizations that require accelerating (Adams, Gearhart, Miller, and Roberts, p. 438 in this volume), scaling back (Bernstein, p. 85), or ending "remediation" as part of their funding requirements (Otte and Mlynarczyk, p. 427). Basic writing, considered to be part of the social good in educational experiments of the late 1960s and early 1970s (Shaughnessy, p. 7; Rich, p. 12), often has been redefined, forty years later, as a set of basic skills over which students must demonstrate mastery before they are allowed to move to for-credit composition courses.[2]

Although some courses require that students master sentence-level skills and paragraph writing before attempting a complete essay, current best practices suggest that this step-by-step approach can lead to inattention and a lack of critical thinking, which is deeply detrimental to students just beginning to write for academic purposes. Students need to practice critical thinking throughout the writing process in order to develop and sustain ideas in depth and detail. When students learn this practice early on, they have an opportunity to transition with more facility to writing in college-level courses and in workplace settings. Conceiving of writing beyond basic skills also gives students a chance to experience "a sense of the power of learning new things and, through that learning, redefining who you are" (Rose, p. 27). For these reasons, many of the authors in *Teaching Developmental Writing* suggest that students in basic writing need practice writing full-length essays and can learn to understand rules of grammar, syntax, and style in rhetorical terms—that is, in terms of the writer's intended audiences and purposes for composing a particular text (Micciche, p. 220).

Many of the authors in this volume give detailed descriptions of Basic Writing curricula that integrate academic writing with reading, multimedia, and grammar and style, providing alternatives to a modular or basic skills approach (see Charlton, p. 102; Sanchez and Paulson, p. 113; Carter, p. 161; Klages and Clark, p. 183; and Bruch, p. 309).[3] These authors argue that such curricula offer writers extensive practice with the kinds of writing that they will encounter in more advanced writing courses. The authors believe that students will continue to grow and change as writers throughout their years in college and that students in basic writing are better served by writing complete essays.

Still More Change: New Scholarship and Pedagogy

Teacher-based research supports these assumptions,[4] and the rapid change we are experiencing in the field can foster conditions for new, creative approaches to addressing long-standing issues as well as contemporary concerns. Such has unquestionably been the case for basic writing scholarship and pedagogy as presented in *Teaching Developmental Writing*, Fourth Edition. The majority of articles in this new edition were first published in the twenty-first century, many of them within the last five years. The currency of the articles demonstrates even more significant changes since 2007, as authors deal with up-to-date issues that evolve from the material realities of our classrooms, our writing centers, and our program administrative offices — issues that were perhaps seedlings in 2007 and now have grown significantly. In basic writing, change has indeed created fertile ground.

The fourth edition of *Teaching Developmental Writing* offers a rich sampling of new scholarship in basic writing, rhetoric and composition, writing studies, second language writing, English education, disability studies, and other fields that impact and inform our basic writing classrooms. Recent innovations such as acceleration, multimedia studies, antiracist pedagogy, immigrant concerns, and first-year transitions also receive attention. In addition, *Teaching Developmental Writing* continues to provide historical contexts for framing current situations (Davis, p. 306) and also includes articles published in previous editions (Jordan, p. 255; Anzaldúa, p. 245; and hooks, p. 270).

The structure of *Teaching Developmental Writing* has undergone some reconstruction as well. This edition is divided into four parts, each with a general subject heading. Under each of those subject headings, the reader will find more specific chapter headings that connect to the larger general subject, for a total of twelve chapters, each related to a significant aspect of teaching basic writing. Part One, Basic Writing: Perspectives from the Field, presents a variety of views from teachers and students on the classroom and the profession. Part Two, Literacy and Literacies, offers approaches on the multiple and ever-changing literacies that constitute writing in the twenty-first century: the complexities of the writing process, the inextricable links between reading and critical thinking, the connections of writing and everyday life to multimedia and new literacies; and the significance of context for lessons in grammar and style. Part Three, Engaging Difference, addresses diversity, not as a surface feature but as questions of difference that can lead to systemic biases and inequalities inside and outside the classroom. Articles in Part Three cover a range of multicultural and antiracist pedagogies, past and present, as well as learning differences and English language learning. Part Four, Collaboration, Assessment, and Change, examines the collaborations outside the classroom that can lead to changes and reforms inside the classroom. Writing centers, assessment, accelerated courses, and stretch courses are included in these recent innovations for basic writing.

Teaching Developmental Writing also features an extended apparatus called Resources for Teaching and Research, which invites the reader to participate in the long, multifaceted, and ongoing discussion of basic writing and its particular triumphs and challenges. This apparatus includes suggestions for keeping a teaching journal and a classroom archive, ideas for turning classroom events into conference proposals and articles for publication, springboards for addressing diversity and social justice in the classroom, and a sample syllabus based on the innovations of writing studies. The hope is that new and experienced basic writing educators alike will find not only activities for Monday morning (or Saturday morning, or Thursday night, or asynchronously online), but also a space for our own reflections on and insights about the students and the courses we teach.

Alternative Contents

The questions and challenges of basic writing educators may fall under a variety of headings not covered by the main table of contents for this book. For that reason, *Teaching Developmental Writing* includes an alternative contents that reorganizes the readings under additional subject headings and helps to extend the usefulness of readings that may fall into multiple categories. For instance, Justin Hudson's essay in Part One, Amy Winans's article in Part Three, and Condon, Geller, Eodice, Carroll, and Boquet's appendix in Part Four could be read together as part of a thematic unit on gaining greater awareness of the systemic impact of racism on teaching and learning. The potential for categorizing similar themes and for the cross-fertilization of ideas holds endless possibilities.

Conclusion: Basic Writing and Responsibility

> I thought, I have responsibility to these students. How am I going to speak to them? How am I going to tell them what I want from them — literally, [I felt] that kind of terror [before I entered the classroom].
>
> —Audre Lorde

Whether we are veteran teachers of basic writing or we are teaching our first basic writing class with only a day's notice; whether we are writing center tutors or writing program administrators; we all face that grave sense of responsibility that Audre Lorde describes. We may teach basic writing in challenging times or comfortable ones, but whatever circumstances we face, no matter how isolated we may feel, we are never quite alone.

A couple of years after our beginning Basic Writing course ended, Devin and Helen and a few other students from our class "friended" me on Facebook. I still hear from them from time to time. If we reminisce about our work together, I remind them of the commitment and perseverance they brought to their writing, of their ability to work collaboratively and to inspire and to motivate their peers. They remind me of my responsibility to remember that every student has the potential to learn, that every student—no matter where he or she begins—deserves a chance to move forward. *Teaching Developmental Writing* reflects that perspective, and remains a tool to help teachers and our students, no matter what our situations.

Welcome to this new edition.

Notes

1. "Authentic reflection considers neither abstract man nor the world without people, but people in their relations with the world. In these relations consciousness and world are simultaneous: consciousness neither precedes the world nor follows it" (Freire 32). Also see the footnote on the same page that references Jean Paul Sartre, from whom Freire draws this existentialist relationship between individual consciousness and the world. In this sense, "authentic reflection" may be defined as a reflection that is subject to transformation based on changing conditions. An authentic reflection is not stagnant or fixed, but always already in the process of finding meaning. This story of multimedia learning and the writing process is told more fully in my article in Chapter 3. For a compelling example of the ways in which learning continues after college, see the award-winning article on writer center tutors' postcollege experiences by Hughes, Gillespie, and Kail in Chapter 11.
2. See Greene and Alexander.
3. For different models and approaches to basic writing, see Lalicker and Uehling.
4. Sternglass (1997); also see Sternglass (2000). Sternglass's analysis still proves relevant for the trajectories of students' lives today. Students who cannot meet time requirements are often either denied admission or shifted to vocational programs that offer few opportunities to develop nascent abilities into forms of critical thinking and democratic participation. These notions were near and dear to early, influential advocates of pedagogical experimentation like Mina Shaughnessy and the writers she hired to teach in her program, such as Adrienne Rich, Audre Lorde, and June Jordan. In Shaughnessy's and Sternglass's eras, as in this current historical moment, students may begin their college careers with hope and enthusiasm, only to encounter economic exigencies that interrupt their studies. In Sternglass's research, as in our own classrooms, we meet stu-

dents who, encumbered with multiple jobs and family responsibilities, must drop the course before the end of the term, or stop for a semester or a year or two or more to work to raise money to finish their education.

Works Cited

Freire, Paulo. *Pedagogy of the Oppressed*. New York: Continuum, 1993. Print.

Greene, Nicole Pepinster, and Patricia J. Alexander, eds. *Basic Writing in America: The History of Nine College Programs*. New York: Hampton, 2008. Print.

Lalicker, William B. "A Basic Approach to Basic Writing Program Structures." *BWe: Basic Writing e-Journal*. 19 Nov. 1999. Web. 14 Mar. 2012.

Lorde, Audre. Interview with Adrienne Rich. *Signs* 6.4 (1981). Republished in *Sister Outsider*. Print.

Sternglass, Marilyn. "The Changing Perception of the Role of Writing: From Basic Writing to Discipline Courses." *BWe: Basic Writing e-Journal*. 7 July 2000. Web. 14 Mar. 2012.

———. *Time to Know Them: A Longitudinal Study of Writing and Learning*. Mahwah: Erlbaum, 1997. Print.

Uehling, Karen. "Creating a Statement of Guidelines and Goals for Boise State's Basic Writing Courses: Content and Development." *Journal of Basic Writing* 22.1 (2003): 22–34. Print.

Contents

PART ONE: BASIC WRITING: PERSPECTIVES FROM THE FIELD   1

1   Basic Writing: Teachers' Perspectives   7

Mina Shaughnessy
Some Needed Research on Writing   7

Shaughnessy presents four seminal questions—first printed in 1977—that are still relevant for contemporary teachers/scholars of basic writing. Her explanations of the significance of each question provide an insightful guide to scholarly inquiry in the field.

Adrienne Rich
Teaching Language in Open Admissions   12

Feminist poet and essayist Rich reflects on the joys and challenges of teaching basic writing in the early years of open admissions at City College of New York, where she taught under the direction of Mina Shaughnessy.

Rose argues that remediation is a puzzle consisting of "interlocking pieces" which scholars cannot see all at once because "our disciplinary and methodological training and public policy toolkit work against a comprehensive view of the problem."

Maher provides an update of her experiences teaching basic writing at Bedford Hills Correctional Facility, a women's maximum-security prison that she first wrote about in "'You Probably Don't Even Know I Exist': Notes from a Prison College Program."

Hill employs hip-hop pedagogy to critique the difficulties that arose in his classroom as students and teachers presented difficult personal stories during class discussion.

In his graduation speech from Hunter High School in New York, Hudson addresses his school's discouragement of faculty introducing readings or discussions on educational inequality. Hill also explains his reasons for addressing this controversial matter during what many consider a celebratory occasion.

PART TWO: LITERACY AND LITERACIES   81

3   Processes of Writing and Research   85

Susan Naomi Bernstein
Basic Writing: In Search of a New Map   85

Bernstein presents Martin Luther King Jr.'s "Beyond Vietnam: A Time to Break Silence" speech to students enrolled in the beginning course of a two-course basic skills writing sequence. The students use a variety of meaning-making, multimodal processes to understand and deal with the speech.

Jonikka Charlton
**Seeing Is Believing: Writing Studies with
"Basic Writing" Students**   102

Charlton writes about students enrolled in a basic writing course paired with first-year composition at a university in Texas near the Mexican border. In this successful curriculum, students read and engage with the same rhetoric and composition texts that teachers/scholars read.

4   Intersected Literacies: Reading, Writing, and Critical Thinking   113

Deborah M. Sánchez and Eric J. Paulson
**Critical Language Awareness and Learners
in College Transitional English**   113

Sánchez and Paulson provide examples of studies that show students in transition reading, critically thinking about, and learning from more complex materials—and learning the ways in which language awareness can help them to unpack the underlying themes of texts.

David A. Jolliffe and Allison Harl
**Texts of Our Institutional Lives: Studying the
"Reading Transition" from High School to College:
What Are Our Students Reading and Why?**   126

Jolliffe and Harl conducted a study to discover the contexts and contents of first-year students' reading. This article reports the findings of their study, which include some surprising results that not only challenge faculty perceptions, but may also help to inform curriculum development—especially in terms of technology.

PART THREE: ENGAGING DIFFERENCE   239

8 Transforming Pedagogies   277

Valerie Purdie-Vaughns, Geoffery L. Cohen, Julio Garcia,
Rachel Sumner, Jonathan C. Cook, and Nancy Apfel
Improving Minority Academic Performance:
How a Values-Affirmation Intervention Works   277

Purdie-Vaughns, Cohen, and their team of researchers investigated
likely causes of and remedies for the achievement gap between students of color and white students. Working in a northeastern suburban
school, the research team found that a values intervention can serve as
a powerful antidote to internalized stereotypes and can help to sustain
student achievement.

Amy E. Winans
Cultivating Racial Literacy in White Segregated Settings:
Emotions as Site of Ethical Engagement and Inquiry   284

In order to complicate and interrogate the perception that race problems exist outside the racially homogenous, rural university at which
she teaches, Amy Winans analyzes the intersections of emotions and
ethical values with white students' writing about race.

9 Learning Differences   306

Lennard Davis
From "The Rule of Normalcy"   306

Davis reexamines the difference between the terms *normality* and
normalcy through linguistic and cultural history, drawing significant
conclusions about the language and terminology used to assess ability,
disability, and standards. As part of this history, Davis presents the
differences between the concepts of *ideal* and *normal* and how these
notions continue to shape standardized testing.

Patrick L. Bruch
Interpreting and Implementing Universal Instructional
Design in Basic Writing   309

Bruch demonstrates the link between social justice work and universal
instructional design for basic writing pedagogy. He discusses how this
theory works in practice and offers a writing assignment that features
inclusive participation for students with (and without) apparent learning disabilities.

Rodriguez and Cruz offer an informative review of recent research on English learners' and undocumented students' transitions to college. Most significantly, they offer recommendations for needed research that would have a direct, proactive impact on policies toward and available resources for students whose linguistic backgrounds cannot be easily generalized and who often have been underserved in their previous experiences with education.

Cummings and her ESL students grapple with writing, language, and identity as they read *Someday This Pain Will Be Useful to You*, Peter Cameron's young adult novel about a wealthy New York teenager who is questioning his sexual orientation. Cummings also deals with the question of whether or not to come out to her students after her experiences of living closeted for four years while teaching in Japan.

Using three case studies and teacher-based research, Christina Ortmeir-Hooper explores immigrant students' experiences in first-year college writing courses.

PART FOUR: COLLABORATION, ASSESSMENT, AND CHANGE 389

11 Writing Centers 395

Brad Hughes, Paula Gillespie, and Harvey Kail
**What They Take with Them: Findings from the
Peer Writing Tutor Alumni Research Project** 395

Hughes, Gillespie, and Kail conducted a twenty-five-year survey—
spanning from 1982 to 2007—of alumni peer tutors from their institutions for which alumni were invited to respond to a series of open-ended
questions about their experiences. The researchers sought to understand the long-term impact of peer tutoring on the alumni tutors.

International Writing Centers Association
Position Statement on Two-Year College Writing Centers 421

This position statement presents a list of guidelines and best practices
for developing and sustaining writing centers in two-year institutions.
It was composed after writing center directors asked for an IWCA professional statement to help represent writing center work to institutional administrators and other colleagues and stakeholders who make
funding and programmatic decisions at two-year colleges.

*Anne Ellen Geller, Michele Eodice, Frankie Condon,
Meg Carroll, and Elizabeth H. Boquet*
**Anti-Racism Work (Appendix to Everyday Racism:
Anti-Racism Work and Writing Center Practice)** 423

In a book chapter titled "Everyday Racism: Anti-Racism Work and
Writing Center Practice," Geller, Eodice, Condon, Carroll, and Boquet
describe scenes of systemic racism at the writing center and argue for
actions that promote racial justice. This appendix to that chapter provides practical resources for addressing such issues.

12 Access, Placement, Assessment, and Retention: Models and Challenges 427

George Otte and Rebecca Williams Mlynarczyk
Assessment 427

In this excerpt from their book *Basic Writing*, Otte and Williams
Mlynarczyk take on the vexed history of assessment of students in basic

writing, from the 1970s to the first decade of the twenty-first century. The authors offer the sobering assertion that basic writing assessment is subject to the changes and whims of an ever-shifting political climate.

Peter Adams, Sarah Gearhart, Robert Miller, and Anne Roberts
The Accelerated Learning Program: Throwing Open the Gates 438

Adams, Gearhart, Miller, and Roberts discuss the creation of the Accelerated Learning Program at the Community College of Baltimore County (CCBC), a program that evolved out of increasing concerns about attrition rates for students who did not complete either the basic writing or college composition sequences at the college.

Gregory R. Glau
Stretch at 10: A Progress Report on Arizona State University's Stretch Program 456

Glau recounts the high pass rate of Arizona State University's *Stretch Program* for students in basic writing over a ten-year period from 1994–1995 to 2004–2005. If the future of the *Stretch Program* seemed vulnerable to changing times, this ten-year overview provides teachers and writing program administrators an exemplary model for success in basic writing.

Alternative Contents

Transitions from High School to Higher Education, from Community to College

Classroom Practices—Practical Pedagogies

Questions and Conundrums for Research and Administration

PART ONE

Basic Writing: Perspectives from the Field

By making limited, ahistorical assertions about the places in which basic writers have existed, we ignore the rich models—and powerful lessons — we can take to our classrooms and programs in search of equal institutional status and opportunity for all writing students. In order for research in basic writing to truly contextualize its origins, we must consider all sites of instruction when assembling a social history of the basic writer or student whose writing is outside what is considered standard/acceptable to the institution at hand and the culture in which it operates.

—Kelly Ritter, *Before Shaughnessy: Basic Writing at Yale and Harvard, 1920–1960* (143)

What is basic writing? Postsecondary institutions might call this course "developmental writing," "remedial writing," "basic skills writing," "introduction to college writing," "pre-college composition," or another title to indicate its status as a course for students at the very beginning of their journey as writers in postsecondary education. Yet the histories of basic writing are multiple and complicated (Soliday; Ritter). The course has been vilified as an inappropriate offering for college students who ought to know how to write because they have presumably already acquired this skill from prior education. Basic writing also has been championed as an entry point for students who otherwise might not have access to a college education, because their "development as writers has been delayed by inferior preparation" (Shaughnessy; see p. 9 in this volume). For many years, the course has been a political battleground with a variety of stakeholders, including philanthropists, state legislators, the federal government, postsecondary institutional administrators, faculty, and students (Greene and McAlexander). Once offered in four-year institutions and many research universities, basic writing courses are now shifting primarily to community colleges and even to high schools as part of dual enrollment programs for high school students. As Ritter has suggested, the students enrolled in the course have been "variously defined, but uniformly stigmatized over the past eighty years" (143).

However, rather than focus on stigma, Part One of this book directly addresses the differences between a course called "Basic Writing" and the students enrolled in that course (Adler-Kassner; see also Gray-Rosendale). For this reason, Part One concentrates on teachers' perspectives of the course (Chapter 1) and on students' perspectives of education (Chapter 2). The teachers in question are Mina Shaughnessy and Adrienne Rich, who taught at City College of CUNY in the 1960s and 1970s, and Mike Rose, who teaches at the University of California, Los Angeles. Mina Shaughnessy, who was the driving force behind the Basic Writing program at the City College of CUNY, poses four research questions for teachers/scholars of the Basic Writing course. Her questions focus on the course itself, on "what goes on or ought to go on in the composition classroom" (p. 12). Shaughnessy demonstrates her respect for students throughout the essay, emphasizing the lack of equitable schooling for "adults whose development as writers has been delayed by inferior preparation" (p. 9). Although Shaughnessy first published this essay in 1977, her research questions remain highly relevant for writing studies in the second decade of the twenty-first century.

The poet and feminist theorist Adrienne Rich was hired by Mina Shaughnessy to teach basic writing in the first years of open admissions at City University of New York. Rich's essay offers necessary historical context not only for her curriculum choices but also for the reasons why she chose to teach in CUNY's open admissions program. Rich came to City College in the wake of the 1968 assassination of civil rights leader and activist Martin Luther King Jr., and her reasons are linked to addressing her "white liberal guilt," her politics, and "a need to involve myself with the real life of [New York City]." Indeed, it is critical to note that Rich and Shaughnessy are part of the same generation as King and Malcolm X (Bernstein), and that urban open admissions education at City College began in the same decade as the most transformative work of these two activists (Branch; Marable)—and in the aftermath of their assassinations.

Although Mina Shaughnessy and Adrienne Rich wrote these essays more than thirty-five years ago, the questions they ask and the conflicts they describe have only intensified over time. Mike Rose, author of *Lives on the Boundary*, an auto-ethnographic study of public schooling and social class privilege in the United States, draws similar connections in an essay published in *Inside Higher Education* in 2011, which he first gave as an address to the 2011 American Educational Research Association Convention.

The essays in Part One all draw a clear connection between poverty and inadequate access to equitable preparation for college. Rose argues that students in basic writing do not need oversimplified lessons, but rather an intellectually challenging program that honors the people who they are capable of becoming. The students' perspectives in the second chapter adhere to that perspective. All of the students are poor, with complicated family lives. The students Jane Maher teaches are incarcerated in a maximum-security women's prison in upstate New York. Marc Lamont Hill's students attend an alternative high school in Philadelphia and study Hip-Hop Lit, with mixed results. Justin Hudson gives a graduation speech at his exclusive New York City public high school that clearly and poignantly details the lack of choices available to the children of poor and working-class parents and the consequences of lack of equitable access to public education on the future of those children.

These essays were chosen because each one, in its own way, argues against what University of Texas educator Richard R. Valencia calls "deficit thinking." Valencia deconstructs the stated and unstated assumptions that constitute deficit thinking. He equates deficit thinking with blaming the victim, rather than locating the causes of inadequate preparation within the schools themselves. At the same time, he argues that students and their families must play an active role in education, because of these very same systemic weaknesses. For a brief time in the first thirty years of the twentieth century, Basic Writing attempted to play that role at City College. Indeed Attewell and Lavin and Marilyn Sternglass have both documented that, over time, students who gained access to basic writing through open admissions improve their intellectual and economic lives. The chapter on students' perspectives demonstrates students struggling with those intellectual efforts and the benefits and costs of educational access.

Taken together, the essays in Part One provide a counterargument to the current trend of downsizing and outsourcing basic writing courses. The essays suggest that historical context is critical for understanding what basic writing can become, amid the complexities and exigencies of the students who are required to enroll in the course.

Works Cited

Adler-Kassner, Linda. "Just Writing, Basically: Basic Writers on Basic Writing." *Teaching Developmental Writing*. Ed. Susan Naomi Bernstein. New York: Bedford, 2001. 27–35. Print.

Attewell, Paul, and David E. Lavin. *Passing the Torch: Does Higher Education for the Disadvantaged Pay Off Across the Generations?* New York: Russell Sage Fdn., 2007. Print.

Bernstein, Susan Naomi. "Beyond the Basics: The 3 Rs of Summer: Reading, Reflection, and Renewal." *Bedford Bits*. Bedford/St. Martin's, 23 May 2011. Web. 10 Feb. 2012.

Branch, Taylor. *At Canaan's Edge: America in the King Years 1965–1968*. New York: Simon, 2007. Print.

Gray-Rosendale, Laura. *Rethinking Basic Writing: Exploring Identity, Politics, and Community in Interaction*. Mahwah: Erlbaum, 2000. Print.

Greene, Nicole Pepinster, and Patricia J. McAlexander. *Basic Writing in America: The History of Nine College Programs*. New York: Hampton, 2008. Print.

Marable, Manning. *Malcolm X: A Life of Reinvention*. New York: Viking, 2011. Print.

Ritter, Kelly. *Before Shaughnessy: Basic Writing at Yale and Harvard, 1920–1960*. Carbondale: Southern Illinois UP, 2009. Print.

Soliday, Mary. *Politics of Remediation: Institutional and Student Needs in Higher Education*. Pittsburgh: U of Pittsburgh P, 2002. Print.

Sternglass, Marilyn S. *Time to Know Them: A Longitudinal Study of Writing and Learning at the College Level*. Mahwah: Erlbaum, 1997. Print.

Valencia, Richard R. *Dismantling Deficit Thinking: Educational Thought and Practice*. New York: Routledge, 2010. Print.

Basic Writing:
Teachers' Perspectives

Some Needed Research on Writing

Mina Shaughnessy

"We cannot hope," Mina Shaughnessy states in this 1977 essay from College Composition and Communication, *"to solve the problems that arise out of vast inequities in public education by arguing that when those problems were* not *being solved, or even thought about higher education was in excellent shape" (p. 12). Shaughnessy's scholarship evolved from her work as teacher and administrator of Basic Writing. Reprinted in 1980 in the* Journal of Basic Writing, *this article presents four questions still contemporary for teachers/scholars in the 2010s. Shaughnessy's questions, as well as her explanations of the significance of each question, guide the reader toward scholarly inquiry in basic writing. In these questions, Shaughnessy clearly foregrounds the strengths and needs of her students and their writing. For Shaughnessy, students in basic writing are "adults whose development as writers has been delayed by inferior preparation but who are then exposed to intensive instruction in writing" (p. 9). In her germinal study,* Errors and Expectations: A Guide for the Teacher of Basic Writing, *Shaughnessy takes up the questions that she asked in this essay.* *

*Similarly, Marilyn Sternglass's book *Time to Know Them: A Longitudinal Study of Writing at the College Level* (Mahwah: Erlbaum, 1997) also may be read as a response to Shaughnessy's questions, with focused attention to the material conditions that allow for students to attend and develop their writing. Each teacher/scholar based her ideas on the belief that students are not unskilled, but instead inexperienced. Indeed, Shaughnessy and Sternglass both made a case for the possibilities of students' growth and development through intensive practice with writing, and extensive and multiple experiences with writing.

Among most of the arts and skills people attempt to acquire in this society, the sequences and goals of instruction are far more stable and specific than they seem to be for writing. Most students of piano, wherever they study, make their way through similar types of scales and exercises (many are still apprenticed to Czerny's exercises for finger dexterity, now over one hundred years old). Ballet students still practice their *pliés* and *rond de jambes* in much the same order and according to similar developmental timetables, whether their studios are in Kansas City or New York. And athletes have familiar training rituals, known to coaches from big leagues to little. For such skills, teachers need not invent whole pedagogies as they go, nor return with debilitating regularity to fundamental questions about their purpose and procedures. They continue a vital tradition of instruction in which their roles are of unquestioned importance. It is assumed that to learn to play the piano or to dance or to play football, a person must generally become someone's student. And that someone, a teacher, understands what comes after what and what constitutes an acceptable level of performance at each step along the way.

Teachers of reading and writing, particularly those who teach ill-prepared freshmen, enjoy no such stability. In a culture that has been engaged in reading and writing for centuries, the pedagogies of literacy are in a puzzling state of discord, with theorists and practitioners and taxpayers all arguing about how people become literate or why they don't.

The reasons for this discord are clearly complex. It cannot be simply a matter of English teachers' having failed to do their homework. I have been the beneficiary, as both a writer and a teacher, of too many fine texts and theoretical works about rhetoric, grammar, style, and so on to be ready now to condemn the profession as roundly as it is being condemned for the state of literacy in America.

Still, I must admit that those pedagogies that served the profession for years seem no longer appropriate to large numbers of our students, and their inappropriateness lies largely in the fact that many of our students these days are exactly in the same relation to writing that beginning tennis students or piano students are to those skills: they are adult beginners and depend as students did not depend in the past upon the classroom and the teacher for the acquisition of the skill of writing.

Most of us learned to write through such a long, subtle process of socialization that we cannot remember how it happened. For some, freshman composition played an insignificant part of their maturation as writers, and for most, it was at best a helpful rather than an essential course. But the students we have now will be able to say—if they are fortunate in their teachers—that they learned to write in such a year, with such a teacher, and that their courses in writing were crucial to their advancement in college.

This is a tremendous responsibility for English teachers. But my own experience with unprepared—severely unprepared—students persuades me that it is a responsibility we can meet if we are willing to give our energies to the development of a pedagogy for writing that respects, in its goals and methods, the maturity of the adult, beginning writer and at the same time admits to the need to begin where the beginning is, even if that falls outside the traditional territory of college composition.

If we accept this responsibility, we are committed to research of a very ambitious sort—so ambitious that I have not been able to suggest its boundaries. What I will do instead is simply raise four questions that have concerned me lately and that might in turn generate specific research plans that would move us toward the pedagogy I speak of.

My first question is *"What are the signs of growth in writing among adults whose development as writers has been delayed by inferior preparation but who are then exposed to intensive instruction in writing?"* Just how, that is, at what pace and in what manner, do such students get to be better at the skills? From a managerial perspective, it would be convenient if the writing of such students were to advance regularly, on all fronts, preferably within one semester, in response to instruction, paralleling the developmental patterns that have been observed among younger learners over longer periods.

Yet experience with the unprepared adult writer suggests that the pattern of development is marked by puzzling plateaus and even retreats in some areas and remarkable leaps into competence in others, producing very different writing records from those we are accustomed to in better-prepared students, refusing throughout to bring the unprepared writers into parallel courses with their better-prepared peers. Thus, while the most dramatic difference between the prepared and unprepared writer is probably the incidence and quality of error in each group, errors, particularly the errors that are deeply rooted in linguistic habit and not simply the result of inattentiveness, may be more resistant to direct instruction than other seemingly more complex problems that are traditionally taken up after the slaying of the dragon error. I have in mind the skills of elucidation and validation and sequencing in expository writing or the management of complex sentence patterns (which are usually ripe for development among adult students even though their early writings produce many tangled and derailed sentences, a reality which complicates the use of measures of maturity such as the T-unit). I would guess that by the criteria for improvement now common in many remedial programs, the developing writer is likely to be penalized for his or her growth simply because the phenomenon of growth in writing for this population has not been looked at directly, through case studies, for example, over four-or-five year stretches.

My second question is *"What sub-skills of writing, heretofore absorbed by students over time in a variety of situations, can be effectively developed through direct and systematic instruction at the freshman level?"* Here I raise the question of whether some of the slow-growing skills, such as spelling, vocabulary, and syntax, which in ordinary development are acquired gradually and inductively, might not be approached through effective paradigms and conceptual keys appropriate for adult learners although inaccessible to young learners. Teachers' fatalistic views about many of their students' difficulties may well arise out of a failure so far to have found the most productive generalizations about those features of written language that give students the most difficulty, generalizations that may be already available to us in research literature or that lie around the corner, were English teachers inclined or encouraged to turn in that direction. It should not be difficult, for example, to link great improvements in the teaching of spelling at the elementary levels to the major work of Hanna and others in the analysis of phoneme-grapheme correspondences as clues to spelling improvement. There is much still to be drawn from that work, now a decade old, for the instruction of adult learners as well. Or, as another example, there is the recent work of Sandra Stotsky on vocabulary development, which not only gives special attention to the mastery of prefixes among young learners but suggests a systematic approach to vocabulary development that has applications for older students.

My third question is *"What skills have we failed to take note of in our analysis of academic tasks?"* "The aim of a skillful performance," Polanyi has written, "is achieved by the observance of a set of rules which are *not known as such* to the person following them." In my few attempts to work contrastively with experienced and inexperienced academic writers on the same assignments in order to discover hidden features of competency, I have been surprised by the emergence of certain skills and orientations I had not thought to isolate or emphasize as subjects of instruction. I have noted, for example, that the craft of writing has a larger measure of craftiness in it than our instruction seems to suggest. Experienced academic writers, for example, appear to spend little time deliberating over their main intent in answering a question or developing an essay; this conviction evidently reaches them through some subtle, swift process of assessment and association that has doubtless been highly cultivated after years of writing in academic situations. But after this recognition of intent, there follows a relatively long period of scheming and plotting during which the writer, often with great cunning, strives to present his or her intent in a way that will be seductive to an academic audience, which, while it aspires among other things to high standards of verification and sound reason, is nonetheless subject to other kinds of persuasion as well—to the deft manipulation of audience expectations and biases, to shrewd assessments of what constitutes "adequate proof" or enough examples in specific situations, to the stances of fairness, objectivity, and formal courtesy that smooth the surface of academic disputation. One has but to re-read such brilliant academic performances as Freud's introductory lectures on psychoanalysis to observe this craftiness at work.

Now, beginning adult writers are without protection in such situations. They do not know the rituals and ways of winning arguments in academia. Indeed, so open and vulnerable do they appear in their writing that teachers often turn sentimental in their response to it, urging them into the lion's den of academic disputation with no more than an honest face for protection. Furthermore, the traditional formulations of expository writing too easily lead to the conviction that only certain kinds of writing (poetry, for example, or fiction) are concerned with seduction, whereas the formal writing of academics and professionals is carried out at more spiritual (i.e., rational) levels of discourse where the neutral truth is thought to dwell.

This view not only inhibits students from joining in the academic contest but takes much of the fun and competition out of the sport. "The greatest minds," Leo Strauss has remarked, "do not all tell us the same things regarding the most important themes; the community of the greatest minds is rent by discord and even by various kinds of discord." College prepares students—or ought to prepare them—to survive intellectually in this atmosphere of discord. It teaches them, or should teach them, in the words of a Master of Eton in the 1860's, "to make mental efforts under criticism."

But the emphasis in writing instruction over the past years has not encouraged a close look at academic discourse nor favored such images as the contest or the dispute as acceptable metaphors for writing, with the result that too many students, especially at the remedial level, continue to write only or mainly in expressive and narrative modes, or to work with worn and inaccurate formulations of the academic mode.

As part of this exploration of academic discourse I am recommending, we need above all else to take a closer look at vocabulary, which is of course critical to the development of complex concepts, the maturation of syntax, and the acquisition of an appropriate tone or register. This is probably the least cultivated field in all of the composition research, badly, barrenly treated in texts and not infrequently abandoned between the desks of reading teachers and writing teachers. We lack a precise taxonomy of the academic vocabulary that might enable us to identify those words and those features of words that would lend themselves to direct instruction or that might allow us to hypothesize realistic and multi-dimensioned timetables for vocabulary growth. We have done little to distinguish among the words in disciplines, except to isolate specialized terms in lists or glossaries, and we have done even less to describe the common stock of words teachers assume students know—proper names, words that have transcended their disciplines, words that initiate academic activities (*document*, *define*, etc.), words that articulate logical relationships, etc. In short, the territory of academic rhetoric—its vocabulary, its conventions, its purposes—is waiting for an Aristotle.

Finally, I must ask a fourth question, which is embarrassingly rudimentary: *"What goes on and what ought to go on in the composition classroom?"* The classroom, as I have said, has become a more important place than ever before. For some students, almost everything that is going to happen will happen there—or through work that is generated there. Yet we know surprisingly little about what goes on there. We know what teachers do by our own recollections of what our teachers did, by what teachers tell us they do (which opens up a vast territory of imaginative literature), and by the periodic observations of peers and students that are largely managerial in intent and that pose rather crude sorts of questions about teaching effectiveness.

But we have evolved no adequate scheme for observing precisely the classroom behavior of students and teachers nor for classifying the models of association between student and teacher that govern different styles of teaching. That is, we can perhaps locate metaphors that describe the orientations of teachers and students—the theatre, the courtroom, the clinic, the editorial office, the couch—but we have not analyzed them nor related them to the teaching of discrete subskills in writing. Nor have we entertained or adequately tested any bold departures from the familiar classroom configurations and timetables, even though teaching the skill of writing may be more like coaching football than teaching literature or history or biology.

What I am suggesting through this question and others is that we have as yet no sociology or psychology (not even an adequate history) of teaching the advanced skills of literacy to young adults who have not already acquired them. Yet many such students are now in college classrooms. We cannot hope to solve the problems that arise out of vast inequities in public education by arguing that when those problems were *not* being solved, or even thought about higher education was in excellent shape.

Teaching Language in Open Admissions

Adrienne Rich

First published in 1972 and informed by the political struggles of its era, feminist poet and essayist Adrienne Rich's article "Teaching Language in Open Admissions" is a testimony to the necessities and possibilities of teaching students in basic writing. With a nod to the liberatory philosophies of Paulo Freire and Jean-Paul Sartre, Rich analyzes both the philosophical and the practical issues of teaching open admissions students at the City College of CUNY in the late 1960s and early 1970s—the same time and place in which Mina Shaughnessy began the inquiry that would lead to

Errors and Expectations. *"Teaching Language in Open Admissions,"* dedicated to Shaughnessy, stands as a companion piece to the foundational work of Errors and Expectations.*

To the memory of Mina Shaughnessy, 1924–1978

I stand to this day behind the major ideas about literature, writing, and teaching that I expressed in this essay. Several things strike me in re-reading it, however. Given the free rein allowed by the SEEK program (described in the text of the essay) when I first began teaching at the City College of New York, it is interesting to me to note the books I was choosing for classes: Orwell, Wright, LeRoi Jones, Lawrence, Baldwin, Plato's *Republic*. It is true that few books by black women writers were available; the bookstores of the late sixties were crowded with paperbacks by Frederick Douglass, Malcolm X, Frantz Fanon, Langston Hughes, Eldridge Cleaver, W. E. B. Du Bois, and by anthologies of mostly male black writers. Ann Petry, Gwendolyn Brooks, June Jordan, Audre Lorde, I came to know and put on my reading lists or copied for classes; but the real crescendo of black women's writing was yet to come, and writers like Zora Neale Hurston and Margaret Walker were out of print. It is obvious now, as it was not then (except to black women writers, undoubtedly) that integral to the struggle against racism in the literary canon there was another, as yet unarticulated, struggle, against the sexism of black and white male editors, anthologists, critics, and publishers.

For awhile I have thought of going back to City College to ask some of my former colleagues, still teaching there, what could be said of the past decade, what is left there of what was, for a brief time, a profound if often naively optimistic experiment in education. (Naively optimistic because I think the white faculty at least, those of us who were most committed to the students, vastly underestimated the psychic depth and economic function of racism in the city and the nation, the power of the political machinery that could be "permissive" for a handful of years only to re-trench, break promises, and betray, pitting black youth against Puerto Rican and Asian, poor ethnic students against students of color, in an absurd and tragic competition for resources which should have been open to all.) But it has seemed to me that such interviews could be frag-mentary at best. I lived through some of that history, the enlarging of classes, the heavy increase of teaching loads, the firing of junior faculty and of many of the best and most dedicated teachers I had known, the efforts of City College to reclaim its "prestige" in the media; I know also that dedicated teachers still remain, who teach Basic Writing not as a white man's—or woman's—burden but because they choose to do so. And, on the corner of Broadway near where I live, I see young people whose like I knew ten years ago as college students "hanging-out," brown-bagging, standing in short skirts and high-heeled boots in

*See Halasek and Highberg (xvi), who provide a similar context for "Teaching Language in Open Admissions." Halasek, Kay, and Nels P. Highberg. "Introduction: Locality and Basic Writing." *Landmark Essays on Basic Writing*. Landmark Essays Vol. 18. Ed. Kay Halasek and Nels P. Highberg. Mahwah: Erlbaum, 2001. xi–xxix. Print.

doorways waiting for a trick, or being dragged into the car of a plumed and sequined pimp.

Finally: in reprinting this essay I would like to acknowledge my debt to Mina Shaughnessy, who was director of the Basic Writing Program at City when I taught there, and from whom, in many direct and indirect ways, I learned—in a time and place where pedagogic romanticism and histrionics were not uncommon—a great deal about the ethics and integrity of teaching.

This essay was first published in *The Uses of Literature*, edited by Monroe Engel (Cambridge, Mass.: Harvard University, 1973).

My first romantic notion of teaching came, I think, from reading Emlyn Williams's play *The Corn Is Green*, sometime in my teens. As I reconstruct it now, a schoolteacher in a Welsh mining village is reading her pupils' essays one night and comes upon a paper which, for all its misspellings and dialect constructions, seems to be the work of a nascent poet. Turning up in the midst of the undistinguished efforts of her other pupils, this essay startles the teacher. She calls in the boy who wrote it, goes over it with him, talks with him about his life, his hopes, and offers to tutor him privately, without fees. Together, as the play goes on, they work their way through rhetoric, mathematics, Shakespeare, Latin, Greek. The boy gets turned on by the classics, is clearly intended to be, if not a poet, at least a scholar. Birth and family background had destined him for a life in the coal mines; but now another path opens up. Toward the end of the play we see him being coached for the entrance examinations for Oxford. I believe crisis strikes when it looks as if he has gotten one of the village girls pregnant and may have to marry her, thus cutting short a career of dazzling promise before it has begun. I don't recall the outcome, but I suspect that the unwed mother is hushed up and packed away (I would be more interested to see the play rewritten today as *her* story) and the boy goes off to Oxford, with every hope of making it to donhood within the decade.

Perhaps this represents a secret fantasy of many teachers: the ill-scrawled essay, turned up among so many others, which has the mark of genius. And looking at the first batch of freshman papers every semester can be like a trip to the mailbox—there is always the possibility of something turning up that will illuminate the weeks ahead. But behind the larger fantasy lie assumptions which I have only gradually come to recognize; and the recognition has to do with a profound change in my conceptions of teaching and learning.

Before I started teaching at City College I had known only elitist institutions: Harvard and Radcliffe as an undergraduate, Swarthmore as a visiting poet, Columbia as teacher in a graduate poetry workshop that included some of the best young poets in the city. I applied for the job at

City in 1968 because Robert Cumming had described the SEEK program to me after Martin Luther King was shot, and my motivation was complex. It had to do with white liberal guilt, of course; and a political decision to use my energies in work with "disadvantaged" (black and Puerto Rican) students. But it also had to do with a need to involve myself with the real life of the city, which had arrested me from the first weeks I began living here.

In 1966 Mayor John Lindsay had been able, however obtusely, to coin the phrase "Fun City" without actually intending it as a sick joke. By 1968, the uncollected garbage lay bulging in plastic sacks on the north side of Washington Square, as it had lain longer north of 110th Street; the city had learned to endure subway strikes, sanitation strikes, cab strikes, power and water shortages; the policeman on the corner had become a threatening figure to many whites as he had long been to blacks; the public school teachers and the parents of their pupils had been in pitched battle. On the Upper West Side poor people were being evicted from tenements which were then tinned-up and left empty, awaiting unscheduled demolition to make room for middle-income housing, for which funds were as yet unavailable; and a squatter movement of considerable political consciousness was emerging in defiance of this uprooting.

There seemed to be three ways in which the white middle class could live in New York: the paranoiac, the solipsistic, and a third, which I am more hesitant to define. By the mid-sixties paranoia was visible and audible: streets of brownstones whose occupants had hired an armed guard for the block and posted notices accordingly; conversations on park benches in which public safety had replaced private health as a topic of concern; conversion of all personal anxieties into fear of the mugger (and the mugger was real, no doubt about it). Paranoia could become a life-style, a science, an art, with the active collaboration of reality. Solipsism I encountered first and most concretely in a conversation with an older European intellectual who told me he liked living in New York (on the East Side) because Madison Avenue reminded him of Paris. It was, and still is, possible to live, if you can afford it, on one of those small islands where the streets are kept clean and the pushers and nodders invisible, to travel by cab, deplore the state of the rest of the city, but remain essentially aloof from its causes and effects. It seems about as boring as most forms of solipsism, since to maintain itself it must remain thick-skinned and ignorant.

But there was, and is, another relationship with the city which I can only begin by calling love. The city as object of love, a love not unmixed with horror and anger, the city as Baudelaire and Rilke had previsioned it, or William Blake for that matter, death in life, but a death emblematic of the death that is epidemic in modern society, and a life more edged, more costly, more charged with knowledge, than life elsewhere. Love as one knows it sometimes with a person with whom one is locked in struggle, energy draining but also energy replenishing, as when one is fighting for life, in oneself or someone else. Here was this damaged, self-destructive organism, preying and preyed upon. The streets were rich with human possibility and vicious with human denial (it is breathtaking to walk through a street in East Harlem, passing among the lithe, alert, childish bodies and attuned, observant, childish faces, playing in the spray of a hydrant, and to know that addiction awaits every brain and body in that block as a potential killer). In all its historic, overcrowded, and sweated poverty, the Lower East Side at the turn of the century had never known this: the odds for the poor, today, are weighted by heroin, a fact which the middle classes ignored until it breathed on their own children's lives as well.

In order to live in the city, I needed to ally myself, in some concrete, practical, if limited way, with the possibilities. So I went up to Convent Avenue and 133rd Street and was interviewed for a teaching job, hired as a poet-teacher. At that time a number of writers, including Toni Cade Bambara, the late Paul Blackburn, Robert Cumming, David Henderson, June Jordan, were being hired to teach writing in the SEEK program to black and Puerto Rican freshmen entering from substandard ghetto high schools, where the prevailing assumption had been that they were of inferior intelligence. (More of these schools later.) Many dropped out (a lower percentage than the national college dropout rate, however); many stuck it out through several semesters of remedial English, math, reading, to enter the mainstream of the college. (As of 1972, 208 SEEK students—or 35 to 40 percent—have since graduated from City College; twenty-four are now in graduate school. *None* of these students would have come near higher education under the regular admissions programs of the City University; high-school guidance counselors have traditionally written off such students as incapable of academic work. Most could not survive economically in college without the stipends which the SEEK program provides.)

My job, that first year, was to "turn the students on" to writing by whatever means I wanted—poetry, free association, music, politics, drama, fiction—to acclimate them to the act of writing, while a grammar teacher, with whom I worked closely outside of class, taught sentence structure, the necessary mechanics. A year later this course was given up as too expensive, since it involved two teachers. My choice was to enlarge my scope to include grammar and mechanics or to find a niche elsewhere and teach verse writing. I stayed on to teach, and learn, grammar—among other things.

The early experience in SEEK was, as I look back on it, both unnerving and seductive. Even those who were (unlike me) experienced teachers of remedial English were working on new frontiers, trying new methods. Some of the most rudimentary questions we confronted were: How do you make standard English verb endings available to a dialect-speaker? How do you teach English prepositional forms to a

Spanish-language student? What are the arguments for and against "Black English"? The English of academic papers and theses? Is standard English simply a weapon of colonization? Many of our students wrote in the vernacular with force and wit; others were unable to say what they wanted on paper in or out of the vernacular. We were dealing not simply with dialect and syntax but with the imagery of lives, the anger and flare of urban youth—how could this be *used*, strengthened, without the lies of artificial polish? How does one teach order, coherence, the structure of ideas while respecting the student's experience of his or her thinking and perceiving? Some students who could barely sweat out a paragraph delivered (and sometimes conned us with) dazzling raps in the classroom: How could we help this oral gift transfer itself onto paper? The classes were small—fifteen at most; the staff, at that time, likewise; we spent hours in conference with individual students, hours meeting together and with counselors, trying to teach ourselves how to teach and asking ourselves what we ought to be teaching.

So these were classes, not simply in writing, not simply in literature, certainly not just in the correction of sentence fragments or the redemptive power of the semicolon; though we did, and do, work on all these. One teacher gave a minicourse in genres; one in drama as literature; teachers have used their favorite books from *Alice in Wonderland* to Martin Buber's *The Knowledge of Man*; I myself have wandered all over the map of my own reading: D. H. Lawrence, W. E. B. Du Bois, LeRoi Jones, Plato, Orwell, Ibsen, poets from W. C. Williams to Audre Lorde. Sometimes books are used as a way of learning to look at literature, sometimes as a provocation for the students' own writing, sometimes both. At City College all Basic Writing teachers have been free to choose the books they would assign (always keeping within the limits of the SEEK book allowance and considering the fact that non-SEEK students have no book allowance at all, though their financial need may be as acute.) There has never been a set curriculum or a required reading list; we have poached off each others' booklists, methods, essay topics, grammar-teaching exercises, and anything else that we hoped would "work" for us.[1]

Most of us felt that students learn to write by discovering the validity and variety of their own experience; and in the late 1960s, as the black classics began to flood the bookstores, we drew on the black novelists, poets, and polemicists as the natural path to this discovery for

---

[1]What I have found deadly and defeating is the anthology designed for multiethnic classes in freshman English. I once ordered one because the book stipends had been cut out and I was trying to save the students money. I ended up using one Allen Ginsberg poem, two by LeRoi Jones, and asking the students to write essays provoked by the photographs in the anthology. The college anthology, in general, as nonbook, with its exhaustive and painfully literal notes, directives, questions, and "guides for study," is like TV showing of a film—cut, chopped up, and interspersed with commercials: a flagrant mutilation by mass technological culture.

SEEK students. Black teachers were, of course, a path; and there were some who combined the work of consciousness-raising with the study of Sophocles, Kafka, and other pillars of the discipline oddly enough known as "English." For many white teachers, the black writers were a relatively new discovery: the clear, translucent prose of Douglass, the sonorities of *The Souls of Black Folk*, the melancholy sensuousness of Toomer's poem-novel *Cane*. In this discovery of a previously submerged culture we were learning from and with our students as rarely happens in the university, though it is happening anew in the area of women's studies. We were not merely exploring a literature and a history which had gone virtually unmentioned in our white educations (particularly true for those over thirty); we were not merely having to confront in talk with our students and in their writings, as well as the books we read, the bitter reality of Western racism: we also found ourselves reading almost any piece of Western literature through our students' eyes, imagining how this voice, these assumptions, would sound to us if we were they. "We learned from the students"—banal cliché, one that sounds pious and patronizing by now; yet the fact remains that our white liberal assumptions were shaken, our vision of both the city and the university changed, our relationship to language itself made both deeper and more painful.

Of course the students responded to black literature; I heard searching and acute discussions of Jones's poem "The Liar" or Wright's "The Man Who Lived Underground" from young men and women who were in college on sufferance in the eyes of the educational establishment; I've heard similar discussions of *Sons and Lovers* or the *Republic*. Writing this, I am conscious of how obvious it all seems and how unnecessary it now might appear to demonstrate by little anecdotes that ghetto students can handle sophisticated literature and ideas. But in 1968, 1969, we were still trying to prove this—we and our students felt that the burden of proof was on us. When the Black and Puerto Rican Student Community seized the South Campus of C.C.N.Y. in April 1969, and a team of students sat down with the president of the college and a team of faculty members to negotiate, one heard much about the faculty group's surprised respect for the students' articulateness, reasoning power, and skill in handling statistics—for the students were negotiating in exchange for withdrawal from South Campus an admissions policy which would go far beyond SEEK in its inclusiveness.

Those of us who had been involved earlier with ghetto students felt that we had known their strength all along: an impatient cutting through of the phony, a capacity for tenacious struggle with language and syntax and difficult ideas, a growing capacity for political analysis which helped counter the low expectations their teachers had always had of them and which many had had of themselves; and more, their knowledge of the naked facts of society, which academia has always, even in its public urban form, managed to veil in ivy or fantasy. Some were indeed chronologically older than the average college student; many, though eighteen or twenty years old, had had responsibility for themselves and their families for years. They came to college with a greater insight into the actual workings of the city and of American racial oppression than most of their teachers or their elite contemporaries. They had held dirty jobs, borne children, negotiated for Spanish-speaking parents with an English-speaking world of clinics, agencies, lawyers, and landlords, had their sixth senses nurtured in the streets, or had made the transition from southern sharehold or Puerto Rican countryside to Bedford-Stuyvesant or the *barrio* and knew the ways of two worlds. And they were becoming, each new wave of them, more lucidly conscious of the politics of their situation, the context within which their lives were being led.

It is tempting to romanticize, at the distance of midsummer 1972, what the experience of SEEK—and by extension, of all remedial freshman programs under Open Admissions—was (and is) for the students themselves. The Coleman Report and the Moynihan Report have left echoes and vibrations of stereotypical thinking which perhaps only a first-hand knowledge of the New York City schools can really silence. Teaching at City I came to know the intellectual poverty and human waste of the public school system through the marks it had left on students—and not on black and Puerto Rican students only, as the advent of Open Admissions was to show. For a plain look at the politics and practices of this system, I recommend Ellen Lurie's *How to Change the Schools*, a handbook for parent activists which enumerates the conditions she and other parents, black, Puerto Rican, and white, came to know intimately in their struggles to secure their children's right to learn and to be treated with dignity. The book is a photograph of the decay, racism, and abusiveness they confronted, written not as muckraking journalism but as a practical tool for others like themselves. I have read little else, including the most lyrically indignant prose of radical educators, that gives so precise and devastating a picture of the life that New York's children are expected to lead in the name of schooling. She writes of "bewildered angry teenagers, who have discovered that they are in classes for mentally retarded students, simply because they cannot speak English," of teachers and principals who "behaved as though every white middle-class child was gifted and was college material, and every black and Puerto Rican (and sometimes Irish and Italian) working-class child was slow, disadvantaged, and unable to learn anything but the most rudimentary facts." She notes that "81 elementary schools in the state (out of a total of 3,634) had more than 70 percent of their students below minimum competence, and 65 *of these were New York City public schools!*" Her findings and statistics make it clear that tracking begins at kindergarten (chiefly on the basis of skin color and language) and that nonwhite and working-class children are assumed to have a maximum potential which fits them only for the so-called general diploma, hence are not taught, as are their middle-class contemporaries, the math or languages or writing skills needed to pass college entrance examinations or even to do academic-diploma high-school work.[2] I have singled out these particular points for citation because they have to do directly with our students' self-expectations and the enforced limitation of their horizons years before they come to college. But much else has colored their educational past: the drug pushers at the school gates, the obsolete texts, the punitive conception of the teacher's role, the ugliness, filth, and decay of the buildings, the demoralization even of good teachers working under such conditions. (Add to this the use of tranquilizing drugs on children who are considered hyperactive or who present "behavior problems" at an early age.)

To come out of scenes like these schools and be offered "a chance" to compete as an equal in the world of academic credentials, the white-collar world, the world beyond the minimum wage or welfare, is less romantic for the student than for those who view the process from a distance. The student who leaves the campus at three or four o'clock after a day of classes, goes to work as a waitress, or clerk, or hash-slinger, or guard, comes home at ten or eleven o'clock to a crowded apartment with TV audible in every corner—what does it feel like to this student to be reading, say, Byron's "Don Juan" or Jane Austen for a class the next day? Our students may spend two or three hours in the subway going to and from college and jobs, longer if the subway system is more deplorable than usual. To read in the New York subway at rush hour is impossible; it is virtually impossible to think.

How does one compare this experience of college with that of the Columbia students down at 116th Street in their quadrangle of gray stone dormitories, marble steps, flowered borders, wide spaces of time and architecture in which to talk and think? Or that of Berkeley students with their eucalyptus grove and tree-lined streets of bookstores and cafés? The Princeton or Vassar students devoting four years to the life of the mind in Gothic serenity? Do "motivation" and "intellectual competency" mean the same for those students as for City College undergraduates on that overcrowded campus where in winter there is often no place to sit between classes, with two inadequate bookstores largely filled with required texts, two cafeterias and a snack bar that are overpriced, dreary, and unconducive to lingering, with the incessant pressure of time and money driving at them to rush, to get through, to amass the needed credits somehow, to drop out, to stay on with gritted teeth? Out of a graduating class at Swarthmore or Oberlin and one at

[2]Ellen Lurie, *How to Change the Schools* (New York: Random House, 1970). See pp. 31, 32, 40–48.

C.C.N.Y., which students have demonstrated their ability and commitment, and how do we assume we can measure such things?

Sometimes as I walk up 133rd Street, past the glass-strewn doorways of P.S. 161, the graffiti-sprayed walls of tenements, the uncollected garbage, through the iron gates of South Campus and up the
driveway to the prefab hut which houses the English department, I
think wryly of John Donne's pronouncement that "the University is a
Paradise; rivers of Knowledge are there; Arts and Sciences flow from
thence." I think that few of our students have this Athenian notion of
what college is going to be for them; their first introduction to it is a
many hours' wait in line at registration, which only reveals that the
courses they have been advised or wanted to take are filled, or conflict
in hours with a needed job; then more hours at the cramped, heavily
guarded bookstore; then perhaps, a semester in courses which they
never chose, or in which the pace and allusions of a lecturer are daunting or which may meet at opposite ends of an elongated campus stretching for six city blocks and spilling over into a former warehouse on
Broadway. Many have written of their first days at C.C.N.Y.: "I only
knew it was different from high school." What was different, perhaps,
was the green grass of early September with groups of young people in
dashikis and gelés, jeans and tie-dye, moving about with the unquench-
able animation of the first days of the fall semester; the encounter with
some teachers who seem to respect them as individuals; something at
any rate less bleak, less violent, less mean-spirited, than the halls of
Benjamin Franklin or Evander Childs or some other school with the
line painted down the center of the corridor and a penalty for taking
the short-cut across that line. In all that my students have written
about their high schools, I have found bitterness, resentment, satire,
black humor; never any word of nostalgia for the school, though sometimes a word of affection for a teacher "who really tried."

The point is that, as Mina Shaughnessy, the director of the Basic Writing Program at City, has written: "the first stage of Open Admissions
involves *openly admitting* that education has failed for too many students."[3] Professor Shaughnessy writes in her most recent report of the
increase in remedial courses of white, ethnic students (about two-
thirds of the Open Admissions freshmen who have below-80 high school
averages) and of the discernible fact, a revelation to many, that these
white students "have experienced the failure of the public schools in
different ways from the black and Puerto Rican students." Another
City College colleague, Leonard Kriegel, writes of this newest population: "Like most blue-collar children, they had lived within the confines

---

[3]Mina P. Shaughnessy, "Open Admissions—A Second Report," in *The City College Department of English Newsletter*, vol. II, no. 1., January 1972. *A. R., 1978:* See also Shaughnessy's *Errors and Expectations: A Guide for the Teacher of Basic Writing* (New York:
Oxford, 1977), a remarkable study in the methodology of teaching language.

of an educational system without ever having questioned that system. They were used to being stamped and categorized. Rating systems, grades, obligations to improve, these had beset them all their lives. . . . They had few expectations from the world-at-large. When they were depressed, they had no real idea of what was getting them down, and they would have dismissed as absurd the idea that they could make demands. They accepted the myths of America as those myths had been presented to them."[4]

Meeting some of the so-called ethnic students in class for the first time in September 1970, I began to realize that: there *are* still poor Jews in New York City; they teach English better to native speakers of Greek on the island of Cyprus than they do to native speakers of Spanish on the island of Manhattan; the Chinese student with acute English-language difficulties is stereotyped as "nonexpressive" and channeled into the physical sciences before anyone has a chance to find out whether he or she is a potential historian, political theorist, or psychologist; and (an intuition, more difficult to prove) white, ethnic working-class young women seem to have problems of self-reliance and of taking their lives seriously that young black women students as a group do not seem to share.

There is also a danger that, paradoxically or not, the white middle-class teacher may find it easier to identify with the strongly motivated, obviously oppressed, politically conscious black student than with the students of whom Kriegel has written. Perhaps a different set of prejudices exists: if you're white, why aren't you more hip, more achieving, why are you bored and alienated, why don't you *care* more? Again, one has to keep clearly in mind the real lessons of the schools—both public and parochial—which reward conformity, passivity, and correct answers and penalize, as Ellen Lurie says, the troublesome question "as trouble-making," the lively, independent, active child as "disruptive," curiosity as misbehavior. (Because of the reinforcement in passivity received all around them in society and at home, white women students seem particularly vulnerable to these judgments.) In many ways the damage is more insidious because the white students have as yet no real political analysis going for them; only the knowledge that they have not been as successful in school as white students are supposed to be.

Confronted with these individuals, this city, these life situations, these strengths, these damages, there are some harsh questions that have to be raised about the uses of literature. I think of myself as a teacher of

[4]"When Blue-Collar Students Go to College," in *Saturday Review*, July 22, 1972. The article is excerpted from the book *Working Through: A Teacher's Journal in the Urban University* (New York: Saturday Review Press, 1972). Kriegel is describing students at Long Island University of a decade ago; but much that he says is descriptive of students who are now entering colleges like C.C.N.Y. under Open Admissions.

language: that is, as someone for whom language has implied freedom, who is trying to aid others to free themselves through the written word, and above all through learning to write it for themselves. I cannot know for them what it is they need to free, or what words they need to write; I can only try with them to get an approximation of the story they want to tell. I have always assumed, and I do still assume, that people come into the freedom of language through reading, before writing; that the differences of tone, rhythm, vocabulary, intention, encountered over years of reading are, whatever else they may be, suggestive of many different possible modes of being. But my daily life as a teacher confronts me with young men and women who have had language and literature *used against* them, to keep them in their place, to mystify, to bully, to make them feel powerless. Courses in great books or speed-reading are not an answer when it is the meaning of literature itself that is in question. Sartre says: "the literary object has no other substance than the reader's subjectivity; Raskolnikov's waiting is my waiting which I lend him. . . . His hatred of the police magistrate who questions him is my hatred, which has been solicited and wheedled out of me by signs. . . . Thus, the writer appeals to the reader's freedom to collaborate in the production of his work."[5] But what if it is these very signs, or ones like them, that have been used to limit the reader's freedom or to convince the reader of his or her unworthiness to "collaborate in the production of the work"?

I have no illuminating answers to such questions. I am sure we must revise, and are revising, our notion of the "classic," which has come to be used as a term of unquestioning idolatry instead of in the meaning which Sartre gives it: a book written by someone who "did not have to decide with each work what the meaning and value of literature were, since its meaning and value were fixed by tradition."[6] And I know that the action from the other side, of becoming that person who puts signs on paper and invokes the collaboration of a reader, encounters a corresponding check: in order to write I have to believe that there is someone willing to collaborate subjectively, as opposed to a grading machine out to get me for mistakes in spelling and grammar. (Perhaps for this reason, many students first show the writing they are actually capable of in an uncorrected journal rather than in a "theme" written "for class.") The whole question of *trust* as a basis for the act of reading or writing has only opened up since we began trying to educate those who have every reason to mistrust literary culture. For young adults trying to write seriously for the first time in their lives, the question "Whom can I trust?" must be an underlying boundary to be crossed before real writing can occur. We who are part of literary culture come up

---

[5]Jean-Paul Sartre, *What Is Literature?* (New York: Harper Colophon Books, 1965), pp. 39–40.
[6]Ibid., p. 85.

against such a question only when we find ourselves writing on some frontier of self-determination, as when writers from an oppressed group *within* literary culture, such as black intellectuals, or, most recently, women, begin to describe and analyze themselves as they cease to identify with the dominant culture. Those who fall into this category ought to be able to draw on it in entering into the experience of the young adult for whom writing itself—as reading—has been part of the not-me rather than one of the natural activities of the self.

At this point the question of method legitimately arises: How to do it? How to develop a working situation in the classroom where trust becomes a reality, where the students are writing with belief in their own validity, and reading with belief that what they read has validity for them? The question is legitimate—How to do it?—but I am not sure that a description of strategies and exercises, readings, and writing topics can be, however successful they have proven for one teacher. When I read such material, I may find it stimulating and heartening as it indicates the varieties of concern and struggle going on in other classrooms, but I end by feeling it is useless to me. X is not myself and X's students are not my students, nor are my students of this fall the same as my students of last spring. A couple of years ago I decided to teach *Sons and Lovers*, because of my sense that the novel touched on facts of existence crucial to people in their late teens, and my belief that it dealt with certain aspects of family life, sexuality, work, anger, and jealousy which carried over to many cultures. Before the students began to read, I started talking about the time and place of the novel, the life of the mines, the process of industrialization and pollution visible in the slag heaps; and I gave the students (this was an almost all-black class) a few examples of the dialect they would encounter in the early chapters. Several students challenged the novel sight unseen: it had nothing to do with them, it was about English people in another era, why should they expect to find it meaningful to them, and so forth. I told them I had asked them to read it because I believed it was meaningful for them; if it was not, we could talk and write about why not and how not. The following week I reached the classroom door to find several students already there, energetically arguing about the Morels, who was to blame in the marriage, Mrs. Morel's snobbery, Morel's drinking and violence—taking sides, justifying, attacking. The class never began; it simply continued as other students arrived. Many had not yet read the novel, or had barely looked at it; these became curious and interested in the conversation and did go back and read it because they felt it must have something to have generated so much heat. That time, I felt some essential connections had been made, which carried us through several weeks of talking and writing about and out of *Sons and Lovers*, trying to define our relationships to its people and theirs to each other. A year or so later I enthusiastically started working with *Sons and Lovers* again, with a class of largely ethnic students—

Jewish, Greek, Chinese, Italian, German, with a few Puerto Ricans and blacks. No one initially challenged the novel, but no one was particularly interested—or, perhaps, as I told myself, it impinged too dangerously on materials that this group was not about to deal with, such as violence in the family, nascent sexual feelings, conflicting feelings about a parent. Was this really true? I don't know; it is easy to play sociologist and make generalizations. Perhaps, simply, a different chemistry was at work, in me and in the students. The point is that for the first class, or for many of them, I think a trust came to be established in the novel genre as a possible means of finding out more about themselves; for the second class, the novel was an assignment, to be done under duress, read superficially, its connections with themselves avoided wherever possible.

Finally, as to trust: I think that, simple as it may seem, it is worth saying: a fundamental belief in the students is more important than anything else. We all know of those studies in education where the teacher's previously induced expectations dramatically affect the learning that goes on during the semester. This fundamental belief is not a sentimental matter: it is a very demanding matter of realistically conceiving the student where he or she is, and at the same time never losing sight of where he or she *can* be. Conditions at a huge, urban, overcrowded, noisy, and pollution-soaked institution can become almost physically overwhelming at times, for the students and for the staff: sometimes apathy, accidia, anomie seem to stare from the faces in an overheated basement classroom, like the faces in a subway car, and I sympathize with the rush to get out the moment the bell rings. This, too, is our context—not merely the students' past and my past, but this present moment we share. I (and I don't think I am alone in this) become angry with myself for my ineffectualness, angry at the students for their apparent resistance or their acceptance of mediocrity, angriest at the political conditions which dictate that we have to try to repair and extend the fabric of language under conditions which tend to coarsen our apprehensions of everything. Often, however, this anger, if not driven in on ourselves, or converted to despair, can become an illuminating force: the terms of the struggle for equal opportunity are chalked on the blackboard: this is what the students have been up against all their lives.

I wrote at the beginning of this article that my early assumptions about teaching had changed. I think that what has held me at City is not the one or two students in a class whose eyes meet mine with a look of knowing they were born for this struggle with words and meanings; not the poet who has turned up more than once; though such encounters are a privilege in the classroom as anywhere. What has held me, and what I think holds many who teach basic writing, are the hidden veins of possibility running through students who don't know (and strongly doubt) that this is what they were born for, but who may find it out to their own amazement, students who, grim with self-depreciation and prophecies of their own failure or tight with a fear they cannot express, can be lured into sticking it out to some moment of breakthrough, when they discover that they have ideas that are valuable, even original, and can express those ideas on paper. What fascinates and gives hope in a time of slashed budgets, enlarging class size, and national depression is the possibility that many of these young men and women may be gaining the kind of critical perspective on their lives and the skill to bear witness that they have never before had in our country's history.

At the bedrock level of my thinking about this is the sense that language is power, and that, as Simone Weil says, those who suffer from injustice most are the least able to articulate their suffering; and that the silent majority, if released into language, would not be content with a perpetuation of the conditions which have betrayed them. But this notion hangs on a special conception of what it means to be released into language: not simply learning the jargon of an elite, fitting unexceptionably into the status quo, but learning that language can be used as a means of changing reality.[7] What interests me in teaching is less the emergence of the occasional genius than the overall finding of language by those who did not have it and by those who have been used and abused to the extent that they lacked it.

The question can be validly raised: Is the existing public (or private) educational system, school, or university the place where such a relationship to language can be developed? Aren't those structures already too determined, haven't they too great a stake in keeping things as they are? My response would be, yes, but this is where the *students* are. On the one hand, we need alternate education; on the other, we need to reach those students for whom unorthodox education simply means too much risk. In a disintegrating society, the orthodox educational system reflects disintegration. However, I believe it is more than simply reformist to try to use that system—while it still exists in all its flagrant deficiencies—to use it to provide essential tools and weapons for those who may live on into a new integration. Language is such a weapon, and what goes with language: reflection, criticism, renaming, creation. The fact that our language itself is tainted by the quality of our society means that in teaching we need to be acutely conscious of the kind of tool we want our students to have available, to understand how it has been used against them, and to do all we can to insure that language will not someday be used by them to keep others silent and powerless.

---

[7]Compare Paulo Freire: "Only beings who can reflect upon the fact that they are determined are capable of freeing themselves." *Cultural Action for Freedom*, Monograph Series No. 1 (Cambridge, Mass.: Harvard Educational Review and Center for the Study of Development and Social Change, 1970).

Remediation at a Crossroads

Mike Rose

In his life's work, Mike Rose has focused on the lives, works, and education of poor and working-class people. His book Lives on the Boundary: The Struggles and Achievements of America's Educationally Underprepared *(1989), has often been used as a text for students in basic writing courses, as well as in graduate classes for training teachers of basic writing.* Rose's other books include* Possible Lives: The Promise of Public Education in America *(1995),* The Mind at Work: Valuing the Intelligence of the American Worker *(2005), and* Why School: Reclaiming Education for All of Us *(2009). Rose is professor of education at UCLA, in the division of Social Research Methodology. He blogs at http://mikerosebooks .blogspot.com/.*

In the following essay on remediation and postsecondary education, Rose argues that "to make significant change, we'll need to understand all the interlocking pieces of the remediation puzzle, something we're not oriented to do, for our disciplinary and methodological training and public policy toolkit work against a comprehensive view of the problem." After this essay was published in Inside Higher Education, *Rose added a further comment that serves to foreground his major concerns:*

> *Remediation of some kind is not at all a new phenomenon in higher education. From the mid-nineteenth century on, the American college has had preparatory departments, catch-up courses, remedial classes, etc. to maintain enrollment and to bring entering students up to speed. In 1841 the president of Brown lamented that "students frequently enter college almost wholly unacquainted with English grammar." In 1898 U.C. Berkeley instituted its Subject A English proficiency examination and was soon designating 30–40% of entering students as not proficient in English—and offering Subject A (remedial) English to prepare them for English Comp. And so it goes.*
>
> *If you have social inequality but also have an open educational system, then you'll need some sort of remedial function to compensate for unequal pre-college educational opportunity. The numbers of students currently being held for one or more remedial courses may be higher than the norm right now, particularly at the community college level. But the reasons for that do not signal either cultural armageddon or an out-of-control remedial industry, but, rather, the fact that the nation is urging more and more people to go to college, that a lot of workers are seeking some small educational advantage in a bad economy, that inequality (by any measure, by liberal or conservative opinion) is growing in the United States, and so on.*

---

*See Susan Naomi Bernstein's "*BWe* 2007: Practice, Professional Development, and Favorite Books" and Shannon Carter's "Graduate Courses in Basic Writing Studies: Recommendations for Teacher Trainers." Both articles are available at *BWe: Basic Writing e-Journal* 6.1 (2007): n. pag. Web. 10 Feb. 2012. <http://faculty.tamu-commerce.edu /scarter/BWe2.htm#BWe_2007>.

> *Academic underpreparation is a signification educational problem*
> *and a civil and moral blight on our nation's best vision of itself. But it*
> *is a complex issue and can't be understood as a single thing with a*
> *single cause.*

The young woman in the hoodie behind me whispers "cried" to her friend, whose head is resting on her folded arms. "Wrote," head-resting woman whispers to herself as the teacher goes down a list of sentences on an overhead screen. "Repeated," "ate," "swam," they and the two other students in their row answer softly, in between light chatter.

I am visiting the most basic class of a community college remedial English sequence, and the teacher is reviewing verb tense by having her students convert a list of verbs from present tense to past. No one seems to be having any trouble with the exercise. The quartet behind me does it under-breath while catching up on their day-to-day. They might make errors in tense in their writing, but they won't be writing anything longer than a paragraph until they take the next course in the remedial sequence. Unfortunately, a number of students in such classes won't make it through the series to get to fuller writing assignments of the kind they have to do in their other classes.

This little episode reveals some of the problems with college remediation as it is typically executed. It is built on a set of assumptions about language and cognition that have long ago been proven inadequate, like the belief that focusing on isolated grammar exercises will help students write better prose. The work students are doing isn't connected to the writing they are required to do in their other courses, academic or vocational.

Going beyond the standard remedial playbook—if the instructor were so inclined—would be a big challenge, not only because she lacks training, but also because she has no time; like so many of her peers, she is teaching at two other colleges to try to make a living. The sequence of three, even four, lockstep non-credit courses established to help students build proficiency is based on the same flawed notion of language growth that limits the curriculum of the courses in the sequence. The textbook market, college requirements, and departmental structures all further reinforce the standard remedial model.

For quite a while some teachers of basic or remedial writing have been working against the grain, creating challenging curriculums that directly foster the kinds of writing skills and habits of mind needed for success in college. Or developing programs that link a writing course to a content course to provide a meaningful context for writing. Or placing those students who test low into credit-bearing freshman composition and providing additional support.

But now we are at a watershed moment when not only are individuals and programs trying to do something fresh with remediation, but national attention—public and philanthropic—is focused on the issue as well.

The big question is whether we will truly seize this moment and create for underprepared students a rich education in literacy and numeracy, or make some partial changes—more online instruction, shortened course sequences—but leave the remedial model intact. To make significant changes, we'll need to understand all the interlocking pieces of the remediation puzzle, something we're not oriented to do, for our disciplinary and methodological training and public policy toolkit work against a comprehensive view of the problem.

Most higher education policy research on remediation does not include historical analysis of the beliefs about cognition and instruction that inform curriculums. In fact, there's not a lot of close analysis of what goes on in classrooms, the cognitive give-and-take of instruction and what students make of it. And I'm not aware of any policy research crafted with the aid of people who actually teach those classes. Finally, we don't get much of a sense of the texture of students' lives, the terrible economic instability of some of them, but even less of a sense of the power of learning new things and, through that learning, redefining who you are. Profiles of students in remedial classes, when we do get them, are too often profiles of failure rather than of people with dynamic mental lives.

Most of us are trained and live our professional lives in disciplinary silos. Let me give you one example of how mind-boggling, and I think harmful, this intellectual isolation can become. In all the articles I've read on remediation in higher education journals, not one cites the 40 years' worth of work on basic writing produced by teachers and researchers of writing. There is even a *Journal of Basic Writing* that emerged out of the experiments with open admission at CUNY in the 1970s. Not a mention of any of it. Zip.

In addition to disciplinary silos, there are methodological silos. You won't find a randomized control trial in the 130-plus issues of the *Journal of Basic Writing*, and that for some is sufficient reason for many people to ignore them. But if we hope to really do something transformational with remediation, we'll need all the wisdom we can garner, from multiple disciplines and multiple methodologies, from multiple lines of sight.

Along with a wider scope of inquiry we will need a bountiful philosophy of education—and the leadership to enact it. At the same time that there is a push to get more low-income people into postsecondary education, cash-strapped states are cutting education budgets, leading colleges to limit enrollments and cut classes and student services.

In my state of California (and I'm sure in other states as well) some policy makers are wondering—not fully in public—if we can no longer afford to educate everybody, if we should ration our resources, directing them toward those who are already better prepared for college.

We have here the makings in education of a distinction the historian Michael Katz notes in the discourse on poverty, a distinction between those deserving and undeserving of assistance. In the midst of a powerful anti-government, anti-welfare-state climate, will there be the political courage to stand against the rationing of educational opportunity?

The democratic philosophy I envision helps us to see in basic skills instruction the rich possibility for developing literacy and numeracy and for realizing the promise of a second-chance society. Such a philosophy affirms the ability of the common person and guides instruction that goes beyond the acquisition of fundamental skills and routine toward an understanding of their meaning and application, the principles underlying them, and the broader habits of mind that incorporate them. In such instruction, error becomes an intellectual entry point.

If a young adult is having trouble with fractions, for example, how did his misunderstandings and flawed procedures develop? What formal or informal mathematical knowledge does he have that can be tapped? How does one access that cognitive history and lead the student to analyze and remedy it?

The de facto philosophy of education we do have is a strictly economic one. This is dangerous, for without a civic and moral core it could easily lead to a snazzy 21st-century version of an old and shameful pattern in American education: working-class people get a functional, skills-and-drills education geared toward lower-level work. To be sure, the people who are the focus of current college initiatives are going to school to improve their economic prospects. As one woman put it so well: "It's a terrible thing to not have any money."

But people also go to college to feel their minds working, to remedy a poor education, to redefine who they are. You won't hear any of this in the national talk about postsecondary access and success. For all the hope and opportunity they represent, our initiatives lack the kind of creativity and heartbeat that transform institutions and foster the unrealized ability of a full sweep of our citizenry.

Basic Writing:
Students' Perspectives

Raw Material

Jane Maher

In this selection, Jane Maher provides an update of her experiences teaching basic writing at Bedford Hills Correctional Facility, a women's maximum-security prison.* Maher's writing clearly evokes the material realities of the prison and emphasizes the necessity of a college education in the lives of the inmates. When state and federal support for higher education for prisoners ended in the mid-1990s, the women's morale greatly deteriorated and prospects for containing recidivism declined. Private funds, while remaining precarious, were raised to reinstate the college program and Maher was subsequently invited to teach the basic writing course.

It is November1998, and I have arranged for James McBride, author of *The Color of Water*, to visit the college composition course I am teaching at the Bedford Hills Correctional Facility for Women in Westchester, NY. McBride's book was already on best-seller lists before he and his mother appeared on Oprah, and he has already begun work on another project, but still he agrees to come. I am delighted. He lives in

---

*Readers may be familiar with Maher's article "'You Probably Don't Even Know I Exist': Notes from a Prison College Program," which appeared in the previous edition of *Teaching Developmental Writing*, and featured a full-length essay by Kecia Pittman, one of Maher's students at Bedford Hills. The earlier version is from *Journal of Basic Writing* 23.1 (2004). Print.

Westchester, so although the class meets in the evening, it will not be too much of an inconvenience for him, and he'll be home by 9:30.

The students have already read several books, all of which address in some way the theme of motherhood, but McBride's book is hands down their favorite. Most of them have come from poor homes and have young children, so they relate to the struggles Ruth McBride endured raising twelve children. This is the first course I have taught in a prison, so I don't know the procedure to bring in a guest speaker. When I ask the academic director of the program, she is somewhat helpful, but it is her first semester as well.

College programs had been a booming business in the United States for many years until both federal and state governments decided that prisoners should no longer be eligible for Pell and TAP grants, reasoning that they do not deserve to attend college using public funding. The program that had existed at Bedford Hills, sponsored by Mercy College, had closed down by the end of 1996. A college program sponsored by Marymount Manhattan College has been reinstated only because Bedford's superintendent, scores of inmates,[1] community volunteers, and several female presidents of colleges in the area worked together to bring college back, using donations of money, time, and equipment.

I am one of the first teachers in the "new" college program; in addition I help administer the program. I teach full time at Nassau Community College, and I have already gotten one speeding ticket trying to navigate from my job on Long Island to my home in Greenwich, CT, to the prison. Inviting a guest speaker has only complicated an already difficult schedule, yet I feel myself getting drawn more deeply into the college program.

Although I had never been in a prison before I started teaching, I feel very comfortable "inside." Many of the women had their college careers interrupted when Mercy's program closed down; they are so grateful college courses are again available to them that they treat us volunteers as if we are heroes. They send me letters thanking me for teaching them; they even write little notes of gratitude at the bottom of their essays. When I tell one of the older students to call me Jane, she looks at me with indignation and says: "I've been waiting all my life to attend college. If you don't mind, I'm going to call you Professor Maher."

The facility is located in a beautiful area of Westchester County (surrounded by huge estates), but the prison itself is ugly. Despite the fact that the women are always scraping and painting and cleaning and repairing as part of their work assignments, nothing can make up for the fact that it is an old and decaying facility. Chainlink fences surrounding the compound are topped with thick rolls of concertina wire, and feral cats roam the perimeter. Sometimes when I arrive to teach an

---

[1] All inmates' names in this memoir have been removed or changed to protect their privacy.

evening class, I see huge buses pulling up, carrying inmates. I soon grow accustomed to the appearance of the prison, even to the buses, but I never adjust to the heat in the summer; it is so intense that the women's perspiration turns their state-issued uniforms a darker shade of green.

Soon after I confirm a date with James McBride, the academic director suggests that we contact the *New York Times* and ask them to cover McBride's visit, reasoning that it will garner support for the program. I think it's a good idea, not altogether for altruistic reasons: I like the possibility of having my name, even my photograph, in the *Times.* The director tells me I must get permission from Elaine Lord, the superintendent, before I can contact the media, so I make an appointment. Knowing she is overworked, I resolve to be brief, but in my mind, superintendents don't read; therefore, I bring a copy of the book so at least she'll know who James McBride is.

She already knows, has read the book, along with thousands of others, and I begin to realize she has met volunteers like me before and has decided to be nice to them. She hears me out, asks if I've contacted anyone yet, and looks relieved when I say no. We talk for a while, and she explains that the "new" program is tenuous at best, that she had to struggle to get her superiors to agree to bring a college program back. Most politicians had voted for the elimination of funding even though prisoners received only .06 percent of the more than $6 billion in Pell grants. I scoff at their narrow mindedness. She swivels her chair around for a moment, and then turns back to face me, holding a handwritten letter.

She explains that she received the letter a few days after an article about the reinstated college program had appeared in an Upstate New York newspaper. It was from the mother of an eighteen-year-old girl who had been murdered in 1995, two days before she was scheduled to leave home to attend college. The woman convicted of the girl's murder is serving a twenty-five-year-to-life sentence at Bedford Hills, and the mother was writing to ask if her daughter's murderer is participating in the college program.

"Is she?" I ask, thinking of my two daughters, already graduated from college, on their own, in good relationships, with good careers.

"You don't need to know," the superintendent responds. "You don't need to know why any of the women are here. Just do a good job teaching them so when they are released, they stand a better chance of not coming back." I apologize for taking her time. She tells me it is good to meet me, that she appreciates what I am doing, and not to worry, I'll learn as I go.

I've already been advised by several people, some of whom work for the Department of Correctional Services and some of whom are "civilians" (the term used for anyone who is not a DOCS employee or an inmate), not to ask the women why they are in prison. "It's just not polite," a long-time volunteer in the Children's Center explains. I follow this advice, but it has little to do with manners. I have always hated when other teachers warn me about students; there is something inherently unfair in this practice. The way I figure it, if I don't want to know that the students I teach on the outside are absent a lot or don't do their homework or fall asleep in class or have an attitude, I certainly don't want to know what the students in the college program did to warrant being sent to the only maximum-security prison for women in New York State.

I have, however, developed a truly warped attitude about the length of the women's sentences. The expense of reinstating the college program (I beg friends and colleagues for donations, as do all of the other volunteers), and the labor involved in getting the women enrolled in the college program is daunting: testing, advisement, registration, applications, proof of GED or high school diploma. I actually get angry when a woman is transferred out to a medium-security facility soon after her paperwork has been completed and she is officially admitted to the college program. As a result, I added to our student questionnaire a space where the women can fill in the number of years they will be at Bedford. My colleague just shakes her head when she hears me whispering "hooray" as I review the questionnaires and notice sentences of at least ten years.

Although a long sentence (fifteen years or more) usually means "there's a body" in corrections jargon, I am beginning to realize that in order for a student to be able to earn even an associate's degree, she needs at least seven years at Bedford—and that's only if she already has a high school diploma or a GED when she comes into the prison, and only if she does not have to take non-credit courses. Given the women's mandatory work and program schedules, and given the space limitations in the prison (we use the GED classrooms after those classes end for the day), the women can only take classes in the evening, and we have already realized that even our best students cannot handle more than six or nine credits under these conditions.

In the past, if a woman was transferred out of Bedford into a medium- or minimum-security facility, she could continue her college education, but now that more than 350 college programs in prisons have shut down across the United States, we have come to be known as the only show in town. One of our teachers heard that a student who had earned thirty credits was going to be transferred to an Upstate facility to complete her sentence, but she was so desperate to continue college that she was considering committing another crime in prison so she would be kept at Bedford.

The James McBride visit is truly wonderful. He tells me on our way out of the prison that my students asked better questions than any he's been asked on college campuses. He talks in particular about the thoughtful discussion started by one of the students who asked if his book would have been such a success if his mother had been a black woman. I tell him that almost 80 percent of the women at Bedford are African American and are from some of the worst neighborhoods—and have attended some of the worst schools—in New York City.

Although I never talk to the women about their crimes, I know a lot of them involve drugs—buying, using, selling; their sentences are long enough for them to wind up in a max because of the Rockefeller Drug Laws. And from my own experience raising two daughters in a white, affluent suburb of Connecticut, I know that if my or my neighbors' kids had been arrested on some of the same charges, they wouldn't have spent one day, maybe not even one hour, in jail.

I am proud of my students, not only on this special evening, but at most other times as well—they are often more attentive and mature than students I have on the outside. They benefited from and enjoyed McBride's visit; when the officer came to the classroom door to announce that it was time for the women to return to their units, they actually groaned. I reminded myself at that moment that the extra work and effort to bring a guest speaker into the prison was worth it, and that I should try to do it more often. On the long dark drive home, however, I realize why it is so important for me not to know what my students did to wind up in prison: I cannot help but wonder if one of the students who so impressed James McBride had murdered that woman's daughter.

The notes from the students keep coming, and I begin to save them— first because many of them are so flattering. Later, when I no longer need the flattery, I save the ones that will help me remember, because from the very beginning I know someday I will write about teaching in the prison. I now have three large boxes of these notes, and most of them still break my heart when I reread them: They are either full of hope or full of despair—there is rarely an in-between in prison, and there is far more despair than hope.

> Dear College staff,
> The Reason of this letter is because of my interest in going to college. How do I sign up for classes, When do classes start & How/what do I go about getting into School, Very soon—A.S.A.P. Thank You!

> Dear Jane,
> I will pass GED exam this time. Your extra help. I just read the book you loan me when I was puerto rican I remember when I in puerto Rican and I was there with my father. I want to school down there. I miss it a little but not that much. I need some more math worksheets.

> Dear Dr. Maher,
> Enclosed please find the proof of Melissa's high school graduation. I'm glad she wants to attend college. Thanks for taking the trouble to call me at work and thanks for taking care of my rather foolish child.

Happy Mother's Day Ms. Maher
Hoping you enjoy this poem.

Capuccino and Crosaint
Mother of mine
Wish I could take you out to dine
To a fancy restaurant
For cappuccino and crosiant
Treat you to your favorite meal
And to music that heal
Mother I'll try to make your
Day happy hour after hour.

Dear Jane,
    Now that I am released I know I am not supposed to write to you unless it is about academic matters, but I miss you and the other teachers, and especially the women. And I just wanted to say thank you. I honestly appreciate you as a person. I went to Macy's and bought a nice dress. I already have a nice pair of shoes. I went to fill out some applications for jobs. I've been doing that for weeks. I went to Victoria's Secret and four other stores. They never call me back and I'm not sure how much longer I'll be able to afford my cell phone. I love you,

When I first started teaching at Bedford Hills, I had never heard the term "cutting." In an e-mail I sent to a friend during my second semester at the prison, I told her I had been at the prison until 9:00 p.m. that evening testing thirty-five new students. "As I sat there watching them struggle with their entrance exams, I couldn't help but notice their scars," I wrote — rather dramatically it seems to me now. One of the women had a two-inch scar on her cheek; the skin was discolored and shiny; it seemed to be pulled tight, as if it still hurt. Another had a long pinkish scar down the length of her arm, with Frankenstein-like scars from the stitches running parallel on both sides.

"Those are the scars you can see," my friend, a social worker, e-mailed back the next day. "They usually cut where the incisions can't be seen." I was not entirely sure what she was talking about, but one of my students had referred to cutting in a note she had written to me — explaining that she had been under observation in the satellite unit for "cutting" and was filing a complaint because she believed she had been overmedicated — and thus unable to attend class.

I began to feel like Queen Elizabeth who responded, upon learning that Diana had an eating disorder, that it was a waste of perfectly good food. I did not remain ignorant for long. A facility counselor whom I had come to trust called to say we could not permit the professors in the college program to show "whatever movie they felt like." The movie in question, *The Sweet Hereafter*, portrays an incestuous relationship between a father and his daughter, and the counselor explained that three of the women who viewed it had "cut up" over the next four days.

This was not the first time the issue had been raised. I had intuitively refrained from asking the women to write about personal issues, and the first time I taught a basic writing course at the prison, I chose the theme of education. I had the women write about some of their own educational experiences, or the experiences of their children, explaining that I would copy and distribute what they wrote to form a "text" from which we could observe, analyze, interpret. I asked the students to recall and describe a typical school experience and reflect on it—figuring that such an assignment was relatively safe. Sheila wrote the following passage:

> Even though I wasn't accepted as popular by the other students, I stayed at school and joined up in all the extracurricular activities. Then I would not get home until 6 p.m. when my aunt got home. Then my uncle couldn't bring me into his bedroom and rape me and tell me that he would kill my puppy if I told.

That night, after Sheila returned to her unit, she went on such a rampage that she was "locked," kept in her cell until a disciplinary hearing could be held. Her counselor suspected that something had triggered the behavior, and she called me to ask what had happened in class the night before. I brought Sheila's essay to the counselor, and she later told me that when she showed it to Sheila, Sheila had absolutely no recollection of writing it.

I started to become afraid for the women, afraid for the program, afraid that I had already said or done the wrong thing in my classes and not even known it. All of us felt this way, so the teachers and tutors decided that we would use our next faculty development meeting to talk about the need to balance a strong academic curriculum with the possibility of unintended consequences. I did some research on women in prison (something I was doing more and more lately) and ordered two books through interlibrary loan: *Self-Injurious Behaviors* and *Women Living with Self-Injury*—the Greenwich librarian smiled perkily as she reviewed my request. *Women Living with Self-Injury* arrived a week before the meeting, and, as I read it, the logic of the counselor's concern became obvious to me almost immediately: Chapter Two, "From Childhood Abuse to Adult Behavior," is a primer on the lasting effects of childhood sexual abuse. The statistics are staggering—65 percent of women in prison have been abused before the age of twelve; the abuse begins in many cases between the ages of two and seven; the abuser often convinces the child that she was "asking for it"; it is not uncommon for women who have been abused to engage in vaginal cutting; some women cut in response to seemingly minor stresses. The women also engage in picking at the wound. I have seen the women doing this, and as I read, I tried to convince myself that *I didn't* say to them something I would intuitively say to one of my daughters or one of my students on the outside: "Stop doing that, you'll get a scar."

I am over my head now; there is no doubt about it, and for the first time, I wish I had never started teaching at the prison. I had begun to take on more responsibility, had made successful presentations and had three articles published about the reinstated program. I was beginning to think I was really something. But suddenly everything I had said and written seemed sentimental, *was* sentimental. At about the same time, I was also beginning to come to terms with the fact that a lot of students were not succeeding—the drop-out rate was higher than on the outside, and it couldn't be explained away entirely by the fact that the women were transferred or released or had medical emergencies. Self-injury, I was coming to learn through my reading and my conversations, is only one effect of trauma. Women who have been abused think of themselves as worthless; they cannot *endure* success.

I turn to Karen, an inmate who works in our program as a "peer tutor." (We try to avoid using the word inmate as much as possible in the college program, but this is a civilian hangup—the women are used to it.) I know that Karen has a history of mental illness (her scars are visible), but she has also been invaluable in helping me understand the workings of the prison. I ask her if she would write something about the issue of cutting for me to read aloud at the faculty meeting, which will be held at a nearby college.

Karen agrees immediately, as she always does. She is one of about eight inmates who are on our facility-approved "payroll"; they earn about twenty cents an hour. All inmates must work a certain number of hours per week in some capacity in the prison, in addition to participating in mandated programs, unless they have a medical exemption. I have come to realize that the concept of inmates having nothing but "time" on their hands is ludicrous. Almost all of the inmates' "modules" are filled, leaving them little time to do the things that everyone, whether in prison or not, needs to do: laundry, calling or writing home, personal hygiene. I conduct the same kind of time management workshops in the prison as I do at Nassau Community College, but given that every activity is scheduled for a specific time—from showering to eating to exercise to lights out, it is truly difficult for the inmates to find time to do their homework.

Working in the college program is quickly becoming a coveted job among the inmates because, as Karen has told me hundreds of times, when she is working in the college learning center, surrounded by books and computers (without Internet access), tutors and students, teachers and (two overworked) administrators, she can almost forget she is in a prison.

I am unable to get to the prison the day before the faculty meeting, so I ask my colleague to bring Karen's presentation where I will read it to the other teachers. She hands me a sealed envelope, and I do not think about it until we reach that item on our agenda, one that my colleague has diplomatically described as "Conditions that may impede our students' performance and success." As the teachers begin to talk about the emotional issues that seem to be affecting their students, I open the envelope and glance at what Karen has sent me. It seems to be a *compacted* version of her handwriting: Every inch of six lined pages is covered; she had used a heavy pencil; there is very little space between the words. The pages are still connected by the thin hardened strip of glue that holds the pad together. I wonder what I am supposed to do with these pages, but then I notice that Karen has attached two double-spaced typewritten pages. She has also attached Post-it notes telling me which sections to read, and I read them:

> When I looked at my hand I saw the instrument that would set me free from emotional suffering. I heard voices chanting commands into the right side of my brain. The message was the same. If I obey their commands, I would find release from guilt and release from my emotional suffering. I stared at the razor and tried to engage it in conversation, but it was not interested in cheap talk.
>
> The voices started to get louder, and they started to flash blazing orbs in front of my eyes. The orbs turned into visages of suffering people I did not know. I felt that I was the cause of their suffering. What followed was a type of silence that only the mentally disorganized can recognize. I felt like I was in a vacuum. The only thing that existed was my intense guilt and my desire to get rid of that guilt. I know that the only way to stop the flow of guilt was to cut myself.
>
> I raised my razor high, and slowly dragged the tip of the razor across my arm. My guilt and emotional suffering started to drip to the floor. I sat back and watched my pain escape. It was like an orgasm; so complete. I knew who I was and knew what I had done. I began to feel connected.
>
> Self-mutilation is an art form: Only the brave and crazy do it. I am brave and I am crazy. Toward the end of practicing self-mutilation, I discovered blood art. I would cut myself and then dab my blood onto a piece of paper. Next, I started using a pin and drawing with my blood. Some of my drawings looked like ideograms, and that gave me an idea. I started to practice the alphabet, and then I started writing short sentences. I still have the letter scars. I realized that I had a great deal to say, and that I did not have enough blood to write with, so instead of blood writing, I decided to write about cutting myself. I found that it was easier to pour my thoughts onto paper than to put my blood onto paper. So, instead of carving with a razor I started writing with a pencil.
>
> This happened a long time ago. I do not practice self-mutilation anymore, but the urge to cut myself is still there, still in the back of my mind. But instead of cutting, I write. On paper. Long sentences. I leave the scars of the alphabet behind.

I am following three strands of thought almost simultaneously: How will the tutors and teachers react to what I just read? Will this lead to repercussions with the prison administration given that I had not gotten written permission from Karen to use it? Karen already knows she is a talented writer, but how can I encourage her to continue to write while avoiding the same sort of issues that such writing had caused Sheila? Or was it already too late? Would I find out when I next went to the prison that Karen had been admitted to the satellite unit for observation?

The discussion that ensues is almost identical to the kind teachers have all the time: Should we encourage students to write autobiographically as a first step in helping them learn and practice the process of writing? Or must we concentrate on the kind of academic writing students need to survive/succeed in college—assign a grade to the product, because the way the essay came to be created is not a concern of ours at this stage of the students' education?

As usual, I have a lot to say. But I actually stop myself: "Be quiet, Jane. These are good and smart and experienced people who know what they are talking about. You don't have all the answers. In fact, you have already unwittingly created a problem for Sheila and you may have caused one for Karen as well. Her writing has not shocked or frightened the teachers. It has done exactly what it was supposed to do—direct the conversation toward a pedagogical issue. Sit quietly, read Karen's handwritten pages."

They are hard to read, and some of the passages do, in fact, scare me: references to her crime, painful memories of her childhood, descriptions of a distant and cruel mother, two poems that I cannot understand on first reading. But by the end of the sixth page, I smile to myself as I see the note Karen has scribbled to me. "Dear Jane, I did what you tell your writing students to do. I just kept writing until I figured out what I wanted to say."

Karen and I are both okay, for now.

If the officers are not too busy, they make small talk with me as I'm being processed in the visitors' area (scanned with a metal detector and having the contents of my pockets, purse, and book bags searched), or simply as I wait for a count to clear. There are "counts" in all New York State prisons—they occur five times a day, and during these counts every inmate is required to be in a cell or on a unit. If I arrive during a count, I must wait in the visitors' area until it is complete. On one of these occasions, I am reading an essay written by one of my students, and the officer on duty, one of my favorites because of his patience and sense of humor, looks over my shoulder.

"How is Valerie doing?" he asks in a voice so gentle that if I didn't know better, I would think he was a father asking about his daughter. I am a little surprised, and I ask the officer how he knows her.

"I worked on her unit for a couple of years," he replies. "She's got it rough. She eats state and wears state." He goes on to tell me that she struggled academically but was one of the hardest workers he had ever seen. He told me there had been a celebration on her unit when she finally passed the GED exams on her third try.

She was struggling in my class as well (the pre-college, non-credit writing course), but she was still working hard and I was pretty sure she would make it. Both of us heard the crackly announcement coming from the radio on his belt saying the count had cleared, so there was no time to continue the conversation. He had other volunteers to process, and I wanted to get to the school building before my class began.

When I went out that evening, the same officer was on duty, and I asked him what he had meant about eating and wearing state. He explained that many of the inmates receive help from home: food items, money deposited in their commissary accounts, articles of clothing. (There are truly mind-boggling rules and regulations concerning these packages and gifts: weights, amounts, colors, fabric, hermetic seals; every package is searched thoroughly before the women can pick them up from the package room.) He then explained that some of the women either have families who are too poor to send anything or they just don't have family—they are either dead or they have chosen not to keep in touch. "Valerie's doing her time alone," he said. "All she's got is what the state issues her."

I think back over all of my interactions with Valerie. She has never asked me to bring her anything or to do anything for her (I would have refused—petrified that I'd be permanently banned from entering the prison if I break this most basic rule). Although I don't know exactly how old Valerie is, she looks far older than most of the other women in the college program. I do know how long she has been in prison: Every inmate has her last name, her first initial, and her DIN (Department Identification Number) printed on a small white cloth label pressed onto the chest pocket of her state-issued green uniform. The DIN begins with the year the inmate arrived at the prison—Val's number begins with 88. I wonder if she had received packages at first; but then, as the years passed, they tapered off as one after another relative died or as she faded from their consciousness. Or perhaps there were no packages from the start; maybe her crime was so reprehensible that her family resolved to have nothing to do with her.

I get my answer about a month later when an argument breaks out in the learning center. I know the women fight from time to time, and I have heard of women being injured and/or receiving severe punishments for these fights, but such incidents are truly rare in the college program. It's no different than on the outside—the inmates in the college program tend to be more mature, more able to control their impulses and emotions.

I have no idea why the argument started, but at the sound of screaming, I came out of the small alcove where the staff desks are located and into the open area where the women do their work. Valerie and another inmate named Josie are positioned across from each other with a table between them. I hear snatches of insults being screamed: "You grew up in a piss-stained hallway"; name calling: "whore," "slut," "fucking bitch"; followed by accusations about something that had been stolen or was missing, but the words are so garbled and loud that I cannot understand them. Everyone is quiet, looking at the two women. I know from my training that I am supposed to go directly into the hall to summon the officer who is stationed less than ten yards away, and as the screaming continues, I rush past Valerie and Josie, both of whom are oblivious to my presence. As I reach the door, Valerie screams at Josie: "Baby killer." Josie, without missing a beat, retorts: "Yeah, well at least I didn't kill my own parents."

The officer has already spotted me. He is in the learning center immediately, and the instant he arrives, the women stop screaming. Everyone tries to pretend that nothing has happened. I know the rules: I am supposed to tell the officer exactly what transpired, and then let him take over. I am a civilian, a volunteer; in matters like these, I have absolutely no say. He asks me what is the matter and I say that two of the women were arguing, but it was nothing serious. I do not name names. I don't tell him what they were arguing about because I truly have no idea, and I do not tell him what they said because I don't want to repeat it. I almost tell him that I'm sorry I attracted his attention, but I stop myself.

The officer, a young, gentle, wise man who has often given me good advice, talks to me softly in the entrance to the learning center. "Look," he says, "if I write these inmates up, there will be a hearing. They'll be confined. They will lose their college privileges." I almost laugh out loud as I realize that the officer is trying to convince *me* that he shouldn't file a misbehavior report. "No one is hurt, right? There was nothing physical, right?" he asks. "The holidays are coming; tempers flare at this time." I agree and he seems genuinely relieved.

It is almost time for the women to return to their units, so I ask them to turn off the computers and put the library books away. I remind them which tutors will be available that evening and the next afternoon. I think I am doing a good job pretending everything is okay. Valerie and Josie have moved farther away from each other; the other women are keeping an eye on them, and the officer is standing inside the door. As the students file out of the learning center, no one looks at me. Ordinarily, they make small talk, remind me to bring in a book or an article, tell me to drive home safely, thank me for being there. We are all off balance. The women know how fragile the college program is, and if anyone wanted to close it down, this fight could be reason enough.

But there is something else: I have already noticed the way the inmates try to insulate the civilians, to keep them from knowing too much. The women are often overly polite; they pay close attention to the stories the civilians tell, and they pretend to be interested even when the stories are truly deadening. On one occasion when I brought in a guest lecturer who droned on for almost an hour, the women managed to rouse themselves enough to give him a hearty round of applause. I realize that the women are, quite literally, trying to keep up appearances, and at least in terms of the college program, they have succeeded. Almost every volunteer had said to me at one time or another that the women are so normal, friendly, comely, intelligent—in short, like them, or like their children, or like their students on the outside, or like their neighbors' kids. As I lock up the learning center, I realize why the women avoided making eye contact with me as they were leaving—I had seen what they had been trying to hide. Our children, our students, our neighbors' kids do not murder their own offspring and parents.

The next day four of the inmate staff members come into the office as soon as I arrive and say they want to talk to me. It is almost as if they know what I had been thinking. They thank me for handling the situation well. They know my behavior, perhaps even more than that of Valerie and Josie, could have jeopardized the program. Later that day, Sharon, one of the most serious students, comes into the office and asks if we can speak in private. "I heard what happened yesterday," she says," and I want you to know what it is like being in prison for committing a terrible crime. There is the cruelty and humiliation, of course. You saw that yesterday. But that's not the hardest part. All day long, I am with inmates and staff, going to programs, eating, working, attending my college classes. I can almost pretend that everything is okay. But every night, when it is quiet and dark, I am alone in my cell with my victim."

My friendship with the superintendent and the officers continues to deepen. I like their company—perhaps it is because of my own background. Although I am a college professor living in Greenwich, CT, I was born and raised in Brooklyn, NY, in a neighborhood and from a family not much different from those of a lot of the officers. My father was a firefighter and my mother worked as a school crossing guard. Both of my parents were Italian Americans, and my aunts and uncles used to ask them if maybe they took the wrong kid home from the hospital given that I liked to read so much. By the time I was seven, they had nicknamed me Einstein, and not in a flattering way. My brother-in-law is a retired New York City police officer; my sister worked in the Manhattan district attorney's office for more than twenty years.

It was the superintendent who told me, very early on, that these men and women were to be called officers, not guards. They are not "guarding" anything, she says every time she hears the word; "they are entrusted with the care and well-being of 800 inmates, and it is one of the most difficult and complex jobs in the world, one for which they get paid far less than they should." Most of the officers respect her as much as she respects them.

One of the officers, Joe, has read, at my recommendation, *Newjack: Guarding Sing Sing* by Ted Conover. I love the book. Conover captured the difficulties and ironies that exist in prison with an accuracy that is extraordinary. And I had especially admired the fact that when Conover couldn't get permission to go into Sing Sing as a journalist, he went through officer training and then spent a year as an officer there. Joe doesn't like the book very much, but he can't really say why. I begin to realize he feels a deep resentment of Conover.

Joe protests so much about Conover's book that I tell him he should write his own book, starting with an essay. After all, Conover has described a male facility, and if there is anything that needs to be written, it's an officer's firsthand account of the differences between a male and female facility. Before coming to Bedford, Joe had worked in some of the toughest male prisons in New York, and the women say he is one of the fairest officers they've ever met. I tell Joe I will be his editor, and he replies, only half jokingly, "Oh, so you're willing to help the officers. I thought you only helped the inmates."

Joe is verbalizing what a lot of the officers feel. Often, as I would wait in the visitors' area, officers would ask me if I could get them scholarship applications so that their children could attend college. Or they would ask why we didn't offer college classes for the officers as well as the inmates. One evening in class, one of the women bragged that she had "beaten a ticket" because the officer had done such a poor job writing it up—whatever he was charging her with was described so incoherently that the inmate had talked her way out of it "in five minutes." At the time, I may have sided with the inmate, but as I got to know the officers better, I began to realize they were all too often doing this job because they had no other choice.

At the end of a year, Ted Conover left Sing Sing and wrote his book. These officers count the years till they can retire, and because of the location of Bedford Hills, in one of the most affluent and expensive communities not only in New York but in the nation, they cannot even afford to rent an apartment. There is a dilapidated housing unit for the officers provided by the state, located behind the prison. The rooms are small, and they are cold in the winter and hot in the summer. The common kitchen area is decrepit. To add insult to injury, there are not enough rooms for all of the officers, and even these inadequate accommodations are not cheap.

Most of the officers who live there are "newjacks," forced to work in Westchester because the more senior officers have won their bids for positions in the Upstate prisons. The officers often compare their living conditions with that of the inmates, with the inmates having "more hot water and three squares." Some officers actually live out of their cars and work double and triple shifts so they can make the ten-hour drive home and be with their families for a few days before having to return to work.

Most of the professors in the program make a better living than the officers, but some of the other volunteers, particularly those who come

from the immediate area, are truly wealthy. I have been in the entrance
when some of them arrive. They are mostly women, and they are kind-
hearted, sincere, effective, and devoted to the prisoners' well-being.
They certainly do not flaunt their wealth, but when they remove their
coats and jackets to be searched, I can see the designer labels. Just
one of those jackets or coats costs far more than the officers earn in a
month, including overtime.

Joe does write a draft for me to read. It is typed in single space and
it gets off to a slow start. I realize he is doing the same thing most inexperienced writers do, trying to impress at the expense of clarity: "There
is no amount of training," Joe wrote in his opening paragraph, "that
could prepare anyone to walk into a female correctional facility and
function as a professional law enforcement agent should. Your job,
should you choose to accept it, is to apply good judgment, without consideration of sex or the promise thereof, when dealing with your clien-
tele group. To operate in good faith, without looking at the female in
front of you as a woman, when you decide whatever it is you have to
decide, when it concerns the daily duties you are charged with, in the
normal operations of the facility on any given day."

As I read, I realize that there's a book here, or at least an essay. But
what will it take to get it into readable form? How much time is Joe
willing to give it? How much time am I willing to give it? Joe had said
to me when he handed me his draft that he was "a macho man" and
proud of it. But as I read, I begin to think that if men are from Mars
and women are from Venus, then Joe is operating from an as-of-yet un-
discovered galactic collision of planetary assumptions about gender:
"In the middle of the chaos is me. The man. It isn't always a good thing
to be a man in a female correctional facility. They look at you as the
cause of their pain. They are women. I am expected to sort out the non-
sense and do the right thing. Deal with the issues and resolve the problems. Discipline them as I deem necessary and use compassion as my
guide. What a thing to ask a man. Do what is reasonable to a woman.
I'm the man in their lives. Yes, they love me. They are women."

I had asked some of the women about Joe, and they didn't seem to
be describing the same man who has written, "On any given day, half
of them have their period, a built in excuse for acting out." Instead,
they tell me that Joe takes no bullshit, but he doesn't hand it out either.
He's fair, he's smart; he follows the rules consistently, unlike some officers who apply the rules arbitrarily. Most important, one of the women
tells me, "Joe doesn't take sex, and he doesn't give sex." I don't ask her
to explain; I've already heard it all: There are women who want to have
sex with an officer so they can provide a semen sample and sue the
state; there are officers who want sex for their own pleasure and will
use their power to get it.

Another woman tells me that Joe spends hours helping the women
on her unit with their GED and college homework assignments. "He's

really smart," she says, "and if he doesn't understand it, he keeps our books and reads the assignments, then when he comes back on shift, he explains it to us."

I am beginning to realize that Joe is struggling to understand the same issues that confuse me—how can these women who "are articulate, some very beautiful, some very intelligent," who "dress impeccably, wear make up and jewelry, smell nice and laugh at stupid jokes," who seem to "have nothing threatening about them," commit the crimes they commit. He then offers a litany of crimes that makes Josie and Valerie seem downright ordinary: "67 stab wounds, 13 gunshots, severing of genitalia, burning, smothering, slashing their children, allowing their so-called lover to mutilate and kill their children, execution of their parents who abused them." Joe pulls back: "Don't let me make you think they are all crimes of passion. We have our drug dealers, armed robbers, extortionists, forgers, thieves, and the like. But they are all usually connected to a man who got them into the predicament that caused them to be incarcerated."

I prepare a four-page double-spaced memo for Joe. I choose my words carefully; I reread my words to make sure I am not being too critical—I don't want to scare Joe off. I recommend that he recall and record anecdotes until some themes emerge. On the evening that Joe and I meet to talk about his essay, several other officers join us at the restaurant. I am confused, then annoyed, as I realize that Joe had actually invited them. He cannot possibly think I am going to "conference" with him in front of six officers, all of whom are in serious kick-back mode after a long, hard week.

I let Joe bring up the subject. I hand him the memo and tell him we should meet again after he reads it. The other officers just want to know if Joe is going to include them in his book; they start suggesting material, telling stories, wondering who will play the role of Joe when the blockbuster movie is made. I like these officers; I know several of them suffer from PTSD as a result of the Vietnam War, and I know they are the same officers the women who also suffer from PTSD most like and respect. But I don't want to talk about Joe's writing in front of his colleagues. I talk instead about corrections officers in general so Joe can see what I've learned from Conover's book, can see what readers could learn from his book, and can see that I respect the work he does. I talk about some of the points Conover made: Inmates appreciate it most when the officers are consistent because doing time is difficult enough without having the rules enforced differently every day; it takes five years before an officer can really do the job well. I quote Conover: It is a job "full of discretionary power, and the decisions about how to use it are often moral."

The superintendent arrives just as I begin to talk about Conover's discovery that although most people believe the officer wields all the power in a prison, the inmate has power, too. It turns out Joe had invited her earlier in the day; it is now clear to me that Joe believes writing is a social activity—the more people the better. The superintendent overhears part of my conversation and smiles approvingly. "I see you've been doing some reading," she says, referring to two books she had recommended, seminal works in the field: *A Society of Captives* and *The Asylum*, and referring to a conversation we had had several weeks earlier in which she explained that in order for a prison to maintain equilibrium, there must be a form of "healthy collusion" between the inmates and the officers, a willingness to work together. "Good for you, you're learning: she says. I had gotten the two books through interlibrary loan, but they had sat in my briefcase untouched until I finally had to return them to avoid the dollar-a-day fine. I don't tell her this, and as the officers tease me about scoring brownie points with the boss, I feel guilty, as if I had aced an exam by reading the CliffsNotes.

The superintendent is actually more pleased that I am helping Joe with his writing. She is a trained sociologist, and she knows the academic work that floods the field of corrections needs to be supplemented by first-person accounts from "insiders." Furthermore, she takes great pride in the accomplishments of both the inmates and the staff. I had helped Karen submit one of her poems to a literary journal, and when it was published, the superintendent had made a special trip to the learning center to congratulate Karen in front of the other students. I can only imagine what she would do if Joe got something published. She makes sure that Joe and I set a time to talk about his writing, and I gently suggest that we do it alone.

But less than a month later, before Joe has a chance to show me any more drafts, he suffers a massive heart attack, and after using up all of his sick days and comp time, he takes early retirement. When news of his heart attack spreads through the prison, the women are bereft—asking for updates, requesting permission to send him get-well cards. One of the women said he was the closest thing she ever had to a father. Another woman said the inmates on her unit were getting "reckless" with Joe gone, finding themselves engaged in a battle of wits with a new officer who goaded them for the sheer fun of it.

I meet Joe one more time for dinner, but a book is the furthest thing from his mind. He has to lose weight; his life literally depends on it. He is not sure what he'll do to earn money to supplement his retirement income; he has scores of ideas, all of which sound like a poor substitute. Joe had, quite simply, loved being a corrections officer. He spent most of the time we were together asking how particular inmates were doing, and he finally admitted that more than anything else, what he missed most was the women themselves. "I think about them and worry about them a lot," he said. "If I had been at a female facility from the start, I probably wouldn't have had a heart attack. I think the women cared about me as much as I cared about them." I tell Joe that if, at the end of my tenure at Bedford Hills, the women have benefited half as much from my being there as they did from his presence, I'll be very proud of myself.

"You women are all alike," Joe replies. "You talk too much."

The program has been in existence long enough at this point for some of our graduates to be released, and we are thrilled when so many of them find jobs quickly—the most essential component to getting one's life back in order after prison. Michelle Fine, a CUNY professor, had used our program to conduct a study on the impact of college on prisoners, and the results were extraordinary—recidivism rates dropping in direct proportion to the number of years of post-secondary education. These statistics are good for our program, but actually seeing and hearing from our former students on the outside is good for me. I am exceedingly pleased when Shakira sends me a draft of a report she has to do for her job and asks me to review it for her." I used to hate your comments and corrections on my drafts," she wrote, "but now I am glad you were such a tough bitch. Let loose with your red pen on this one; it's going to the big suits in the company."

But a college degree can't fix everything, and I am unbearably saddened when I am given a copy of a blanket e-mail from a former inmate announcing Sharon's death and providing information about funeral arrangements. Sharon, who had told me that she spent her nights alone in her cell with her victim, had been released a year before, and although I knew she had AIDS, I did not realize how sick she was. I am further saddened but not surprised as I read that "there was no insurance, so any donations of any amount will be appreciated. We will try to take up a little collection there, so bring your dough and your checkbooks." I take to heart the closing line of the e-mail: "Easy everyone—life is really short." I do not go to the funeral because I have already scheduled a weekend visit to my granddaughter. The visit is wonderful, but I cannot stop thinking about Sharon.

Many of the women in the college program are very smart; a few are truly brilliant. One of our math instructors, a retired IBM executive, used to say to me every week as we left the prison that some of the students in his Introduction to Algebra class could be CEOs of a Fortune 500 company. (We both know, of course, that these women will probably not even get entry-level positions in such companies once they check the "Yes" box under the criminal record question.) But for some reason, I gravitate toward the students who don't do well, who in some cases won't make it, even with extra help and support. I had agreed to develop the pre-college program because of the way some of these women struggled to gain admittance to the college program; their perseverance was almost painful to witness.

But there is something about these women that I like—an honesty and humor and savvy that the better students often do not exhibit.

Once when I told one of the pre-college students that her homework assignment was so easy she "was getting away with murder," she retorted without a second's delay, "No I'm not." While reviewing another student's essay, I told her that her sentence was too long. "I agree wholeheartedly," she replied.

These women are also serious and introspective as they examine, perhaps for the first time, the reasons why they wound up in the pre-college program. One of them describes the way her confidence had been eroded after years of being called "fat house" by her stepfather. Another explains that she had been unable to do her homework because she had been responsible for her four younger siblings, but when they were finally taken away by child protective services, she was unable to do her homework because she was too depressed.

They are not afraid to disagree. As we read the opening scene of Richard Wright's *Black Boy*, I question the way Wright's grandmother brutally beat him after he accidentally set her house on fire. The women look at me in amazement. They had received far worse beatings for far less serious infractions, and they were convinced they deserved the punishment. As we discuss Cedric Jennings from Ron Suskind's *Hope in the Unseen*, I praise what I thought was Jennings' amazing ability to gain entry into an Ivy League college given his circumstances: He had come from one of the worst neighborhoods of Washington, D.C.; he lived in poverty; for all intents and purposes he was fatherless. The women retort: He had a mother, he had never been shot or stabbed; he had never gone without food for more than a day. When the women read that his mother had forbidden him to work after school because she didn't want him out of the apartment in such a dangerous neighborhood, they insist that he was being pampered—that maybe he didn't need an Ivy League education as much as he needed a kick in the ass. I would drive home from these sessions questioning everything I taught, every one of my interpretations. At the next class, it would begin all over again. Finally I ask the women if they think I am naive. "Of course you are," they all respond, incredulous that I even ask.

I have slowly taken on the responsibility for students with physical and learning disabilities. I suspect that all of the students in the pre-college program have undiagnosed learning disabilities, but given the descriptions they have written about their educational experiences, I understand why none of them has been tested or classified. Many of them stop attending school at fourteen or fifteen years old. When I protest and say they aren't allowed to drop out of school in New York until they are sixteen, one of them corrects me. "I didn't say I dropped out, I said I stopped attending." Those who stayed in school describe high schools where the teachers were terrorized in the classrooms and the weaker students were terrorized in the bathrooms. Apparently the halls were more democratic, a place where everyone was free to terrorize everyone else. The admissions essays the applicants write don't horrify me anymore, but they should: The women describe scenes of brutality and cruelty with the same tone that my students on the outside use to describe their high school proms. English teachers have a standard (sick) joke about reacting to essays that contain personal information: "I'm sorry your mother died, but this is a sentence fragment." As I grade the essays of the incoming students, I am beginning to engage in an English teacher's version of jailhouse humor—"I'm sorry your mother's body was riddled with bullets, but this essay is riddled with run-on sentences." I keep these sick jokes to myself.

I spend hours making taped recordings of material for Barbara, a student who had slowly lost her vision in prison as a result of macular degeneration. When I first started working with Barbara, she was able to read large bold print, but now she has lost even that ability. On the weekends, I often set my alarm clock for 5:00 a.m., brew coffee, and sit at my kitchen table recording Barbara's reading assignments for her courses. I love the stillness of the morning, and because Barbara often takes the courses I am teaching, I am able to review my own reading assignments as I make the tapes.

At first, I would read exactly what was printed, imitating as best I could the voice and manner of the professionals I had heard on books on tape. But after a while, I begin to talk to Barbara directly—telling her how I feel that day, when I will be at the prison to meet with her, asking her what she thought of a particular assignment and telling her what I thought of it.

I know that Barbara never has visitors, never gets packages from home, and I also know she annoys the other women: She can be brusque, even rude, and her mental health seemed to be deteriorating along with her vision. But I like being with Barbara; I am amazed at her memory, her intelligence, her love of literature, her talent as a writer. She loves to talk about books, about my students on the outside, about my life. When I told her it had taken me more than eight years to earn my college degree as a part-time evening student, she leaned over, gave me a hug, and congratulated me—as if I had earned the degree the day before instead of thirty years ago. In short, we are becoming friends.

One particular morning, while reading Jhumpa Lahiri's short story "The Third and Final Continent," I started to cry as I recorded the scene in which the narrator discovers that Mrs. Croft has died. As I read the words "when I learned of her death I was stricken, so much so that when Mala looked up from her knitting she found me staring at the wall, the newspaper neglected in my lap, unable to speak," I was also unable to speak. I simply left the tape recorder running as I composed myself, and then I apologized to Barbara and continued to read. I was crying over the sadness of the story, of course, but I was crying for Barbara as well. I know she will probably never leave Bedford, and even if she does, her life will be severely circumscribed not only by her disability but by the fact that she has spent more than half her life in prison.

I had been at the Greenwich Library the day before, choosing books on tape for Barbara and picking up research and reference books for the other students. I had told a few of the librarians about my work at the prison, and they had begun to help me. When I explained to one of the librarians why nine books were almost a month overdue (after three renewals)—the student who was using them had been hospitalized and wanted to read them—the librarian forgave my overdue fines.

The library has recently been renovated as a result of an unexpectedly large endowment: It is now truly grand and magnificent, filled with light from floor-to-ceiling windows, with a wide wooden staircase rising majestically up to the second floor. There is always a huge vase of fresh flowers on one of the information desks in the entry. On this day, there were scores of people on the main floor: mothers helping their children select books for school projects, retired men reading and dozing in the overstuffed chairs, a group of middle-aged men and women gathering for their weekly book club. Suddenly I felt more comfortable and secure and relaxed than I had in a long time; it was as if I was on some sort of emotional vacation. I usually head straight for the second floor where the books on tape are located, but I found myself simply standing in the midst of this scene wondering if an audiotape existed that would somehow compensate for the fact that Barbara would never have such an experience, for the fact that Barbara has no idea such an experience is even possible.

I often feel sad that the women cannot participate in this "outside" public life—to see a particular movie or documentary, attend a lecture or exhibit. One of the women told me she wanted to visit the site of the World Trade Center where she had worked for several years; until she saw it, she still could not believe what had happened. But this particular feeling was different. I was overcome, perhaps for the first time, with the realization that one of the effects of imprisonment is the inability to be with people who are not imprisoned. I suddenly better understood the rage that Josie and Valerie had exhibited that day in the learning center.

I also understood better why the women were so grateful to the volunteer teachers and tutors and visitors: A string of engaging and brilliant writers and artists had followed James McBride's visit: Adrienne Rich, Eve Ensler, Blanche Boyd, Liz Swados, Alfred Uhry, Paula Allen, Howard Zinn, A'Lelia Bundles, Tonya Bolden, Helen Lester, Ron Suskind, Stanley Nelson, Philip Lopate, Grace Paley, Debra Dickerson, Paule Marshall, Nicholas Lemann, Saidah Ekulona, Hazelle Goodman, Lynn Nottage—they came simply because I or another teacher asked in the name of the students. But there are limitations to such visits—it is a mere glimpse of the life that exists outside, and it is comprised only of those willing to take the time and trouble to come into a prison.

I know the Greenwich Library is not a typical public place; in fact, it is a stark contrast to the public places that most of the women frequented before they were imprisoned. As I sat at my kitchen table, I wished I could bring Barbara to the Greenwich Library. I suddenly felt so tired that I went back to bed.

I have had dreams about the women in the prison before, but this time my dream is so vivid I wake up wondering if it actually happened. I am standing at the top of the staircase as two buses arrive at the Greenwich Library. As the passengers file off the bus, I realize they are the college students from Bedford Hills, and each woman is carrying books in her arms. I am very happy to see them, but they don't seem to recognize me. I look at every face, but Barbara is not among them.

I get up and start my day for the second time. As I brew more coffee, I ask myself how much longer I will be able to endure the intensity of the work I am doing with the women at Bedford Hills.

Wounded Healing: Forming a Storytelling Community in Hip-Hop Lit

Marc Lamont Hill

Marc Lamont Hill, a hip-hop intellectual, speaker, writer, and activist, is an associate professor of education at Teacher's College, Columbia University, and affiliate faculty member in African American studies at the Institute for Research in African American Studies at Columbia University. His commentary has appeared in the Washington Post, *the* New York Times, Essence, *and elsewhere. Hill's study of the Twilight Schools program first appeared in* Teachers College Record *and also is part of Hill's book* Beats, Rhymes, and Classroom Life: Hip-Hop Pedagogy and the Politics of Identity *(2009). In this excerpt from the initial article, Hill provides a thick description of Hip-Hip Lit, a course he co-taught in the evening program of a small, public, comprehensive high school in Philadelphia. In the abstract of the article, Hill defines the term* wounded healing *as a practice in which "students were able to recognize the commonality of their experiences, challenge various ideologies, and produce new knowledge. In doing this, the members of the class forged a cohesive community replete with multiple roles and relations of power." This knowledge is produced through close readings of the narratives of selected hip-hop songs, and the students' own stories that directly connect to the narratives. However, rather than merely celebrate the success of this culturally relevant pedagogy, Hill employs hip-hop pedagogy to critique the difficulties that arose as students and teacher participated in difficult personal in-class discussions. Students' voices (through journals and interviews) permeate this article, as Hill provides detailed qualitative evidence from his study of the complexity of students' lives inside and outside the classroom.*

Wounded Healing

[O]ne of the principal features of the Hip-Hop Lit curriculum was its focus on personal narratives. These narratives came primarily from two sources: the course texts and the members of the class. Because of the content of our thematic units (e.g., Love, Despair, Family), the course texts frequently took narrative form and were most often autobiographical in nature. For example, the unit on despair featured texts in which the authors described their personal circumstances to substantiate their feelings of hopelessness. In addition to their autobiographical focus, the course texts typically reflected what Forman (2002) calls the "extreme local," or hip-hop's narrative preoccupation with specific cities, area codes, neighborhoods, housing projects, and so on, within its texts. As Khaleef, a regular from Hip-Hop Lit noted, it was this focus on geographic specificity and local knowledge within the texts that enabled many of the class conversations:

> The stuff we be readin' get us talking 'cause it's more real than other stuff. . . . Like, I can tell that [the stories] really happened to [the authors] because they tell us where they from and stuff about they 'hood. Plus the [stuff] they be goin' through is the same as we go through.

Khaleef's comment, which was echoed by many students throughout the semester, speaks to the importance of hip-hop's narratives for humanizing urban experiences by appending names and faces to otherwise distant and abstract narratives about urban ghettos (Hill, 2008). It also demonstrates, as critical race theorists have argued (e.g., Delgado Bernal, 2002; Guinier & Torres, 2002), how such narratives enable oppressed people to recognize the commonality of their experiences. With regard to Hip-Hop Lit, the course texts served as counternarratives that contributed largely to the formation of a storytelling community in which students felt comfortable sharing their own personal stories.

As the school year advanced and students increased their level of engagement with the course texts, the practice of wounded healing began to take form. Through wounded healing, members of Hip-Hop Lit engaged in storytelling practices that challenged assumptions, assuaged various forms of pain, and produced new knowledge. I use the term *wounds* to refer to those narratives of pain, suffering, and injustice that mediate an individual's understanding and negotiation of the world; *healing* alludes to those storytelling practices that enabled students to recognize the commonality of their experiences, gain insight into their problems, and access new ideological perspectives. As such, to engage in wounded healing was to participate in a storytelling community in which members both exposed their wounds and tended to the wounds of others. It is important to note, however, that the term *healing* does not imply or infer a notion of completed recovery. Such a circumstance was neither an expressed goal nor a reasonable expectation for a space like Hip-Hop Lit. Rather, *healing* refers to an ongoing *process* of negotiating various personal and ideological struggles in reflective, collective, and productive fashion.

"I Got a Story to Tell"

Although the students in Hip-Hop Lit expressed interest in the course from the beginning, they were generally reluctant to speak about their own personal experiences at the beginning of the school year. For the first month, classroom conversation was primarily limited to analysis of the course texts, with little explicit connection to students' personal experiences or stories. Although this reluctance was partly due to the impersonal nature of our first unit, Roots of Hip-Hop and Literature, which contained only one autobiographical narrative, their discomfort with sharing personal information in front of strangers seemed to be the most important reason. As Jay, one of the students in the class, later told me,

> It's like, at the beginning ain't nobody wanna talk . . . 'cause they ain't know nobody. You don't know who listenin' or what they gonna do. If my enemies is in here and I don't even know it, how I'm gon' tell them [something] that they could use against me? . . . But then it got cool when everybody started talking and it was like "oh, you gon' tell me this, then I'm gon' tell *you* this."

Dorene, Lisa, and Kristina, three other Hip-Hop Lit students with whom I later spoke, were even more specific about when and why the class began to talk:

> *Dorene:* I know I wasn't gonna say nothin' if ain't nobody else say nothin'. I was like . . . "y'all ain't gonna be talking 'bout me when I leave." Then I remember Robin said something about love and it was deep and then everybody wanted to start saying stuff.
>
> *Lisa:* Exactly!!
>
> *Kristina:* True!!
>
> *Lisa:* When Robin started talking, I felt like I could say whatever I had to say.
>
> *Kristina:* I mean. I don't say much about myself. But if nobody else would talk, I wouldn't say *nothing*. Then she came with some ol' personal stuff and I was like "damn"! I could talk in here.

The moment to which these students alluded occurred early in October, as the class moved from the Roots of Hip-Hop and Literature unit to the Love unit. Our first reading from the unit was "Manifest" by Lauryn Hill, a first-person narrative about a bad relationship:

You see I loved hard once, but the love wasn't returned
   I found out the man I'd die for, he wasn't even concerned
   And time it turned
He tried to burn me like a perm
Though my eyes saw the deception, my heart wouldn't let me learn
For um, some, dumb woman, was I,
And every time he'd lie he would cry and inside I'd die.
My heart must have died a thousand deaths
Compared myself to Toni Braxton thought I'd never catch my breath
Nothing left, he stole the heart beating from my chest
I tried to call the cops, that type of thief you can't arrest
Pain suppressed, will lead to cardiac arrest
Diamonds deserve diamonds, but he convinced me I was worth less
when my peoples would protest,
I told them mind their business, cause my shit was complex
More than just the sex
I was blessed, but couldn't feel like it when I was caressed
I'd spend nights clutching my breasts overwhelmed by God's test
I was God's best contemplating death with a Gillette
But no man is ever worth the paradise manifest

                                              (Fugees, 1996)

After reading "Manifest," we engaged in a spirited conversation about the meaning of particular parts of the song. Like other classes in the past, there was much debate over the meaning of the last two lines of the text. Although most students (along with Mr. Colombo and me) assumed that Lauryn Hill was contemplating suicide, several students emphatically argued that Hill was considering killing her lover with a razor. After debating over the meaning of the lines for a few minutes, one of the students who was vigorously advocating for the second interpretation rhetorically asked, "I mean, who would kill they *self* over somebody else?" I decided that his question provided a perfect segue for a more personal discussion of the text and responded, "That's an interesting question. Has anyone felt like Lauryn does in 'Manifest'? Not just the suicide part, either." The class suddenly grew quiet as heads began to shake left and right, indicating No. A few minutes later, class ended.

The following day, I began the class with a journal question that picked up where we had left off the previous day. The board read: "'I loved hard once but the love wasn't returned.' Can you relate to this? If so, how?"

As soon as they entered the classroom, most of the students, as well as Mr. Colombo and I, sat down and wrote what appeared to be detailed responses to the question. After 15 minutes, I signaled the end of the writing period by asking, "So who wants to share?" Two full minutes of nearly complete silence passed before being interrupted by Robin's half-raised hand and soft voice.

"I do. I got a story to tell," Robin said, without moving her eyes from her notebook. Robin is a short, heavy-set Cambodian girl with big bright cheeks and a quiet demeanor. She is 23 years old and has lived on her own since she became pregnant at 16 and her parents forced her to leave home. She works full time at a local supermarket and raises her 2-year-old biracial son without help from his father, whom she hasn't seen in 18 months. When she leans forward, the slightly under-sized velour sweatsuit that she wears almost daily reveals the bottom half of a large red tattoo written across her back that reads, "LOVE HURTS." Robin is the oldest student in the class and hasn't been to school since she dropped out 7 years ago. Unable to find a steady job, she decided to return to school to obtain her diploma and continue on to college to better provide for her son. She doesn't say much to the other students, which gives her an air of mysteriousness that causes them to listen to her with curious attention whenever she speaks.

"I loved hard once," she said, barely above a whisper. After a deliberate but unpretentious pause she continued,

> I mean, I know exactly what she talking about. I was in love with this boy when I was young. I gave him everything. I put him above everybody including my father. Everybody told me I was trippin' but I ain't listen. I gave him everything and he didn't love me for real for real. I got pregnant and he just left. If it wasn't for my son, I don't know what I would've did to myself. I knew he needed me. Otherwise, I don't know.

Robin's personal narrative, which many of the students, Mr. Colombo, and I all recollect as the first one articulated within the class, represents the most important and difficult component of wounded healing: *personal disclosure.* As she later told me, her willingness to expose her wounds by sharing a personal and painful story was animated by a desire to "help somebody else through they own shit." Although there was no indication that the story that Robin shared related to another student's personal experience, it nonetheless facilitated the development of a classroom community in which students shared their own stories and responded to others.

Robin's decision to tell her story marked a watershed moment in the Hip-Hop Lit school year because it encouraged other students to engage in similar storytelling acts. As Kristina noted above, Robin's disclosure showed the other members of the class that they "could talk in here." Kristina's use of *could* is critical because it refers not to the students having official permission to tell their stories, because the course was explicitly designed to encourage storytelling. Rather, *could* refers to the construction of new possibilities for members of Hip-Hop Lit. By offering her story, Robin enabled the other students in Hip-Hop Lit to begin imagining the classroom as a potentially safe site for sharing their stories. After her disclosure, many students began to explore the possibilities of the classroom for storytelling by increasing the frequency, depth, and personal nature of their stories.

Like Robin's story, the most personal and engaging narratives that were shared in class typically emerged unexpectedly during normal classroom instruction. Students would insert their stories into the conversation and, after they received a response, return to their previous activity. These events typically lasted no more than a few minutes and rarely subverted the rhythm of the class despite their apparent disconnection from the formal curriculum. An example of this occurred as I was teaching a lesson on mood and tone using Tupac's "Dear Mama":

Me: [S]o what is the mood of this piece?

Joe: Sad.

Me: Why?

Joe: After all . . . he went through with his moms, he had to be sad.

Me: But isn't he thanking her for being a good mom in spite of everything?

Joe: Yeah but you gotta be sad going through that. Me and mom and my brother went through the same shit.

Jay: Me too. More me than my brother but my pop wasn't there so shit gonna be sad. But you still happy 'cause you made it through.

Me: I know he might've been sad thinking about everything they went through. Just like y'all probably did. But if you made it and everybody was listening to your story, how you think they would feel?

Joe: I think they would feel better. Like "Joe went through that and became a rapper or whatever so it don't gotta turn out f-ed up."

Jay: Exactly. Like "y'all could learn from my pain."

Me: OK. OK. That's what mood is all about. Not so much what the writer is feeling but how might the reader feel when he [sic] reads it. So what would be a good word to describe how you might feel when you read this?

Jay: Better

Kenef: Happy. Like y'all said, you might feel better knowing it ain't gotta end up all crazy.

Me: What might be a good word for that?

Mr. Colombo: How about hopeful?

Me: Hopeful! That sounds good. Let's say the mood is hopeful. Now, y'all really answered this, but what would you say is the tone of the piece?

From my perspective, two things were happening simultaneously during this interaction. After I solicited a response to my question about the mood of the text, Joe and Jay answered by saying that the mood was sad and offered personal stories to justify their response. For them, "Dear Mama" was sad because they had similar personal stories that they relied on to understand how Tupac was feeling; the mood was sad because they remembered being sad in their own respective experiences. Although I challenged their interpretation because I was unsatisfied with their answer, which appeared to conflate mood (the atmosphere of the narrative) and tone (the character's state of being)— Tupac's "Dear Mama" is a tribute to his mother that, despite its often disturbing content, was presumably written to invoke joy, not sadness, from the audience—the personal narratives that informed their reading of the text nonetheless provided a critical point of entry for teaching the day's lesson. Equally important, the Hip-Hop Lit classroom enabled a space for wounds to be exposed and healed through the acts of cosigning and challenging.

Cosigning

One of the primary ways that members of the classroom community responded to personal disclosures was through the act of *cosigning*, in which members of the community would provide affirmation for the person exposing his or her wound. Cosigning served two functions: substantiating the truth-value of the narrative and encouraging the speaker to continue. Cosigning practices included nonverbal cues (e.g., head nods, empathetic facial gestures), interjections (e.g., "Exactly!" or "Mm hmm"), and, most important, complementary stories. Such narrative practices can be located within the homiletical tradition of the Black church, where call-and-response interactions are engaged by the preacher and the congregation to stimulate the listener and encourage the speaker (Smitherman, 1977). These practices are equally apparent during the act of "testifyin'," in which a member of the congregation shares a personal story within the formal church service as a means by which to affirm the goodness of God (Smitherman). Within this space, personal stories are often buttressed by an additional story from another member of the church community, thereby acknowledging both the commonality and the legitimacy of the narrative.

In the above interaction, Jay cosigned Joe's narrative by offering a complementary story that articulated the commonality of their respective experiences with their fathers. Although such interactions may have served a therapeutic purpose, they also served the additional (and with regard to the classroom, primary) purpose of enabling a "teachable moment" wherein we were able to make an effective bridge between student narratives and the curriculum. Although I could have disregarded their narratives and simply explained the differences between mood and tone, I instead attempted to validate their stories by using them as a part of the lesson. As many of the students noted, this approach yielded enormous personal and practical benefits:

> *Jay:* The stuff we be learning is interesting even if we ain't talk about hip-hop. But the fact that we get to talk about our own stories make it easier to relate to everybody.
>
> *Robin:* Plus, sometimes in school stuff can get boring and you don't even try to understand it. When you be connecting it to our lives it's easier to follow and better to understand.
>
> *Dorene:* Exactly. I learn stuff easier when I could relate to it. Plus, when you get to know everybody better, with their stories and everything, it's easier to relax and pay attention.

As the students' comments suggest, it was these acts of individual disclosure and our collective response to them—both of which occurred on a daily basis—that enabled the construction of the classroom community and served as a suitable hook for sustaining student interest.

Challenging

In addition to cosigning, students often responded to personal disclosures through the act of challenging. Unlike cosigning, which was a common response to all types of stories, challenging only occurred when members of Hip-Hop Lit exposed wounds that were explicitly ideological. In my use of the term *ideological wounds*, I am not alluding (as do many critical pedagogues; Ellsworth, 1989) to "false consciousness" or a dogmatic neo-Marxian belief that the students' conceptions of the world were "damaged" by their personal experiences and therefore in need of repair. Rather, many of the beliefs about the world that were articulated within Hip-Hop Lit were largely shaped by painful encounters with forces of inequality and marginalization that had not been previously articulated or critically examined. The conversations that emerged from these ideological narratives were therefore not less personal but less *personalized*, because the entire class was able to use a particular narrative to challenge individual and collective worldviews within a relatively safe space.

Like cosigning, challenging took both verbal and nonverbal forms, the most significant being the offering of a competing narrative. Unlike personal wounds, the exposure of ideological wounds frequently led to longer, more inclusive conversations that took the class away from the planned lesson. Although the conversations that emerged from challenging were often intense, they rarely became antagonistic. The following example of this type of conversation came on the day that we read "Project Window" by Nas as part of a lesson about imagery. After discussing Nas's use of imagery in his description of the Queensbridge Housing Projects, I initiated a conversation about the relationship between "Project Window" and the students' ideas about neighborhoods:

Me:	So how does the imagery that Nas uses connect to your own ideas about neighborhoods?
Kia [Af-Am]:	It reminded me about how neighborhoods turn into "hoods."
Me:	What do you mean?
Kia:	Black people don't know how to keep they neighborhoods. Look at where we live. Every time I come outside people be selling drugs and they be shooting all the time. The same stuff that Nas talkin' about.
Dorene [Af-Am]:	Exactly. White people keep they house clean on the outside. Black people throw stuff everywhere. That's why the hood look like it do. It don't be crackheads and stuff around White people neighborhoods.
Maggie [White]:	Shiiiit. That ain't true. It's crackheads and trash and stuff in my neighborhood too!
Kia:	But it's different though. Y'all got silver spoons in y'all mouths. Y'all dads got companies that y'all can work at and we gotta start from the bottom. It's different when you don't got money.
Maggie:	I ain't got no money!
Lisa [White]:	Me neither. . . . Plus, I live two blocks from y'all!

This interaction represents a frequent occurrence when students explicitly linked their ideological positions to personal disclosures. In this instance, Kia explained that her conception of the Black neighborhood was informed by her experiences within her own neighborhood. Dorene cosigned the story by explaining the relationship between race and the quality of neighborhoods. Maggie, a White student in the class, then pushed the conversation into a different direction by challenging Kia with a competing story.

For Maggie, the students' romantic conception of "White neighborhoods" contradicted her own experiences as a White person living under circumstances similar to those of Dorene and Kia. Lisa cosigned Maggie's challenge by pointing out that all the students in the conversation lived in the same neighborhood, thereby complicating Dorene's and Kia's arguments about the relationship between racial identity and class position. As was usually the case, this exchange quickly ended, and we returned to our formal lesson. Nevertheless, the ideas discussed became reference points for further conversations, because the students,

Mr. Colombo, and I would use future class conversations and course texts to cosign or challenge earlier claims. Through this practice, students would engage in closer readings of the texts, as well as sustained analyses of the issues raised in class.

Healing

Through the acts of personal disclosure, cosigning, and challenging, members of Hip-Hop Lit were able to engage in processes of healing. It is worth reiterating, however, that my use of *healing* neither presumes nor suggests a completed medical, psychological, or ideological recovery. Rather, it refers to the process by which members of Hip-Hop Lit were able to find varying levels of insight, relief, support, empathy, and critique within the Hip-Hop Lit community for their personal and ideological wounds.

For many students, the process of healing was primarily linked to the act of personal disclosure. Although they benefited from the community's response to their narratives, students in Hip-Hop Lit often mentioned how important it was to offer their stories in full public view, regardless of the particular response that they received. This sentiment was captured by Robin, who remarked, "Even though people say good stuff to each other, sometime it just feel good to say stuff out loud." Other students in the class offered a similar perspective about the importance of "saying stuff out loud":

> *Lisa:* When you tell a story in front of everybody, sometimes it feel good just to get it off your chest.
>
> *Dorene:* Me too! Sometimes I don't even need nobody to say nothing. I just need get something off my chest. Like the time I was talking about all the drama with my baby father. Just talkin' about how he hurt me made me feel better because I never said it out loud before.

Although the benefits of public disclosure did not always hinge upon the community's response, the relative safety of the classroom space was nonetheless crucial for enabling such disclosures. In an interview, Lisa and Dorene explained the importance of the classroom community:

> *Me:* Now that you know how good it feels to get stuff off your chest, do you find yourself doing it more often?
>
> *Lisa:* Yes and no. I be trying but it's hard because even though it feel good just to say it sometimes, you can't just say it *anywhere*. I can say it in here cause I know everybody and that's how we get down.

> *Dorene:* Exactly. Even if don't nobody say nothing, you gotta know that if you *need* some support or whatever, somebody gon' be there. Plus you gotta know people ain't gonna tell all your business.

> *Lisa:* Plus I don't be thinkin' about this stuff until we be readin'.

Lisa's and Dorene's observations underscore the importance of the Hip-Hop Lit community in facilitating the healing process. Even when people found healing primarily in the act of disclosure, Hip-Hop Lit served as a safe space in which people felt that their disclosures could be heard, responded to, and protected. In addition, the narratives within the course texts often connected to students' experiences in ways that created organic opportunities for disclosure.

Although many students found relief in personal disclosures, most students, including those mentioned above, often spoke about the value of engaging with the stories of their classmates. In the case of Joe and Jay, understanding the commonality of their experiences with their fathers was a critical part of their healing process. As Joe explained,

> It just feel good sometimes to hear that other people is goin' through the same [stuff]. Me and Jay not even that cool. I mean we don't got beef or nothin' but I don't know him like that. . . . But he still was like "I been through the same bullshit with my pops." That shit is so real because sometimes you be like "Why this had to happen to me?" Then you realize that it happens to everybody.

In a separate conversation, Jay added, "It's crazy cause you might not even know somebody but you could still feel they pain. You don't be *happy* 'cause they goin' through it but it feel good to know it's not just you." For Joe and Jay, the usefulness of their interaction rested upon its ability to expose the commonality of their experiences.

In addition to providing personal pleasure for students, the process of healing also informed students' performance of classroom assignments. For example, Joe and Jay used class assignments to negotiate their issues with their absentee fathers. As part of a creative writing assignment in our Despair unit, Jay and Joe began to work collaboratively on a rap about a young boy in the ghetto who contemplates suicide after finding out that his "deadbeat" father lived around the corner from him but did not want to meet him. Other students, such as Robin, Dorene, and Lisa, frequently used their journal assignments to write about abusive relationships. At the end of the semester, they spoke about the importance of class activities for the healing process:

> *Lisa:* Even though we were learning literature and writing, we also got to deal with personal stuff. By the end of the year I felt a lot better.

> *Dorene:* Yeah, like every time we wrote about our triflin' boyfriends, I learned how to avoid [them] in the future.

Lisa: Plus we got cool with each other because we was all in the same boat!

Dorene: Yeah, 'cause I used to think it was all my fault. By the end it was all good.

In a separate interview, Joe expressed a similar feeling:

When Joe and I made that song about the kid who lost his pop, we got real cool. Before that, we didn't really know each other but after that we became like family. It was mad cool to learn that everybody has struggles and, by the end of the class, I wasn't as mad anymore. Don't get me wrong, I'm not over it but I'm dealing better.

Although some of the students may have overstated the transformative effects of the class, they nonetheless speak to the possibilities of Hip-Hop Lit for enabling the healing process.

Teaching (as) Wounded Healers (or Not)

As indicated earlier, many roles developed in the classroom community in relationship to the practices of wounded healing. With respect to Mr. Colombo and me, these roles were further complicated by the teacher-student power relationships within the class. Despite our common position as coteachers, each of us responded to our position within the storytelling community in drastically different ways.

My position within Hip-Hop Lit underwent dramatic shifts throughout the year. Like many of the students, I was extremely apprehensive at the beginning of the semester about sharing my personal stories in full public view. As such, my primary role at the beginning of the year was that of a listener. Because of my position as a teacher, I was often favorably positioned in a relationship of *one-sided storytelling*, in which a person or group offers personal narratives as the other person or group is empowered to listen, judge, and respond based on their assessment of the narrative. In the case of Hip-Hop Lit, the students would tell their personal stories while Mr. Colombo and I listened and responded.

Like in most urban schools, one-sided storytelling extended beyond the bounds of the formal curriculum and into other "hidden" dimensions of the classroom. For example, early in the year, Robin approached me and told me that she had been absent the previous day because she could not find child care. She told me that she could not afford her usual babysitter because she did not have enough money, and her son's father was not providing financial support. Although she did not have to provide as much personal detail as she did, the program's allegedly strict attendance policy forced students to provide "an *acceptable* [italics added] excuse for all absences" (Twilight Program Memo). By positioning teachers and administrators as arbiters of acceptability, students who were unable to attend class or stay for the entire period because of court appearances, child care issues, or other personal problems were forced to disclose these deeply personal parts of their lives to relative strangers who offered judgment (approval, dismissal, and so on) in exchange.

The one-sided nature of this relationship first became apparent to me in mid-October when I entered the class wearing a "North Philly" T-shirt. One of the students immediately said to me, "What you doin' with a N.P. shirt on?" I explained to their amazement that "I was born on Luzerne Street," a well-known street in North Philadelphia. Up to that point, the students did not know that I was born and partly raised in North Philadelphia, even though I knew the neighborhoods, streets, and often the houses in which they lived. Such events were extremely common in Hip-Hop Lit, just as they are in other traditional and non-traditional educational settings, where students are explicitly or implicitly coerced into exposing their personal selves while teachers and other authority figures are empowered to decide which stories they want to reveal.

The practice of one-sided storytelling was equally evident, though far more complicated, as Mr. Colombo and I began to teach Hip-Hop Lit. As students wrote in their daily journals, Mr. Colombo and I, per our agreement with the class, would respond to the question of the day in our own journals. Although we responded to each question— at times, however, teaching demands allowed us only enough time to give an oral response—our early responses were, like the rest of the class, relatively impersonal. By the time the Love unit began, however, my responses became increasingly personal. During the love unit, in response to the question "I loved hard once . . . ," I read the following response from my journal after Robin shared hers:

> I loved a girl once when I lived in Atlanta for college. We were friends since I was seventeen and I fell in love with her, although I didn't realize it until later. She loved me as a friend but not in a romantic way. I never told her how I felt until I saw her . . . the summer before last. She gave me the impression that we had a chance but when I got home she fronted on me. I was sick about that for a minute.

Disclosures like this one became common for me within the class. Despite their personal appearance, however, these stories required little effort for me to share. It was not until later in the year that I became comfortable enough to share the stories in which I had a personal, emotional investment and a genuine need for healing. One of the first occasions occurred as we began the Family unit.

During the Family unit, we read "Ms. Jackson" by Outkast, in which Big Boi and Andre 3000 (the group's members) write letters to Ms. Jackson, the fictional grandmother (whom they call the "baby's momma's momma") of their children. We began a discussion of Andre 3000's use of imagery in the second verse of the song:

> Ten times out of nine
> Now if I'm lyin', fine
> The quickest muzzle throw it on my mouth and I'll decline
> King meets queen, then the puppy love thing, together dream
> 'Bout that crib with the Goodyear swing
> On the oak tree, I hope we feel like this forever
> Forever, forever, ever? Forever, ever?
> Forever never seem that long until you're grown
> And notice that the day-by-day ruler can't be too wrong
> Ms. Jackson my intentions were good I wish I could
> Become a magician to abracadabra all the sadder
> Thoughts of me, thoughts of she, thoughts of he
> Askin' what happened to the feelin' that her and me
> Had, I pray so much about it need some knee, pads
> It happened for a reason one can't be, mad
> So know this, know that everything's cool
> And yes I will be present on the first day of school, and graduation
>
> (Benjamin, 2000)

We performed a text rendering of the song and many of the students read "Forever, forever, ever. Forever, ever?" and others, including me, read "Forever never seem that long until you grown" as the line that stood out to them. I asked the students to talk about why those two lines were so significant, and several responded with stories about relationships that they thought would last forever but abruptly ended. While I nodded with approval as the students told their stories, Dorene stared at me quizzically before finally asking, "What *you* know about this, Mr. Hill?" I fought the urge to ignore or playfully dismiss her question, as I had often done up to that point when faced with a personal question. Instead, I responded,

> That line, "Forever never seem that long until you're grown" is deep to me. I mean, I'm thinking about the song and how I can feel that in my own life. I have a baby on the way right now that I didn't expect. Her mom is 6 months pregnant and I'm really stressin' about it. I ain't worried about money or nothin' like that. It's just . . . I wasn't expecting this and she and I not together and she [the mother] gotta be in my life forever. So I'm like *"Forever*, ever? *Forever* ever?" That's a long ass time! [class laughs] This just wasn't how I thought about it back when I was a kid. I thought I'd end up married to the person that I have kids with and even when she told me she was pregnant the thought crossed my mind to just get married but I knew that wasn't right because I would've been miserable.

The class suddenly grew quiet as the students and Mr. Colombo stared at me to see if I was done sharing. When they seemed confident that I was, they began to respond:

Hakeem: I feel you. Baby moms be trippin'.

Kanef: You should know! All them kids you got!!

Hakeem: Shut up! I'm serious. Mr. Hill, I went through the same . . . I thought I was gonna be wit' my baby mom and then [it] got crazy.

Me: It's not that I wanted to be with her. It just crossed my mind. . . .

Dorene: That's 'cause everybody act like it's what you supposed to do but you gotta do what's best for you. It's like the song say, forever is a long time.

Me: Yeah you right. "Forever never seem that long until you grown."

Hakeem: You just gotta make sure that she don't get mad . . . about money or 'cause you not messin' with her and not let you see the kids.

Me: [looking at the entire class] I feel you. Based on what we've read, how do you y'all think Andre and Big Boi feel about their situations?

This brief interaction, which I deliberately ended by posing a question about the text, is significant because it was the first time that I exposed my own wounds in front of the students. After class I wrote,

> I told the students about my situation with the baby. I was surprised at how thoughtful and helpful they were when they heard about my story. Even more surprising to me is how much better I felt about the situation after talking to them. Although they didn't tell me anything that I didn't already know, there was something special about sharing that particular experience with my students.

Hakeem, who was 17 years old with two children born 1 month apart, and Dorene, who was 18 years old with a 6-month-old baby, both listened to my story and responded with advice that was thoughtful, helpful, and informed by their own personal experiences. For the first time, I felt like I was not in complete control of the class as a teacher, but another member of the storytelling community. Although my power to end the conversation when I deemed it appropriate affirms that I never completely ceded my authority as teacher, there was nonetheless a moment in class when I felt as if my story was no more or less important than the others.

According to Keneka, one of the most engaged regulars in Hip-Hop Lit, it was this type of practice that strengthened the bond between the students and me. She told me, "[the] only reason how you . . . get with us is because you be tellin' us your lifetime stories. You don't lie. You keep it real." As Keneka's quote suggests, it was not only my willingness to expose my wounds but also the coherence of my particular wounds with their own that helped legitimate my status within the community. To many of the students in Hip-Hop Lit, my life was "real" enough to warrant entry into the community.

Mr. Colombo, however, experienced great difficulty joining the community of wounded healers. Like several of the students, Mr. Colombo was extremely uncomfortable sharing his stories in class. He also saw his position as teacher as prohibitive with regard to storytelling. After the students left class on the day that I told the students my story about the baby, Mr. Colombo said to me, "Wow. You told them a *lot*." I asked if he could share such a personal story, and he replied, "I mean. I don't mind telling them stuff but some stuff I think teachers shouldn't tell students. You want them to see you in a certain way and they're lookin' for stuff to use against you." As Mr. Colombo was telling me this, I felt as if he was both explaining his own stance and subtly offering advice that he hoped would dissuade me from further such disclosures.

Mr. Colombo's position on personal disclosure quickly became apparent to the students as the school year persisted. Whereas students who were designated as "listeners" were met with a mix of empathy and wariness, Mr. Colombo's silence was uniformly rejected by the students, who would frequently request that he share "real" stories. By the middle of the year, the students' disdain for Mr. Colombo's reticence was reflected in their interactions with him. For example, when Mr. Colombo would ask a question, Dorene (a regular) and Angel (an extra), would mockingly ask (in a caricaturesque middle-American White male voice), "How do *you* feel about this Colombo? What does this remind *you* of?" Mr. Colombo would typically respond by laughing and changing the subject or saying, "I'm more interested in what *you* guys think."

One day, when Mr. Colombo did not come to school and I was teaching the class by myself, Dorene sparked the following conversation:

Dorene: How come Mr. Colombo don't never tell us nothing?

Me: What do you mean?

Dorene: You know what I'm talkin' about, Mr. Hill. You be talkin' and telling us stuff but if you ask him something, he don't wanna say nothin'.

Keneka: I know! He act like he too good to talk.

Me: I don't think it's that. . . . Maybe he's just not comfortable yet.

Keneka: How you gonna ask us to do all this talkin' and [in a mocking voice] "sharing our feelings" and you don't say nothing. That shit is corny.

Josh: I don't he think he do it on purpose. He just, y'ah mean, he can't relate 'cause he's from, you know, a different culture so he don't want to say nothin'.

Dorene: N'aah. Other people can't relate too but they try [pauses]. And he a *teacher*.

As Dorene pointed out, Mr. Colombo's position as teacher created a different set of expectations with regard to his participation. Whereas other "listeners" were excused for their lack of participation or at worst viewed skeptically, Mr. Colombo was expected to offer more of himself because of his extraordinary access to students' stories and his perceived power in relation to the students.

Despite his refusal to offer personal narratives, Mr. Colombo did not express any dissonance about listening to other students' stories. In fact, hearing student stories was a critical part of the agenda that largely informed our curriculum development process. Nevertheless, Mr. Colombo was at his quietest when students offered their own stories. Typically, Mr. Colombo would listen as students shared their ideas, beliefs, and personal stories and offer little in response except for a perfunctory nod of his head or an empathetic "thank you." He rarely discussed student stories within our curriculum meetings, and he admittedly did not attempt to let the stories inform his teaching. He told me,

> I feel like we're helping the kids by listening to them. I'm guessing that a lot of the stuff that they tell us they don't get to tell anybody else. And to be honest, I think it's interesting what they're telling us. I'm learning a lot about kids . . . not just the kids in class but other kids like them.

As his comment suggests, Mr. Colombo was often positioned within the class as a voyeur who engaged in one-sided storytelling for the purpose of what Foucault (1990) called "the pleasure of analysis," or a self-centered obsession with the sources of pleasure (or in this case pain) of another person. It was this type of surveillance, or at least its perception, that further marginalized Mr. Colombo within the class.

The relationship between Mr. Colombo, me, and the rest of the Hip-Hop Lit community with regard to storytelling is critical for understanding the power dynamics of the class. Although teachers can never relinquish classroom power (Gore, 1998; O'Reilly, 1993), the willingness to render oneself vulnerable can reorganize classroom power relations in ways that allow for more democratic, engaged, and productive practices. Such a gesture is particularly important in spaces like Hip-Hop Lit, where students are being asked to confess desires, share secrets, or otherwise offer aspects of themselves that have been traditionally excluded from the formal schooling process. By contrast, the failure to do so can further marginalize and silence both students and teachers in ways that undermine the spirit of wounded healing.

Open(ing) Wounds: Acts of Silencing and Hurting

Despite the collective success of Hip-Hop Lit in creating a community of wounded healers, there were clear tensions that appeared as the conversations became more personal. Because of the high level of intimacy within the community, members occasionally took the liberty of asking questions and telling stories that were potentially uncomfortable to others. When it became clear that a question was "too much" for someone, Mr. Colombo and I (and sometimes other regulars within the class) would redirect the conversation to another person or topic. The success of our attempts, however, was dependent on the students' ability and desire to expose their discomfort and our ability to respond effectively. What we often failed to do, however, was listen to the silences and acts of silencing (Fine, 1991; Schultz, 2003) that our conversations created. The most memorable example of this came through the following vignette. Although it represents the most extreme instance, the vignette nonetheless serves as a telling case that illustrates some of the fundamental tensions and problems that developed within the Hip-Hop Lit community.

Keneka

As was our daily practice, I sent the day's journal question as a cellular text message to Mr. Colombo as I rushed to Howard High so that the students could begin writing before I arrived. We were beginning the second section of our unit on family, which dealt with abortion, and I did not want my tardiness to cause us to lose any discussion time for what I expected to be a very spirited and engaged conversation. No sooner had I walked through the classroom door did I hear the voice of Keneka, who demanded that I tell her why I had chosen the day's journal question.

Keneka was a tall 18-year-old African American girl whose bright smile often betrayed the tough front that she offered her classmates and teachers. Before returning to graduate school, I had been Keneka's Spanish teacher during day school, and I also had been her summer school Spanish teacher for the past two summers. During that time, Keneka and I had developed a playfully antagonistic relationship that, to the uninitiated, would look like blatant and mutual disrespect. In front of other people, she and I would argue, tease each other, and even feign irritation at the sound of the other's voice. Mr. Colombo once remarked that he had never seen two people, much less a student and teacher, interact with each other the way Keneka and I did. His remark, which seemed to reflect the attitude of most of our audiences, did not matter to us. Our relationship was an unspoken inside joke that only we shared, and it was my understanding of our relationship that mediated my interactions with her on this day.

I responded to Keneka by joking that Mr. Colombo had picked the question and that I was as surprised as she was at the nature of the question. Unfazed by my attempts at humor, she sternly replied "No he didn't. He already showed us the text [message] you had sent him.

Why did *you* pick *that*??!!!" She then pointed to the day's question and read each word with such disgust that it seemed as if she could taste the words: "Do you believe in abortion? Explain. If you have a story, please share." As I scrambled to think of an appropriate response to Keneka's question, I looked around the room and noticed that several students, all female, were not writing anything. Because the students were frequently resistant to journal writing, I dismissed their inactivity as coincidental and decided that Keneka's concerns were not reflective of the rest of the class. I also assumed that Keneka was not angry but merely upping the stakes in our daily game of the verbal sparring.

After the students finished writing in their journals, I asked them to share their responses. One by one, each student answered the question and provided an explanation for why he or she believed in or disapproved of abortions. When I got to Keneka, the following exchange occurred:

> *Me:*   What do you think?
>
> *Keneka:* Yeah.
>
> *Me:*   What do you mean, "yeah"???
>
> *Keneka:* Yeah!!!!!!

As was our daily ritual, Keneka gave a one-word answer to a question ("Do you believe in abortion?") for which I clearly wanted and asked for a detailed response. Normally, after a bit of prodding, Keneka would follow with a long and thoughtful response to the day's question. This time, however, she closed her book and turned to the person next to her, signifying that she was done participating in the activity. I decided not to push her further and moved on to the next student.

After the rest of the students read their entries, Mr. Colombo distributed our reading for the day, "Retrospect for Life" by Common (1997). Through text rendering, we read the entire piece:

> Knowin' you the best part of life, do I have the right to take yours
> 'Cause I created you, irresponsibly
> Subconsciously, knowin' the act I was a part of
> The start of somethin', I'm not ready to bring into the world
> Had myself believin' I was thorough
> I look into mother's stomach, wonder if you are a boy or a girl
> Turnin' this woman's womb into a tomb
> But she and I agreed, a seed we don't need
> You would've been much more than a mouth to feed
> But someone, I woulda fed this information I read
> To someone, my life for you I woulda had to lead
> Instead I led you to death
> I'm sorry for takin' your first breath, first step, and first cry
> But I wasn't prepared mentally nor financially
> Havin' a child shouldn't have to bring out the man in me

Plus I wanted you to be raised within a family
I don't wanna, go through the drama of havin' a baby's momma
Weekend visits and buyin' J's ain't gon' make me a father
For a while bearing a child is somethin' I never wanted to do
For me to live forever I can only do that through you
Nerve I got to talk about them niggaz with a gun
Must have really thought I was God to take the life of my son
I could have sacrificed goin' out
To think my homies who did it I used to joke about, from now on
I'ma use self control instead of birth control
Cause $315 ain't worth your soul
$315 ain't worth your soul
$315 ain't worth it

Seeing you as a present and a gift in itself
You had our child in you, I probably never feel what you felt
But you dealt with it like the strong black woman you are
Through our trials and tribulations, child's elimination
An integration of thoughts I feel about the situation
Back and forth my feelings was pacin'
Happy deep down but not joyed enough to have it
But even that's a lie, in less than two weeks, we was back at it
Is this unprotected love or safe to say it's lust
Bustin', more than a sweat in somebody you trust
Or is it that we don't trust each other enough
And believe, havin' this child'll make us have to stay together
Girl I want you in my life cause you have made it better
Thinkin' we all in love cause we can spend a day together
We talkin' spendin' the rest of our lives
It's too many black women that can say they mothers
But can't say that they wives
I wouldn't chose any other to mother my understanding
But I want our parenthood to come from planning
It's so much in my life that's undone
We gotta see eye to eye, about family, before we can become one
If you had decided to have it the situation I wouldn't run from
But I'm walkin', findin' myself and my God
So I can, discipline my son with my Rod
Not have a judge tellin' me how and when to raise my seed
Though his death was at our greed, with no one else to blame
I had a book of African names, case our minds changed
You say your period hasn't came, and lately I've been sleepy
So quit smokin' the weed and the beadies and let's have this boy

(Lynn, 1997)

After doing a text rendering of "Retrospect for Life," I attempted to start a class discussion about the song by posing several questions: Who is Common addressing in this text? What is the tone of the piece? What did Common mean by "Three hundred and fifteen dollars ain't worth your soul?" Instead of the normal blend of waving hands and competing voices, I was met with a curious silence that intensified as my questions persisted. Determined to keep the class moving, I began to look for regulars to call on to answer my questions. As my eyes scanned the room, students' heads and bodies began to turn to avoid making eye contact with me.

Finally, after several long minutes passed with little progress, I wondered out loud, "How come y'all not answering the questions?" Keneka, who had been slumped in her seat and seemingly inattentive, jumped to attention as if she had been waiting all day for the question. Without hesitation, she said, "Because they didn't like the song!" Although slightly relieved that she was paying attention, I was more annoyed by the confidence with which she spoke for the entire class. "Retrospect for Life" was one of my favorite songs, and its discussion of a regretted abortion seemed extremely provocative. I was convinced that either Keneka was having a bad day and being belligerent (which was not uncommon for her) or that she was simply mistaken about the class's opinion. Determined to prove that she was in the minority, I responded to her comment:

> *Me:* Well, don't speak for everybody. But why don't *you* like the song?"
>
> *Keneka:* Because I didn't.
>
> *Me:* I need a more elaborate response to than that. We're in a. . . .
>
> *Keneka:* [much louder and seemingly annoyed] Because I *didn't*!

I was now sure that Keneka was merely being oppositional and had no desire to be a productive participant in the class. Although I was growing increasingly frustrated and mildly angry at her now not-so-cute resistance, I was equally determined not to let the other students see me lose my composure:

> *Me:* [in a low voice] I understand that you don't like it but I need your help in explaining to me why the text was bad so that we don't got to read other stuff like this in the future.
>
> *Keneka:* Don't pick stuff like *this* anymore!
>
> *Me:* What is it about *this* that that I should consider when picking a song?

At this point, Haneef, a student who rarely comes to class and speaks even less, is unable to tolerate my ignorance any further and exclaims, "She don't like it because it's about abortion." Without missing a beat, Keneka adds, "Basically!" to punctuate Haneef's declaration of the apparently obvious.

Finally, I had managed to feel as dumb as I must have looked to my students. A sick feeling came over me as I stumbled through the remainder of the class, speaking vaguely about tone and mood while attempting to find meaning in Keneka's distant expression. Although Keneka and two other female students assured me that we could continue to read and analyze "Retrospect for Life" as long as I didn't "make them talk," I felt the most uncomfortable and embarrassed that I ever had as a teacher. Part of my discomfort came from my overestimation of Hip-Hop Lit's ability to facilitate such personal conversations, as well as my unwitting invocation of male privilege. More important, however, I worried that I had ruined my relationship with Keneka. After class, I read Keneka's journal entry for the day:

> I think if your not ready to have a baby or just don't want to have get a abortion but nine out of ten people would say its bad you do what you want to. So I would say abortion ok with me. Fuck it only you can make [several words scratched out] up your own mind.

Keneka's journal entry, which she represented in class simply by saying "yeah," provides further evidence that her resistance to the classroom activities of the day was not enacted to mask her lack of interest or effort. It seemed that Keneka had reflected a great deal about the topic and, as I would later find out, was putting forth great effort simply by remaining in the classroom.

I arrived at school early the following day hoping to catch Keneka in between classes so that we could talk about what had happened the previous day. I wanted to explain to her that much of what happened was a misunderstanding and I wanted to apologize for any discomfort that I may have caused. I asked Ms. Blount, her first period teacher, if Keneka had come to her class, and she told me that Keneka was absent. Although it was not uncommon for students to miss their first class and still come to Hip-Hop Lit, I was not optimistic. We were scheduled to discuss "Retrospect for Life" for another day and then move to "La Femme Fatal" by Digable Planets, in which the narrator politicizes and ultimately supports abortion, for 2 more days. Keneka, however, did not return to class for 7 days.

Because of unexpected scheduling issues, we were still reading "La Femme Fatal" when Keneka returned to school. Although Keneka did not express any dissonance with staying in the class, she was noticeably subdued. Even the normally vacant Mr. Colombo noted after the class, "Keneka was awful quiet today." I repeatedly looked at Keneka as I taught the lesson to see if she was engaged in the activities. I found no answers in her face, as she scribbled in her notebook and stared at her desk. Embarrassed and saddened by the experience, I canceled the remainder of the abortion section of the unit.

As several weeks passed, Keneka and I resumed our normal playful relationship. Nevertheless, I felt compelled to discuss the ordeal with her to express my apologies and understand her perspective. During one of our "make-up days," when students spent the entire period completing old assignments, I brought Keneka into the adjacent classroom and explained to her that it was not my intention to make her uncomfortable or force her to talk about overly personal information. She responded,

> I wasn't mad at you or nothin'. I just didn't want to talk. Remember in the summer time when you asked me if I was pregnant because I was getting fat? [I nodded] Well, I had got pregnant and I ain't wanna tell you. So when we was talking about it in class it just made me think. I had always said that it wouldn't happen to me, and so I couldn't see myself like that.

Although our relationship was restored, this incident provided me with what I considered to be my greatest failure as an educator. Unbeknownst to me, I had created a painful situation for one of my students, completely undermining the goals of wounded healing. Further, the fact that another student, Haneef, had to intervene for me to recognize the silent suffering of Keneka forced me to consider the other ways that Hip-Hop Lit potentially silenced all members of the community, even those who were typically willing to speak.

The story of Keneka represents the potential underside of Hip-Hop Lit and other sites of culturally relevant pedagogy. By linking the curriculum to the lived realities of students, particularly those from marginalized groups, we position ourselves to hear stories of pain, disappointment, and oppression that are often difficult to hear and even more difficult to tell. Given the commonality of many of these experiences among students and teachers, we must constantly consider how the articulation of their accompanying narratives can affect members of the storytelling community. Such a consideration demands that we listen not only to what is said in class but also for silences and acts of silencing within the classroom.

Conclusion

In this article, I have shown how Hip-Hop Lit operated as a space in which members offered and responded to various types of individual and group narratives through the practice of wounded healing. Through this practice, students were able to recognize the commonality of their experiences, challenge various ideologies, and produce new knowledge. In doing this, the members of the class forged a cohesive community replete with multiple roles and relations of power. To be certain, the unique context in which Hip-Hop Lit operated created a particular set of circumstances that stand in sharp relief to the spaces occupied by many K–12 educators. Despite these differences, as well as those that undoubtedly exist even within more traditional schooling contexts, this article points to the need for critically interrogating the ostensible virtues of hip-hop based education and critical and culturally relevant pedagogics more broadly.

To make an effective case for various forms of culturally relevant pedagogy, particularly hip-hop-based education, we must do more than substantiate claims that such approaches "work" vis-à-vis quantitative outcome measures and qualitative assessments of teacher/student motivation and engagement. We must also expand our empirical resources and critical vocabularies to account for the complex relations of power that operate concomitantly within any educational space that draws on the personal and cultural resources of its students. Through close ethnographic investigations, we are better equipped to understand the nuances and contradictions of such spaces—many of which defy the a priori textualist interpretations of many critical pedagogues—and craft appropriately responsive theories and practices.

Even in the absence of an explicit focus on wounded healing, the effective use of culturally relevant curriculum and pedagogy inevitably creates new relationships between teachers, students, and the classroom context. Despite the well-documented virtues of such a shift, we must resist the urge to romanticize the relocation of previously marginalized cultural artifacts, epistemologies, and rituals into formal academic spaces. Although such processes can yield extraordinary benefit, we must also take into account the problematic aspects of "culture" and the underside of "relevance." In particular, we must keep track of the ways in which many of our connections to culturally relevant texts are underwritten by stories of personal pain, forces of structural inequality, and sources of social misery. Although these realities should not necessarily disqualify such texts from entering the classroom, they demand that we move beyond merely hortatory approaches and adopt more critical postures.

Finally, the insights from this article force us to reimagine the classroom as a space in which teachers and students can "risk the self" through individual and collective storytelling. Although scholarship in fields such as composition theory and critical race theory advocate the use of storytelling, there remains a need to develop educational theory and practice that prepares us for the benefits, challenges, and consequences of enabling personal disclosures within the classroom. As this article demonstrates, the failure to take such considerations seriously severely undermines our ability to transform the classroom into a more safe, democratic, productive, and culturally responsive space.

References

Benjamin, A. (2000). Ms. Jackson. On *Stankonia* [CD]. Atlanta: LaFace Records.

Delgado, Bernal, D. (2002). Critical race theory, Latino critical theory, and critical raced-gendered epistemologies: recognizing students of color as holders and creators of knowledge. *Qualitative Inquiry, 8,* 105–126.

Ellsworth, E. (1989). Why doesn't this feel empowering? Working through the repressive myths of critical pedagogy. *Harvard Educational Review, 59,* 297–324.

Fine, M. (1991). *Framing dropouts: Notes on the politics of an urban public high school.* Albany: State University of New York Press.

Forman, M. (2002). *The 'hood comes first: Race, space, and place in rap and hip-hop.* Middletown, CT: University Press of New England/Wesleyan University Press.

Foucault, M. (1990). *History of sexuality.* New York: Vintage.

Fugees. (1996). Manifest. *The score* [CD]. New York: Columbia Records.

Gore, J. (1998). Disciplining bodies: On the continuity of power relations in pedagogy. In T. Popkewitz & M. Brennan (Eds.), *Foucault's challenge: Discourse, knowledge, and power in education* (pp. 231–255). New York: Teachers College Press.

Guinier, L., & Torres, G. (2002). *Miner's canary: Enlisting race, resisting power, transforming democracy.* Cambridge, MA: Harvard University Press.

Hill, M. L. (2008). Toward a pedagogy of the popular. Bourdieu, hip-hop, and out-of-school literacies. In A. Luke & J. Albright (Eds.), *Bourdieu and literacy education* (pp. 136–161). New York: Routledge.

Lynn, L. R. (1997). Retrospect for life. *One day it'll all make sense* [CD]. Los Angeles: Relativity.

O'Reilly, M. R. (1993). *The peaceable classroom.* Portsmouth, NH: Boynton-Cook.

Schultz, K. (2003). *Listening: A framework for teaching across difference.* New York: Teachers College Press.

Smitherman, G. (1977). *Talkin and testifyin: The language of Black America.* Detroit, MI: Wayne University Press.

The Brick Tower

Justin Hudson

As part of basic writing lore, faculty are warned against introducing readings or discussion on educational inequality because the subject matter is too depressing and/or too volatile for students to handle. Yet students are often passionately aware of the social inequalities reproduced in public schools. Justin Hudson, who is African American and matriculated to Columbia University, addressed these issues in his high school graduation speech, published in the New York Times. *His speech provides an unmediated student voice that addresses issues presented by Mina Shaughnessy and Adrienne Rich in an earlier era. Hudson states:*

> *It is certainly not Hunter's fault that socioeconomic factors inhibit the educational opportunities of some children from birth, and in some ways I forgive colleges and universities that are forced to review eighteen year-olds, the end results of a broken system. But, we are talking about eleven year-olds. Four year-olds. We are deciding children's fates before they even had a chance. (p. 78)*

Besides taking on a difficult problem, Hudson faces a complicated rhetorical situation that may be useful to discuss with students in basic writing. Hudson's audience was not only graduating students, their families, and high school faculty, but also college administrators. Hudson directly addresses his purposes in giving this particular speech for what many consider to be a celebratory occasion.

Ladies and gentlemen, family, faculty and my fellow classmates of the class of 2010, before I begin I would like to thank those teachers who chose this modest speech among the outstanding collection of speeches written by my highly competent peers. I would also like to thank all the people who have expressed their support for me and their anticipation for this speech. To be told "You are the best person in the grade to give this speech," or some variation of that statement, more than once is truly humbling, and you all are either the most polite people I know, or the kindest people I know. It is a great honor to give this address, and I promise I do not take it lightly. I have chosen every word quite carefully because I am fully aware of the responsibility you all have bestowed upon me.

Today, I stand before you as a personification of conflictedness. I find myself on this podium experiencing numerous warring emotions, and I am certain many of you here empathize with me on that point. Firstly, and perhaps most obviously, I am filled with a great sense of happiness and accomplishment. My peers and I have put much effort for the last six years—a third of our lives thus far—into being able to stand here today and say that we've earned the right to stand here. It was by no means easy, and there were many times when I thought I would not reach this finish line. But those struggles have only made this moment sweeter. The people who are on this stage survived four years of Latin, or 8th grade swim class, or English with Ms. D'Amico, or BC Calculus, or the 25% rule, and I think all of us can take some pride in that.

Yet, my ambivalence on this day stems from the very fact that this ceremony is the end of an arduous journey. While I am ready to continue my academic endeavors, knowing that Hunter has thoroughly prepared me for them, I am also filled with a deep sense of anxiety and sadness. Hunter has been my second home for the last six years, and it has bordered on becoming my first home. Between my time diligently taking notes in the classroom, playing Chinese Poker in the hallway, taking a nap in the G.O. office, frantically rehearsing for a cultural show or theater production in the auditorium, cheering for an undefeated basketball team in the gymnasium, or simply sitting outside on the senior steps, listening to a boom box and enjoying nice weather in the courtyard, Hunter has truly become a sanctuary for me. My life has revolved around the four-story brick building that stands on East 94th Street and Park Avenue, and Hunter's intimate class size means that I have become as connected to the people of this school as I have to the building itself. It may sound disingenuous to say that I will miss each and every one of you, but all of you in some small way have shaped me into the person I am today, so I thank you all for that.

Of course, the comfort that I have attained at Hunter makes this departure a rather anxious one, but with anxiety comes excitement, and the end of this journey signifies the start of a brand new one. As I leave behind the warmth that I have experienced at Hunter to enter a vastly new and quite frightening terrain, I can only help but think back to the last time I was in this situation, as a fresh-faced, wide-eyed twelve-year-old entering the foreboding, windowless Brick Prison for the first time. Every aspect of my life since that point has been overwhelmingly positive, so all my fears about what lies ahead are slightly tamed by the idea that I will at least come close to experiencing in my future what I have already experienced at Hunter.

However, ladies and gentlemen, more than happiness, relief, fear, or sadness, I feel a very strong emotion that I cannot ignore today. More than anything else, today I feel guilty.

I feel guilty because I don't deserve any of this. And neither do any of you. We received an outstanding education at no charge based solely on our performance on a test we took when we were eleven-year-olds, or four-year-olds. We received superior teachers and additional resources based on our status as "gifted," while kids who naturally needed those resources much more than us wallowed in the mire of a broken system. And now, we stand on the precipice of our lives, in control of our lives, based purely and simply on luck and circumstance. If you truly believe that the demographics of Hunter represent the distribution of intelligence in this city, then you must believe that the Upper West Side, Bayside, and Flushing are intrinsically more intelligent than the South Bronx, Bedford-Stuyvesant, and Washington Heights, and I refuse to accept that. It is certainly not Hunter's fault that socioeconomic factors inhibit the educational opportunities of some children from birth, and in some ways I forgive colleges and universities that are forced to review eighteen-year-olds, the end results of a broken system. But, we are talking about eleven-year-olds. Four-year-olds. We are deciding children's fates before they even had a chance. We are playing God, and we are losing. Kids are losing the opportunity to go to college or obtain a career, because no one taught them long division or colors. Hunter is perpetuating a system in which children, who contain unbridled and untapped intellect and creativity, are discarded like refuse. And we have the audacity to say they deserved it, because we're smarter than them.

As students, we throw around empty platitudes like "deserve" and "earn," most likely because it makes us feel better about ourselves. However, it simply isn't the case. I know for a fact that I did not work as hard as I possibly could have, and I think the same is true for everyone on this stage. Nevertheless, people who work much harder than we ever could imagine will never have the opportunities that lie in front of us.

I apologize if this is not the speech you wanted to hear, but you will have the rest of your lives to celebrate your accomplishments. I apologize if I have not inspired you, or uplifted you, but we have failed to inspire and uplift an entire generation of children. That being said, let me make it very clear that I am not giving anyone here a moral lecture, for I am as complicit in the system we are a part of as anyone else in this room. If anything, I only make these remarks to further emphasize how much Hunter has meant to me, because I am acutely aware of where I would be now without it. As recipients of fortune, we more than anyone else should be able to understand and respect what our high school experience has meant to us, and has done for us.

My guilt ultimately stems from my awareness of the academic, social, emotional, and psychological tools that Hunter has blessed us with. Therefore, I believe the best way to assuage this guilt is to use those fortuitous tools to not only better myself, but also improve the society that surrounds us outside these oh, so narrow walls. I do not know the capacity in which I will be able to make this world a better and more just place, but I strongly believe that education is the most effective means of creating social improvement, which is precisely why this is a battle we cannot concede.

My experiences at Hunter have left me with one final emotion; the last sentiment I will share with you today is hope. I hope that I will use the tools that Hunter has given me as a means to provide opportunities to others, not out of a sense of paternalistic philanthropy, but out of a sense of duty to give to other people what Hunter has given to me. I also hope that you all will do the same, in whatever way you see fit. Even more so, I hope that in the near future, education itself will not be a privilege for the few in this world. I hope that a quality education will not be a privilege for the few in this country. I hope that the Hunter community will descend from its ivory tower made of brick, and distribute its tools evenly to the mass of humanity that is the City of New York. I hope that, despite its problems, Hunter can prove to be the rule, and not the exception, to what can exist as a school. Finally, I hope from the bottom of my heart that someday a class speaker can stand on this podium and look into an audience of his closest and dearest friends whom he never would have met without Hunter and whom he'll never forget, an audience of faculty members he has a deep respect and admiration for, an audience of family members who have supported him throughout his entire life without asking for anything in return. I hope this child can stand on this very stage, look at the most important people in his life, and feel happy, sad, relieved, scared, accomplished, or whatever his heart desires, without feeling guilty about a damn thing. Thank you for your time.

PART TWO

Literacy and Literacies

For some, literacy is a technology; for others, a cognitive consequence; for still others, a set of cultural relationships; yet for others, a part of the highest human impulse to think and rethink experience in place. Literacy is a complex phenomenon, making problems of perspective and definition inevitable. Literacy is also something of real value, making struggle around it unlikely to end.

—Deborah Brandt, *Literacy as Involvement:*
The Acts of Writers, Readers, and Texts (1)

The readings in Part Two explore the complexities of understanding literacy for students in basic writing in the twenty-first century. Each of the separate chapters in this section explores a component part of literacy—in other words, one of the many literacies that form the building blocks for a definition of literacy that is bigger than the sum of its parts. The terms *integrating* and *intersecting* play an important role in this section, because these literacies overlap each other, and often appear inseparable (CCCC).

I have chosen this approach for Part Two because of the intersections of skills and knowledge that constitute literacy in the twenty-first century (Executive Committee). To succeed in twenty-first-century postsecondary literacy, students need to understand each separate piece—and to have a sense of how the whole structure works together. These separate pieces include but are not limited to: processes of writing and research, reading, writing, and critical thinking, digital technologies (called "new literacies" here), and grammar and style. The articles in this section don't separate these components from one another. Rather, they show the intersections and interconnections between the component parts. Yet there still exists a tension in this section between traditional academic literacies and the literacies of "digital natives," students who came of age in the midst of the vast technological changes that continue to unfold with Web 2.0 in our more interactive Internet-based environment. Chief among these tensions is the familiar question of how and why students claim agency for their own writing, and the newer conundrum of what counts as "writing" in this digital age.

Bernstein and Charlton depend on students reading contextually rich and complex texts, even as they focus on processes of research for writing. Sánchez and Paulson, and Jolliffe and Harl show the necessities and purposes of entwining critical thinking with paired reading and writing courses. Carter, Kinloch, and Klages and Clark demonstrate the significance of digital technologies in transforming students' knowledge, and the possibilities for new configurations of teaching and learning. Micciche, and Fearn and Farnan present suggestions for teaching grammar that move students beyond "drill and kill"—and into the rich contexts of process-based classrooms.

Teachers'/scholars' suggestions for course activities, and students' writing based on those activities, permeate this section. We gain a sense that "what works" has as much to do with teachers'/scholars' high expectations for students, as it does with specific exercises implemented in selected classrooms. Whether studying basic writing in the Rio Grande Valley or in Harlem, the students highlighted here share a hunger for coming to understand themselves and their global world—with literacy as both medium and message.

Works Cited

Brandt, Deborah. Introduction. *Literacy as Involvement: The Acts of Writers, Readers, and Texts.* Carbondale: Southern Illinois UP, 1990. Print.
CCCC. "Poster Page: Literacy/Literacies." *College Composition and Communication* 62.2 (2010): 400. Print.
Executive Committee. "The NCTE Definition of 21st Century Literacies." National Council of English Teachers. NCTE, 15 Feb. 2008. Web. 10 Feb. 2012.

Processes of Writing and Research

Basic Writing: In Search of a New Map

Susan Naomi Bernstein

Susan Naomi Bernstein presents Martin Luther King's "Beyond Vietnam: A Time to Break Silence" speech to students enrolled in the beginning course of a two-course basic skills writing sequence at an urban northeastern community college. The students use a variety of meaning-making processes to grapple with the speech, including but not limited to: identifying key words and other critical uses of language, listening to an audio recording of the forty-one-minute speech as they read along, and engaging in a kinesthetic group learning activity. The students discover that the speech, given on April 4, 1967 (a year to the day before King was assassinated), holds many parallels to their own lives, late in the first decade of the twenty-first century. While in the midst of the kinesthetic learning activity, the class discovers that one student has been using his telephone to record the group presentations. Collectively, the students and the professor decide to incorporate this new media into that day's course activities. Rather than existing as ancillary to basic skills, these multimodal interpretive strategies become a key feature of the writing process, offering students opportunities to shape the learning of their classmates, their professor, and themselves.

Writing reflects a daily struggle with language and belief, with learning to understand what we want to say and the many ways we can choose to say it. Writing remains an existential struggle, potentially transformative and profoundly connected to the developing perspectives of the writer. Writing is critical engagement and embodied engagement with the word and the world, to borrow Paulo Freire's often-cited (29–36), but still arresting, terms for the constantly changing processes of literacy development.

Writing pedagogy, I argue, should mirror that critical engagement regardless of who our students are or what their experiences with writing have been. Indeed, we urgently need close readings of Basic Writing classrooms, the term I will use to describe potential attributes of beginning courses in college writing.[1] The students enrolled in such courses often linger precipitously at the margins of higher education, and the courses themselves are consistently underfunded and in constant danger of elimination.[2] Examinations of Basic Writing classrooms remain vital for effectively interrogating—and ultimately re-envisioning—the premises of "remedial" and "basic skills" education.

If we wish to end the need for and the existence of "remedial" courses in higher education, we cannot simultaneously demand the uniformity of standards in high stakes placement and exit assessments; this demand for uniformity contradicts our concurrent goal for critical engagement that English educators value in student writing. My search for a new map is a quest to make sense of this seminal contradiction that undermines many Basic Writing courses before the semester even begins. The writing pedagogy I advocate here grows out of the bureaucratic minefield that Basic Writing has become at many institutions and the impact that this minefield continues to have on students and teachers alike.

Boundaries and Limitations of the Current Map

What is Basic Writing and why does Basic Writing often exist as a separate, segregated space on the margins of the rest of the institution? Perhaps the responses to these questions seem simple at first, but it seems almost impossible to define our understanding of Basic Writing by what it *is*, rather than by what it is not. Basic Writing often focuses on the knots of difference that make writing unacceptable or incomplete; in other words, Basic Writing is everything that is "not" College Writing. Most of us are familiar with this litany of nots:

- Basic Writing is not grammatically correct.
- Basic Writing is not clearly organized.
- Basic Writing does not have a thesis.
- Basic Writing does not feature any or many paragraphs.
- Basic Writing does not have topic sentences.

- Basic Writing does not include sufficient supporting evidence or examples.

- Basic Writing is not complex.

- Basic Writing is not College Writing.

But what would happen if we defined Basic Writing by accentuating its most positive features? Basic Writing would be, through this lens, a series of opportunities for students. Basic Writing exists because our system of public schooling is fraught with unequal opportunities. Basic Writing, however, is an opportunity to hold our commitment to public education accountable. If the academic world said YES to Basic Writing and approached it as critical engagement, a course description might look something like this:

- Basic Writing creates a space—physical and/or virtual—for students to develop as writers.

- Basic Writing provides an opportunity for students to discover the kinds of writing they will encounter throughout college and in the workplace.

- Basic Writing offers time to practice writing intensively and extensively.

This second list is much shorter and presents a more accurate view of Basic Writing's potential to honor the recursive nature of the writing process in creating a written product for a variety of audiences and purposes. Such opportunities frame Basic Writing as non-deficient; the lenses of the frame allow us to see that "remedial" is an inappropriate label for a college course and for students who find themselves in the difficult situation of taking this course. This re-seeing can become a first draft of our new map, a map linked by time and place to the advent of open admissions college education in New York City.

For a very brief moment in history, educators such as Mina Shaughnessy, who designed the Basic Writing program at the City College of New York (CUNY) in the late 1960s and early 1970s, were able to create a vision of Basic Writing as a social change movement. The history of open admissions in the decades following the social movements of the 1960s is much rehearsed. Instead of reiterating that history,[3] I will concentrate instead on Shaughnessy's approaches to pedagogy and the implications of those approaches for drawing a new map.

Shaughnessy envisioned a pedagogy that would provide students with equal access to a democratic education and that would enable teachers to experiment with pedagogy that would facilitate equal access for students. Various stakeholders did not believe that "remedial" courses belonged at City College or other public universities; they worked continually to undercut the efforts of educators and students involved with Basic Writing, as Jane Maher has described in her groundbreaking biography *Mina P. Shaughnessy: Her Life and Work.* Then, as now, many stakeholders inside and outside of public higher education identified Basic Writing as "remedial."[4] Nonetheless, Shaughnessy and a diverse community of students and teachers struggled to establish a foothold for Basic Writing, and for a while they managed to succeed. Because of the urgency surrounding the beginning of open admissions at CUNY and because of the experimental nature of those first courses at CUNY, Mina Shaughnessy was able to hire teachers with wide varieties of experiences, among them the feminist poets Audre Lorde and Adrienne Rich.

In a conversation conducted in 1981, Lorde and Rich discussed their pedagogy for teaching Basic Writing ("Interview"; see also Rich's "Teaching Language in Open Admissions"). Lorde and Rich used literary and sociological texts to teach Basic Writing, texts that challenged students' previous experiences with reading and writing. Lorde and Rich believed that students enrolled in these courses were capable of engaging with the complexity of these texts; these educators created a pedagogy that would break complexities into manageable component parts for the students. Lorde, in particular, discussed her joy at learning, along with the students, the power and possibilities of studying grammar and sentence structure. In these ways, students could gain more access to the texts and to the purposes and potential of writing thus embodying the principles of democratic education that Shaughnessy envisioned (723–27).

Contexts for Reading the Basic Writing Classroom: Understanding Constrictions and Restrictions

What Jean Anyon has called the "hidden curriculum" (68) has, to some extent, come out of hiding and is now more visible to students under extreme financial and academic pressures. In other words, the intellectually invigorating reading and writing courses described by Lorde and Rich now recede into the background as explanations of course policies take up more syllabus space and class time. The hidden curriculum of Basic Writing as an institutional gate-keeping mechanism is revealed when assessment criteria for placement and exit must be explained, as well as rules for credit/no credit courses and financial aid. Students rightly have questions about these issues, since failure to follow a specific policy may well result in failure for the course and failure to thrive in higher education.

The limits and boundaries of "remediation" have haunted me often in the last several years as I have participated in the rise and fall of new programs and in the failed hopes and crushed dreams of far too many students. Students are usually required to enroll in "remedial" courses because they have failed a writing placement test; the test is generally given before the term begins. Often, as Ira Shor has observed (1–10), students have not been fully informed about the institution's expectations for college-level writing. Indeed, many students also have not absorbed the unstated assumptions behind the placement test, that the test determines how the institution views students as writers. Given these circumstances, "remediation" always already carries the stain of failure for students.

"Remediation" also contains the seeds of its own failure to find a sustainable place in higher education. In the current period of diminished public funding for post-secondary institutions, "remedial" courses are often eliminated, as recent examples from California and Ohio make clear (Jaschik n.p.; Hand n.p.). Institutional policies for "remediation" also grow more restrictive, as institutions raise "educational standards" to enforce "academic rigor."

These restrictions carry the consequence of limiting access to higher education. As Janice L. Bloom's research with urban high school students suggests, young people often eliminate themselves from the pool for higher education (363–64). This elimination often happens when potential students face life circumstances exacerbated by economic emergencies. Placement tests and "remedial" courses figure into this equation because they generally cost the same amount of money as college-level courses. However, "remedial" courses usually do not carry credit for graduation. Educational opportunity, under these circumstances, morphs into a separate-but-equal world of "remediation," and its bureaucratic restrictions and constrictions to the material bodies of human beings.

"A Better Place to Live for the Next Generation"

The classroom narrative that follows grows out of these material consequences of "remediation" and the responses of students to working with the kinds of pedagogical challenges with which Audre Lorde and Adrienne Rich and their students struggled (Lorde and Rich; Rich)—and found intellectual gratification. I examine an open admissions, beginning Basic Writing course classroom in a large northeastern city. The students would not earn graduation credit for this course, and they would have to take a second, more advanced (but also non-credit) Basic Writing course. This second non-credit course would determine their eligibility to take the test to "exit remediation." The backdrop for this classroom suggests the "conflict and struggle" (Lu 33–55) of institutional definitions of and purposes for remediation as always already embedded in the material realities of unequal educational opportunity. In this highly contested and ever-diminishing space, students and their teachers are increasingly under the gun to produce visible, if not quantifiable, results.

I present this class as exemplary—an exception to business as usual. This exception helps me to plot the coordinates of a new map that foregrounds students' strengths and presents possibilities for a collaborative journey toward critical engagement with academic writing. Students are represented as composite figures; writing is paraphrased; and names, details, and backgrounds have been changed to protect privacy.

In the first week of our Basic Writing class, a student named Helen asked me: "Why are we beginning with 'I Have a Dream?' What about King's later speeches? What about reading something by Thurgood Marshall or Fannie Lou Hamer?" Helen had emailed me after watching "I Have a Dream" on YouTube in class on the first day of the term. She wrote, "My name is Helen, I sit in the front of your class I wore a bright orange shirt today, anyway I'm hoping that you will be the one to unleash the missing writer inside of me." Helen's concerns would motivate me to think and rethink about this class long after the term had ended. Our shared concerns about writing helped us to form an unusual classroom community—unusual because of our commitment to making collective, if sometimes chaotic, decisions about course curriculum and assignments. In perhaps the most significant decision of the course, we voted to drop a short novel from the syllabus and to focus instead on one of King's most rhetorically complex and intricate texts: "Beyond Vietnam: A Time to Break Silence."

King presented "A Time to Break Silence," a groundbreaking speech against the War in Vietnam, on April 4, 1967, at Riverside Church in New York City. A year later, on April 4, 1968, King was assassinated during a sanitation workers' strike in Memphis, Tennessee. Most significantly, however, my students and I were studying King's work in the same spring that Barack Obama was running for President of the United States; for the first time in many years, I would bear witness to a classroom of young people engaged in a critical historical moment.

We approached working with "A Time to Break Silence" through analyzing how King used grammatical structure and word choice to create a persuasive text. Often our work took the form of keyword analysis in single paragraphs of the text, as exemplified by an excerpt from a whole class participatory lesson on how King used binary oppositions to create a connection to his audience—Concerned Clergy and Laity (see Appendix 1). We also listened to the entire speech (over an hour long) and took part in an exercise that involved kinesthetic learning and an investigation of learning styles. In this sense, our class implemented principles of universal instructional design; universal instruction design provided students with opportunities to select resources from a variety of learning styles. With a text as rich as "A Time to Break Silence," I suggested that students would benefit from a class project on kinesthetic learning; the speech would allow students to grapple with language and rhetorical issues through small and large motor movements. The goal was for students to learn how to analyze a passage through an embodied, kinesthetic investigation of the text (see Appendix 2). This investigation was designed to enhance their interpretive strategies for examining text. They eventually would translate their interpretations into persuasive writing.

Each group had approximately twenty-five minutes to select, discuss, and carry out its project. Some groups drew individual pictures clearly connected to the themes of their excerpts, and one group wrote and presented a skit based on King's list of strategies for achieving peace in Vietnam. One group chose to construct a mural with deliberate placement of text and images. Our next step in this process was to move from group work to group presentations. Because I was observing the presentations at the front of the room, I did not know that Devin, sitting in the last row, was photographing and videotaping the presentations with his cell phone. When his group rose to give the final presentation, Devin's role as class photographer and videographer was revealed. The class and I invited Devin to lend his phone to another class member who would record the proceedings. Another student offered to videotape while Devin's group presented their mural, and I took notes. The video excerpt and the mural have been published on the National Conversation on Writing website (see Appendix 3 and Appendix 4).

These artifacts represent the collective work that becomes possible when, in Marilyn Cochran-Smith and Susan Lytle's terms, the teacher and the students approach classroom-based research as both process and as product. Students themselves become active researchers on the question of what constitute "best practices" for teaching and learning in basic writing courses; they take a primary role in co-creating an environment in which "best practices" can flourish. This research seems particularly vital in the current material realities of our students' lives and in the lives of our institution, in a historical moment when "remedial" courses at colleges and universities are threatened by legislative intervention and funding cuts that make sustaining such courses a low institutional priority.

Perhaps the "risk" of disengagement lessens when students have an opportunity to share responsibility for their own success, when the motivation is intrinsic rather than extrinsic, and when students share responsibility for each other's learning. Vincent Tinto has noted that collectivity and collaboration can contribute to successful retention of students categorized as "at-risk" (173). In this case, the students' involvement extended from the kinesthetic activities and group work to their writing for the course.

Their classroom-based inquiry gave them an opportunity to turn the embodied experiences of their observations into writing. The final in-class high-stakes essay assignment invited students to respond to one of two writing prompts about "A Time to Break Silence." Writing in the midst of the whirlwind of events surrounding the spring presidential primaries of the 2008 US elections, students seemed to be particularly inspired by the following prompt:

> In his 1967 speech "A Time to Break Silence," Dr. Martin Luther King states, "A time comes when silence is betrayal." Several times he repeats the phrase "we must speak." Do you think that Dr. King's commitment "to break the silence of the night" is still meaningful in 2008? Why or why not? Refer to "A Time to Break Silence" as support for your own ideas. Write an essay of at least 250 words and refer to "A Time to Break Silence" as support for your own ideas. [N.B. 250 words was our program's minimum length requirement for the course; students' final essays in the course were generally 500 words or longer.]

The students who wrote the three paragraphs below took part in the mural/video project as participant observers. The following paragraphs served as the conclusions for their final in-class essays, representing the last words that the students would write for the beginning Basic Writing course:

> Dr. Martin Luther King, Jr. gave this speech "A Time to Break Silence" in 1967 but it's still applying for 21st century. Just like Dr. Martin Luther King Jr. said "We must speak." We must speak up right now to save our country and put stop on war. We must speak up to improve America. It is the time to break silence, otherwise most of the college students will not get a better education and the American economy will go down and down and we could be facing another great depression.
>
> John

> The reason that Dr. King's commitment "to break the silence of the night" is still meaningful in 2008 is because by speaking out and standing up you can make a change in the world. At times it could become hard but if we stick together as a nation we would become stronger as a group. Martin Luther King is a very strong example of why "we must speak." United we stand as a strong country. Remember if we speak out now we can make the world a better place to live in for the next generation.
>
> Michael

> King is all about keeping people united as one. One quote that he uses where he says that we all must stay together to "create a beautiful symphony of brotherhood." This quote suggests how he believed that people should stand up for what they believed in. I also believe that his commitment is still alive today because learning about him made me want to be a better person and always fight for what I believe to be true.
>
> Sarah

I was particularly intrigued by the ways in which technology played a significant role in this classroom and the ways in which students turned their engagement with technology into writing. As happens in many contemporary classrooms, we watched YouTube videos together to study history and to make connections between history and the present moment. Not only did the students agree to spend a significant amount of time studying a single text, they also used technology to aid their comprehension of the text and its historical and contemporary contexts. Students also created their own multimedia presentations to move from a familiar technology to a difficult and unfamiliar text, what Shannon Carter calls "rhetorical dexterity" (142). For instance, students responded to visual and kinesthetic presentations with photography and videography, framing their responses to peers' multimedia work by creating additional multimedia texts.

Valerie Kinloch, drawing on her research with Harlem youth, understands multimodal learning as a means of creating reciprocity and enacting transformative learning for both educators and students. Through referencing the work of her own students, she affirms the critical need for students and educators to co-create their learning environments (186). Such learning is not a one-way, top-down process, but builds reciprocity for everyone involved. As Kinloch states, "[multimedia learning] brings us closer to witnessing how youth understand education, experience learning, and make meaning from a variety of encounters ..." (187). Indeed, Devin gave the class an opportunity to keep a record of our own learning through digital media, something that I had not considered when I had planned the lesson for that day. Because of Devin's initiative in creating a more inclusive definition of multimedia, our class has a much fuller record of the ways in which we made meaning that day.

This record includes (perhaps most obviously) visuals and sound, but also the kinesthetic and the emotional. We hear the camcorder changing hands and watch its quickly shifting angles as its first-time videographer, who also serves as an impromptu narrator, learns to focus; we observe the shift of subject positions as professor and students move from teachers to learners, from audience members to performers. We also can see and hear the emotions in the room, from body language to the moments of making meaning. At three minutes and forty-seven seconds into the video, for example, a muralist describes his symbol of "chickens kissing" to signify happiness. The videographer laughs, and we watch as the muralist moves his fingers down to pictures of soldiers "killing one another." At four minutes and thirty-five seconds, the videographer finds connection in the work of another muralist. "Oh, that's symbolism. That's symbolism. I like that," the videographer enthuses. "That—that's good. I like that." As our class experienced making meaning through multimedia, we reconnected to "A Time to Break Silence" and the rhetorical tropes that we had encountered as we studied the key words of the text.

Indeed, students in this beginning Basic Writing class grew more engaged with persuasive writing in relation to, rather than in isolation from, multimedia; this engagement also included listening to and watching available recordings of King's speeches. Of the many endeavors of the co-created curriculum in our Basic Writing classroom, perhaps the most exciting remained our class's movement through the visual, aural, and kinesthetic literacies of multimedia through the literacies of writing for an academic audience. In other words, the students' writing and multimedia, cited above, serve as examples of the critical skills involved in learning to write for an academic audience. The students' persuasive writing might appear to be the most crucial example, as students would need to write a persuasive essay to pass the test for "exiting remediation."

Another writing sample from earlier in the course suggests the complexity of the processes involved in learning to write for an academic audience. In the following sample, Robert experiments with persuasive writing in a rough draft of his second essay; he writes to make meaning for a twenty-first century reader of "Beyond Vietnam: A Time to Break Silence" and focuses especially on the theme of violence:

> I believe the 21st century audience would capture about this theme all the horrible and awkward experiences that harm or damage the life of the Vietnamese people and shock the whole world. The actions that the 21st century audience should take as a result of paying attention to this theme might be learning the reasons and consequences that a war would always bring. Consequences like the economy, prices of food, gas, more people unemployed, more homeless people, low paying jobs, lack of education, and lack of healthcare. These are reasons and consequences that a war would always bring. Because all the money is used to buy machine guns, and transport the soldiers to the war zone.

Educators in beginning Basic Writing classes often present the concepts of developing ideas and using supportive evidence as crucial skills for writing for academic audiences. Students may interpret these skills as adding more details to their essays but may not have experience with implementing such details in their own writing practice. The multimedia of kinesthetic learning offers an embodied experience of adding detail through voice, body language, color, and digital videography, as students learned through creating the video and then replaying that experience on YouTube. Robert drafted this essay not only in the context of reading "Beyond Vietnam: A Time to Break Silence," but also in the context of student-driven multimedia projects and through watching and listening to recordings of King's speeches. Traditional and new media worked together to create the context for learning the critical skills involved in composing a persuasive essay.

Such work holds the promise of turning basic writing into an engaging and challenging academic course that offers students new opportunities to develop their abilities as writers. "Exiting remediation" is a finite, institutionally imposed goal, with punitive consequences for non-compliance. Yet a curriculum which foregrounds students' prior and developing knowledge presents exciting possibilities for basic writing pedagogy.

What Is Basic Writing? What I Believe to Be True

We as teachers also have an opportunity to develop and to grow, to remove ourselves from our own comfort zones so that we may learn again. This learning may indeed become a difficult task, and we may feel stymied by too many papers to grade, too little time for grading and preparing lessons, and too many additional responsibilities to clearly hear our own voices speaking back to us. Nonetheless, as educators we need to examine our own implicit notions that we are always already aware of students' abilities, needs, and behaviors within the complex communities that constitute our classrooms.[5] We may need to go against the grain of what we think we already know from our own experiences as teachers and students so that our approaches to teaching and learning do not stagnate or calcify. Along with our students, we can refuse to accept their predefined status as institutional failures.

As the students themselves suggest, following King's model of speaking out "against the silence of the night" can bring its own powerful rewards. John and Robert's concerns appear to foreshadow the Wall Street crash of September 2008. Yet students in tenuous financial and academic circumstances have long struggled with the intersections of economics and education; their concerns are not new and have not been adequately addressed or ameliorated.[6]

Although high stakes tests may seem to offer a snapshot of how students perform on a single measurement of skills that are uniformly normed and evaluated, the test results are less reliable for determining individual characteristics of a cohort of students.

The tests do not measure motivation for learning beyond high school, persistence for learning in challenging situations, or potential for future achievement. The tests do not measure the bureaucratic system of barriers that a new college student must negotiate, or the damage done by marking Basic Writing courses as "remediation" and misidentifying students and their teachers as "failures." As stated earlier, this demand for uniformity (via standardized testing) contradicts our concurrent goal for critical engagement that English educators value in student writing.

Indeed, the tests also do not account for the support systems that students with more educational privilege can take for granted. Students with educational privilege in high school, as Bloom found in her research, often have better access to information about college, including financial aid and career counseling; their preparation for college may be more strongly supported by teachers and administrators at their school and by their families.

Students that are the first members of their families to attend college may not have these support systems; such students may not be aware of the need to consciously prepare for college, and they may not know how to find information that will help them to prepare. These issues may be exacerbated by the financial needs of students who must work full time to support themselves and their families. The learning gaps of unequal access to cultural and financial capital are not measured by standardized tests and cannot be easily "remediated." Yet unequal access seems inextricably linked to students' "failed" performance on high stakes tests and their placement in "remediation." Given the high stakes exigencies surrounding our students' lives, the search for a new map becomes even more significant.[7]

It is equally significant to document our own search for a new map, whether that means writing with students, or contributing to scholarly discourse, or initiating or adding to discussions in our own institutional and other communities. If we remain silent, we risk losing time in the endless activity of reinventing the wheel. When we do not keep a record, there is no writing, reading, or thinking—and silence stands in the place of active and deeply embodied learning. This silence and the absence of embodied lives is what we risk when we reinscribe institutional practices of placement and assessment that were NOT always natural or normal. Our records can help to create educational spaces that remove us from our comfort zones as learners (and as teachers) and that help to address the risks of burnout and disengagement. The act of recording itself can help us to become reflexive. Yet self-reflexivity remains only one part of an ongoing process. As Cochran-Smith and Lytle remind us (calling attention to the work of Dwayne Huebner), we must "responsibly take action to improve the educational choices and life chances of [our] students" (84).

This "transformation of silence into language and action," as Lorde suggests elsewhere ("Transformation" 40), can be compared to the difference between having a dream and learning to break silence to enact the dream in material reality. We must continue to embody the hope and the potential for learning. We continue to "always fight for," as King would have it, "what I believe to be true." There is a world of writing waiting to be born and we must start by writing a new map for this leg of the journey. Let us begin together—and let us begin now.[8]

Notes

Thanks to my students enrolled in beginning Basic Writing in Spring 2008, and my colleagues Adam Vine, Amy Winans, Steve Cormany, Shannon Carter, and Ken Monteith who read, discussed, and debated with me the many drafts of this essay.

1. Mina Shaughnessy introduced the term "Basic Writing" to the general public in her 1977 book *Errors and Expectations: A Guidebook for Teachers*

of Basic Writing. For *Errors and Expectations*, Shaughnessy studied writing examples of students that were placed in beginning writing courses in the early 1970s, the first years of open admissions at the City University of New York (CUNY). The appropriate name for beginning writing courses has been debated and contested frequently in the thirty-three years since *Errors and Expectations* was first published. George Otte and Rebecca Williams Mlynarczyk provide an especially succinct version of this history in their recent book *Basic Writing.* I use "Basic Writing" here to affirm germinal connections to the introduction of open admissions at CUNY, and to the work of Mina Shaughnessy at CUNY.

Many state legislatures and other post-secondary education stakeholders prefer the term "remedial," and tellingly, these stakeholders generally do not cite or acknowledge Shaughnessy's work in their arguments against beginning writing courses. I will enclose "remedial," "remediation," and other variants of the term in quotes to indicate its misappropriation for educational reforms that seek to eliminate (or have already eliminated) open admissions and beginning writing courses at post-secondary educational institutions. See Thomas Bailey for specific examples of this usage. Although Bailey notes that "the terms developmental education and remediation are used interchangeably" in this work (11), the first term, according to the *Oxford English Dictionary Online* (2nd edition) suggests "Of, pertaining, or incidental to development; evolutionary," while the second term's first suggestions "the action of remedying, *esp.* the giving of remedial teaching or remedial therapy." While the first term presents education as evolutionary process, the second term draws a direct connection to remedies and therapies for illness or other conditions that deviate from the norm. (Also see Rose, "Colleges Need," A76, cited in Otte and Mlynarczyk).

In June 2010, Thomas Bailey was appointed by United States Secretary of Education Arne Duncan to chair the Committee on Student Success. This committee, as charged under the Higher Education Equal Opportunity Act,

> will develop recommendations for two-year degree-granting institutions of higher education to comply with the law's graduation and completion rate disclosure requirements. The committee will also develop recommendations regarding additional or alternate measures of student success that are comparable alternatives to the completion or graduation rates, taking into account the mission and role of two-year degree-granting higher education institutions. (United States Department of Education)

2. Indeed, many institutions across the United States have already eliminated courses called Basic Writing, as well as courses in beginning college reading and basic mathematics. See Greene and McAlexander, and Otte and Mlynarczyk, for specific histories surrounding this issue.
3. In addition to the histories cited above, also see Sternglass; Laurence, Rondinone, Gleason, Farrell, Hunter, and Lu; Horner and Lu; Soliday; Maher; Lewiecki-Wilson and Sommers; and Ray for histories that present specific detail, and differing perspectives on the fraught relationship of CUNY and Basic Writing. I am also indebted to my colleague Victor Rosa for his insights regarding CUNY in the early years of its open admissions policy

and the hopes of social change that this policy engendered for students and professors alike. In addition, see Ritter for a history of Basic Writing at elite selective enrollment institutions.

4. See Rose's eloquent arguments in defense of providing higher education for students that, because of education inequity in economically underserved communities, may lack adequate preparation for college. Rose sees access to higher education as a critical necessity for creating a more just society. Also see Traub, who argues that college is "too late" for many of the students that he observed in "remedial" courses at City College in the early 1990s, and Danzig, who in 1976 suggested that "egalitarian education has been developed with little regard for the realities of the world of work" (12).

5. I am grateful to my colleague Adam Vine for offering this insight.

6. See Gutierrez and Rogoff, and Royster and Taylor (cited in Lewiecki-Wilson and Sommers) for critical work on teaching and learning, and the complexities of embodied identities.

7. At the time of this writing, CUNY has just announced that it has closed admissions for first-year students applying to all of its campuses (including the community colleges), for the 2010–2011 academic year. Students who applied after the first week of May 2010 would be put on a waiting list, the first ever in CUNY's history. See Foderaro and Christ. At the end of 2008–2009, the college that I refer to in the article eliminated its beginning Basic Writing course, but in the spring of 2010 several of the students from the 2008 class had moved well beyond their "remediation" requirements in writing. In subsequent meetings, in the cafeteria and in my office, these students spoke passionately of their love for writing and of their current academic interests in urban studies, theater, and politics.

8. At the 2010 meeting of the American Association of Community Colleges, philanthropist Melinda Gates, co-founder of the Bill and Melinda Gates Foundation, stated, "If you start in a remedial class, the odds are that you will never finish a credit-bearing course in that subject" (Amario). The Gates Foundation is one of many stakeholders involved in reforming higher education, and Melinda Gates, in these remarks, reiterated many stakeholders' low expectations for students to succeed beyond "remediation."

Gates Foundation research (completed by the firm Public Agenda) also suggests that a key reason that students do not graduate from college has nothing to do with intelligence or ability to learn, but with the material realities of economic inequality. According to the research, more than 50% of college dropouts have household incomes of less than $35,000 a year, and 70% had not received loans or scholarships to help pay for college costs. Because they need to work to support themselves and their families, many of these former students attended college part time and were not eligible to receive financial aid (Lewin). In the popular media, however, "remediation" and economic inequality seldom, if ever, were reported in the same context. Stories of "success" in courses called "Basic Writing" also are rarely reported to a wider audience.

Appendix 1

Key Word Analysis

- **Keyword**
- *Opposite of key word*
- Definitions of key words [and opposites]

This call for a worldwide fellowship that lifts neighborly concern beyond one's tribe, race, class, and nation is in reality a call for an all-embracing and unconditional love for all mankind. This oft misunderstood, this oft misinterpreted concept, so readily dismissed by the Nietzsches of the world as [a weak and cowardly force,] has now become an absolute necessity for the survival of man. When I speak of **love** I am not speaking of some sentimental and weak response. I am not speaking of that force which is just emotional bosh. I am speaking of that force which all of the great religions have seen as the supreme unifying principle of life. **Love** is somehow the key that unlocks the door which leads to ultimate reality. This Hindu-Muslim-Christian-Jewish-Buddhist belief about ultimate reality is beautifully summed up in the first epistle of Saint John: "Let us **love** one another, for love is God. And every one that **loveth** is born of God and knoweth God. He that **loveth** not knoweth not God, for God is love." "If we **love** one another, God dwelleth in us and his love is perfected in us." Let us hope that this spirit will become the order of the day.

We can no longer afford to worship the god of *hate* or [bow before the altar of retaliation.] The oceans of history are made [turbulent by the ever-rising tides] of *hate*. And history is cluttered with [the wreckage of nations and individuals] that pursued this self-defeating path of *hate*. As Arnold Toynbee says: "**Love** is the ultimate force that makes for the saving choice of life and good against the [damning choice of death and evil.] Therefore the first hope in our inventory must be the hope that **love** is going to have the last word."

Appendix 2

Group Work with Learning Styles

Directions:

- A member of each group picks a passage from the hat.
- The group creates a presentation from one of the learning styles listed below; your presentation must show why King's speech is still relevant in 2008.
- The group presents a 5–7 minute presentation to the class; audience questions and discussion can be included as part of the presentation.

Visual:

- Create a collage that analyzes the passage
- Create a mural that analyzes the passage
- Something else?

Oral/Aural:

- Create a musical presentation that analyzes the passage.
- Create a play that analyzes the passage.
- Something else?

Kinesthetic:

- Create a dance that analyzes the passage.
- Create a pantomime (silent movement piece) that analyzes the passage.
- Something else?

Appendix 3

Mural

"Mural for Dr. Martin Luther King's 'A Time to Break Silence.'" National Conversation on Writing. 8 July 2008. Web. 28 November 2008. <http://dmc.tamu-commerce.edu/cdm4/document.php?CISOROOT=/ncow&CISOPTR=71&REC=13>

Appendix 4

Video

See "A Mural for Martin Luther King's 'A Time to Break Silence.'" <http://www.youtube.com/watch?v=RNg3tOn2bio>

Works Cited

Amario, Christine. "Nation Has High Remedial College Education Rate." *Associated Press.* 11 May 2010. Web. 29 May 2010.

Anyon, Jean. "Social Class and the Hidden Curriculum of Work." *Journal of Education* 162.1 (1980): 67–92. Print.

Bailey, Thomas. "Challenge and Opportunity: Rethinking the Role and Function of Developmental Education in Community College." *New Directions for Community Colleges* 2009.145 (2009): 11–30. *Education Research Complete. EBSCO.* Web. 7 May 2010.

Bloom, Janice L. "(Mis)Reading Social Class in the Journey Towards College: Youth Development in America." *Teachers College Record* 109.2 (2007): 334–68. Print.

Carter, Shannon. *The Way Literacy Lives: Rhetorical Dexterity and Basic Writing Instruction*. Albany: SUNY P, 2008. Print.

Christ, Lindsay. "CUNY Sets Up Wait List for Fall 2010." *NY1 Online*. 5 May 2010. Web. 6 May 2010.

Cochran-Smith, Marilyn. and Susan Lytle. *Inside/Outside: Teacher Research and Knowledge*. New York: Teachers College P, 1993. Print.

Danzig, Martin E. "An Appraisal of Open Admissions." *Community College Review* 4 (1976). 8–14. Print.

Foderaro, Lisa W. "Two-Year Colleges. Swamped, No Longer Welcome All." *New York Times Online*. 12 Nov. 2009. Web. Retrieved 8 Dec. 2009.

Freire, Paulo. "The Importance of the Act of Reading." Paulo Freire and Donalda P. Macedo. *Literacy: Reading the Word and the World*. Critical studies in education series. South Hadley: Bergin & Garvey, 1987. 29–36. Print.

Greene, Nicole Pepinster and Patricia J. McAlexander, editors. *Basic Writing in America: The History of Nine College Programs*. Cresskill: Hampton UP, 2008. Print.

Hand, Greg. "UC Admissions Changes Align with State Strategic Higher Education Plan." *University of Cincinnati News*. 7 Aug. 2009. n. pag. Web. 17 May 2010.

Horner, Bruce and Min-Zhan Lu. *Representing the "Other": Basic Writing and the Teaching of Basic Writing*. Urbana: NCTE, 1999. Print.

Huebner, Dwayne, "The Vocation of Teaching." *Teacher Renewal: Professional Issues, Personal Choices*. Eds. Frances S. Bolin and Judith McConnell Falk. New York: Teachers College P, 1987. 17–29. Print.

Jaschik, Scott. "Sophie's Choice for Two-Year Colleges." *Inside Higher Education*. 5 Oct. 2009. Web. 17 May 2010.

King, Martin Luther. "Beyond Vietnam: A Time to Break Silence," *American Rhetoric*. n.d. Web. Retrieved 30 Nov. 2008.

Kinloch, Valerie. *Harlem on Our Minds: Race, Place, and the Literacies of Urban Youth*. New York: Teachers College P, 2010. Print.

Laurence, Patricia, Peter Rondinone, Barbara Gleason, Thomas J. Farrell, Paul Hunter, and Min-Zhan Lu. "Symposium on Basic Writing, Conflict and Struggle, and the Legacy of Mina Shaughnessy." *College English* 55.8 (1993): 879–903. Print.

Lewiecki-Wilson, Cynthia and Jeff Sommers. "Professing at the Fault Lines: Composition at Open Admissions Institutions." *College Composition and Communication* 50.3 (1999): 97–121. Print.

Lewin, Tamar. "College Dropouts Cite Low Money and High Stress." *New York Times Online*. 10 Dec. 2009. Web. 23 Dec. 2009.

Lorde, Audre. "The Transformation of Silence into Language and Action." *Sister/Outsider: Essays and Speeches*. Berkeley; Ten Speed P, 1984. 40–44. Print.

Lorde, Audre and Adrienne Rich. "An Interview with Audre Lorde." *Signs* 6.4 (1981): 713–36.

———. "An Interview: Audre Lorde and Adrienne Rich." *Sister/Outsider: Essays and Speeches*. Berkeley: Ten Speed P, 1984. 81–109. Print.

Lu, Min-Zhan. "Conflict and Struggle: The Enemies or Preconditions of Basic Writing?" *Representing the "Other": Basic Writing and the Teaching of Basic Writing*. Eds. Bruce Horner and Min-Zhan Lu. Urbana: National Council of Teachers of English, 1999. 30–55. Print.

Maher, Jane. *Mina P. Shaughnessy: Her Life and Work*. Urbana: NCTE, 1997. Print.

McNeil, Linda M. *Contradictions of School Reform: Educational Costs of Standardized Testing.* New York: Routledge, 2000. Print.

Otte, George and Rebecca Williams Mlynarczyk. *Basic Writing.* Reference Guides to Rhetoric and Composition. Ed. Charles Bazerman. Lafayette: Parlor-WAC Clearinghouse, 2010. Print.

Ray, Brian. "A New World: Redefining the Legacy of Min-Zhan Lu." *Journal of Basic Writing* 27.2 (2008): 106–27.

Rich, Adrienne. "Teaching Language in Open Admissions." (1912). *On Lies, Secrets, and Silence: Selected Prose, 1966–1978.* New York: Norton, 1995. 51–68. Print.

Ritter, Kelly. *Before Mina Shaughnessy: Basic Writing at Yale and Harvard, 1920–1960.* Carbondale: Southern Illinois UP, 2009. Print.

Rose, Mike. *Lives on the Boundary: The Struggles and Achievements of America's Underprepared.* New York: Free Press, 1989. Print.

———. *Why School?: Reclaiming Education for All of Us.* New York: New P, 2009. Print.

Royster, Jacqueline Jones, and Rebecca Greenberg Taylor. "Constructing Teacher Identity in the Basic Writing Classroom." *Journal of Basic Writing* 16.1 (1997): 27–50. Print.

Russell, Alene. "Enhancing College Student Success Through Developmental Education." *Policy Matters.* ASCU: August 2008. Web. 18 July 2009.

Shaughnessy, Mina P. *Errors and Expectations: A Guide for the Teacher of Basic Writing.* New York: Oxford UP, 1977. Print.

Shor, Ira. *Empowering Education: Critical Teaching for Social Change.* Chicago: U of Chicago P, 1992. Print.

Soliday, Mary. *The Politics of Remediation: Institutional and Student Needs in Higher Education.* Pittsburg: U of Pittsburgh P, 2002. Print.

Sternglass, Marilyn. *Time to Know Them: A Longitudinal Study of Writing and Learning.* Mahwah: Erlbaum, 1997. Print.

Tinto, Vincent. "Colleges as Communities: Taking Research on Student Persistence Seriously." *The Review of Higher Education* 21.2 (1997): 167–77. Print.

Traub, James. *City on a Hill: Testing the American Dream at City College.* Reading: Addison-Wesley, 1994. Print.

Valenzuela, Angela. *Subtractive Schooling: U.S.-Mexican Youth and the Politics of Caring.* New York: SUNY P, 1999. Print.

Seeing Is Believing: Writing Studies with "Basic Writing" Students ↟

Jonikka Charlton

Jonikka Charlton writes about students enrolled in a basic writing course paired with first-year composition at a Texas university located near the Mexican border. The students are immersed in the process of writing about writing, also known as writing studies. In this successful curriculum, students read the same rhetoric and composition articles that teachers/ scholars read. Since the students focus on studies of writing processes,

*products, and context, writing about writing proves to be immediately
helpful to their own work. As they are introduced to the theory and practice
of composition, students discover research questions that arise out of their
own writing pasts or that pertain to their own writing futures. Additionally
students realize that their instructors hold them to high expectations, and
use those expectations to propel them through the challenges presented by
writing about writing.*

> *Sé el cambia que quieres ver en el mundo.*
> Be the change you want to see in the world.
> —Gandhi

To believe you can be the change, sometimes you have to see it.

When I entered the room, an outside observer for the day, it was the second hour of class. The students were already circled up and talking about where they were in their research processes. They each talked about their research questions, how the questions had evolved as they researched, read, and thought about them, and they shared the challenges they faced in pursuing answers to their questions.

Izzy[1]

Izzy, a graduate of one of the more successful charter schools in Texas' Rio Grande Valley, hasn't done much with her project, so her turn begins with a number of excuses for why she isn't further along. When she started her project, she was confident about her question, something about whether AP classes prepare students for college. As a student who had taken a number of AP classes herself in high school, she seems convinced of their value, and her plan is to interview a couple of students, one who had had AP classes, one who didn't. But she is having trouble finding additional information. So, Marlene, her teacher, turns the conversation over to the class. Did her peers have any questions/comments for Izzy? A couple of students begin to question her about the purpose of her surveys, what data she would collect and how she could sort it and use it, and within a few minutes, they and Marlene have convinced Izzy that she should be focusing on *English* AP classes, and her survey participants should be college students since they are the ones who would know for sure if their high school AP classes had any impact on their success in their college classes. Izzy realizes she had a perfect survey group in her own classmates as they fit her profile, and they brainstorm ways that AP English classes for them were different than "regular" ones. Marlene suggests she do some research into AP materials online to see if the stated goals of the AP English classes correspond to their own first-year writing class goals. Her turn ends with students suggesting specific databases for Izzy to continue her research with, and then it's on to another student.

Vanessa

Vanessa's research question has evolved from "Does having an ability to read music affect the ability to read rhetorically?" to "Is there a connection between learning how to read music and learning how to read texts?" She claims that her one success in the project thus far has been changing her question to something she can find sources for. Before this class, she says research was like a foreign language to her. She didn't know what to look for or what would be useful, so she just used whatever sources she could find quickly. Most of her peers in the class seem to have had the same experience. Now, she says, she realizes she needs patience to do research, that you should take the time to look for the right sources rather than using any old thing. She has learned a new way of reading research, as a way to see if the sources are reliable and relevant. She thinks she can finish her project in two to three weeks, and she has an answer to her question.

César

César began his project by trying to find out whether employers have a better perception of a college graduate than they do of a high school graduate with years of experience. A returning student with a full-time job, César is having a really hard time squeezing in even a few minutes a day for his research. He now wants to know what the influence of a parent's educational level is on his/her children going to college. Jorge, from across the circle, jumps in with a suggestion for doing more efficient research: "When you pull up a source, do a CTRL-F and use a keyword from your research to see how many times it shows up in the article. For me, I use 'parents' because my research is about parents helping their kids to write. Read through some of the sentences where the key word is found and if it's not pertaining to what you're interested in or it doesn't show up enough, throw that source out." He then goes on to offer a source he found that wasn't quite right for his research, but sounds like it fits really well with César's. Another student, sensing César's unease with where he is in focusing his project, asks him specific questions to help him clarify and further explain why he's interested in it. He wants to interview students who dropped out (like him, it turns out) and find out why they did. Cynthia, who had been relatively quiet until now, suggests that everyone put their research question on the class blog and then, if anyone might be able to help by offering a source or potential survey/interview subject, they can add a comment there.

Background

Two years ago, I began my graduate course on teaching first-year writing with an article which had just been published in the summer *CCC*: Douglas Downs and Elizabeth Wardle's "Teaching about Writing, Righting Misconceptions: (Re)Envisioning 'First-Year Composition' as 'Introduction to Writing Studies.'" I did so as part of a grander scheme to disrupt common assumptions about the purpose(s) of first-year writing classes and to make the familiar—in this case, the almost universally required first-year writing course—strange again. My students were a microcosm of almost any English department in the country. Many of them had primarily a literature background, a fair number were creative writers, and a smaller percentage were rhetoric and composition students. About half wanted to be TAs in our writing program and were thus required to take the course. Class discussion of this article, generally speaking, elicited more favorable responses than I imagined. Most read a "writing about writing" approach as legitimate, even mildly intriguing, though they had serious concerns about how it might be enacted and what they might lose by teaching it. Some, for instance, clearly valued a cultural studies approach to teaching FYC. Such a curriculum allowed them to teach what they loved, and cultural studies' focus on critical reading and analysis fit well with many of the goals and outcomes we shared for FYC courses. They worried, legitimately, about where students would be taught to interrogate cultural assumptions and think critically about issues of gender, ethnicity, etc. But there were two bigger concerns shared by some teachers in our program. First, the curriculum described in the "Introduction to Writing Studies" approach in Downs and Wardle's article asked students to read scholarly articles from the discipline of rhetoric and composition—some of the same articles, in fact, that I was asking the graduate students to read. Many are long, hard, and students are clearly not the audience for them, so there was some question of how much sense the average freshman could make of them. And getting students to read *anything* was already hard enough. Second, few of the graduate students and faculty could believe that first-year students would be engaged by such work either. Most students hate writing anyway—who in their right mind would want to ask them to read, research, and write about the very thing they hate? They thought surely the students would revolt.

When I asked one of our lecturers in the program, a woman with a literature background, but solid grounding in rhetoric and composition as well, what her original ideas about the approach were, she recalled thinking that "the entire idea of using articles written by and for professional compositionists in FYC was wrongheaded. . . . [T]he length, complexity, and the background needed in order to be an engaged reader was suited to grad school, not freshmen." But, perhaps more interestingly, she was "suspicious of the motives of Downs and Wardle . . . wonder[ing] if the approach would benefit students or if it was a way to carve out a new niche in a department." "Empire building to gain academic capital" is how she described it.

At that point in my tenure as WPA, I was trying to build a program, a sense of shared values and vision for the first-year writing program at UTPA, and I wasn't interested in trying to convince anyone to use what many of my faculty would probably consider a pretty radical approach to teaching FYC. We are an Hispanic-Serving Institution (HSI) located in the Rio Grande Valley, home to the poorest county in America, and most of our students come from the area. Just over 53 percent of the freshman class of 2009 graduated in the bottom 75 percent of their high school class (Office 17), and it is common to hear faculty, administrators, and others describe our student population as underprepared and at-risk. So, I knew it would be a hard sell to get faculty to bring thirty-plus page articles written for scholarly journals into their classrooms, particularly with freshmen. Particularly with *our* freshmen.

But it wasn't long before one of my TAs who had been in my graduate class the year before decided to give the writing studies approach a try. I gave her a lot of leeway to develop her own syllabus, and she actually drew heavily on the readings we had done for our graduate class to design the course. She asked students to develop their own writing-related research questions, which they pursued both through primary and secondary means, and they ended the semester by taking their work public, transforming their traditional research papers into projects in a variety of forms, with meaningful purposes, and for real audiences. Over the course of the semester, I could see that the other TAs were a little shocked by her success. Students were engaged and were developing research questions and projects that rivaled my own senior-level composition theory class, both in terms of complexity and overall quality of finished products. Eventually, I saw the other TAs incorporating a few writing studies articles into their own classes. I think they wanted to know if it was just her or whether there was something to this particular approach. Last summer, a couple of our faculty tried teaching the curriculum, and they had great success as well, and, as word spread, four or five more took it on, including some of our new lecturers (with a 5/5 load). So, when we completely redesigned our developmental program this last fall, we decided to take a chance and use the very same writing studies curriculum that we use with our first-semester FYC class with our developmental writing students.

And it has worked better than we ever imagined.

The Redesign

For the past few years, we had been offering the top-scoring, developmentally-placed writing students the opportunity to take what we called a fast-track developmental writing course. Students would sign up for both English 1320-Basic Writing (the non-credit-bearing developmental writing course) and 1301 (the first-semester credit-bearing writing course) in the same semester. (On the books, 1320 would run the first half of the semester while 1301 would run the last half.) Students would meet every day of the week for an hour, do the work of a 1301, and, hopefully, at the end of the semester, pass both 1320 and 1301. This program had been a success—more students passed the developmental course than normal and, in our English 1302, end-of-year program assessment, fast-track students usually performed better than "regular" students who hadn't taken developmental writing. But Colin, the developmental coordinator, and I believed that these results weren't just limited to the fact that they were the best testers of the developmentally placed students. We knew that the intensity of the course (meeting, in essence, twice as often as other developmental students), the pedagogy and curriculum being employed, and the students' investment in the course (knowing they would get credit for a "real" college course at the end of the semester) were key factors in these students' successes.

We wanted to go further, and last fall we got the opportunity to make some changes that would affect the entire developmental program. We allowed any developmental writing student to take both English 1320 and 1301, meeting for two class periods back to back two or three times a week. We use the same writing studies curriculum that we use for regular 1301 classes, and the extra hours each week are dedicated to a studio environment with more one-on-one and small group conferencing, peer response groups, and time to write/revise with the teacher close by.

The Curriculum

Our developmental writing students read the following:

- Doug Downs and Elizabeth Wardle's "Teaching about Writing, Righting Misconceptions: (Re)Envisioning 'First-Year Composition' as 'Introduction to Writing Studies'"

- Christina Haas and Linda Flower's "Rhetorical Reading Strategies and the Construction of Meaning"

- Luis Moll and Norma Gonzalez's "Lessons from Research with Language-Minority Children"

- Gloria Neubert and Sally McNelis's "Peer Response: Teaching Specific Revision Strategies"

- Alice Gillam's "Research in the Classroom: Learning through Response"

- Margaret Kantz's "Helping Students Use Textual Sources Persuasively"

- Nancy Sommers's "Revision Strategies of Student Writers and Experienced Adult Writers"

Instructors could add pieces of their own choosing, some about gender or specific second language/bilingual issues, sometimes additional readings about inquiry-based research. Regardless of the resulting mix, the number, length, and complexity of the readings is daunting, particularly in light of the fact that these are students who, in many cases, have felt left out of or uninterested in academic work. But there are important reasons why this set of readings works really well:

- *Because students read Downs and Wardle first, they begin the class with a philosophical overview of why their teachers are asking them to do the work they are.* Most of our students are used to teachers telling them to do stuff, and they do it—or don't, as is the case with many developmental students—without ever knowing why. Each assignment or task is another in a long line of (to them) useless busy work, which usually reveals their flaws and reinforces their ideas that good writing ability is a gift few possess. But when they read about Jack, a student in the Downs and Wardle piece, they begin to realize that (1) there are people out there who study students like them, which they think is pretty cool and buys our discipline a little cultural capital, and (2) they realize that they, like Jack, can learn something about writing even if they've never been very good at it.

- *Embedded in the readings are tools students can use to get through the work.* When they read Sommers's piece on revision, they see their own ideas about revision reflected in the language of the "inexperienced" writers. The Gillam article offers a brief, but important, rationale for why peer response work matters, what students can *learn* and how they can *benefit* from doing it well. Neubert and McNelis argue for and gives real examples of feedback of varying quality. Kantz shows them how and why to incorporate source material into their writing. And they do so in ways that don't water the concepts down into bold-able key terms whose complexities have been erased.

The strength of the curriculum for our developmental students has been, however ironic this might seem, its *rigorous, academic nature*. Students have never been asked to do anything like it, and that's a good thing given most of their past relationships with education in general and "school writing" in particular.

A Testing Culture

It is now commonplace to note that our educational institutions are shaped by a test-obsessed culture. In the Valley, this is particularly true in many, if not most, school districts. In the years when writing is tested on the state-mandated exams, you'll see students practicing often in the genre of that exam, writing narratives in response to prompts like "Write about a time you were surprised" (readers might also be interested in the fact that those prompts change very little from fourth to eleventh grade). In the years when there is no writing exam, attention is shifted elsewhere. They're asked to read, but mostly literary texts, and not necessarily in ways that are useful to them when applied to other reading situations. And the testing culture, as it is wont to do, breeds a find-the-right-answer mentality that too often stifles inventive, creative approaches to thinking through problems. It doesn't help that students are tracked into pre-AP classes starting in sixth grade. Those who don't look like they can cut it are shifted to the side *very* early on.

So, when students enter our classroom, the kind and amount of reading, thinking, and writing we ask them to do seems radically at odds with their past experiences, and many of them develop research questions designed to help them (1) make sense of their past experiences in high school, and (2) understand how they can relate to their current and future learning experiences. As I said earlier, that's a good thing.

The Difference a Curriculum Can Make

Marlene recently passed out a survey to her developmental students, asking them to reflect on their experiences in the class. All of them said the class was fast-paced, more so than any class they'd ever taken, but one student said something very telling: "Usually when I'm asked to do this much work this fast, I give up. But, I didn't this time." And the question is, why not? Part of the answer is *confidence*. We have confidence in their ability to do rigorous work, and they begin to have confidence in their own abilities to do it, not just in our classes, but in their other academic work as well.

I asked the teachers who use the writing studies approach in my program what was different for their students in this curriculum versus others, and a few of their comments bear repeating:

- "Writing studies changes the dynamic of the classroom in the sense that the instructor is not an authoritative figure telling students what to do, but a facilitator helping students make sense of what's going on in college and in their brains as they read and write, a process they never considered" (Regine).

- "The idea that I was left with was that dealing with the articles gave them more confidence, because of the points made by the authors about students owning their work, and I think, also because they were able to get into the articles and discuss them—this was not high school work" (Mary Anne).

- "Students can clearly see a correlation between the work they're doing in the classroom and how it relates to larger conversations taking place amongst scholars.... When they read writing studies articles (although they're lengthy) it's easier to understand the concepts in terms of how it relates to them as FYC students. When I taught ENG 1302 [the second-semester FYC course] with a non-writing studies approach, I don't think that at the end of the semester any of my students were able to clearly define rhetoric or rhetorical awareness. My English 1320/1301 students this semester use the terms rhetorical reading and rhetorical writing almost daily. They're comfortable with these terms. And as the semester progresses, I can see their confidence grow in their abilities to actually perform this type of reading and writing" (Marlene).

- "The writing studies approach asks a lot from students, but it gets a lot from students.... When I ask them to reflect on things they are proud of, the most common answers are that they're proud they read a thirty page article (some of them even read it twice, even if it took them two or three days), they're proud they wrote a four-page essay for Project 1, they're amazed when they go beyond the six to eight page requirement for Project 2 and it still feels unfinished to them. Generally, they're proud they survive the course" (Marlene).

We're really proud, too.

The Take-Aways

Beatrice Mendez Newman writes in "Teaching Writing at Hispanic-Serving Institutions" that "[t]he composition classroom, potentially one of the most student-centered, social sites in the students' early academic experience, could figure prominently in the HSI students' decision to persist or drop out, to cross the 'threshold' or to retreat from the institution" (23). That, of course, is true for the FYC classroom in most institutions and for the developmental writing classroom especially. We have had the opportunity to radically alter the content and delivery of our "basic writing" curriculum to facilitate our students' abilities to cross that threshold, and our students have risen to our admittedly high expectations. Here's how we think they did it.

- *Immersion.* Because students met for two hours each class day, they were immersed in the work of the class for long enough periods of time that they could try out ideas, get feedback, revise, and try them out again—all before leaving for the day. As they were trying to become more effective and efficient writers and readers, they were reading, writing, and reflecting on their own experiences doing those activities. They came to see how their past experiences with these activities affected their current challenges as readers and writers, and they learned that they can take some measure of control over becoming better at it. What they were reading and researching directly applied to them and what they were trying to do for class.

- *An Enriched Knowledge Base.* Asking students to become researchers from the moment they enter a college writing classroom (as opposed to waiting until the second-semester writing course to introduce research), and asking them to focus that inquiry on meaningful questions about writing that impact them, has led the majority of our students to produce work that is informed, engaged, rhetorical, and not just bland evidence of information-gathering.

- *Networks.* What I see in the opening scene of this article is a class that has built a network that rivals any graduate student cohort. Those students are asking questions of one another, almost everyone is talking and contributing in ways that go well beyond the superficial comment, and they help each other further their thinking, research, and writing.

- *Engagement.* Those networks emerged not just because the students needed one another's support (which they did, of course), but because they were engaged with their work and knew enough about their issues that they could share sources and ask relevant questions. With this approach, our students seem to have more control over and connection to their problems with reading and writing, and they see ways to do something about them.

Some of our students do give up, though most of the time it has nothing to do with the rigor of the work we ask them to do. I was so excited when I visited Marlene's class and heard Izzy, Vanessa, César, and their peers talking. I wanted to stand up and say, "Do you have any idea how fantastic this is?" None of these students will be English majors, and they may never read another article in rhetoric, composition, or literacy studies again, but the ways they see writing, reading, and researching are fundamentally changed, the familiar strange and the strange now more familiar. For these students and teachers, for myself, and hopefully for others who try to work with this type of curriculum, lasting change is possible. And seeing the differences in student engagement, confidence, and writing is certainly believing.

Note

1. All the names of real students have been changed to protect their anonymity.

Works Cited

Downs, Douglas, and Elizabeth Wardle. "Teaching about Writing, Righting Misconceptions: (Re)Envisioning 'First-Year Composition' as 'Introduction to Writing Studies.'" *CCC* 58.4 (2007): 552–84. Print.

Gillam, Alice M. "Research in the Classroom: Learning through Response." *The English Journal* 79.1 (1990): 98–99. Print.

Haas, Christina, and Linda Flower. "Rhetorical Reading Strategies and the Construction of Meaning." *CCC* 39.2 (1988): 167–83. Print.

Kantz, Margaret. "Helping Students Use Textual Sources Persuasively." *College English* 52.1 (1990): 74–91. Print.

Moll, Luis C., and Norma Gonzalez. "Lessons from Research with Language-Minority Children." *Journal of Reading Behavior* 26.4 (1994): 439–56. Print.

Neubert, Gloria A., and Sally J. McNelis. "Peer Response: Teaching Specific Revision Suggestions." *The English Journal* 79.5 (1990): 52–56. Print.

Newman, Beatrice Mendez. "Teaching Writing at Hispanic-Serving Institutions." *Teaching Writing with Latino/a Students: Lessons Learned at Hispanic-Serving Institutions.* Ed. Cristina Kirklighter, Diana Cárdenas, and Susan Wolff Murphy. Albany: SUNY P, 2007. 17–35. Print.

Office of Institutional Research and Effectiveness. "Stats at a Glance: Fall 2009." Edinburg: U of Texas-Pan American, 2009. Print.

Sommers, Nancy. "Revision Strategies of Student Writers and Experienced Adult Writers." *CCC* 31.4 (1980): 378–88. Print.

Intersected Literacies: Reading, Writing, and Critical Thinking

Critical Language Awareness and Learners in College Transitional English

Deborah M. Sánchez and Eric J. Paulson

Critical language awareness curricula allow students to understand the implications of language for critical thinking, beyond reading for merely banking model informational purposes. Students become aware of the ways in which language can be used against them to diminish academic access and possibilities for educational growth. For this reason, labeling students as "remedial" shrinks expectations for achievement, resulting in basic skills curricula that assume low cognitive capabilities. Deborah Sánchez and Eric Paulson provide examples of studies that show students in transition reading, critically thinking about, and learning from more complex materials—and learning the ways in which crucial awareness of language can help them to unpack the underlying themes of texts, leading to more acute reading comprehension and increased academic cognition.

One of us (Deborah) recently received an e-mail from a colleague who expressed dismay at the increasing disappearance of transitional English at four-year universities. The e-mail said: "somewhere along the way basic writing became remedial, became punitive, became business as usual" (Susan N. Bernstein). The "business as usual" sentiment seems to be true at many institutions of higher education. For example, one Midwestern urban university recently published an academic plan for the twenty-first century which foregrounds academic preparedness for incoming students. The president's report card to the board of trustees lists "elite entry" as one of the university's achievements — citing an increase in enrolled National Merit Scholars. It also lists an increase in ACT scores of entering students as an achievement in academic excellence (UC 21: The President's Report Card to the Board of Trustees).

The increased efforts of the university to "achieve academic excellence" and "elite entry" seem to have coupled with the passing of Ohio Senate Bill 311, which proposed phasing out all state-operated funding to developmental education at four-year universities. As a result, the combined effect has trickled down to the classroom level in the form of loss of access to the university for students who have traditionally been excluded (McNenny and Fitzgerald).

The "business as usual" sentiment, in which higher education acts in the interests of corporations and economic gains (Emery and Ohanian), and increases in the amount of standards work to exclude more students rather than provide access (Fox 7), have unfortunately become the norm at many previously open-access institutions, with ACT and SAT scores providing convenient measures for deciding who enters and who is rejected.

Despite, and also because of, these obstacles, research that continues to counter deficiency assumptions about students and demonstrates the value of open-admissions programs is indispensable. Owing to Mina Shaughnessy's legacy, we find her question still relevant: "What goes on and what *ought* to go on in the composition classroom?" [emphasis added] (*CCC* 320). What *ought* to go on is still quite relevant amid the changing face of what it means to be academically and technologically literate in today's world, in addition to the systemic inequalities of old that continue to affect students in transition in negative ways.

In this article, we use the term *transitional English*, rather than remedial or developmental English, in order to foreground the idea that literacy for all students develops over time. We also use *students in transition* (see Armstrong) where appropriate, rather than remedial or developmental students, because the latter terms often reflect negative assumptions about students' cognitive abilities. Year after year, students in transition continue to arrive at two-year colleges and four-year universities and enter transitional English courses. According to a 2000 report from the National Center for Education Statistics (NCES), almost 30% of freshmen entering American colleges and universities enrolled in a transitional course in English, reading, or mathematics (*Remedial Education at Degree-Granting Postsecondary Institutions, Fall 2000*, Table 4). Although institutions vary in how they approach curriculum in these courses — from grammar drills to experimental writing to critical analytical writing—basic skills remediation still exists (Shor, "Our Apartheid"). In some cases, accountability testing in higher education is required of students in transitional English courses, as Bernstein ("Writing and White Privilege: Beyond Basic Skills") recounted in her experience of teaching basic writing in Texas, where students had to pass an accountability test before their junior year. It is this skills-based approach—the point of view that academic literacy is a technical skill to be quickly acquired rather than a complex set of practices that take years to develop—that is most problematic.

Students who are in transitional English courses—often as a result of inferior schooling conditions (see Kozol), unequal funding (see Shor, "Errors and Economics" 31), and the miseducation (see Shor, "Errors and Economics" 33) that they receive because of a zealous reliance on one test score (Meier and Wood)—come from working-class backgrounds and racial and ethnic minority groups. Statistics from a report on remedial education at higher education institutions in fall 2000 revealed that minorities are overrepresented in remedial courses: "At institutions with high minority enrollment, 43 percent of first-time freshmen were enrolled in remedial reading, writing, or mathematics, compared with 26 percent at institutions with low minority enrollment" (20). As these discouraging statistics demonstrate, minority students' underprepared status often serves to compound their marginalization and oppression. A more progressive and democratic pedagogical approach to teaching academic literacy would be one in which students learn not only how to read and write academic texts, but also how to examine critically the discourse that makes up their world(s). Paulo Freire asserted that teachers and students could use literacy to examine the themes that emerge from texts and look critically at the "limit situations"— the situations or myths that maintain the status quo and prevent them from fulfilling goals for their lives (99). One such limit situation might be the inequality of schooling conditions that results in students being underprepared (see Kozol). More than thirty years ago, Shaughnessy wondered "what had gone wrong" (*Errors and Expectations* vii) as she read students' writings; in the same way, students and teachers in transitional English courses need to examine what has gone wrong in regards to systemic issues mired in language practices and policies that result in inequality. This examination should not originate from a stance in which students are positioned as being in need of basic skills remediation or, even worse, as not belonging in higher education at all, but rather from one that examines the socially constructed dominant "Discourse," to use James Gee's big "D" notion (26), of the academy and how that impacts the perceived success of transitional students in college.

Critical Language Awareness (CLA) is one literacy tool that students need in order to examine limit-situations or "what went wrong." Norman Fairclough defines CLA as an awareness of the ways in which ideas become naturalized or taken for granted as "truths" about the natural and social world and how these "truths" are tied up with language in use (14–15). The purpose of CLA is to encourage students to uncover the ways that the language of texts is socially constructed and how language may position students in negative ways, both purposefully and inadvertently.

Therefore, reading and writing instruction should not be concerned only with basic skills, but rather it should focus on how students use reading and writing to analyze language — in various textual forms — in order to understand the ways in which texts, and the Discourse that makes up texts, may impose certain ideas about the world onto readers. Students would benefit from an awareness of how language functions to impose certain beliefs and values about society. The premise we are developing is that the teaching of CLA and critical analysis should begin in transitional English courses, in order to prepare students fully for college-level literacy, democratic citizenship, and the realities of work; it should not be deferred for later composition courses, as is frequently the case.

Historical Context of Remediation

Glynda Hull, Mike Rose, Cynthia Greenleaf, and Brian Reilly trace the historical perspective of the discourse surrounding the concept of remediation, providing the analysis that labels given to poor-performing students at the beginning of the nineteenth century — such as "dunce," "loafer," "wrongdoer," and "incorrigible" — blamed their poor performance on an inherently flawed character (6). During the latter half of the nineteenth century, the labels changed and terms such as "born late," "sleepy minded," and "slow" revealed a change from placing the blame on a flawed character to placing the blame on a developmental or cognitive problem (6). The advent of intelligence quotient (IQ) testing at this time fueled the idea that students who performed poorly in school were cognitively inferior (7). Although the twentieth century brought new and more progressive theories of learning, which included social and cultural aspects, Glynda Hull, Mike Rose, Kay Losey Fraser, and Marisa Castellano demonstrate in their study, through an analysis of classroom discourse, the ways that teachers inadvertently reify deficiency assumptions about students in transition (317). Their discourse analysis of teacher-student talk in a developmental English class illustrates the contradictions that teachers carry with them in regards to students who are in transition. While teachers desire a progressive and liberatory curriculum, the talk used by the teacher in the study revealed deeply ingrained deficiency assumptions about students labeled "underprepared."

The problem is that a reliance on grammar instruction and basic skills remediation, which comes from socially constructed deficiency assumptions about students' work, can hold them back further from equality in schooling and from fulfilling their desires for their lives. The significance of Hull, Rose, Fraser, and Castellano's research study is that, although teachers may espouse sociocultural theories of language learning, contradictions still exist in how teachers view and educate students in transition, and these negative assumptions are often played out in the discourse of the classroom (318). Socially constructed deficiency assumptions, as illustrated in Hull, Rose, Fraser, and Castellano's research study, may translate into a pedagogy based on a deficiency model in transitional English classes and open-admissions programs in higher education.

On the other hand, Allan Luke, a literacy teacher and theorist, argued that, "Criticism [. . .] is not a genre, not a skill, not a later developmental moment, not a reading position. It is [. . .] a constitutive and available element of every sign, utterance, and text" (334). The tool of critique, as Luke argues, should not be postponed until students have learned the basics or until they have reached a perceived level of cognitive maturity.

Through CLA pedagogy, a curricular aim is that students access the discourse of academic literacy—the dominant discourse—but also learn to critique the issues related to power, access, and equality that are entrenched in language practices (see Clark and Ivanic). Students can learn to use the language of academic literacy while learning to ask critical questions about language, such as "Whose interests are being served by the language in a text?" Although CLA is part of the curriculum in various settings in the United Kingdom and in South Africa (Clark and Ivanic), according to H. Samy Alim, few recent research studies in the United States employ a CLA curricular approach.

CLA Studies

In the following section, the term CLA is not used in all of the research; nevertheless, these studies are significant because of their focus on instruction that encourages students in transitional English courses to critique dominant messages about societal issues, such as access to education and the world of work—issues that are endemic to the situations of many students in college transitional English courses. In addition, all of the studies in the following section provide evidence that students develop academic literacy skills while they learn critical literacy skills.

Nicholas Coles and Susan Wall employ discourse analysis of students' discussion, reading, and writing in order to illustrate how students in a transitional English class talk, write, and read about the tensions and contradictions between their ideas and the critical ideas in texts. All of the students in the course came from working-class backgrounds and had been in work settings where they had problems, so the authors chose the subject of work as the course theme. The issue of work was inextricably tied to the students' experiences and the reasons for their participation in the course—all were enrolled in the course in order to find better jobs or to improve the situation in their current jobs. Coles and Wall engaged the students with texts that included built-in critiques about the world of work, such as George Orwell's *Down and Out in Paris and London*, Studs Terkel's *Working*, Richard Wright's *American Hunger*, Thomas Bell's *Out of This Furnace*, Robert Coles and Jane Hallowell Coles's *Women of Crisis*, and Rosabeth Moss Kanter's *Men and Women of the Corporation*. The researchers encouraged the students to rely on their own background knowledge, experiences, and interests during their reading, which allowed them the authority to identify with people and issues. In addition, the texts embodied built-in critique, allowing students to make connections between their own struggles with work-related issues and the struggles of others. Students became more effective readers, as evidenced by their ability to identify and make generalizations linking their own experiences, the experiences of others, and the systemic issues involved in their problems with work. Coles and Wall's study demonstrated how students were able to "see," that is, to analyze, the language and the messages in dominant and oppositional texts. This is the critical language awareness that Fairclough discussed. Not only were students engaged in analysis of the literary theme of work, but they were also engaged in analysis of how power and ideology are tied up in the dominant messages about the world of work. The students evolved from being readers who read the texts exclusively from the perspective that the author has the ultimate authority and that they, as readers, must submit to that authority into readers who could comprehend and also be critical of the message. In this way, they became more effective and critical readers, a skill that would help them in both academic and workplace contexts.

Glynda Hull's case study ("Critical Literacy") reported on community college students enrolled in a banking and finance program. All of the students in the course were minorities: African American, Hispanic, and Asian, and 95% were women. The program curriculum consisted of basic skills necessary to find a job as a bank proof operator or teller. Hull described the working conditions of a bank proof operator as high stress, in the sense that the "high demands to produce and be accurate [. . .] and strict rules of tardiness" (383), compounded with the monotony of unskilled work, amounted to the kind of work that Vygotsky would see as intellectual crippling (178). To this end, the job had a high turnover rate. Therefore, although the basic skills that the students received in the program got them a job, it did not help them keep the job. The significance of this study comes from Hull's illustration of these contradictions and is two-fold: that basic skills are not sufficient for the world of work and that students from nondominant backgrounds need critical literacy skills in order to access personal empowerment and social change.

Ernest Morrell's descriptive case study was conducted with a population of "at-risk" first-year college students. Students came from underrepresented schools and communities serving racial, ethnic, and socioeconomic minority groups in urban Los Angeles (10). Students learned the language of academic literacy through research on critical themes that included the media's negative portrayal of urban youth, the potential role of hip-hop music and culture in school curricula, teen access to a livable wage, teacher quality, school safety, and the digital divide (14). Morrell demonstrated that students deemed "at-risk" engaged in sophisticated critical thinking and critiqued and composed texts that provided both liberating counternarratives and evidence of academic literacy growth.

Bernstein's study ("Writing and White Privilege") asks students in a college transitional English course to read and write about the contradictions inherent in preparing for high-stakes testing and for learning to be critical readers, writers, and thinkers. She uses the case study of Michael, a student in her developmental English course. Bernstein describes Michael, the only white working-class student in the class, as being an "insider/outsider" (130) in that, although his race may have allowed him the benefits of white privilege, because of his working-class background he shared some of the same negative experiences with schooling and standardized testing as his fellow nonwhite classmates. She includes his writing, which illustrated the way that Michael was able to critique the zealous overreliance on high-stakes testing and its implications for his presence in a developmental course. Similarly, Bernstein ("Teaching and Learning") illustrates how developmental students in an English class use reading and writing to advocate for social change. In particular, she includes Noah's writing to illustrate his engagement with critical themes, those having to do with the problematic notion of high-stakes testing and its implications for himself as a Latino student and for other students of color like himself. Bernstein was able to cultivate academic literacy in a developmental classroom while engaging with texts, such as "Theme for English B" by Langston Hughes, that embodied the experiences of the students. Therefore, the texts were both personally and critically relevant to the students' access to academic literacy.

June Jordan chronicles the awareness of language—Black English in particular—that students in an undergraduate English course gained when she worked with the tensions of students who encountered Black English in Alice Walker's *The Color Purple*. When her students translated passages from *The Color Purple* from Black English to Standard English, she notes that "the students pushed me to explain their own negative first reactions to their spoken language on the printed page" (343). Rather than ignore the social and critical aspects of literacy, she collaborates with students to foster an awareness of how language is tied up with identity, values, and power, reflecting an important component of CLA.

The culmination of this work came when the students chose to write a letter of protest to newspapers after a fellow classmate's brother was killed by police. Although Jordan did not use the term CLA in the article, her decision to make visible the politics of language and to give students the choice of whether to use Black English or Standard English in the letter illustrates a CLA pedagogical approach. An explicit awareness of Black English was not separate but, rather, inextricably tied to the social situations of Black English speakers in the course because Jordan foregrounded the issue of police violence—an issue that she argues is "endemic to Black life" (351). That Jordan chose to foreground the literacy work that students did around a societal theme that was authentic and pertinent to the students seems to be an essential principle in critical pedagogy and critical literacy work, respectively.

The question that she posed to her students—"Should the opening, group paragraph be written in Black English or Standard English?"—makes explicit to the students the rhetorical choices and the real-life consequences that those choices have. To be sure, the students understood the ramifications of their choice to write the letter in Black English. They knew that their voices would not be heard, but they chose to write in Black English anyway, to honor the young man who had been killed. With Jordan's help, the students discovered how language is connected with social reality and issues of justice, and they were conscious of their rhetorical choices available.

Lesley Lancaster and Rhiannan Taylor adopted a CLA curricular approach in a study of working-class students in a secondary English classroom in the United Kingdom. Their study is grounded in a sociocultural and critical perspective on literacy learning, in that they based the curriculum on the great deal that they assumed the students already knew about language, as opposed to what they assumed students did not know. This sociocultural approach opposed a deficit view of students' language abilities and looked instead to explore the ways in which their existing knowledge of language could bring about a bridge to a better awareness of critical themes. Two of the goals of the course were "to explore the way language is used in school, at home, in the street and in the community, and to encourage students to explore attitudes to language and dialects" (268). Lancaster and Taylor raised questions such as the following: Why has language changed? Who determines those changes? How have those changes taken place? (268). Through these questions, the authors hoped to raise the students' awareness of how language is socially constructed and produced and help them understand and challenge why some languages have more prestige than others (268). What they found from the CLA activities implemented in the course was that students developed an increased level of awareness of many different languages. The students also stopped referring to local languages by using pejorative terms, and their attitude toward their own local accent changed. The significance of this study is that, when the tools for critique are fostered in a classroom, students at the secondary level are capable of critiquing and challenging dominant and hegemonic perspectives that negatively affect them. Similar to students in Romy Clark's study, the students left the course with a better awareness of their language choices and how these choices were related to social and critical aspects of language in use. We include Lancaster and Taylor's study (in a high school setting), even though the study was not conducted with a population of underprepared college students, because it might speak to critics who argue that underprepared students are not ready for the cognitive demands of critical analysis (see Traub; D'Souza).

In a qualitative study of underprepared college students in a developmental reading course, Mellinee Lesley investigated how students in a required college study skills course accessed the dominant conventions of academic writing and, at the same time, challenged those conventions. She employed a critical literacy approach with the following justification: "literacy at all levels always begins with the impetus of the context for reading, writing, and speaking. The impetus of the context for students in developmental reading courses exists within a system of social stratification" (184). Therefore, Lesley chose to situate the theme of the course within the reasons why students are in transitional literacy courses in the first place. These reasons include issues of power, such as unequal schooling conditions, resegregation, unequal funding, and tracking. Although Lesley does not cite CLA in the study, it is a component. For example, Lesley provides evidence from students' in-class reader-response essays about excerpts from Mike Rose's *Lives on the Boundary*. She asked students to revise a previously written essay from earlier in the quarter and she asked them to look closely in their revision at the language and respond to the ways that social class is enacted in discourse. Students were learning the language of academic discourse, but they also used this language in their examination and critique of how language is tied to unequal societal issues (186). In this way, CLA was an important curricular component of the course. Lesley demonstrates how students deemed "remedial" can access academic literacy and the tools for critique and how these tools do not have to be deferred for later composition courses. Similar to students in Bernstein's two studies, Lesley's students began to reflect on their own unequal educational experiences and how literacy and language practices play a part in the construction of unequal educational experiences.

Implications for Using CLA as a Curricular Approach to Teaching English to Students in Transition

A few implications for teaching English to students in transition emerge from the previously discussed research studies. Texts of everyday life that illustrate issues endemic to the lives of students should be used as valid objects of analysis in the classroom. Deborah Hicks writes: "In order for working-class students to take up unfamiliar forms of literary practice, they first have to see a place for their voices within the dominant practices of reading articulated by teachers" (78). Many of the studies discussed illustrate how students were able to see a place for their own voices and engage in social critique through literacy assignments that allowed them to connect with texts and through questions that were meaningful to them and came as a result of their own inquiry. In addition, they were able to integrate their own voices within assignments that asked them to use the "basic" academic literacy skills *and* the tools for critique—both of which are necessary for success in a baccalaureate program.

As the studies reviewed demonstrate, students in transitional English courses, often labeled "underprepared," are capable of the critical thinking work necessary for college-level literacy. In addition, as many of the participants in the studies demonstrate, students are capable of engaging in critique of systemic issues, including schooling inequalities, because they have keen experiences that allow for a more critical awareness of how language practices are tied to unequal relations of power. The experiences of students should be validated and used to engage them in critical thinking work and to speak back to texts and language practices that position them in negative ways.

An example of CLA comes from a teacher/researcher study that Deborah Sánchez, the first author, implemented in a college transitional English class. In order to engage their critical thinking skills, she encouraged students to question assumptions or "common-sense knowledge" about the world that is tied to language practices. One CLA activity that she implemented centered on an excerpt from Jonathan Kozol's book *The Shame of the Nation*. As a class and in small groups, students discussed in depth one of the chapters, entitled "Preparing Minds for Markets." In this chapter, Kozol describes a visit to an urban elementary school, serving mostly students from minority backgrounds, in Columbus, Ohio, in which the teachers and administrators at the school used the word "manager" to encourage students to behave and act in certain ways. Kozol criticizes the school's use of the word "manager" and its ties to what he believes are low expectations for the students and their futures after school.

Sánchez asked students to discuss in small groups the following questions: Do you see the word "manager" being used to position the students in a positive, negative, or neutral way? Explain why. What idea is being imposed on the students about their futures? Catherine Wallace asserts that "one advantage of CLA as essentially a classroom procedure is that it takes place within a ready-made interpretive community" (99). From her observational field notes, Sánchez, similar to Wallace, found that the dialogic nature of the classroom was a perfect place for students to engage in discussions about the socially constructed nature of language and the unequal social practices resulting from language practices at play in the real world. In small groups, students responded to the questions about "Preparing Minds for Markets" in lively and critical ways. Sánchez recorded in her observational field notes that, even before class started on the day of the planned discussion of "Preparing Minds for Markets," she had heard students "buzzing" about the text. In addition, Kozol's text, which included a built-in critique of schooling practices, allowed students, in groups, not only to engage in reading with and against the text but also to read their worlds into and onto the text, a tenet of CLA. Sánchez recorded that two students, Kerry and Damon, who both attended area public schools, commented that reading "Preparing Minds for Markets" reminded them of, and made them rethink, a schooling practice from their own childhoods—that of reciting the "seven pillars of character" every morning.

Students also responded to the text in writing. We include the following excerpt from Alex's essay because it demonstrates a growing CLA that resulted from his reading the text, discussing the class questions with his classmates, and reading his world into and onto the text:

> After reading Kozol and talking to fellow classmates about some of the issues going on in this article, I understand some of the things going on in it. In our discussion group we had some controversy over some of the things said in this article [. . .] Kozol's Views on the Students from the Elementary school, made me think about when I was in Elementary. [. . .] I was one of maybe 5 black kids in the class, and the class size was about twenty to twenty-five kids in the class. In this class we moved at a faster pass then the district kids but we still had the manager system going on. We had a line leader, a pencil manager, an Attendance manager, a black board eraser manager. Back then, I thought it was a privilege to be a Manager in the class I never really thought about it in the negative sense. Reading his thoughts and views on the subject made me think maybe the teachers assigned these jobs because of the same reason the schools Kozol visit did. I want to believe that they were trying to teach us responsibility and possibly respect for others. [. . .] But to think the only reason they gave these jobs to us is because they think we might end up being felons is heartbreaking.

This excerpt demonstrates how teachers might encourage students' transactions with the texts as legitimate in order to give students who normally have not had sufficient practice with making assertions in academic writing the authority and confidence to make them.

We return to the beginning of the article in calling on Mina Shaughnessy in order to address the relevance and connection between pedagogy and access. Shaughnessy's foundational research study and guidebook for the teacher of basic writing, *Errors and Expectations*, emerged during a time that was ripe for social change. One of the most profound ideas that resulted from her research was that of the educability of students that she called "basic writers." Also, the implicit idea that resulted from her commitment to teach these students was the value of open-admissions programs at colleges and universities. Just as Shaughnessy wrote during a turbulent time in which there were detractors who did not support open-admissions policies, we are writing amid increasing attempts to remove transitional courses from four-year universities. Despite current detractors, we argue that educators should stay committed to the idea that resulted from Shaughnessy's legacy, namely, that students in transitional courses belong at the university. Although the proposed curricular approach does not address the issue of access at the state or institutional level, we hope that the studies reviewed and the example from Sánchez's classroom might influence how educators view the needs of students in transition at the pedagogical level. In addition, we hope that conversations about students and classroom pedagogies that oppose deficiency models might work interdiscursively to argue for continued access at the institutional level. The example from Alex's essay, along with the studies reviewed in this paper, demonstrate that students in transition can learn the language of academic literacy and, at the same time, use this language in their critique of language practices that may at times position them in negative ways.

Works Cited

Alim, H. Samy. "Critical Language Awareness in the United States: Revisiting Issues and Revising Pedagogies in a Resegregated Society." *Educational Researcher* 34 (2005): 24–31. Print.

Armstrong, Sonya L. "Beginning the Literacy Transition: Postsecondary Students' Conceptualizations of Academic Writing in Developmental Literacy Contexts." Diss. University of Cincinnati, 2007. Discussion.

Bernstein, Susan N. "Re: Chipping Away." E-mail to Deborah M. Sánchez. 5 Dec. 2007. E-mail.

———. "Teaching and Learning in Texas: Accountability Testing, Language, Race and Place." *Journal of Basic Writing* 23 (2004): 4–24. Print.

———. "Writing and White Privilege: Beyond Basic Skills." *Pedagogy* 4 (2004): 128–31. Print.

Clark, Romy. "Principles and Practice of CLA in the Classroom." *Critical Language Awareness*. Ed. Norman Fairclough. London: Longman, 1992. 117–40. Print.

Clark, Romy, and Roz Ivanic. "Raising Critical Awareness of Language: A Curriculum Aim for the New Millennium." *Language Awareness* 8 (1999): 63–70. Print.

Coles, Nicholas, and Susan V. Wall. "Conflict and Power in the Reader-Responses of Adult Basic Writers." *College English* 49.3 (1987): 298–314. Print.

D'Souza, Dinesh. *Illiberal Education: Political Correctness and the College Experience.* Ashland, OH: Ashland UP, 1992. Print.

Emery, Kathy, and Susan Ohanian. *Why Is Corporate America Bashing Our Public Schools?* Portsmouth: Heinemann, 2004. Print.

Fairclough, Norman. *Critical Language Awareness.* London: Longman, 1992. Print.

Fox, Tom. *Defending Access: A Critique of Standards in Higher Education.* New York: Boynton/Cook, 1999. Print.

Freire, Paulo. *Pedagogy of the Oppressed.* New York: Continuum International, 1970. Print.

Gee, James Paul. *An Introduction to Discourse Analysis: Theory and Method.* London: Routledge, 2005. Print.

Hicks, Deborah. "Back to Oz?: Rethinking the Literary in a Critical Study of Reading." *Research in the Teaching of English* 39 (2004): 63–84. Print.

Hull, Glynda. "Critical Literacy and Beyond: Lessons Learned from Students and Workers in a Vocational Program and on the Job." *Anthropology and Education Quarterly* 24 (1993): 373–96. Print.

Hull, Glynda, Mike Rose, Kay Losey Fraser, and Marisa Castellano. "Remediation as Social Construct: Perspectives from an Analysis of Classroom Discourse." *College Composition and Communication* 42 (1991): 299–329. Print.

Hull, Glynda, Mike Rose, Cynthia Greenleaf, and Brian Reilly. "Seeing the Promise of the Underprepared." *Quarterly of the National Writing Project and the Center for the Study of Writing and Literacy* 13 (1991): 6–15. Print.

Jordan, June. "Nobody Mean More to Me Than You and the Future Life of Willie Jordan." *Teaching Developmental Writing.* Susan N. Bernstein, Ed. Boston: Bedford/St. Martin's, 2007. 340–55. Print.

Kozol, Jonathan. *Savage Inequalities.* New York: Harper Perennial, 1991. Print.

Lancaster, Lesley, and Rhiannan Taylor. "Critical Approaches to Language, Learning and Pedagogy: A Case Study." *Critical Language Awareness.* Ed. Norman Fairclough. London: Longman, 1992. 256–84. Print.

Lesley, Mellinee. "Exploring the Links between Critical Literacy and Developmental Reading." *Journal of Adolescent and Adult Literacy* 45 (2001): 180–89. Print.

Luke, Allan. "When Basic Skills and Information Processing Just Aren't Enough: Rethinking Reading in New Times." *Teachers College Record* 97 (1995): 95–115. Print.

McNenny, Gerry, and Sallyanne H. Fitzgerald, eds. *Mainstreaming Basic Writers: Politics and Pedagogies of Access.* Mahwah: Erlbaum, 2001. Print.

Meier, Deborah, and George Wood, eds. *Many Children Left Behind.* Boston: Beacon Press, 2004. Print.

Morrell, Ernest. "Writing the Word and the World: Critical Literacy as Critical Textual Production." ERIC document # ED475208, 2003. Print.

Ohio Senate. 126th Assembly. *Amended Substitute Ohio Senate Bill Number 311.* Legislative Information Systems, n.d. Web. 2006. <http://www.legislature.state.oh.us/bills.cfm?ID=126_SB_311>.

Remedial Education in Degree-Granting Postsecondary Institutions in Fall 2000. Ed. National Center for Education Statistics. Washington, D.C., 2000.

Rose, Mike. *Lives on the Boundary.* New York: Free P, 1989. Print.

Shaughnessy, Mina. *Errors and Expectations: A Guide for the Teacher of Basic Writing.* New York: Oxford UP, 1977. Print.

———. "Some Needed Research on Writing." *College Composition and Communication* 28 (1977): 317–20. Print.

Shor, Ira. "Errors and Economics: Inequality Breeds Remediation." *Mainstreaming Basic Writers: Politics and Pedagogies of Access.* Ed. Gerri McNenny. Mahwah: Erlbaum, 2001. 29–54. Print.

———. "Our Apartheid: Writing Instruction and Inequality." *Journal of Basic Writing* 16.1 (1997): 91–104. Print.

Traub, James. *City on a Hill: Testing the American Dream at City College.* Reading, MA: Addison-Wesley, 1994. Print.

UC 21: The President's Report Card to the Board of Trustees. U of Cincinnati, Sep. 2007. Web. 15 Sept. 2007. <http://www.uc.edu/reportcard/>. September 15, 2007.

Vygotsky, Lev. "The Socialist Alteration of Man." *The Vygotsky Reader.* Ed. René Van Der Veer and Jaan Valsiner. Oxford, UK: Blackwell. 1994. 175–84. Print.

Wallace, Catherine. "Critical Language Awareness: Key Principles for a Course in Critical Reading." *Language Awareness* 8 (1999): 98–110. Print.

Texts of Our Institutional Lives: Studying the "Reading Transition" from High School to College: What Are Our Students Reading and Why?

David A. Jolliffe and Allison Harl

David Jolliffe and Allison Harl note a common faculty perception that first-year students transitioning from high school to college "don't read." However, as they consulted results from national surveys, Jolliffe and Harl did not find enough specific evidence to support curricular adjustments and changes for reading-based composition and general education courses. Jolliffe and Harl wanted to find out more about the "reading lives" of their students at the University of Arkansas, so they conducted a study to discover the contexts and contents of first-year students' reading. The twenty-one randomly selected students in this study filled out a questionnaire about their own perceptions of their reading habits, kept a reading-intensive journal for two weeks, and completed an exit interview that included a think-aloud protocol of their textbook reading. In the following article, Jolliffe and Harl report the findings of their study. They include some surprising results that not only challenge faculty perceptions but also help to inform curricular development, especially in terms of technology.

More than our colleagues in other departments, English department faculty members and administrators need to know what, how, and why students read. Most composition programs and assignments are grounded in reading, and, of course, so are English majors' curriculums.

English department faculty members are nearly always major players in general education, most of which requires substantial reading. We need to know how students are learning to read before they come to college, how we continue to foster close, critical reading throughout the college years, and how our students develop reading abilities and practices that they will continue to inhabit and improve after college.

If the scuttlebutt about reading is true, the Visigoths are at the door. An array of national surveys and studies suggests that neither high school nor college students spend much time preparing for class, the central activity of which we presume to be reading assigned articles, chapters, and books. Similar studies argue that college students spend little to no time reading for pleasure and that adults in the United States are devoting less and less of their free time to reading fiction, poetry, and drama. Books lamenting the decline in the reading of great literature in our culture[1] find an eager and ardent audience. The water-cooler conversation in English departments and indeed throughout the university seems to confirm the reports and corroborate the end-of-reading treatises and memoirs: legions of students apparently come to class ill prepared, not having done the assigned reading at all or having given it only cursory attention. Professors admit that students can actually pass exams if they come to the lectures and take (or buy) good notes, whether or not they have read the assigned material. In short, careful reading seems have become a smaller blip on the higher educational radar screen or dropped off it altogether.

Despite the attention paid to student reading in the national surveys, relatively little scholarship has examined empirically what, how, and whether college students actually do read and how reading thus figures in the transition from high school to college. We set out to address this knowledge gap in a local way during a recent fall semester at our institution, the University of Arkansas. We wanted to know how our first-year students taking college composition, a course in which students mostly write about their reading, perceived and effected the transition from high school to college as readers. Therefore, we studied the reading habits and practices of twenty-one first-year composition students during the first two weeks of October, at which time they were in their sixth and seventh weeks of a fifteen-week semester. In some ways, our study provides a remarkably accurate local representation of the data about student reading as reported in the national surveys: first-year students at the University of Arkansas spend just about the same amount of time reading and preparing for class as students at other research universities—probably not as much time as their instructors and institutional administrators think they should. In other ways, however, our study offers insights into the reading environments of first-year college students that neither the national surveys nor the status-quo chatter hints at. We found students who were actively involved in their own programs of reading aimed at values clarification, personal enrichment, and career preparation. In short, we discovered students who were extremely engaged with their reading, but not with the reading that their classes required.

We offer our study as an example of local institutional research, aimed at helping our faculty understand salient aspects of our students' reading experiences and develop key strategies for addressing our students' reading histories. We hope, however, that what we found might help other institutions' faculty members and administrators think more carefully about how they meet and understand their students as readers.

What Do We Know about Reading?: High School, College, and the Transition

Any faculty member who wonders how and whether students prepare for class can probably find sources of consternation and concern in two national surveys. Since its inception in 1999, the National Survey of Student Engagement (NSSE), directed by George Kuh at Indiana University, has provided valuable data to college and university administrators and faculties about first-year and senior-year students' practices and beliefs as related to the survey organization's five "national benchmarks of effective educational practice": "level of academic challenge, active and collaborative learning, student-faculty interaction, enriching educational experiences, and supportive campus environments" (12). Although the answers to questions engendered by each of the benchmark categories might interest faculty members who want to understand their students better, we believe that the questions generated under the rubric of "levels of academic challenge" are most germane to anyone concerned about student reading. The eleven questions in this category ask students about the number of textbooks, books, and book-length packs of course readings that they were required to read; the number and length of the papers that they were required to write; their perceptions of course emphases (for example, analyzing, synthesizing, making judgments, and applying theories or concepts); and the amount of time that they spent preparing for class.

Under the traditional rule of thumb of two hours' preparation time for every one hour in class, this average full-time student should be devoting 24 hours per week to studying, reading, writing, and so on. However, in the 2005 NSSE, taken by about 130,000 first-year students and a similar number of seniors from 523 colleges and universities, 66 percent of first-year students and 64 percent of seniors at all participating colleges and universities reported spending fewer than sixteen hours during a typical seven-day week preparing for class—"studying, reading, writing, doing homework or lab work, analyzing data, rehearsing, and other academic activities."[2]

If one concludes that college students are spending too little time preparing for class, one would also have to deduce that the situation in high school is even more dire. In 2004, five years after NSSE's debut, the High School Survey of Student Engagement (HSSSE) emerged from the same organization. In the inaugural HSSSE, over 90,000 high school students from grades 9 through 12 completed the survey, providing information about who is planning to go to college and how well students are prepared for college (*Getting Students Ready for College* 3). Among the seniors completing the survey, 94 percent of all respondents and 90 percent of respondents taking "college credit/prep/honors" courses reported spending six hours or fewer per week on "assigned reading." These data notwithstanding, a large majority of all of the respondents agreed with the statement, "I have the skills and abilities to complete my work." (*What We Can Learn from High School Students* 12). In other words, although the large majority of high school students spend less than one hour a day on assigned reading, they feel as though they are good enough readers to get by—perhaps *because* their schoolwork does not challenge them very much.

The NSSE and HSSSE data find an ominous counterpart in a study reported by Alvin Sanoff in 2006. Nearly 800 high school teachers and about 1,100 college faculty members were surveyed to determine their perceptions of how well students were prepared for college in reading, writing, science, mathematics, and oral communication, as well as in more attitudinal domains such as "motivation to work hard," "study habits," and "ability to seek and use support services." Only one-quarter of high school teachers and one-tenth of college faculty members thought that entering first-year students were "very well prepared" to read and understand difficult materials.

Consider the NSSE, HSSSE, and Sanoff data alongside two widely hailed studies of adult reading in the United States and the situation seems even more portentous. The 2004 report *Reading at Risk* from the National Endowment for the Arts found that literary reading among adult readers in the United States declined by ten percentage points between 1982 and 2002, representing a loss of 20 million readers, a decline mirrored, somewhat less precipitously, in the diminishing numbers of adults who read books of any kind (ix).[3] More recently, the NEA's 2007 report, *To Read or Not to Read*, maintained that "Americans are spending less time reading, reading comprehension skills are eroding," and "[t]hese declines have serious civic, social, cultural, and economic implications" (5).

Although the NSSE, the HSSSE, and NEA studies provide fodder for the perception that college-bound and college students can't and/or don't read extensively, critically, or even sufficiently, the surveys and reports did not provide us with a rich enough perspective as we planned how to engage in conversations with our institution's faculty members about designing, adjusting, and delivering reading-based composition and general-education curricula to our students. Very few scholars have actually investigated the quality or quantity of college students' reading.[4] We wanted to know more about the reading lives of our students.

How We Studied Student Reading

In that semester, we randomly selected twenty-one full-time freshmen from a volunteer pool of about one hundred students and paid the participants to complete three tasks. First, they filled out a questionnaire about their perceptions of their own reading abilities and habits in high school and college. Students provided information and opinions in response to the following questions:

- Approximately how many hours per week did you spend reading in your senior year of high school?

- Approximately what percentage of those hours were devoted to reading for your courses, in contrast to reading for your own interest or pleasure?

- Did you consider the amount of time you spent reading during your senior year in high school excessively high, moderately high, moderately low, or excessively low? Explain why.

- Did you consider yourself an excellent, above average, below average, or poor reader in high school? Explain why.

- So far this year [as of October 2], approximately how many hours per week are you spending on reading?

- Approximately what percentage of those hours are devoted to reading for your courses, in contrast to reading for your own interest or pleasure?

- Do you consider the amount of time you spend reading this year excessively high, moderately high, moderately low, or excessively low? Explain why.

- Do you now consider yourself an excellent, above average, below average, or poor reader? Explain why.

The second task required them to keep a reading journal for two consecutive weeks. We asked them to write for at least thirty minutes daily, describing in detail everything they read that day, and to produce at least ten full entries over the two weeks. For each entry, we asked the students to provide the title and author and the number of pages of each reading, indicating whether each text was read for a class, for a job, or for their interest or pleasure. Additionally, we asked students to indicate approximately how many minutes they spent reading during each day. Finally, we asked participants to focus specifically on *one* of the texts they read for each day and write about that text, responding to a series of questions. These questions were divided into five major categories: 1.) Focusing on One Specific Text, 2.) Reading Critically, 3.) Drawing Relationships: Text to Self, 4.) Drawing Relationships: Text to Text, and 5.) Drawing Relationships: Text to World.[5] The following are the actual questions that we asked students to answer in response to their one "chosen" text:

Focusing on One Specific Text

1. What was the title of the text you read?

2. What was the purpose of reading this text? Why did you read it?

3. Did you choose to read this text or was it assigned? If assigned, who assigned it?

4. If assigned the text, did whoever assign it give you instructions on how to read it? If so, what were the instructions?

5. If you chose this text for pleasure, why did you choose it?

6. How long did it take you to read the text?

7. Were you engaged in any other activity as you read the text (cooking, watching TV, etc.)?

8. Did you take a break or read straight through?

Reading Critically

1. What was the most important point the text made?

2. What were its most important secondary or supporting points?

3. Did you agree or disagree with the writer on any points?

4. Did you draw any inferences or conclusions that weren't directly stated in the text?

5. How difficult was the text to read?

6. Did you underline, highlight, or make comments in the margins? If so, describe the kinds of things you noted.

7. Did you ask questions of the text as you read? If so, describe your questions.

8. Did you look at headings and subtitles before you began to read? If so, what did they teach you?

9. What part of the reading, if any, did you skip over?

10. Why did you skip over this part, if you did?

Drawing Relationships: Text to Self

1. Did you find that what you read relates to your life in any way? If so, how?

2. Did this work inspire you in any way or stimulate your creativity? If so, how?

3. Did the text relate to your current job or a future job in any way? If so, how?

4. Did you discover anything new about your personal opinions, beliefs, or values in response to reading this text? If so, how?

5. How do you think your life experiences influence the way you read the text?

Drawing Relationships: Text to Text

1. Did you make any connections between this text and other texts you have read?

2. Does this text relate to other texts assigned in your classes? If so, how?

3. Does this text relate to other texts you have read outside of class? If so, how?

4. Did reading other texts help you understand this one? Or do you feel you needed more background information to understand the material?

5. How do you foresee this text helping you understand texts you expect to read in the future?

Drawing Relationships: Text to World

1. Did you discuss what you read with anyone? If so, with whom?

2. Who else read this text?

3. How is others' response similar to or different from your own?

4. How does this text relate to the world, to the "bigger picture" in general?

For the third task in the study, students participated in an exit interview, in which they provided a think-aloud protocol about a self-selected 250-word portion of a textbook that they were currently reading for one of their classes. In the remainder of this article, after a brief comment on data from the intake questionnaires, we focus on what the students' reading journals taught us.

The data generated by the intake questionnaires did not suggest that the students see the reading transition from high school to college as all that dramatic. The first-year students at the University of Arkansas were reading a bit more in college than they did during their last year of high school, and they were reading a bit less for pleasure than they did during the previous year.

Students characterized the time that they spent reading during their senior year in high school as "moderately low," about 7.6 hours per week, 70 percent of which was for their classes. Nevertheless, their general perception of their reading abilities in high school was in the "above average" range.[6] Not much seemed to change for these students when they came to college. According to the intake questionnaires, as first-year students they were still spending what they characterized as a moderately low amount of time reading, about 12.9 hours per week, 84 percent of which was for their classes, and they still perceived themselves as above-average readers.

What We Learned from the Journals, Part I: Toeing the NSSE Line

The students' two-week intensive journals in some ways fleshed out the students' self-perceptions from the intake questionnaires, but in other ways they contradicted them. Above all else, the journals offered a considerably richer picture of the students' reading lives than we had anticipated—the journals turned out to be a bountiful data source. One could certainly drop into them like an anthropologist and find several aspects of the late-adolescent reading culture that are worthy of note and, from an educationally conservative viewpoint, perplexing. For example,

- All of the students spent lots of time reading online documents.

- A substantial majority of them read their Facebook sites almost daily, sometimes for extended periods.

- Most of them read while doing something else: listening to music, checking emails and sending instant messages, watching television, and so on.

But, as fascinated as we were by the minutiae of the students' rituals, we wanted to look for bigger patterns in the journals. Initially, we simply wanted to see how our first-year students stacked up against the national numbers reported in the NSSE.

For each journal entry, we asked the participants not only to list everything they read during the course of each day but also to estimate the amount of time they had spent reading each item. All of the participants provided at least ten full entries, but only half of them were faithful recorders of texts and time. As we made a first pass through the journals of these accurate respondents, we tried to categorize the texts that they read as either "academic"—that is, texts that they read for their courses—or "nonacademic"—that is, texts that they read for pleasure, leisure, personal interest, or work. Given our interest in technologically mediated writing, moreover, we found it interesting to subdivide the "nonacademic" category into "nonacademic/

technological"—reading done on a computer screen—and "non-academic/nontechnological." The students who were faithful recorders of their texts and time spent an average of 1 hour and 24 minutes per day on academic reading, some of which—a surprisingly small proportion—was done using technology. The faithful recorders devoted an average of 54 minutes a day to nonacademic reading involving technology—Facebook profiles, emails, instant messages, Internet sites, and so on. They spent an average of 25 minutes per day on nonacademic reading that did not involve technology—magazines, books, newspapers, and so on. Thus, the faithful, categorizing respondents reported spending an average of 2 hours and 43 minutes per day on all types of reading, almost evenly divided between academic and nonacademic reading.[7]

If we assume, however, that the faithfully categorizing respondents and the summative respondents were devoting roughly the same proportion of time to academic and nonacademic reading, their reports place these University of Arkansas first-year students right smack in the middle of that 66 percent of first-year students in the NSSE who spent fewer than 16 hours per week "preparing for class."[8]

What We Learned from the Journals, Part II: Hints of a Reading Life

In addition to telling us how much and roughly what kinds of reading our students did, the journals also provided a fascinating window into why and how they read. Because we asked students to include in their journal entries everything that they read during the course of a day and gave them the freedom to write their "focusing-on-one-specific-text" entry in response to anything they might choose, we were quite interested in the types of texts that they selected. We found an abundant and varied array.

The journals contained a grand total of 210 daily entries. Within this number, about half of the "focused" entries were about texts that students were reading for their classes, and the other half were about texts that we categorized as "nonacademic." Among the nonacademic responses, the large majority were about texts that students were reading for their personal pleasure or interest, such as employee manuals and job instructions. A smaller number were about texts they were reading either for work or for personal "business" as a student, such as documents about academic advising, academic progress, and so on. Another small percentage of nonacademic responses dealt with texts that students were reading as part of a personal program to support and, in some cases, explore their religious faith.

Considering that all of the participants in the study were full-time students, one might expect the reading that they were doing for their courses to occupy the top position in their list of intellectual priorities.

Moreover, considering that the participants had reported spending 84 percent of their reading time during the first six weeks of the semester occupied with academic reading, one might expect that their nonacademic reading was done primarily for rest and relaxation.

The journal entries do not support these presumptions. Like the students in the Stanford Study of Writing, who reported having actively "performative" writing lives that transcended the writing they must do for courses (Fishman et al.), many of the students in our study described having regular, steady, full reading lives in which they engaged with a wide variety of texts for reasons both academic and nonacademic. We encountered students who, during the two-week period, were reading novels (examples: *The Fellowship of the Ring*, *A Handmaid's Tale*, and *Angels and Demons*), nonfiction books (*Guns, Germs, and Steel* and *Under the Banner of Heaven*), magazines (*Seventeen* and *Cosmopolitan* were favorites among the females; exercise and hunting magazines prevailed among the males), and newspapers (both the campus paper and the statewide one) for personal interest and pleasure. We found students, perhaps because of our prompting, drawing solid connections between the texts that they were reading and their emerging sense of themselves as adults in the world. One student unpacked her connection to a magazine article about the untimely death of young woman who had had an unresolved argument with her father; the journal entry described the student's own estrangement from her father following her parents' divorce. Another student noted that she connected to *The Diary of Anne Frank* because, as a Jew, she had experienced racial slurs herself. A third student described her memory of training a puppy to help her connect to part of her psychology textbook about behavioral conditioning. A fourth student explained his connection between Plato's *Republic* and Marxist governments: "Karl Marx and socialist and communist societies tried to use many of Plato's ideas in their writings and governments, but they all consistently failed, while democracy thrived and continues to spread today."

The following three brief case studies offer slightly more extended profiles of students who defy the status-quo thinking that portrays first-year college students as incapable of and uninterested in reading. Angela, Pauline, and Corey have come to college as readers of texts that speak to their own exigencies and interests.

Angela Ivy[9] was taking four courses during the study—Italian, algebra, composition, and sociology—and she devoted some reading time to each of them. But the reading activity that occupied most of her time during the two weeks involved the Bible, plus books and articles from the popular press about contemporary issues of Christian faith. Her reports of reading experiences showed, on the one hand, a young person who was looking for confirmation of religious principles that she grew up with but, on the other hand, questioning how these principles fit into the new culture in which she was immersed at the university.

The number of minutes that Angela devoted to reading for her four courses is interesting in itself. Over the two weeks, she reported spending 325 minutes reading and studying for algebra, 215 minutes reading and studying vocabulary items for her composition class, 175 minutes reading and studying Italian, and 35 minutes reading for sociology. Compare these times with her reports for three other activities: she spent 345 minutes reading the *Bible* and books and articles dealing with Christian faith—texts that she chose to read for "interest/personal benefit." She devoted 330 minutes to reading email messages, websites (at least one of which was related to her coursework), and Facebook entries. She spent 210 minutes reading articles in magazines and newspapers for "personal interest," but at least three of these articles were about topics that frequently emerge in contemporary discussions of religion and faith: creationism versus intelligent design, homosexuality and tolerance, and the legalization of marijuana.

Angela's journal opened with a long, questioning entry on a book called *Show Me, God* by Fred Heeren, a text that Angela says she read "by choice." The main point of the text, she wrote, "was concerning the Law of Cause and Effect—that logic demands a cause for every effect and that world/universe is an effect that demands a very great cause." She added:

> The sun, moon, and stars could not have come from nothing—that's <u>irrational</u>. Every observable fact around us can be explained in terms of something else that caused it, but when the question is about the existence of the universe itself, there is nothing in the universe to explain it— no <u>natural</u> explanation. I understood where the author was coming from, but just because we haven't found a natural explanation for creation doesn't mean we should just throw up our hands and say 'God did it.' (Emphasis in original)

Angela's last journal entry provided a fascinating summary of her commentary on reading texts that lead to theological questioning. She read an article entitled "The Bible Is Still Number One" in a magazine called *A Matter of Fact*. She encapsulated the main point of the article: "Prophesy and scientific foreknowledge are repeated in the Bible—giving evidence of its credibility as The Word of God." She drew a powerful connection between this text and herself: "If I could go into apologetics for a career," she wrote, "it [the article] would definitely relate to my future job." Tacitly conceding that she probably won't have this option as a career, she added, "Regardless, it's good to have a rational foundation in what you're trying to put your trust in." She saw possible connections between this text and others she might read for courses or personal interest: "The more I read about this, the more I'll have to implement into other texts I have read. It helps to have a well-rounded approach so you can look at things more objectively."

Pauline Rosario offers a powerful counterexample to those who believe that first-year students don't engage with their reading. Pauline had become fluent in English, her second language, but read regularly in her first language, Spanish, to maintain her fluency in it. She belonged to a book club, undertook a considerable amount of reading outside of class, and showed a strong ability to draw connections between her reading and her growing sense of self, the texts she has previously read, and the larger world beyond academia.

During the two-week journaling period, Pauline spent a lot of her spare time reading for pleasure. For instance, she read *One Hundred Years of Solitude* in Spanish, her native language, for the book club that she belonged to as an extracurricular activity. She commented that she read it slowly because she had difficulty with reading Spanish now that she was used to reading in English. Apparently, Pauline still valued her first language enough to put forth the effort to read the text in Spanish rather than in its translated form. She wrote, "There is one factor that is hindering my reading speed and comprehension, the book is in Spanish. Spanish was my first language but after 12 years in school, using English, it has become difficult to understand Spanish as I read it. In total I spent about an hour and a half reading the book and accomplished one and a half chapters."

Pauline even saw possibilities for drawing connections in her reading using technology. Commenting on reading emails and Web logs, she wrote, "This text obviously does not involve any academic reward, but it is very important as far as my social life goes. I did make connections with other texts (e-mails) that I've read, though, mainly because e-mails are an ongoing conversation with friends that I do not see as often. Reading this text did in fact make me understand other e-mails a little better." Pauline did not discredit the value of her personal reading or the use of electronic media because she believes that they help her explore her ideas. "As far as discovering anything about my personal opinions, this text succeeded. Because these e-mails were of a personal subject, they did relate to my life 100%. After reading these e-mails, I called a friend, so I did discuss the reading with someone else."

Finally, Pauline included this note at the end of her journal:

> I am aware that this study is to figure out the "jump" from high school to college reading; however the fact is that most of my required reading (which is not much) has nothing to do with this "jump" because what is different is not the amount of reading, but the level and wording of the text. The college text jumps to a level of reading exponentially higher than high school texts, and this is what causes the struggles for the students.

Corey Essene was enrolled in the College of Arts and Sciences Honors Program at the time of our study, and, as such, was the type of student that one might expect to take his class preparation very seriously.

A superficial reading of his journal entries might lead one to question that expectation. In short, Corey seemed to blow off his required reading. On the other hand, however, his journal entries show a young man devoted to reading fantasy fiction and learning French—not so much to do well in his French class, but instead to communicate with a friend he met while traveling the previous summer and to fulfill his goal of getting a job working in the American Embassy in Paris.

Corey's first journal entry was one of only two in which he had anything substantial—or positive—to say about his assigned reading. He described his admittedly superficial reading of an essay, "The Genocidal Killer in the Mirror," simply because he and some classmates in his Honors Composition class had to meet and collectively come up with a thesis statement for an essay about it. In his next entry, however, he focused at some length on a chapter entitled "Celbedeil" in a book called *Eldest* by Christopher Paolini, which he chose to spend thirty minutes reading "to break the monotony of studying and doing homework for all of my classes." *Eldest* is clearly mainstream fantasy, the second book in a trilogy, Corey reported: "It's a story about dragons in a mythical setting. It is kind of like books I have read including Tolkien's books because it has many of the same mythical races and similar settings." Corey offered a connection-filled thought to conclude this entry: "This really relates to the real world because this symbolizes bigotry that still exists across the planet. I think that because I am aware of bigotry in society that I was able to see Paolini's throwback and symbology [sic] of these ancient grudges and beliefs. This text basically reaffirmed my passion against the ignorance of bigotry, whether it be in fiction novels, or real life and history."

In another entry, Corey turned his attention to French and made an explicit text-to-self connection, referring directly to his employment goal. He reported studying his French textbook for "about a half an hour" in his dorm room: "I read this because I am currently learning French as my second language and it is my minor. I read this also for pleasure because I enjoy learning the French language. This relates to me personally because I hope to get a job at the American embassy in Paris." Two entries later, Corey returned to the French project, describing his reading of a "long email from a friend in Paris." He added, "I read the entire text in French and it took me about ten minutes. I understood most of the letter, but I was forced to look up a few words that were not in my French vocabulary." Corey explained that he had struck a deal with Axel, a French friend whom he met traveling last summer. They agreed they would write to each other only in French: "I actually made this arrangement with Axel, most importantly, for educational purposes. Axel is fluent in English, so he is doing this as a favor to me to strengthen my French vocabulary and grammar."

In his next-to-last entry, Corey returned to some assigned reading, this time for his Fundamentals of Communication class: "The text was the basic dry, boring textbook type text, but it was highly informative. I read it in about an hour. This relates to me because I know it will help me give my assigned speech and later speeches I am to give throughout my college career and life."

We don't want to argue that Angela, Pauline, and Corey are necessarily representative of any particular population, but they do evince a strong interest in personal reading, something that status-quo thinking would assert that college students lack. Angela, Pauline, and Corey engage thoughtfully with texts; however, most of the texts that they value and connect with are not those assigned in their courses.

Rethinking Reading in College Courses

Although neither of us had Angela, Pauline, or Corey as a student in class, when we read their journals, we tended to think we might like to. Here were three students, all engaged readers, all capable to some degree of connecting their reading to their own growing sense of self and to the world around them. We venture, however, that, although Pauline might be seen as a successful college student reader, many instructors would find Angela and Corey to represent the kinds of students that they normally encounter in their courses—not very interested in the assigned course readings, not eager to "participate" in a discussion, not inclined to read any more deeply than the assignment requires.

So what did we learn about these kinds of students by reading their journals? What kinds of readers are these randomly selected University of Arkansas students? Let us unpack those questions before turning to the issue of how we urged faculty members and program administrators at our institution to think differently about reading in their courses.

First of all, our students were reading, but they were not reading studiously, either in terms of the texts they were engaging with or the manner in which they read them. Like the high school boys whose literate practices Michael Smith and Jeffrey Wilhelm describe in *Reading Don't Fix No Chevys*, the University of Arkansas students often manifested a passion for reading that was not connected to their courses. Instead, they saw the reading that they had to do for school as uninspiring, dull, and painfully required. Here was Angela's response to her sociology text: "I completely agree" with it and it "raises no questions." Corey assessed his Fundamentals of Communication reading as being self-evident, and said that he rapidly perused "The Genocidal Killer in the Mirror" just in order to generate a thesis about it. Although Angela's and Corey's responses to school-based reading, typical of those of many of the participants, were rather neutrally dismissive, other students were more adamantly critical. One student, Jennifer Respighi, described how she took only five minutes to read a sample biology lab report "because it was so boring." Another student, Katherine Quick, characterized her psychology textbook as "a brutally boring overwad" and wrote that she skipped sections "because there was no reason to read a bunch of bullshit." A third student, Walter Hope, simply opined that "my chemistry book sucks."

Many of the participants clearly rushed through their required reading simply to get it done and then move on to reading that they found more engaging. In the journals, we found daily reading schedules such as the following:

- Andrea Less, Day 5: 30 minutes reading an article for an English assignment, 20 minutes reading email and Ebay ads.

- Kathy Gravette, Day 1: 30 minutes total for reading an English assignment and the essay it required her to read, plus her art assignment, and *Cosmopolitan* magazine; Day 5: 30 minutes total for reading her English assignment ("It was difficult to read") plus *Cosmopolitan* and the newspaper.

- Fred Borg, Day 1: 45 minutes reading a selection from Descartes's *First Meditation*, during a lecture in a math class; Day 3: 20 minutes reading an essay for English.

- Tony Richardson, Day 2: 30 minutes reading an essay for English; Day 5: 96 minutes reading *The Boater's Handbook*.

In many of these reports, we would be hard pressed to find reading experiences that we would characterize as focused and contemplative.

Second, although the students generally showed some ability to draw the three types of connections that we urged them to create with our leading questions, their reported connections were not evenly distributed among the three categories. Our students seemed quite capable of making text-to-self connections—Lindsey James, for example, related her response to an article about cults to her own religious upbringing—and text-to-world connections—recall Angela's repeated connections between texts that she was reading and campus/community/world events. But it was the rare student who, like Pauline, would draw connections between and among texts that she was reading for her classes, or like William Hope, who described the connections that he drew between *Helter Skelter* and *Under the Banner of Heaven*, two books that he read for his own pleasure and interest.

Third, students are motivated by and engaged with reading, but the texts that they interact with most enthusiastically are technologically based. In addition, students have become proficient in the art of multitasking as they navigate in and out of electronic media. Virtually all of the students indicate in their journals that they spend a substantial amount of time reading online. Although some of the students' academic assignments require online research or reading on the computer, their journal entries indicate that they interact with electronic media primarily when reading for pleasure. The majority of their time reading for pleasure is spent reading and writing emails, instant messaging, or creating and perusing Facebook and MySpace profiles. In these examples, technology encourages reading for personal communication and social networking, and these purposes overlap in many ways that relate to academic study. For instance, Corey became inspired to learn French, so he emailed back and forth with a friend in France to help him acquire and enhance his reading skills. Without this incentive, Corey may not have pursued his study of French with the same enthusiasm. Pauline wrote in her journal that the significant amounts of time she spends blogging and networking with friends may have no academic reward; nevertheless, she values this kind of reading for its ability to help her network and stay connected socially. As a result of the amount of time that students spend with electronic media, their reading practices and habits have shifted with influence of these technologies. Their journal entries consistently refer to the myriad ways in which they multitask as they read. For instance, many students email and instant message their friends while surfing the Internet and reading texts on the computer. Many watch television, listen to music, or talk on their cell phones as they read their textbooks.

Given that our students seem to engage with some types of reading, what did we suggest that faculty members the University of Arkansas do to help their students engage more fully with, and read more critically, the material that they need to read for their classes? Both in campus forums sponsored by our university's Teaching and Learning Center and in internal publications, we suggested three avenues.

First, we argued that faculty members need to teach students explicitly how to draw the kinds of connections that lead to engaged reading, particularly text-to-world and text-to-text connections. It's not that we think text-to-self connections are not important. We do think, however, that, as valuable as these kinds of personal connections are for initiating engaged reading, students ultimately need to be stretched beyond the boundaries of their own personal reactions. As Wayne Booth contended in *Modern Dogma and the Rhetoric of Assent*, one major function of college is to drag students "kicking and screaming, out of infantile solipsism into adult membership in an inquiring community" (13). As they read, students need to be walked through demonstrations of mature, committed, adult readers who draw connections to the world around them, both historical and current, and to other texts. One relatively easy teaching technique, the think-aloud protocol, is particularly useful. The instructor simply focuses on a passage—say, 250 words or so—from the required reading and reads it aloud to students, pausing regularly to explain to the students what connections he or she is making to his or her own life and work, to the world beyond the text, and, most important, to other texts that he or she has read. (For more on the think-aloud protocol, see Daniels and Zemelman, Chapter 5.)

Second, we suggested that faculty members and administrators need to create curriculums, co-curriculums, and extra-curriculums that invite students to engage in their reading and to connect texts that they read to their lives, their worlds, and other texts. Certainly, learning-community programs—in which students are taking two or three courses together, focusing on a common theme—foster this kind of curricular connectivity, as do service-learning and community-outreach programs, in which students accomplish necessary and useful projects that reflect principles and ideas from their reading. But even in the absence of such curricular innovations, instructors can take relatively simple steps to foster students' making connections between their courses. An instructor might ask his or her students to list and offer a one-sentence description on an index card of every other class that they are taking. Perusing the other subjects that his or her students are studying, the instructor could make an explicit effort to show how the class readings might evoke themes, issues, and motifs being raised in the other classes. In addition, the instructor might adapt and follow guidelines developed by Christopher Thaiss for first-year writing courses with a writing-across-the-curriculum orientation ("A Rubric for Understanding Writing in Different Classes and Disciplines"; see also Thaiss and Zawacki). An instructor dedicated to improving connected, engaged reading throughout the curriculum could explain explicitly to students how the documents that they must read relate directly to the aims and methods of learning that are most valued in the course environment, show clearly how the students' reading for the course should be manifest in projects and examinations, and demonstrate specifically *how* students should read the course material.

Third, we urged faculty members to look for ways to incorporate more technology into their reading assignments. It is becoming common knowledge that students engage effectively with reading done in interactive electronic contexts. For example, Gail E. Hawisher and her colleagues point out that all students have different "cultural ecologies" and therefore experience different "technological gateways" for acquiring and developing literacy, but many students have developed literacies in electronic contexts that instructors overlook or ignore. "As a result," according to Hawisher et al., "we fail to build on the literacies students already have" (676). We suggested that faculty members could enhance student learning through better engagement with reading by incorporating assignments that achieved two primary goals:

- They would provide students with opportunities to interact with electronic hyperlinked texts.

- They would engage student readers through reflection in electronic public spheres.

We urged faculty to consider incorporating such components as discussion forums through WebCT or Blackboard to help students reflect on and respond to reading assignments with their classmates, and we argued that students could also benefit from online conversations with larger discourse communities and professionals in the field of study to enhance their reading about certain topics. Setting up a Web blog or posting to an established Usenet group could help get students interested. In short, we noted that supplementing course instruction with technological materials would allow students to navigate information and to multitask in ways that would ultimately enhance their reading.

Although our study was most useful for motivating and shaping discussions at our own institution, we see merit in faculty members and administrators conducting similar studies on their own campuses; reporting the results to groups of students, instructors, and administrators; and discussing the implications of the results for teaching and learning on the campus. Indeed, we would urge any college or university serious about improving undergraduate composition and general education to examine student reading on its own campus. While the outcomes of such studies would vary according to context and region — some of our conclusions are related to the high number of fundamentalist evangelicals who attend our university — the results would generate very useful intra- and inter-institutional discussions about teaching and learning.

Should the English department take the lead in conducting such studies? Not necessarily. Every English department faculty member who has been involved with writing-across-the-curriculum or writing-in-the-disciplines programs knows that they succeed best when faculty members throughout the university buy into the notion of improving learning by increasing the amount and complexity of student writing and by teaching writing consciously and explicitly in all courses. The same must be true in efforts to examine and improve student reading.

There will be resistance to such efforts. People will wonder why colleges and universities admit students who "can't read." Faculty members will opine that they lack time to teach students how to read material carefully in their courses "because there is so much I have to cover already." To anticipate and counter this resistance, any institutional effort to study whether, how, how much, and why students read must be initiated and championed by faculty members and administrators directly responsible for overseeing curriculum, instruction, and assessment of general education.

There's no need for any college or university to be apologetic about looking at students' reading habits and practices. The transition from high school to college must entail a transition to different types of reading, different amounts of reading, and different approaches to success with reading. If we intend to continue basing assignments, syllabi, and entire academic programs on student reading, then we need to know more about it.

Notes

1. See, for example, Sven Birkerts's *The Gutenberg Elegies* and Mark Edmundson's *Why Read?*
2. The responses about the "number of assigned textbooks, books, or book-length packs of course readings" that students reported reading are also instructive: 64 percent of first-year students and 56 percent of seniors reported reading ten or fewer textbooks, books, or course packs during the academic year (38).
3. *Reading at Risk* was not without its naysayers. In *Black Issues Book Review*, Wayne Dawkins questions the "dire picture" painted by the NEA.
4. A 1991 study by Charlene Blackwood and her colleagues examined the pleasure reading habits of 333 college seniors in a small, public liberal arts university. Although 88 percent of the respondents reported that they read for pleasure, they did so for only about two and a half hours per week while school was in session and slightly more during vacations. In 1999, Jude Gallik surveyed the recreational reading habits of 139 first-year and upper-level students at a private, liberal arts college in Texas. Gallik found that 87 percent of the respondents devoted fewer than six hours per week to recreational reading while school was in session, a number that dropped to 75 percent during school vacations. A 1994 study by Ravi Sheorey and Kouider Mokhtari investigated the reading habits of 85 college students enrolled in an elective developmental reading course at a large public university, finding that the students read about 4.75 hours per week. In a study conducted in 2000 at Texas A&M Corpus Christi, but never published, Richard Haswell and his graduate students examined practices of, and attitudes toward, "self-sponsored" and "school-sponsored" reading among 100 ninth-graders and 100 first-year college students. Haswell found that the two groups spent slightly different amounts of time each week on reading and writing: The ninth-graders reported reading 163 pages and spending 23 hours per week; the first-semester college students read 141 pages and devoted 18 hours per week. However, the ninth-graders reported reading almost twice as many pages per week of self-chosen material than did the college students, although the college students said they read one-fifth more pages of school-sponsored material per week than the ninth-graders (5). Under the auspices of the Henry J. Kaiser Family Foundation, Victoria Rideout, Donald Roberts, and Ulla Foehr studied the daily media use of more than 2,000 8- to 18-year-olds. The researchers found that subjects spent an average of 6.5 hours daily with "media": 4 hours and 16 minutes watching television and/or movies, 1 hour and 44 minutes listening to music, 1 hour and 2 minutes using the computer, and 49 minutes playing video games. Although three-quarters of the survey participants reported reading something for pleasure every day, the average time spent daily reading books, magazines, and newspapers was 43 minutes.
5. The "drawing-relationships" questions were motivated by the types of connections that Ellin Keene Oliver and Susan Zimmerman teach students to draw in *Mosaic of Thought: Teaching Comprehension in a Reader's Workshop*, a widely used resource for teacher-development programs in high schools.
6. When examining the students' evaluations of how much time they devoted to reading in high school and college, we coded a response of "excessively

high" as a 4, "moderately high" as a 3, "moderately low" as a 2, and "excessively low" as a 1. When examining the students' perceptions of their own abilities as readers, we coded a response of "excellent" as a 4, "above average" as a 3, "below average" as a 2, and "poor" as a 1.

7. Over a seven-day week, therefore, these students devoted about 19 hours per week to reading—in other words, somewhat more than they had reported on their intake questionnaires, perhaps because the act of listing *everything* that they read during a day turned "reading" into a larger activity for these students. In contrast, the students who did not record how much time they spent reading each item, but simply provided a total number of minutes of reading per day, reported spending an average of 1 hour and 41 minutes daily on all types of reading, or about 11.8 hours per week—a bit less than they had reported on their intake questionnaires.

8. The largest subgroup within that 66 percent is the students who reported spending 6 to 10 hours per week preparing for class—27 percent. Because the participants in our study included *everything* that they read in their daily tallies, we think it's safe to assume that the amount of time that they spent on reading *in preparation for class* probably lies within this 6-to-10-hours-per-week category.

9. By agreement with the participants, all names have been changed to pseudonyms.

Works Cited

Birkerts, Sven. *The Gutenberg Elegies: The Fate of Reading in an Electronic Age.* New York: Fawcett, 1994. Print.

Blackwood, Charlene, et al. "Pleasure Reading by College Students: Fact or Fiction?" Paper presented at the annual meeting of the Mid-South Educational Research Association, Lexington, KY, Nov. 1991.

Booth, Wayne. *Modern Dogma and the Rhetoric of Assent.* Chicago: U of Chicago P, 1974. Print.

Daniels, Harvey, and Steven Zemelman. *Subjects Matter: Every Teacher's Guide to Content-Area Reading.* Portsmouth: Heinemann, 2004. Print.

Dawkins, Wayne. "Is Anybody Out There? A Closer Look at the Dire Picture Unearthed in the NEA's Reading at Risk Study Turns Up Some Hopeful Signs." *Black Issues Book Review* 7.3 (May 2005): 110. Print.

Edmundson, Mark. *Why Read?* New York: Bloomsbury, 2004. Print.

Fishman, Jenn, Andrea Lunsford, Beth McGregor, and Mark Otuteye. "Performing Writing, Performing Literacy." *CCC* 57 (2006): 224–52. Print.

Gallik, Jude D. "Do They Read for Pleasure: Recreational Reading Habits of College Students." *Journal of Adolescent and Adult Literacy* 42 (1999): 480–88. Print.

Haswell, Richard. Personal correspondence. 1 Dec. 2006. E-mail.

Hawisher, Gail E., Cynthia L. Selfe, Brittney Moraski, and Melissa Pearson. "Becoming Literate in the Information Age: Cultural Ecologies and the Literacies of Technology." *CCC* 55 (2004): 642–92. Print.

High School Survey of Student Engagement, 2005. *Getting Students Ready for College: What Student Engagement Data Can Tell Us.* CEEP, n.d. Web. 15 Dec. 2007.

High School Survey of Student Engagement, 2005. *What Can We Learn from High School Students.* CEEP, n.d. Web. 15 Dec. 2007.

National Survey of Student Engagement. *Exploring Different Dimensions of Student Engagement: 2005 Annual Survey Results.* CEEP, n.d. Web. 15 Dec. 2007.

Oliver, Ellin Keene, and Susan Zimmerman. *Mosaic of Thought: Teaching Comprehension in a Reader's Workshop.* Portsmouth: Heinemann, 1997. Print.

Reading at Risk: A Survey of Literary Reading in America. Washington, DC: National Endowment for the Arts, 2004. Web. 15 Dec. 2007. <http://www.nea.gov/pub/ReadingAtRisk.pdf>.

Rideout, Victoria, Donald F. Roberts, and Ulla G. Foehr. *Generation M: Media in the Lives of 8–18 Year Olds.* Menlo Park, CA: Kaiser Family Foundation, 2005. Print.

Sanoff, Alvin P. "What Professors and Teachers Think: A Perception Gap over Students' Preparation." *Chronicle of Higher Education.* 10 Mar. 2006. Web. 15 Dec. 2007. <http://chronicle.com/free/v52/i27/27b0091.htm>.

Sheorey, Ravi, and Kouider Mokhtari. "The Reading Habits of College Students at Different Levels of Reading Proficiency." *Reading Improvement* 31 (1994): 156–66. Print.

Smith, Michael W, and Jeffrey Wilhelm. *Reading Don't Fix No Chevys: Literacy in the Lives of Young Men.* Portsmouth, NH: Heinemann, 2002. Print.

Thaiss, Christopher. *A Rubric for Understanding Writing in Different Classes and Disciplines.* McGraw-Hill, n.d. Web. 15 Dec. 2007.

Thaiss, Christopher, and Terry Myers Zawacki. *Engaged Writers/Dynamic Disciplines.* Portsmouth: Boynton/Cook, 2006. Print.

To Read or Not to Read: A Question of National Consequence. Washington, DC: National Endowment for the Arts, 2007. Web. 15 Dec. 2007. <http://ww.nea.gov/research/ToRead.pdf>.

Teaching and Learning with New Literacies

Harlem, Art, and Literacy *and* Documenting "Harlem Is Art"/"Harlem as Art"

Valerie Kinloch

Valerie Kinloch presents an action research project on digital literacies, producing video walk-throughs of the gentrification of Harlem with her students Phillip and Khaleeq. The gentrification of Harlem absorbs the lives of Phillip and Khaleeq, as they experience rent increases at home and higher prices in the new chain stores in the neighborhood. They also comment on the displacement of long-time Harlem residents, and consider the implications of displacement for themselves and the histories of their historically African American community. This project, Kinloch explains, grew out of Phillip and Khaleeq's concerns that school-based literacies they encountered at their public high school did not address these changes or the impact of these changes on the community, a topic of immediate significance to themselves and their peers. With Kinloch as participant-observer, Phillip and Khaleeq begin to explore this disconnect through digital literacies using audio, video, and photographs. Kinloch's mini-documentary of this project is available on YouTube at <http://www.youtube.com /watch?v=XoupQBrME8U>.

Harlem, Art, and Literacy

Many times, we do not critically observe the communities through which we travel as we go to school, to work, shopping, or even home. What can we learn from the everyday of urban landscapes? From architectural designs to cultural activities to the role of local communities in civil rights movements, urban places and spaces are rich in history. We can study how communities function as sites of conflict, or, according to Mary Louise Pratt (1991), as "contact zones," as well as how they serve as spaces of safety, what bell hooks (1990) describes as "homeplaces." I believe we can engage in this learning by listening to what people, especially youth, have to say about their neighborhoods.

On a Sunday afternoon in Harlem, I observed Phillip and Khaleeq's observations of the community. I was compelled to document their conversations on the stereotypes they believed people have about urban communities. Many complex ideas about Harlem as art were revealed, ideas that I believe connect to 21st-century literacy learning. I had not considered many of these ideas until I started working with Phillip and Khaleeq and intimately listening to their feelings about community and change. Here is an excerpt:

Khaleeq: Harlem as art.

Phillip: Harlem is art, ya' heard!

Khaleeq: People shouldn't be talking 'bout places like Harlem like it's some bad, dangerous area or something. Harlem's not to be criticized but appreciated.

Phillip: People talk 'bout Harlem, our Black community with its crowded streets and our Black schools with its crowded seats. They don't know 'bout the rhythm that's our madness. It's the art in how we walk, baby, and the art in how we talk, man. Harlem is art. This thing they call gentrification can't take that from Harlem. It might separate people like Black people from White people because of who can stay here, but Harlem's always gonna be art to me.

Khaleeq: Harlem is art. . . . Harlem's literacy even if we ain't like the other side of town, like how rich White people live on the east side. Harlem's art and literacy, well, at least for the Black kids I know living here.

Phillip: Man, see what's gonna happen is we'll have a New York City with Black students/Black communities like Harlem that'll soon be gentrified and White students/White communities like the Upper East Side that's a different world.

Khaleeq: It's a different world, but Harlem's still art.

Concerned with disparities between "Black students/Black communities like Harlem that'll soon be gentrified and White students/White communities like the Upper East Side," Phillip, Khaleeq, and I initiated a conversation on how art in Harlem can serve as yet another literacy response to gentrification. With our shared rhyme books, or journals, which served as our paper space to pose questions about community change, we routinely exchanged ideas on the art within Harlem, including architectural designs, murals painted on the sides of buildings, and the poetic sounds of words we heard spoken by people on the streets. From our rhyme books, community observations, and participation in community meetings, Phillip and Khaleeq continuously practiced ways to engage in data member checking sessions (Lincoln & Guba, 2000) at the same time that they were becoming comfortable using language to search for deeper meanings of gentrification. Doing so encouraged them to critically consider their conflicting responses to community change (e.g., "separate people"; "what's gonna happen"; "even if we ain't like the other side of town"; "it's a different world").

Phillip and Khaleeq both had a strong fondness for Harlem's famous 125th Street. They focused on 125th Street as a site where "art is in constant process" (Phillip). In a clip from his video documentary of the community, Khaleeq made the comment., "Harlem is already art. It has been for decades, although the community is now being gentrified to create a sense of art [Phillip interrupted: "A fake sense of art"]. If this new art and new Harlem gon' to improve our community, why's it displacing so many Black residents who've lived here for years?" Phillip could not help but respond, "it's time that young people stand up and talk about the value of Harlem. Look, where else can you find so many symbols of Blackness in one community?"

I have described some of the symbols of Blackness that Phillip alluded to, such as the Apollo Theater, the Studio Museum of Harlem, the Adam Clayton Powell Jr. State Building, the Schomburg Center for Research in Black Culture, the Harriet Tubman Gardens, the Frederick Douglass Houses, and local high schools and enrichment centers. He also referred to inscribed passages from speeches by Malcolm X that appeared on the sides of buildings just as much as they appeared on T-shirts worn by young and adult residents of Harlem. Phillip also saw the value of stories "as art" embedded in local and national histories of people's struggles for rights (e.g., education; housing; voting; economics; political).

By turning to art forms to make sense of community changes, Phillip, Khaleeq, and other urban youth were able to create honest, descriptive stories to challenge negative images of urban space (Beauregard, 1993) and inform adult learning and activism. Khaleeq's sentiments, "people got their stories," was not just a call for youth to tell their stories, but for youth and adults to exchange their stories "with a purpose." Khaleeq's emerging ways of looking at the power of stories and their meanings can lead to intergenerational collaborations in which people exchange narratives, whether shared or competing ones, about identity, belonging, and struggle. Such exchanges can serve to protect, preserve, and privilege the histories of understudied communities.

Khaleeq's belief that "people shouldn't be talking 'bout places like Harlem like it's some bad, dangerous area or something" connected with Phillip's argument that "Harlem is art, ya' heard." They "stand up and talk about the value of Harlem" (Phillip) by recognizing struggles, socio-political tensions, and the transformation of people in changing spaces. They read the local newspapers, attended tenants' association meetings, and took pictures of historical community landmarks. At the same time, they struggled to understand why schools do not readily account for the literacies within local communities. Then, they questioned why people, including former President Bill Clinton and New York City Councilman Bill Perkins, would want to live or open offices in Harlem. For Phillip: "Clinton moving to Harlem looks good, but then our rent goes up . . . and Perkins, he another story." On this latter point, Khaleeq shook his head in agreement before inquiring, "Don't Perkins got an office off 125th?" Phillip continued, "He had space like around 121st [Street] when he was running for election. Now ask if I seen him around since then. See, that's the thing. Where's the real commitment? People come in, but do they stay?" As Phillip and Khaleeq discussed the transformation of Harlem space, I took it upon myself to listen to their voices, stories, experiences, and points of disagreement in much the same ways that I wanted them to listen to me: with an open heart, a critical mind, and a questioning soul that was always in pursuit of more stories. It is this pursuit that convinced me, in the words of Khaleeq, that "Harlem is art. . . . Harlem's literacy."

Phillip stated, "It's the art in how we walk . . . the art in how we talk." This art that makes up Harlem is not simply about the artifacts of art (e.g., drawings; books), but the people of Harlem themselves. He refers to the knowledge and power that made Harlem a mecca of Black life for people of color at the brink of the 1920s Harlem Renaissance. During this time, meanings of literacy (e.g., writing about pain, reading literature by people of color, interpreting history, and engaging in apprenticeships) and experiences of human struggles (e.g., racism; discrimination) took an artistic turn. "People," according to Phillip, "from what I know, were making music of their lives, out in the community with action, not just sitting waiting for something they don't like to up and happen." For Khaleeq, people were not "like machines waiting on a button to be pushed so they could get up." Instead, they were teaching one another about living in the world in ways that beckoned action. On this latter point, I can still hear Phillip say, "See, schools try to create us into machines. Gentrification is a machine. With schools and gentrification I can't sing my own art."

Feelings of confusion mixed with the desire to really understand forced me to contemplate Phillip's statement of defeat: "I can't sing my own art." As an educator and researcher, I was dismayed by the argument that schools produce student "machines," given my observations of Phillip and Khaleeq when working with Ms. L at Harlem High. Initially, they both appeared to be going through the motions involved with the routine nature of traditional school-sponsored learning. When they eventually recognized Ms. L's passion for teaching and working with students, they gravitated toward critical literacy opportunities. Yet this was just one of many classes and teachers they had encountered during their educational journey, and for them, the "bad" far outweighed the "good." Additionally, I recalled their ongoing insistence that I read the words "can't sing" silently and then aloud over and over again so that I understood the larger points being made. In doing so, I realized that all along Phillip wanted to sing his own song, make his own art, and dance to the meanings that emerged from those multiple experiences.

Extensive follow-up conversations with Phillip and Khaleeq taught me new ways to see art as "action you don't get permission to create" (Phillip) and as "what we got inside us that wanna get out" (Khaleeq). Seeing art as action signified their processes of making sense of the changing world by exploring meanings of freedom and expression in Harlem. It also helped them question the purposes of schooling that, for Phillip and Khaleeq and their peers, "don't be teaching about public spaces" (Phillip) and "what's happening where people live, go to school, stuff like that" (Khaleeq). As Phillip and Khaleeq examined "Harlem as art" and "how schools try to create us into machines," they were beginning to see how other people metaphorically described spaces of interaction: "global-local," "location," "third space," and "the city" (Keith & Pile, 1993, p. 1). Examining spatial descriptions, reflecting on their schooling experiences, and arguing that "Harlem is art" contributed to how they approached gentrification through a literacy framework.

When they decided to cross 125th Street, Phillip and Khaleeq were aware of how one's cultural practices and identities—especially for people of color in poor and working-class urban and rural communities—are often negatively portrayed by mass media. They agreed with Soja's (1990) insistence that space is created to conceal consequences—that is, space often functions to hide human reality, differences, and diversities that exist throughout the world—because "relations of power and discipline are inscribed into the apparently innocent spatiality of social life" (p. 6). In Phillip and Khaleeq's acceptance of Soja's belief, they pondered ways to encourage adult members of the community to use art (e.g., billboard campaigns, local museums, historical buildings, and avenues and boulevards) to improve and protect the area. These ways included displaying works by local artists at community festivals and in the windows of local businesses, as well as requesting that neighborhood museums and theaters devote the first or last Friday of each month to celebrating Harlem's literacy heritage and its contemporary street artists. They wanted adults, including teachers, business owners, shoppers, and longtime residents, to have positive community identities. They wanted them to willingly cross borders by understanding that the historical construction of borders—cultural, physical, and psychological—can both prohibit and permit "particular identities, individual capacities, and social forms" (Giroux, 1992, pp. 29–30). Phillip and Khaleeq did not want to be prohibited from living and/or participating in the community, even if it is gentrified. Additionally, they did not want the cultural practices and identities of the residents of color in Harlem to be ignored, erased, and forgotten. One way that Phillip and Khaleeq exerted influence over their urban communities was by using photography and video interviews to capture Harlem's changing conditions.

Documenting "Harlem Is Art"/"Harlem as Art"

> See, the hard part of this project on Harlem and art is facing them new people who ain't from Harlem and think this community is all about new things popping up: the Disney Store [now closed], Magic Johnson Theater, Old Navy, Aerosoles [shoe store], and Mac [cosmetic store]. By the way, I wonder how many people now coming into Harlem know that right around the corner from Aerosoles and Mac is the Hotel Theresa. They don't know. They overlook these things that we see on a regular basis, important things that part of our history like the Theresa. (Phillip)

Located at the intersection of West 125th Street and Adam Clayton Powell Jr. Boulevard, the Hotel Theresa opened in 1913. After the hotel was desegregated in the 1940s, numerous African Americans stayed there, including Louis Armstrong and Lena Horne. The hotel is now an office space and an official New York City landmark. It is popularly known as the location where Malcolm X held meetings for the Organization of Afro-American Unity (OAAU), where Fidel Castro of Cuba stayed during his first visit to the city and the United Nations (Castro also met with Malcolm X at the Theresa), and where boxer Joe Louis celebrated his various victories. Upon discovery of the history of the Theresa, both Phillip and Khaleeq found this site to be a historical marker that represented Black power and activism.

After Phillip explained to Khaleeq and me the value of historic sites throughout the community that people "overlook," Phillip and Khaleeq exchanged perspectives on Harlem as art:

> *Khaleeq:* Yeah, like the way the old Apollo was before the glitzy lights and expensive tickets. You think we [Black people] can afford to go there now?
>
> *Phillip:* You mean before all the White people started feeling safe enough to take over Harlem and community spots? The new Apollo is their new "art space" in what they think's an exotic Black neighborhood. That's funny!
>
> *Khaleeq:* But what other people think is . . . art in Harlem isn't the real of . . . the everyday.

Phillip: Not the conditions we have to live in. Why do I have to live in an apartment building with a cheap fire escape when right around the corner is a new building with real balconies for all the new apartments? Why do I have to deal with trash and signs of crime and drugs when they don't have to? And we all right here.

Khaleeq: Yeah, and across the street from my projects are condos with balconies. Right across the street! It's so different across there. These are the things people don't want to see. They believe what's going on here in the community is like a second renaissance . . . another Harlem Renaissance.

Phillip: A second what . . . Harlem Renaissance? Don't get me wrong, there's a lot of newness in Harlem, some for the good, some for the bad, some I just don't understand yet. But how can the new replace the old: condos versus projects; Whites versus Blacks; balconies versus fire escapes; silence versus community gatherings; not knowing neighbors versus having people's backs. And this is a renaissance?

Khaleeq: Clean surroundings versus trash and crime, drugs, funky smells.

Phillip: It's an either-or situation we're living in, so to say Harlem is going through a second renaissance ain't right. Don't get me wrong: There's art underneath all this rubble. You just gotta look really hard for it.

Khaleeq and Phillip's exchange echoed Haymes's (1995) discussion of how a "pedagogy of place" should focus on issues of race and struggle in urban communities. This pedagogy involves the physical area, material conditions, and changing landscape of Harlem, or the "old versus new." For Khaleeq and Phillip, the relationship of "old" versus "new" included visual images of and spatial changes occurring throughout Harlem. The Theresa Hotel, the Schomburg Center, community cultural events, and the crowds of people on the streets talking with street vendors represented the "old." Conversations among community residents, business owners, and activists about who and what belongs in Harlem—such as, Whites versus Blacks and other minority groups, condos versus housing projects, and balconies versus fire escapes—pointed to signs of the "new." When I asked them to talk about art in Harlem, or as Phillip called it, "Harlem as art," their concern became one of belonging to a community undergoing rapid changes associated with gentrification, shifting demographics, and forgotten histories.

Khaleeq, Phillip, and I documented stories of change through photography, mapping, and video documentaries, beginning with the areas surrounding their home spaces. Khaleeq's documentation began with a reflexive look at art in his community. He grappled with how to document art in "the Frederick Douglass Projects when all around me are people who don't seem to care, who throw paper [trash] on the ground, who sell drugs, who just hang out." He added, "I get tired of seeing this. I know the art's there, since Harlem is a history landmark of African culture and struggle . . . and that history trickles into the Upper West Side." Here, I believe that Khaleeq is expressing a desire for community normalization—he wants his neighborhood to "be okay, clean, safe, you know, like how it is across the street." However, his position shifts away from normalization to contradiction when he expresses angst over the visible changes that the neighborhood is experiencing— "the too expensive [stores] redone for White people," and "the signs of history that's vanishing." Nevertheless, Khaleeq eventually pointed out to me the name of his housing complex, Frederick Douglass, as he directed Phillip to get a video shot of the signs that bear this ex-slave's name. Although Khaleeq was unable to tell Phillip and I on the spot the significance of the name of his housing development, he did remark: "When I think of Harlem as art, I gotta look around where I live, to get a better handle of history here."

A few days later, after he had researched Frederick Douglass, Khaleeq said, "Douglass was a slave and then an abolitionist. That's important for Black people to know. That's art through, um, struggle." After a long pause, Khaleeq composed himself, silently struggled with the words he wanted to use to convey his true feelings, and continued: "That's art and history. That's what we don't learn in school. I never studied [these connections] in my history class, geography class, English class, or nothing. I never had a standardized test ask me what I think about that, either." In fact, teachers at Harlem High School do include Douglass as well as other important figures in their curriculum. Khaleeq's comments, however, point to disconnections between *teaching* Douglass and *establishing relationships* between Douglass (e.g., life; struggle) and local history in the curricular lessons being taught in the space of classrooms. Khaleeq then went into his backpack in search of his rhyme book. "I bet he looking for his rhyme book," Phillip said, to which Khaleeq responded, "I'm looking. Something I wrote relates to what we talking 'bout. Valerie, you got my notebook, I think." I did have his rhyme book, and Khaleeq told me to "just look in it later for the passage talking 'bout the things students see in their community that's signs of history, but we don't study in school." Khaleeq wanted to say more, as indicated by his body language, and both Phillip and I waited until Khaleeq found the words that he wanted to use: "We talk about how things so separate: poor from rich communities, Blacks from Whites, gentrification and White pride [Phillip corrected, "White privilege"]. Why don't teachers ask us about this? These things scary for me and people my age, but no one's asking our opinions."

As we stood there with Khaleeq's powerful words going into our ears and moving through our hearts, noises from the crowded M100 bus on one side and hard hat construction workers on the other side brought us back to the changing space of New York City. Despite the noise, I thought what Khaleeq had said: "Harlem as art," "art in Harlem," and also "signs of history," "struggle," "why don't teachers ask us." When I did locate Khaleeq's rhyme book, I quickly turned to the passage that he was referring to:

> I talk to Val and Phil . . . all the time. We talk about things going on that matter. I see the community going thru lots of changes I don't understand. It makes me scared. . . . I don't have a place to think about these things but when we together. I try talking to teachers, they seem interested, but "gotta move on with the business of the day." I'd like just to have one day in a class that we talk about real signs of history in front of us. Maybe write about what the signs mean, how they make us feel. I can support that writing by drawing on evidence in the community: gentrification's a sign that new [things] coming. How I know? Look at how many new, high-price apartments going up we [poor and working-class Black residents in Harlem] can't buy or rent. We should force schools to talk about this and history, teach us to tell stories about that.

As Khaleeq recognized signs of history in the community and acknowledged that *some* schools do not engage students in critical discussions of such signs—"gotta move on with the business of the day"—he also told a story of belonging through art forms. With a digital camera, he took pictures of the Frederick Douglass projects, the row of abandoned storefronts adjacent to the projects, and the condominiums with balconies across the street—"why the apartments where White people live have balconies and right across from them you have Black people like my family with apartments that have raggedy fire escapes?" (Khaleeq). He then took Phillip and me on another video walk-through of the area. As he described his negative feelings toward gentrification, he pointed out how the creation of newness (e.g., new condominiums, new residents, and new businesses that will enter the community) often occurs without regard to the local schools, small businesses, and housing projects that quickly fall into disrepair. Khaleeq's visual texts (e.g., photographs; video interviews) represented what linguistic modes of communication could not fully capture: "aesthetically communicative power" (Vasudevan, 2006, p. 214) of a youth using art forms to create stories of community. His stories were about spatial, or geographical, struggle, and they contributed to his emerging definitions of art, community, and power.

Much like Khaleeq, Phillip had a story about art in his immediate surroundings, particularly the art of the new (e.g., renovated apartments; balconies; influx of White people) versus the art of the old (e.g., old apartments; fire escapes; longtime Black residents). Phillip accepted Khaleeq's acknowledgment of "signs of history" just as much as he related to Khaleeq's feelings about local sites left in disrepair: "There are projects, abandoned lots, in the center of this new art, and nobody seems to think this crazy? If nobody stands up to this to show people how Harlem is art, has been for years, what's going to be left? Will they take away the Adam Clayton Powell Building cause they need that block of space for more high rises?" Phillip continued by talking about the Apollo Theater as a local space where new talents performed on "Amateur Night" and where one could get an inexpensive ticket to see famous acts "do their thing on stage." This was no longer a reality for Phillip, who expressed shock at seeing a long line of White people going into the Apollo on a Wednesday night in May 2006. He commented:

> We [Phillip and Valerie] were walking from the Powell Building, just left a meeting where activists were complaining about living conditions, increased rent, unfair conditions by management in their housing complexes. Next thing I know, we approach the Apollo, and there they are . . . claiming our community art spot as their own. Probably not even realizing that the artwork on the concrete and fenced walls next to the Apollo was created by a local working Black artist. I'm glad I had the digital [camera].

With the camera, Phillip took pictures of "White people in front of the redone Apollo." In our shared rhyme book and in subsequent interview sessions, he compared the pictures to those he took of Black people going into the Studio Museum of Harlem and waiting for the bus in front of the Powell building, and of construction sites for new condominiums near where he lived—just eight blocks south of 125th Street. In his comparison, he highlighted the race of the "White people in front of the redone Apollo" as an indication of a changing, soon-to-be gentrified community: "They were never here when I was growing up. They were too afraid to come to Harlem, and at night! Never would've happened." Phillip admitted that the presence of "lines of White people" in Harlem made him uncomfortable because "they change the face of this community and take away the real meaning of art in a place like the Apollo. Blacks always been going to the Apollo, the museum, whether they live in Harlem or just visiting." He continued: "Most Blacks know Harlem or live in a similar space. We share that struggle. But Whites know Harlem as an artsy place because of gentrification. It's not the same kind of knowing." Contrary to his initial understanding of Black-ification and White-ification, Phillip's sentiments were now grounded in critical thinking and pointed to a more developed articulation of these terms. That is, Black-ification is not just about middle- to upper-class Black people moving back into and changing Harlem. It is about Black people, across individual experiences and class statuses, recognizing their long history of civil and political struggle in the United States in comparison to White (mainstream) values. This is an important distinction to make because it demonstrates Phillip's increasing understanding of connections among race, place, and identity for Black people. That is, acts of place-making (e.g., creating safe spaces and fostering positive social encounters) for Black people, historically, are directly connected to a shared struggle for the creation and preservation of safe spaces, which Phillip and Khaleeq are beginning to acknowledge.

During one of his video walk-through sessions near the intersection of Frederick Douglass Boulevard and 117th Street, Phillip pointed out the renovated apartment building on one corner, the new drugstore on another, and the "crazy priced" new dry cleaners. He spoke of an abandoned Laundromat in the same breath that he talked about a vacant lot that is now barricaded, the latter where many community members met for social events:

> This is what I see on the regular. I didn't pay much attention to it before, but now I do. And do I see any art in all this rubble? New condo over here, old apartment building over there! New dry cleaners there, closed Laundromat here! Right here in Harlem. Yeah, I have to, if I want to remember history. I believe the old is more of art than the temporary new. But nobody, except you and Khaleeq, asked me. Nobody else really wants me to tell my story about what I think I want in the area.

I told Phillip that I believed he was already engaging in critical literacy as he theorized ideas around struggle, art, community change, and gentrification. I also encouraged him to find ways to think through these same ideas in the context of his high school. During an independent reading and writing session in Ms. L's English class, I walked over to Phillip and asked him, with his teacher's permission, to begin describing with words and visuals what he talked about in his community walk-through video: what he would want and what he was willing to fight for as the debate around gentrification in Harlem increased. Over three separate independent reading and writing sessions, we collaborated (with input from other students and Ms. L) to create a visual representation of what he wanted. Figure 1 is an illustration of the result of that particular school-based collaboration.

Phillip's visual depiction, in his own words, "is about not getting rid of the old because new things coming. Like I said in my video, the old is important, it's more art than the temporary new. I'm struggling to embrace the old art and not get caught in the new." Phillip's struggle speaks beyond education in the classroom to include local literacies. Clearly, "to embrace the old art" is rarely considered in public debates over the corporatization of schools and the gentrification of urban communities. Yet I firmly believe that "the old art" should be embraced and critiqued alongside the new as Harlem and other communities across the United States undergo major spatial, racial, and economic changes that have dire consequences for the youth and adult residents who cannot afford to stay. Thus, the idea of crossing—whether that means crossing the physical borders of 125th Street or crossing the emotional

Figure 1. The Struggles of Youth Participants

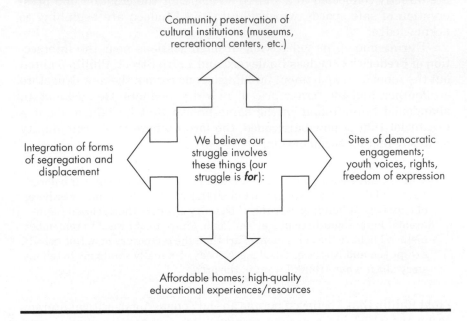

and psychological barriers associated with change—greatly impacts one's level of involvement and activism in the community. Phillip and Khaleeq know this reality all too well.

To speak of this struggle more widely, Phillip, Khaleeq, and I met Vivian, Barbara, Thelma, John, and a host of other adults at a community action meeting held at the Adam Clayton Powell Jr. State Building. The meeting focused on "saving the community" from gentrification, increased rent, and the displacement of Black residents as well as preserving "the old." In this case, for Phillip, Khaleeq, and many long-time Black residents in the area "the old" signified a spatial history of struggle and survival. In this moment, documented representations of art and community captured by youth influenced adult learning. By engaging in conversations with and explaining their perspectives on gentrification to adults (i.e., residents; teachers; me) who were invested in protecting the community, Phillip and Khaleeq encouraged them to question current community practices (e.g., the value of gatherings and meetings and taking care of/protecting the community) and assumptions (e.g., young people have no voice, and they do not care about the community). At the same time, the adults encouraged Phillip and Khaleeq to study the community's long history of struggle (e.g., segregation; fights for civil rights) and political leadership (e.g., Malcolm X; Adam Clayton Powell Jr.). In this context, learning became reciprocal, active, and transformative for both the youth and the adults. Youth

Figure 2.   The Struggles Against Gentrification of Youth Participants

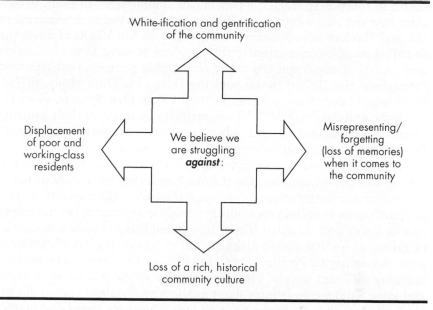

activism was met with adult learning. With this point in mind, Khaleeq, Phillip, and I created a diagram during a session in my university office that describes what we are working "against." We presented it to other adults.

The diagram serves as a response to Phillip's diagram on, "We believe our struggle involves these things (our struggles are *FOR*)." At the same time, it speaks to what Phillip and Khaleeq, and some of their friends, including Damen, were struggling to prevent, such as gentrification, displacement, and White-ification (see Figure 2). In creating the diagram, Phillip and Khaleeq recalled brief conversations they had with Vivian and other adult members of the community, adults who either lived or worked within the immediate neighborhood or whom they met at local tenants' association meetings. Those conversations helped the young men understand how their words and actions influence adult activism: "When we presented the maps and pictures and things at the meeting, they [adults] had lots of questions for us. They asked things like, what can we as adults do? How can we help you keep up the work y'all doing? What can our stories offer?" (Phillip). Khaleeq then recalled, "They were listening to us and seem like they believed we serious about this. We showed the maps, talked about the pictures . . . told them about some community stories. They were learning. We were teaching."

Phillip and Khaleeq spent the next few weeks examining their digital pictures of Harlem. They also began to imagine, as Vivian asked them to do, the untold stories of adults in both the community and school in relation to Harlem's past. Their imaginings led them to consider how the past—"what was here before"—served as a precursor to the *real* Harlem Renaissance (which began in the 1920s, and not the so-called renaissance currently taking place leading to gentrification and spatial change) and the many civil rights protests that occurred throughout the United States and the Diaspora. Their study of Harlem's long history was captured in their many photographs, video interviews, and conversations. These artifacts attested to their growing interest in collaborating with adults to document stories and protect Harlem from gentrification and commercialization.

How did the youth view "Harlem as art" in relation to the influx of newness in the community? On the one hand, they were curious to see the new chain drugstores; on the other, they were dismayed to no longer participate in certain community rituals that occurred in the empty spaces stores now occupied. Their dismay led them to view newness as negative, as an attempt to disguise and/or ignore the art of Harlem's past. According to Phillip, "Lots of stores in this area have opened, bringing different people. This changes the whole feeling of Harlem, including what we be talking about as the arts. Khaleeq agreed, insisting that Harlem has always been a place where art forms dominated, even on "less than popular [neighborhood] streets, even the ones on the edge of Harlem like mine." Both Phillip and Khaleeq believed that before the new stores, there were a lot of conversations, museums, parades, festivals, and block performances, a point corroborated by longtime adult residents in the community. However, "We don't have them as much because lots of people left since they can't afford to stay" (Phillip). Even with this reality, Phillip and Khaleeq still insisted that Harlem is art and "gentrification can't take it away" (Khaleeq). Khaleeq and Phillip's pictures of the Cotton Club, the Studio Museum of Harlem, the Harlem YMCA, the Audubon Ballroom, Abyssinian Baptist Church, Duke Ellington Statue, and Marcus Garvey Park reiterated this point. Their pictures captured a legacy of artistic and political action in Harlem and throughout the African Diaspora. Their images portrayed art as a vehicle that opened the doors to African, African American, and Latino expression of the Harlem Renaissance to contemporary times.

The pictures spoke volumes to their emerging definition of "art as experience" (Dewey, 1959) and as visible signs of everyday life. For Phillip and Khaleeq, the pictures were connected to what they called the 1920s "youth and adult arts movement" of the Harlem Renaissance. In their photo collages, they referenced the likes of African American literary scholars Langston Hughes, Zora Neale Hurston, and James Weldon Johnson. Their collages and journals recognized the value of young artists apprenticing with adult members of the community, which helped make Harlem a major site of Black cultural expression.

In the 1920s, the significance of art in Harlem paralleled the community's historical struggle with representation, racism, and socioeconomic strife. Now that today's Harlem is undergoing gentrification, I wonder, "Where are the adults, the Black and White and Latino/a and Puerto Rican residents and political leaders, the people who are supposed to protect the community? The social activists, the politicians, the teachers, the artists? The people we are told to follow? Where's everybody, the other Vivians? And where are the apprenticeship models from the Harlem Renaissance?" (Khaleeq, Phillip, & Valerie, inquiry questions).

References

Beauregard, R. (1993). *Voices of decline: The power of fate in US cities.* Oxford: Blackwell.

Dewey, J. (1959). *Art as experience.* New York: Perigee Trade.

Giroux, H. (1992). *Border crossings: Cultural workers and the politics of education.* New York: Routledge.

Haymes, S. (1995). *Race, culture, and the city: A pedagogy for black urban struggle.* Albany: State University of New York Press.

hooks, b. (1990). *Yearning: Race, gender, and cultural politics.* Boston: South End Press.

Keith, M., & Pile, S. (1993). *Place and the politics of identity.* New York: Routledge.

Lincoln, Y. S., & Guba, E. (2000). Paradigmatic controversies, contradictions, and emerging confluences. In N. K. Denzin & Y. S. Lincoln (Eds.), *Handbook of qualitative research* (2nd ed., pp. 163–188). Thousand Oaks, London, and Delhi: Sage Publications.

Pratt, M. L. (1991). Arts of the contact zone. *Profession, 91.* 31–40.

Soja, E. (1990). *Postmodern geographies: The reassertion of space in critical social theory.* London: Verso.

Vasudevan, L. (2006). Making known differently: Engaging visual modalities as space to author new selves. *E-Learning 3*(2), 207–216.

The Way Literacy Lives

Shannon Carter

Shannon Carter introduces the term rhetorical dexterity *as a means of describing how students in basic writing move from out-of-school communities of practice (plumbers, fan fiction writers, basketball players, video gamers, etc.) to the school-based literacies needed to become successful with academic writing. Students in Carter's study struggle with a plethora of constantly changing and evolving rules for writing, rules of which students cannot easily keep track, and which present writing as a series of constraints rather than as an academic practice necessary for college success. To address these issues, Carter created a curriculum based on the notion of rhetorical dexterity, in which students examine the rules for communities of practice with which they are already familiar, and how to adapt those rules to the literacies required for academic writing. A guiding question for this curriculum asks students to consider, "how is who you are shaped by your experiences within [your] community of practice?" (p. 163). In the five essays that students write for this basic writing course, students move from considering school-based rules for writing, to analyzing out-of-school literacies, to connecting out-of-school literacies to in-school literacies, learning and performing the practices of rhetorical dexterity. Examples of students' writing from these assignments are included throughout Carter's selection.*

What does the world look like outside of school? What do the people do or say or even write outside of this school community? There are many different things that shape up a community. It's not only about the rules for the system, but the people who share certain use of language, clothing, or even style. Instead it can be a group of people who are passionate about the same thing.

For me, art is everything. I started drawing ever since I learned how to hold a pencil. I'm not good at talking or expressing myself in words and sentences, so I put my feelings into figures. And no matter what happen, I will always be a part of this community, unknowingly. . . .

Artists express their feelings through lines and shapes. . . . A painting . . . with lots of curve lines express confusion. A man with his face covered represents mystery. . . . Through all the graphics and colors, we communicate in our own language. (Marian, "The Language of Figures")

Rhetorical dexterity treats learning new literacies as a situated activity; thus, in a sense, this means the basic writing classroom with rhetorical dexterity as its goal offers learners the "legitimate peripheral participation" Jean Lave and Etienne Wenger contend is a necessary prerequisite for joining any community of practice. As they explain,

Learning viewed as a situated activity has as its central defining characteristic a process that we call legitimate peripheral participation. By this we mean to draw attention to the point that learners inevitably participate in communities of practitioners and that the mastery of knowledge and skills requires newcomers to move toward full participation in the socioeconomic peripheral practices of a community. "Legitimate peripheral participation" provides a way to speak about relations between newcomers and old timers, and about activities, identities, artifacts, and communities of knowledge and practice. It concerns the process by which newcomers become part of a community of practice. (29)

A curriculum shaped by a pedagogy of rhetorical dexterity thus asks students to examine the "process by which newcomers become part of a community of practice" as they have experienced it in an out-of-school context and apply that process to the ones required of newcomers in

academic communities of practice. In doing so, we ask students to consider questions like the following: What are the activities that make up
a community of practice with which you are deeply familiar? How did
you learn them? What identities are constructed via these activities?
In other words, how is who you are shaped by your experiences within
this community of practice? What artifacts are produced via the activities of this community of practice and how might those compare with
the artifacts produced in academic communities of practice?

An approach like this forces participants to pay attention to the
inequitable ways literacy is represented and how that representation
paralyzes many already-marginalized writers, but, as I will try to make
clear in the current chapter, it does not stop there. Certainly, such
inequities must be acknowledged before students can gain control over
the academic literacy measures shaping their student lives. As writing
teachers, we represent and are most often proficient users of standard
edited English; thus, it is imperative that we recognize these inequities
and speak to them—with our students and *for* our students—especially
given that inequities among literacies and among literate users largely
determine how one learns new literacies. However, as I discovered myself via different curricular choices (especially ones deeply informed
by critical literacy)[1] and as I have argued elsewhere, pointing out and
giving students the space to speak back to those inequities will not
be enough to enable them to subvert them—or even, in many cases, to
begin to represent literacy differently to and for themselves. Instead, we
must give them the tools they need to *experience* literacy differently—
to look again at the ways in which literacy functions in the multiple and
intellectually viable lifeworlds in which they are already full-fledged
members.

The Curriculum

> I really do not know who I am as a writer, but I know I am a bad writer.
> (Dominique, "Thoughts of a Troubled Writer")

In working with the writers in our program and in training new educators to do the same, we begin by working against the myths that
shape common sense understandings of what basic writers need, but in
keeping with the findings of the New Literacy Studies, we do so within
the context of what we know about how literacy functions in the world
beyond the largely artificial "school" literacies we often celebrate. In
other words, we teach basic writing by articulating and helping our
students articulate the way literacy actually lives, which, as Brandt
explains in "Accumulating Literacy," places greater pressure on Americans "not to meet higher literacy *standards* as has been so frequently
argued elsewhere but rather to develop a *flexibility and awareness*"
(651, emphasis mine).

Like many programs, we begin by asking students to articulate the ways in which they have experienced literacy and learning thus far, especially how they understand the "rules" for writing in school and whether those rules have changed over time, from subject to subject, from classroom to classroom, from project to project. Many basic writing students tell us that such rules do change, and these changes often confuse and frustrate them. As one writer explained it recently, "I've been told one thing I did in a previous class was wrong in another. When it was said, I became very upset because I'd been doing what I was taught. Once that barrier was broken I had to *start from scratch*" (emphasis mine). As we know, when literacy is understood as a matter of "correctness," the "standards" by which "correctness" is judged can cause writers much confusion, especially those who, like this student, witness the standard mutating right before their eyes.

In the next three essays, students investigate "vernacular" or familiar literacies. We discuss the concept of "communities of practice," reading a brief essay called "What Is a Community of Practice?" (Carter) that articulates the ways in which "communities of practice" may function as an appropriate framework for investigating familiar literacies and learning new ones. They are then asked to explore the "rules" that all literate users must come to know, understand, and be able to negotiate in order to be heard, understood, and taken seriously in that particular community of practice (as a plumber, a deer hunter, or a fan fiction writer for example).

In the second writing assignment, they are asked to investigate a familiar literacy of their choice. Students have selected everything from quilting to playing dominoes to creating Anime, and these early essays are often quite general in their descriptions of "literate ability" within this target community of practice. The writers are surprised to find that someone could be as "football illiterate" or "Christian illiterate"[2] as they learn I am, as they learn other readers who are not members of that community of practice tend to be. The primary objective at this point is to learn how expertise (i.e., "literacy") functions when trying to communicate among people whose experiences, interests, and expertise may differ in some rather substantial ways.

Essays 4 and 5 require a more detailed and sophisticated analysis of two different categories of communities of practice: workplace literacies and those more closely associated with leisure. In preparation for the third essay on workplace literacies, students read and present to one another chapters from Mike Rose's book *The Mind at Work: Valuing the Intelligence of the American Worker* (2004)—a series of case studies that articulate the cognitive abilities required of electricians, plumbers, carpenters, welders, waitresses, hairstylists, and other similar occupations. In doing so, they consider the special tools, terminology, values, and body movements that might be required of users to be accepted as members of these communities of practice (the literacies associated with waiting tables, styling hair, installing a light fixture). Many students draw upon their own expertise in the fields they investigate (the daughter of a plumber, for example, a Mexican immigrant with fifteen years experience as a building inspector, among others). Reading and analyzing Rose's book in the ways we did was a new experience for many of these writers, and several found working in these ways with this text and their groups to be particularly enlightening. As one basic writing student and art major put it,

> Reading for me used to be just about finding out what happened at the end of the story. Did the bad guys die? Did the hero save the world? The storyline in the book was the thing I value most. When I read Mike Rose's *The Mind at Work* through the summer, I found that [he] has a way of putting down a lot of specific details. The writing itself was brilliant. But when we were doing the assignment in the class over the book, we did it chapter by chapter, and then different little parts like terminology, tools, and body movements. That assignment forced us to look into the text and read not only the words, but the context also. . . . I had fun breaking down the text and the meaning in it. All the stuff from the book might one day be able to help create our own social circle because it gave us the idea of how to fit into a different community of practice. It didn't just GAVE us the details and need-to-know facts about different discourse communities, but also TAUGHT us how it works for a person to learn something entirely new. (2–3, 4)

In preparation for Essay 4 (on literacies associated with "play"), we examine and discuss excerpts from Steven Johnson's *Everything Bad Is Good for You: How Today's Popular Culture Is Actually Making Us Smarter* (2005) and James Paul Gee's *What Video Games Have to Teach Us About Literacy* and *Learning* (2003), both of which treat video games as intellectually rigorous spaces that demand much of players—not only those learning to play the game for the first time but also those already highly literate players.[3] Previous students have examined the "rules" for membership in communities of practice like skateboarding, photography, basketball, *Halo 2*, and cheerleading. Again, they analyze the specific strategies literate users employ to be heard, understood, and taken seriously among other literate members of this community of practice. Here, they begin to really articulate the specific events that taught them what they needed to know to become insiders in the target community. At this point, many students even begin to think of one another in terms of the familiar communities of practice with which they most identify. Gretna describes her writing group this way: "Our [group] was made up of: Kailey the cheerleader, Markwen the rapper/construction worker, Bryson the . . . hunt[er], Sincar the gamer . . . Maria the . . . cook[er] of authentic Mexican food, Dorothy the basketball player, and me, the softball player" (Final Reflections).

The next two essays are revisions of earlier ones. In Essay 5, we return to the literacies the students associate with school, asking them to "think about all we've done in class thus far and consider what it might have to teach us about the 'rules' for writing in school and how they might be established, upheld, and perpetuated. What special terminology is embedded in these rules? How does it change from context to context? How do we learn these rules? What special knowledge do we need to have before we can embark on a new reading/writing project? Why?" In doing so, we hope they will begin to represent their experiences with school literacies in less "autonomous" and more situated terms. Most do. Essay 6 is a revision of one of the three essays that explore vernacular literacies.

The final essay asks students to compare and contrast a community of practice seemingly unrelated to school with those literacies required of writers at the college level. Ideally, students can merely combine and rework Essays 5 and 6, as Essay 5 examines in-school literacies and Essay 6 explores an out-of-school literacy. In preparation for this essay, writers develop a one-page handout comparing these two literacies, which they then present to the class. The presentation itself serves as fodder for the final essay.

The genre these writers use to report their findings (WA1–WA7) is important as it forces them to develop a meta-analysis of a given community of practice in terms those illiterate in that community might need to make sense of it and perhaps even learn what they need to join it, if possible. Reporting on the findings of his 1985 study of the effects of writing on learning, Cheryl Geisler shares Copeland's "warning":

> [I]n using writing to help students learn, one should structure writing activities so that they help students incorporate in their writing those particular ideas they are expected to learn. If students write about a topic but are not asked to do so in a way that helps them focus upon the targeted information, writing may nor help students achieve the learning goals set forth. (Copeland qtd. in Geisler 115)

The "targeted information" in rhetorical dexterity is the way literacy lives within a variety of communities of practice; thus, the genres themselves ask writers to consider what someone unfamiliar with that community of practice might need to know. According to Marian, the basic writer and art major quoted earlier, this meta-awareness is very useful. As she explains, in investigating familiar literacies in this way, it forced her to articulate things about them that she instinctively knew in some ways but not enough to make use of them in new contexts. Communities outside of school and those related to work

> don't usually have written rules like academic communities of practice, so we had to look beyond words to find out what the rules were. . . .

> After all the assignments we've done so far . . . I felt like I know myself
> better than before. All the rules in the . . . communities we all know that
> they are there, but writing them down and analyzing them sort of marks
> their existence in our mind. (3, 5)

Each community of practice is made up of, among other things, behaviors shaped by ideologies particular to that community that may seem odd to outsiders but to members of the community are merely common sense. From the ideologies informing a particular community emerge the "rules" one should know and apply before one will be considered "literate" by other members. The problem is that without working consciously against those things we instinctively assume to be plain common sense, the real "rules" will remain largely unavailable to outsiders and unteachable by insiders; ideology, as Marilyn Cooper explains, "just sits there, making the world we think we know" (159). The genres by which these writers are asked to communicate the invisible "rules" users must know and make use of in order to be heard, understood, and taken seriously "marks their existence in our mind," which enables them to analyze and make deliberate use of that knowledge base in new, largely unfamiliar contexts.

The curricular choices that might effectively make use of a pedagogy of rhetorical dexterity extend well beyond the ones described earlier. What I offer here is just one option, and we will continue to rework our own curricula as interest and student needs demand it. In the remaining pages of this chapter, I will attempt to describe student responses to this particular curriculum in ways that I hope will enable readers to see what they were able to gain from this incarnation of it. I will end with a discussion of the ways in which we will likely alter future versions of the curriculum to enable students to develop a deeper understanding of the ways in which literacies differ across the curriculum.

School Literacies (WA1, WA2, and WA6)

> They are outrageous with the rules. They've even gotten to the point
> where they've started combining shit. Like combining a period with a
> comma and calling it a semi-colon. They even use two upside down com-
> mas beside each other known as quotations.
>
> I interviewed my friend Jessica. She says, "I don't like semi-colons.
> Why can't they just be a damn comma[?]" (Lamanda)

Student representations of school literacies largely replicate what Adler-Kassner and Harrington describe in *Basic Writing as a Political Act* and "Just Writing, Basically" as a "huge gulf" between "being a writer" and "learning to write." In other words, few saw themselves as real writers, despite the fact that many write quite often in their lifeworlds beyond school. Holly, a theatre major who describes herself as an "avid reader with severe dyslexia," reads and writes pages of fan fiction each and every day. Fan fiction, as I learned from Holly, is fiction developed to extend the story lines created and reproduced in media outlets like comic books, Hollywood films, television, and even video games. Fans of particular television shows/books/video games/films extract their favorite characters and develop stories around them, stories that must be consistent with the "universe" in which this character first emerged but can take liberties that may not have occurred in the original. Holly describes the appeal of fan fiction this way: "Fan fiction has now become quite a habit for me. In high school, I'd come home as fast as I could, sit down in front of the computer, and read for hours on end, getting drawn into these stories. It takes me away from reality and I find myself becoming a character in one of the many stories." The stories themselves are generated by fans and circulated among these same fans via Internet sites devoted to the subject. Thus, as Holly is a fan of the Anime series *Techni Muyo!*, she frequents fan fiction sites devoted to that series and its key characters.

Like many students in our basic writing program, however, Holly has never found reading and writing for school at all appealing. Thus, many begin the term by describing themselves as "bad writers" who "hate" writing, a self-assessment they attribute to either a lack of familiarity with "the" rules for writing or an "obsession" with the rules. As one writer puts it, "Beginning writers often want to know what hard and fast rules are, the rules we simply must follow. Sometimes writing teachers and books of advice even provide us with the rules, which we then get obsessive [about]" (Dominique). In his second essay, another basic writing student concurs: "Sometimes when I am writing, I get frustrated by minor things .... For example: when I'm writing a sentence, I still have ideas or words that still go with that sentence. But I can't finish it, because then it becomes a run-on sentence. *Once again, I become a victim of the rules*" (emphasis mine).

The rules for writing, it seems, are both mysterious and confining. Many express frustration at their inability to learn "the rules" of writing, as well as the ways in which they feel that once learned, these rules continue to distance what they *want* to say from what they feel they *can* say. Ruben offers an incredibly generous portrayal of the function of the writing "rules," but finds that they often "tend to stop me from expressing everything I want to say." The disconnect between home and school felt all the more profound for Ruben because, as he explains, "I was raised in a Spanish speaking community, so you can only imagine how difficult this is for me." Another ESL student (from Korea) describes his previous writing experiences this way: "I didn't know how to learn Standard English and everything I wrote was wrong" (Wong).

In her sixth writing assignment, Emilia makes a similar argument; "If you are given certain ... rules to follow, that limits your ability to express yourself as an individual writer, stripping you of your creative rights." In her second essay, "No Rules, No Pass," Ashley concurs, arguing that the rules, especially what she calls "the five paragraph rule . . . limits my ability to express how I feel about the writing assignment." In fact, "I think that rule sucks and should be removed from wherever the rules of writing are made. I suggest that teachers of the future should: first, open children minds that there are many different ways of writing . . . and never teach a child that their teaching of the rules is the only way we should know."

They understand, instinctively, that the rules change, but the changes seem unpredictable and largely arbitrary. Steven asserts that "the . . . rules, for some reason, seem to change according to the person grading." Others, like Emilia and Caroline, locate the source of this change in the circumstances in which school writing takes place. Writing near the end of the semester, Emilia explains that

> Before taking this class, I thought writing was pointless, boring, frustrating, confusing, and had too many rules to follow. All those feelings came from many years of being taught so many different rules and being penalized for using them. The most recent case of that happen was my sophomore year in high school when we had to take a practice test of the new standardized state test, the TAKS. Now we were not given any previous warning of how the test was to be graded or what was expected to be written. . . . [Before the test], I had been making super grades in my English class because I had mastered the art of whatever rules for writing we were expected to follow, so I thought I had that test grade in the bag. When it came down to it, I had scored a one (the lowest grade possible) out of a possible four *because I was following rules that no longer applied to the new writing styles of the present time*. . . . I began to realize the severity of how these rules were affecting my grades as well as my knowledge as a student. (emphasis mine)

In her sixth essay entitled "Stupid Rules for Stupid Writers," Caroline puts it this way: "There are so many rules, rules, rules, and more rules when it comes to writing. With so many rules to follow there are also consequences in writing. Like a bad grade, red marks all over the paper, and hearing the teacher telling the student to redo it until it's better. And than it take like forever to be revised until it's better." Another writer offers a similar reading of his experiences with writing "rules": "There are so many different ways of writing. I learn one way then have to learn another. What I mean by this is what I write really depends on my teacher and my surrounding." From this experience, he likely learned what Emilia describes as "the severity of how these rules were affecting my grades as well as my knowledge as a student." For Emilia, thank goodness, the consequences of not knowing the new rules for the latest high-stakes context would not continue to be quite as negative, at least as far as TAKS was concerned. As she explains,

Later on in my sophomore and beginning of my senior year of high school, I learned the "correct" way to write for TAKS, and went in knowing what was expected to know in order to pass the writing portion of the test. From taking this English 100 class, I know there really isn't a "correct" way to write and it isn't always pointless.

Like Ashley who argues that the "five paragraph rule sucks" and should be changed, many of the writers in our program view this rule-making dynamic as mutable, but they have difficulty locating the persons or institutions responsible for making these decisions. Shatavia asks, "Who created these rules, the government? It's funny how these rules come up but no one knows who created them." Among those who grew up in Texas where writing "rules" are largely upheld by high-stakes tests—preparation for the tests and the test itself—many hypothesize that these rules were, in fact, made up by the government itself. In his fourth essay, Ruben tells us that "the government plays a big role in the creation of the rules of writing because of all the tests they make for us to go to college," tests, he explains, "the government was making . . . harder and harder as time was passing" (3). Desmond reminds us how intricately connected are the "rules for writing" as enforced via state-mandated tests like TAKS and THEA and the very courses in which he must enroll: "As the years continue to go by, the government seems to keep enforcing more and more rules, and laws that you must write a certain amount of essays each year you are in school. Some college classes and high school classes are taken due to requirements of the government even though they might not be needed." He ends on a note that succinctly expresses the powerlessness writers often feel in the face of further marginalization via institutionalized oppression like this: "if you were to try and fight the government about this issue, then they would probably try to take whatever you already have away and not even give it to anyone else." Caroline responds to this hopelessness with biting humor: "Who invented these rules? The government? If a writer messes up, would the FBI come and arrest them? How dumb can that be? It's like an unexplainable mystery waiting to be solved."

It was not until we began exploring other literacies that writers like these would began to speak of literacy in terms that seemed to free them from the frustrations imposed on them via artificial and arbitrary writing rules.

Out-of-School Literacies

Every now and then I am given the opportunity to write about something I am passionate about. If feel like I can express my thoughts in an orderly fashion and feel good about it. I do not think of it as a waste of time or a blow-off assignment to make a passing grade in class. It is a chance like this, which makes me feel like I am able to write and get my point across effectively. It is the only time I really enjoy writing. (Gretna, "Writing's Hold on Me")

Mike began our program, as he explains in his final reflections near the end of the term, "a very frustrated twenty-six year old man." His frustration was, in part, a natural consequence of returning to school after several years in the manufacturing sector of the workforce, but it was amplified considerably by our requirement that his first paper for us speak directly to his experiences with writing in school. As he remembers his response to the first-day writing assignment several weeks earlier, "writing in school was just a very sore subject for me at the time that paper was written." In the second week of the class, he came to the writing center for assistance with his paper about the "rules" for writing in school; he was understandably frustrated: "Look, I haven't been in school for almost ten years," he said, growing obviously and increasingly more agitated. "I never knew the rules then, and I certainly can't talk about them now."

"Okay, so talk about what you *do* know," I said. "There are no wrong answers." He remained unconvinced. I asked him to tell me what he did in his spare time. "I don't know. Why does it matter?" He finally told me he did a lot of hunting, so I asked him to talk about the "rules for hunting." How did you come to learn them? Are they written down somewhere? Can you break them? What is their purpose? After quite a bit of discussion about hunting, we returned to his experiences in school. "Tell me a story," I requested. "What's the first thing you remember about school—not necessarily the rules associated with writing but with your experiences as a student." He started to write. Later in the term, Mike would describe our exchange this way: "Dr. Carter and I went back and forth for at least an hour about why she thought I could write this paper. Finally, I gave in and began writing. I didn't stop until I had three pages. Something happened inside me [that day] and I knew I was going to love to write." But it would not be until he started to unpack the literacies associated with his workplace experiences that things would really begin to change for him as a writer.

When I started Literacies at Work, I was so excited. I had a lot of work experience to draw from for this paper . . . [b]ut after brainstorming for a while I decided that the most interesting job to write about would be injection molding. . . .

This paper was about my employment with R___ Tool Company and all the processes that were involved in manufacturing carbide parts using injection molding equipment. I had several people read this paper and I revised it three times before turning it in to my teacher. When [my teacher] returned the paper back to me, I could tell that she was impressed with my work. She had probably never heard about most of the information in this paper because this type of work is unique and there are only three company's in the world that have been able to perfect making carbide using low-pressure injection molding techniques.

That paper about the literacy requirements of R___ Tool Company would make the greatest difference for him as a writer. "After writing" the essay about his workplace literacies, he argues, "I had pretty well figured out that English writing class was not the only literate community on the planet" (8).

Younger writers may have had fewer workplace experiences from which to draw, but most found the experience of investigating a familiar community of practice associated with the workplace nonetheless useful to them in rethinking the way literacy lives in communities of practice beyond school. Many drew from their experience with part-time jobs as a cashier at McDonald's, a shift leader at Jack in the Box, a waitress at IHOP, or a grocery clerk at the local supermarket. As Derek describes it, his position as a "courtesy clerk" at Brookshire's can be summed up this way: "What I do at my job is talk to people, make them feel comfortable where they are at, and pack the hell out of their groceries while talking to them." Steven chooses to describe his job as a cashier at the same grocery store as decidedly more complex. At first glance, he explains, the job of the cashier may seem simple enough: "The cashier . . . must . . . make sure he hands back the correct change and [that] you walk out with everything you have paid for." However, while this may seem "easy . . . there are many things that are in a cashier's mind while checking out a customer," things like "his scan time" ("how many items he can scan per minute is crucial. A top scan time could earn honors like Employee of the Month"), keeping the cash drawer accurate, and "memorizing the produce codes."

As Derek describes his position, the primary value-sets in the community of practice that is "packing groceries" are activities that make the customer feel "comfortable" and get the groceries packed quickly. The customer's "comfort" is important to Brookshire's management as they must compete with the lower prices Wal-Mart offers just down the road. "Courtesy," according to employees like Steven and Derek, is "what sets us apart." An awareness of the, in Gee's words, "external design grammar" of a given community of practice thus enables Derek and Steven to prioritize activities within their positions: Wal-Mart offers "low prices" but not the "courtesy" available to shoppers at Brookshire's (no one carries out a shopper's groceries at Wal-Mart, for example). Steven knows that a quick "scan time" and an accurate cash drawer are valuable activities in this particular community of practice, as well—a value established and reinforced within this community of practice via "honors" like "Employee of the Month" based on criteria like "scan time" and "accuracy." He is also aware of the "internal design grammar" that affects his ability to meet the objectives valued within this community; things like "memorizing produce codes" are important because looking up these produce codes would reduce his "scan time" considerably.

Speed and accuracy are valuable in Paola's work as a waitress as well, and this community of practice also requires "good social skills" a "good memory," and the capacity "to do two or more things at the same time." As she explains, "every job has its own rules, ideas, and its own way to get the job done." The activities required to "get the job done" are reproduced organically by virtue of the "tips" that work as incentive within this community of practice, but they are also reproduced more formally by the specific tools made available to them via the restaurant in which they serve and the systems by which the supervisors and the corporation of which the specific location is a part have in place. For Paola, this meant that

> when I started to work as a waitress, my boss explained to me what I should have to do, how to serve the customers, used the register machine, and write the tickets, that way the cook would not get confused with the order. I had to follow one of the waitresses with more experience to see how to serve, take people's orders, ask for drinks, and give to the customer an appetizer while they are waiting for their food.

Thus, it appears that several of the activities reproduced in this community of practice are learned by newcomers via what Lave and Wenger call "legitimate peripheral participation." While training, Paola "participated" in this community of practice by shadowing a full-fledged member to learn what she does so she can, in turn, begin performing the activities of waiting tables in many of the same ways. Again, the values guiding work as a server appear to be courtesy, accuracy, and speed. She needs a system for approaching the tables in order to keep the customers happy (drinks refilled, food ordered in a timely manner and in such a way that "the cook would not get confused," etc.). Her "legitimate peripheral participation" in this community of practice while training enabled her to develop fluency in the "internal design grammar" of this system.

Some value-sets are reproduced via more formal training materials, as is the case with the large and highly regulated company McDonald's. As Courtney explains, the activities reproduced in McDonald's are much more formalized than they seem to have been for servers at IHOP. According to Courtney,

> When working at McDonald's you must be train before [being] put in a specific area. You have to watch videos on everything a McDonald's worker have to do. The video might take all day or make two day. You must watch video on how to cook the food from fries, to meat, breakfast item. . . . Also you must know how to clean. You can not clean a McDonald's restaurant like you clean your house. You must have cleaning item that McDonald's get from a company. Such as special Windex, sanitizer for towel and dishes as well.

Thus, the systems McDonald's employees must adhere to when completing tasks within this context are deeply dependent on the corporate structure of which their particular location is but a part. The values reproduced within this community of practice may be accuracy and speed, but of primary importance here is uniformity—in methods, in tools, in the artifacts produced. As Courtney puts it, "McDonald's is a fast food business, but that does not mean we are always fast. Sometimes we might take the wrong order, put the wrong things in the bags, or might not give the right change back." As Steven describes his work as a cashier at Brookshire's, these activities would be grounds for dismissal in the communities of practice with which he is most familiar. At McDonald's, however, at least according to Courtney, they are quite commonplace.

What Out-of-School Literacies Have to Teach Us about Academic Ones

Derek doesn't play many video games because of his visual impairment. As he explains, "I cannot see the detail that is needed to play some of them." He does play a lot of Madden 2003, however—a football simulation video game. Derek is drawn to this particular video game, he says, because he's a football player and, according to Derek, "the ethics and terminology is about the same. I have found that it is a lot easier to play a game that you will already have some kind of understanding to. It has so much to do with past experiences." In many ways, then, this game parallels for him more traditional education. As he explains, "I feel that video games are very educational, because you have to take time to learn them meaning of the game . . . the purpose of the game, and . . . the combinations of codes that will have to be used to successfully beat the game." Likewise, approaching a new writing assignment requires writers to take time to learn the internal and external design grammars limiting and shaping the relevant rhetorical spaces, the "purpose" of the assignment itself as understood by the key evaluators responsible for it, and "the combinations of codes" (language use, special terminology, rhetorical moves) that will be required of him as he negotiates this complex writing task. Thus, a familiarity with similar activities—particularly as the similarity is based on the new literacy being a simulated version of the one already well known to him—enables him to adapt quickly to this new environment. Derek understands, however, that many times the new literacy being learned will depend on codes, conventions, and rules that are largely unfamiliar to him. While this budding awareness does worry him a bit, he tells us that he is much happier thinking of literacy as "different" everywhere rather than always the same.

In his final essay (entitled "Knuckle Grinding"), Brad argues that his learning new literacies depends not so much on familiarity—as

Derek contends—but on a willingness to take risks. Accordingly, as Brad explains, "writing is a lot like playing extreme paintball: When you're on the field and you don't know the game, you're going to get shot down, and it hurts. . . . So when this happen all you can do is sit out that once and wipe the paint off and jump back in, and use the skills you learned from the last game like what to do and not to improve your skills that much more."

Likewise, a pedagogy of rhetorical dexterity requires that the learner not only redefine literacy in terms more consistent with the ideological model Street advocates, but also to develop a willingness to take risks to determine the limits and possibilities available within the new context and weigh the consequences of adherence with any desire to resist doing so. The value of risk-taking behavior in learning new literacies is often much more visible in communities of practice associated with video games than those associated with school, however. In the strange but provocative weblog *The Dancing Sausage*, a contributor makes clear that the "video game literate" are those who are "willing to die."

> The ultimate test of video game literacy is this: Are you willing to die? The video game literate generally are. . . . They'll try any button until they figure out what works. They will walk over the shimmering circle which may be a land mine, may be a warp portal; they will chase after the bouncing ball which may turn out to be a health restorative, may turn out to be a bomb. They'll try anything once. If it proves to be lethal, they'll try not to do it again.

According to her argument, literate players are willing to die for at least two reasons. First, they know "death" is the likely consequence of taking the risks necessary to learn what's possible in this new context; second, because in video games, "death" is relatively insignificant. Each player usually has multiple "lives" available to her. If her ship sustains too much battle fire to go on, she's simply issued a new one. No questions asked. If she "dies" more times than the number of "lives" allocated to a given player, she simply starts a brand new game. They risk death in order to learn from it, and they are willing to "die" because death in this context is relatively meaningless.

It is important to note, however, that to the video game literate, a willingness to "die" is not the same as finding no value in "living." Quite the contrary. Actually, death in a video game is no more (and no less) than the ultimate threat—a danger one immediately takes charge of when one is willing to die. "Death" for the literate gamer is a necessary risk; otherwise the user can never really learn what's possible within that virtual context and which activities are too deadly to ever try again. For Brad, "death" in a game of paintball offers him the same opportunity to learn, and in comparing this important prerequisite for learning in playing paintball with the need for risk-taking behavior in developing print-based texts in school, he learns to embrace risk there, too, rather than continue to, in his words, "play it safe." In order to develop enough familiarity with a new video game to eventually "beat it," literate gamers know they can't be "afraid to screw up." According to the blogger cited earlier, "[t]hey'll try any button until they figure out what works. . . . They'll try anything once. If it proves to be lethal, they'll try not to do it again." Learning new literacies thus becomes a process energized by the excitement of what may be possible in this new context rather than a chore stifled by a constant fear of "death." Thus, transference from a familiar literacy to an unfamiliar one is easiest for Derek when the new literacy is not completely unlike the old one; for Brad, this transference is possible once he learns to value and again make use of risk-taking behavior.

Gretna also chose to compare out-of-school literacies with writing as a learner, paying particular attention to the ways in which she became a "legitimate" member of more familiar communities of practice and how she planned to make use of these lessons in this new context. You may recall that one of the key issues that continued to affect Gretna's perception of herself as a writer was her concerns about the constraints of time. But in developing her presentation that compared gaming literacies to what she called "writing literacies," she began to consider the ways in which her success in the video game *Dance Dance Revolution* (DDR) also depended on her ability to think fast. As she explains, throughout the game you must think "the steps through," much like she discovered she had to when writing her timed response to the high-stakes test that placed her in basic writing. DDR is a console game that uses a floor pad on which players "dance" rather than a control unit with obvious buttons or a joystick. The player (or players) selects a song, then attempts to step where the signals on the television screen tell her to step (signals on screen are color-coded, as is the floor pad).

According to Gretna, this experience requires lots of quick thinking. Apparently, when playing DDR, players must ask themselves, "Which foot will they have to move their bodies to dance as efficiently as possible? It's the same thing with writing. The topic you are writing about requires thinking it through and finding the best way to explain something. Timing is everything [too]. Being able to pace yourself according to the time given to you and the length of a song are definitely a big part of both activities." Thus, in making these comparisons, Gretna was required to consider the ways in which she had been able to successfully negotiate time constraints in some rather complex spaces (like DDR), a revelation that helped her develop much more confidence as a writer in unfamiliar rhetorical spaces. Interestingly enough, she does point out at least one advantage "writing literacies" have over gaming literacies: "While writing, you are able to think about what you are going to write about. Unfortunately, you are not able to plan out or predict the steps you will be making while playing DDR. The screen only shows you a small amount of what you will be dancing to at a time" and you get no choice in the dance steps you are required to mimic.

Rather than examining the "in-the-moment" experiences of playing/writing in contexts like school and video games, Desmond compared the *processes* involved. In comparing training for a game of football with writing a paper for school, he focused on writing and football as processes that take place in phases and over time. As he describes it,

> A rough draft would be considered a full practice day because you are giving it all that you have to give. When a person makes a rough draft, they should write it like it is a final draft. In football when it is a full practice, the coach wants his players to play like they are going to play in the big game. So therefore when a rough draft is written, it would be written like its ready to be presented at that very moment.
>
> . . . The next step in writing is letting others read what you come up with. This is what we call an open practice in football, which is when you allow people to come in and watch you practice.

In a similar way, Adrian, an avid player of what he tell us is "futbol" (not "soccer," he tells me), chose to compare team "formations" to rhetorical traits of writing like "organization." As he explains,

> when you use formations in futbol you use it so that you have organization on the field in order to develop a play. . . . A formation is all about placement and it does affect all the other player[.] If one player doesn't know it doesn't work. A formation is chosen by seeing what formation an opponent is bringing on the field and then you use a formation that will hurt them. . . . Well with writing you can use formations in order to organize your paper and even develop a well organized paper.

Sports were a common choice among many writers in our program. "Danny" compares reading for school with his position on the football field as a linebacker.

> In my mind there are many ways of reading. . . . When I played as a linebacker, I would have to read plays. First I would have to tell if it was a passing or a running play. If it was a passing play, I would have to drop back into my zone and cover whoever entered it. If it was a running play, I would have to figure out which side the play was going to, who was carrying the ball, which hole it was going to go through, and what my job was. I had to read all this all within three seconds. I found this very difficult.

Danny "read" the football field in many of the same ways Adrian and his teammates "read" (current formations) and "wrote" (new formations) in response to this reading. As players (of football, in Danny's case, of "futbol" in Adrian's case), they had to anticipate where the players were going—the logic guiding their plays so Danny/Adrian could know how he should behave. They had to do this quickly, and only the football/futbol literate know how. Danny continues: "In a way this is also how we read books. When you read a book you have to be able to tell who was telling the story, where the story was taking place, when the story was happening, and what the story was about."

In making these comparisons, then, these writers were able to redefine literacy in terms more in keeping with the way literacy lives, (re)produced within a given community of practice with a deeply situated, people-oriented set of behaviors considered "literate" and very specific consequences for not following these rules. As Marion puts it in her response to WA6 assigned late in the term, "No matter what we think of these rules, obey is the only option. Every community formed its own language.... If we are in school, this community of practice, then we have to follow the[ir] rules, because that's how this community works. People who can't follow the rules will be left out of the community, no matter how intelligent they are."

By the end of the term, most writers understand that these rules change as context changes. Marion offers the interesting example of the common elementary school lesson "ain't ain't a word." According to Marion, students are taught early and often that "[t]he word 'ain't' can never be seen in a formal paper." She finds this lesson highly problematic; as she explains, "[t]he word 'ain't' might not need to be defined as non verbal but" instead as "a word that belongs to another community." This statement alone reveals the ways in which she is beginning to treat literacy as a social practice rather than a universal norm.

In effect, the real objective of the course is not to get the students to produce sophisticated academic discourse that is well organized, concrete, and convincing. That is certainly *an* objective, but as one reviewer for an earlier draft of an article-length version of this project (in the *Journal of Basic Writing*) pointed out, "What makes you believe that it is this particular sequence of essay/readings/coursework that helps students toward rhetorical dexterity, rather than the simple fact that they write six college-level essays, with the support of studio-type peer- and mentor-feedback"? From our analysis, it appears that the students do, indeed, learn how to produce academic discourse that may be judged effective in even the most traditional of contexts. I agree, however, that their abilities to do so are more likely the result of smart, constructive "peer- and mentor-feedback" than the curriculum alone.

What they do gain from a pedagogy of rhetorical dexterity and this particular curriculum, I argue, is a new understanding of the way literacy actually lives—a meta-cognitive ability to negotiate multiple literacies by understanding that "literacy is not literacy is not literacy" (Hull 19). The course did not, necessarily, give them "literate strategies" that they could easily translate from one community to the next, at least not automatically or without rereading the unfamiliar community of practice in similarly rigorous ways. In the end, then, making relevant the communities of practice with which they were already quite familiar (often even experts in) helped them redefine literacy for themselves in more productive ways. As one writer puts it in her final reflections for the course, "Overall, I learned that academics can be related to everything we do. . . . Some people find it as hard as I did at first to relate their [familiar] communities to academics. As I found out by doing so, everything we do or say is related to academics in some way or else how do we learn to do or say these things?" In other words, how we learn in *any* community of practice is necessarily going to help us understand how to learn new literacies in academic ones. It appears obvious, once we make it obvious.

Reflections

As previously stated, two hours each week English 100 students meet with a group of five to seven other writers led by a peer tutor—this in addition to the three hours each week they spend with their English 100 classroom instructor. In these writing groups, students workshop papers and challenge themselves and one another to think of reading and writing in new ways ("reading/writing the world") via their Dialogue Journals (as suggested by Ann Berthoff) and their Dialogue Journal Conferences (as suggested in *The Journal Book: For Teachers of At-Risk College Writers*), all of which inform their development of a reflective essay in which they articulate the ways the work they generated this term meets the following objectives:

> The student will (1) understand that literacy is context-dependent, (2) validate and investigate one or more familiar communities of practice, (3) articulate the unwritten rules participants must obey in that community of practice if they want to remain/become accepted as members, (4) investigate new literacies in order to articulate the unwritten rules participants must likewise obey (or at least acknowledge), (5) locate and articulate the *points of contact* between familiar literacies and unfamiliar ones, (6) examine and articulate the *points of dissonance* between different literacies, and (8) put *rhetorical dexterity* to use in a variety of contexts for a variety of purposes. (English 100 syllabus)

At midterm, the students submit a draft of this project (Critical Reflections), which their tutors then bring to a panel of readers made up of all the English 100 group tutors, the graduate administrator(s) of the writing center, and . . . myself (the director). Readers assess this draft according to a rubric I've developed for just this purpose (built on the objectives outlined above), and the assessment (provided by two different readers) guides the writer in her revisions of her critical reflections.

The rubric helps these new educators determine the effectiveness of the current draft in meeting the above objectives via prose that meets the demands of this particular academic community (effectively organized, filled with what the community might consider "relevant" evidence, focused on the issue at hand, clear, and relatively free of surface-level concerns). Readers ask themselves questions like the following: Does the writer understand what other literacies may have to offer her as she attempts to learn new ones? Can she articulate this understanding and reveal the ways in which the work she has produced this term (her essays, her presentations, etc.) serves as evidence of this understanding and her ability to apply what she has learned here to new contexts?

The final portfolio for each English 100 student should include a revised draft of these critical reflections, as well as deeply revised drafts of the essays and presentations the student completed (as articulated above). It, too, is graded by a panel of readers. The following information is included on their English 100 syllabus: "Your Final Portfolio will be reviewed by a panel of experienced English 100 instructors. This panel will be looking for things like this: How evident is your growth as a writer? Is there evidence here that you understand the importance of deep revision? Is there evidence of your ability to effectively rework these writing assignments to meet (or exceed) specified criteria? Are you ready for the demands of English 101?" Thus, the specific educational benefits of this program are determined by the student's ability to articulate these benefits in the critical reflections and to provide evidence of the applicability of this *pedagogy of rhetorical dexterity* via the final portfolio.[4]

Changes

Though we have found the curriculum described above to be effective in teaching basic writing students and new educators to think of literacy in new, more productive ways, many of our students have found making comparisons to school literacies more difficult than I expected them to and, while most have begun to rethink literacy in terms much more closely approximating the ideological model Street advocates, they continue to speak of school literacies in monolithic terms. The major reason for this may be that they have had so few experiences with college-level literacy. Thus, future versions of this curriculum will include an additional group project. This project, assigned early in the semester and completed in their English 100 writing groups, would require students to explore the disciplinary differences among literacy requirements as represented in a set of journals and books collected and placed on reserve by a campus librarian.[5] That is, students would share their majors with their group tutors, then pair up with someone declaring a major unlike their own (a history major may pair up with someone interested in the health sciences, for example). Again in pairs, they would analyze the literacy requirements of each discipline as represented in one or two journals and books. The analysis should follow a set of criteria that might include use of informal language (personal pronouns, contractions, etc.), graphs, charts, surveys, polls, statistics, interviews, and special terminology. Finally, they would compare and contrast each, articulating the points of contact and points of dissonance between each discipline and, finally, presenting those findings to their writing group. My hope is that in doing so even more students will discover the number of ways in which "correctness" is context and, in fact, discipline specific (see especially Geisler and Russell). Of course many of our students have not yet declared majors. Thus we ask these "undecided" students and suggest a discipline from there.

Portability

Given public perceptions of this always new "literacy crisis," those of us hoping to "make basic writing a political act" would do well to represent literacy in more appropriate and contextualized ways. However, given that policies like "No Child Left Behind" show no signs of fading and that state-mandated "remediation" mirrors public perception of what "basic writers" need, it seems unlikely that many of us will be able to do so beyond the learning spaces for which we are responsible, at least not immediately or directly.

In the short term, I seem to be without the power to make major changes to the institutionalized oppression that regularly represents the way literacy functions and measures it in inappropriate ways. I suspect I am not alone in this. Thus, a *pedagogy of rhetorical dexterity* seems to lend itself to application in other institutions and contexts, especially as such a philosophical perspective enables us to work toward social justice by making changes within basic writing programs at the levels of curriculum, tutor training, and teacher training—in my case, all within the confines of the system my predecessors established in response to the TASP law almost twenty years ago (enacted in 1989). It is my hope that such moves will extend far beyond the classroom—into conversations with colleagues about what basic writing students need, into forums that allow us to confront reticent colleagues and administrators (perhaps even politicians and the general public) with what basic writing students can already do (abilities they had long before attending our programs), maybe even into a series of colloquia in which former "basic writers" speak with the general public about literacy in smart, flexible ways (perhaps within the presence of those who define it in much less informed ways). At an area conference in 2007, one of our former basic writing students did just this.

Overturning the institutional, political, social, and economic infrastructure invested in the autonomous model of literacy requires time, patience, and—above all—diplomacy. Taking that ideological model of literacy public through the mouths and texts of current and former basic writing students seems to me the sweetest revenge possible for the many ways in which that autonomous model has stigmatized them. Not only do I think such publicity is (eventually) possible; I think it is, in fact, inevitable.

Notes

1. As described in chapter three, a prior sequence included excerpts from Elspeth Stuckey's *The Violence of Literacy* and Deborah Brandt's "Sponsors of Literacy" and focused on the ways in which the autonomous model that shapes standardized tests like TASP and TAAS is largely inappropriate and even unfair to many marginalized populations. In many ways, the sequence was a great success; however, while many students did seem empowered by this perspective, a large percentage continued to define literacy in terms no less problematic and were, therefore, unable to display the linguistic and rhetorical flexibility required to succeed in the variety of rhetorical contexts extending beyond the basic writing classroom.
2. In a recent presentation for CCCC and an article for *College English*, I explore the ways in which my own Christian illiteracies have complicated my work with some of my most religious students (see "Living Inside the Bible (Belt)").
3. We also viewed Trekkies as an interesting example of how fandom functions as a community of practice, as well as an episode of the British reality show *Faking It* in which a fry cook learns what he needs to pass as a master chief at a top restaurant in London. Future sequences may make use of the cult film *Heavy Metal Parking Lot* as it examines the value-sets, activities, language, clothing, and other elements that mark the activities associated with heavy metal fandom (at least in the mid-1980s). The film is a strange documentary in which an amateur filmmaker simply records the activities of fans "hanging out" in the parking lot before a Judas Priest concert.
4. Again, this system appears to me to be in keeping with Edward White's suggestions for portfolio assessment at the programmatic level.
5. In the past, the librarians on our campus have been incredibly helpful with similar activities. I have already spoken with at least one librarian about our curriculum change, and he tells me that what I suggest can be easily accommodated.

Works Cited

Carter, Shannon. "Living Inside the Bible (Belt)." *College English* 69.9 (2007): 572–595. Print.

Berthoff, Ann. *The Making of Meaning: Metaphors, Models, and Maxims for Writing Teachers*. Montclair: Boynton/Cook, 1981. Print.

Brandt, Deborah. "Accumulating Literacy: Writing and Learning to Write in the Twentieth Century." *College English* 57 (1995): 649–668. Print.

———. "Sponsors of Literacy." *College English* 49.2 (1998): 165–185.

Carter, Shannon. "What is a Community of Practice?" *Texas A&M University-Commerce.* Texas A&M University-Commerce, 30 Nov. 2006. Web. 30 Mar. 2012.

Cooper, Marilyn. *Writing as Social Action.* Portsmouth: Boynton/Cook, 1989. Print.

Gardner, Susan, and Toby Fulwiler. *The Journal Book: For Teachers of At-Risk College Writers.* Portsmouth: Boynton/Cook, 1999.

Gee, James Paul. *What Video Games Have to Teach Us About Literacy and Learning.* New York: Palgrave, 2003. Print.

Geisler, Cheryl. *Academic Literacy and the Nature of Experience: Reading, Writing, and Knowing in Academic Philosophy.* Mahwah: Erlbaum, 1994. Print.

———. "Writing and Learning at Cross-Purposes in the Academy." *Reconceiving Writing, Rethinking Writing Instruction.* Ed. Joseph Petraglia. Mahwah: Erlbaum, 1995. 101–120. Print.

Hull, Glynda, and Katherine Schultz, eds. *School's Out!: Bridging Out-of-School Literacies With Classroom Practice.* New York: Teachers College P, 2001. Print.

Johnson, Steven. *Everything Bad Is Good for You: How Today's Popular Culture Is Actually Making Us Smarter.* New York: Riverhead Books, 2005. Print.

Lave, Jane, and Etienne Wagner. *Situated Learning: Legitimate Peripheral Participation.* Cambridge: Cambridge UP, 1991. Print.

Rose, Mike. *The Mind at Work: Valuing the Intelligence of the American Worker.* New York: Penguin, 2005. Print.

Russell, David R. "Activity Theory and Process Approaches: Writing (Power) in School, and Society." Post-Process Theory: Beyond the Writing Process Paradigm. Ed. Thomas Kent. Carbondale: Southern Illinois UP, 1999.

———. "Activity Theory and Writing Instruction." *Reconceiving Writing, Rethinking Writing Instruction.* Ed. Joseph Petraglia. Mahwah: Erlbaum, 1995. 51–77. Print.

Stuckey, Elspeth J. *The Violence of Literacy.* Portsmouth: Heinemann, 1991. Print.

New Worlds of Errors and Expectations: Basic Writers and Digital Assumptions

Marisa A. Klages and J. Elizabeth Clark

Marisa Klages and J. Elizabeth Clark discuss the promise and practice of ePortfolios as implemented in their basic writing classrooms at the City University of New York's LaGuardia Community College. Their students are digital natives, young people coming of age in the midst of Web 2.0 ubiquity. Yet as students "who come from 163 different countries and speak 118 different languages" enrolled in basic writing, they still face obstacles that can hamper their possibilities for success, including jobs, family responsibilities, and lack of sufficient preparation for college. Klages and Clark also suggest that their students are more acclimated to informal

*uses of digital media (social networking sites, texting, etc.) than employing
digital media for academic writing. In order to bridge this new digital
divide, Klages and Clark demonstrate three specific uses of ePortfolios for
their students in basic writing classes: to revise, to reflect, and "to explore
the full possibilities of the digital platform the ePortfolio provides" (p. 190).
Student ePortfolios offer direct audiences and purposes for producing academic writing, and students learn to negotiate the divide between formal
and informal writing via digital media.*

In an age when 8 million American adults have blogs (Rainie), e-mail
is ubiquitous, cyber-communities like YouTube, Twitter, Facebook,
and MySpace are already passé among the teen and college-age set,
and the use of computers in composition is a given, technology is part of
the academic zeitgeist. While in the 1980s and 1990s, much was made
of "the digital divide," documenting the economic and educational
injustice of access to computers, those arguments are largely erased,
or forgotten, in a culture where computers are everywhere. With the
advent of Web 2.0 and social media, however, a new digital divide is
emerging. Concomitant with the idea of the "digital native" is the idea
that all students will come to the classroom proficient in new technologies, cyber-literate, and comfortable with the discourse of digital rhetoric. But this expectation presumes of its "digital natives" a literacy
which they have absorbed uncritically or which they cannot produce
(Prensky 1).

While many basic writers come to us today with the fluency of
digital natives, they still have the same need for learning writing and
critical thinking skills that has traditionally marked basic writers.
Moreover, while most basic writers are adept at accessing information
digitally, they are not as proficient when it comes to producing digital
information, nor are they able to code-switch between informal cyber-
situations and the more formal academic and professional expectations
of cyber-literacy. They also need to deepen their understanding of the
role writing can play in developing digital texts. In order to be effective
users of digital media, students must know how to write for a multimodal environment; they are adrift in a world of instant publishing
without the skills of proficient writers and thinkers. Where in previous
eras, one might argue that basic writers were almost invisible, today
basic writers are often audaciously demonstrating their lack of understanding of edited American English online. Furthermore, the digital
environment encourages this showcasing of ungrammatical writing
with the widespread use of texting, emoticons, and popular websites
like "I Can Has Cheezburger." While these modalities are appropriate
for digital environments promoting social networking, they confront
basic writers, and in fact all students, with one more code from which
they need to switch when intersecting with academic and professional
realms of writing.

The virtual world is process-less: writing becomes an act of moving from immediate composing to instant publishing. What, then, are the ramifications for basic writers? How do we teach process in a process-less world of digital media? How do we engage students and help them to value process as a necessary tool for becoming more articulate in their writing? How can we engage students so that they can navigate both digital and traditional writing? How do we help students to code switch between their use of technology with friends and its use in academic and professional situations?

As teachers at a large, urban community college where pen and paper are often the only classroom technology, we believe that ePortfolios are an ideal pedagogical tool for engaging basic writers and teaching them to merge Web 2.0 digital literacies and multimodal composing strategies at this critical juncture of digital and traditional writing. In its most basic iteration, the ePortfolio is a digital version of the traditional paper portfolio, in which students collect written work during the term, select key pieces, and write reflections about those pieces. In contrast with paper portfolios, however, ePortfolios are available online to employers, admissions officers, and the international friends and families of students. While the ePortfolio adds portability and the possibility of using multimodal composing, it also builds on a considerable legacy of portfolio pedagogy and teaching with technology in the field of composition studies. More importantly, the ePortfolio is beginning to radically change our students' understandings of their relationship to the written word in an era of digital literacy and the power of authority hidden within that authorship. Through the use of ePortfolio and other Web 2.0 tools, students implement critical digital literacy skills as they learn how to write for real audiences and find an authentic voice.

Recontextualizing the Digital Native: Writing and ePortfolios

Clocks change themselves on the weekend of daylight savings time. Coffee makers can be set to turn on automatically in the morning. We bank online. We know what our friends and family members are doing throughout the day by following their Twitter and Facebook updates. And yet, our classrooms remain largely the same as they were twenty or thirty years ago. We have not radically changed our practices or our academic expectations of students. In *Born Digital: Understanding the First Generation of Digital Natives* (published in 2008), John Palfrey and Urs Gasser outline recent shifts in culture and explain how the youngest generations of global citizens exist in a digital world that bears little similarity to the world their parents and teachers grew up in. In a conversation with students in a digital rhetoric course, DigiRhet.org created an impressive catalogue of the shifts in our daily lives caused by an increased reliance on technology and the ways that students understand the world. Almost every aspect of our lives today is permeated by a reliance on seemingly invisible technology:

> The list we generated was extensive, ranging from a digital alarm clock; an interactive mapping and direction-giving device one student had in her car; a device for runners to clip onto their shoes that digitally records their progress at time markers set for a marathon; a digital meat thermometer with an alarm that ran through a student's oven; a "virtual girlfriend" a student was "dating" that sent text messages via cell phone and e-mail; a digital audio recorder that allowed a student to record notes and thoughts as she commuted to campus, which she could then connect to her computer to transcribe her voice to text notes with the software that came with the recorder; a networked PlayStation console with a headset so that geographically distant players could not only compete against one another online but also speak to each other while gaming; a grocery store keychain card, which promised access to savings and specials but which students recognized quite quickly as a tracking device to monitor purchases; a USB drive that worked as a portable miniature hard drive and virtually replaced all other media (e.g., floppy disks, CDs); and digital cable and TiVo, which several students had in their homes. The infiltration of these different technologies in students' lives varied greatly; for instance, when the student who brought in her USB drive to show and talk about separated it from her keychain and held it in the air, at least ten other students immediately grabbed their keychains or dug in their bags to show their own USB drives and talk about common practices, different uses, storage capacities, cost, and so on. (236–37)

Students are clearly acquiring new types of literacy in their engagement with technology. With the acquisition of new hardware and software, new technological gadgets and devices, and the invisible ways that technology has become embedded in everything from our ovens to our cell phones, the emerging digital world is a vastly different place, one of connectivity and fast pace, than the one in which many college professors were educated.

However, just because students have and use technology, this does not mean that they are proficient in creating it or in code switching for different audiences. As we transition to this new culture as citizens and as teachers, we are simultaneously challenged with learning new media ourselves and bringing them into the classroom, wrestling with what this cultural shift means for our classrooms and our pedagogy. What is real writing in our new technologically rich world? How have the roles of teachers and students been reversed by the fact that our students are often more techno-savvy than we are?

In her 2004 address to the Conference on College Composition and Communication, Kathleen Blake Yancey characterized this cultural change as "tectonic." Likening this increasing technological dependence, which represents a massive change in daily life, to the shifting of the plates that undergird the continents, Yancey believes, as do increasing numbers of educators, that our new digital culture calls for a significant shift in the classroom. Yancey argues, "Literacy today is in the midst of a tectonic change. Even inside of school, never before have writing and composing generated such diversity in definition" ("Made Not Only in Words" 298). Yancey examines the impact of these different modes of writing and the situations in which that writing occurs: "The members of the writing public have learned—in this case, to write, to think together, to organize, and to act within these forums— largely without instruction and, more to the point here, largely without our instruction. They need neither self-assessment nor our assessment: they have a rhetorical situation, a purpose, a potentially worldwide audience, a choice of technology and medium—and they write" ("Made Not Only in Words" 301–302). No longer do writing instructors struggle to present the idea of audience to the students in their classrooms. Their students already write publicly on blogs, wikis, and social networking sites, and often, to a large audience of readers connected by cell phones, texting, and the Internet. However, embedded in Yancey's analysis is an assumption that there are culturally and academically valued forms of this new writing, which many basic writers have yet to master.

A 2008 Pew Internet and American Life report, "Writing, Technology and Teens," highlights the distinction between public and private writing: "At the core, the digital age presents a paradox. Most teenagers spend a considerable amount of their life composing texts, but they do not think that a lot of the material they create electronically is *real* writing. The act of exchanging emails, instant messages, texts, and social network posts is communication that carries the same weight to teens as phone calls and between-class hallway greetings" (Lenhart et al.). While many students recognize the difference between academic and professional writing and virtual writing, they are not adept at code switching between the virtual world and the world of academia. In academic and professional discourse, there are assumptions about "acceptable modes of communication" for a particular context. This hidden world of literacy presumes that students and writers in general are able to make the necessary transitions between differing contexts. How, then, do faculty help students to use the technological medium they are conversant in to learn and engage with more traditional forms of writing? How do we transform the paper and pen classroom to a digitally saturated environment? And, most importantly, how do we adjust our own understanding of "good" writing from traditional print literacy to a definition that includes digital literacy—and in ways that are continually shifting? In our next section we discuss the use of ePortfolios at LaGuardia Community College as one way to help shift the classroom to include digital literacy.

Texting Isn't Writing: Today's Basic Writer

Located in Long Island City in Queens, LaGuardia Community College is one of six community colleges in the City University of New York (CUNY). It serves a student body of 15,169 matriculated students who come from 163 different countries and speak 118 different languages ("LaGuardia Community College Institutional Profile"). Our classrooms are a fabulous cacophony of difference, divergence, and often, dislocation. Students come to us with varying degrees of familiarity with the American educational system. Classes at LaGuardia include students from underperforming American high schools, students who were trained in Caribbean schools based on the British-colonial model, students who have come to the United States as refugees with very little educational preparation, and students with advanced degrees from their native countries. Because of their diverse educational histories, these students present a complicated mix of expectations about their interactions with teacher-authorities. And, like all students, they arrive in our classrooms informed by the ideologies that have guided their upbringing. LaGuardia students also face socioeconomic risk, often unable to afford the "affordable" community college tuition (tuition and fees for full-time students at LaGuardia range from $1,545.85 to $2,424.85 per semester depending on the student's residency status). Many students have family members to support and care for, and they often work full time while maintaining full-time student schedules. They are at risk on many levels, teetering on the edge of that ever-elusive American dream.

Nearly half of all students entering LaGuardia (44 percent in 2006) are placed in basic writing. Like most basic writers, they are uncomfortable with writing and experience high levels of writing anxiety in academic situations. They have little or no confidence in their writing, reading, and critical thinking abilities. For most of these students, academic writing is seen as a one-way communication in which they seek to demonstrate acquired knowledge to a teacher-authority. In an era of No Child Left Behind, students educated in American public schools often understand writing as high-stakes and test-driven. These students often have little investment in education as a means toward cultural and social empowerment, rather seeing it as an end to economic advancement.

In most situations, including their placement into a basic writing course in college, writing has served as a basis for punishment. Within the City University of New York system, students are placed in basic writing based on their score on a placement exam. Once in the basic writing sequence, students at some CUNY colleges are prevented from beginning their college-level studies. Additionally, basic skills courses (including reading, math, and writing) no longer carry credit. Students perceive the basic writing course as an academic ghetto, preventing them from pursuing their educational goals. Exit from this course is based on a high-stakes examination. Thus, students regard academic writing as the means by which they are judged and found lacking.

Many LaGuardia students also face the challenge of negotiating writing in a second, third, or fourth language, which becomes a daunting obstacle. Despite success in English language acquisition courses preceding their work in basic writing or ESL courses, these students come to us as hesitant writers, concerned about their fluency and often frustrated by their inability to communicate as eloquently or persuasively as they might in their native languages.

Although basic writing and ESL students do not usually think of themselves as writers, they maintain a considerable online presence through texting, e-mail, and social networking. However, this online presence falls outside of their understanding of writing. Indeed, it exists outside of their discomfort with writing. Digitally, they exist happily in a mix of slang and imperatives and patois that richly captures their everyday lives.

Facebook, MySpace, and various journaling communities all privilege personal narrative as a powerful means to construct political, entrepreneurial, and entertainment personalities. Our students, however, have repeatedly learned that their stories are not important. Throughout their educational careers they have been given impersonal, prescriptive writing assignments that punish them for incorrect grammar. Their conception of academic writing is limited to the rigidly constructed five-paragraph essay, something that spelled success in high school writing assignments and on the SAT writing examination. So, while presidential candidates make much of the opportunity to connect with voters through personal stories that make them seem more "real" or "down to earth," and affluent teens and young adults keep blogs that offer their opinions on everything from fashion to sex to politics, our community college students are silenced in this larger cultural milieu, believing that their stories and their lives are unimportant. Their online presence is a means of everyday, survival communication that happens on the go, in short bursts as they connect with others in their community. They do not see this online communication as a connection to the larger world of "writing."

ePortfolios: "What We Ask Students to Do Is Who We Ask Them to Be"

At LaGuardia, the use of digital portfolios, or ePortfolios, offers the opportunity to merge the best of Web 2.0 and the tectonic shifts Yancey identifies with a process-based writing approach that teaches students to think about their writing and what is at stake when they publish that writing (for more information about LaGuardia's use of ePortfolios, go to http://www.eportfolio.lagcc.cuny.edu/). As students create and refine their ePortfolios, they work toward a new digital literacy while using their already well-defined technological skills, and in the process they begin to understand the expectations of a digital culture.

Too often, basic writers are asked to write simple essays that don't engage their intellectual interests or their critical thinking abilities. For some, "developmental skills" is a phrasal code for "not college able." And all too often, basic writers are marginalized within a larger college curriculum that uses the issue of "standards" as a weapon against them. Yancey writes, *What we ask students to do is who we ask them to be*" ("Postmodernism" 738, emphasis in original). In our classrooms, we seek to use the ePortfolio as a tool to suggest to students that the world they write is the world they will claim, as authors and as citizens. In our basic writing classrooms, we strive to shift students' perspectives of themselves as non-writers as they compile ePortfolios documenting their development as writers and reflecting on the tangible progress as evidenced by their collected writing. This practice significantly challenges the other measures of student achievement in the course—two high-stakes exams imposed by the university system and our department—to help students document their emerging authorship and to claim authority over their own writing, and, ultimately, their own education. The ePortfolio, and students' understanding of their progress and their limitations as writers, serves to provide them with a powerful counternarrative within an otherwise anonymous and punitive writing context. As they develop rich multimodal ePortfolios characterized by an intensive use of visual rhetoric to complement their written and oral productions in the course, students build on their technological dexterity and begin to understand their emerging writing skills as equally important components of their digital literacy.

The ePortfolio serves as a locus to teach developmental writing over the course of a semester while also using what Yancey calls a "web sensible portfolio, where students can explore their emerging literacy in a wide range of digital media ("Postmodernism" 745). The heart of our ePortfolio pedagogy revolves around three key practices: (1) asking students to demonstrate revision in essays, (2) asking students to reflect on their development as writers, and (3) encouraging students to explore the full possibilities of the digital platform the ePortfolio provides. In basic writing courses, the first two often take priority because, as students work on their writing and their reflections, they are also often learning to use the ePortfolio system. Accordingly, their first ePortfolios are often less technologically sophisticated. However, since we share the mantra, "If you can do it on paper, why reproduce paper in the ePortfolio?" we find that students are increasingly creative in their use of digital media. They create movies, Power-Points, and audio files that allow them to express themselves and to demonstrate their critical inquiry in courses as varied as writing, history, math, and science.

To this end, the practice of writing in an ePortfolio fully embodies what DigiRhet.org identifies as a culture where "Writing is no longer a purely text-driven practice," but one where

> [w]riting requires carefully and critically analyzing and selecting among multiple media elements. Digital writers rely on words, motion, interactivity, and visuals to make meaning. Available computer software applications, for instance, allow writers to more easily manipulate and embed visual information in their documents. Even basic word-processing applications come with fairly large clip-art collections and offer the ability for writers to create data displays like charts, graphs, and diagrams. Most Web search engines allow writers to search for photographs, animations, and video clips to download and use in documents, Web pages, and digital movies. These tools shift the ways in which composing takes place: they change the way we do research, the way we produce texts, the way we deliver our writing. (240)

Student ePortfolios become public artifacts in the course, accessible to all of their classmates as well as their instructors. Long before the evolution of the ePortfolio, our writing classes were all based on paper portfolio models. However, in many ways, the paper portfolio reinscribes the teacher-student relationship as students hand in a portfolio at the end of the term to a professor. The ePortfolio, among its many possibilities, makes writing more public than any other technique or tool we have tried in the classroom. Gone are the days of peer review groups restricted by the number of copies a student makes of his/her paper (and complicated by broken copiers, printers needing toner, or students without money to pay for photocopies).

The ePortfolio allows easy access for all students enrolled in a course, or even among several courses, depending on the instructor's course design. The ePortfolio is also a good platform to allow students to showcase their use of other technologies like blogs, wikis, digital stories (mini-movies based on essays students write), PowerPoint presentations, and a public discussion thread (through Blackboard course management software). The ePortfolio serves as the locus for all of a student's digital production in our courses. And, because of the very public nature of all of these technologies, students come to think of all writing in our courses as public. Because anyone in the class, or sometimes in other classes, might comment on their work, they work harder to make their writing impressive. During the basic writing course, students begin to combine their increased proficiency in using technology with their own broadened expectations of traditional writing, producing a new investment in their own writing and literacy. That someone else might read their writing is no longer a possible abstraction; it's an expectation. Students also inspire and teach one another with their discoveries, their reflections, and their critical analyses of texts we read in class.

Throughout the semester, students increasingly complicate their understanding of authorship as they write the drafts and reflections that appear on the ePortfolio. Coupled with this new public writing, students begin to enter into an academic conversation about intellectual property and the value of ideas. They engage with new forms of rhetoric as they combine digital imagery with prose. They use film and social networking sites as ways to further experiment with their work and with their development. The ePortfolio, and student work showcased therein, has limitless possibilities for revision, for invention, and for imagination. In class, we discuss their public writing, designing activities and exercises to address the questions around crafting public writing.

ePortfolios offer the most recent iteration of a basic writing pedagogy that seeks to claim space for basic writers' voices within the cacophony of university classrooms, to address issues of audience and voice, to teach about the important role of revision in writing, and to tackle the questions of writing in a modern world, contextualizing and providing a laboratory for exploring writing in the world of Web 2.0 and its varying manifestations of authorship.

Defining New Culture: Acculturation on Many Levels

In her article "Personal Genres, Public Voices," Jane Danielewicz asks, "How might we move students toward public voices?" We have found that using ePortfolios is one way to move students from their personal writing to public writing. As explained earlier, students in basic writing classes at LaGuardia are tentative and often timid in their approach to writing. They barely have a private voice, let alone a voice "that enters the ongoing conversation to change, amend, intervene, extend, disrupt, or influence it" (Danielewicz 425). For our students, it is the ePortfolio that provides a gateway to this type of public academic discourse.

Much of what we do with at-risk writers is help them acculturate to a larger college experience, preparing them for future successes. In the discussion that follows, all student names are pseudonyms. Student writing is used with permission and appears exactly as it was submitted. Liz's student, Maria, a graduate of an underperforming New York City High School, writes this of her initial performance in class:[1]

> When I first came to college, I was under the false assumption that it would be a more slightly difficult, but extremely similar high school experience. Little did I know about the extreme culture shock that was awaiting as I walked through the doors of LaGuardia Community College. Where I was once that perfect student that all the teachers knew and loved, I was now that student who was struggling to keep that reputation in college. That struggle began with my very first formal college

paper. This paper challenged and successfully changed my entire per-spective of that "mildly difficult" college life that I imagined I would have.

This paper was about how something personal to you, something that you feel strong about could become in a sense political. When I first recieved the assignment, I assumed I would breeze by this paper and recieve an A just like in high school. As I recieved the first draft of my paper back, I didn't know what to do as a huge NP (which happened to be a very small NP in the corner of my paper), stared me in my face, making a mochary of the effort that I put forth to impress my english teacher. (NP means Not Passing). With my hurt ego, I took the remainder of the time before the final draft was due and feverishly worked to re-write the paper, even neglecting my other classes. In my mind, the hard work seemed to be to no prevail as I somberly handed in what I thought would be a F.

This paper captures the disconnect between high school and college life that many students experience. While this student expected easy As, she was surprised by being placed in a basic writing class and found herself struggling to meet the demands of that course. In this first re-flective letter, she also begins to discover the importance of revising in a process-based approach to writing.

When writing reflective pieces for their ePortfolios, students often discuss how they want people to see and understand them. Of her expe-rience with ePortfolio, Marisa's student Emma writes, "My wish is to make people know more about my personality and the way I'm seeing myself as a writer. Eng 099 class made me to write as a free motivated person. I had so much fun practicing my writing as well as having a hard time in my assignments." Emma, who had started the semester with extreme writing anxiety and who often failed to produce in-class essays because they taxed her so badly, eventually found motivation in writing for her ePortfolio. The knowledge that this document was going to be public was the catalyst for her to write. Another student, Analise, reports, "I feel my EPortfolio its appropriate for public view because I show improvement in all my areas. Also in my opinion I know I could have done a better job but I feel it's a well done project that is present-able." Analise recognizes and finds it necessary to defend what she sees as sub-standard work because she understands the public nature of this writing. Thus, the ePortfolio adds an element to the writing class-room that allows students to safely explore themselves as writers while they turn an eye to a public audience.

Developing their public voice goes further when students begin to provide links in their ePortfolios to the blogs they keep during the se-mester. The blogs are motivated by our pedagogical assumption that students need to understand their writing as something they are in-vested in. In the blogs, students write about topics that are important to them, and as contextualized for an audience, understanding that their writing is public. Both the ePortfolio and the blog are integrated into the course as part of our larger pedagogical methodology. Students' blogs are already accessible to their classmates, but by providing links to their blogs in their ePortfolios, they make them public to those in their academic community who might not otherwise have read them. Student ePortfolios are password protected. While they are available to faculty and classmates, the general public cannot see them without a password; however, including the blog URL in the ePortfolio allows teachers and students other than the ones who were in the initial class with the student to access these very public blogs.

In one class that focused on environmental issues, students blogged about the connections they were noticing as popular TV shows focused on the environment. Marisa's student, Karissa, writes a brief analysis of Bravo TV's "Green Is Universal" campaign: "In this campaign many bravo tv's stars, who are Tim Gun, Lee Ann Wang from Top chef 1, and Jesse Brune from Work out, are sharing their experience and tips for keeping our nature being Green." She continues: "For me it is awesome and desirable that the people in the shows-actually they're competetors and kind of masters in their field, so what they do is powerful to persuade people who want to be like them—because it has corrected my thoughts of what I eat, how I wash the laudaries, and why I should work out." This analysis, while not rhetorically sophisticated (or grammatically correct) enables Karissa to share her understanding of this program with her professors, her peers, and strangers who may have surfed onto her blog because she profiles herself as "the Christian who doesn't ignore what is going on in the world." Karissa is beginning to develop a public voice, even as a basic writer. She is entering into the existing conversation about the environment and media, and she is intervening in this conversation. Perhaps, in her future classes, Karissa will attempt to disrupt or amend the conversations in which she is participating.

Our students regularly keep blogs on issues related to cyberspace and technology. A standard part of that assignment is asking students in each class to comment on the blogs of the students in another class. Each week, we ask students to choose an article from the online versions of *The New York Times*, *The Washington Post*, the *BBC*, or the *Guardian*. Students link to the article and then write brief reflections on why the piece interests them and relates to the themes of our class. In her ePortfolio, Serena, one of Liz's students, linked to her blog entry on hybrid cars as an example of how she was able to write an informal, persuasive piece on the question "Can technology make our lives better?" Her resolute answer, as a future computer and information systems major, was yes.

The ePortfolio also allows, in the development of that emerging academic voice, an opportunity to reflect on changes in a student's writing. Serena, who had been in the United States for less than a year, writes in her mid-term reflective letter:

I never thought I would improve this much in my writing skill. When I first wrote my diagnostic essay it was very poor. It had red ink on most every sentence.[2] It was mess to look at. The problem I faced in my writing class was because of the way of teaching in this college is totally different from what I used to learn in my place. It's really hard for me to adjust the new changes going through my studies. So maybe this is the reason why I am always back in my studies. Going through my paper I found that my essays needed a totally new look. There were changes to be made in the introduction, body paragraph and in the conclusion. Since the introduction attracts the reader, I tried to make improvements in the introduction. If the intro is interesting, engaging and clear, it is sure that the reader will definitely go through your 400 word essay. The common mistake you marked on both of my essays was unclear thesis and how do the paragraphs relate to the main idea. In order to make my essay outstanding and engaging, the 1st thing I needed to do was understand what the essay was about and what it was asking? So when I revised the paper I jotted down my new ideas that came to my mind and rewrote the essay again. Later when I read the essay I found that this revision plan has really helped me.

By mid-term, Serena had moved beyond her initial disappointment at being placed in a basic writing class to fully engaging the course objectives, understanding and articulating how to improve her writing. She shares important cultural information about how different this class was for her than classes in her native Nepal and then recontextualizes her understanding of education in an American educational setting. She explains her understanding of what an essay should do, how it should connect to a reader, and how its structure allows the reader to better understand an argument. Moreover, she demonstrates an increasing awareness of the importance of revision in this process. "I needed to . . . understand what the essay was about and what it was asking," she writes. Isn't this the essential question that all writers should ask of themselves? Serena moves from focusing on errors that her teacher identifies to situating herself as an author and trying to crystallize what she wants to say.

Serena's ePortfolio provided readers with even greater access to personal and reflective information. In another course, she had written an "About Me" essay (one of the important features of a LaGuardia ePortfolio, where students write their personal narrative) complete with pictures and a discussion of Nepal. Like other students, Serena wanted to teach her instructors and her classmates about her native country and her background, so she asked Liz to read and comment on her "About Me" essay. Here, Serena assumed a dominant role as she instructed us through her narrative. Understanding Serena's cultural background allowed Liz to construct their one-on-one conferences in a different way not with Serena's essays, but with the differences in educational expectations. Her ePortfolio led to many rich conversations about how culture shapes us and our expectations.

Serena's reflective essay demonstrates a clear understanding of the academic expectations of the course and the requirements for a passing essay. She marks her dominant writing challenge as learning to identify the main idea of her own essay, "the 1st thing I needed to do was understand what the essay was about and what it was asking." In her letter, she discusses the two essays she had selected to showcase. Her strategy was to choose essays that had significant structural and grammatical errors and to rewrite those essays, showing what she had learned. Moreover, in her letter, she comments on Liz's comments, showing where they helped her to improve and where she felt confident enough to follow her own ideas about the structure and content of the essay. In her conclusion to the letter, she writes, "I revised my essay again and again. I used to write essays at home and bring them to your office hours. My final revision for this essay was 750 words with full proofreading and not a single grammatical error."

At mid-term, this student was already writing essays that exceeded our first-year college level composition requirements (600 words). She understood the process of revision and how to make her essays stronger. She also demonstrates a clear understanding of our class discussions about the structure and content of effective essays. More importantly, she confidently recounts her choices and her process. Like other students in this class, she writes with the confidence that someone is reading her writing, and that makes it more important than an abstract academic exercise because she knows that her teacher, her classmates, and possibly eventually strangers might be reading her work.

Serena's ePortfolio is also a good example of how students work to use the digital possibilities of the ePortfolio. Each of her final drafts is illustrated. She selected images from the online photograph archive Morguefile and learned how to cite them. Images and digital representations of students form an important visual rhetoric in ePortfolios. She chose to use seventeen different thumbnail images of herself on her ePortfolio's welcome page, displaying herself in several different versions of her everyday life: as a student in jeans and a sweatshirt, in her native Nepali dress, in a headscarf and "Western" clothing, sitting while studying, and standing on the Staten Island Ferry. These images, coupled with her "About Me" introductory essay, allow her to shape the ePortfolio as a powerful autobiographical narrative, coupling her academic and personal life. She suggests that her experiences and prior education have an important place in her educational autobiography and that her previous life is not disconnected from her current academic and career goals. For Serena, and many other LaGuardia students, the ability to demonstrate many different sides of their personalities and identities is a key way in which the ePortfolio encourages the emerging authorship of the at-risk writer.

In the course of 12 short weeks, the students whose work is quoted here began to transform their relationship to writing, emerging as confident writers with a new sense of how they can translate their authority onto the page. For us, this represents the possibility of ePortfolios in the classroom. Basic writers emerge with a new relationship to the written word, understanding how and why writing can help them in their academic journeys. Additionally, this emerging sense of self is a significant step in our students' educational careers. All too often, the power of the individual voice is negated in a preference for facts and statistics. Students who have yet to learn the power of their own voices are told not to use them. Yet the power of story, the power of narrative, the compelling details of personal experience have always been what captures the imagination. Without the power of personal voice, leaders like Martin Luther King, Malcolm X, or Gloria Steinem wouldn't have begun their revolutions. This is our expectation: we push students to believe that their voices matter and they start to see their voices matter in public presentations of their writing. ePortfolio makes this possible as they engage in very public notions of writing in the classroom and on the Web.

Possible Classrooms: ePortfolios' Impact on the Basic Writing Classroom

DigiRhet.org points to a new digital divide involving "problems specific to digital literacies and rhetorical abilities. We see a divide where students may download complex, multimodal documents but lack the training to understand how to construct similar documents. . . . The new, emergent digital divide we will negotiate as teachers will be between those with and without access to the education and means to make use of multimodal civic rhetorics" (236). The ability to make meaning from these multimodal civic rhetorics, according to DigiRhet.org, will create a significant civic and social gulf. Without significant work in digital literacies, as outlined here, basic writers face double jeopardy. They will have the traditional markers and challenges of basic writers coupled with an inability to critically engage and produce in the digital medium. Just as literacy has always been linked to social, cultural, and economic power, so too does this new digital literacy mean access to our newest forms of cultural power. The digital divide is no longer about access to technology, but rather a more complex divide of those who have had the educational access, training, and critical engagement to use technology well as literate cyber-citizens. In our classrooms, we are aware that ePortfolios shape this kind of new writing instruction by engaging students in an awareness of digital literacies and the ways in which writing is both produced and owned traditionally and as we move forward into an increasingly digital world. Through ePortfolio and our use of other Web 2.0 technologies, our basic writing students, for whom writing has often been a means of punishment and restriction within the academic community, come to understand that writing can be a powerful means of social and cultural transformation. By using the ePortfolio as a platform for multimodal work in the basic writing course and for showcasing revision, we believe that we make visible the expectations of a digital culture and help our students to become proficient authors of a twenty-first century narrative.

Notes

1. All student work is used with permission and appears as the author submitted it. Although we have changed student names in this article, we have not edited student work for grammatical correctness or precision.
2. Although this does not make it into Serena's final draft of her reflective letter, we had several conversations about the fact that I [Liz] don't mark student papers in red ink. She was shocked when I asked her to pull out the paper. She literally didn't realize that the paper was marked in green. However, her reaction to seeing comments and marks on her paper was so overwhelming that she perceived the questions and comments on her paper as having been written in "red ink," a further testament to negative student perceptions of teacher authority.

Works Cited

Danielewicz, Jane. "Personal Genres, Public Voices." *College Composition and Communication* 59.3 (2008): 420–50. Print.

DigiRhet.org. "Teaching Digital Rhetoric: Community, Critical Engagement, and Application." *Pedagogy: Critical Approaches to Teaching Literature, Language, Composition, and Culture* 6.2 (2006): 231–59. Print.

Lenhart, Amanda, Sousan Arafeh, Aaron Smith, and Alexandra Rankin Macgill. "Writing, Technology and Teens." *Pew Internet and American Life Project.* Pew Research Center, 2008. Web. 24 Apr. 2009. <http://pewresearch.org/pubs/808/writing-technology-and-teens>.

LaGuardia Community College Institutional Profile. LaGuardia Community College. November 2008. Web. 29 May 2009. <http://www.laguardia.edu/facts/facts03/PDFs_profile/Complete.pdf>.

Palfrey, John, and Urs Gasser. *Born Digital: Understanding the First Generation of Digital Natives.* New York: Basic Books, 2008. Print.

Prensky, Marc. "Digital Natives, Digital Immigrants." *On the Horizon 9.5* (2001): 1–6. Print.

Rainie, Lee. "The State of Blogging." *Pew Internet and American Life Project.* Pew Research Center, 2005. Web. 24 Apr. 2009. <http://www.pewinternet.org/Reports/2005/The-State-of-Blogging.aspx>.

Yancey, Kathleen Blake. "Made Not Only in Words: Composition in a New Key." *College Composition and Communication* 56.2 (2004): 297–328. Print.

———. "Postmodernism, Palimpsest, and Portfolios: Theoretical Issues in the Representation of Student Work." *College Composition and Communication* 55.4 (2004): 738–61. Print.

6

Learning Academic English: Approaches to Grammar and Style

When Is a Verb? Using Functional Grammar to Teach Writing

Leif Fearn and Nancy Farnan

Leif Fearn and Nancy Farnan explain the significance of understanding functional grammar for development and improvement in writing. They discuss two different modes of writing instruction. The first instructional mode teaches grammar through identification, description, and definition (IDD) of parts of speech, and offers separate instruction in the writing process. The second mode presents how parts of speech function in students' writing, focusing especially on verbs, nouns, adjectives, dependent clauses, and independent clauses. Writing prompts (offered in Keeping Journals and Building a Course Archive on p. 473) related directly to how grammar functions in writing (emphasis in the original) and in the construction of sentences. For example, students learning functional grammar were instructed to "Write a nine-word sentence with the verb in the seventh position." As students wrote longer pieces, they were asked to become more conscious of verbs as they wrote, and to count their verbs when they had finished writing. Fearn and Farnan present details of their study comparing tenth-grade students taught functional grammar versus students taught IDD and writing process skills. They found that there was no difference between these groups' knowledge of grammar terminology. However, the students who learned functional grammar earned higher scores in holistically scored writing samples. Fearn and Farnan suggest that this difference can be attributed to the students "using grammar to think about writing."

Twenty years ago, Arthur Stern's article "When Is a Paragraph?" posed a revealing challenge to graduate-level Education students: identify the number of paragraphs into which a piece should be divided and show where the paragraph divisions should occur. Stern's students divided the 500-word essay into two, three, four, and five paragraphs, and provided credible justifications for their various paragraph arrangements, not all the same but logical, based on ideational shifts. At the same time, when Stern's English-teacher students self-reported their definitions of a paragraph, they presented a traditional view—a paragraph is a unit of discourse made of several sentences that develop a central idea around an identifiable topic sentence. In essence, their English-teacher conception of a paragraph was as a composition in miniature, based on structural design, rather than the ideational shifts that guided them in the exercise. Stern had uncovered a discrepancy between the operational understanding of the paragraph and student/ teacher beliefs about it.

This study is not about the paragraph; it is about the sentence. However, the disconnect that Stern found operating between definition— and function-based understandings of grammar is quite similar—a difference between how we understand grammar and how we teach it. We began with the premise, just as Stern might, that there is a mismatch between how we routinely *describe* something (in this case, a sentence) and approach instruction, and the operational reality of sentence grammar. We hypothesized that the operational reality is instructive to help students understand sentences and, more to the point, to write them more effectively.

Hillocks and Smith's review of the literature twenty years ago highlighted the idea that teaching grammar and grammatical structures does not enhance writing proficiency. However, we continue to teach traditional grammar definitions, and ask students to identify grammatical elements, under the guise of teaching writing. Descriptive knowledge is further entrenched in the curriculum because of its inclusion in high-stakes tests. The English language arts course of study includes, and will continue to include, grammar. Many teachers are trained for, and believe in, the grammar they teach. Tests feature it. Education policy-makers believe it belongs. It can be tested objectively. We would not claim that descriptive grammatical knowledge in itself is useless or nonproductive. However, we do argue that the ability to define and identify grammatical elements is not related to writing skills. Furthermore, contrary to Mellon's claim that grammar instruction does no harm, we would point out that time committed to descriptive and definitional grammar impedes the development of writing skills precisely because time committed to grammar is not available for writing.

We posed a question relative to grammar instruction which responds to a call by Hartwell for research questions in "more productive terms" (108). Our question focuses on how to articulate the grammar issue more productively: *Is there a way to teach grammatical structures that will satisfy high-stakes tests and teachers' needs, and at the same time, positively affect writing performance?* We looked pragmatically at what "productively" means. As we argue, the grammar we teach in school is not going away. Therefore, the research focus should be on how to satisfy the reasons for its existence, and, at the same time, help our students write better.

Definitions and Descriptions vs. Functions and Applications

Definition and Description

The verb is a useful place to begin, but we could just as well begin with nouns, adverbs, or adjectives, for the routine instructional approach is the same: identify, describe, define. For example, in 1979, Weaver states, "A verb is traditionally defined as a word that expresses action or a state of being or becoming" (*Grammar for Teachers* 111). Seventeen years later, Weaver's definition is essentially the same: "Traditionally, a verb is said to show action or a state of being" (*Teaching Grammar in Context* 258–59). The assumption is that a verb is a verb is always a verb.

Student handbooks are another good source for the descriptive tradition. Hacker tells students, "the verb in a sentence usually expresses action (*jump, think*) or being (*is, become*)" (267), and Raimes, "Verbs tell what a person, place, thing, or concept does or is, or what people, places, things, or concepts do or are: *smile, throw, think, seem, become, be*" (237). Mulderig tells readers, "verbs not only present an action or a condition, but also indicate a time frame within which that action or condition occurs — at present, in the past, in the future" (59). Gordon writes, "a verb is the momentum in the sentence. It asserts, moves, impels, reports on a condition or situation. What the verb asserts may be an action or an identity or a state of being" (18). Finally, in a grammar text for K–12 students, we have Carroll describing a verb as "a word that shows action or state of being" (87). In all the texts and handbooks we examined, the descriptive essence of "verb" changes little, save for adjustments in wording or phraseology. Carroll's description in 2001 is precisely the same, down to the word, as the one required on junior high grammar tests handed to students many years ago, for example as in the tests by Leif's junior high teacher, Miss Bessie Ott, in

1952. Miss Ott taught IDD grammar through endless diagramming exercises because she believed her instruction would make Leif and his seventh-grade classmates better writers. In 1952, she reflected what the profession knew. In 2007, we know better.

A Different View: It Is All in the Preposition

Does this all mean that we should not teach sentence parts any more? Of course not. What we know is that such instruction *for* writing wastes students' and teachers' time, and deludes both into believing they are doing something useful. The preposition is wrong. A different perspective would have us shift the preposition to sentence parts in writing, helping us reframe our productively oriented question: *Will teaching sentence parts in writing affect students' writing performance?* We recognize students' experience of grammar as traditional, tending toward the *descriptive*, that is, as young writers have been taught definitions, and that this knowledge has not influenced students' writing. In this study, we probed the influence on students' writing when teaching focused on how sentence parts *function*.

The second reason for what we taught and studied is that grammar instruction also tends to be separate from student writing, even when we claim it is in the context of writing. Typically, students learn grammatical elements in one portion of English language arts class, experience literature in another portion, and write in still another. Just as this practice flies in the face of modern instructional theory that calls for contextualized instruction, we acknowledge that much of what occurs in classrooms flies in the face of modern instructional theory.

Thus, the idea to feature *prescriptive* rather than *descriptive* instruction. Students wrote in the grammatical functions (i.e., prescriptions), studying them rather than defining them, and searching for them in what other people wrote. We studied the influence, if any, of functional instruction *in* the writing performance of tenth graders. And as we acknowledge the educational value in knowing sentence parts, we also tested students' knowledge of traditional grammar when the instruction occurred in functional context.

A Functional Perspective: The Verb We Taught

We asked tenth graders in two class periods, *What is a verb?* The response was immediate and consistent: "It shows action or state of being."

"What is an action word?"

Student: "Running."

We wrote a sentence on the board: *A horse is running around the track* and asked the student, or anyone else who wanted to respond, "What is the verb?

Student: "Running."

We wrote another sentence on the board: *Our new running track is rubberized* and asked for the verb.

Student: "Running."

When we asked what kind of track is around the new football field, they agreed it is rubberized. We asked how else they could describe the track. They said "new" and "red." We asked what people do on the track, and when they said kids run on it, we said that would make it a running track. They agreed. We asked what kind of word "track" is. Noun. "So what kind of word describes that noun?" we asked. They said "running." We asked if "running" could be the verb if it is a describing word for the noun "track."

They looked as though they had just been told the earth is flat. We asked what we call a word that does what "running" does in that sentence. Another student said it has to be an adjective, but the -ing at the end shows action so it has to be a verb. We asked if "running" acts like an adjective, what would be the verb? Still another student knew the answer. She said it has to be "is" because it shows a state of being.

These tenth graders were quick with the opening definition, but not because they were special; they were merely well-schooled in the definitions of sentence parts. They knew the definition of verb in the second grade and were reminded of it in every grade thereafter. By the middle of the tenth grade, they had "action and state of being" taught, reinforced, and tested for nine years. They had it cold. They didn't understand it, they couldn't use it, they couldn't apply it, and, therefore, it was of no use to them when they talked, read, wrote, or, for that matter, answered questions from someone who didn't stick to the script. But our script was functions, not definitions and descriptions. Function identifies verbs as they occur in sentences, not lists. "Running" is an adjective in the sentence because it does what adjectives do; "is" is a verb because it does what verbs do.

Some may argue that "running" is not an adjective in the sentence; rather, it is part of a hyphenated noun (*running-track*) and is, therefore, more gerund in the sentence than adjective. And all of the students in that tenth grade who grow up to be linguists or English teachers will have to grapple with that distinction. On that day, in that classroom, there were a couple dozen fifteen-year-olds who didn't understand what a verb is, or an adjective, because they depended on definitions. Rather than confuse them further with a new definition (gerund), we took all their definitions away.

We went back to our sentence and asked for words that fit between "new" and "track," and as they called out words, we wrote them in a column between "new" and "track." They suggested "fast," "red," "pretty," "bigger," "spongy," "lined."

Teachers: "Do you know what these words are?"

Student: "They're describing words. Adjectives."

Teachers: "Why?"

Student: "Because they tell about the noun."

Teachers: "Yes, maybe, but the best answer is that they are adjectives because they fit in that hole between "new" and "track." Any word you put in there will describe the track, so it will do the work of an adjective. And verbs? Think of words instead of 'is' for the sentence."

They suggested "was, will be, used to be, can be." They laughed. We agreed it is funny to think about the kinds of words that do certain work in sentences rather than to try to identify words by dictionary definitions. Our lesson on verbs allowed us to offer, "We are going to do something different here for several weeks."

Methodology

Sample

Treatment and control students attended an urban high school. In this overcrowded high school of 2,300 students, the average student scores below grade level in both reading and mathematics, and research shows that score patterns in reading and mathematics hold for writing as well (Smagorinsky 55). The school's average student tests in the lowest 10% of all high school students in the state. Year to year, an average of 65% of the school's students are classified as limited English proficient, and nearly 100% are eligible for free or reduced lunch. Forty percent of the adult residents in the larger neighborhood have not graduated from high school; 5% have graduated from college. The demographics seem to signify a complex teaching/learning situation.

For five weeks, for ten to twelve minutes twice a week, on Mondays and Wednesdays, one of the investigators (both university professors who work regularly in K–12 classrooms) conducted intentional instruction (Fearn and Farnan *Interactions* 74) of grammar *in* writing in each of two treatment classes. On Tuesdays and Thursdays, the classroom teacher followed upon the Monday/Wednesday instruction with eight to ten minutes of review and writing practice in the grammatical elements. Thus, students received approximately twenty-two minutes of intentional instruction and eighteen minutes of guided practice during each of the five weeks of the treatment for approximately two hundred minutes of instruction. A similar amount of time was committed to traditional grammar instruction in a control group of tenth graders in the same school.

All three classes contained twenty-four to twenty-six tenth graders who worked on a similar grammar unit: noun, verb, adjective, dependent clause, and independent clause. Immediately prior to the initial instructional session, we collected a cued and timed writing sample from all three classes (see Appendix A). In the same session, all students responded to test items that covered several grammatical items and structures. This test included eighteen items (see Appendix B). The pre-grammar test was administered to establish equivalency among the three groups.

The Process: Teaching Grammar in Writing

The instructional emphases in the two treatment classes were function and writing. Function refers to what a grammatical element *does* in a sentence. To the extent that definitions were used at all, they were functional.

Basic function instruction in the two treatment classes was limited to ten to fifteen minutes throughout the five weeks because in most instances, we did precisely what we did with verbs in the rubberized running track example, for the same reason—to replace the definitions with roles and functions. The preponderance of the treatment emphasized writing. For example, following the verb-in-rubberized-running-track opener explained earlier, we posed a thinking and writing task. *Select one of the verbs on the list and write a sentence in your mind that uses that word as a verb.* They all started scrambling for paper in their backpacks. We stopped the action. *Forget the paper and pens. Think of a sentence and write it in your mind.* We used the oral foundation of writing (Fearn and Farnan *Interactions* 79). *Now think of a sentence in which one of the words on the list appears as a verb.* We listened to several mental sentences read aloud, e.g., *The old track* used to have *dirt and cinders. The new track* will be great *to run on. Rubberized tracks* are *better.*

We posed another sentence-thinking and -writing prompt. *Think of a six-word sentence in which another of the words on the list appears as a verb* (Fearn and Farnan *Interactions* 87–95). Several hands went up to share. We waited until about half of the students indicated they had a sentence. *Write your sentence on your paper. You have one minute.* We listened to several read aloud, e.g., *Our old track* was *really bad. I* like *our new track now. The new track* can be *great.* They all read sentences. We expected to have to help someone make a revision to accomplish a sentence, but there were no nonsentences read aloud. It is rare, in our experience, that students write nonsentences when sentence-writing prompts direct students to think in an explicit manner.

We posed the next prompt in the series. *Think of an eight-word sentence in which one of the words on the list appears as a verb in the fifth position.* When a student posed a question about two-word verbs, we assured everyone that they could consider their verb as one word for this activity. We directed them to write their sentence on paper and to read aloud. We commented occasionally. One student wrote, *"A yellow spotted bird will be in its nest."* We asked why he wrote *yellow spotted* instead of *spotted yellow.* He said because it just seemed better to say *yellow spotted.* We made a pronouncement to the class. *During the sessions when we are here teaching grammar, you may trust your instincts about what seems right. If we hear it differently, we will explain why and help you understand how we hear it.*

When our pre-service teacher candidates saw one of the videos from our sessions in those classes, several expressed indignation. *Why do you say that your instinct is the one they have to learn; is not their instinct just as valuable as yours?* We explained that a fundamental part of any language instruction is to value and capitalize on the "internal" grammar (Hartwell) that students bring with them, their sense of how language works. Of course, their sense is not always conventional. It is teachers' responsibility to help students recognize how distinctions between students' internal grammar and the attributes of convention work. Usually, those distinctions become most clear in oral language.[1]

Our instructional scenario about verbs consumed two sessions. The sentence-thinking and -writing tasks varied greatly, but they stayed focused on using verbs intentionally in sentences. Before changing the focus to nouns, we prompted writing beyond a single sentence. We used "Short Cues" (Fearn and Farnan *Interactions* 230) at least weekly throughout the treatment. An example of a Short Cue is Power Writing (Fearn *Thinking for Teaching* 124; Fearn and Farnan *Interactions* 167–69),where the focus is fluency (Fearn "Individual Development" 55–64; Guilford 444–54) and promotes automaticity (Fearn and Farnan *Interactions* 27–28). We wrote two words on the board (*mosquito—taxi*), directed each student to *select one of the two, and use it as the topic about which to write as much as you can as well as you can. Oh, and include as many verbs as you can.* At exactly one minute, we called time, directed them to count their words, and recorded their totals on a chart on the board (Fearn and Farnan *Interactions* 168). We called that *round one.* We directed *rounds two* and *three,* each time with a different pair of cue words, each time one-minute writes, and each time telling them to include as many verbs as they could. After *round two,* we asked them to count their verbs, as well. We didn't record the number of verbs; we cared only that students were thinking about verbs as they wrote.

Over the remaining four weeks, we moved very quickly through the grammatical elements. We taught noun, verb, adjective, and dependent and independent clause. We remained within the limits of what the control teacher taught in the five-week unit.

Teaching Grammar Traditionally

In another class during the same five-week period, an English teacher on the other side of the school campus taught grammar to demographically similar tenth graders. He agreed to cooperate with every aspect of the study, confident in the appropriateness of what he taught and how. He taught nouns, verbs, adjectives, and dependent and independent clauses during the five-week period of the study. His students read aloud daily and responded to his identification questions that focused on nouns, verbs, adjectives, and both dependent and independent clauses. He led his students through identification worksheets that contained sentences he wrote and others he cut from literature anthologies and pasted onto worksheets. He supplied cloze procedure worksheets that contained sentences with missing nouns, verbs, and adjectives so students could write the words they thought made the best sense into the blanks. In most class sessions, his students edited prepared sentences to make nouns and verbs agree, and completed nonsentences (dependent clauses) by adding independent clauses. They also wrote extended discourse every day, following writing process stages depicted on a wall chart. The control class used the entire forty-seven minute period for grammar instruction and process writing, partly because the writing they did took so much more time than did the treatment students' writing, and partly because the worksheet activities were so time-intensive.

Data Collection

Having established general grammar knowledge equivalency between the two treatment groups and between the treatment groups and the control group before the treatment began (see Table 4), the post-test included grammar applications as well as writing. There were seven items on the grammar applications test, each beginning with the stem: "Write a sentence . . ." Item one read "Write a sentence that contains exactly two nouns, one of which is modified by a prepositional phrase" (see Appendix C).

Pre- and post-writing samples were scored both analytically and with a general impression rubric (see Appendix D). Analytic scoring quantified fluency and mechanical control (Fearn and Farnan, *Interactions* 343). General impression scoring (G-score) occurred on a six-point scale in consideration of four attributes: the writing is on-point, elaborative, organized, and textured (for example, figurative language). The six-point general impression scale is absolute; that is, a 1 is rudimentary, no matter students' grade level, ethnicity, primary language, or socioeconomic class, and a 6 is as well as the piece is likely to be written by an experienced writer.

The writing samples reflected first-draft writing. While anecdotal criticism of assessing first-draft and teacher-prompted writing was not lost on the authors, we used first-draft writing in the absence of empirical evidence of an interaction between writing quality and the source of writing prompt (Hidi and McLaren 187–97). The writing samples were also timed at five minutes, again in the absence of evidence of any interaction between writing quality and available time. In fact, a contrary conclusion relative to prompt-source and time appears more sound.[2]

We scored the writing samples analytically and independently in a double-blind procedure, having had a colleague mix the treatment and control grammar tests and writing samples. Inter-rater reliability on analytic scoring is traditionally very high, given that the analytic protocol is largely objective. In this study it was 97%.

Three trained raters conducted the general impression scoring. Inter-rater reliability on G-scoring was 96%. Finally, the seven-item grammar test was scored by the investigators. Because each item on the grammar test was clearly correct or incorrect, there was no need to cross-check the scoring process.

Results

What is the effect of teaching grammar *in* writing rather than *for* writing? Results show that the effect, as measured by both writing performance and grammar application, is two-fold. Students in the treatment groups demonstrated enhanced writing performance, while students in treatment and control groups showed no difference in their knowledge of grammatical elements in the testing situation. Table 1 shows the pre- and post-writing effects using a holistic rubric in both treatment and control groups.

Treatment students in both Periods 1 and 2 wrote significantly better on the post-writing sample based on the holistic (G-score) criterion. While the instructional emphasis in the treatment classes was writing, i.e., teaching grammatical elements *in* writing, the control teacher also emphasized writing. Control students wrote extended discourse every day, always following a process writing protocol. In fact, control

Table 1. Pre-Writing and Post-Writing G-scores

	Pre-Writing Scores			Post Writing Scores		
	Mean	*SD*	*P value*	*Mean*	*SD*	*P Value**
Treatment Class: Period 1 N=18	2.94	.938	P < .621	3.61	1.09	**P < .002**
Control Class N=18	2.78	1.06		2.61	.698	
Treatment Class: Period 2 N=21	2.95	.805	P < .563	3.48	.928	**P < .003**
Control Class N=18	2.78	1.06		2.61	.698	

*Bold face indicates significant differences between treatment and control groups.

Table 2. Frequency of Post-writing Sample G Scores

G-Scores	Treatment Group (Period 1)	Control Group
5	1	0
4	3	3
3	11	7
2	7	10
1	0	0

students wrote more each day (extended discourse) than treatment students, who wrote directed sentences each day in response to grammar-driven prompts, and additional extended discourse at least weekly, though never more than twice per week. The evidence appears to show that grammar instruction and process writing, as two distinct activities, though occurring during the same instructional period, do not positively influence the quality of writing performance as powerfully as does directed writing practice driven by grammar content. It is not the grammar instruction, then, nor the process writing; rather, the more powerful influence on student writing comes from *directed writing*, where students' attention is focused on using grammar to think about writing. This is what grammar *in* writing appears to accomplish.

Another way to look at the post-test differences is to compare the holistic scores themselves (see Table 2) and look at sample papers as exemplars (see Appendix E).

In the treatment group Period 1, fifteen writing samples were scored at 3 or above, while in the control group, only ten scored in that range, with no paper receiving the highest score of 5. In other words, five fewer papers received an average score or above in the control group, with three more papers scoring below the average possible score. Exemplary papers from treatment and control students show what the scores tend to mean in the students' writing.

Analytic scores showed remarkable post-writing sample stability among the three groups with respect to fluency and mechanical control (see Table 3), where fluency refers to the number of words written in five minutes, and mechanical control refers to average number of errors per sentence (i.e., punctuation, capitalization, spelling, tense agreements).

While more is not necessarily better when it comes to writing, young writers tend to become more fluent over time—with increasing practice and expertise. That is the case with these students in both

Table 3. Pre- and Post-writing Sample Data on Fluency and Mechanical Control

	Fluency Pre-Test	Fluency Post-Test	Mechanical Control Pre-Test	Mechanical Control Post-Test
Period 1 Treatment Group	75.6	93.1	1.3	1.3
Period 2 Treatment Group	64.5	88.0	1.6	1.3
Control Group	62.4	88.1	1.3	1.2

treatment and control groups. Interestingly, their error rates per sentence are not only stable from pre- to post-test, they are also stable between treatment and control classes. Neither instructional procedure influenced writing fluency, positively or negatively. The tenth graders' ability to generate ideas and produce text that explicated those ideas was neither enhanced nor compromised by the mode of instruction, either traditional/descriptive or functional/grammar-driven writing instruction. Likewise, neither mode of instruction seemed to influence students' use of mechanics and the conventions of written text. Even the seeming difference in the treatment group Period 2 (1.6 errors per sentence) represents, on the average, only two additional errors in every ten sentences.

To summarize, the grammar-driven writing instruction enhanced writing performance as measured by holistic criteria, while traditional grammar instruction, separate from writing instruction, did not influence writing performance. Furthermore, the more traditional grammar instruction had no greater influence on students' error rate than did the grammar-driven writing instruction that was not directed at reducing error rate. And neither form of grammar instruction was superior with regard to students' fluency, not even in the control class where "process" writing emphasized ideational fluency during prewriting.

Part of this investigation was grammar knowledge itself. The evidence appears to show that time committed to grammar instruction need not compromise students' writing development, if grammar is taught in the context of writing, as part of writing instruction, but what about students' grammar knowledge? Table 4 shows differences in student performance on the grammar test.

Results show no significant differences between treatment and control students, in either of the two comparisons (treatment 1 vs. control and treatment 2 vs. control), at either pre- or post-testing. The students were equivalent when the investigation began, and they were equivalent when it was finished. The formal, more traditional, grammar instruction in the control class did not produce significantly

Table 4. Pre- and Post-Test Scores on the Grammar Test

	Pre-Writing Scores			Post Writing Scores		
	Mean	SD	P value	Mean	SD	P Value*
Treatment Class: Period 1 N=18	3.67	2.03	P < .492	4.00	2.14	P < .324
Control Class N=18	3.17	2.28		4.72	2.19	
Treatment Class: Period 2 N=21	3.05	2.01	P < .863	4.00	2.35	P < .330
Control Class N=18	3.17	2.28		4.72	2.19	

superior grammar test performance for control students. If the ability to define, identify, and use sentence parts (parts of speech) is the objective, then grammar-driven writing and formal grammar study appear to be equally influential. Teaching grammar *in* writing had a similar effect on grammar knowledge as did the more traditional grammar *for* writing. This research suggests that there is a critical difference in the two approaches to grammar instruction. The emphasis on writing did not compromise grammar knowledge, but it did enhance overall writing performance.

In addition, in every comparison, fluency was neither enhanced nor compromised by the form of instruction. Neither was error rate reduced or increased due to the form of grammar instruction. Whether teaching grammar *in* writing or *for* writing, students in treatment and control classes performed equally well on grammar knowledge.

Conclusions

Is there a way to teach grammatical structures that will satisfy high-stakes tests and teachers' needs, and at the same time, positively affect writing performance? Evidence from this research indicates there is. Take the two purposes in turn.

High-stakes grammar tests reinforce the ability to define and identify. We may not agree that define-and-identify is grammar, but that is what students must do to perform well on today's achievement tests. Define-and-identify is also what many teachers value. But define-and-identify is just as likely what most teachers know because they have rarely seen grammar as a branch of study within linguistics and an area within linguistics that focuses on the organization and reorganization of words and inflections to construct larger meaning (Francis 223), and how that occurs, in this case, in American English.

The evidence in this investigation indicates that if students think deliberately about how sentences are constructed, and the prompt for their thinking is grammatical terminology, they learn to define and identify as well as do students who study define-and-identify in isolation. The reason why is likely more cognitive than linguistic. While it is possible to work with definitions and attributes without attending deliberately to the content and function those definitions and attributes describe and organize, it is impossible to fail to deliberately attend when the content and function are embedded in a writing task. We can do most things in school with our attention elsewhere, but few people can write while thinking of something else. It is probably the deliberate attention (Neisser 90–91), mobilized when students must focus on both verb and verbness, over and over, every time "verb" is used as a sentence-thinking and sentence-writing prompt, that promotes verb learning. For these tenth graders, it was used every day, over and over, with noun, verb, adjective, and dependent clause.

The power of functional grammar instruction is seen in treatment students' performance on the grammar test. Treatment students equaled control students' test scores, even though they did not have formal grammar instruction of the traditional type. What treatment students received was a functional "definition" ("It's a verb because it fits in the verb hole and does what verbs do"), and then they wrote scores of sentences prompted by verbs ("Write a nine-word sentence with a verb in the seventh position"). Five weeks of that was sufficiently powerful for them to perform as well as their control peers who learned definition and identification in traditional form.

That there is no discernible difference in effect relative to grammar for the two groups documents the power of using grammar *in* writing, where grammar is used as the prompting device, rather than *for* writing on the assumption that grammar is supposed to transfer to writing. It does not transfer (Hillocks and Smith). Grammar instruction influences writing performance when grammar and writing share one instructional context. The field of *situated cognition* rests on the proposition that the context in which something is learned is fundamental to its application (Brown, Collins, and Duguid 32–42). When grammar is taught and learned in a define-and-identify context, that becomes the context in which the grammar can be applied. So we find students who can identify and define verbs but do not use verbs adroitly when they write because they did not learn verbs in sentence thinking and writing. When we see verbs used badly, or not at all, in sentence writing, we teach verbs, again, and then we teach the writing, again. The general impression (holistic) scores reflect the significance of the differences between treatment and control students' writing performance.

Teaching grammar *in* writing rather than *for* writing, over a relatively short treatment time, five weeks, resulted in both superior writing and equal grammar test scores for treatment students in a four-attribute rubric. We draw several important conclusions from these results.

- One: Writing can be the context when we teach grammar. We can use writing to teach the grammar we want to teach.

- Two: Traditional grammar instruction did not affect error rate; both groups committed about an equal number of errors when they wrote.

- Three: If the purpose of grammar instruction is to satisfy standards and prepare for high-stakes testing, we can teach sentence parts and enhance students' writing at the same time without compromising either. The instruction about adjectives, for example, focused on the function of adjectives in sentences, so students learned to understand adjectives' purpose and to use them properly when they wrote sentences. Moreover, the learning transferred to writing itself, for holistic scores were heavily affected by elaboration (i.e., modification and qualification).

Shall we teach grammar? Of course. This study does not call into question grammar instruction; it calls into question how we teach grammar. It shows how a certain kind of grammar study establishes grammar knowledge as it positively affects writing performance. If the point is writing, perhaps it is reasonable to ask why teach grammar at all? We think the reason is similar to the reason why we teach the Periodic Table of Elements in chemistry. The table is not chemistry, and knowledge of the table does not make chemists. But the table is chemistry's taxonomy, its explanation, its elemental foundation. The table provides a context for the content. Music has a taxonomy, as well, and while mastery of the taxonomy does not make musicians, it is a rare musician who functions without it. It is a rare chemist whose background does not include mastery of the taxonomy.

It is a rare writer, novice or expert, whose background does not include the taxonomy, the grammar. We do not mean that writers know the definitions. We mean that writers have to be able to rub nouns and verbs together when they write, and rub nouns and verbs together with modifiers and qualifiers to enhance meaning, so images and ideas emerge in readers' minds and souls. We mean that grammar is the terminology of syntactic concepts, the words and ideas for talking about sentences. Grammar knowledge is the elemental foundation for writing. Certainly we should teach grammar, *in* writing, so learners understand better how the language works, and *functionally*, so learners can use what they understand about language when they write.

Notes

1. There is evidence to show young writers write well, or not well, because that is how they write, irrespective of whether or not they selected their topic or dictated their writing time (Fearn and Farnan "Writing Instruction"; "Writing on Demand").
2. There is a sizeable literature on interactions between oral language and writing (Sperling 53–86).

Works Cited

Brown, John S., Allan Collins, and Paul Duguid. "Situated Cognition and the Culture of Learning." *Educational Researcher* 18 (1989): 32–42. Print.

Carroll, Joyce A. *Writing and Grammar: Communication in Action.* Upper Saddle River: Prentice Hall, 2001. Print.

Fearn, Leif. *Teaching for Thinking.* San Diego: Kabyn Books, 1980. Print.

———. "Individual Development: A Process Model in Creativity." *Journal of Creative Behavior* 10 (1976): 55–64. Print.

Fearn, Leif, and Nancy Farnan. *Interactions: Teaching Writing and the Language Arts.* Boston: Houghton Mifflin, 2001. Print.

———. "Writing Instruction: Theories and Responsibilities." *California English* 8 (2003): 13–15. Print.

———. "Writing on Demand: The Influence of Time." *California English* 11 (2005): 6–7. Print.

Francis, Nelson. *The Structure of American English.* New York: The Ronald Press, 1958. Print.

Gordon, Karen E. *The Deluxe Transitive Vampire: The Ultimate Handbook of Grammar for the Innocent, the Eager, and the Doomed.* New York: Pantheon Books, 1993. Print.

Guilford, J. P. "Creativity." *American Psychologist* 5 (1950): 444–54. Print.

Hacker, Diana. *A Writer's Reference, Second Edition.* Boston: Bedford Books of St. Martin's Press, 1992. Print.

Hartwell, Patrick. "Grammar, Grammars, and the Teaching of Grammar." *College English* 47 (1985): 105–27. Print.

Hidi, Suzanne, and John A. McLaren. "Motivation Factors in Writing: The Role of Topic Interestingness." *European Journal of Psychology of Education* 6 (1991): 187–97. Print.

Hillocks, George, and Michael J. Smith. "Grammar." *Research on Written Composition: New Directions for Teaching.* Urbana, IL: Educational Resources, 1986. 134–41. Information Center and National Council on Research in English. Print.

Mellon, John C. "A Taxonomy of Compositional Competencies." *Perspectives on Literacy.* Ed. Richard Beach and P. David Pearson. Minneapolis: University of Minnesota College of Education, 1979. 247–72. Print.

Mulderig, Gerald P. *The Heath Guide to Grammar and Usage.* Lexington, MA: D.C. Heath, 1995. Print.

National Assessment of Educational Progress. *The Nation's Report Card: Writing 2002.* Washington, DC: National Center for Educational Statistics, 2002. Print.

Neisser, Uric. *Cognition and Reality: Principles and Implications of Cognitive Psychology.* San Francisco: W. H. Freeman, 1976. Print.

Noguchi, Rei R. *Grammar and the Teaching of Writing.* Urbana, IL: National Council of Teachers of English, 1991. Print.

Raimes, Ann. *Keys for Writers: A Brief Handbook, Second Edition.* Boston: Houghton Mifflin, 1999. Print.

Smagorinsky, Peter, ed. *Research on Composition: Multiple Perspectives on Two Decades of Change.* New York: Teachers College P, 2006. Print.

Sperling, Melanie. "Revisiting the Writing-Speaking Connection: Challenges for Research on Writing and Writing Instruction." *Review of Educational Research* 66 (1966): 53–86. Print.

Stern, Arthur S. "When Is a Paragraph?" *College Composition and Communication* 27 (1976): 109–13. Print.

Weaver, Connie. *Grammar for Teachers: Perspectives and Definitions.* Urbana, IL: NCTE, 1979. Print.

———. *Teaching Grammar in Context.* Portsmouth: Boynton/Cook, 1996. Print.

Appendix A

Direct Writing Assessment

Writing assessment takes two forms: analytic to inform instruction, and G-score to better inform students and the larger public. This assessment will score for both forms, and that is the reason for the following directions. The assessment must control for both task and time. Students must write to the same prompt and for the same amount of time.

There is a belief that if students are to write as well as they are able, they should select their topics and write for as long as they feel necessary. This belief, while widely held, enjoys little or no confirming evidence. In fact, students write about as well as they are able when they write, irrespective of time or prompt. They write well because they can.

Please follow these directions to ensure equivalence.

1. Everyone has a sheet of paper and a writing implement, preferably 8 ½ × 11 lined paper and dark lead or ink.

2. You will write as much as you can, as well as you can, for five minutes. Think of a place where you feel comfortable, safe, at ease. It could be inside or outside, a park, a room. It could be that you feel most comfortable in the company of friends or family. This is probably a place to which you return often because it feels good. Think about that place, what is there, and why you selected it. Write as much as you can as well as you can about that place. You have five minutes. Go.

3. At exactly five minutes, students should stop and count their words. They write the word-count at the top of the paper and turn in the papers.

Appendix B

Grammar Pre-Assessment

In the following sentences, underline the **subject** once and the **verb** twice.

1. Running across the lawn, the excited puppy raced to greet his owner.

2. I would like to go to the next Olympic Games.

3. Are you going to the birthday party?

4. Ellie fell over the toys and landed on her sore shoulder.

5. After dinner, we saw a movie about the life of a brilliant mathematician.

6. In some neighborhoods, people do not know the names of their neighbors.

7. My favorite book is *Harry Potter and the Sorcerer's Stone*.

8. The weatherman predicted heavy rain through the evening.

In the following sentences, underline each **adjective** once, each **adverb** twice, and put an X over each **pronoun**.

9. Running across the lawn, the excited puppy raced to greet his owner.

10. I would like to go to the next Olympic Games.

11. Are you going to the birthday party?

12. Ellie fell over the toys and landed on her sore shoulder.

13. After dinner, we saw a movie about the life of a brilliant mathematician.

14. In some neighborhoods, people do not know the names of their neighbors.

15. My favorite book is *Harry Potter and the Sorcerer's Stone*.

16. The weatherman predicted heavy rain through the evening.

Appendix C

Grammar Applications

Name: _____   Date: _____

1. Write a sentence that contains exactly two nouns, one of which is modified by a prepositional phrase.

2. Write a sentence that contains two pronouns, one of which is neither male or female.

3. Write a sentence that contains a verb that does not end in "ing" or "ed," and use a prepositional phrase to modify your verb.

4. Write a sentence that contains an adjective and an adverb, but the adverb is not the last word in the sentence.

5. Write a sentence in which the subject is "old shoes."

6. Write a complex sentence in which the first word is "because."

7. Write a sentence that uses "but" to connect two independent clauses.

Appendix D

G-score Rubric

This rubric generates a G-score that transcends analytic scores. The rubric features four attributes of good writing.

- The writing is on-point. The writing focuses on the prompt or the requirement.

- The writing is elaborative. There are descriptive elements and explanations such as, "It is a hot and sunny day so the sun is shining brightly in the blue sky." And "I feel the cool water on my toes."

- The writing is organized/sequenced: There is a recognizable system of organization in the paper.

- The writing contains relevant extensions (texture). The rubric gives credit for figurative statements such as, "When you look at the grass and the sun's reflection on it, the shine in your eyes is like if you saw a silver coin on the ground."

Mechanical control is not scored in this rubric unless the writing is so far out of control that the four primary attributes are severely compromised.

Score each sample on an absolute **6-point scale**. "Absolute" means "as well as the paper can be written." Fully literate writing would be scored a 6. In this rubric, good writing is scored 4–5–6; poorer writing is scored 1–2–3.

Appendix E

Sample Exemplars

These writing samples appear exactly as drafted in response to the prompt (favorite place) and in exactly five minutes from statement of the prompt to pencils down and papers collected.

Treatment, Score 5

I would like to have a house in a tropical land. I want to feel the fresh air go threw my window and blow my air to the sides. I want to go to the river and swim when it's hot. I want to heard the small birds sing when I wake up. And I want to see the beautiful green leaves that are outside. Also on special occasions I want to go outside and take a bunch of flowers to give to special someone. I want to feel free to scream and I want at night camp outside make a small fire and eat marshmallows. I want a clam place where I don't have to think about my problems. I want a place where I can relax and grow old but happy. I want my house in a tropical island. But until then I'm going to enjoy my life in the city where I am allowed to work and worry about other things.

Treatment, Score 4

I'm singing in the choir stand and I'm, singing one of the songs we sing every time we practice on Thursdays "Oh Magnify the Lord." It was the first thing that popped into my head because I love tossing. Another place that I went in my head is when I write in my poetry book journal and it doesn't matter where I'm at because I write wherever, whenever. It is so relaxing and peaceful to me. It is the best time to think, especially when it's quiet and peaceful and it makes me happy.

Treatment, Score 3

My favorite place is a place where nobody can be except me, which is my closet it like a little room where there's light. I don't lave a lot of things in this closet so there's a lot of space for me to sit. Well in this closet I get a lot of ideas of what to do during the weekend and I also like this place because I have my own stars to where I could look which even day I would like to even in the day. These stars are glow in the dark stars.

Treatment, Score 2

The place I'm describing is a place from Mexico is a street. around that street there is a big building all around you on the walls of the street ther's grafitti everywhere all over the walls of the buildings. Friends all over the place drawing more pictures, sketing, drinking or dancing.

Control, Score 4

The majestic blue water slaps the Shore line ever so softly. While the sun reflects perfectly of the ocean. The Sand warm, with my towle in a perfect rectangle. I am in a place of comfort and total relaxation. A bare beach except for me and the few palm trees that layed scattered in irregular spots of grass. I smell the animals salty bodies threw the gentle breezes of the water.

Control, Score 3

I like to go to my Aunts house. She lives in Los Angeles. The reason why I like going over there is because it's a nice place to think & relax. When you tire you could just lay there and no one will bother you.

Control, Score 2

My favorite place would be my old school. I went there for 3 years and one semester. I grew up there. I had to change schools. That is one of my favorite places in the whole world. I always go when I have a chance.

That school is my most favorite place in the world.

Making a Case for Rhetorical Grammar

Laura R. Micciche

Laura Micciche presents pedagogy for studying grammar rhetorically, by analyzing how and why texts are constructed through syntax and punctu-ation for specific audiences, purposes, and contexts. In conceptualizing grammar as a rhetorical choice, Micciche argues, we move beyond prescrip-tive "drill-and-kill" lessons that divorce the study of grammar from an understanding of the writing process. Indeed, advice that students focus on grammar only during revision ignores important opportunities for learning to read closely and think critically about language and its uses. Drawing on the work of Kolln and Lazere, Micciche argues that rhetorical grammar can serve as a liberatory pedagogy as well. She presents two major activities that introduce students to the possibilities of rhetorical grammar: large group discussions of texts that focus on how writers use grammar and style to help shape audience; and commonplace books in which students analyze a passage for rhetorical uses of grammar and style, and then imitate the style, but not the content of the passage, in their own writing. Examples of students' writing throughout Micciche's article dem-onstrate the ways in which these rhetorical grammar activities work in classroom practice.

Grammar makes people anxious, even—perhaps especially—writing teachers. Just as writing teachers dread when, our iden-tities discovered, strangers announce that they had better "watch their grammar," we also recoil at the idea of teaching grammar, often con-sidered a mind-numbing pedagogical task that offends our rhetorical sensibilities. In composition studies, grammar instruction is unques-tionably unfashionable. It is frequently associated with "low-skills" courses that stigmatize and alienate poor writers while reproducing their status as disenfranchised. This association emerges naturally from teaching methods that present grammar as a fix-it approach to weak writing rather than, as Martha Kolln describes, "a rhetorical tool that all writers should understand and control" (*Rhetorical Grammar* xi). As a result, students' understanding of the tight weave between what we say and how we say it often gets short shrift as we reserve in-struction on grammar for the very final stage of drafting.

In composition's disciplinary discourse (and perhaps in practice, though it's hard to know), teaching grammar and teaching writing are separate enterprises. While teaching style, the "extraordinary" use of language, is a familiar enough focus in disciplinary scholarship, teach-ing the "ordinary" use of language—grammar—is often constructed as ineffective because, it is widely believed, grammar knowledge out of context doesn't translate to grammatical correctness in context.[1] Fur-ther complicating the problematic place of grammar in writing instruction is the matter of what *kind* of grammar we're talking about. Often *grammar* is used in a way that assumes we all understand and agree upon its meaning—and, in fact, grammar referred to loosely seems to signify traditional "school grammar" and its focus on repetitive, decontextualized, drill-and-kill exercises. However, grammar has a range of referents (i.e., prescriptive, descriptive, rhetorical) that describe very different kinds of intellectual activities, differences that matter tremendously. These differences evaporate, reducing the issue of grammar instruction to a rather simple rejection of a banal practice, when we fail to specify just what kind of grammar we're rejecting.

My aim in this paper is to establish grounds for teaching grammar rhetorically and for linking this pedagogical effort to larger goals of emancipatory teaching. Teaching grammar is not *necessarily* incompatible with liberatory principles; binaries that suggest otherwise constrain our teaching and our thinking, solidifying and casting as unquestionable rehearsed assumptions about writing. The absence of a sustained contemporary conversation about grammar instruction at the college level does not eclipse the practical reality that nearly every writing teacher struggles with at one time or another: how to teach students to communicate effectively. And effective communication, which entails grammar knowledge, is essential to achieving many of the goals regularly articulated in composition studies. Chief among them are teaching students to produce effective writing that has some relevancy to the world we live in, to see language as having an empowering and sometimes transformative potential, and to critique normalizing discourses that conceal oppressive functions.

Rhetorical grammar instruction, I argue here, is just as central to composition's driving commitment to teach critical thinking and cultural critique as is reading rhetorically, understanding the significance of cultural difference, and engaging in community work through service-learning initiatives. Yet, teaching students grammar skills is rarely associated with the political programs that characterize our disciplinary rhetoric and is seldom linked with rhetorical education or the practice of cultural critique. Grammar instruction, in short, is decidedly not sexy but school-marmish, not empowering but disempowering, not rhetorical but decontextualized, not progressive but remedial.

I hope this study of rhetorical grammar will contribute to our collective thinking about the work of rhetorical education, its possibility and its promise. Donald Bryant, in "Rhetoric: Its Functions and Its Scope," offers an instructive description of the need for rhetorical education:

> If enlightened and responsible leaders with rhetorical knowledge and skill are not trained and nurtured, irresponsible demagogues will monopolize their power of rhetoric, will have things to themselves. If talk rather than take is to settle the course of our society, if ballots instead of bullets

> are to effect our choice of governors, if discourse rather than coercion is
> to prevail in the conduct of human affairs, it would seem like arrant folly
> to trust to chance that the right people shall be equipped offensively and
> defensively with a sound rationale of informative and suasory discourse.
> (291)

The construction of "informative and suasory" discourse includes knowing one's audience, responding appropriately to a particular situation,
and drawing on relevant examples and illustrations. As I suggest here,
it also requires an ability to communicate effectively, using grammatical devices that enable us to respond appropriately and effectively to
a situation. Like Bryant, I believe that rhetoric—including rhetorical
grammar—should occupy a place of "uncommon importance" in general education (291). While this emphasis is consistent with that of
some ancient rhetoricians,[2] contemporary rhetoricians, by omission
rather than vocal opposition, tend to construct grammar as outside the
realm of rhetoric.

   We need a discourse about grammar that does not retreat from the
realities we face in the classroom—a discourse that takes seriously the
connection between writing and thinking, the interwoven relationship
between what we say and how we say it. In addition, we need to ask
questions about the enabling work of grammar instruction alongside
composition's view of writing and its instruction as social practices that
have the potential to both reproduce and challenge cultural values,
truths, and assumptions. Can grammar knowledge be conceived as extending the work of cultural critique? How might we teach grammar
in a way that supports rhetorical education? I believe that the examinations of language made possible through rhetorical grammar pedagogy encourage students to view writing as a material social practice
in which meaning is actively made, rather than passively relayed or
effortlessly produced. In this sense, rhetorical grammar instruction can
demonstrate to students that language does purposeful, consequential
work in the world—work that can be learned and applied.

Rhetorical Grammar as a Way of Thinking

> Let no man, therefore, look down on the elements of grammar as small
> matters; not because it requires great labor to distinguish consonants
> from vowels, and to divide them into the proper number of semivowels
> and mutes, but because, to those entering the recesses, as it were, of this
> temple, there will appear much subtlety on points, which may not only
> sharpen the wits of boys, but may exercise even the deepest erudition
> and knowledge.
>
> —Quintilian (in Murphy 29)

The chief reason for teaching rhetorical grammar in writing classes
is that doing so is central to teaching thinking. The ability to develop

sentences and form paragraphs that serve a particular purpose requires a conceptual ability to envision relationships between ideas. Such relationships involve processes of identification with an imagined or real reader and reflection on the way our language invites and/or alienates readers. The grammatical choices we make—including pronoun use, active or passive verb constructions, and sentence patterns—represent relations between writers and the world they live in. Word choice and sentence structure are an expression of the way we attend to the words of others, the way we position ourselves in relation to others. In this sense, writing involves cognitive skills at the level of idea development *and* at the sentence level. How we put our ideas into words and comprehensible forms is a dynamic process rather than one with clear boundaries between what we say and how we say it.

Of course, linking grammar and conceptual thinking is not the first thing that comes to mind when we think of teaching grammar. Usually, our minds go to those unending rules and exceptions, those repetitive drills and worksheets, perhaps even to diagramming sentences with a ruler, performing a quasi-scientific operation on language (one that I found particularly satisfying while in middle school). These are the hallmarks of formal grammar instruction, the deadening effects of which are widely known. A familiar argument against teaching formal grammar, particularly forceful since the rise of process pedagogies, insists that integrating grammar instruction would dangerously reduce time spent on higher-order concerns like invention and arrangement. Another argument contends that if students can't articulate their ideas in a comprehensible form, correct grammar does nothing to improve their writing. Both lines of argument rely on the faulty assumption that grammar instruction means only *formal* grammar instruction, the deadly kind that teaches correctness divorced from content and situation. Both lines of argument keep intact the binary that defines grammar instruction in opposition to composing and thinking, a binary that reproduces the notion that grammar-talk is most appropriate for the end stage of drafting.

When grammar is reserved for end-stage drafting, it is most often a version of formal grammar or "school grammar." The following passage, excerpted from the *Instructor's Manual and Answer Key to Accompany The Writer's Harbrace Handbook*, provides a familiar, though not an isolated, example of just what generates fear and paranoia in students and teachers alike:

> Once we diagnose and show students how to correct errors, then they must correct them consistently. Making comments about errors on drafts and then requiring students to turn in revisions provide immediate practice. However, only through subsequent assignments, however [sic], can we assess students' mastery over errors. Therefore, instructors and students should record errors, and instructors should hold students accountable for correcting those errors. (Winchell 21)

The orientation to grammar here is error driven and disciplinary, as evidenced in the description of efforts to "diagnose," "record," and "correct" errors. The goal is student "mastery over errors," resulting in self-conscious correction. Intentionally or not, the framework is one of finding and fixing errors rather than of active choice making for a purpose. Rhetorical grammar instruction, in contrast, emphasizes grammar as a tool for articulating and expressing relationships among ideas. The purpose of learning rhetorical grammar is to learn how to generate persuasive, clear thinking that reflects on and responds to language as work, as *produced* rather than evacuated of imperfections.

How we think and give shape to ideas is intimately tied up with the forms, patterns, and rhythms of spoken and written language. Thus, writing is profoundly reflective of the deep grammars that we absorb as inhabitants of a particular place and time. For this reason, when we reserve grammar-talk for the end of the drafting stage, I think we miss opportunities to discuss with students how the particulars of language use show us something about the way we figure relationships among people, ideas, and texts. Writing teachers need to be able to talk about how a well-coordinated sentence can keep your reader breathlessly moving with you, how techniques that create rhythm and emphasis heighten the feeling being conveyed, how subordination expresses relationships among ideas, how someone like Eminem uses repetition and power words—or words of emphasis—to create culturally relevant and, for some people, resonant stories.

More than a systematic application of rules, Mina Shaughnessy reminds us, grammar involves "a way of thinking, a style of inquiry," as opposed to "a way of being right" (129). For instance, we learn through Quintilian's excerpt above that *men* and *boys* are the subjects of education; his word choice reveals his "way of thinking" about who is entitled to an education. His male referents point to the real exclusion—as opposed to functioning as convenient placeholders for all people—of women and girls from the educational enterprise in the eighteenth century. When we broaden the goals of rhetorical grammar, it's possible to see how the intimate study of language it encourages has enormous potential for studying language as central to constructions of identity and culture. Rhetorical grammar enables such readings because it is "grammar in the service of rhetoric," which means that grammar is never divorced from ideological functions (Kolln, "Rhetorical Grammar" 29).

I am talking about rhetorical grammar as an integral component of critical writing, writing that at minimum seeks to produce new knowledge and critique stale thinking. One of the key operations of critical writing is that it locates an object of discourse in space and time, thereby placing it in a system of relationships. Joan Didion, in "Why I Write," describes this function when commenting on grammar's "infinite power": "All I know about grammar is its infinite power. To shift the structure of a sentence alters the meaning of that sentence, as definitely and inflexibly as the position of a camera alters the meaning of the object photographed" (7). As Didion's comment suggests, grammar is a positioning tool, a way of framing and presenting ideas that influences how and what we see.

This shaping of meaning through writing is intimately connected with a writer's grammatical choices. Elizabeth Bruss illuminates this idea in her brilliant study of the discourse of literary theory, *Beautiful Theories*. She suggests that the rhetoric of grammar is an important factor in the construction and consumption of theoretical discourse, and it tells us something about the "mind" in the writing. She explains, "In reading theory, one often notes where the energy of the writing seems to have been expended—in lush diction or well-turned phrases, in the juxtaposition between sentences or organization of larger episodes. From this, one receives a first (if not always a lasting) impression of the power or delicacy of mind that informs the theory" (117). She notes that the "manipulation of syntax" in theoretical writing creates a "disturbing sense of disorientation," a point that nicely describes the way grammar and content work together in theoretical writing to disturb settled or "natural" ways of thinking (122).

Referring to language as "conceptual machinery," Bruss observes: "One comes to know the nature of this machinery through watching how it functions and using it for oneself, rather than by visualizing or possessing it as a set of properties" (131). Bruss's emphasis on *use* as a way to test and experiment with the possibilities of language informs my commonplace book assignment, designed for teaching rhetorical grammar. As demonstrated in the student writing samples in the next section, the study of rhetorical grammar encourages students to experiment with language and then to reflect on the interaction between content and grammatical form. While this approach entails study of sentence slots, structures like participial phrases and adverbials that add information to a sentence, and the difference between independent and dependent clauses, rhetorical grammar more generally requires students to think about the work these aspects of grammar achieve for a writer's message. In practical terms, as well as identifying a dependent clause, students are asked to construct a sentence with a dependent clause in it and to explain the discursive effects of subordinating one idea to another.

Among other things, I want students to consider how such a sentence-level choice might reflect configurations of power in a more general sense. Explaining how discursive practices signify more than technical skill, Michel Foucault writes, "Discursive practices are not purely and simply ways of producing discourse. They are embodied in technical processes, in institutions, in patterns for general behavior, in forms for transmission and diffusion, and in pedagogical forms which, at once, impose and maintain them" (128). To illustrate just how language practices are embodied in cultural institutions, I have asked students to read a variety of texts that bring this issue to life. Selections have included George Orwell's "Politics and the English Language," bell hooks's "Language," excerpts from Robin Lakoff's *Language and Woman's Place*, and James Baldwin's "If Black Language Isn't a Language, Then Tell Me, What Is?" In different ways, each reading offers students a framework for understanding how grammar and language practices are schooled and maintained in culture. In addition, we learn that grammar use can sometimes function as a form of resistance, a point that bell hooks discusses in relation to slave songs. She writes that the English in these songs "reflected the broken, ruptured world of the slave. When the slaves sang 'nobody knows de trouble I see —' their use of the word 'nobody' adds a richer meaning than if they had used the phrase 'no one,' for it was the slave's *body* that was the concrete site of suffering" (170). hooks argues that the syntax of the songs did not change over the years because "the incorrect usage of words" expressed "a spirit of rebellion that claimed language as a site of resistance" (170). hooks's essay, along with the readings named above, encourages my students to think about grammar as a crucial tool for both communication and the expression of identity. This way of thinking about grammar often challenges students' preconceptions about grammar as a rigid system for producing correctness, preparing them for the commonplace book assignment described below.

Getting Close to Language

I emphasize the rhetorical aspects of grammar by asking students to focus on connections between grammar and concepts such as audience and purpose, paying particular attention to grammar as an art of selection. I want students to consider how and why discourses take the form they do, seeing discourse as a production that involves work and intention and craft. In setting up a classroom study of grammar as rhetorically produced, I use Kolln's *Rhetorical Grammar* as the primary theoretical framework, supplemented by excerpts on figures of thought from Sharon Crowley's *Ancient Rhetorics for Contemporary Students*. My course[3] is based on the assumption that learning how to use grammar to best effect requires lots of practice and a good deal of exposure to varied writing styles. To this end, students maintain a commonplace book throughout the semester in which they imitate and record passages of their own choosing. In *Ancient Rhetorics* Crowley explains the history of commonplace books as follows: "In pre-modern times, most rhetors kept written collections of copied passages; these were called *florilegia* (flowers of reading) in medieval times, and **commonplace books** during the Renaissance and into the eighteenth century" (250; emphasis in original). She defines such a book as "a notebook kept by a rhetor as a storehouse of materials to be remembered or quoted" (335).

As I have conceived the commonplace book, students follow each entry with at least one paragraph of analysis in which they identify the work achieved by specific grammatical techniques in the passage. I ask students to look critically at writing by analyzing passages from their favorite authors, literature and textbooks they are reading in other courses, syllabi, Web-based texts, television advertisements, segments from presidential debates—in short, any text that students find interesting. I have two goals for the commonplace books: first, to emphasize the always entangled relationship between *what* and *how* we say something; second, to designate a place where students document and comment on their evolving relationship to writing and grammatical concepts. Both goals circulate around the idea that learning how to recognize and reflect on language as *made* and *made to work on* people's lives is central to being able to use language strategically.

Commonplace books encourage students to read and analyze texts as skillfully crafted documents that convey and perform different kinds of meanings—among them, aesthetic, rhetorical; and political. Students are able to tinker with language, seeing how it is crafted and directed rather than as simply "correct" or "incorrect." Thinking of language as correct or incorrect distorts it into an objective medium consisting of ahistorical rules and truths, obscuring the living quality of language. This aliveness—the changing, transforming capacity of language—is what makes the study of rhetorical grammar especially relevant and necessary. Rhetorical grammar offers a perspective on the way people purposefully use language to describe problematic or possible new realities. It presents students with a framework and a vocabulary for examining how language affects and infects social reality, as it also provides them with tools for creating effective discourse.

Understanding how language is made and then deployed for varying effects has the potential to highlight the important work of language in our culture. This goal is especially important at the present time, as political dissent is increasingly under suspicion, and the USA Patriot Act of 2001 threatens speech acts both within and beyond the classroom. An ability to examine closely and carefully the work of language could influence discussions of political texts in the classroom. For instance, in my fall 2002 Functional Grammar class, students analyzed the grammar of President Bush's speech to the United Nations on 12 September 2002. The speech, printed in the *New York Times on the Web*, sought to present evidence to the U.N. that would make a case for moving "deliberately and decisively to hold Iraq to account" for its harboring of weapons of mass destruction. In a large-group discussion, my students analyzed Bush's use of hedging, or qualification of claims. They noted the following language choices: "U.N. inspectors *believe* Iraq has produced two to four times the amount of biological agents it declared"; "United Nations inspections also reveal that Iraq *likely* maintains stockpiles of VX, mustard, and other chemical agents . . ."; if not for the Gulf War, "the regime in Iraq would *likely* have possessed a nuclear weapon no later than 1993" ("Bush's Speech"; emphasis added).

The students' examination of hedging, demonstrated by Bush's word choice, evolved into a lively discussion about what counts as evidence in the context of declaring war; indeed, more recently, critics worldwide have begun asking questions about the "facts" regarding Iraq's weapons development program. This example is meant to suggest that rhetorical grammar analysis can form the basis for wider analyses of civic discourse, enabling students to hone in on the specific grammatical choices that give shape and meaning to content. While the following student applications of rhetorical grammar analysis do not take this sort of politicized focus, the close study of how grammar enhances and conceals meaning can certainly be applied in this way.

I ask students to make a variety of entries in their commonplace books. Recordings are entries that require students to record a passage of their own choosing and then analyze how grammar and content work together to convey meaning. In the following recording,[4] the student writer illustrates how language works on her as a reader. She records a passage from Washington Irving's "Rip Van Winkle," Rip comes down the mountain after being asleep for twenty years and is confused by the amount of time that has elapsed and by the figure, which turns out to be his son, who looks remarkably like Rip himself. "'God knows,' exclaimed [Rip], at his wit's end; 'I'm not myself—I'm somebody else— I'm somebody else—that's me yonder—no—that's somebody else got into my shoes—I was myself last night, but I fell asleep on the mountain, and they've changed my gun and everything's changed, and I'm changed, and I can't tell my name, or who I am!'" In her analysis, this student writes,

> I think Irving does a great job of showing the puzzlement Rip Van Winkle feels when he comes down the mountain and doesn't know himself or anyone else. The use of dashes in this text is effective, which is sometimes hard to accomplish. If dashes are overused, the reader can get confused and have a hard time grasping the feeling the author is trying to convey. But in this passage, Irving uses dashes to help the reader understand how Rip is feeling. Rip is disoriented, confused, and he feels lost. The dashes break up his thoughts, and the reader can hear the panic he is feeling.
>
> The structure of the sentence also conveys the alarm Rip feels. As I read the passage out loud, I found that my voice got higher and I read faster as I got toward the end. The emphasis is put on the end of the sentence, and this lets the reader know that Rip is getting more and more upset as his thoughts go on.

This analysis explains how grammatical techniques intertwine with meaning to convey Rip's confusion. When the writer points out that the dashes help the reader to experience Rip's fragmented sense of identity, she demonstrates her ability to see that meaning emerges from the very specific marks a writer chooses. The writer's analysis offers a reading of how feeling is suspended in this passage, which creates, to borrow from Bruss, an "impression of the power or delicacy of mind" that shapes the narrative (117).

Other commonplace entries include imitations of a writer's form — not, it should be noted, imitations of content.[5] In these entries, the student writer must not only mimic the writer's syntax, but must also identify the specific effects created by the syntax. In an example from Brian's commonplace book, he begins with a quotation from Harper Lee's *To Kill a Mockingbird*. In this scene, Atticus, a lawyer, is questioning Mr. Ewell to determine why he failed to retrieve a doctor to examine his daughter who was allegedly raped. "'Mr. Ewell,' Atticus began, 'folks were doing a lot of running that night. Let's see, you say you ran to the house, you ran to the window, you ran inside, you ran to Mayella, you ran for Mr. Tate. Did you, during all this running, run for a doctor?'" In his analysis, Brian writes,

> Lee, through Atticus, uses parallelism to emphasize that Mr. Ewell seemed to be running everywhere. By beginning each clause with *you ran*, he adds emphasis each time as he builds to the final point. Lee uses an asyndeton series style sentence to add emphasis to the final point. By using this type of series, there is no *and* used between each item in the series. This absence says to the reader that I could go on and on. This type of series is important in the underlying motive of the statement. Atticus is trying to emphasize that Mr. Ewell should have run for a doctor. By using the asyndeton series, he is saying that you ran here, you ran there, and I could go on and on pointing out where you did run, but the most important thing is that you didn't run to the doctor.

Having decided that Lee's passage is similar to "the kinds of speeches a coach might give his team for motivation," Brian creates the following imitation: "'Boys,' the coach began, 'this team has been doing a lot of scoring on us today. Let's see, they scored on a free kick, they scored on a header, they scored on a penalty kick, they scored on a cross, they scored on a nice shot. Did you, during all their scoring, score any of your own?'"

A similar attention to the grammatical work of a passage characterizes Chris's analysis of one passage in Kurt Vonnegut's *Breakfast of Champions*. Explaining Vonnegut's use of the word *charm* in a passage, Chris writes,

> In his definition, Vonnegut uses the word "charm" in one form or another six times within five sentences, and he uses the word "oodles" three times. He also uses the same basic sentence structure for the last three sentences. These repetitions convey the satirical nature of the explanation. That is, Vonnegut is mocking the word by overdoing its definition. Rather than combining the subjects in the last three sentences and making one

compound sentence, Vonnegut chooses to repeat the same sentence format three times in a row. This has the effect of enforcing each separate subjects place in the explanation. In this case the word comes out as being somewhat discredited. Vonnegut's point is that lots of people have charm and those who don't can usually fake it.

Drawing on descriptions of sentence structure and repetition that Kolln describes in *Rhetorical Grammar*, Chris shows us how Vonnegut reinforces the idea of the passage through grammatical techniques. He chose to examine Vonnegut's work because he had always admired it and wanted to get a better look at how Vonnegut creates such an effective tone. By requiring students to select texts to record or imitate in their commonplace books, this assignment can work well to get students to look closely at language that pleases or disturbs them. Students are pushed to think in unfamiliar ways about texts to which they have developed familiar responses. Or, in some cases, students analyzed texts that they come into contact with on a regular basis but never read attentively.

Getting close to a passage in order to reveal the technical processes that make it work forms the basis of another student's reading of Ambrose Bierce's story," An Occurrence at Owl Creek Bridge," This excerpt, taken from a student's grammatical analysis paper,[6] was originally a recording in her commonplace book. In her discussion of Bierce's use of parallelism, she writes,

> Bierce masters this technique, and seems to understand the effects that it has on the rhythm: "The water, the banks, the forest, the now distant bridge, fort, and men—all were commingled and blurred" (86). To achieve parallelism, Bierce repeats "the," followed by a noun phrase, four times. He opts not to use it, though he has the opportunity, a fifth and sixth time—doing this may make the parallelism redundant or gratuitous. Bierce thoughtfully controls the rhythm of this sentence. The reader is made to slow down where the word "the" appears—it takes more time to say "the water" than to say "water." Furthermore, the sentence gets progressively slower as we push through "the now distant bridge" and then are set free by the sleek, and fast flow of "fort, and men." This control of rhythm relates to control of emphasis, and thus drama. We emphasize the words following "the" simply because we slow down and have more time to absorb the image. Correspondingly, we pass over words without the "the" in front of them and do not have time to savor their meanings.

This writer's analysis highlights Bierce's use of momentum and rhythm to mirror the feeling of the passage. As I think her reading illustrates, the closeness to language encouraged by the commonplace book assignment requires students to dig around in the writing of others and really think about what makes it tick. This intimacy with the language of others can be an enormously powerful way to impress upon students that writing is made and that grammar has a role in that production. In addition, the commonplace book assignment offers a productive space where students document their sense of writing as reflecting intentional choices that have consequences.

While the examples I've included draw from literary texts, I want to note that my students have selected a variety of texts as the basis for commonplace book entries. These have included billing information accompanying phone bills and credit card bills, instruction manuals for appliances, text on food packaging, advertisements, textbooks, and syllabi. Whatever the textual source for entries, the model of rhetorical grammar pedagogy described here can be an asset to teaching practices that view analytical thinking as a necessary component of any socially engaged pedagogy.

Rhetorical Grammar and Empowering Pedagogies

Composition scholars have yet to map out the potentially productive connections between rhetorical grammar and composition's disciplinary commitment to cultural difference and ethical rhetoric. What's notable about liberatory pedagogies of the 1980s and 1990s is not that they reject grammar instruction but that grammar is largely absent from their descriptions of critical education. The higher level concerns of liberatory pedagogies focused on creating social change by teaching students skills with which to challenge cultural norms (Berlin; Fitts and France; Luke and Gore) and by articulating teaching and writing as cultural practices that transmit and produce cultural meanings (Giroux and McLaren; Sullivan and Qualley). Internal analyses of composition's identity as a discipline have revealed the troubling working conditions and wages of part-time teachers (Schell); the gender, race, and class politics of composition studies (Bullock and Trimbur; Jarratt and Worsham); and the relationship between pedagogy and diverse student populations (Ashton-Jones; Severino et al.).

This body of work has profoundly shaped my intellectual and political orientation in composition studies, and I believe that its politicized dimensions can provide insights about teaching grammar as a study of how language does work *in* (and sometimes *against*) the world. Gary Olson's "Encountering the Other" offers a framework for considering this claim. Olson notes that composition studies has increasingly come to focus on "issues of gender, race, or 'contact zones'" as an ethical commitment to foregrounding "interaction with an Other" (92). Ethics, for him, deals with "how we balance our own needs, desires, and obligations with those of the Other" (92). This balancing act, which requires careful consideration of self/other relations, is relevant to grammatical choices that writers make because it is part of the conceptual work that we do as writers. We envision and construct an audience through diction, tone, and the selection of examples; and as writers we seek to reach across the space that separates us from our audience, using techniques that engender trust, establish credibility, and sometimes build connection.

A student in my sophomore-level Writing with Style course demonstrates how attention to grammatical choices dovetails with an understanding of self/other relations in his analysis of the grammar and style that typifies Malcolm X's writing. He argues that Malcolm X's use of "you" in "Not Just an American Problem but a World Problem" involves his African American audience in an intimate way:

> Speaking in the second person helps urge audience members to personally take responsibility for creating a political change and becoming active participants in the revolt for racial equality. . . . By constantly using words and phrases that signify "togetherness" to refer to himself and his audience, Malcolm urges African-Americans to organize and unify.

Throughout his paper, this student examines how grammatical choices reinforce Malcolm X's emphasis on black unity as a necessary component of meaningful social change, a focus that centers on the relations between the speaker and conditions in the world. Like other forms of textual analysis, grammatical analysis can yield engaged political and cultural insights about language as "the carrier of culture, the facilitator of humanity, and the most powerful of the means of social control" (Sledd 62).

Such insights form the basis of critical pedagogy, which reveals how language constructs and reproduces oppressive cultural discourses that naturalize inequality. For instance, Ira Shor describes critical pedagogy as a teaching method that "questions the *status quo*," and is consistent with democratic values, political activism aimed at eliminating inequalities, and efforts toward "desocializing" (3). Critical pedagogy, for Shor, entails a questioning "posture towards the construction of the self in society" (16), a model of inquiry that is also key to Krista Ratcliffe's conceptualization of feminist composition pedagogy. This pedagogy "foregrounds the functions of gender as it intersects with other categories (e.g., race, class, sexual orientation, nationality); as such, it attempts to empower real historical students, particularly real historical women students, by helping them to recognize their own politics of location and negotiate such positions" (58). This kind of cultural work associated with liberatory pedagogical efforts is not incompatible with analyses that foreground rhetorical grammar analysis. In fact, such analysis can enrich our understanding of how writers use language to construct identity—both that of self and other—and to position themselves alongside or in opposition to the status quo.

In a large-group discussion of Gertrude Stein's grammatical inventions and subversions, for instance, my students commented on the way Stein uses language to deconstruct prescribed subject positions. Stein, the students argued, constructs something like a new language, using repetition and alliteration of words to do the work of punctuation. She constructs herself as a builder of meaning who uses the conventional tools of language in unconventional ways. My students were interested in how Stein, rather than duplicating moves that characterize "good writing," uses language to assert her identity as a different kind of writer; in addition, they made links between Stein's disruption of language conventions and her disruption of sexual categories and desires (portrayed especially in *Tender Buttons*).

As I'm suggesting, rhetorical grammar analysis promises to offer students more tools for analyzing culture. Cultural studies scholars, according to Pamela Caughie, make "the construction of the subject in cultural institutions and social discourses central to their investigations" (111–12). Interdisciplinary approaches to cultural studies share a common goal of investigating "the complex ways in which identity itself is articulated, experienced, deployed" (Nelson et al. qtd, in Caughie 112). By looking at practices of representation in various discursive forms, cultural studies methodologies tell us something about the way desires are fabricated and reproduced in order to construct certain kinds of subjects. Rhetorical grammar analysis can work in concert with these goals by making available to students a vocabulary for thinking through the specificity of words and grammatical choices, the work they do in the production of an idea of culture and an idea of a people.

This insight is revealed not only in studies of grammar use but also in studies that make visible the cultural attitudes and assumptions informing grammar instruction itself. Miriam Brody's *Manly Writing*, for instance, examines gendered metaphors in advice texts from the Enlightenment through the twentieth century that liken good writing to manliness and virility. Brody's study reveals what she calls the "hidden curriculum" of writing instruction—a curriculum that, mirroring the shift from a rural to an industrialized culture, ennobled masculine virtues and repelled feminine "vice," or the arts of deception, emotion, and flowery language. Brody discusses early grammar texts, in which a "fusion of patriotic, linguistic, and gendered issues forged an ideology for an age that frankly and reasonably imagined itself as perfectible, if only young boys learned their mother tongue well" (96). In this context, Brody argues, writing was gendered as a male activity that signaled a boy's civility, intelligence, and cleanliness. In addition, grammar texts from the late-1700s and early-1800s compared writing to men's work, just as the increasing industrialization during the period was seen as male labor requiring strength, forcefulness, and muscular achievement. Brody contends that the grammar exercise was the method by which young boys learned their trade: "The grammatical exercise assumed that the student was like a master builder with words, which, like so many levers and bolts, became tools for production" (105). The simplicity and cleanliness of grammar exercises, while no longer gendered in the same way that Brody describes, continue to provide students with a sense of achievement and mastery and, perhaps most satisfying of all, finality. Yet, as many have noted, when correcting language outside a meaningful context, students and teachers alike are often frustrated by the lack of transfer from the exercise to the rhetorical situation (see note 1).

The point I want to emphasize is that grammar skill and instruction are linked to cultural attitudes, beliefs, and assumptions. But an absence of attention to grammar instruction prevents us from considering productive links. Instead, we adhere to a normalized reflex against teaching grammar in the context of writing instruction. David Lazere makes a similar point in "Back to Basics" when he questions leftists' automatic reflex against "basic skills" instruction. "Basic skills," for him, refers to a somewhat amorphous "factual knowledge" and to the more explicit "mechanical and analytic skills (including remedial instruction in reading and writing standard English)" (19). While he does not utter the *g*-word here, it seems that Lazere's focus on mechanical skills and Standard English is connected to teaching grammar. He finds that a lack of "basic skills and factual knowledge" among students and teachers creates obstacles "to autonomous critical thinking and to openness toward progressive politics," a point largely overlooked or simplified by leftist educators (9). By rejecting "basic skills" as dogmatically as conservatives endorse it, leftists err, Lazere contends, in failing to see that basic skills instruction "might be a force for liberation—not oppression—if administered with common sense, openness to cultural pluralism, and an application of basics toward critical thinking, particularly about sociopolitical issues, rather than rote memorizing" (9). Although the particulars of basic skills instruction are never made clear, Lazere poses a useful challenge to binaries that refuse to see skills instruction—including grammar instruction—as anything other than conservative and dehumanizing, a position that bespeaks the already achieved privileges of rhetorical skill and the cultural capital that accompanies it (see Delpit). The opposition between teaching grammar and teaching writing—which depends on an understanding of grammar instruction in the traditional, formal sense—limits and forecloses productive discussion about rhetorical grammar as a tool for supporting and extending cultural analysis.

Grammar competency has always been linked with social power or the lack thereof. As a component of written literacy, grammar knowledge often functions to "draw lines of social distinction, mark status, and rank students in meritocratic order" (Trimbur 279). In addition to its association with class markers that lock people into social place, grammar competency also raises difficult questions concerning second-language learners and the teaching of grammar as a skill (not a craft, an art, or a tool for cultural critique) that serves the dominant economic order (i.e., see Giroux). We can challenge these associations, exploring what it might mean to teach grammar in a way that promotes composition's goals to equip students to be active citizens of the worlds they inhabit. Rather than abandon grammar instruction, I'm suggesting that writing teachers seek avenues from which to revitalize practice, positioning rhetorical grammar as a necessary component of rhetorical education.

Acknowledgments

An earlier version of this paper was delivered at the 2000 NCTE Conference in Milwaukee. I want to thank Alice Gillam for introducing me to rhetorical grammar in her Teaching Composition seminar; thanks go also to Gary Weissman, Martha Kolln, and an anonymous reader for their generative feedback on earlier drafts. In addition, I want to acknowledge my graduate research assistant, Sean Memolo, who so carefully gathered and summarized research materials for this project. His assistantship was supported by the English Department at East Carolina University.

Notes

1. A number of studies questioning how formal grammar instruction translates into writing improvement have been influential in composition studies (Braddock et al.; D'Eloia; Hartwell; Hillocks; Meckel; Sutton; Tabbert). For useful reviews of this work, see Bonnie Devet, Susan Hunter and Ray Wallace, and Rei Noguchi.
2. On ancient rhetoricians and grammar instruction, see Gina Claywell, Cheryl Glenn, or Jon Olson.
3. In this section, I describe and draw examples from two different courses in which I taught the same material. One is Writing with Style, a sophomore-level course that I taught in spring 1999 while a graduate student at the University of Wisconsin–Milwaukee. This course integrated rhetorical grammar study with issues of style, a pairing that reflects the frequent blurring of distinctions between grammar and style in composition scholarship (see Zemliansky).

   The other course described in this section is a sophomore-level course entitled Functional Grammar, which I have taught during three noncontiguous semesters at East Carolina University since fall 2000. Like several of the linguists in my department, I teach the course as rhetorical grammar because this terminology highlights grammar as integral to persuasive speech acts. As an approach to studying language, however, rhetorical grammar shares several principles with functional grammar, including the idea that language *does* something, language use varies according to context, and learning grammar entails sentence-level and larger discursive-level knowledge. See Charles Meyer for a useful overview of functional grammar with specific attention to M. A. K Halliday's functional theory of language.
4. I'd like to extend special thanks to those students who gave me permission to quote from their commonplace books; those whose names are not given

wished to remain anonymous. All student writing appears here exactly as it was written.

5. Resources on using imitation exercises in the writing classroom are plentiful. For a sampling, see Robert Connors on rhetoric and imitation, Frank D'Angelo on "strict" and "loose" imitations, and Winston Weathers on "creative imitation."

6. Students wrote an eight-page analysis of the grammar of any text of their choosing. For more information on this and other assignments, visit the following links on my Web site: <http://personal.ecu,edu/miccichel /grammar02.htm> and <http://personal.ecu.edu/miccichel/2730.htm> and <http://personal.ecu.edu/miccichel/style.htm>. Send me an e-mail at miccichel@mail.ecu.edu regarding suggestions and/or comments about the ideas discussed in this article.

Works Cited

Ashton-Jones, Evelyn. "Collaboration, Conversation, and the Politics of Gender." *Feminine Principles and Women's Experience in American Composition and Rhetoric.* Ed. Louise Wetherbee Phelps and Janet Emig. Pittsburgh: U of Pittsburgh P, 1995. 5–26. Print.

Baldwin, James. "If Black English Isn't a Language, Then Tell Me, What Is?" *Ten on Ten: Major Essayists on Recurring Themes.* Ed. Robert Atwan. Boston: Bedford, 1992. 321–24. Print.

Berlin, James A. "Rhetoric and Ideology in the Writing Class." *College English* 50.5 (1988): 477–94. Print.

Braddock, Richard, Richard Lloyd-Jones, and Lowell Schoer. *Research in Written Composition.* Champaign, IL: NCTE, 1963. Print.

Brody, Miriam. *Manly Writing: Gender; Rhetoric, and the Rise of Composition.* Carbondale, IL: SIUP, 1993. Print.

Bruss, Elizabeth W. *Beautiful Theories: The Spectacle of Discourse in Contemporary Criticism.* Baltimore: Johns Hopkins UP, 1982. Print.

Bryant, Donald C. "Rhetoric: Its Functions and Its Scope." *Professing the New Rhetorics: A Sourcebook.* Ed. Theresa Enos and Stuart C. Brown. Englewood Cliffs, NJ: Prentice Hall, 1994. 267–97. Print.

Bullock, Richard, and John Trimbur, eds. *The Politics of Writing Instruction: Postsecondary.* Portsmouth, NH: Boynton/Cook, 1991. Print.

"Bush's Speech to U.N. on Iraq." *New York Times*, Web. 12 Sept. 2002. 12 Sept. 2002.

Caughie, Pamela L. "Let It Pass: Changing the Subject, Once Again." *Feminism and Composition: In Other Words.* Ed. Susan C. Jarratt and Lynn Worsham. New York: MLA, 1998. 111–31. Print.

Claywell, Gina. "Reasserting Grammar's Position in the Trivium in American College Composition." Hunter and Wallace 43–53. Print.

Connors, Robert J. "The Erasure of the Sentence," *College Composition and Communication* 52.1 (2000): 96–128. Print.

Crowley, Sharon. *Ancient Rhetorics for Contemporary Students.* New York: Macmillan, 1994. Print.

D'Angelo, Frank. "Imitation and Style." *The Writing Teacher's Sourcebook.* 2nd ed. Ed. Gary Tate and Edward P. J. Corbett. New York: Oxford UP, 1988. 199–207. Print.

D'Eloia, Sarah. "The Uses—and Limits—of Grammar." *Journal of Basic Writing* 1.3 (1977): 1–20. Print.

Delpit, Lisa, *Other People's Children: Cultural Conflict in the Classroom.* New York: The New P, 1995. Print.

Devet, Bonnie, "Welcoming Grammar Back into the Writing Classroom." *Teaching English in the Two-Year College* 30.1 (2002): 8–17. Print.

Didion, Joan. "Why I Write." *Joan Didion: Essays and Conversations.* Ed. Ellen G. Friedman. Princeton, NJ: Ontario Review P, 1984. 5–10. Print.

Fitts, Karen, and Alan W. France, eds. *Left Margins: Cultural Studies and Composition Pedagogy.* Albany: SUNY, 1995. Print.

Foucault, Michel. *Language, Counter-Memory, Practice.* Ed. Donald F. Bouchard. Ithaca: Cornell UP, 1980. Print.

Giroux, Henry A. *Teachers as Intellectuals: Toward a Critical Pedagogy of Learning.* Granby, MA: Bergin and Garvey, 1988. Print.

Giroux, Henry A., and Peter McLaren, eds. *Critical Pedagogy, the State, and Cultural Struggle.* Albany: SUNY, 1989. Print.

Glenn, Cheryl. "When Grammar Was a Language Art." Hunter and Wallace 9–29. Print.

Hartwell, Patrick. "Grammar, Grammars, and the Teaching of Grammar." *College English* 47.2 (1985): 105–27. Print.

Hillocks, George, Jr. *Research on Written Composition: New Directions for Teaching.* Urbana, IL: NCRE/ERIC, 1986. Print.

hooks, bell, "Language." *Teaching to Transgress: Education as the Practice of Freedom.* New York: Routledge, 1994. 167–75. Print.

Hunter, Susan, and Ray Wallace, eds. *The Place of Grammar in Writing Instruction: Past, Present, Future.* Portsmouth, NH: Boynton/Cook, 1995. Print.

Jarratt, Susan C., and Lynn Worsham, eds. *Feminism and Composition Studies: In Other Words.* New York: MLA, 1998. Print.

Kolln, Martha. "Rhetorical Grammar: A Modification Lesson." *English Journal* 85.7 (1996): 25–31. Print.

———. *Rhetorical Grammar: Grammatical Choices, Rhetorical Effects.* 4th ed. New York: Longman, 2003. Print.

Lakoff, Robin. *Language and Woman's Place.* New York: Harper & Row, 1975. Print.

Lazere, David. "Back to Basics: A Force for Oppression or Liberation?" *College English* 54.1 (1992): 7–21. Print.

Luke, Carmen, and Jennifer Gore, eds, *Feminisms and Critical Pedagogies.* New York: Routledge, 1992. Print.

Meckel, Henry C. "Research on Teaching Composition and Literature." *Handbook of Educational Research.* Ed. N. L. Gage. Chicago: Rand McNally, 1963. 966–1006. Print.

Meyer, Charles F. "Functional Grammar and Discourse Studies." *Discourse Studies in Composition.* Ed. Ellen Barton and Gail Stygall. Cresskill, NJ: Hampton P, 2002. 71–89. Print.

Murphy, James J., ed. *Quintilian on the Teaching of Speaking and Writing.* Carbondale, IL: SIUP, 1987. Print.

Noguchi, Rei R. *Grammar and the Teaching of Writing: Limits and Possibilities.* Urbana, IL: NCTE, 1991. Print.

Olson, Gary A. "Encountering the Other: Postcolonial Theory and Composition Scholarship." *Ethical Issues in College Writing*, Ed. Fredric G. Gale, Phillip Sipiora, and James L. Kinneavy. New York: Peter Lang, 1999. 91–105. Print.

Olson, Jon. "A Question of Power: Why Fredrick Douglass Stole Grammar." Hunter and Wallace 30–42. Print.

Orwell, George, "Politics and the English Language." *Ten on Ten: Major Essayists on Recurring Themes.* Ed. Robert Atwan. Boston: Bedford, 1992. 309–20. Print.

Ratcliffe, Krista. *Anglo-American Feminist Challenges to the Rhetorical Traditions: Virginia Woolf, Mary Daly, Adrienne Rich.* Carbondale, IL: SIUP, 1996. Print.

Schell, Eileen E. *Gypsy Academics and Mother-Teachers: Gender, Contingent Labor, and Writing Instruction*, Portsmouth, NH: Boynton/Cook, 1998. Print.

Severino, Carol, Juan C. Guerra, and Johnnella E. Butler, eds. *Writing in Multicultural Settings*, New York: MLA, 1997. Print.

Shaughnessy, Mina P. *Errors and Expectations: A Guide for the Teacher of Basic Writing.* New York: Oxford UP, 1977. Print.

Shor, Ira. *Empowering Education: Critical Teaching for Social Change.* Chicago: U of Chicago P, 1992. Print.

Sledd, James. "Grammar for Social Awareness in Time of Class Warfare." *English Journal* 85.7 (1996): 59–63. Print.

Sullivan, Patricia A., and Donna J. Qualley, eds. *Pedagogy in the Age of Politics: Writing and Reading (in) the Academy.* Urbana, IL: NCTE, 1994. Print.

Sutton, Gary A. "Do We Need to Teach a Grammar Terminology?" *English Journal* 65.9 (1976): 37–40. Print.

Tabbert, Russell, "Parsing the Question 'Why Teach Grammar?'" *English Journal* 73.8 (1984): 38–42. Print.

Trimbur, John. "Literacy and the Discourse of Crisis." *The Politics of Writing Instruction: Postsecondary.* Ed. Richard Bullock and John Trimbur. Portsmouth, NH: Boynton/Cook, 1991. 277–95. Print.

Weathers, Winston. "Teaching Style: A Possible Anatomy." *The Writing Teacher's Sourcebook.* 2nd ed. Ed. Gary Tate and Edward P. J. Corbett. New York: Oxford UP, 1988. 187–92. Print.

Winchell, Donna A. "Teaching the Rhetoric of Grammar and Style." *Instructor's Manual and Answer Key to Accompany The Writer's Harbrace Handbook.* Ed. Robert K. Miller, Suzanne S. Webb, and Winifred B. Horner. New York: Harcourt College Publishers, 2001. 16–58. Print.

Zemliansky, Pavel. "Mechanical Correctness." *Composition Forum* 10.2 (2000): 1–19. Print.

PART THREE

Engaging Difference

But I think there is really a larger picture that includes disability along with other nonstandard behaviors. Language usage, which is as much a physical function as any other somatic activity, has become subject to an enforcement of normalcy, as have sexuality, gender, racial identity, national identity, and so on.

   —Lennard Davis, *Disability and the Teaching of Writing* (207)

What is normal, what is different, and who decides? These questions, which Lennard Davis addresses in his essay in Chapter 9, provide the connecting theme for Part Three. For students in basic writing, often someone else has decided what constitutes a "normal" college writer: a person or a machine that scores writing placement tests; a long-standing institutional policy that separates native speakers and nonnative speakers for writing instruction; an educational system that perpetuates segregation and inadequate college preparation for students classified as "nonmainstream" or "at risk," such as students of color, students from low-income households, students with learning disabilities, or students with linguistic differences. Because they deal with consequences of decisions made by often-faceless and nameless bureaucracies, students may feel as if they have no choice in their own education, or that they do not possess the means to create positive change.

The readings in Part Three offer examples for creating more presence and ownership in education for students—and for educators across a wide spectrum of issues that seem constantly in flux inside and outside our institutions. Davis calls this presence "agency," and suggests that through claiming agency, we "begin to move away from the victim-victimizer scenario" (p. 309 in this volume). From exploring processes of writing and identity formation, to research on paradigms of successful learning, these readings do *not* call for "color blindness," or even for "tolerance." Instead, these articles collectively suggest the promise of honoring and engaging difference in all of its many, ever-changing forms.[1]

Chapter 7, "Classic Perspectives on Multicultural Teaching and Learning," focuses on the early years of formal inclusion of multicultural pedagogies in postsecondary education in the 1980s and 1990s. By demonstrating the intersections of language and culture, Gloria Anzaldúa, June Jordan, and bell hooks document the persistence of systemic and institutionalized racism, classism, sexism, and homophobia as challenges to achieving equitable and democratic education. These writers suggest that calling attention to and naming these challenges remains a starting point for working toward social justice and engaging difference through teaching and writing.

Chapter 8, "Transforming Pedagogies," presents pedagogies that take ethos, the appeal to values, and pathos, the appeal to emotions, as significant and necessary starting points for creating successful learning conditions for all students. Valerie Purdie-Vaughns, Geoffrey Cohen, and their team invite students to respond to a series of writing prompts that affirm students' values about subjects such as relationships or the arts. The researchers suggest that "the affirmation reduces stress, allowing people's skills to be more completely displayed and the institution's resources to have greater impact" (p. 281). Amy E. Winans teaches at a segregated rural university, and finds that white students believe that racial "problems" exist elsewhere. Winans provides students with opportunities to write about race, and offers insights about the ways in which white students' writing about race is tied to emotions and ethical values.

Chapter 9, "Learning Differences," questions conceptions of difference and suggests pedagogies that have the potential to benefit *all* students. Alleviating the need for "tips" or "helpful hints," Lennard Davis and Patrick Bruch offer perspectives for creating a more equitable environment for students with visible and invisible learning differences. Davis, an extensively published disability studies scholar, compares "ability" and "disability" to "standard" and "nonstandard" English grammar. He reminds readers than Standard English grammar is not a fixed or permanent entity, but transforms through active usage. Similarly, definitions of *disability* and *ability* can be understood as fluid, continuing to evolve over place and time. Patrick Bruch extends this idea through a classroom narrative of teaching with universal design, a concept borrowed from architecture, and references structural adaptations to building that initially were intended to comply with the Americans with Disabilities Act (ADA), and also benefit people not covered by ADA.

Chapter 10, "English Language Learners," focuses on the notion of continuums, which Martha Clark Cummings defines through the words of her student "Nila," as "Connected. In chemistry. Like rainbow" (p. 355). In her article, Cummings movingly describes her reflections disclosing her lesbian identity to her ESL class, and presents the notion of "continuum" in a discussion about heterosexuality and homosexuality with her students. Christina Ortmeir-Hooper suggests that the idea of a continuum is more helpful for English learners than the either–or categories of "ESL" or "Generation 1.5." She presents case studies of three students based on the notion of the continuum of learning to write in English, and addresses whether each student identifies him or herself as "ESL." Gloria M. Rodriguez and Lisceth Cruz review recent research on English Learner and undocumented students and transitions to college, and provide recommendations for research that would have a positive and direct impact on policies and resources. Rodriguez and Cruz point to inappropriate stereotypes that contribute to "perpetual victim" status; instead, the authors advocate, educators and researchers must recognize skills not often measured by standardized tests, especially the intelligence and self-efficacy of English Learners and undocumented students, who must utilize "agency and self-reliance," in order "to support their own educational goals."

Note

1. Villanueva suggests that "our work is tied to how racism can be denied while the language of exclusion and hate dominates in the talks of wars, the representation of immigrants, the tie to gays, and other such matters." The readings in Part Three are intimately connected with this work.

Works Cited

Davis, Lennard. *Disability and the Teaching of Writing: A Critical Sourcebook.* Boston: Bedford/St. Martin's, 2008. Print.

Villanueva, Victor. "2009 CCCC Exemplar Award Acceptance Speech." *College Composition and Communication* 61.3 (2010): 581–82. Print.

Classic Perspectives on Multicultural Teaching and Learning

How to Tame a Wild Tongue

Gloria Anzaldúa

In her book of cultural criticism, narrative, and poetry Borderlands/La Frontera: The New Mestiza *(1987), the Chicana, Tejana, lesbian feminist writer and teacher Gloria Anzaldúa (1942–2004) explored the metaphors and material realities of growing up in south Texas's Río Grande valley on the U.S.-Mexican border. In this selection, a chapter from* Borderlands/La Frontera, *Anzaldúa recounts how growing up Chicana continues to shape her life, especially in terms of language. She writes in "Spanglish," a combination of Spanish and English, both to help the reader understand the rich cultural conditions of the borderlands and to demonstrate to Anglo and non-Spanish-speaking readers what it means to be the "other"— outside of so-called mainstream language and culture. Certainly, many ESL students may have shared Anzaldúa's childhood experience of the teacher who did not care to understand how Anzaldúa pronounced her name. "If you want to be American, speak 'American,'" (p. 246) her teacher tells her. In this essay, Anzaldúa reminds us that there are many ways of speaking "American."*

> "We're going to have to control your tongue," the dentist says, pulling out all the metal from my mouth. Silver bits plop and tinkle into the basin. My mouth is a motherlode.

The dentist is cleaning out my roots. I get a whiff of the stench when I gasp. "I can't cap that tooth yet, you're still draining," he says.

"We're going to have to do something about your tongue," I hear the anger rising in his voice. My tongue keeps pushing out the wads of cotton, pushing back the drills, the long thin needles. "I've never seen anything as strong or as stubborn," he says. And I think, how do you tame a wild tongue, train it to be quiet, how do you bridle and saddle it? How do you make it lie down?

Who is to say that robbing a people of
its language is less violent than war?
                                    —Ray Gwyn Smith[1]

I remember being caught speaking Spanish at recess—that was good for three licks on the knuckles with a sharp ruler. I remember being sent to the corner of the classroom for "talking back" to the Anglo teacher when all I was trying to do was tell her how to pronounce my name. "If you want to be American, speak 'American.' If you don't like it, go back to Mexico where you belong."

"I want you to speak English. *Pa'hallar buen trabajo tienes que saber hablar el inglés bien. Qué vale toda tu educación si todavía hablas inglés con un* 'accent,'" my mother would say, mortified that I spoke English like a Mexican. At Pan American University, I and all Chicano students were required to take two speech classes. Their purpose: to get rid of our accents.

Attacks on one's form of expression with the intent to censor are a violation of the First Amendment. *El Anglo con cara de inocente nos arrancó la lengua.* Wild tongues can't be tamed, they can only be cut out.

Overcoming the Tradition of Silence

Abogadas, escupimos el oscuro,
Peleando con nuestra propia sombra
el silencio nos sepulta.

En boca cerrada no entran moscas. "Flies don't enter a closed mouth" is a saying I kept hearing when I was a child. *Ser habladora* was to be a gossip and a liar, to talk too much. *Muchachitas bien criadas*, well-bred girls don't answer back. *Es una falta de respeto* to talk back to one's mother or father. I remember one of the sins I'd recite to the priest in the confession box the few times I went to confession: talking back to my mother, *hablar pa' 'tras, repelar. Hocicona, repelona, chismosa*, having a big mouth, questioning, carrying tales are all signs of being *mal criada*. In my culture they are all words that are derogatory if applied to women—I've never heard them applied to men.

The first time I heard two women, a Puerto Rican and a Cuban, say the word *"nosotras,"* I was shocked. I had not known the word existed. Chicanas use *nosotros* whether we're male or female. We are robbed of our female being by the masculine plural. Language is a male discourse.

> And our tongues have become
> dry   the wilderness has
> dried out our tongues   and
> we have forgotten speech.
> —Irena Klepfisz[2]

Even our own people, other Spanish speakers *nos quieren poner candados en la boca.* They would hold us back with their bag of *reglas de academia.*

Oyé como ladra: el lenguaje de la frontera

> *Quien tiene boca se equivoca.*
> —Mexican saying

"Pocho, cultural traitor, you're speaking the oppressor's language by speaking English, you're ruining the Spanish language," I have been accused by various Latinos and Latinas. Chicano Spanish is considered by the purist and by most Latinos deficient, a mutilation of Spanish.

But Chicano Spanish is a border tongue which developed naturally. Change, *evolución, enriquecimiento de palabras nuevas por invención o adopción* have created variants of Chicano Spanish, *un nuevo lenguaje. Un lenguaje que corresponde a un modo de vivir.* Chicano Spanish is not incorrect, it is a living language.

For a people who are neither Spanish nor live in a country in which Spanish is the first language; for a people who live in a country in which English is the reigning tongue but who are not Anglo; for a people who cannot entirely identify with either standard (formal, Castillian) Spanish nor standard English, what recourse is left to them but to create their own language? A language which they can connect their identity to, one capable of communicating the realities and values true to themselves—a language with terms that are neither *español ni inglés,* but both. We speak a patois, a forked tongue, a variation of two languages.

Chicano Spanish sprang out of the Chicanos' need to identify ourselves as a distinct people. We needed a language with which we could communicate with ourselves, a secret language. For some of us, language is a homeland closer than the Southwest—for many Chicanos today live in the Midwest and the East. And because we are a complex, heterogeneous people, we speak many languages. Some of the languages we speak are:

1. Standard English

2. Working-class and slang English

3. Standard Spanish

4. Standard Mexican Spanish

5. North Mexican Spanish dialect

6. Chicano Spanish (Texas, New Mexico, Arizona and California have regional variations)

7. Tex-Mex

8. *Pachuco* (called *caló*)

My "home" tongues are the languages I speak with my sister and brothers, with my friends. They are the last five listed, with 6 and 7 being closest to my heart. From school, the media, and job situations, I've picked up Standard and working-class English. From Mamagrande Locha and from reading Spanish and Mexican literature, I've picked up Standard Spanish and Standard Mexican Spanish. From *los recién llegados*, Mexican immigrants, and *braceros*, I learned the North Mexican dialect. With Mexicans I'll try to speak either Standard Mexican Spanish or the North Mexican dialect. From my parents and Chicanos living in the Valley, I picked up Chicano Texas Spanish, and I speak it with my mom, younger brother (who married a Mexican and who rarely mixes Spanish with English), aunts, and older relatives.

With Chicanas from *Nuevo México* or *Arizona* I will speak Chicano Spanish a little, but often they don't understand what I'm saying. With most California Chicanas I speak entirely in English (unless I forget). When I first moved to San Francisco, I'd rattle off something in Spanish, unintentionally embarrassing them. Often it is only with another Chicana *tejana* that I can talk freely.

Words distorted by English are known as anglicisms or *pochismos*. The *pocho* is an anglicized Mexican or American of Mexican origin who speaks Spanish with an accent characteristic of North Americans and who distorts and reconstructs the language according to the influence of English.[3] Tex-Mex, or Spanglish, comes most naturally to me. I may switch back and forth from English to Spanish in the same sentence or in the same word. With my sister and my brother Nune and with Chicano *tejano* contemporaries I speak in Tex-Mex.

From kids and people my own age I picked up *Pachuco*. *Pachuco* (the language of the zoot suiters) is a language of rebellion, both against Standard Spanish and Standard English. It is a secret language. Adults of the culture and outsiders cannot understand it. It is made up of slang words from both English and Spanish. *Ruca* means girl or woman, *vato* means guy or dude, *chale* means no, *simón* means yes, *churro* is sure, talk is *periquiar, pigionear* means petting, *que gacho* means how nerdy, *ponte águila* means watch out, death is called *la pelona*. Through lack of practice and not having others who can speak it, I've lost most of the *Pachuco* tongue.

Chicano Spanish

Chicanos, after 250 years of Spanish/Anglo colonization, have developed significant differences in the Spanish we speak. We collapse two adjacent vowels into a single syllable and sometimes shift the stress in certain words such as *maíz / maiz, cohete / cuete*. We leave out certain consonants when they appear between vowels: *lado / lao, mojado / mojao*. Chicanos from South Texas pronounce *f* as *j* as in *jue (fue)*. Chicanos use "archaisms," words that are no longer in the Spanish language, words that have been evolved out. We say *semos, truje, haiga, ansina*, and *naiden*. We retain the "archaic" *j*, as in *jalar*, that derives from an earlier *h* (the French *halar* or the Germanic *halon* which was lost to Standard Spanish in the sixteenth century), but which is still found in several regional dialects such as the one spoken in South Texas. (Due to geography, Chicanos from the Valley of South Texas were cut off linguistically from other Spanish speakers. We tend to use words that the Spaniards brought over from Medieval Spain. The majority of the Spanish colonizers in Mexico and the Southwest came from Extremadura—Hernán Cortés was one of them—and Andalucía. Andalucians pronounce *ll* like a *y*, and their *d*'s tend to be absorbed by adjacent vowels: *tirado* becomes *tirao*. They brought *el lenguaje popular, dialectos y regionalismos*.)[4]

Chicanos and other Spanish speakers also shift *ll* to *y* and *z* to *s*.[5] We leave out initial syllables, saying *tar* for *estar, toy* for *estoy, hora* for *ahora* (*cubanos* and *puertorriqueños* also leave out initial letters of some words). We also leave out the final syllable such as *pa* for *para*. The intervocalic *y*, the *ll* as in *tortilla, ella, botella*, gets replaced by *tortia* or *tortiya, ea, botea*. We add an additional syllable at the beginning of certain words: *atocar* for *tocar, agastar* for *gastar*. Sometimes we'll say *lavaste las vacijas*, other times *lavates* (substituting the *ates* verb endings for the *aste*).

We use anglicisms, words borrowed from English: *bola* from ball, *carpeta* from carpet, *máchina de lavar* (instead of *lavadora*) from washing machine. Tex-Mex argot, created by adding a Spanish sound at the beginning or end of an English word such as *cookiar* for cook, *watchar* for watch, *parkiar* for park, and *rapiar* for rape, is the result of the pressures on Spanish speakers to adapt to English.

We don't use the word *vosotros / as* or its accompanying verb form. We don't say *claro* (to mean yes), *imagínate*, or *me emociona*, unless we picked up Spanish from Latinas, out of a book, or in a classroom. Other Spanish-speaking groups are going through the same, or similar, development in their Spanish.

Linguistic Terrorism

> *Deslenguadas. Somos los del español deficiente.* We are your linguistic
> nightmare, your linguistic aberration, your linguistic *mestisaje*, the sub-
> ject of your *burla.* Because we speak with tongues of fire we are culturally
> crucified. Racially, culturally, and linguistically *somos huérfanos*—we
> speak an orphan tongue.

Chicanas who grew up speaking Chicano Spanish have internalized the
belief that we speak poor Spanish. It is illegitimate, a bastard language.
And because we internalize how our language has been used against
us by the dominant culture, we use our language differences against
each other.

Chicana feminists often skirt around each other with suspicion and
hesitation. For the longest time I couldn't figure it out. Then it dawned
on me. To be close to another Chicana is like looking into the mirror. We
are afraid of what we'll see there. *Pena.* Shame. Low estimation of self.
In childhood we are told that our language is wrong. Repeated attacks
on our native tongue diminish our sense of self. The attacks continue
throughout our lives.

Chicanas feel uncomfortable talking in Spanish to Latinas, afraid
of their censure. Their language was not outlawed in their countries.
They had a whole lifetime of being immersed in their native tongue;
generations, centuries in which Spanish was a first language, taught in
school, heard on radio and TV, and read in the newspaper.

If a person, Chicana or Latina, has a low estimation of my native
tongue, she also has a low estimation of me. Often with *mexicanas y
latinas* we'll speak English as a neutral language. Even among Chicanas we tend to speak English at parties or conferences. Yet, at the
same time, we're afraid the other will think we're *agringadas* because
we don't speak Chicano Spanish. We oppress each other trying to out-
Chicano each other, vying to be the "real" Chicanas, to speak like Chicanos. There is no one Chicano language just as there is no one Chicano
experience. A monolingual Chicana whose first language is English or
Spanish is just as much a Chicana as one who speaks several variants
of Spanish. A Chicana from Michigan or Chicago or Detroit is just as
much a Chicana as one from the Southwest. Chicano Spanish is as diverse linguistically as it is regionally.

By the end of this century, Spanish speakers will comprise the biggest minority group in the U.S., a country where students in high schools
and colleges are encouraged to take French classes because French is
considered more "cultured." But for a language to remain alive it must
be used.[6] By the end of this century English, and not Spanish, will be
the mother tongue of most Chicanos and Latinos.

So, if you want to really hurt me, talk badly about my language. Ethnic
identity is twin skin to linguistic identity—I am my language. Until I

can take pride in my language, I cannot take pride in myself. Until I can accept as legitimate Chicano Texas Spanish, Tex-Mex, and all the other languages I speak, I cannot accept the legitimacy of myself. Until I am free to write bilingually and to switch codes without having always to translate, while I still have to speak English or Spanish when I would rather speak Spanglish, and as long as I have to accommodate the English speakers rather than having them accommodate me, my tongue will be illegitimate.

I will no longer be made to feel ashamed of existing. I will have my voice: Indian, Spanish, white. I will have my serpent's tongue—my woman's voice, my sexual voice, my poet's voice. I will overcome the tradition of silence.

> My fingers
> move sly against your palm
> Like women everywhere, we speak in code . . .
> —Melanie Kaye/Kantrowitz[7]

"Vistas," corridos, y comida: My Native Tongue

In the 1960s, I read my first Chicano novel. It was *City of Night* by John Rechy, a gay Texan, son of a Scottish father and a Mexican mother. For days I walked around in stunned amazement that a Chicano could write and could get published. When I read *I Am Joaquín,*[8] I was surprised to see a bilingual book by a Chicano in print. When I saw poetry written in Tex-Mex for the first time, a feeling of pure joy flashed through me. I felt like we really existed as a people. In 1971, when I started teaching High School English to Chicano students, I tried to supplement the required texts with works by Chicanos, only to be reprimanded and forbidden to do so by the principal. He claimed that I was supposed to teach "American" and English literature. At the risk of being fired, I swore my students to secrecy and slipped in Chicano short stories, poems, a play. In graduate school, while working toward a Ph.D., I had to "argue" with one advisor after the other, semester after semester, before I was allowed to make Chicano literature an area of focus.

Even before I read books by Chicanos or Mexicans, it was the Mexican movies I saw at the drive-in—the Thursday night special of $1.00 a carload—that gave me a sense of belonging. *"Vámonos a las vistas,"* my mother would call out and we'd all—grandmother, brothers, sister, and cousins—squeeze into the car. We'd wolf down cheese and bologna white bread sandwiches while watching Pedro Infante in melodramatic tearjerkers like *Nosotros los pobres*, the first "real" Mexican movie (that was not an imitation of European movies). I remember seeing *Cuando los hijos se van* and surmising that all Mexican movies played up the love a mother has for her children and what ungrateful sons and daughters suffer when they are not devoted to their mothers. I remember the singing-type "westerns" of Jorge Negrete and Miquel Aceves Mejía. When watching Mexican movies, I felt a sense of homecoming as well as alienation. People who were to amount to something didn't go to Mexican movies, or *bailes* or tune their radios to *bolero, rancherita*, and *corrido* music.

The whole time I was growing up, there was *norteño* music sometimes called North Mexican border music, or Tex-Mex music, or Chicano music, or *cantina* (bar) music. I grew up listening to *conjuntos*, three- or four-piece bands made up of folk musicians playing guitar, *bajo sexto*, drums and button accordion, which Chicanos had borrowed from the German immigrants who had come to Central Texas and Mexico to farm and build breweries. In the Rio Grande Valley, Steve Jordan and Little Joe Hernández were popular, and Flaco Jiménez was the accordian king. The rhythms of Tex-Mex music are those of the polka, also adapted from the Germans, who in turn had borrowed the polka from the Czechs and Bohemians.

I remember the hot, sultry evenings when *corridos*—songs of love and death on the Texas-Mexican borderlands—reverberated out of cheap amplifiers from the local *cantinas* and wafted in through my bedroom window.

Corridos first became widely used along the South Texas/Mexican border during the early conflict between Chicanos and Anglos. The corridos are usually about Mexican heroes who do valiant deeds against the Anglo oppressors. Pancho Villa's song, *"La cucaracha,"* is the most famous one. *Corridos* of John F. Kennedy and his death are still very popular in the Valley. Older Chicanos remember Lydia Mendoza, one of the great border *corrido* singers who was called *la Gloria de Tejas.* Her *"El tango negro,"* sung during the Great Depression, made her a singer of the people. The everpresent *corridos* narrated one hundred years of border history, bringing news of events as well as entertaining. These folk musicians and folk songs are our chief cultural mythmakers, and they made our hard lives seem bearable.

I grew up feeling ambivalent about our music. Country-western and rock-and-roll had more status. In the fifties and sixties, for the slightly educated and *agringado* Chicanos, there existed a sense of shame at being caught listening to our music. Yet I couldn't stop my feet from thumping to the music, could not stop humming the words, nor hide from myself the exhilaration I felt when I heard it.

There are more subtle ways that we internalize identification, especially in the forms of images and emotions. For me food and certain smells are tied to my identity, to my homeland. Woodsmoke curling up to an immense blue sky; woodsmoke perfuming my grandmother's clothes, her skin. The stench of cow manure and the yellow patches on the ground; the crack of a .22 rifle and the reek of cordite. Homemade white cheese sizzling in a pan, melting inside a folded *tortilla*. My sister Hilda's hot, spicy *menudo, chile colorado* making it deep red, pieces of *panza* and hominy floating on top. My brother Carito barbequing *fajitas* in the backyard. Even now and three thousand miles away, I can see my mother spicing the ground beef, pork, and venison with *chile*. My mouth salivates at the thought of the hot steaming *tamales* I would be eating if I were home.

Si le preguntas a mi mamá, "¿Qué eres?"

> Identity is the essential core of who
> we are as individuals, the conscious
> experience of the self inside.
> —Kaufman[9]

Nosotros los Chicanos straddle the borderlands. On one side of us, we are constantly exposed to the Spanish of the Mexicans, on the other side we hear the Anglos' incessant clamoring so that we forget our language. Among ourselves we don't say *nosotros los americanos, o nosotros los españoles, o nosotros los hispanos*. We say *nosotros los mexicanos* (by *mexicanos* we do not mean citizens of Mexico; we do not mean a national identity, but a racial one). We distinguish between *mexicanos del otro lado* and *mexicanos de este lado*. Deep in our hearts we believe that being Mexican has nothing to do with which country one lives in. Being Mexican is a state of soul—not one of mind, not one of citizenship. Neither eagle nor serpent, but both. And like the ocean, neither animal respects borders.

> *Dime con quien andas y te diré quien eres.*
> (Tell me who your friends are and I'll tell you who you are.)
> —Mexican saying

Si le preguntas a mi mamá, "¿Qué eres?" te dirá, "Soy mexicana." My brothers and sister say the same. I sometimes will answer "*soy mexicana*" and at others will say "*soy Chicana*" o "*soy tejana*." But I identified as "*Raza*" before I ever identified as "*mexicana*" or "Chicana."

As a culture, we call ourselves Spanish when referring to ourselves as a linguistic group and when copping out. It is then that we forget our predominant Indian genes. We are seventy to eighty percent Indian.[10] We call ourselves Hispanic[11] or Spanish-American or Latin American or Latin when linking ourselves to other Spanish-speaking peoples of the Western hemisphere and when copping out. We call ourselves Mexican-American[12] to signify we are neither Mexican nor American, but more the noun "American" than the adjective "Mexican" (and when copping out).

Chicanos and other people of color suffer economically for not ac-
culturating. This voluntary (yet forced) alienation makes for psychological conflict, a kind of dual identity—we don't identify with the
Anglo-American cultural values and we don't totally identify with the
Mexican cultural values. We are a synergy of two cultures with various
degrees of Mexicanness or Angloness. I have so internalized the borderland conflict that sometimes I feel like one cancels out the other and
we are zero, nothing, no one. *A veces no soy nada ni nadie. Pero hasta
cuando no lo soy, lo soy.*

When not copping out, when we know we are more than nothing,
we call ourselves Mexican, referring to race and ancestry; *mestizo* when
affirming both our Indian and Spanish (but we hardly ever own our
black ancestry); Chicano when referring to a politically aware people
born and/or raised in the U.S.; *Raza* when referring to Chicanos; *teja-
nos* when we are Chicanos from Texas.

Chicanos did not know we were a people until 1965 when Cesar
Chavez and the farmworkers united and *I Am Joaquín* was published
and *la Raza Unida* party was formed in Texas. With that recognition,
we became a distinct people. Something momentous happened to the
Chicano soul—we became aware of our reality and acquired a name
and a language (Chicano Spanish) that reflected that reality. Now that
we had a name, some of the fragmented pieces began to fall together—
who we were, what we were, how we had evolved. We began to get
glimpses of what we might eventually become.

Yet the struggle of identities continues, the struggle of borders is
our reality still. One day the inner struggle will cease and a true integration take place. In the meantime, *tenémos que hacer la lucha. ¿Quién
está protegiendo los ranchos de mi gente? ¿Quién está tratando de cer-
rar la fisura entre la india y el blanco en nuestra sangre? El Chicano, si,
el Chicano que anda como un ladrón en su propia casa.*

Los Chicanos, how patient we seem, how very patient. There is the
quiet of the Indian about us.[13] We know how to survive. When other
races have given up their tongue, we've kept ours. We know what it is to
live under the hammer blow of the dominant *norteamericano* culture.
But more than we count the blows, we count the days the weeks the
years the centuries the eons until the white laws and commerce and
customs will rot in the deserts they've created, lie bleached. *Humildes*
yet proud, *quietos* yet wild, *nosotros los mexicanos-Chicanos* will walk
by the crumbling ashes as we go about our business. Stubborn, perse-
vering, impenetrable as stone, yet possessing a malleability that ren-
ders us unbreakable, we, the *mestizas* and *mestizos*, will remain.

Notes

1. Ray Gwyn Smith, *Moorland Is Cold Country*, unpublished book.
2. Irene Klepfisz, "*Di rayze aheym*/The Journey Home," in *The Tribe of Dina: A Jewish Women's Anthology*. Melanie Kaye/Kantrowitz and Irena Klepfisz, eds. (Montpelier, VT: Sinister Wisdom Books, 1986), 49.
3. R. C. Ortega, *Dialectologia Del Barrio*, trans. Hortencia S. Alwan (Los Angeles, CA: R. C. Ortega Publisher & Bookseller, 1977), 132.
4. Eduardo Hernandéz-Chávez, Andrew D. Cohen, and Anthony F. Beltramo, *El Lenguaje de los Chicanos: Regional and Social Characteristics of Language Used by Mexican Americans* (Arlington, VA: Center for Applied Linguistics, 1975), 39.
5. Hernandéz-Chávez, xvii.
6. Irena Klepfisz, "Secular Jewish Identity: Yidishkayt in America," in *The Tribe of Dina*, Kaye/Kantrowitz and Klepfisz, eds., 43.
7. Melanie Kaye/Kantrowitz, "Sign," in *We Speak in Code: Poems and Other Writings* (Pittsburgh, PA: Motheroot Publications, Inc., 1980), 85.
8. Rodolfo Gonzales, *I Am Joaquín / Yo Soy Joaquin* (New York, NY: Bantam Books, 1972). It was first published in 1967.
9. Gershen Kaufman, *Shame: The Power of Caring* (Cambridge, MA: Schenkman Books, Inc., 1980), 68.
10. John R. Chávez, *The Lost Land: The Chicano Images of the Southwest* (Albuquerque, NM: University of New Mexico Press, 1984), 88–90.
11. "Hispanic" is derived from *Hispanis* (*España*, a name given to the Iberian Peninsula in ancient times when it was a part of the Roman Empire) and is a term designated by the U.S. government to make it easier to handle us on paper.
12. The Treaty of Guadalupe Hidalgo created the Mexican-American in 1848.
13. Anglos, in order to alleviate their guilt for dispossessing the Chicano, stressed the Spanish part of us and perpetrated the myth of the Spanish Southwest. We have accepted the fiction that we are Hispanic, that is Spanish, in order to accommodate ourselves to the dominant culture and its abhorrence of Indians. Chávez, 88–91.

Nobody Mean More to Me Than You[1] and the Future Life of Willie Jordan

June Jordan

For the late writer and teacher June Jordan, language and literacy issues remained inseparable from social justice work. In the following essay, first published in her collection On Call: Political Essays *(1985), Jordan chronicles her experiences with teaching Black English to undergraduates at SUNY–Stony Brook. Intertwined with Jordan's narrative is the story of her student Willie Jordan, who struggles with events surrounding the murder of his brother by New York City police officers. Throughout the essay, Jordan intersperses examples of student writing, such as the "Guidelines to Black English" on which her class collaborated, and Willie Jordan's end-of-semester essay on "racism, poverty, and the abuse of power." Noting that "Willie's writing needed the kind of improvement only intense practice will yield," Jordan looked forward "to see[ing] what happened when he could catch up with himself, entirely, and talk back to the world." The story of Willie's progress—as well as the stories of the writing processes of Jordan's students in the Black English course as they struggled with questions of audience and purpose—make for compelling reading and pose many questions about the political and cultural implications of language.*

B lack English is not exactly a linguistic buffalo; as children, most of the thirty-five million Afro-Americans living here depend on this language for our discovery of the world. But then we approach our maturity inside a larger social body that will not support our efforts to become anything other than the clones of those who are neither our mothers nor our fathers. We begin to grow up in a house where every true mirror shows us the face of somebody who does not belong there, whose walk and whose talk will never look or sound "right," because that house was meant to shelter a family that is alien and hostile to us. As we learn our way around this environment, either we hide our original word habits, or we completely surrender our own voice, hoping to please those who will never respect anyone different from themselves: Black English is not exactly a linguistic buffalo, but we should understand its status as an endangered species, as a perishing, irreplaceable system of community intelligence, or we should expect its extinction, and, along with that, the extinguishing of much that constitutes our own proud, and singular identity.

What we casually call "English," less and less defers to England and its "gentlemen." "English" is no longer a specific matter of geography or an element of class privilege; more than thirty-three countries use this tool as a means of "intranational communication."[2] Countries as disparate as Zimbabwe and Malaysia, or Israel and Uganda, use it as their non-native currency of convenience. Obviously, this tool, this "English," cannot function inside thirty-three discrete societies on the basis of rules and values absolutely determined somewhere else, in a thirty-fourth other country, for example.

In addition to that staggering congeries of non-native users of English, there are five countries, or 333,746,000 people, for whom this thing called "English" serves as a native tongue.[3] Approximately 10 percent of these native speakers of "English" are Afro-American citizens of the U.S.A. I cite these numbers and varieties of human beings dependent on "English" in order, quickly, to suggest how strange and how tenuous is any concept of "Standard English." Obviously, numerous forms of English now operate inside a natural, an uncontrollable, continuum of development. I would suppose "the standard" for English in

Malaysia is not the same as "the standard" in Zimbabwe. I know that standard forms of English for Black people in this country do not copy that of whites. And, in fact, the structural differences between these two kinds of English have intensified, becoming more Black, or less white, despite the expected homogenizing effects of television[4] and other mass media.

Nonetheless, white standards of English persist, supreme and un-questioned, in these United States. Despite our multi-lingual population, and despite the deepening Black and white cleavage within that conglomerate, white standards control our official and popular judgments of verbal proficiency and correct, or incorrect, language skills, including speech. In contrast to India, where at least fourteen languages co-exist as legitimate Indian languages, in contrast to Nicaragua, where all citizens are legally entitled to formal school instruction in their regional or tribal languages, compulsory education in America compels accommodation to exclusively white forms of "English." White English, in America, is "Standard English."

This story begins two years ago. I was teaching a new course, "In Search of the Invisible Black Woman," and my rather large class seemed evenly divided between young Black women and men. Five or six white students also sat in attendance. With unexpected speed and enthusiasm we had moved through historical narratives of the nineteenth century to literature by and about Black women, in the twentieth. I had assigned the first forty pages of Alice Walker's *The Color Purple*, and I came, eagerly, to class that morning:

"So!" I exclaimed, aloud. "What did you think? How did you like it?"

The students studied their hands, or the floor. There was no response. The tense, resistant feeling in the room fairly astounded me.

At last, one student, a young woman still not meeting my eyes, muttered something in my direction:

"What did you say?" I prompted her.

"Why she have them talk so funny. It don't sound right."

"You mean the language?"

Another student lifted his head: "It don't look right, neither. I couldn't hardly read it."

At this, several students dumped on the book. Just about unanimously, their criticisms targeted the language. I listened to what they wanted to say and silently marvelled at the similarities between their casual speech patterns and Alice Walker's written version of Black English.

But I decided against pointing to these identical traits of syntax; I wanted not to make them self-conscious about their own spoken language—not while they clearly felt it was "wrong." Instead I decided to swallow my astonishment. Here was a negative Black reaction to a prize-winning accomplishment of Black literature that white readers across the country had selected as a best seller. Black rejection was aimed at the one irreducibly Black element of Walker's work: the language—Celie's Black English. I wrote the opening lines of *The Color Purple* on the blackboard and asked the students to help me translate these sentences into Standard English:

> *You better not never tell nobody but God. It'd kill your mammy.*
> Dear God,
>   I am fourteen years old. I have always been a good girl. Maybe you can give me a sign letting me know what is happening to me.
>   Last spring after Little Lucious come I heard them fussing. He was pulling on her arm. She say it too soon, Fonso. I aint well. Finally he leave her alone. A week go by, he pulling on her arm again. She say, Naw, I ain't gonna. Can't you see I'm already half dead, an all of the children.[5]

Our process of translation exploded with hilarity and even hysterical, shocked laughter: The Black writer, Alice Walker, knew what she was doing! If rudimentary criteria for good fiction include the manipulation of language so that the syntax and diction of sentences will tell you the identity of speakers, the probable age and sex and class of speakers, and even the locale—urban/rural/southern/western—then Walker had written, perfectly. This is the translation into Standard English that our class produced:

> *Absolutely, one should never confide in anybody besides God. Your secrets could prove devastating to your mother.*
> Dear God,
>   I am fourteen years old. I have always been good. But now, could you help me to understand what is happening to me?
>   Last spring, after my little brother, Lucious, was born, I heard my parents fighting. My father kept pulling at my mother's arm. But she told him, "It's too soon for sex, Alfonso. I am still not feeling well." Finally, my father left her alone. A week went by, and then he began bothering my mother, again: Pulling her arm. She told him, "No, I won't! Can't you see I'm already exhausted from all of these children?"

(Our favorite line was "It's too soon for sex, Alfonso.")

Once we could stop laughing, once we could stop our exponentially wild improvisations on the theme of Translated Black English, the students pushed me to explain their own negative first reactions to their spoken language on the printed page. I thought it was probably akin to the shock of seeing yourself in a photograph for the first time. Most of the students had never before seen a written facsimile of the way they talk. None of the students had ever learned how to read and write their own verbal system of communication: Black English. Alternatively, this fact began to baffle or else bemuse and then infuriate my students. Why not? Was it too late? Could they learn how to do it, now? And, ultimately, the final test question, the one testing my sincerity: Could I teach them? Because I had never taught anyone Black English and, as far as I knew, no one, anywhere in the United States, had ever offered such a course, the best I could say was "I'll try."

He looked like a wrestler.

He sat dead center in the packed room and, every time our eyes met, he quickly nodded his head as though anxious to reassure, and encourage, me.

Short, with strikingly broad shoulders and long arms, he spoke with a surprisingly high, soft voice that matched the soft bright movement of his eyes. His name was Willie Jordan. He would have seemed even more unlikely in the context of Contemporary Women's Poetry, except that ten or twelve other Black men were taking the course, as well. Still, Willie was conspicuous. His extreme fitness, the muscular density of his presence underscored the riveted, gentle attention that he gave to anything anyone said. Generally, he did not join the loud and rowdy dialogue flying back and forth, but there could be no doubt about his interest in our discussions. And, when he stood to present an argument he'd prepared, overnight, that nervous smile of his vanished and an irregular stammering replaced it, as he spoke with visceral sincerity, word by word.

That was how I met Willie Jordan. It was in between "In Search of the Invisible Black Woman" and "The Art of Black English." I was waiting for Departmental approval and I supposed that Willie might be, so to speak, killing time until he, too, could study Black English. But Willie really did want to explore Contemporary Women's Poetry and, to that end, volunteered for extra research and never missed a class.

Towards the end of that semester, Willie approached me for an independent study project on South Africa. It would commence the next semester. I thought Willie's writing needed the kind of improvement only intense practice will yield. I knew his intelligence was outstanding. But he'd wholeheartedly opted for "Standard English" at a rather late age, and the results were stilted and frequently polysyllabic, simply for the sake of having more syllables. Willie's unnatural formality of language seemed to me consistent with the formality of his research into South African apartheid. As he projected his studies, he would have little time, indeed, for newspapers. Instead, more than 90 percent of his research would mean saturation in strictly historical, if not archival, material. I was certainly interested. It would be tricky to guide him into a more confident and spontaneous relationship both with language and apartheid. It was going to be wonderful to see what happened when he could catch up with himself, entirely, and talk back to the world.

September, 1984: Breezy fall weather and much excitement! My class, "The Art of Black English," was full to the limit of the fire laws.

And, in Independent Study, Willie Jordan showed up, weekly, fifteen minutes early for each of our sessions. I was pretty happy to be teaching, altogether!

I remember an early class when a young brother, replete with his ever present pork-pie hat, raised his hand and then told us that most of what he'd heard was "all right" except it was "too clean." "The brothers on the street," he continued, "they mix it up more. Like 'fuck' and 'motherfuck.' Or like 'shit.'" He waited. I waited. Then all of us laughed a good while, and we got into a brawl about "correct" and "realistic" Black English that led to Rule 1.

Rule 1: *Black English is about a whole lot more than mothafuckin.*
As a criterion, we decided, "realistic" could take you anywhere you want to go. Artful places. Angry places. Eloquent and sweetalkin places. Polemical places. Church. And the local Bar & Grill. We were checking out a language, not a mood or a scene or one guy's forgettable mouthing off.

It was hard. For most of the students, learning Black English required a fallback to patterns and rhythms of speech that many of their parents had beaten out of them. I mean *beaten.* And, in a majority of cases, correct Black English could be achieved only by striving for *incorrect* Standard English, something they were still pushing at, quite uncertainly. This state of affairs led to Rule 2.

Rule 2: *If it's wrong in Standard English it's probably right in Black English, or, at least, you're hot.*
It was hard. Roommates and family members ridiculed their studies, or remained incredulous, "You *studying* that shit? At school?" But we were beginning to feel the companionship of pioneers. And we decided that we needed another rule that would establish each one of us as equally important to our success. This was Rule 3.

Rule 3: *If it don't sound like something that come out somebody mouth then it don't sound right. If it don't sound right then it ain't hardly right. Period.*
This rule produced two weeks of compositions in which the students agonizingly tried to spell the sound of the Black English sentence they wanted to convey. But Black English is, pre-eminently, an oral/spoken means of communication. *And spelling don't talk.* So we needed Rule 4.

Rule 4: *Forget about the spelling. Let the syntax carry you.*
Once we arrived at Rule 4 we started to fly because syntax, the structure of an idea, leads you to the worldview of the speaker and reveals her values. The syntax of a sentence equals the structure of your consciousness. If we insisted that the language of Black English

adheres to a distinctive Black syntax, then we were postulating a profound difference between white and Black people, *per se.* Was it a difference to prize or to obliterate?

There are three qualities of Black English—the presence of life, voice, and clarity—that testify to a distinctive Black value system that we became excited about and self-consciously tried to maintain.

1. Black English has been produced by a pre-technocratic, if not anti-technological, culture. More, our culture has been constantly threatened by annihilation or, at least, the swallowed blurring of assimilation. Therefore, our language is a system constructed by people constantly needing to insist that we exist, that we are present. Our language devolves from a culture that abhors all abstraction, or anything tending to obscure or delete the fact of the human being who is here and now/ the truth of the person who is speaking or listening. Consequently, *there is no passive voice construction possible in Black English.* For example, you cannot say, "Black English is being eliminated." You must say, instead, "White people eliminating Black English." The assumption of the presence of life governs all of Black English. Therefore, overwhelmingly, *all action takes place in the language of the present indicative.* And every sentence assumes the living and active participation of at least two human beings, the speaker and the listener.

2. A primary consequence of the person-centered values of Black English is the delivery of voice. If you speak or write Black English, your ideas will necessarily possess that otherwise elusive attribute, voice.

3. One main benefit following from the person-centered values of Black English is that of *clarity.* If your idea, your sentence, assumes the presence of at least two living and active people, you will make it understandable because the motivation behind every sentence is the wish to say something real to somebody real.

As the weeks piled up, translation from Standard English into Black English or vice versa occupied a hefty part of our course work.

> Standard English (hereafter S.E.): "In considering the idea of studying Black English those questioned suggested—"
> (What's the subject? Where's the person? Is anybody alive in there, in that idea?)
> Black English (hereafter B.E.): "I been asking people what you think about somebody studying Black English and they answer me like this:"

But there were interesting limits. You cannot "translate" instances of Standard English preoccupied with abstraction or with nothing/nobody evidently alive, into Black English. That would warp the language into uses antithetical to the guiding perspective of its community of users. Rather you must first change those Standard English sentences, themselves, into ideas consistent with the person-centered assumptions of Black English.

Guidelines for Black English

1. Minimal number of words for every idea: This is the source for the aphoristic and/or poetic force of the language; eliminate every possible word.

2. Clarity: If the sentence is not clear it's not Black English.

3. Eliminate use of the verb *to be* whenever possible. This leads to the deployment of more descriptive and therefore, more precise verbs.

4. Use *be* or *been* only when you want to describe a chronic, ongoing state of things.

   He *be* at the office, by 9. (He is always at the office by 9.)

   He *been* with her since forever.

5. Zero copula: Always eliminate the verb *to be* whenever it would combine with another verb, in Standard English.

   S.E.: She is going out with him.

   B.E.: She going out with him.

6. Eliminate *do* as in:

   S.E.: What do you think? What do you want?

   B.E.: What you think? What you want?

   Rules number 3, 4, 5, and 6 provide for the use of the minimal number of verbs per idea and, therefore, greater accuracy in the choice of verb.

7. In general, if you wish to say something really positive, try to formulate the idea using emphatic negative structure.

   S.E.: He's fabulous.

   B.E.: He bad.

8. Use double or triple negatives for dramatic emphasis.

   S.E.: Tina Turner sings out of this world.

   B.E.: Ain nobody sing like Tina.

9. Never use the –*ed* suffix to indicate the past tense of a verb.

   S.E.: She closed the door.

   B.E.: She close the door. Or, she have close the door.

10. Regardless of intentional verb time, only use the third person singular, present indicative, for use of the verb *to have,* as an auxiliary.

>   S.E.: He had his wallet then he lost it.

>   B.E.: He have him wallet then he lose it.

>   S.E.: We had seen that movie.

>   B.E.: We seen that movie. Or, we have see that movie.

11. Observe a minimal inflection of verbs. Particularly, never change from the first person singular forms to the third person singular.

>   S.E.: Present Tense Forms: He goes to the store.

>   B.E.: He go to the store.

>   S.E.: Past Tense Forms: He went to the store.

>   B.E.: He go to the store. Or, he gone to the store. Or, he been to the store.

12. The possessive case scarcely ever appears in Black English. Never use an apostrophe ('s) construction. If you wander into a possessive case component of an idea, then keep logically consistent: *ours, his, theirs, mines.* But, most likely, if you bump into such a component, you have wandered outside the underlying worldview of Black English.

>   S.E.: He will take their car tomorrow.

>   B.E.: He taking they car tomorrow.

13. Plurality: Logical consistency, continued: If the modifier indicates plurality then the noun remains in the singular case.

>   S.E.: He ate twelve doughnuts.

>   B.E.: He eat twelve doughnut.

>   S.E.: She has many books.

>   B.E.: She have many book.

14. Listen for, or invent, special Black English forms of the past tense, such as "He losted it. That what she felted." If they are clear and readily understood, then use them.

15. Do not hesitate to play with words, sometimes inventing them: e.g. "astropotomous" means huge like a hippo plus astronomical and, therefore, signifies real big.

16. In Black English, unless you keenly want to underscore the past tense nature of an action, stay in the present tense and rely on the overall context of your ideas for the conveyance of time and sequence.

17. Never use the suffix –*ly* form of an adverb in Black English.

>   S.E.: The rain came down rather quickly.

>   B.E.: The rain come down pretty quick.

18. Never use the indefinite article *an* in Black English.

>   S.E.: He wanted to ride an elephant.

>   B.E.: He want to ride him a elephant.

19. Invariant syntax: in correct Black English it is possible to formulate an imperative, an interrogative, and a simple declarative idea with the same syntax:

>   B.E.: You going to the store?
>   You going to the store.
>   You going to the store!

Where was Willie Jordan? We'd reached the mid-term of the semester. Students had formulated Black English guidelines, by consensus, and they were now writing with remarkable beauty, purpose, and enjoyment:

> *"I ain hardly speakin for everybody but myself so understan that."*
> —Kim Parks

Samples from student writings:

> "Janie have a great big ole hole inside her. Tea Cake the only thing that fit that hole . . .
> "That pear tree beautiful to Janie, especial when bees fiddlin with the blossomin pear there growin large and lovely. But personal speakin, the love she get from starin at that tree ain the love what starin back at her in them relationship." (Monica Morris)

> "Love is a big theme in, *They Eye Was Watching God.* Love show people new corners inside theyself. It pull out good stuff and stuff back bad stuff . . . Joe worship the doing uh his own hand and need other people to worship him too. But he ain't think about Janie that she a person and ought to live like anybody common do. Queen life not for Janie." (Monica Morris)

> "In both life and writin, Black womens have varietous experience of love that be cold like a iceberg or fiery like a inferno. Passion got for the other partner involve, man or woman, seem as shallow, ankle-deep water or the most profoundest abyss." (Constance Evans)

> "Family love another bond that ain't never break under no pressure." (Constance Evans)

> "You know it really cold/When the friend you/Always get out the fire/Act like they don't know you/When you in the heat." (Constance Evans)

"Big classroom discussion bout love at this time. I never take no class where us have any long arguin for and against for two or three day. New to me and great. I find the class time talkin a million time more interestin than detail bout the book." (Kathy Esseks)

As these examples suggest, Black English no longer limited the students, in any way. In fact, one of them, Philip Garfield, would shortly "translate" a pivotal scene from Ibsen's *A Doll House*, as his final term paper.

Nora: I didn't gived no shit. I thinked you a asshole back then, too, you make it so hard for me save mines husband life.

Krogstad: Girl, it clear you ain't any idea what you done. You dont exact what I once done, and I losed my reputation over it.

Nora: You asks me believe you once act brave save you wife life?

Krogstad: Law care less why you done it.

Nora: Law must suck.

Krogstad: Suck or no, if I wants, judge screw you wid dis paper.

Nora: No way, man. (Philip Garfield)

But where was Willie? Compulsively punctual, and always thoroughly prepared with neatly typed compositions, he had disappeared. He failed to show up for our regularly scheduled conference, and I received neither a note nor a phone call of explanation. A whole week went by. I wondered if Willie had finally been captured by the extremely current happenings in South Africa: passage of a new constitution that did not enfranchise the Black majority, and militant Black South African reaction to that affront. I wondered if he'd been hurt, somewhere. I wondered if the serious workload of weekly readings and writings had overwhelmed him and changed his mind about independent study. Where was Willie Jordan?

One week after the first conference that Willie missed, he called: "Hello, Professor Jordan? This is Willie. I'm sorry I wasn't there last week. But something has come up and I'm pretty upset. I'm sorry but I really can't deal right now."

I asked Willie to drop by my office and just let me see that he was okay. He agreed to do that. When I saw him I knew something hideous had happened. Something had hurt him and scared him to the marrow. He was all agitated and stammering and terse and incoherent. At last, his sadly jumbled account let me surmise, as follows: Brooklyn police had murdered his unarmed, twenty-five-year-old brother, Reggie Jordan. Neither Willie nor his elderly parents knew what to do about it. Nobody from the press was interested. His folks had no money. Police ran his family around and around, to no point. And Reggie was really dead. And Willie wanted to fight, but he felt helpless.

With Willie's permission I began to try to secure legal counsel for the Jordan family. Unfortunately Black victims of police violence are truly numerous while the resources available to prosecute their killers are truly scarce. A friend of mine at the Center for Constitutional Rights estimated that just the preparatory costs for bringing the cops into court normally approaches $180,000. Unless the execution of Reggie Jordan became a major community cause for organizing, and protest, his murder would simply become a statistical item.

Again, with Willie's permission, I contacted every newspaper and media person I could think of. But the William Bastone feature article in *The Village Voice* was the only result from that canvassing.

Again, with Willie's permission, I presented the case to my class in Black English. We had talked about the politics of language. We had talked about love and sex and child abuse and men and women. But the murder of Reggie Jordan broke like a hurricane across the room.

There are few "issues" as endemic to Black Life as police violence. Most of the students knew and respected and liked Jordan. Many of them were from the very neighborhood where the murder had occurred. All of the students had known somebody close to them who had been killed by police, or had known frightening moments of gratuitous confrontation with the cops. They wanted to do everything at once to avenge death. Number One: They decided to compose personal statements of condolence to Willie Jordan and his family written in Black English. Number Two: They decided to compose individual messages to the police, in Black English. These should be prefaced by an explanatory paragraph composed by the entire group. Number Three: These individual messages, with their lead paragraph, should be sent to *Newsday*.

The morning after we agreed on these objectives, one of the young women students appeared with an unidentified visitor, who sat through the class, smiling in a peculiar, comfortable way.

Now we had to make more tactical decisions. Because we wanted the messages published, and because we thought it imperative that our outrage be known by the police, the tactical question was this: Should the opening, group paragraph be written in Black English or Standard English?

I have seldom been privy to a discussion with so much heart at the dead heat of it. I will never forget the eloquence, the sudden haltings of speech, the fierce struggle against tears, the furious throwaway, and useless explosions that this question elicited.

That one question contained several others, each of them extraordinarily painful to even contemplate. How best to serve the memory of Reggie Jordan? Should we use the language of the killers—Standard English—in order to make our ideas acceptable to those controlling the killers? But wouldn't what we had to say be rejected, summarily,

if we said it in our own language, the language of the victim, Reggie
Jordan? But if we sought to express ourselves by abandoning our language wouldn't that mean our suicide on top of Reggie's murder? But if
we expressed ourselves in our own language wouldn't that be suicidal
to the wish to communicate with those who, evidently, did not give a
damn about us/Reggie/police violence in the Black community?

At the end of one of the longest, most difficult hours of my own life,
the students voted, unanimously, to preface their individual messages
with a paragraph composed in the language of Reggie Jordan. *"At least
we don't give up nothing else. At least we stick to the truth: Be who we
been. And stay all the way with Reggie."*

It was heartbreaking to proceed, from that point. Everyone in the
room realized that our decision in favor of Black English had doomed
our writings, even as the distinctive reality of our Black lives always
has doomed our efforts to "be who we been" in this country.

I went to the blackboard and took down this paragraph, dictated by
the class:

". . . You cops!
We the brother and sister of Willie Jordan, a fellow Stony Brook student
who the brother of the dead Reggie Jordan. Reggie, like many brother
and sister, he a victim of brutal racist police, October 25, 1984. Us appall,
fed up, because that another senseless death what occur in our community. This what we feel, this, from our heart, for we ain't stayin' silent no
more:"

With the completion of this introduction, nobody said anything. I
asked for comments. At this invitation, the unidentified visitor, a young
Black man, ceaselessly smiling, raised his hand. He was, it so happens,
a rookie cop. He had just joined the force in September and, he said, he
thought he should clarify a few things. So he came forward and sprawled
easily into a posture of barroom, or fireside, nostalgia:

"See," Officer Charles enlightened us, "Most times when you out on
the street and something come down you do one of two things. Over-
react or under-react. Now, if you under-react then you can get yourself
kilt. And if you over-react then maybe you kill somebody. Fortunately
it's about nine times out of ten and you will over-react. So the brother
got kilt. And I'm sorry about that, believe me. But what you have to
understand is what kilt him: Over-reaction. That's all. Now you talk
about Black people and white police but see, now, I'm a cop myself.
And (big smile) I'm Black. And just a couple months ago I was on the
other side. But see it's the same for me. You a cop, you the ultimate
authority: the Ultimate Authority. And you on the street, most of the
time you can only do one of two things: over-react or under-react. That's
all it is with the brother: Over-reaction. Didn't have nothing to do with
race."

That morning Officer Charles had the good fortune to escape without being boiled alive. But barely. And I remember the pride of his smile when I read about the fate of Black policemen and other collaborators, in South Africa. I remember him, and I remember the shock and palpable feeling of shame that filled the room. It was as though that foolish, and deadly, young man had just relieved himself of his foolish, and deadly, explanation, face to face with the grief of Reggie Jordan's father and Reggie Jordan's mother. Class ended quietly. I copied the paragraph from the blackboard, collected the individual messages and left to type them up.

Newsday rejected the piece.

The Village Voice could not find room in their "Letters" section to print the individual messages from the students to the police.

None of the tv news reporters picked up the story.

Nobody raised $180,000 to prosecute the murder of Reggie Jordan.

Reggie Jordan is really dead.

I asked Willie Jordan to write an essay pulling together everything important to him from that semester. He was still deeply beside himself with frustration and amazement and loss. This is what he wrote, un-edited, and in its entirety:

"Throughout the course of this semester I have been researching the effects of oppression and exploitation along racial lines in South Africa and its neighboring countries. I have become aware of South African police brutalization of native Africans beyond the extent of the law, even though the laws themselves are catalyst affliction upon Black men, women and children. Many Africans die each year as a result of the deliberate use of police force to protect the white power structure.

"Social control agents in South Africa, such as policemen, are also used to force compliance among citizens through both overt and covert tactics. It is not uncommon to find bold-faced coercion and cold-blooded killings of Blacks by South African police for undetermined and/or inadequate reasons. Perhaps the truth is that the only reasons for this heinous treatment of Blacks rests in racial differences. We should also understand that what is conveyed through the media is not always accurate and may sometimes be construed as the tip of the iceberg at best.

"I recently received a painful reminder that racism, poverty, and the abuse of power are global problems which are by no means unique to South Africa. On October 25, 1984, at approximately 3:00 p.m. my brother, Mr. Reginald Jordan, was shot and killed by two New York City policemen from the 75th precinct in the East New York section of Brooklyn. His life ended at the age of twenty-five. Even up to this current point in time the Police Department has failed to provide my family, which consists of five brothers, eight sisters, and two parents, with a plausible reason for Reggie's death. Out of the many stories that were given to my family by the Police Department, not one of them seems to hold water. In fact, I honestly believe that the Police Department's assessment of my brother's murder is nothing short of ABSOLUTE BULLSHIT, and thus far no evidence had been produced to alter perception of the situation.

"Furthermore, I believe that one of three cases may have occurred in this incident. First, Reggie's death may have been the desired outcome of the police officer's action, in which case the killing was premeditated. Or, it was a case of mistaken identity, which clarifies the fact that the two officers who killed my brother and their commanding parties are all grossly incompetent. Or, both of the above cases are correct, i.e., Reggie's murderers intended to kill him and the Police Department behaved insubordinately.

"Part of the argument of the officers who shot Reggie was that he had attacked one of them and took his gun. This was their major claim. They also said that only one of them had actually shot Reggie. The facts, however, speak for themselves. According to the Death Certificate and autopsy report, Reggie was shot eight times from point-blank range. The Doctor who performed the autopsy told me himself that two bullets entered the side of my brother's head, four bullets were sprayed into his back, and two bullets struck him in the back of his legs. It is obvious that unnecessary force was used by the police and that it is extremely difficult to shoot someone in his back when he is attacking or approaching you.

"After experiencing a situation like this and researching South Africa I believe that to a large degree, justice may only exist as rhetoric. I find it difficult to talk of true justice when the oppression of my people both at home and abroad attests to the fact that inequality and injustice are serious problems whereby Blacks and Third World people are perpetually short-changed by society. Something has to be done about the way in which this world is set up. Although it is a difficult task, we do have the power to make a change."

—Willie J. Jordan Jr.
EGL 487, Section 58, November 14, 1984

It is my privilege to dedicate this book to the future life of Willie J. Jordan Jr.
August 8, 1985

Notes

1. Black English aphorism crafted by Monica Morris, a Junior at S.U.N.Y. at Stony Brook, October 1984.
2. *English Is Spreading, But What Is English?* A presentation by Professor S. N. Sridahr, Dept. of Linguistics, S.U.N.Y. at Stony Brook, April 9, 1985: Dean's Conversation Among the Disciplines.

3. Ibid.
4. *New York Times*, March 15, 1985, Section One, p. 14: Report on study by Linguistics at the University of Pennsylvania.
5. Alice Walker, *The Color Purple* (1982), p. 11, Harcourt Brace, N.Y.

Embracing Change: Teaching in a Multicultural World

bell hooks

bell hooks, author of Belonging: A Culture of Place *(Routledge, 2008), has written extensively on social class, race, and gender. She is Distinguished Professor in Residence in Appalachian Studies at the Loyal Jones Appalachian Center at Berea College in Kentucky. The following essay is taken from her 1994 book,* Teaching to Transgress: Education as the Practice of Freedom, *in which hooks addresses issues of race, social class, and gender as they pertain to multicultural education. "When we, as educators, allow our pedagogy to be radically changed by a recognition of a multicultural world," hooks suggests, "we can give students the education they desire and deserve" (p. 276). In her work, hooks offers strategies for classroom teachers working with a diverse student body; moreover, the author provides insights about teaching in multicultural environments. She remains inspired by the work of the Brazilian educator Paulo Freire, who influenced hooks to interrogate her notions of critical pedagogy, liberatory education, and student-centered learning.*

Despite the contemporary focus on multiculturalism in our society, particularly in education, there is not nearly enough practical discussion of ways classroom settings can be transformed so that the learning experience is inclusive. If the effort to respect and honor the social reality and experiences of groups in this society who are nonwhite is to be reflected in a pedagogical process, then as teachers—on all levels, from elementary to university settings—we must acknowledge that our styles of teaching may need to change. Let's face it: most of us were taught in classrooms where styles of teaching reflected the notion of a single norm of thought and experience, which we were encouraged to believe was universal. This has been just as true for nonwhite teachers as for white teachers. Most of us learned to teach emulating this model. As a consequence, many teachers are disturbed by the political implications of a multicultural education because they fear losing control in a classroom where there is no one way to approach a subject—only multiple ways and multiple references.

Among educators there has to be an acknowledgment that any effort to transform institutions so that they reflect a multicultural standpoint must take into consideration the fears teachers have when asked to shift their paradigms. There must be training sites where teachers have the opportunity to express those concerns while also learning to create ways to approach the multicultural classroom and curriculum. When I first went to Oberlin College, I was disturbed by what I felt was a lack of understanding on the part of many professors as to what the multicultural classroom might be like. Chandra Mohanty, my colleague in Women's Studies, shared these concerns. Though we were both un-tenured, our strong belief that the Oberlin campus was not fully facing the issue of changing curriculum and teaching practices in ways that were progressive and promoting of inclusion led us to consider how we might intervene in this process. We proceeded from the standpoint that the vast majority of Oberlin professors, who are overwhelmingly white, were basically well-meaning, concerned about the quality of education students receive on our campus, and therefore likely to be supportive of any effort at education for critical consciousness. Together, we decided to have a group of seminars focusing on transformative pedagogy that would be open to all professors. Initially, students were also welcome, but we found that their presence inhibited honest discussion. On the first night, for example, several white professors made comments that could be viewed as horribly racist and the students left the group to share what was said around the college. Since our intent was to edu-cate for critical consciousness, we did not want the seminar setting to be a space where anyone would feel attacked or their reputation as a teacher sullied. We did, however, want it to be a space for constructive confrontation and critical interrogation. To ensure that this could hap-pen, we had to exclude students.

At the first meeting, Chandra (whose background is in education) and I talked about the factors that had influenced our pedagogical practices. I emphasized the impact of Freire's work on my thinking. Since my formative education took place in racially segregated schools, I spoke about the experience of learning when one's experience is rec-ognized as central and significant and then how that changed with de-segregation, when black children were forced to attend schools where we were regarded as objects and not subjects. Many of the professors present at the first meeting were disturbed by our overt discussion of political standpoints. Again and again, it was necessary to remind ev-eryone that no education is politically neutral. Emphasizing that a white male professor in an English department who teaches only work by "great white men" is making a political decision, we had to work consistently against and through the overwhelming will on the part of folks to deny the politics of racism, sexism, heterosexism, and so forth that inform how and what we teach. We found again and again that almost everyone, especially the old guard, were more disturbed by the overt recognition of the role our political perspectives play in shaping pedagogy than by their passive acceptance of ways of teaching and learning that reflect biases, particularly a white supremacist standpoint.

To share in our efforts at intervention we invited professors from universities around the country to come and talk—both formally and informally—about the kind of work they were doing aimed at transforming teaching and learning so that a multicultural education would be possible. We invited then-Princeton professor of religion and philosophy Cornel West to give a talk on "decentering Western civilization." It was our hope that his very traditional training and his progressive practice as a scholar would give everyone a sense of optimism about our ability to change. In the informal session, a few white male professors were courageously outspoken in their efforts to say that they could accept the need for change, but were uncertain about the implications of the changes. This reminded us that it is difficult for individuals to shift paradigms and that there must be a setting for folks to voice fears, to talk about what they are doing, how they are doing it, and why. One of our most useful meetings was one in which we asked professors from different disciplines (including math and science) to talk informally about how their teaching had been changed by a desire to be more inclusive. Hearing individuals describe concrete strategies was an approach that helped dispel fears. It was crucial that more traditional or conservative professors who had been willing to make changes talk about motivations and strategies.

When the meetings concluded, Chandra and I initially felt a tremendous sense of disappointment. We had not realized how much faculty would need to unlearn racism to learn about colonization and decolonization and to fully appreciate the necessity for creating a democratic liberal arts learning experience.

All too often we found a will to include those considered "marginal" without a willingness to accord their work the same respect and consideration given other work. In Women's Studies, for example, individuals will often focus on women of color at the very end of the semester or lump everything about race and difference together in one section. This kind of tokenism is not multicultural transformation, but it is familiar to us as the change individuals are most likely to make. Let me give another example. What does it mean when a white female English professor is eager to include a work by Toni Morrison on the syllabus of her course but then teaches that work without ever making reference to race or ethnicity? I have heard individual white women "boast" about how they have shown students that black writers are "as good" as the white male canon when they do not call attention to race. Clearly, such pedagogy is not an interrogation of the biases conventional canons (if not all canons) establish, but yet another form of tokenism.

The unwillingness to approach teaching from a standpoint that includes awareness of race, sex, and class is often rooted in the fear that classrooms will be uncontrollable, that emotions and passions will not be contained. To some extent, we all know that whenever we address in the classroom subjects that students are passionate about there is always a possibility of confrontation, forceful expression of ideas, or even conflict. In much of my writing about pedagogy, particularly in classroom settings with great diversity, I have talked about the need to examine critically the way we as teachers conceptualize what the space for learning should be like. Many professors have conveyed to me their feeling that the classroom should be a "safe" place; that usually translates to mean that the professor lectures to a group of quiet students who respond only when they are called on. The experience of professors who educate for critical consciousness indicates that many students, especially students of color, may not feel at all "safe" in what appears to be a neutral setting. It is the absence of a feeling of safety that often promotes prolonged silence or lack of student engagement.

Making the classroom a democratic setting where everyone feels a responsibility to contribute is a central goal of transformative pedagogy. Throughout my teaching career, white professors have often voiced concern to me about nonwhite students who do not talk. As the classroom becomes more diverse, teachers are faced with the way the politics of domination are often reproduced in the educational setting. For example, white male students continue to be the most vocal in our classes. Students of color and some white women express fear that they will be judged as intellectually inadequate by these peers. I have taught brilliant students of color, many of them seniors, who have skillfully managed never to speak in classroom settings. Some express the feeling that they are less likely to suffer any kind of assault if they simply do not assert their subjectivity. They have told me that many professors never showed any interest in hearing their voices. Accepting the decentering of the West globally, embracing multiculturalism, compels educators to focus attention on the issue of voice. Who speaks? Who listens? And why? Caring about whether all students fulfill their responsibility to contribute to learning in the classroom is not a common approach in what Freire has called the "banking system of education" where students are regarded merely as passive consumers. Since so many professors teach from that standpoint, it is difficult to create the kind of learning community that can fully embrace multiculturalism. Students are much more willing to surrender their dependency on the banking system of education than are their teachers. They are also much more willing to face the challenge of multiculturalism.

It has been as a teacher in the classroom setting that I have witnessed the power of a transformative pedagogy rooted in a respect for multiculturalism. Working with a critical pedagogy based on my understanding of Freire's teaching, I enter the classroom with the assumption that we must build "community" in order to create a climate of openness and intellectual rigor. Rather than focusing on issues of safety, I think that a feeling of community creates a sense that there is shared commitment and a common good that binds us. What we all ideally share is the desire to learn—to receive actively knowledge that enhances our intellectual development and our capacity to live more fully in the world. It has been my experience that one way to build community in the classroom is to recognize the value of each individual voice. In my classes, students keep journals and often write paragraphs during class which they read to one another. This happens at least once irrespective of class size. Most of the classes I teach are not small. They range anywhere from thirty to sixty students, and at times I have taught more than one hundred. To hear each other (the sound of different voices), to listen to one another, is an exercise in recognition. It also ensures that no student remains invisible in the classroom. Some students resent having to make a verbal contribution, and so I have had to make it clear from the outset that this is a requirement in my classes. Even if there is a student present whose voice cannot be heard in spoken words, by "signing" (even if we cannot read the signs) they make their presence felt.

When I first entered the multicultural, multi-ethnic classroom setting I was unprepared. I did not know how to cope effectively with so much "difference." Despite progressive politics, and my deep engagement with the feminist movement, I had never before been compelled to work within a truly diverse setting and I lacked the necessary skills. This is the case with most educators. It is difficult for many educators in the United States to conceptualize how the classroom will look when they are confronted with the demographics which indicate that "whiteness" may cease to be the norm ethnicity in classroom settings on all levels. Hence, educators are poorly prepared when we actually confront diversity. This is why so many of us stubbornly cling to old patterns. As I worked to create teaching strategies that would make a space for multicultural learning, I found it necessary to recognize what I have called in other writing on pedagogy different "cultural codes." To teach effectively a diverse student body, I have to learn these codes. And so do students. This act alone transforms the classroom. The sharing of ideas and information does not always progress as quickly as it may in more homogeneous settings. Often, professors and students have to learn to accept different ways of knowing, new epistemologies, in the multicultural setting.

Just as it may be difficult for professors to shift their paradigms, it is equally difficult for students. I have always believed that students should enjoy learning. Yet I found that there was much more tension in the diverse classroom setting where the philosophy of teaching is rooted in critical pedagogy and (in my case) in feminist critical pedagogy. The presence of tension—and at times even conflict—often meant that students did not enjoy my classes or love me, their professor, as I secretly wanted them to do. Teaching in a traditional discipline from the perspective of critical pedagogy means that I often encounter students who make complaints like, "I thought this was supposed to be an English class, why are we talking so much about feminism?" (Or, they might add, race or class.) In the transformed classroom there is often a much greater need to explain philosophy, strategy, intent than in the "norm" setting. I have found through the years that many of my students who bitch endlessly while they are taking my classes contact me at a later date to talk about how much that experience meant to them, how much they learned. In my professorial role I had to surrender my need for immediate affirmation of successful teaching (even though some reward is immediate) and accept that students may not appreciate the value of a certain standpoint or process straightaway. The exciting aspect of creating a classroom community where there is respect for individual voices is that there is infinitely more feedback because students do feel free to talk—and talk back. And, yes, often this feedback is critical. Moving away from the need for immediate affirmation was crucial to my growth as a teacher. I learned to respect that shifting paradigms or sharing knowledge in new ways challenges; it takes time for students to experience that challenge as positive.

Students taught me, too, that it is necessary to practice compassion in these new learning settings. I have not forgotten the day a student came to class and told me: "We take your class. We learn to look at the world from a critical standpoint, one that considers race, sex, and class. And we can't enjoy life anymore." Looking out over the class, across race, sexual preference, and ethnicity, I saw students nodding their heads. And I saw for the first time that there can be, and usually is, some degree of pain involved in giving up old ways of thinking and knowing and learning new approaches. I respect that pain. And I include recognition of it now when I teach, that is to say, I teach about shifting paradigms and talk about the discomfort it can cause. White students learning to think more critically about questions of race and racism may go home for the holidays and suddenly see their parents in a different light. They may recognize nonprogressive thinking, racism, and so on, and it may hurt them that new ways of knowing may create estrangement where there was none. Often when students return from breaks I ask them to share with us how ideas that they have learned or worked on in the classroom impacted on their experience outside. This gives them both the opportunity to know that difficult experiences may be common and practice at integrating theory and practice: ways of knowing with habits of being. We practice interrogating habits of being as well as ideas. Through this process we build community.

Despite the focus on diversity, our desires for inclusion, many professors still teach in classrooms that are predominantly white. Often a spirit of tokenism prevails in those settings. This is why it is so crucial that "whiteness" be studied, understood, discussed—so that everyone learns that affirmation of multiculturalism, and an unbiased inclusive perspective, can and should be present whether or not people of color are present. Transforming these classrooms is as great a challenge as learning how to teach well in the setting of diversity. Often, if there is one lone person of color in the classroom she or he is objectified by others and forced to assume the role of "native informant." For example, a novel is read by a Korean American author. White students turn to the one student from a Korean background to explain what they do not understand. This places an unfair responsibility onto that student. Professors can intervene in this process by making it clear from the outset that experience does not make one an expert, and perhaps even by explaining what it means to place someone in the role of "native informant." It must be stated that professors cannot intervene if they also see students as "native informants." Often, students have come to my office complaining about the lack of inclusion in another professor's class. For example, a course on social and political thought in the United States includes no work by women. When students complain to the teacher about this lack of inclusion, they are told to make suggestions of material that can be used. This often places an unfair burden on a student. It also makes it seem that it is only important to address a bias if there is someone complaining. Increasingly, students are making complaints because they want a democratic unbiased liberal arts education.

Multiculturalism compels educators to recognize the narrow boundaries that have shaped the way knowledge is shared in the classroom. It forces us all to recognize our complicity in accepting and perpetuating biases of any kind. Students are eager to break through barriers to knowing. They are willing to surrender to the wonder of relearning and learning ways of knowing that go against the grain. When we, as educators, allow our pedagogy to be radically changed by our recognition of a multicultural world, we can give students the education they desire and deserve. We can teach in ways that transform consciousness, creating a climate of free expression that is the essence of a truly liberatory liberal arts education.

Transforming Pedagogies

Improving Minority Academic Performance: How a Values-Affirmation Intervention Works

*Valerie Purdie-Vaughns, Geoffery L. Cohen,
Julio Garcia, Rachel Sumner, Jonathan C. Cook,
and Nancy Apfel*

Valerie Purdie-Vaughns, Geoffrey Cohen, and their team of researchers investigated likely causes of and remedies for the achievement gap between students of color and white students. Working in a suburban northeastern school, the research team found that a values intervention can serve as a powerful antidote to internalized stereotypes, and can help to sustain student achievement. Students at this middle-class and working-class school responded to prompts that invited them to write about values that were most important to them, such as family relationships or artistic interests. Learning, as defined by this research, becomes possible — and powerful — for students as they write and become aware of their own values, and how those values connect to success in high-risk academic situations.

The researchers suggest that "the affirmation reduces stress, allowing people's skills to be more completely displayed and the institution's resources to have greater impact" (p. 281). Moreover, the attitudes of teachers may begin to change as well: "The effects of teacher expectancies could then assert themselves, acting as channels that carry forward and amplify the effects of the intervention" (p. 281). In other words, through writing, students may become more confident of their own abilities, and teachers may become more aware of students' capabilities for sustainable achievement.

Closing the racial achievement gap is a national imperative in the United States. Academically at-risk minority students, such as African Americans and Latino Americans, perform almost a standard deviation below European American students on standardized intelligence tests (Jencks & Phillips, 1998). They also have lower grades than their European American and Asian American peers.

To the concern of all involved, the authors included, the gains made since 1990 in closing the gap have not been proportional to the resources and commitment devoted to it (Dillon, 2006; Neal, 2005). A National Assessment of Educational Progress (NAEP) report found the difference in average reading and math scores of African American and European American eighth-graders to be virtually unchanged between 2007 and the early 1990s (Vanneman, Hamilton, Baldwin Anderson, & Rahman, 2009). Moreover, between the years 2004 and 2007, of every hundred African Americans, ten had not received a high school diploma or its equivalent, while for every 100 Latino Americans 22 had not. By contrast, during this period the number of European Americans not receiving a high school diploma or its equivalent was six out of every 100 (U.S. Department of Education, 2009).

Racial differences in socioeconomic status were long thought to be at the heart of these performance gaps (Hacker, 1995; Jencks & Phillips, 1998). However, at every level of socioeconomic status academically at-risk minority students score lower on standardized tests such as the SAT and earn lower grade point averages than their European Americans counterparts (Bowen & Bok, 1998; Steele, 1997). While it is undeniable that such socioeconomic factors have a substantial role in academic performance, there is a clear imperative to examine other factors that may also be undermining minority achievement.

We focus on how social psychological factors influence these academic outcomes. These include students' group or "social" identity, particularly among those ethnic groups that have historically faced prejudice in school and the larger social context. For these minority students, school can evoke concerns that they will be judged on the basis of a negative stereotype about the intellectual ability of their race— that is, confront stereotype threat (Steele & Aronson, 1995; Steele, Spencer, & Aronson, 2002). Due to the living legacy of discrimination in the U.S., which includes negative stereotypes, members of these groups are more likely to experience psychological threat in school and work and to display lower performance as a result. In situations where the stereotype is relevant, such as taking a test, the fear that they or another group member may confirm the stereotype in the minds of others can cause stress (Blascovich, Spencer, Quinn, & Steele, 2001; Steele et al., 2002; Cohen & Garcia, 2005). Stress in turn can undermine performance, as when people choke under pressure. This threat may occur even if students cannot articulate the source of this stress and regardless of the objective level of discrimination or prejudice in a school.

Given the pervasiveness of stereotype threat and its negative impact on students' sense of security, one effective way to buffer students against such stressors is to provide them with opportunities to shore up their sense of self. One way to do so is to allow them to affirm core personal values that they deeply care about (Sherman & Cohen, 2006; Steele, 1988). Not only do self-affirmations secure students' sense of self-integrity in a threatening environment, but they also reduce stress (Creswell et al., 2005; see also Martens, Johns, Greenberg, & Schimel, 2006; Sherman et al., in press; Sherman & Cohen, 2006). When people reflect on important values that transcend a stressful situation—for instance, their relationships or religion—they feel less stressed and are better equipped psychologically to cope with the threatening situation. The series of values-affirmation exercises, or "self-affirmations," that we administer as structured writing assignments during our intervention reduce the stress of being the target of a negative racial stereotype by having students reflect on self-defining values, such as relationships with friends, sports, or religion, over the course of the school year.

Putting Our Money Where Our Theory Is: Testing a Values-Affirmation Intervention

Our work found that a self-affirmation intervention improved the grades of middle-school African American students (Cohen, Garcia, Apfel, Masters, 2006; Cohen, Garcia, Purdie-Vaughns, Apfel, Brzustoski, 2009). Follow-up data indicate similar positive effects on state achievement test scores (Garcia, Cohen, Purdie-Vaughns & Cook, 2009). In this work, we conducted three double-blind field experiments at a suburban Northeastern middle school whose student body was divided almost evenly between African Americans and European Americans (two experiments in the original 2006 paper, an additional study in the 2009 follow-up). As children are randomly assigned to receive the intervention and both they and their teachers are unaware of their assignment to an intervention, its nature, and expected effects (double-blind experiments), we can be extremely confident that differences observed between children receiving the intervention and those that do not are not due to some spurious occurrence, teacher expectancies, student selection effects, or so-called placebo effect, but are in fact genuine differences caused by the intervention.

Seventh-graders from middle- to lower-middle-class families completed a series of values-affirmations—structured-writing assignments designed to bolster their sense of self-integrity and thus reduce their stress over the possibility of confirming negative stereotypes. In-class exercises, presented as part of the regular classroom curriculum, instructed students to complete a packet in which they were first presented with a list of values, such as relationships with friends or family, music, or artistic interests (McQueen & Klein, 2006; Sherman & Cohen, 2006). Students who had been randomly assigned to receive the self-affirmation circled their most important values and, in response to a series of prompts, wrote a brief essay about why those values were important to them. By contrast, students who had been randomly assigned to the control condition completed neutral exercises such as writing about an unimportant value or their morning routine.

Our results revealed that affirmed African American students earned higher fall-term grades and GPA from official school records, in the affirmation condition than those not affirmed. Moreover, the affirmation intervention cut the percentage of African American students receiving a D or F grade in the course in which it was administered from 20% for students not receiving the affirmation to 9% for those receiving it, cutting the poor performance rate approximately in half. The intervention's effect was on average .30 grade points in this class (on a grade metric "A" = 4.0, "B" = 3.0, etc.). The greatest benefit to African American students of the intervention was that it eliminated roughly 40% of the achievement gap in the class that had existed between the races prior to the intervention. Additionally, the intervention's benefits were apparent across all levels of performance for African Americans. Its impact was significant for those students classed as low and moderate in achievement prior to its administration, and nearly so for those high in prior achievement. Finally, the effects of the intervention spilled over to benefit African Americans' grades in their other core courses.

A two-year follow-up to the study assessed whether the affirmation intervention buffered these same minority students from the effects of psychological threat over the long term (Cohen et al., 2009). If it did, would this lead to academic benefits beyond those that were found in a single academic term? The answer is yes.

The academic performance of three separate cohorts was observed for a period running from the first term of seventh grade to the end of eighth grade. The performance data during this period showed that the intervention effect on overall GPA persisted for at least two years (average of grades in math, English, social studies, and science). Interestingly, on closer examination, the intervention's effect on two-year GPA for African American students was largely driven by those classified as low achievers prior to its administration, a group often least responsive to intervention. Given the costs in terms of the time and resources dedicated to low-achieving students by schools, teachers, and society, these latter results were particularly encouraging. Moreover, our affirmation intervention lessened the typical downward performance trend found in middle school for African American students. It thus prevented the race gap from growing with time.

How Does It Work? What Processes Lead to Apparently Small Interventions Having Such Long-Term Effects?

The value-affirmation intervention acts like a *catalyst*. It permits the positive forces in school to assert a fuller impact (Garcia & Cohen, in press). In many schools the teachers are skilled and concerned, and the children not only have the motivation and ability to achieve, but have acquired new knowledge and skills. The impact of these forces, however, is blunted by other factors, such as stress, that prevent people from performing to their potential. This is akin to a skilled athlete underperforming while under pressure, despite his or her training and supportive coaches. The affirmation reduces stress, allowing people's skills to be more completely displayed and the institution's resources to have greater impact.

Moreover, *recursive processes acting like chain reactions* then carry forward the initial effects of the intervention (Cohen et al., 2009). A small improvement early in the year due to the intervention might, for example, give children a little extra confidence, and this confidence might lead to further gains in performance, in a potentially repeating cycle that sustains their performance for a long time. Likewise, a small intervention early in the school year might only raise children's performance by a modest amount. But, if their teachers had not expected this, then they may come see such students as more able and worthy of attention and mentoring. The effects of teacher expectancies could then assert themselves, acting as channels that carry forward and amplify the effects of the intervention.

It will be important to test the intervention in more diverse and less privileged environments, for instance urban and economically poor schools. However, our use in our original research of a relatively middle-class suburban school has two key merits. First, given the prevalent idea that the primary source of the achievement gap is socioeconomic status, if racial differences still exist in relatively advantaged schools, as they do, such gaps provide fodder to those who would attribute the race gap to some inherent and persistent difference in ability. In this respect such an environment as the school where this research was conducted provides a strong test of our hypothesis that racial differences are not due solely to socioeconomic status and are not due to inherent fixed differences between groups, but rather due to dynamic social-psychological factors. Second, to be effective, our intervention requires the presence of other key resources in the school and classroom environment. This is because the intervention acts as a catalyst. In environments where such resources are of poor quality or non-existent, the intervention's benefits, if they occur at all, will be less pronounced and most likely of shorter duration. Nevertheless, if whatever existing factors in the school can carry forward any improvement, small effects could matter in the long run. In closing we note that we are currently testing the intervention in a more disadvantaged school whose student body is nearly equally divided between Latino Americans and European Americans. Our initial findings are both positive and promising. As Latino Americans are the fastest growing population in the United States (U.S. Census 2000), if our findings prove robust they would provide another hopeful possibility for future intervention.

In Conclusion

We believe that our research advances an understanding not only of the achievement gap but also of school achievement in general. Identifying remedies of the racial achievement gap may improve the school achievement of all students by shedding light on the performance processes that affect us all. The effects of psychological threat and stress may help explain when and why people in general perform below their potential. Given that many adolescent students, regardless of race, begin a downward trend in middle school, a scientific understanding of under-performance will help teachers and policy-makers improve the lives of young children during their vulnerable transition to adulthood.

References

Blascovich, J., Spencer, S. J., Quinn, D., & Steele, C. (2001). African Americans and high blood pressure: The role of stereotype threat. *Psychological Science*, *12*, 225–229.

Bowen, W. G., & Bok, D. (1998). *The shape of the river: Long-term consequences of considering race in college and university admissions.* Princeton, NJ: Princeton University Press.

Cohen, G. L., & Garcia, J. (2005). I am us: Negative stereotypes as collective threats. *Journal of Personality and Social Psychology*, *89*, 566–582.

Cohen, G. L., Garcia, J., Apfel, N., & Master, A. (2006). Reducing the racial achievement gap: A social-psychological intervention. *Science, 313*, 1307–1310.

Cohen, G. L., Garcia, J., Purdie-Vaughns, V., Apfel, N., & Brzustoski, P. (2009). Raising minority performance with a values-affirmation intervention: A two-year follow-up. *Science, 324*, 400–403.

Creswell, J. D., Welch, W., Taylor, S. E., Sherman, D. K., Gruenewald, T., & Mann, T. (2005). Affirmation of personal values buffers neuroendocrine and psychological stress responses. *Psychological Science, 16*, 846–851.

Creswell, J. D., Lam, S., Stanton, A. L., Taylor, S. E., Bower, J. E., & Sherman, D. K. (2007). Does self-affirmation, cognitive processing, or discovery of meaning explain cancer-related health benefits of expressive writing? *Personality and Social Psychology Bulletin, 33*, 238–250.

Dillon, S. (2006, Nov. 20). Schools slow in closing gaps between races. *The New York Times*, p. A1.

Garcia, J., & Cohen, G. L. (in press). A social psychological perspective on educational intervention. In E. Shafir (Ed.), *The Behavioral Foundations of Policy*.

Garcia, J., Cohen, G., Purdie-Vaughns, V., & Cook. (2009). Self-affirmation and achievement test performance among middle school students. Manuscript forthcoming.

Hacker, A. (1995). *Two nations: Black and white, separate, hostile, unequal.* New York: Ballantine.

Jencks, C., & Phillips, M. (1998). *The black-white test score gap.* Washington, DC: The Brookings Institution.

Martens, A., Johns, M., Greenberg, J., & Schimel, J. (2006). Combating stereotype threat: The effect of self-affirmation on women's intellectual performance. *Journal of Experimental Social Psychology, 42,* 236–243.

McQueen, A., & Klein, W. (2006). Experimental manipulations of self-affirmation: A systematic review. *Self and Identity, 5,* 289–354.

Neal, D. A. (2005). *Why has black-white skill convergence stopped.* NBER Working Paper No. W11090. Available at SSRN: http://ssrn.com/abstract=657602.

Sherman, D. K., & Cohen, G. L. (2006). The psychology of self-defense: Self-affirmation theory. In M. P. Zanna (Ed.), *Advances in experimental social psychology* (Vol. 38, pp. 183–242). San Diego, CA: Academic Press.

Sherman, D. K., Cohen, G. L., Nelson, L. D., Nussbaum, A. D., Bunyan, D. P., & Garcia, J. (in press). Affirmed yet unaware: Exploring the role of awareness in the process of self-affirmation. *Journal of Personality and Social Psychology.*

Steele, C. M. (1988). The psychology of self-affirmation: Sustaining the integrity of the self. In L. Berkowitz (Ed.), *Advances in experimental social psychology* (Vol. 21, pp. 261–302). New York: Academic Press.

Steele, C. M., & Aronson, J. (1995). Stereotype threat and the intellectual test performance of African Americans. *Journal of Personality and Social Psychology, 69,* 797–811.

Steele, C. M. (1997). A threat in the air: How stereotypes shape the intellectual identities and performance of women and African Americans. *American Psychologist, 52,* 613–629.

Steele, C. M., Spencer, S. J., & Aronson, J. (2002). Contending with group image: The psychology of stereotype and social identity threat. In M. Zanna (Ed.), *Advances in experimental social psychology* (Vol. 34, pp. 379–440). New York: Academic Press.

U.S. Census Bureau. (2000). *National population projections, Components of change.* Retrieved July 7, 2009, from http://www.census.gov/population/www/projections/natdet-D3.html.

Vanneman, A., Hamilton, L., Baldwin Anderson, J., & Rahman, T. (2009). Achievement gaps: How black and white students in public schools perform in mathematics and reading on the National Assessment of Educational Progress (NCES 2009-455). National Center for Education Statistics, Washington, DC.

Cultivating Racial Literacy in White Segregated Settings: Emotions as Site of Ethical Engagement and Inquiry

Amy E. Winans

Amy Winans teaches at a segregated rural university, with a generally homogenous white, middle-class faculty and student body. "The perception of many White students that race and racial issues are located elsewhere," Winans suggests, "is reflected in descriptions of their rural hometowns" (p. 292). In order to complicate and interrogate this perception, Winans analyzes the intersections of emotions and ethical values with white students' writing about race. As questions for guiding her inquiry, Winans asks, "How do emotions motivate, curtail, or otherwise impact beliefs and ethical inquiry surrounding race? How is identity (especially in terms of ethics) represented, negotiated, or interrogated in the context of race?" (p. 293).

In the wake of the 2007 United States Supreme Court decision overturning voluntary school desegregation programs in public school districts of Louisville, Kentucky, and Seattle, Washington, Gary Orfield, director of the Civil Rights Project, has reminded us that in public schools across the United States White students are in fact the most racially isolated students. Indeed, drawing on the research of Amanda Lewis (2004), Jennifer Seibel Trainor (2008b) observes that "most white students in the United States attend all white schools; most live in highly racially segregated neighborhoods and have little regular, substantial contact with people of other races" (p. 130). Unfortunately, in the movement from high school to college, levels of segregation and racial isolation—as well as the beliefs and practices that support them—remain too similar. Numerous colleges remain overwhelmingly white institutions, places whose racial demographics differ markedly from those in the United States as a whole: the rural college where I teach, for example, is located in one of the whitest counties in Pennsylvania, and the school's student population is 92% White.[1] For many White students and parents, the racial demographics and the cultural, historical, and institutional factors that sustain them do not present a problem; indeed, they are implicitly valorized. Yet as the work of scholars like Henry Giroux (1988) and William Pinar (1993) suggests, the dominant discourses in racially segregated environments have a significant impact upon the nature of learning that occurs there, and these discourses lay the groundwork for a sort of racial illiteracy.

In this article I argue that instructors, especially White instructors like me, should seek to cultivate students' racial literacy, the ability to examine critically and recursively the ways in which race informs discourses, culture, institutions, belief systems, interpretive frameworks, and numerous facets of daily life. An ideal place for addressing racial literacy is in a first-year writing class, in part because a key dimension of students' analytical writing skills entails their recognizing the situated nature of their experiences and the interpretive lenses through which they engage with the world, our readings, and their writing. Thus, as part of a unit in my composition class, I assign a racial literacy narrative in which students write an essay analyzing some of their experiences of race. In this article, I consider how White, first-year students in a rural, private, liberal arts college in the United States address race and racial identity in this assignment, one of the four main writing assignments they complete over the course of a semester-long composition class focused on memoir. I am interested in understanding more fully how White students in a segregated setting describe and analyze their experiences as they begin to move from seeing themselves as innocent and raceless to understanding and experiencing themselves as raced/White. More specifically, I want to explore the role that emotions play in White students' accounts of their experiences with race because I believe that this is a fundamental, yet often overlooked, aspect of students' learning.

We might assume that the main challenge that White students would experience in cultivating racial literacy would be their limited knowledge of race and racism. Indeed, models of White identity development posit a direct correlation between White people's knowledge of race and racism and their stage of identity and racial awareness (Carter, 1997; Tatum, 2003). Yet classroom experience—both my own and others' (Schneider, 2005)—illustrates that simply offering students more or different information about race and racism isn't what cultivates racial literacy. Instead, I argue that we need to shift our attention from considering what White students know about race and racism to analyzing their experiences of knowing and coming to know, especially in a setting whose very nature depends upon people *not* cultivating racial literacy. To this end, it is essential to consider how ethical questioning and emotions inform students' experiences. After all, when we ask White students to grapple with their experiences of race, we are implicitly asking them to grapple with a difficult ethical question: What are the meanings and implications of being White in a highly racialized culture, one that is historically and currently marked by racism? This uncomfortable ethical question is both propelled and informed by emotions, emotions that are bound up with students' beliefs about race and identity.

Traditionally scholars have understood emotions primarily as manifestations of White students' resistance (Ringrose, 2007), and even scholarship that has looked more critically at the function of emotions has emphasized understanding them as obstacles to analysis and critical reflection (Trainor, 2008a, 2008b). Yet theory in the interdisciplinary field of critical emotion studies allows us to understand more fully the nature, function, and expression of emotions that inform White students' writing about race. Thus, when I analyze students' papers from my first-year writing class through the lenses of critical race theory, critical emotion studies, and many years of teaching first-year writing, my primary emphasis is less on considering what White students know about race and racism and more on better understanding how emotions impact their beliefs and their experiences of knowing and learning. As Marilyn Cochran-Smith and Susan L. Lytle (1993) discuss in their definition of conceptual teacher research, the kinds of questions that inform my research "emanate neither from theory nor practice alone but from the critical intersection of the two" (p. 15). Ultimately, I argue that to understand and cultivate racial literacy more effectively, we need to address how students' emotions inform their experiences of and responses to the ethical challenges of racial literacy.

Racial Literacy, Color Blindness, and Ethical Questioning

Racial literacy entails critically examining and continually questioning how race and racism inform beliefs, interpretive frameworks, practices, cultures, and institutions. It has usefully been defined within the framework of critical race theory (CRT), an approach grounded in critical legal studies, yet one that has increasingly been applied to many other disciplines, including education (Dixson & Rousseau, 2006). CRT recognizes racism as "endemic to American life" (Dixson & Rousseau, 2006, p. 33) and suggests that it should be understood not only in personal and interpersonal terms, but also in structural and institutional ones. That is, racism needs to be understood as a systemic problem that informs dominant discourses, culture, and institutions, including the demographics of those institutions. Understanding racial literacy in concrete, daily terms is essential if we are to illuminate the connections between individuals (students, parents, instructors) and institutions. As France Winddance Twine and Amy C. Steinbugler (2006) propose, we might define racial literacy as "a critical analytical lens" (p. 341) informed by race, one that is "developed through everyday microcultural practices" (p. 357). By attending to such practices—the language that we use, the jokes that we tell—in essence, how we interact with others—we are impacting, if incrementally, the larger culture that constitutes our lives.

Given the varied ways that race and racism operate within and across time, it is also essential that we understand racial literacy as a process as opposed to equating it with a particular body of knowledge. Critical race theorist Lani Guinier (2004) proposes that we understand racial literacy as "an interactive process in which race functions as a tool of diagnosis, feedback, and assessment" (p. 115). By approaching race as a critical category of analysis, we continually frame new questions about how it is working (individually, socially, culturally, and/or institutionally). Ultimately, Guinier (2004) suggests, racial literacy is about "learning rather than knowing" (p. 115), an argument that makes particular sense given her description of racial literacy as "contextual rather than universal" (p. 114). The implications of understanding racial literacy as a process and of focusing upon "learning rather than knowing" challenge common approaches to racial literacy.

Indeed, scholars seeking to understand the racial literacy of White students often focus upon identifying the substantial body of knowledge that students lack. Consider, for example, how some have approached the common use of color blindness by White students and the value that these students place on this discourse in White segregated settings. In many instances, color blindness has been offered up as a key example of the limits of White students' understanding of race and racism (Guerrero, 2008). Granted, assertions of color blindness are pervasive in contemporary culture; CRT scholars have long highlighted the problem of color blindness being understood as one of "the official norms of racial enlightenment," as "an ideal" approach to race (Dixson & Rousseau, 2006, p. 39). Indeed, most White students in my overwhelmingly White first-year composition classes define themselves as raceless, innocent, color-blind individuals in their writing: Echoing the discursive norms of their home and school settings, they assert that racism is a relic of the past, that they themselves see beyond race, that they try to live by the Golden Rule, and that they are not racist. One response to such expressions of color blindness is to critique students' ignorance and to highlight the substantial body of content knowledge that is absent.

Yet I argue that much of the scholarship that critiques color blindness within the framework of CRT or from other theoretical frameworks is both necessary but also insufficient if we are to understand student learning and the racial literacy of White students. Clearly, scholarship that unpacks the meanings of color blindness is vital because the dominance of this discourse in our culture means that its implications are seldom articulated fully (Bonilla-Silva, 2003; Bonilla-Silva & Embrick, 2006; Lewis, 2004). In particular, this scholarship helps us better understand the many, varied ways in which color blindness masks the ongoing functioning of structural racism (Vaught & Castagno, 2008). Yet when some scholars reflect on White students' uses of color blindness, color blindness is presented as simply a "cover" for racism. Color blindness is not only wrong but also bad in the sentiment captured in much scholarship, including writing that defines color blindness as "color-blind racism" (Bonilla-Silva, 2003; Rodriguez, 2008). Indeed, instructors might be tempted to approach White students' color-blind discourse with a stance of ethical judgment.

Such critiques of White students' uses of color blindness fail to consider students' ethical desires and goals because they focus primarily upon the problematic way that those goals are expressed within this discourse. Ironically, the sort of moral high road that instructors might claim for themselves ignores the ethical questions with which their students are struggling, and it ignores what Laura Micciche (2007) terms "the emotional content of ethical questions" (p. 163). In fact, when White students assert that they see beyond race, treat everybody the same, and thus define themselves as color-blind, they are seeking to define themselves as good, moral people in an environment in which direct interaction with people of other races is limited.

In the segregated setting where I teach, color blindness often functions as a sort of ethical shorthand, a simplified vocabulary that emerges as White students struggle to understand and express what it means to connect meaningfully and morally with people who differ from them racially. We need to take students' ethical motivations seriously—along with the emotions that inform their ethical views and their efforts to express and develop those views—even if their conclusions about race and racism are erroneous. We must consider the extent to which *what* students know and believe about race is bound up with *how* they know and learn; this entails recalling Guinier's (2004) assertion that racial literacy "is about learning rather than knowing" (p. 115). Thus, if we are to understand better the racial literacy and experiences of White students in segregated environments, we need to read students' writing about race in context, and we need to recognize several things. First, we must consider the importance and implication of understanding racial literacy as a process as opposed to identifying it as a stable knowledge base or a skill that will necessarily bring about certain antiracist actions on the part of students. Second, we need to understand that when we bring the subject of race and racism into our classrooms, we are establishing a context in which students will be implicitly and explicitly struggling with difficult ethical questions as they grapple with growing awareness of racial inequalities and their relationship to them. Third, we need to recognize that when students engage with ethical questions they are also engaging with strong emotions that motivate and inform the process of questioning. Instructors need to understand better the varied ways emotions inform students' writing and beliefs about race and identity.

Understanding Racial Literacy through the Lens of Critical Emotion Studies

To understand and cultivate racial literacy, we must recognize that emotional learning is an often-overlooked yet fundamental aspect of students' thinking. Although traditionally emotions have been understood in opposition to reason or thought, in fact emotion, reason, and thought are inseparable.[2] When emotions are referenced in scholarship about teaching race, they are typically identified as obstacles to effective learning, as illustrations of students' resistance to change (Ring-rose, 2007, pp. 325–326). Yet I argue that students' emotional responses to ethical questions regarding race might offer sites of opening and possibility, not only means of reinforcing the status quo. Scholarship within the field of critical emotion studies offers new ways to help us understand the nature, function, and implications of emotions, not simply for individuals but also for social groups, societies, and institutions (Abu-Lughod & Lutz, 1990; Micciche, 2005, 2007; Sommers, 1988; Trainor, 2006, 2008a, 2008b; Worsham, 1998, 2003). This scholarship challenges common assumptions that emotions exist in opposition to reason and critical thought, and that emotions are best understood through a psychological framework that defines them as simply natural, personal, or individual.

Scholarship that addresses Lynn Worsham's (2003) call that we "make emotion a critical category" (p. 163) approaches emotions not through a psychological lens that might locate them principally as a manifestation of an individual's psychological experience, but instead through an interdisciplinary lens that recognizes emotions as profoundly social and cultural in nature. This approach understands expressions of emotions "as mediated rather than natural responses to a situation" (Micciche, 2007, p. 6) and proposes that "emotions should not be understood as psychological states but as social and cultural practices" (Ahmed, 2004, p. 9). As Megan Boler (1999) and others have argued, these practices are in fact taught in settings including homes, schools, and religious forums. Emotional schooling, to use Lynn Worsham's (1998) term, can function as a means of teaching beliefs and constructing knowledge.

As we attend to emotions within student writing, then, it is useful to recall that emotions are socially constituted, they gain meaning in context, and they emerge "in relation" (Micciche, 2007, p. 50). As such, they inform identities and relationships, between and within individuals and social groups. As Shula Sommers (1988) argues, "Emotions reflect, among other things, knowledge of the valuations of a community, concepts of social relationships as well as attitudes and beliefs held in common by members of a community. It follows that an individual's emotions are embedded in a social framework in which an individual functions" (p. 6). What this suggests, in part, is that emotions are bound up with power relations and that we might usefully explore how they function as a "site of social control" (Boler, 1999, p. xiii). Teaching what constitutes appropriate feelings in a given context can guide and restrict one's beliefs and expression of beliefs in response to the emotional rules.

Considering how emotions might function as a "site of social control" offers one helpful way into considering White students' approaches to race. This strategy has been central to the work of Trainor (2008a, 2008b), who has sought to understand White high school students' uses of racist speech. In particular, Trainor (2008a) considers how the teaching of what she terms emotioned rules (p. 88) at home and school influences White students in ways that make racist speech persuasive to them, regardless of their beliefs and knowledge about race itself. Like Trainor, I am interested in understanding how emotioned rules and learning function in White settings, yet my conceptual framework for understanding White students' learning differs somewhat because I want to understand students' emotions within the context of students' ethical questioning. Unlike Trainor, I do not focus specifically on White students' racist speech. By attending to White students' varied approaches to race in their writing, I am able to understand more fully how emotions inform White students' engagement with race as they address ethical questions. In particular, we must consider their embodied emotional experience of ethical questioning as they reflect upon instances of social and racial injustice.[3] Although we need to understand how emotional learning informs students' ideas about race, an issue I will consider as I explore student writing, it is crucial to recognize that students' emotions don't necessarily reinscribe dominant social beliefs; in fact, they might initiate a challenge to them. Emotions are undoubtedly informed by one's relationships to social groups and the structures of feeling and belief nurtured within those groups and relationships, but they are not reducible to those relationships and those structures. Although we are taught how to feel, our response to that teaching and the beliefs that it seeks to cultivate is not determined.

What is ultimately most important about using critical emotion studies to grapple with the racial literacy of White students is that it provides a very concrete way to ground students in particular contexts, something that is essential and quite difficult for White students — especially those in segregated settings — who frame themselves as innocent, objective observers who stand outside culture or context. Although attending to the emotions of White students might seem to recenter whiteness and to direct attention away from "the consequences [of racism] for people of color" (Rogers & Mosley, 2006, p. 482), I believe that it has the potential to do exactly the opposite. In fact, attending to emotions, a key part of the interpersonal dimension of race, offers a microcosm of or a way into a structural understanding of race. Recognizing how emotions are socially constituted, how they emerge in relation, and how they are taught illustrates that emotions are connected to social structures and institutions rather than existing separately as simply personal phenomena.

Racial Literacy as Ethical Project: Ethical Awareness as a Means of Ongoing Inquiry

I have argued for the importance of exploring how White students' emotions propel and inform their approach to the ethical questions that emerge as they grapple with racial literacy. As another way of understanding the context of my students' writing and the writing itself, I'd like to return briefly to the issue of approaching racial literacy as an ethical project. As noted previously, often scholarship that has critiqued uses of color blindness has adopted a stance of ethical judgment in terms of the way that it has approached "ethics as foundational, static, and objective criteria for 'good' actions" (Micciche, 2005, p. 161). It is useful to consider an alternative approach to ethics as we conceptualize our pedagogy and consider the ethical strategies students use in their work; in particular, we might explore a postmodern model of ethical awareness. Given its attention to process, questioning, and the contingencies of specific locations, ethical awareness offers a productive way for approaching White student writing on race.

Scholars using ethical awareness approach ethics quite differently from those who have adopted a stance of ethical judgment. Because ethical awareness attends carefully to difference, it challenges ethical models such as ethical judgment that suggest universal principles can transcend the particularities of time and place. Those adopting ethical awareness would "reject notions of ethics as hard-and-fast principles, as a kind of checklist of what counts as 'good' or 'bad'" (Micciche, 2005, p. 162). Instead, ethics is understood "as a contingent set of practices that are always in process, localized, and based on principles of difference," and emphasis is placed on the value of understanding "the situated nature of ethics and its capacity to question what counts as right and good in shifting political, cultural, and institutional contexts" (Micciche, 2005, p. 161). What I find especially useful about this approach is that it addresses ethics as inquiry, as "a mode of questioning" (Porter quoted in Fontaine & Hunter, 1998, p. 4), in a way that seems especially appropriate for a definition of racial literacy that emphasizes cultivating an analytical lens as an ongoing process of learning.

Within the context of ethical awareness, then, the goal "is not to change behavior in a predetermined manner, but to see what may not have been seen before, to resist complacency and reconsider what had, heretofore, seemed acceptable" (Fontaine & Hunter, 1998, p. 4). Thus, when we conceptualize our pedagogy we do not have a specific goal of changing our students' actions or racial identities in a particular way. Rather, we are trying to cultivate ongoing questioning about the familiar, the comfortable, and the "acceptable." Bringing ethical awareness to the task of interpreting and cultivating racial literacy thus exists in tension with antiracist scholarship that privileges moving students from awareness/knowledge to action. Conceptualizing racial literacy in terms of ethical awareness entails cultivating ongoing questioning and hence the exploration of alternative ways of being and acting in the world; however, this approach does not presume to script those alternatives for students or to define certain moral and racial identities as ideal.

Locating the Writing of First-Year Students

At the private liberal arts college in the northeast United States where I teach, the rural, predominantly White, middle-class setting is read by many whites as natural. innocent, idyllic, and safe, and it is often framed in opposition to urban spaces that are racialized—typically as Black—and considered poor and dangerous. In a setting whose student population is 92% White, discourses shared by many faculty, staff, students, and their parents obscure the importance of race, even as they implicitly valorize White racial isolation. Indeed, the segregated, small-college setting is often described as an ideal environment for the education of approximately 2,000 traditionally college-aged students. As some White students' parents explain, they approve of the institution *because* of its lack of racial diversity—not in spite of it. For many White students and their parents, the campus looks and feels like home, something that is frequently vocalized when first-year students arrive; strong emotions are bound up with their reading and experience of the campus as comfortable and friendly. Although some White students seem to have unconsciously selected an institution whose racial demographics match those of their hometowns, others make the selection quite consciously. As a White male student from a town in Maine whose population is 99% White explained in his essay, "When it comes to diversity, attending Susquehanna was taking the easy way out for me. . . . If I had been more comfortable with diversity around me, I might have made the decision to go elsewhere."[4]

The factors that led to and sustain the racial demographics and the way that race is lived on campus are largely unacknowledged and unquestioned;[5] there is a sort of inevitability implicit in comments by faculty and administrators about "how hard it is to get minorities to come to such a rural area." Those comments might reflect knowledge of the challenges current faculty of color have experienced finding local housing, yet discussions of housing discrimination have seldom occurred publicly. That no African American students graduated from the institution until 1968 seems unremarkable.[6] Many White students, especially those in my first-year writing class, initially assert that there is simply nothing to say about the topic of race "because everybody's pretty much the same here anyhow." The perception of many White students that race and racial issues are located elsewhere is reflected in descriptions of their rural hometowns. As one White female student wrote, "racial issues seemed to be nowhere in sight. The only racial issues we were aware of were those far away, like in CA where groups of white cops beat black men every now and then." Yet White students also explain their silences surrounding race by explaining that they "don't want to offend anybody" or say the wrong thing" and be seen as racist."

Within this setting, my first-year writing class, traditionally composed exclusively of 18- to 19-year-olds, presents students with memoirs that highlight cultural, racial, linguistic, social class, and gender difference. Prior to the racial literacy narrative assignment, students write an analytical essay about a text grounded in an unfamiliar culture, and they have written about discourse communities within their lives. The readings that surround the racial literacy narrative are short, first-person narratives that address race from varied perspectives. In addition, some course materials, such as selections from the DVD *Race: The Power of an Illusion* (Adelman, 2003), offer examples of structural racism by addressing the emergence of residential segregation in the United States. Within this context I assign students a paper that asks them to analyze race in their lives, an assignment that has typically been broadly framed so that students are able to identify entry points that are most thought provoking to them.

My discussion focuses especially on examples chosen from papers, five to seven pages in length, written in 2008, by a class of 16 self-identified White students and 2 self-identified African American students. I focus on papers written by White students who have grown up in rural, overwhelmingly White areas. In general terms, I sought to understand how rural White students engage or disengage with the challenges of racial inquiry. I selected these examples because they illustrate the range of ways that White students from rural areas conceptualize and respond to the emotions bound up with ethical questioning regarding race. The examples also illustrate the ways that White students rely upon ethical judgment or ethical awareness as they approach race. More specifically, my analysis of student writing was guided by the following questions: How do emotions motivate, curtail, or otherwise impact beliefs and ethical inquiry surrounding race? How is identity (especially in terms of ethics) represented, negotiated, or interrogated in the context of race? These questions were particularly important because I sought to better comprehend the extent to which students understand themselves as racially located, and the extent to which they see themselves as accountable, as bound up with the fate of their location and the social group allegiances that constitute their location.

Approaching Racial Literacy through the Lens of Ethical Judgment: Emotions and Social Control

Alice's essay, entitled "Colorblind," analyzes how she learns color blindness in her overwhelmingly White community and how color blindness functioned in her life after she became aware of racism as a teenager. Alice, a White elementary-education major, has been taught both a way to believe and a way to feel toward others as part of her Catholic identity. She explains that

> Growing up, I attended a Catholic school and was taught that we were all
> created equal and are created in the image and likeness of God. For this
> reason, each and every one of us was made especially by God and there-
> fore demanded a certain kind of respect. No matter what a person's skin
> color, sex, or sexual orientation, we are all the same. Ultimately, we were
> taught to be colorblind, or to be able to look beyond a person's physical ap-
> pearance, so as to gain a better understanding of who the person actually
> is. As students we were expected to follow the Golden Rule. . . .

The Golden Rule teaches her to feel empathy for and to identify
with all; looking "beyond physical appearance" is identified as the best
way to express that empathy. Belief and emotions thus construct identity, a moral and religious identity that offers the comfort of belonging to
a community of fellow believers. Alice recognizes that her identity and
beliefs are informed by a religious context, yet she doesn't consider how
her experience of race is informed by growing up in a highly segregated
area (in which there were only 2 students of color in her elementary
school of 700). Although she has been taught an identity that is grounded
in a specific socio-religious context, the approach she has learned teaches
her to transcend context: The color-blind stance encourages her to look
beyond difference, to a universal status as equal given her belief in the
divine creation of all. Within color-blind discourse she positions herself
as someone who is alternately an outside observer of society and someone who can claim an innocent stance given her beliefs.

As Alice claims a stable, nonracialized identity by means of color
blindness, she adopts a moral identity and a stance of ethical judgment. The ethical stance of color blindness seems to function here as an
instance in which "ethical judgment is applied to situations" based
upon "posit[ing] objective, static, ethical principles as applicable across
situations" (Micciche, 2005, p. 162). Alice's approach to color blindness
suggests that ethics are universal, transcending difference. The ethical
framework within color-blind discourse is often oppositional and seems
to present her with two polarized options: color blindness is good, and
seeing race (read as being racist) is bad. These ethical choices are experienced emotionally—one can be good, safe, and comfortable (and part
of one's community)—or wrong and uncomfortable. For Alice, ethical
judgment also means approaching ethics by claiming a fixed identity
grounded in a particular belief system, rather than approaching ethics
as ongoing inquiry defined by practice.

Alice's commitment to a color-blind stance of ethical judgment, developed during her childhood, remains strong, even as she becomes a
teenager and "realize[s] that there was racial discrimination . . . present in my small town." Within the segregated community of her upbringing, Alice favorably compares her color-blind White identity and
her ability to "look past race," to the racist White identity of some classmates and older relatives; in essence, the presence of racist speech and

actions help her to solidify her moral (White) identity. Accordingly, she folds the questions that emerge about racial discrimination back into her color-blind framework. She argues that

> If people practiced colorblindness, racial discrimination would not be a factor; the color of a person's skin would gain the same type of attention as the color of a person's hair or eyes, which is commonly little to none. The fact that I am able to look past race tells me that the lesson I have learned, to treat others as we would like to be treated and to look inside of a person rather than [at] the outside, is indeed working.

When Alice presents herself as an ethical model, she understands ethics in an individualistic framework whereby one is considered responsible only for the direct, intentional consequences of one's actions. Indeed, those who profess color blindness often dramatically overestimate their control over the impact of their actions. As AnaLouise Keating (2007) has explained, "the majority of my students (especially at the undergraduate level) do not believe that their actions have consequences for anyone but themselves. Nor can they recognize that what affects others—all others, no matter how separate we seem to be—ultimately affects them as well" (p. 31).

Although color blindness seems to protect Alice from understanding herself as connected to (and accountable to) a culture whose racialized nature she is just beginning to recognize, her essay concludes with an implicit and unanswered question: Given that other people are *not* color-blind—a framework she understands as the solution to racism—and racism exists, what happens now? Although her failure to address that question and her description of color blindness as "indeed working" might not seem to hold up logically, within the emotional context of her community, her description makes sense. Alice upholds the system of color blindness by following the emotional rules she has been taught, implicitly solidifying membership in her community; emotions function primarily as social control, not as a site of questioning.

Racial Literacy and Preliminary Ethical Inquiry: Conflicted Emotions, Tentative Questioning

Yet color blindness is not necessarily linked to ethical judgment and to defining identity in terms of belief rather than action; the way that White students approach the emotional learning of color blindness might initiate ethical inquiry, as the next example illustrates. In the following essay, the way in which color blindness coexists with openly racist speech raises questions for a White male business major as he struggles to understand himself as an ethical person based upon his actions as well as upon his beliefs. In Dean's narrative, emotions are linked to questioning and might gesture toward what Timothy J. Lensmire

(2008) describes as "a profound ambivalence . . . at the core of white racial selves" (p. 299).

Initially, Dean's description of his childhood seems to echo Alice's: "As a kid I didn't know much about different races, but I did know that no matter what color your skin was everybody should be treated equally. My parents brought me up with that belief in mind and taught me to treat people with respect and not to judge somebody by the color of their skin." However his approach to understanding race becomes more difficult as he reflects on his high school experiences and the growing popularity of racist speech among his friends. Although he first explains that hearing racist speech made him aware that "some of my classmates were very racist and that they didn't accept the different races the way I accepted them," he later notes that "people would go along with these jokes even if they did not believe in what the jokes were about. Even I was guilty of this and it was almost as if it was the 'cool' thing to be racist. I was afraid that my classmates would think less of me if I didn't go along with their jokes." Emotions both connect Dean to a dominant belief structure within his social environment and propel him to question his acceptance of racist speech. On the one hand, he talks about how he responded to his fears about not belonging to a social group by echoing dominant beliefs surrounding "racial jokes and slurs." On the other hand, as he looks back now and feels "guilty," he notes "that this was not the right thing to take part in, and I tried to stay clear of those jokes and racial slurs as much as I could." When his abstract beliefs about the equality of all are tested, he is uncertain about how to respond. His discomfort and guilt lead to self-questioning as he considers how he constitutes part of the community of his school.

As Trainor (2008a) argues when she considers how White high school students become connected to racist speech, Dean's ambivalent acceptance of racist speech is not necessarily a function of limited knowledge about racism or a desire to protect White privilege. Yet, neither does his relationship to racist humor seem unrelated to his beliefs about race and equity, especially given his assertion that "everybody should be treated equally." Dean's speech demonstrates that emotional learning is linked to the social and ethical identities he is in the midst of negotiating. As he reflects on his conflicted emotions and beliefs, he considers the environmental context for his beliefs and actions, both past and present: "I felt like the lack of diversity in our [high] school was not helping me learn about different races and that if I was not careful I would end up with views and beliefs on race that would be frowned upon in the real world. . . . I still have a lot to learn and understand about race." He concludes his essay with some uncertainty about his beliefs and actions, and importantly, he tentatively positions himself in a social context, one to which he feels some accountability; unlike Alice, he does not seek to claim a stance of innocence or a stable moral identity grounded in a color-blind belief system. Emotions alternately bind him to racist speech and propel inquiry.

Approaching Racial Literacy through the Lens of Ethical Awareness: Emotions as Site of Ongoing Inquiry

Other White students from rural areas such as Tina, a White music-education major, confront questions about their responsibility for challenging racism more directly, and they discover that the emotional turmoil bound up with questioning leads them to reconsider their own identities and the identities of beloved family members. Tina's essay analyzes her struggles to reconcile the practice of her religious beliefs with her strong attachments to two fellow Christians, her grandparents. She begins her essay by explaining that her motivations, actions, and ideas are "grounded in my beliefs as a Christian. The Bible, which teaches unbiased judgment and love for every human being, governs my actions and beliefs. It also explicitly states that all humans are of 'one blood' and reminds Christians that all are 'one' through Jesus Christ." Initially, attending to race does not seem to complicate her actions as a practicing Christian. She finds it easy, even gratifying, to confront the racist speech of two students at her school because she doesn't feel emotionally close to them. Indeed, when the students react critically to her comments, stating that she "definitely wouldn't fit in with our group," she responds "with no trace of regret, 'Oh, no. I definitely wouldn't.'" Tina gladly constructs her identity oppositionally, in relation to her White peers.

Yet when Tina considers the racist words of her grandparents, responding based upon her Christian beliefs proves difficult. When she talks about her grandparents, people she sees as openly loving toward her, but as openly racist toward African Americans, she struggles with a desire to read her grandparents as uniformly moral, innocent people. She seeks to understand them via a stance of ethical judgment, one that she assumed would categorize them as universally loving, yet the ethical complexity and seeming contradictions of their views and practices confuse her. With some frustration, she asks what someone might do "as your eighty-year-old grandmother serves you fresh baked cookies, and makes a blatant racial slur." Her writing reflects her struggles as she realizes that she's a White, family insider—and that not everyone is included within the circle of her grandparents' White, Christian love.

Tina becomes even more conscious of the impact of the situation on her family when she reflects upon her father angrily confronting Tina's grandfather during a meal: "The rest of the table was silent as my grandfather stumbled over his words, a sincere apology mixed with incoherent sounds. I didn't know how to respond. . . . Yes, my grandfather had been speaking in an unacceptable and cruel manner. But by no means is he a bad person." Tina seems torn between her desire to preserve her sense of her grandparents' innocence, an identity that she assumed was fixed, and her desire to adhere to her own beliefs about what is correct behavior, which would encourage her to question her grandparents. It is the connection to her grandparents—the complex space bound up in love—that challenges her most deeply, especially given the way in which her identity is bound up with her relationship to her grandparents. Her conflicted emotions as she considers her interpretation of and response to her grandparents' racist speech are captured by her understated comment that "Those you love are often the hardest to face."

Although Tina decides not to confront her grandparents directly, she does confront herself and her assumptions about identity. The questions that are at the heart of her emotional struggle concerning her grandparents and her understanding of their identities have a profound impact on her. Tina tests her motivations for acting, wondering about her interest in constructing a stable, moral identity for herself, one that might absolve her of the need for ongoing self-questioning. She writes,

> As difficult as it is for me to consider, I wonder if I am so quick to defend [against] racial discrimination because I have an underlying sense that, ultimately, whites still have an advantage in this country? Could this harsh reality of white superiority be an unrecognized force behind my defenses? . . . Is simply the knowledge that the non-white citizens of American have suffered tremendously in the past and continue to suffer today as a result of racial discrimination a reason for me to be all the more proactive in my defenses?

What *are* appropriate motives, Tina wonders? To what extent are motivations important, and to what extent are the consequences of her actions most important? Previously the emotions that bound Tina to her grandparents discouraged her from asking questions about how race informed her beliefs and practices of Christian love; as such, Tina's emotions functioned as what Megan Boler (1999) has termed "inscribed habits of (in)attention" (p. 188) by guiding her away from certain questions. In her essay, Tina considers how her "emotional investments" (Boler, 1999, p. 200) might have protected her from recognizing that her response to White racist speech might emerge from her guilt about racism—and presumably about her White privilege.

Significantly, Tina engages with and interrogates the emotional discomfort associated with recognizing herself as an actor within a racialized culture, rather than trying to position herself as an innocent observer of that culture. Her questioning also helps her grapple with the unexpected ways in which her identity is bound up with her grandparents': she considers how identity might emerge in relation to others, through specific actions and interactions, rather than existing in a stable, unchanging form as she initially hoped. She recognizes that her actions, words, and beliefs are bound up with her family—and those outside her family; thus, there is no neutral place for her to stand where she is simply an impartial "judge" of racist speech. Clearly, Tina's essay does not reflect a very developed understanding of racism or White privilege. Yet within this context, what is more important is that her essay illustrates her approaching racial literacy as ongoing inquiry. A stance of ethical judgment is replaced by the ongoing inquiry of ethical awareness as she questions her beliefs about ethics, identity, race, and acting within the world.

The Possibilities and Challenges of Engaging Emotions and Ethical Inquiry

Students' approaches to ethical questioning within their essays are initiated and informed by emotions that function in several ways. Students might respond to their emotions by solidifying their connection to the status quo in terms of their actions and their assumptions about identity. Or they might find that grappling with emotions leads them to ask new, often unsettling questions. In many cases, emotions seem to move students in both directions: They feel torn between the familiar and the possibility of change. Students like Alice might respond to the ethical questions and any discomfort raised by the assignment by following the emotioned rules that have long guided their behavior and their construction of identity, and these students seem not to pursue further questioning, at least in the context of their papers. In such cases the simplified ethical vocabulary of color blindness defines students as innocent observers, especially when they are in a setting in which some White people use openly racist speech. The stance of innocence allows a White student to transcend the particularities of location and a sense of accountability to location; in such cases racial literacy is not approached as ongoing inquiry but as a finite task.

Yet what the examples of Dean and Tina suggest is that when students do attend directly to emotions (of fear, embarrassment, anger, sadness, or guilt) they are grounding themselves in a specific context in meaningful ways and hence moving away from the stance of innocence; a sense of ethical accountability to themselves and to others propels questioning, a sense that the work of racial literacy is incomplete. When students use difficult emotional experiences to question the meanings of their ethical beliefs and practices, identities that were previously assumed to be stable, innocent and raceless are unsettled. Students might vacillate between a desire to understand ethical identity as core, solid, and fixed—even when race is taken into account—and a recognition that identity emerges in relation and that various experiences of identity may be conflicting and unstable.

Thus, when we understand emotions as cultural practice and as an embodied experience of being located in a specific context and culture, we can better comprehend some students' struggles as they implicitly or explicitly experience themselves as accountable to culture and to the diverse relationships that constitute culture. What student writing aptly illustrates is the value of analyzing closely the emotions bound up with specific experiences so that we can better understand how meanings and identities are created—and how they might be changed. It is within descriptions of specific experiences that students might confront the knowledge that emotions are "not simply something 'I' or 'we' have" (Ahmed, 2004, p. 10), but that emotions, like identity, emerge in relation, in the context of specific relationships. What this means is that interrogating one's emotions and one's response to them entails reconsidering one's identity in profoundly unsettling ways. When Tina confronts the complexity of White identity within the context of her love for her grandparents, she struggles with the uncertainty of how questioning her grandparents' racist speech might threaten her relationship with them—and the identity that emerges in the context of that relationship. The unknown feels profoundly risky and troubling precisely because her identity is so bound up in that loving relationship. Changing her experience of her identity will inevitably be an experience of loss, something that Dean, too, confronts in his essay when he reflects on his relationship with his friends. For a number of White students, deep fears surrounding loss of relationships with other Whites and loss of identity make the ethical project of racial literacy especially fraught.

The struggles linked to loss are illuminated in the writings of feminist memoirist Minnie Bruce Pratt (1984), a White southerner, who writes about the emotional and social struggles she experiences surrounding her identity as she interrogates her White privilege and relationship to racism. Although for Pratt the process of questioning is one that is ultimately about "an expansion, some growth, and some reward for struggle and curiosity" (p. 39), she explains that "we [White people] can experience this change as loss. Because it is: the old likes and ways of living, habitual, familiar, comfortable, fitting us like our skin, were ours. Our fear of losses can keep us from changing. What is it, exactly, that we are afraid to lose?" (p. 39). Pratt's questions are useful as we reflect on the writings of Alice and the ways in which her emotional learning connects her to her family and church. Although various factors might explain Alice's decision not to confront racist speech or actions, the writing of other White students suggests that worries about loss might play a role. Indeed, many White students are sorting out the meanings of White identity within the context of their relationships with White people whom they love deeply. In contrast, racial others can feel distant and abstract. Questioning the meanings and function of whiteness within segregated settings brings with it distinct challenges that are not easily addressed, especially when we recall the feelings of comfort and safety many students and their parents associate with those settings.

Implications: Revisioning Approaches to Emotions

Understanding racial literacy through the lens of ethical awareness encourages instructors to reflect more intentionally on the varied, complex, and often unpredictable ways that emotions function and inform student writing. Doing so is especially important when working with White students in segregated settings because the emotioned rules and dominant discourses within such settings encourage White students to understand themselves as racially innocent and as neutral observers of race and racism that they perceive to be located elsewhere. That White, segregated settings often *feel* comfortable, natural, and normal to White students, their parents, and others on campus highlights the importance and enormous challenge of cultivating racial literacy and addressing emotions in the context of belief, learning, and the creation of knowledge.

How might we teach students to read emotion, a subject that for many seems inappropriate for classroom exploration? We could begin with textual analysis and consider emotions in terms of their meanings, sources, histories, and consequences—for groups and for society, not simply for individuals. Assigning texts that explicitly address individual, social, and cultural functions of emotions such as fear and guilt might open up the topic of emotions in a way that is at once accessible and disorienting for students.[7] Developing a vocabulary for a critical analysis of emotions would then serve as a foundation for a more immediate exploration of experiences and structures of emotion on campus and in classrooms. From there, students could explore the ways that emotions function in the personal narratives they create about their own experiences of race.

Yet analytical approaches to emotions should ideally be complemented with pedagogical approaches that directly confront the fact that emotions and deeply held beliefs are ultimately embodied experiences. As we pursue varied strategies for cultivating racial literacy, I believe we need to return again and again to the experiential, embodied nature of ethical questioning and to learning itself. In so doing we might consider the recent work of scholars in the field of contemplative pedagogy (Hart, 2003; Kirsch, 2008–09; Zajonc, 2009). Tobin Hart (2003) introduces the topic of contemplative pedagogy by explaining that "The contemplative mind is opened and activated through a wide range of approaches—from pondering to poetry to meditation—that are designed to quiet and shift the habitual chatter of the mind to cultivate a capacity for deepened awareness, concentration, and insight" (p. 28). Contemplative approaches might help students become more aware of the workings of emotions by offering them occasions for experiencing varied emotions while gaining reflective distance from them. Hart (2003) describes contemplative practice as "enabling a type of detachment from the contents of our consciousness" (p. 31). Contemplative approaches might help students gain greater awareness, in an embodied sense, of the ways that emotions might consciously and unconsciously inform their beliefs and their responses to the ethical quandaries that emerge when they reflect on experiences of being White in a racist culture. Finally, contemplative pedagogy seems especially appropriate when we understand racial literacy as being about "learning rather than knowing" (Guinier, 2004, p. 115) because this pedagogy often emphasizes inquiry, exploration, and awareness—as opposed to emphasizing acquisition of particular knowledge.

A third approach to addressing emotions is perhaps the most controversial: It involves faculty consciously seeking to change the emotional rules that operate within our classrooms and our society. Trainor (2008a, 2008b) and Worsham (1998, 2003) encourage us to interrogate and intervene in various sites of emotional schooling. Trainor (2008b) urges instructors to ask, "What emotioned rules do we teach, intentionally or not, and what political projects do those rules, again intentionally or not, support?" (p. 28). She questions how we might "begin to teach different emotioned rules" (p. 28) and use emotional rules to "mov[e] white students toward antiracism" (p. 28). Trainor raises important points when she calls for faculty to become more conscious of the emotional rules that they teach and their impact on students. Yet her argument for "teach[ing] different emotioned rules" might overestimate the impact of faculty on students, especially given the role of emotional schooling at home. And I am curious about whether Trainor would tell her students about her goal of schooling them emotionally. Failing to do so would seem to intentionally efface student agency and work at cross-purposes with the goals of critical pedagogy that seem to inform her approach.

Thus I am more drawn to Lynn Worsham's (1998) approach given her attention to individual agency and her argument for connecting individual awareness with broader systemic change. She argues that "if our commitment is to real individual and social change . . . the work of decolonization must occur at the affective level, not only to reconstitute the emotional life of the individual, but also, and more importantly, to restructure the feeling or mood that characterizes an age" (p. 216). If individuals gained greater critical awareness of the varied ways that emotions operate—perhaps by means of the analytical and contemplative approaches have proposed above—this might be the starting point for "restructur[ing] the feeling or mood that characterizes an age" (p. 216). In essence, Worsham proposes that elucidating the functioning of emotions might lay the groundwork for structural change, change that could address racial inequities and, perhaps, the ways that those inequities are informed by other social justice concerns. The scope and difficulty of this project highlight the challenge and the importance of cultivating racial literacy, especially in the segregated contexts in which many of us live and teach. Continuing to explore and address the varied ways that emotions are bound up in the ethical project of racial literacy can help us grapple more effectively with the very real challenges that our students and their instructors continue to confront.

Acknowledgment

I wish to thank Judith Adkins, Susan Naomi Bernstein, Cymone Fourshey, and Ann Green for their feedback on earlier drafts of this article. I am also grateful for the insightful comments offered by the journal's anonymous reviewers.

Notes

1. According to the U.S. Census Bureau, Snyder county's population in 2008 was estimated to be 97.7% White, while across the United States the White population was estimated to be 79.8%. Significantly, demographic trends suggest that by 2050 non-Hispanic Whites will be a minority in the United States.
2. Indeed, neuroscience researchers have found "that reason cannot operate without emotion; the frontal lobes, the site of consciousness, are virtually helpless when they cannot receive input from emotional bodily states" (Crowley, 2006, p. 82).
3. In so doing, we might also recall Spelman's argument that emotions are "revelatory of important parts of our lives as moral agents" (quoted in Quandhal, 2003, p. 18).
4. This quotation, like all quotations from student work, is used by permission of the student. Pseudonyms are used here and throughout.
5. This is one reason I describe the campus as segregated rather than as predominantly White or racially isolated. The campus demographics, discursive norms, and social patterns are neither accidental nor inevitable. With that said, my goal is not to single out my campus as unusual; indeed, many overwhelmingly White campuses should be described similarly. See Massey and Denton's (1993, pp. 1–3) discussion of the evolving use of the term *segregated*.
6. Interestingly, a nearby college, also located in a small, rural town, graduated its first African American student in the mid-19th century.
7. For example, consider Eula Biss's (2009) *Notes From No-Man's Land*, a collection of personal essays that explores a White woman's struggles to navigate racial borderlands. Biss situates emotions historically and in the context of structural racism and White privilege.

References

Abu-Lughod, L., & Lutz, C. (1990). *Language and the politics of emotions.* Cambridge, UK: Cambridge University Press.

Adelman, L. (Producer). (2003). *Race: The power of an illusion* [Motion picture]. (Available from California Newsreel, Order Department, P.O. Box 2284, South Burlington, VT 05407-2284)

Ahmed, S. (2004). *The cultural politics of emotion*. New York: Routledge.

Biss, E. (2009). *Notes from no-man's land: American essays*. St. Paul, MN: Graywolf.

Boler, M. (1999). *Feeling power: Emotions and education*. New York: Routledge.

Bonilla-Silva, E. (2003). *Racism without racists: Color-blind racism and the persistence of racial inequality in the United States*. Lanham, MD: Rowman & Littlefield.

Bonilla-Silva, E., & Embrick, D. G. (2006). Racism without racists: "Killing me softly" with color blindness. In C. A. Rossatto, R. L. Allen, & M. Pruyn (Eds.), *Reinventing critical pedagogy: Widening the circle of anti-oppressive education* (pp. 21–34). Lanham, MD: Rowman & Littlefield.

Carter, R. T. (1997). Is White a race? Expressions of White racial identity. In M. Fine, L. C. Powell, L. Weis, & L. M. Wong (Eds.), *Offwhite: Readings on race, power, and society* (pp. 198–209). New York: Routledge.

Cochran-Smith, M., & Lytle, S. L. (1993). *Inside / outside: Teacher research and knowledge*. New York: Teachers College Press.

Crowley, S. (2006). *Toward a civil discourse: Rhetoric and fundamentalism*. Pittsburgh, PA: University of Pittsburgh Press.

Dixson, A. D., & Rousseau, C. K. (2006). And we are still not saved: Critical race theory in education ten years later. In A. D. Dixson & C. K. Rousseau (Eds.), *Critical race theory in education: All God's children got a song* (pp. 1–54). New York: Routledge.

Fontaine, S. I., & Hunter, S. M. (1998). Ethical awareness: A process of inquiry. In S. I. Fontaine and S. M. Hunter (Eds.), *Foregrounding ethical awareness in composition and English studies* (pp. 1–11). Portsmouth, NH: Boynton/Cook.

Giroux, H. A. (1988). *Schools and the struggle for public life: Critical pedagogy in the modern age*. Minneapolis: University of Minnesota Press.

Guerrero, L. (Ed.). (2008). *Teaching race in the 21st century*. New York: Palgrave Macmillan.

Guinier, L. (2004). From racial liberalism to racial literacy: Brown v. Board of Education and the interest-divergence dilemma. *The Journal of American History, 91*(1), 92–118.

Hart, Tobin. (2003). Opening the contemplative mind in the classroom. *Journal of Transformative Education, 1*, 28–46.

Keating, A. (2007). *Teaching transformation: Transcultural classroom dialogues*. New York: Palgrave Macmillan.

Kirsch, G. E. (2008–09). Creating spaces for listening, learning, and sustaining the inner lives of students. *JAEPL, 14*, 56–67.

Lensmire, T. J. (2008). How I became White while punching de tar baby. *Curriculum Inquiry, 38*(3), 299–322.

Lewis, A. (2004). *Race in the schoolyard: Negotiating the colorline in classrooms and communities*. New Brunswick, NJ: Rutgers University Press.

Massey, D. S., & Denton, N. A. (1993). *American apartheid: Segregation and the making of the underclass*. Cambridge, MA: Harvard University Press.

Micciche, L. (2005). Emotion, ethics, and rhetorical action. *JAC, 25*(1), 161–184.

Micciche, L. R. (2007). *Doing emotion: Rhetoric, writing, teaching*. Portsmouth, NH: Boynton/Cook.

Pinar, W. F. (1993). Notes on understanding curriculum as a racial text. In C. McCarthy & W. Crichlow (Eds.), *Race, identity, and representation in education* (pp. 60–70). New York: Routledge.

Porter, J. (1993). Developing a postmodern ethics of rhetoric and composition. In T. Enos & S. Brown (Eds.), *Defining the new rhetorics* (pp. 207–226). Newbury Park, CA: Sage.

Pratt, M. B. (1984). Identity: Skin, blood, heart. In E. Bulkin (Ed.), *Yours in struggle: Three feminist perspectives on anti-Semitism and racism* (pp. 11–63). Ithaca, NY: Firebrand Books.

Quandhal, E. (2003). A feeling for Aristotle: Emotion in the sphere of ethics. In D. Jacobs & L. R. Micciche (Eds.), *A way to move: Rhetorics of emotion & composition studies* (pp. 11–22). Portsmouth, NH: Boynton/Cook.

Ringrose, J. (2007). Rethinking White resistance: Exploring the discursive practices and psychological negotiations of "whiteness" in feminist, anti-racist education. *Race Ethnicity and Education, 10*(3), 323–344.

Rodriguez, D. (2008). Investing in White innocence: Colorblind racism, White privilege, and the new White racist fantasy. In L. Guerrero (Ed.), *Teaching race in the 21st century* (pp. 122–134). New York: Palgrave Macmillan.

Rogers, R., & Mosley, M. (2006). Racial literacy in a second-grade classroom: Critical race theory, whiteness studies, and literacy research. *Reading Research Quarterly, 41*(4), 462–487.

Schneider, B. (2005). Uncommon ground: Narcissistic reading and material racism. *Pedagogy, 5*(2), 195–212.

Sommers, S. (1988). Understanding emotions: Some interdisciplinary considerations. In C. Z. Stearns & P. N. Stearns (Eds.), *Emotion and social change: Toward a new psychohistory* (pp. 23–38). New York: Holmes and Meier.

Tatum, B. D. (2003). *"Why are all the Black kids sitting together in the cafeteria?" and other conversations about race* (Rev. ed.). New York: Basic Books.

Trainor, J. S. (2006). From identity to emotion: Frameworks for understanding and teaching against anticritical sentiments in the classroom. *JAC, 26*(3–4), 643–655.

Trainor, J. S. (2008a). The emotioned power of racism: An ethnographic portrait of an all-White high school. *College Composition and Communication, 60*(1), 82–112.

Trainor, J. S. (2008b). *Rethinking racism: Emotion, persuasion, and literacy education in an all-White high school.* Carbondale: Southern Illinois University Press.

Twine, F. W., & Steinbugler, A. C. (2006). The gap between Whites and whiteness: Interracial intimacy and racial literacy. *Du Bois Review, 3*(2), 341–363.

Vaught, S. E., & Castagno, A. E. (2008). "I don't think I'm a racist": Critical race theory, teacher attitudes, and structural racism. *Race Ethnicity and Education, 11*(2), 95–113.

Worsham, L. (1998). Going postal: Pedagogic violence and the schooling of emotion. *JAC, 18*(2), 213–245.

Worsham, L. (2003). Moving beyond a sentimental education. In D. Jacobs & L. R. Micciche (Eds.), *A way to move: Rhetorics of emotion & composition studies* (pp. 161–163). Portsmouth, NH: Boynton/Cook.

Zajonc, A. (2009). *Meditation as contemplative inquiry: When knowing becomes love.* Great Barrington, MA: Lindisfarne Books.

Learning Differences

From "The Rule of Normalcy"

Lennard Davis

Lennard Davis, a widely published scholar in disability studies, invites readers to consider the differences between the terms normality *and nor-malcy, in order to explore the conceptual history of the word* normal. *As he reexamines these terms through linguistic and cultural history, Davis draws significant conclusions about the language and terminology used to assess ability, disability, and standards. As part of this history, Davis presents the differences between the concepts of* ideal *and* normal. *An ideal signifies perfection, which no one realistically expects to achieve, but toward which we may reasonably strive.* Normal *or the* norm, *Davis articulates, came into prominent usage at approximately the same historical moment as statistics and the bell curve. In this rhetorical shift away from* ideal, *Davis suggests, came the conceptions of* normal *and* abnormal. *These notions continue to shape the outcomes of standardized testing. People can be easily categorized as superior or failing, able or disabled, in terms of where they stand in relationship to the* norm, *what Davis calls "the main umbrella of the [bell] curve" (p. 308).*

Davis's conclusions hold fascinating possibilities for basic writing, and enrich our understanding of the processes of norming, outcomes assessment, and determining college readiness. What constitutes the history of such language choices, and in what ways does this language shape our notions of students' abilities? Such questions let us reflect on our students not as objects, or as disabilities, problems, and other perceived weaknesses, for us to "fix" through helpful hints and tips. Instead, as we rethink the uses of terms like normal *and* ability, *we can begin to understand our students as subjects, with more complexity, drawing on their resilience and strengths as we engage with them in the processes and products of writing.*

When we say that "normality" is preferred over "normalcy," what exactly do we mean? We mean that some or a preponderance of experts in the field have agreed that a certain word is more "normal" than another word. How is the norm determined? By usage, to an extent. By logic, to an extent. By reference to grammatical patterns worked out from other languages like Latin and Greek. In other words, by social convention. For example, since "normalcy" is credited by the *Oxford English Dictionary* as having an American origin, we can imagine that the neologism would be discounted by some British lexicographers as a colonial malapropism, only another example in the decline of the empire's standards.

If we think of the distinction between prescriptive grammar, the body of didactic rules that tells us how to write and speak, versus descriptive grammar, which aims to describe how language is used in a variety of settings, we can understand how truly socially constructed are grammatical "norms." Prescriptive grammar arose in the seventeenth and eighteenth centuries in an attempt to regularize the English language, which had no grammar, to the level of the revered Latin and Greek, which being dead languages had to have grammars and rules so that they could be taught in schools. Scholars at the time had fretted over the fact that English had no grammar, so the grammatical conventions of Latin were applied in a procrustean way to English, whether they fit or not. During this time, the first English dictionaries were compiled, so that spelling and meaning could be normalized, and so that printers could standardize their productions. In other words, language was regularized, and the effort of speaking and writing came under the jurisdiction and control of a class of scholars, men and women of letters, and other professionals who tried to make spoken language, in its transformational complexity, fit into rather arbitrary, logical categories. As Georges Canguilhem wrote, when French grammarians of the Enlightenment "undertook to fix the usage of the French language, it was a question of norms, of determining the reference, and of defining mistakes in terms of divergence, difference."

Why I am mentioning grammar and language usage in the context of a discussion of disabled or abnormal bodies is worth considering. When we think about normality, people in disability studies have generally made the error, I would say, of confining our discussions more or less exclusively to impairment and disease. But I think there is really a larger picture that includes disability along with any nonstandard behaviors. Language usage, which is as much a physical function as any other somatic activity, has become subject to an enforcement of normalcy, as have sexuality, gender, racial identity, national identity, and so on. As Canguilhem writes, "There is no difference between the birth of grammar ... and the establishment of the metric system. ... It began with grammatical norms and ended with morphological norms of men and horses for national defense, passing through industrial and sanitary norms."

Let me backtrack here for a moment and rehearse the argument I made in *Enforcing Normalcy* so that I can make clear to readers of this essay the direction in which I am going. In that book, I claimed that before the early to mid-nineteenth century, Western society lacked a concept of normalcy. Indeed, the word "normal" only appeared in English about a hundred and fifty years ago, and in French fifty years earlier. Before the rise of the concept of normalcy, I argued, there appears not to have been a concept of the normal, but instead the regnant paradigm was one revolving around the word "ideal." If one has a concept of the "ideal," then all human beings fall below that standard and so exist in varying degrees of imperfection. The key point is that in a culture of the "ideal," physical imperfections are not seen as absolute but as part of a descending continuum from top to bottom. No one, for example, *can* have an ideal body, and therefore no one has to have an ideal body.

Around the beginning of the nineteenth century in Europe, we begin to see the development of statistics and of the concept of the bell curve, called early on the "normal" curve. With the development of statistics comes the idea of a norm. In this paradigm, most bodies fall under the main umbrella of the curve. And those that do not are at the extremes — and therefore are "abnormal." Thus, there is an imperative on people to conform, to fit in, under the rubric of normality. Rather than being resigned to a less-than-ideal body in the earlier paradigm, people in the past hundred and fifty years have been now encouraged to strive to be normal, to huddle under the main part of the curve.

Is it a coincidence, then, that normalcy and linguistic standardization begin at roughly the same time? If we look at that confluence in one area in particular, we see that language and normalcy come together under the rubric of nationalism. As Benedict Anderson has pointed out, the rise of the modern nation took place largely in the eighteenth and nineteenth centuries when the varieties of polyglotism that had made up a politically controlled area were standardized into a single "national" language. Without this linguistic homogeneity, a notion of the modern nation-state would have had great difficulty coming into being. In addition, national literatures, both in prose and poetry, were made possible through the standardization of languages, the prescriptive creation of "normal" language practices.

While few now object to Anderson's thesis that language practices had to be standardized, homogenized, and normalized to allow for the creation of the modern nation-state, I think that the next step, which I want to propose in this essay, might be more objectionable. I would claim that for the formation of the modern nation-state not simply language but bodies and bodily practices also had to be standardized, homogenized, and normalized. In this sense, a national physical type, a national ethical type, and an antinational physical type had to be constructed. Here we see much work done in the nineteenth century on racial studies, studies of pathology, deviance, and so on — all with the aim of creating the bourgeois subject in opposition to all these abnormal occurrences.

This is where I want to return to my putative linguistic solecism. In thinking about the difference, or lack of difference, between normalcy and normality, I began to think of the suffixes which make all the difference in those two words. "-cy" seems to indicate a state of being, as does "-ity," but there are resonating differences. Both "-ity" and "-cy" turn adjectives into nouns—as "sexuality," "ethnicity," "formality," as well as "malignancy," "pregnancy," "immediacy." However, I would suggest, without insisting absolutely, that the use of "-cy" seems more strongly to denote a permanent state, as it does in "idiocy," "complacency," "malignancy." But interestingly enough, many words that describe not simply a corporeal state but a political state use the suffix—"democracy," "autocracy," "plutocracy," or "aristocracy." My thought, then, was to salvage my own oversight by making a valid distinction, much in the way that Jacques Derrida talked about "difference" and "differance." I would call "normality" the alleged physical state of being normal, but "normalcy" the political-juridical-institutional state that relies on the control and normalization of bodies, or what Foucault calls "biopower." Thus, like democracy, normalcy is a descriptor of a certain form of government rule, the former by the people, the latter over bodies.

This distinction allows us to think through ableism in a somewhat different way than we have in the past. Rather than conceptualizing ableism as a trait or habit of thought on the part of certain somatically prejudiced people, we can consider ableism to be one aspect of a far-ranging change in European and perhaps global culture and ideology that is part of Enlightenment thought and part of modernization. Further, and I think this is important, we can begin to move away from the victim-victimizer scenario with which ableism, along with racism, sexism, and the other "isms" have been saddled and which leaves so little room for agency. Instead, one can see ableism as an aspect of modifications of political and social practice that have both positive and negative implications and that can be changed through a political process.

Interpreting and Implementing Universal Instructional Design in Basic Writing

Patrick L. Bruch

In his study Universal Design: Inclusive Post Secondary Education for Students with Disabilities, *Patrick Bruch envisions strong interconnections between universal instructional design and social justice work, especially in basic writing courses for students with (and without) apparent learning*

*differences. Universal instructional design takes its name from the archi-
tectural concept of universal design; for instance, the use of ramps rather
than stairs creates legally mandated access to buildings for people in
wheelchairs and serves "universal" needs as well for children in strollers,
people with backpacks on wheels, and so on.*

*However, Bruch suggests that in composition studies, "universal" access
often implies the goal of assimilation to the status quo, rather than toward
social justice for all students. In order to work for social justice, Bruch
argues, we need to make our pedagogy as equitable as possible and to consider "universality" as a process rather than an outcome. Bruch describes
how these theories work in practice, providing examples of how students
can be involved in shaping activities and assignments, leading to more
equitable conditions for students in basic writing courses.*

In a society that values equality and diversity, the concept of a universally designed curriculum captures a broadly shared ideal. Indeed, education scholarship in the United States might be read as an
ongoing debate about our successes and failures in creating neutral,
universal curricular contexts in which different people can learn together. Ideals of universality have typically assumed that curricula can
escape the relations of power and privilege that shape public life. Dominant strands of current social theory and political philosophy challenge
this way of thinking about what we should be working for as we design
curricula and policy. In this chapter, I offer an interpretation of Universal Instructional Design (UID) informed by this contemporary thinking about justice. I then highlight the implications of this interpretation
of UID for the teaching of writing, discussing my own effort to implement a writing curriculum compatible with UID.

Contemporary Social Theory

In her recent study of political philosophy, Iris Marion Young (1991)
highlights transformations in ideas of justice that have resulted from
the social theories and group movements that emerged in the 1960s
and 1970s. For Young, feminist, anti-racist, gay rights, disability rights,
and other movements drew attention to the shortcomings of those definitions of justice that were understood to be universal in the sense of
being timeless and independent of specific contexts. As an alternative
to pursuit of "a self-standing rational theory . . . independent of actual
social institutions and relations" (p. 4), the social group movements
highlighted the need for understandings of justice that were able to recognize and address unintended consequences of seemingly or actually
neutral policies and practices. As Young explains, rather than searching for a universality good for all people and all times, contemporary
critical theories see justice as rooted in specific social and historical
contexts. Here, rather than be an abstract principle that stands outside

of experience, justice depends upon "hearing a cry of suffering or distress or feeling distress oneself" (p. 5). Where more traditional theories valued detachment and distance, current theories like Young's are participatory and process oriented.

Building on Young's arguments about the need for a more contextual and processual understanding of universal justice, Fraser (1997) has recently drawn attention to the dynamic relationship between two domains, the material and the cultural, in the current social and historical context. For Fraser, listening to the experiences and voices of marginalized social groups suggests that injustice operates in different ways on these two conceptually distinguishable, though overlapping planes. The first understanding of injustice is material. Here, attention to injustice focuses on unequal distribution of things like income, property ownership, access to paid work, education, health care, leisure time, and so on. The second understanding of injustice is cultural and symbolic. Here, injustice refers to "cultural domination . . . nonrecognition . . . and disrespect" (Fraser, p. 14). These forms of injustice often overlap. Physical disability, for instance, is often related to economic disenfranchisement. But the conceptual distinction is useful because it helps draw attention to the fact that economic enfranchisement may not, alone, remedy the unjust relations attached to disability in current institutions. Persons labeled as disabled may still be culturally marginalized, misrecognized, and disrespected.

What is useful about disentangling these overlapping planes of injustice, then, is that by doing so we are equipped with a more robust vocabulary for talking about injustice and suffering in our midst. Thus equipped, we are better able to recognize the need for multiple and perhaps seemingly contradictory remedies for injustice. For, as Fraser highlights, where emphasis on the material view leads people to appreciate injustices rooted in the political-economic structure of society and encourages them to advocate for material equality—remedying injustice by *redistributing* goods and abolishing group difference— the cultural view recognizes the injustice of misrecognition and disrespect and thus leads its proponents to advocate remedying injustice through *recognition* and revaluation of group specificity. Contending with both material and cultural obstacles to equal treatment within significant public contexts like schooling, an adequate conceptual foundation for transforming curriculum must bring together redistribution and recognition.

Summarizing the essential insight that these movements have helped to generate, Catherine Prendergast (1998) has recently argued that, in order to overcome injustices such as White privilege and male privilege, "it will not be simply enough to add women and people of color and stir. Without significant changes to the profession and pedagogy, women and people of color will continue to wind up on the bottom" (p. 50). What is needed are redefinitions of what it means to participate in social practices like work and schooling so that part of the purpose of participating in such practices is to change the practice itself. Within such a view, the universality and thus justness of our practices becomes participatory—they are always in the process of being redefined as we continuously learn more about how our practices relate to material or cultural injustice. Instead of creating a system that applies to any situation, universality means working within concrete contexts to enable more people to participate more fully in defining inequities and better alternatives.

Although Prendergast's (1998) recognition of the need for transformation of "the profession and pedagogy" (p. 50) usefully applies current thinking about justice to the educational context, she concludes her study by explicitly refusing to address classroom issues, pointing to the compromises that, within accepted educational discourses, such attention demands. She concludes that although "at this point articles dealing with composition generally incline toward some pedagogical imperatives," in order to be true to her evidence "[that] not only is an agenda of socialization insufficient for enfranchisement but that it might be detrimental to enfranchisement" (p. 50), she can only reemphasize that "we need to recognize that our rhetoric is one which continually inscribes our students as foreigners" (p. 51). If school curricula are to put into practice recent theories of multicultural justice, they must be transformed to provide marginalized groups meaningful opportunities to participate in and transform educational and other institutions. Our curricula will have to provide a means for expressing and valuing cultural difference in ways that make group difference one of the purposes of knowledge forms like literacy, rather than the foreign element that pollutes literacy. In the absence of such respect and recognition, redistribution fails to fulfill its promise.

Universal Instructional Design

Fulfilling the promise of redistributive measures will involve more fully connecting such remedies to culturally oriented remedies. Growing out of architecture, a field of knowledge in which the connections between material and cultural issues are uniquely visible, Universal Design (UD), in its affirmation of critical revisionary feedback, potentially responds well to our need for new models of participating in knowledge. Universal Design as a professional movement grew out of emerging awareness within architecture of unintended consequences of design features that were thought to be impartial. Specifically, persons with disabilities made building designers aware that their designs were unjust both in terms of the material access they made available and in terms of the cultural and symbolic messages they sent to persons with disabilities and to those temporarily able bodied. Buildings with stairs at each entrance, with doorknobs or other mechanisms that require particular kinds of dexterity not possessed by all, or other features that make the buildings very difficult for some persons to use, materially obstruct equal access. Additionally, such structures and cultural messages about who is expected to participate in public life and who is capable of citizenship, messages that unjustly misrecognize and disrespect certain persons.

Universal Design holds great promise when translated to curriculum design if we remain aware of the central critical capacity that, in practice, UD has placed at the center of the design process—listening to the experiences of those who use the structure, observing the degree to which the structure facilitates equal participation, and continuously revising. In this sense, I see Universal Design as operationalizing a contingent understanding of the term "universal" consistent with the political philosophies I described in the previous section of this chapter. Universal names an ideal and a process rather than a realized outcome or a fixed state of affairs. Seeing universality as a process values participation and discourages those privileged by current structures from ignoring the obligation to listen, learn, and revise. That revisions responsive to particular undesirable effects of designs also enhance the usability of structures in unintended ways is a bonus effect that should help counter arguments against constant revision.

In my view, Universal Design offers educators a chance to design curricula from the position of listener rather than all knowing expert. As Young (1997) has argued, listening plays an important role in identifying and transforming injustice:

> with careful listening able-bodied people can learn to understand important aspects of the lives and perspective of people with disabilities. This is a very different matter from imaginatively occupying their standpoint, however, and may require explicit acknowledgment of the impossibility of such a reversal. (p. 42)

The lesson here for me is that at its best, the design of structures aspires to universal access through listening and learning about how different people understand their experiences in them. With respect to this important process, it seems that curricular designers may have an advantage over building designers because our structures are much more flexible and easily revisable. Thus, there is no reason that curricula need to replicate the situation where buildings meet the letter of laws mandating access but fail to fulfill the spirit of equity.

Connecting UID to Composition Studies: Redefining Writing as Literacy Work

So far, I have offered an understanding of UID as a way of applying the insights of contemporary theories of justice to education. This connection provides a way to practically extend resources developed over the past 30 years within composition studies. It holds promise for addressing issues familiar to compositionists and for broadening attention to issues of access that compositionists have largely ignored. At the heart of the emerging attention to disability is a recognition on the part of composition scholars that assumptions about the physical, emotional, and cognitive norm have negatively impacted the structures we design—our curricula, our profession, and pedagogies.

But composition teachers have tended to separate issues of distribution from issues of recognition. Scholars have recently concentrated attention on the overall failure of redistributive pedagogies that narrowly conceived universality as universal access to a valued set of conventions. Prendergast's (1998) characterization of such efforts as potentially "detrimental to enfranchisement" (p. 50) and Fox's (1993) recent argument that "access through language pedagogy . . . is an unqualifiable failure" (p. 42) both draw attention to the professional tendency to theorize about recognition while emphasizing assimilation in the classroom. The injustice of redistributive pedagogies is less about the limitations of a valued dialect to provide the economic access it promises, though there is that. Additionally, the emphasis on assimilating valued conventions creates an educational context of disrespect in which those who are the beneficiaries of conventions are able to go on without questioning the ways that the structures they are operating within unjustly privilege them. Transforming the teaching of writing in ways that implement the kind of UID I have discussed holds promise for better serving students with disabilities as well as all others, because all are, ultimately, underserved by curricula that concentrate solely on either issues of distribution or issues of recognition.

Applying UID to the teaching of writing means transforming the curriculum to ameliorate cultural and material obstacles to educational equity. Materially, I am speaking of how the class itself operates—the physical layout of activities, the material design of handouts, texts, the environment of the classroom, how much time is spent in different ways, and so on. Culturally, I am referring to questions about the identities students are assumed to have or expected to inhabit by the curricula of the class. As a conceptual framework, UID draws attention to the interrelation of these cultural and material issues. They both become the focus of critical reflection and potential revision in pursuit of the goal of equity.

The practice of UID has resulted in changes in the way that I understand what I want students to learn, in the assignments that I gave, and in the classroom activities through which we work on assignments. UID provides a framework for shifting our attention from literacy as a stable skill that we want to import to a more participatory formulation of writing as a matter of simultaneously doing and shaping in pursuit of equality and difference. A term that, for me, names this understanding of what students learn in writing classes is literacy work. In writing classes students learn to participate in and reflect on the various kinds of work that literacy does. They learn to appreciate that language use is a practice of relating to others and to reflectively navigate those relationships.

Applying the insights of UID to writing classes, the idea of literacy work defines writing as a reflective and revisionary practice. That is, when one writes one simultaneously accomplishes the immediate concrete goal of communicating in a particular context and at the same time, one expresses ideas about communication in that context. As one student, Asante, phrased this insight in a paper for a recent class, "by me writing this paper in this way, I am communicating my thoughts about communication to you, but yet a lot of people may not see it this way at first." In other words, writing includes both participation according to current conventions and reflection on those conventions and the relations of equality and difference they are part of.

As mentioned earlier, a key principle that UID offers to writing teachers is critical participation and revision. The material and cultural issues faced when serving any group are so multifaceted and complex, and the ways that students receive and interpret teachers' messages are so unpredictable, that no design for a class can address all issues and concerns beforehand. Instead, the message of UID is multiple formats supplemented by participatory feedback and redefinition. No single curricular mode can achieve universality and serve all students equally, so classes must be built to work towards contingent universality of serving the students that are actually there.

The role of student feedback is essential here. In one recent class, for example, I learned an important lesson about my practices for introducing new assignments. My method was to extensively describe the new essay assignment on paper, including a discussion of the rhetorical practices I wanted students to recognize and work on, why and how. My introduction to the summary assignment read like this:

> Academic writing is a set of practices for participating in conversation with others. One of the most important of these practices is summarizing. This first project is focused on reading carefully and writing good, strong, summaries. Strong summaries tell your readers what others in the "conversation" you are joining have been saying. Strong summaries convince readers that your view of the conversation has some merit. A strong summary convinces readers that you should be listened to and creates a context for you to add your piece to the conversation.

In an effort to appeal to a broad audience, I contextualized the assignment by linking something I thought students would identify with, conversation, to academic writing. I also offered an in-class overview and provided students with examples to use as models of successful responses that could inspire them in thinking about how they might respond to the assignment. When I asked students for questions, there were none.

When I requested feedback from students on their progress after about a week, one student reported that she had been stuck because she wasn't sure if she understood the assignment "correctly." Although concerns with "giving the teacher what he wants" influence all students, the fact that this student had a learning disability that required a very direct and linear understanding of tasks like writing had made the situation paralyzing for her. In our discussion, I asked her what she thought about the assignment and she said that she thought she could take the authors one at a time and tell readers what they say. We discussed what she thought each of the authors was trying to say and made notes about why she understood them as she did. When I assured her that her understanding was fine she was relieved and said that she was thrown off by my introductory discussion.

I responded to this problem by redesigning the way I introduce new assignments to be much more focused on how the students understand the assignment rather than how I understand it. I now include much more student-generated discussion of how they understand what they are being asked to do and how they anticipate getting to work. One activity that has been very helpful in this regard is simply taking five minutes to let students write the assignment in their own words and then share them. Because I want students to think about the cultural work involved in writing as well as the practical work, I have broken down this process so that students begin by sharing their versions of the assignment in a small group with two or three others. I ask them to share their versions and to talk not so much about who's right or wrong, but about the different kinds of cultural work done by the different kinds of writing that each in the group imagine doing. My role as teacher while these conversations are happening evolves over the course of the term. Early on in the semester I circulate in the groups helping students develop a vocabulary for talking about the work writing does, the consequences of writing in different ways. As students develop confidence in addressing this issue, my role shifts towards helping groups maintain focus and work out difficulties that arise. As a classroom practice, the exercise teaches that rather than being right or wrong, different kinds of writing do different kinds of work. Some of these kinds of work, such as stating and defending an opinion, are more highly valued in some contexts than others.

In addition to operating as material transformations that provide broader and fuller access, such curricular redesigns that evolve from student participation in the design of the class raise and contend with cultural obstacles to equitable access as well. On one level, an activity like the one described above creates a context of greater recognition for students like the one who inspired the change, but also for many others. It creates an opportunity for each student to make an understanding of the assignment that recognizes their needs. Further, it creates a context for beginning to grapple with the cultural work that writing does. For example, in one of the groups I sat in on as students were discussing their understandings of the "strong summary" assignment, two students began to disagree when one African American student compared her understanding of the assignment to another, White, student's understanding by saying that she wanted to make her opinion "plain rather than hidden." The other student responded that a summary shouldn't have an opinion at all. To which the first responded that, for her, a summary is "my view of how I see them." At this point, I intervened to remind the students that the object of sharing was not to decide who in the group was right or wrong, but to try and clarify different understandings and the different kinds of work they do. This encouraged the two students to share their views of the work that their own and each others' interpretations do. Martha explained that she believed her way of understanding a summary would let readers decide how to understand the texts she discussed, using her opinion or not. Mary explained that she believed her way would let readers decide by leaving herself out and just saying what the authors said. Another student here joined in to add that Mary's would, then, be what Mary believed the authors said, which both Mary and Martha agreed to. The value that I hope comes of such exchanges is making each of the students more familiar with how two fundamentally different ways of understanding writing understand themselves and each other. It clarified that one kind of work writing strives to do is to help readers make informed decisions for themselves and that there are different opinions of how best to facilitate this. It provided a basis for each of the students to read and write in a more informed way.

An unexpected outcome of this new activity was that allowing students to take a significant hand in interpreting the assignment required that I clarify for myself the learning objectives and acceptable parameters of responses. In other words, the activity made me more fully reflect on multiple ways of demonstrating learning. In a writing class, flexibility is restricted by the fact that students must write. But the form of that writing is a point of negotiation with profound material and cultural implications. Sarah was most comfortable using writing to communicate stable meanings. Other students I have encountered find that trying to limit themselves to one way of understanding what are invariably complex texts or issues is constraining and demands they limit their writing to acceptable partial versions. In negotiating with students about the range of fully credible responses to the summary assignment, I have had to think about what abilities I want students to work on and demonstrate. For me, what matters is that students learn to read carefully and to help readers see both how they interpret texts and why they think their interpretations are credible in an academic setting. This means linking their summaries directly to what authors say. I think that if students do that, their writing will serve them well in many academic and public situations. As I have learned from student suggestions of how they understand and approach the assignment, this does not demand a thesis based, paragraph oriented, linear, traditional school essay.

An option that one student suggested for herself has become a formal alternative on my assignment sheet. This student was uncomfortable with the idea that she was being asked to be an expert on the various positions making up a conversation that she was previously unfamiliar with. She decided to write out a conversation between the authors that would show readers how she understood their positions. For her, the imaginary context would tell her readers that she was offering one, tentative interpretation of how the authors' opinions related to each other. My assignment sheet now suggests two broad options for completing the assignment as follows:

> Option 1: Find a common thread that emerges across the conversation we've been reading and write an essay in which you present and discuss this common thread by summarizing how at least 3 of the sources relate to it. Feel free to bring in your own experiences or your own senses of the issues, but be sure to concentrate on offering a substantial review of the perspectives offered by each of the authors you discuss, explaining how they each relate to the common thread.

> Option 2: Write a dialogue between four of the authors we've read in which they continue the conversation that their essays are a part of. Incorporate into what each author says your understanding of their view of the issues. Have each speaker use some direct quotes from their pieces to explain what they mean. In the dialogue, each person should talk at least three times, each time speaking at least 85 words. Try to capture some of the voice and style of each of the speakers in what you have them say.

Overall, these curricular transformations shift the emphasis from simple assimilation of conventions to a participatory recognition of the contingency of those conventions and their effects. I say "participatory" in order to call attention to the essential insight of Universal Design that those who inhabit structures have important roles to play in remaking those structures. In terms of a writing class that implements this concept in its instructional design, students are expected to learn that part of the purpose of writing is to call attention to aspects of the structure of writing that "many people may not see" as Asante, my previously quoted student, phrased it. They are learning as well that as writers part of their job is to participate in creating alternative designs for texts. Students in such a class are learning about literacy work by doing the work of literacy. They are interanimating redistributive and recognition-oriented remedies to educational injustice.

References

Fox, T. (1993). Standards and access. *Journal of Basic Writing, 12*(1), 37–45.

Fraser, N. (1997). *Justice interruptus: Critical reflections on the "postsocialist" condition.* New York: Routledge.

Prendergast, C. (1998). Race: The absent presence in composition studies. *College Composition and Communication, 50*(3), 36–53.

Young, I. M. (1991). *Justice and the politics of difference.* Princeton, NJ: Princeton University Press.

Young, I. M. (1997). *Intersecting voices: Dilemmas of gender, political philosophy, and policy.* Princeton, NJ: Princeton University Press.

10

English Language Learners

The Transition to College of English Learner and Undocumented Immigrant Students: Resource and Policy Implications

Gloria M. Rodriguez and Lisceth Cruz

Gloria Rodriguez and Lisceth Cruz offer an informative review of recent research on English learners and undocumented students' transitions to college. Most significantly, they offer recommendations for needed research that would have a direct, proactive impact on policies toward and available resources for these students, whose linguistic backgrounds cannot be easily generalized and who often have been underserved in their previous experiences with education. Indeed, Rodriguez and Cruz emphasize that English learners and undocumented students remain underserved in part because of the stereotypical belief that linguistic deficits will drive down test scores in the current test-driven culture of public schools. "Nevertheless," Rodriguez and Cruz suggest, "it is crucial to this analysis not to relegate ELs and immigrant students to a position of perpetual victim simply because schools may not recognize or assess well the skills and forms of agency and self-reliance the students must deploy to support their own educational goals" (p. 326). From this perspective, the authors affirm, educators and researchers must recognize the intelligence and self-efficacy of English learner and undocumented students.

The Transition to College of English Learners

Linguistic Transition as Part of the Academic Transition to College

The academic transition from K–12 schooling to college for English learner students involves the transition from knowing languages other than English to being bilingual (or multilingual). This process often begins before high school—the commonly assumed starting point of the transition to college—and can last well into the early college years. As has been well established in the literature on second language acquisition, bilingual education scholars have noted that the linguistic transition alone can take between 3–7 [years] (August & Hakuta, 1997; García & Wiese, 2002). The length of time that it might take a student is dependent in part on the literacy levels in his or her native language, but also on the extent to which his or her academic progress in course content beyond English is supported in the native language (Faltis & Wolfe, 1999). Despite the well-supported claim that becoming fluent in English is a transition that could happen concurrently with the overall academic transition to college, it appears that English language acquisition is instead treated as a gatekeeping process for access to college preparatory content.

Language Status as a Gatekeeping Factor: The Secondary/Precollege Schooling Experiences of EL Students

An analysis of ELs' prospects for postsecondary study requires attention to the nuanced differences within this group of students. For example, it is significant to consider the difference between a secondary EL student who is a new arrival to the United States and a student who has attended U. S. schools for much of her or his life without a reclassification[1] of language proficiency status (Gershberg et al., 2004). For example, the reclassification of students from limited English proficient status to fully English proficient status implies that the students are capable of successfully participating in English-dominant classroom environments. However, it also may mean that reclassified students with some remaining (though relatively minor) English language support needs are no longer eligible for any such support whatsoever. The challenges that exist for ELs in their transition to postsecondary education thus do not begin in the ninth grade—or even middle school, for that matter. Indeed, the transition into the status of English proficient is an important parallel process to the broader transition that all students—proficient in English or not—must make to access the knowledge and skills required for success in college. The difficulty in the language proficiency transition is that it is so dependent on what happened in terms of native and/or second language development long before students reach middle or high school age. That is, second language acquisition specialists continue to argue for the maintenance and development of the primary language as a facilitative process for second language acquisition (August & Hakuta, 1997; Faltis & Wolfe, 1999). However, this view presupposes ideal learning and social conditions in which supportive structures and qualified educators are present to ease the transition to English proficiency. Moreover, even under such ideal circumstances, the process would take more time than is permitted by annual high-stakes testing requirements (García & Wiese, 2002). Even more infrequently discussed is the fact that learning conditions are not ideal for most ELs (Higgs, 2005; Rumberger & Gándara, 2004), and the recent focus on test-driven English proficiency as the primary means of accountability has created additional challenges for these students (Gándara et al., 2003; Linquanti, 2001; Olsen & Jaramillo, 1999).

Unfortunately, the no-win situation that the educational system seems to create for EL students within the current accountability environment is either a continued legacy of paying them little to no attention, or a future of directing only negative attention to their presence. In fact, the advice from the bilingual education scholarly community in decades past was to push for the inclusion of ELs in state and local assessments to ensure that their learning needs were monitored regularly and addressed consistently (August & Hakuta, 1997; García & Wiese, 2002). However, rather than view the language acquisition process as moving toward a "value-added" experience, ELs now face the dual stigma of not being proficient in English, which translates into their poor performance on high-stakes measures of academic achievement, and "driving down" their school community's test scores. Thus, for these students, the pressure to perform appears to be considerable and within a context of very little support for their success either in becoming English proficient or in navigating the K–12 system in preparation for higher education.

One study by the Urban Institute (Ruiz-de-Velasco & Fix, 2000) was entitled "Overlooked and Underserved: Immigrant Students in U. S. Secondary Schools," which captures well the general circumstances that immigrants face in their attempts to progress through high school. The authors discuss the particular challenges of immigrants who are in the process of acquiring proficiency in English while in secondary schools. Part of the challenge noted by these and other researchers is that there is a paucity of work that specifically addresses the educational experiences and policy challenges of secondary ELs compared with those in the primary grades (Faltis & Hudelson, 1998; Faltis & Wolfe, 1999; Ruiz-de-Velasco & Fix, 2000).

It appears that the schooling conditions for ELs who are fairly recent immigrants (and usually also from low-income backgrounds) are similar to, but often more acute than, those faced by other low-income students and students of color. Among these limiting conditions are classes taught by teachers who are not fully prepared to facilitate language development or integration into the school community; a lack of courses (for example, in math and science) that incorporate support for EL students; and the within-school segregation of ELs from their English-dominant peers, which can prevent a sense of belonging and full inclusion as learners. Certainly, this is the case with respect to many of the schools in California, a state with a large percentage of ELs among its total student population and with the highest concentrations among their high-poverty city neighborhoods and rural communities (Gándara et al., 2003; Ruiz-de-Velasco & Fix, 2000).

The situation of long-term ELs is an important example of the reality that so-called language barriers are not solely the problem of the students. Rather, there are significant processes within schools and professional judgments and actions that are critical to the successful mastery of English by ELs, about which much is known by researchers. Nevertheless, there continues to be a chasm between what is recommended as "best practices" and what is supported either with policy or material and human resources (Gándara et al., 2005; García & Wiese, 2002; Olsen & Jaramillo, 1999; Rodriguez, 2004; Rumberger & Gándara, 2004). What is most pertinent about this situation is the lack of consistency across state and local school systems in supporting EL students' reclassification as English proficient, which precludes their progress in accessing college preparatory curricular and instructional resources. As long as a student cannot be reclassified—because of delays caused by inefficient assessment systems, inappropriate assessment instruments, lack of school capacity for supporting EL reclassification, or other factors—there exists a considerable obstacle in his or her transition to higher education. We can continue to generally characterize the long-term EL problem as an unfortunate circumstance of the students' inability to perform well on assessments of their language proficiency. However, the growth of the long-term EL population is likewise a reflection of our educational system's insufficient ability to meet the needs of these students by deploying appropriate human and material resources, including the requisite language and instructional skills among teachers (Gándara et al., 2005).

Indeed, although it is undeniable that proficiency in English is critical to students' access to the curriculum, it is a limited perspective to think that students are not capable of acquiring subject matter skills and knowledge, for example, in their native language in an effort to bridge that divide between the designation as an EL and preparation for high school graduation and postsecondary education (Callahan, 2005; Faltis & Wolfe, 1999). As Gándara et al. (2005), Gonzales and Rodriguez (2007), Merino (1999), Olsen and Jaramillo (1999), Padilla and Gonzales (2001), and others continue to argue, the professional development gap that exists for most teachers who serve increasing numbers of ELs, often at varying levels of proficiency, requires serious attention.

Language Status and Its Link to College Preparation

Rather ironically for English learners, it appears that the educational system's overemphasis on language acquisition defined only as English proficiency (García, Kleifgen, & Falchi, 2008) undermines their preparation for college. Although it was a key resource for the students in Rangel's (2001) study of undocumented immigrant students' transition to college, the opportunity to learn English alone was not sufficient to guarantee access to postsecondary study. For example, both Rangel (2001) and Callahan (2005) identified the lack of access to college preparatory courses as a key obstacle to EL students' ability to prepare for study beyond high school.

One feature of public schools that is particularly associated with the underpreparation of EL students for college is academic tracking and the resulting within-school segregation of ELs (Conger, 2005; Schneider, Martinez, & Owens, 2006). For secondary ELs, the track placement decision carries implications not only for access to supports for English language acquisition but also for access to college-required academic coursework. For example, one study shows that the track placement of secondary ELs appears to be a more influential factor in their ability to prepare for postsecondary study than actual English proficiency (Callahan, 2005). This finding should not be misconstrued to mean that support for English language development is unimportant. On the contrary, Padilla and Gonzales (2001) found that instructional support for language development made a significant positive difference in the achievement of EL students at the secondary level. Of course, it is important to note that although our impression of the key challenge for these students centers on acquiring proficiency in English, in fact, English proficiency alone — particularly determined by certain limited standardized assessments — will not guarantee a successful transition into higher education. As indicated by Rumberger and Gándara (2004) in their analysis of the learning conditions for K–12 EL students in California, the school system is not as responsive as it needs to be to foster access to college preparatory curriculum and learning opportunities. Thus, the pathway to college for EL students is diverted by the limited capacity and resultant sorting processes of schools.

It is also helpful to contemplate briefly the longstanding institutional barriers that exist for many ELs in U. S. secondary schools. A huge and persistent concern is with the differential dropout rates among student populations that overlap with the EL student population. For example, as indicated by the demographics of EL students, the majority of this group is Latino, and many are recent immigrants to the United States. The high Latino dropout rate, including the presence of foreign-born students whose early education may not have been in the United States, has been discussed extensively in the literature (Fry,

2003; Rumberger & Lim, 2008; Rumberger & Rodriguez, 2002). When dropout data are disaggregated among Latino groups and between U. S.-born and foreign-born Latino students, it appears that some of the high dropout rate might be explained by the presence of foreign-born Latinos who may not have been as well educated in their early years as their U. S.-born counterparts. Regardless of this consideration, however, it appears that Latinos still experience double the dropout rate as White students, a difference that has persisted for decades (Rumberger & Rodriguez). Recent research (Orfield & Kornhaber, 2001) provides still further evidence that with ever-increasing attention to high-stakes accountability requirements that include high school exit exams for graduation, we might begin to see increases in disengagement with school among ELs, and eventually, higher dropout rates (McNeil & Valenzuela, 2001; Natriello & Pallas, 2001).

The Agency of English Learners in Their Transition to College

Although the literature on secondary ELs is sparse, we can nevertheless draw some insights from the recent studies examining the experiences of immigrant students. One important lesson from them is that social networks play a crucial role in facilitating students' adjustment to their new communities and schools. Secondary ELs who are recent arrivals in the United States rely quite heavily on the social networks that exist in their home communities to navigate the school context (Brittain, 2002; Gibson, Gándara, & Kohama, 2004; Kim & Schneider, 2005; Valenzuela, 1999).

As noted by González et al. (2005) and Yosso (2005, 2006), ELs, low-income students, and immigrant students are often quite skilled at negotiating sophisticated systems on behalf of their families. These researchers explain that the students have skills that enable them to thrive in their rather complicated lives, as well as a work ethic and responsibilities that have been passed down from parents and other caregivers (Glick & White, 2004; Hardway & Fuligni, 2006). They further argued that schools, rather than building on these skills and community resources to support the educational achievement of the students, often construe academic success so narrowly that they diminish the importance of the skills and resources that students bring to the classroom (González et al., 2005; Nieto, 2000; Valencia and Solórzano, 1997; Valenzuela, 1999). This is an important insight to consider relative to EL students, given that they may also face largely "subtractive" processes in their quest to acquire proficiency in English (as theorized by Valenzuela). The processes may include academic tracking, lack of exposure to advanced learning in particular subjects, and limited interactions with adults at the school who might provide information and support to facilitate their broader integration into school and community life (Ruiz-de-Velasco & Fix, 2000). Nevertheless, it is crucial to this analysis not to relegate ELs and immigrant students to a position of perpetual victim simply because schools may not recognize or assess well the skills and forms of agency and self-reliance the students must deploy to support their own educational goals.

Linguistic and Academic (Under)Preparation:
EL Students at the Postsecondary Level

As noted in a quite comprehensive study on immigrants and higher education produced by RAND researchers Gray et al. (1996), data on the presence of EL students are not readily available. This means that we must rely on data that provide much broader English ability and educational attainment figures to get a sense of their presence in higher education. For example, according to a report by the Pew Hispanic Center (2009) based on the Census Bureau's 2006 American Community Survey, of the foreign-born population age 18 and older, 53.8% were reported to speak English less than very well, compared with individuals age 18 or younger, 34.3% of whom speak English less than very well. In the same report, consideration of Mexican foreign-born individuals age 25 or older reveals that 10.3% reported having completed some college, and 3.6% were college graduates. All survey respondents were foreign born, and they were not identified by immigration status, nor were they classified according to their proficiency in English. Still, despite this limitation of the survey, the general sense is that with such a large representation of Mexican immigrants in the sample, it is reasonable to consider that they are generally encountering challenges in acquiring English language skills and in obtaining access to higher education. An added complication to a comprehensive analysis of undocumented immigrant students is that postsecondary institutions are not likely to systematically collect data on this population, and even if they did, they are not likely to publish the information or make it otherwise available to researchers via public media (Gray et al., 1996).

Recent research on the community college experiences of immigrant students, which included groups of English-as-a-second-language (ESL) students, indicates that although students may transition into postsecondary institutions, they still face difficulty in meeting the writing and other demands of their coursework (Bloom & Sommo, 2005; Blumenthal, 2002; California Tomorrow, 2005; Scrivener et al., 2008). There are relatively few resources or services available to support students who are still developing their skills in English. At the community colleges, developmental or "remedial" courses for ESL students are often structured to provide access to English language acquisition in order to support traditional academic language skills. Although such coursework is of great benefit, there are still considerable leaps that must be made by EL students who are using these opportunities to support their transition into postsecondary studies (Blumenthal, 2002).

When academic support services are available for ELs at the post-secondary level, new challenges appear. For example, although it is possible for a student at a community college to proceed with course taking that includes instruction in English language acquisition, such courses are seldom taken for credit, much less transferable for credit at a 4-year institution. In addition, the course content may be geared more toward the needs of "adult education" ESL students whose primary needs are English acquisition for entry-level employment and basic family life, versus preparation for transfer to a 4-year institution (Blumenthal, 2002). Thus, the situation for EL students can involve a cycle of coursework that requires a time investment for which there is no clear payoff in terms of credit accumulation toward either a degree or transfer to a more advanced course of study (Bloom & Sommo, 2005). This is problematic because the gatekeeping practices that students encountered in their precollege schooling experiences can be continued well after they leave high school (or earn a GED). Such a cycle can be discouraging and lead to students' attrition from the higher education pathway altogether (Blumenthal, 2002; Rendón, 2002).

Another important concern is that the majority of the current EL population often must choose between pursuing higher education and contributing to the economic well-being of their families (Rangel, 2001). Although other low-income students must also make this choice, the added vulnerability of immigrant families perhaps makes it even more daunting for EL students, particularly if they continue to face obstacles to their academic development and success.

New research conducted by MDRC (Bloom & Sommo, 2005; Scrivener et al., 2008) indicates that the use of small learning communities at the community college level appears to be a promising initiative for helping students escape a cycle of noncredit coursework that does little to ensure adequate progress in their English language acquisition. The organization is doing its research at nine California community college campuses, and it will likely yield important insights relative to immigrant students' experiences as they transition into higher education. In turn, it should inform our understanding of what happens (and does not happen) for EL students at this stage of their academic careers.

What We Know and Need to Know about the Transition to College of English Learner Students

Returning to the questions guiding this analysis, it is clear that the ability of ELs to successfully prepare for their transition to college is dependent on the educational system's capacity to support its linguistic and academic transitions concurrently. Still, generally speaking, even those states with rather large populations of EL students appear to be hard-pressed to offer the full spectrum of services needed to prepare this group for a transition to higher education. In some cases, we know that the successful linguistic and academic transitions hinge on the schools' capacity to appropriately assess students as they enter the system and to monitor their progress. In other cases, it is a question of whether school personnel (including teachers, counselors, and principals) are prepared professionally to support the students' development of English proficiency, bilingualism/multilingualism, and college preparation. Ultimately, college readiness for EL students depends on the resources of schools—financial and human—that are available to promote not only English language development but also access to and mastery of course content. Tragically, EL students in most U. S. public secondary schools face greater prohibitive than facilitative conditions and processes in their pursuit of higher education. Nevertheless, many educators persist in seeking support for the research-based practices that benefit EL secondary students, even in situations in which the external policy context (e.g., with the emergence of high-stakes accountability) creates barriers to their success.

EL students are not, however, simply to be thought of as victims of an unresponsive educational system. Instead, it is helpful to keep in mind that they have the ability to acquire skills and strategies that promote their sense of agency in pursuing their educational goals. The literature, although certainly providing confirming evidence of schools as unrelentingly bureaucratic and racially and linguistically biased organizations, also documents the sophistication of EL students (and their families) in navigating the school system as just one of many dimensions of American society they confront. Although such linguistic, navigational, and negotiation skills (Yosso, 2005) may go unrecognized as useful to the college preparation/transition process by many educators, the EL students' development of such abilities certainly seems to contribute to the likelihood that they will persist in secondary school and college (Kim & Schneider, 2005; Portes & Rumbaut, 2001).

Perhaps the biggest questions that remain for deepening our understanding of the EL students' transition to college relate to the factors that continue to prevent our educational institutions from being more fully responsive to the needs of these students. It does not appear that secondary schools do not know what needs to be done to respond to the college preparation needs of EL students. Rather, it appears that researchers, educators, and policy makers have yet to fully confront the types of racial, linguistic, and other institutional biases that exist within the inner workings of schools, preventing such a response (Rodriguez, 2007; Valencia & Solórzano, 1997; Valenzuela, 1999; Yosso, 2006). We might also explore the ways that institutions beyond public schools can contribute to efforts aimed at preparing secondary students for college. Although evaluations of precollege "educational pipeline" programs are likely available, the means to incorporate what is learned from them into the core work of schools remains elusive (Phillips, 1991; Rendón, 2002). Finally, it is necessary to find a way to move the concerns for ELs to the center of our thinking instead of treating their educational needs as peripheral to the essence of public schools.

In the section that follows, the analysis turns to the particular concerns for undocumented immigrant students, although there is considerable overlap with the concerns already presented for EL students. Still, as is the case with EL students (immigrant and nonimmigrant), the circumstances of undocumented immigrants also have nuances that add to their vulnerability beyond access to both language development and academic content.

The Transition to College of Undocumented Immigrants

Few studies have been undertaken to consider the specific issue of the transition to college of undocumented immigrant students, but this analysis makes use of the contributions made by the investigations completed thus far. Because of the United States' legal commitment, resulting from *Plyler v. Doe*, to provide access to public schooling regardless of a student's immigration status, it is difficult to know with certainty the magnitude of the demand for educational access for undocumented immigrants at the postsecondary level. However, even conservative estimates indicate that at least 65,000 undocumented immigrant students graduate annually from U. S. public high schools, about 37,000 of whom are Latino (Drachman, 2008; Passel, 2003), so it is essential to be aware of their challenges in realizing their educational goals. In the state of California, it is estimated that between 5,800 and 7,450 undocumented youth are eligible for its in-state tuition, or "AB 540" status, as provided by recent legislative action to make college more affordable for qualifying California high school graduates (Abrego, 2008). Given the policy attention to undocumented immigrants from state legislatures and the Congress, the key argument for promoting their academic transition to college is that college aspirants should not be penalized for circumstances brought on by actions beyond their control. Rather, the efforts of undocumented students to overcome considerable odds (Chávez, 1998) should be rewarded via policies that facilitate their transition into, and persistence in, college.

Student Demographics

This analysis draws from the definitions introduced by Pew Hispanic Center researcher Jeffrey Passel. Specifically, Passel (2005) used the term *unauthorized migrants* to refer to a person "who resides in the United States, but who is not a U. S. citizen, has not been admitted for permanent residence, and is not in a set of specific authorized temporary statuses permitting longer-term residence and work" (p. 2). He went on to elaborate that the term *undocumented immigrant* (Hoefer,

Rytina, & Campbell, 2006) is not as accurate in describing individuals who may be able to reside and work in the United States under counterfeit documentation and/or who are not likely to stay permanently in this country. For purposes of this analysis, the discussion of the distribution of undocumented immigrants will rely largely on Passel's data and thus definitions, as well as other U. S. Census reports that do use the term *undocumented immigrant*.

Passel (2005), using data from the 2000 U. S. Census and the March 2004 Current Population Survey, estimated that of the 35.7 million foreign-born individuals residing in the country in 2004, 10.3 million, or 29%, were "unauthorized migrants." He also noted that most of the unauthorized migrants arrived after 1990, with approximately two thirds of them residing in the country less than 10 years. Pertinent to the discussion of access to, and participation in, postsecondary education is the estimate that roughly 25%–40% of the unauthorized migrants are termed "visa overstayers." These are individuals who entered the country with a temporary visa but stayed beyond its expiration or perhaps violated other conditions of their admission. Unfortunately, there is not adequate information readily available regarding the overstayer population to determine its possible impact on postsecondary institutions.

Of the estimated 10.3 million unauthorized migrants in the United States, 57%, or 5.9 million, are from Mexico (Passel, 2005). Another 24% are from other Latin American countries, representing 2.5 million people. Nine percent (1 million) of unauthorized migrants are from Asian countries, and individuals from European countries and Canada constitute 6% of the total unauthorized migrant population. Finally, an additional 4% of this population are from African countries and other nations (slightly fewer than half a million).

An important note regarding the distribution of undocumented immigrant students is that estimates show that approximately 1.5 million mixed-status families exist, in which there is one or more unauthorized parents and at least one child who is a U. S. citizen by birth (Passel, 2005). This mixed-status group constitutes 58% of the total number of "unauthorized families" with children. In addition, there are nearly half million families with at least one unauthorized parent and a mixture of both U. S. citizen (by birth) and unauthorized migrant children.

Of course, part of the challenge in reporting these figures is the difficulty that educational institutions face in estimating the current distributions of undocumented students, as well as projected growth. The difficulty lies in the institution's necessary reliance on students' willingness to reveal their status and be counted as undocumented. Even in the case of states, such as California, where recent legislative action enables greater numbers of students to be eligible for exemption from nonresident tuition (under AB 540 status), the perceived risks of identifying themselves can still prevent campuses from accurately reporting their current numbers of undocumented students. The University of California, for example, having established the guidelines under which certain students would be eligible for nonresident tuition exemptions in 2002, reported increases in the numbers of students availing themselves of this benefit since that time. In 2006–2007, out of the total 1,246 AB 540 recipients, 265 students were counted as potentially undocumented (University of California, Office of the President, 2008). It is noteworthy that the counts are based on students in the system's database for whom no identifiable documentation status is found. Aside from this form of estimate, there is no direct method to identify students' documentation status. On the one hand, undocumented students can feel that their status can be protected, confidential information; on the other hand, the lack of information about the students' status can mean that a host of student support needs will remain unaddressed by the college or university.

Limited But Growing Scholarship on Undocumented Students

There is scant research available on the transition to college of undocumented immigrant students, but it is useful to offer some findings from a dissertation on this topic. The dissertation used case study methods to analyze the experiences of six female Mexican immigrant students who were attending one of California's three higher education systems in Southern California: the California Community Colleges, the California State University, and the University of California (Rangel, 2001).

Rangel (2001) used an "academic invulnerability" framework, which she explained is a view of students who, despite facing considerably adverse community, home, and/or schooling conditions, are able to succeed academically. The theory, developed by Alva and Padilla (1995, cited in Rangel, 2001), draws on child development studies of the motivation and perseverance of youngsters who experience success as classroom learners even as they navigate high-poverty, violent, unstable, or otherwise psychologically challenging situations.

The students selected to participate in Rangel's study were motivated, high-performing students in Mexico. Rangel's portrayal of her respondents' early educational trajectories provides an important reminder of the within-group diversity that exists among undocumented immigrant students. The families of the students in her study came from a variety of settings and employment backgrounds in Mexico, and all migrated to the United States for economic or family-related reasons. With only one exception, the students' educational potential was nurtured by their parents, and in all cases, there appeared to be broader family and local community support for their educational pursuits. In addition, because at least two of the respondents had one or both parents who held professional positions, there were direct influences and high expectations, not only in terms of the students' performance in school but also regarding the quality of the education they received in both Mexico and United States.

The young women also identified a complex set of circumstances in the U. S. schools that resonate with the literature on the experiences of other immigrants and English learners in K–12 education. At least three noted that although they perceived much greater educational opportunity in the United States, particularly as publicly provided services, their schools were limited in terms of available staff who could help bridge the linguistic divide between them and their peers. However, they also discussed the considerable difference it made when they did encounter teachers and counselors who not only were bilingual but also possessed knowledge and information about higher education options. They further noted that teachers' efforts to provide support via educational pipeline programs helped address some of the unknowns regarding higher education—services that ranged from direct academic support to opportunities to visit campuses and facilitating contact with college representatives.

At the time Rangel conducted her study, California's legislation to provide residency status for in-state tuition purposes to undocumented immigrant students who met certain eligibility criteria for higher education purposes was not yet statute. Thus, for her study participants, the greatest challenge to full participation in their college activities centered on the dual issues of citizenship status and economic class. Although some of the women secured small scholarships that did not depend on their immigration status, they were more likely to have to hide their status in order to enroll in their classes.

The most crucial factors that surfaced as obstacles for Rangel's respondents were educational and financial in nature. They experienced ongoing difficulty if their perceived abilities in English were low, particularly as the rigor of the college coursework increased. Moreover, at the community college level, there was a lack of information and guidance relative to their preparation for transfer to a 4-year institution— an issue that also affects other low-income students of color (Rendón, 2002; Schneider et al., 2006; Shulock & Moore, 2005).

In addition, Rangel's study participants' undocumented status precluded on-campus employment. Their limited employment options compromised their ability to both meet the financial obligations associated with having a nonresident status—usually translating into many times the rate of fees and tuition that a resident student would have to pay—and contribute financially (and in other ways) to the well-being of their families. Even as they were involved in the academic transition from K–12 to college, respondents were also in the process of negotiating their adult caregiver roles as full contributors to their families.

California AB 540 and the Federal DREAM Act

In response to the obstacles faced by undocumented immigrant students in transitioning to college, legislative efforts at the state and federal levels have ensued with a still uncertain future. For example, California's AB 540 legislation was passed by the state legislature in 2001 to provide residency status to undocumented immigrant students meeting strict eligibility criteria—including attendance in and graduation from a California high school—in order to enable them to pay in-state tuition or fees at accredited institutions. Although AB 540 did remove a significant obstacle for many college students, it does not provide eligibility for publicly funded financial aid. Moreover, as this article is being written, a pending challenge in the California courts may lead to a repeal of this legislation. Despite the grim prospects of such an occurrence, recent actions among the undocumented students themselves—and their allies from across various educational and other social institutions—are aimed at remaining proactive in clarifying the positive social benefit of completing their college degrees (UCLA Center for Labor Research and Education, 2008a). It is also important to note that similar legislation has been enacted in several states across the United States, and the impact of such policies is beginning to be examined by researchers as well (Abrego, 2008; Flores & Chapa, 2009).

At the federal level, the proposed Development, Relief, & Education for Alien Minors (DREAM) Act specifies eligibility for both residency for in-state tuition purposes and federal financial aid (National Immigration Law Center, 2006). The DREAM Act was introduced for the second time in 2007, but it has not yet reached a congressional vote. Immigrant and education rights advocates have sought to separate this legislation from the broader concern for immigration reform, both to expedite the process of legislative approval and to sharpen the focus on offering support to academically able students who will graduate from American high schools ready to proceed to college. Approval of the federal DREAM Act is also viewed as an important clarification of the stance of the federal government on granting residency status for students who meet strict criteria for states that are more reluctant to pass legislation that is viewed as being potentially noncompliant with federal law.

Emerging Research and Student Mobilization

As can be seen, the needs of undocumented students overlap with those of ELs in their transition to college. Indeed, although it is possible that a sizeable percentage of undocumented students are fully college eligible, as Rangel's study might suggest, it is also likely that more recent arrivals to the United States are in need of language support services that schools are hard-pressed to provide. Because of the limited access to data and the paucity of available research, what we need to know still far outweighs what we currently know about the college transition experiences of undocumented immigrant students.

Despite the challenge of minimal research on the high school-to-college transition specifically, it is encouraging to note a growing body of scholarship on undocumented students in higher education. With the passage of in-state tuition policies enabling greater numbers of undocumented students to gain access to some forms of higher education, new studies are emerging that help to clarify the variety of issues surrounding the college experiences of these students. Additional dissertation research has been conducted on college preparation, access, and financial aid for undocumented students (Albrecht, 2007; Lopez, 2007; Perry, 2004; Rincón, 2005). These studies have further detailed how educational opportunity for undocumented students involves risk, emotional costs, and a complex balancing of family, work, and student life. Additional new research has attended to the impact of in-state tuition policies and programs that provide greater access to colleges and universities in California, Texas, and other states (Abrego, 2008; Drachman, 2008; Flores & Chapa, 2009; Frum, 2008; R. G. Gonzales, 2007). These studies have revealed a variety of complexities associated with undocumented students' participation in college under these policies, including some important areas of student empowerment and mobilization on their own behalf (Abrego, 2008; Diaz-Strong & Meiners, 2007; Seif, 2004; S.I.N. Collective, 2007; UCLA Center for Labor Research and Education, 2008a, 2008b). Finally, there is a growing concern among higher education practitioners about their responses to the needs of undocumented students, particularly as these students become more openly represented on their campuses. To this end, research and practical resources have emerged to begin to address these issues (e.g., USC Center for Higher Education Policy Analysis, 2006; Miksch, 2005; University of California, Davis, 2008). It remains to be seen how these research efforts will translate (or not) into greater inroads on issues such as the availability of public financial aid for undocumented students—a challenge that nearly all recent studies of undocumented students' experiences in higher education have discussed as a key barrier to their transition to and persistence in college.

Resource and Policy Implications of the Transition to College of English Learners and Undocumented Immigrant Students

If we are to take seriously our national commitment to create greater access to higher education, it is important to move away from conceptualizations of immigrant students as taking up resources and toward a view that they are deserving of an investment of resources. In light of their growing presence in our public schools, our future as a nation is likely better served by the view that it is in our interest to invest in these students' strengths in order to address and overcome their educational needs (Rodriguez, 2007). Given that U. S. schools are required to provide access to public education to children regardless of their immigration status, it is logical to ensure that those resources invested early in their educational process are followed with resources (and systems) that ensure the full realization of their potential as they prepare for entry into higher education.

The findings and conclusions from the research on immigrant education in the United States suggest an obligation to more directly translate research results into changes in practice and policy that make a difference for students. Doing so, however, has proved to be very difficult. Thus, it seems logical that part of our obligation as researchers— particularly those among us who also consider ourselves to be educators and/or policy practitioners—extends to this translation work. That is, an important implication of this analysis for policy and practice is the need to explore methods for going the step further in our work to identify how a particular set of findings interfaces with the great variety of local contexts within which English learners and undocumented immigrants pursue their educational goals. In other words, how can a given school district, with unprecedented numbers of ELs, eliminate its reliance on academic ability tracking that systematically reduces the likelihood that those students will have access to college preparatory courses? It should not be the sole obligation of the educational counselor or, as is more likely the case, the district's English language development (ELD) specialist, to decipher the results of research studies in order to understand how educational institutions are to respond appropriately. Rather, the implication here is toward a closer partnership among all educational entities (K–16), as well as community linkages to the creative application of research-based strategies found to increase the probability for success among ELs (as just one example).

Beyond the notion of identifying new avenues for partnering to translate research findings into action in the practical and policy arenas, there also emerge some important implications for engaging colleagues across disciplinary traditions. Although the use of interdisciplinary research approaches is not new in the research on immigrants in the United States, it is still important to point out that interdisciplinary methodologies and collaborations are invaluable to our grasping what it takes for, say, an undocumented immigrant student to persevere through the transition into the U. S. social and educational system and onward to college. We must consider not only asking new research questions but also revisiting established questions using approaches that tap into the expertise of our colleagues outside of the field of education. In this regard, the universities themselves can be considered resources to be brought to bear in our pursuit of understanding and supporting the transition to college of EL and undocumented immigrant students. The postsecondary institutions in the United States represent, indeed, a multifaceted set of resources. These resources encompass directly applied expertise—as in the case of the teacher education departments that dedicate their programs to increasing the numbers of well-prepared bilingual educators—and the intermediary roles played in partnerships that bring together nonprofit agencies and community-based service organizations aimed at addressing the special circumstances of immigrant students.

Conclusion

Circling back to the opening discussion on the broad lessons we have learned from the literature on the educational attainment of immigrant students, one notes how the particular circumstances of EL and undocumented students further add to the complexity. For example, the generational differences among immigrant students in their overall educational attainment are likely to be complicated relative to students' ability to acquire skills in English and substantive knowledge of college preparatory subjects. Similarly, for undocumented immigrant students whose families are considered "mixed status" or whose type of immigration status differs from their parents, the trajectory that might facilitate their entry to college is fraught with obstacles. In the cases of EL and undocumented students, our task as researchers is to build on the lessons generated by large-scale studies by examining more deeply the ways in which these students are negotiating the processes that form their paths to higher education. The few studies that are available regarding secondary EL students and undocumented immigrants, for example, highlight the need to collect more detailed accounts to fully document not only the students' challenges but also the ways that students are navigating the various educational and social systems that they encounter. The intricate nature of their actions and decision-making processes are critically important contributions to the theories guiding our work.

Much more research on the responsiveness of institutions, pre-K–16 and beyond, to the needs of EL and undocumented immigrant students is also sorely needed. It seems that in the existing literature, which identifies important details about how individual students negotiate their educational success, the educational institutions are often portrayed as rigid, bureaucratic organizations. Thus, the educational innovations that currently serve the needs of these groups successfully should be documented, evaluated, and shared so that important lessons can be drawn for policy and practice from those efforts. Likewise, a better conceptualization of institutional responsiveness to student needs at every level of the educational system would help to expand the literature relative to English learner and undocumented immigrant students. In this spirit, eight areas of future research are outlined:

1. Studies are needed about the role of institutions in facilitating EL and undocumented students' academic achievement. Much of the current literature provides stories that emphasize individual students or groups of students navigating the various educational systems. It does not provide enough information about what the school or university role is in facilitating or hindering students' academic progress, thereby rendering an understanding of students' "success" as based in resiliency factors instead of identifying those aspects—positive and negative—about educational settings that educational policy can actually influence more directly.

2. Studies are needed that illuminate the particular teacher shortages in the midwestern and southern regions of the United States and identify the degree to which EL students there are more vulnerable regarding their ability to realize their academic potential. Similarly, in states with longer histories of large immigrant populations, and thus larger numbers of EL and undocumented students, it is important to know more about the high-growth suburbs and rural communities that may not have the infrastructure to adequately address the needs of ELs and undocumented immigrant students.

3. More research on the secondary EL population is needed, including investigations that distinguish between newly arrived adolescents and long-term ELs, whose educational trajectory occurred in the United States. It is imperative to begin filling the knowledge gap about the capacity of secondary schools (middle and high schools both) to support access to both English language skills and content in college preparatory subjects. Few studies exist that provide insights into students' or teachers' perspectives on the challenges involved in ensuring that EL students have postsecondary options. Likewise, little is known about the role of secondary schools and their districts in providing support and information for undocumented immigrant students whose entire education occurs in those systems but who subsequently face considerable obstacles in pursuing higher education.

4. More research about the factors related to the diminished educational success of immigrants (e.g., the second generation and beyond) over time is needed. What impact might institutional racism and other forms of institutional bias, for example, have on the educational outcomes of 1.5 and second-generation immigrant students? To the degree that English language proficiency is a gatekeeping factor, as well as immigrant status within a growing

"anti-immigrant" context, what are the subtler, hegemonic factors that shape students' experiences in their quest to pursue higher education? These questions remain critically important to understanding how the initial "advantage" of children of immigrants can be bolstered and provide further insights into the tragic educational outcomes noted for the third-plus generation students.

5. Given that the pre-K–12 educational system, particularly in the secondary years, appears to be ill-equipped to meet the challenges of EL students (and, to some degree, undocumented immigrant students) in their transition to college, the role of community colleges becomes increasingly salient. The work of MDRC is likely to yield important insights from programs that carry significant potential to meet the dual challenge of addressing the "remedial" needs of ESL students and increasing the likelihood of transferring to a 4-year institution. However, additional research is required to understand how the funding structures, both for support of the operations of the community colleges and for student access to financial aid, are aligning with the challenges that exist for EL/ESL students as they attempt to pursue higher education. Likewise, the capacity of community colleges appears to be significantly overburdened given the multiple roles and demands ascribed to this segment of higher education (Blumenthal, 2002). Thus, more study is warranted to understand the interconnected roles that pre-K–12, community colleges, and 4-year institutions play (or need to play) in order to respond to the growing EL and immigrant student population.

6. With the current number of states adopting DREAM Act-like legislation to provide undocumented immigrant students with resident status for in-state tuition purposes, it is important to understand both the impact and the challenges of implementing such policies. For example, undocumented immigrant students are already in a very vulnerable position as students; they often experience stress that is due to fear of discovery of their immigration status as they attempt to be full participants in programs and opportunities offered at their college campuses. Key questions that emerge for campuses are: How do such policies affect students' willingness to reveal their status in order to avail themselves of this lowered tuition cost, and how do campuses address unique student support needs (e.g., access to legal counsel regarding immigration status)? In addition, unlike the proposed federal DREAM Act, state tuition policies do not include eligibility for scholarships, grants, or loans. It would be important to understand from the perspectives of students and campus staff how this limitation of in-state tuition policies is shaping student

choices about postsecondary education, including information about experiences of those students who do avail themselves of the in-state tuition policy.

7. Critical to the responsiveness of institutions of higher education to their student populations is the availability of clear and accurate data. Additional efforts are recommended to ensure that accurate data on undocumented students are available. However, of equal importance is the need to safeguard the confidentiality of the students, whose sense of vulnerability unfortunately overshadows their willingness to reveal their status for university purposes. Having better and safe reporting systems would also help inform legislation at both a state and national level.

8. Drawing from the insights emerging from current research on undocumented students, it is recommended that research effort, also extend to examining the information dissemination practices relative to higher education options for students and their parents. Particularly at the secondary levels, it appears that good information for parents on higher educational options and financial aid are two of several areas of need in preparing both undocumented and English learner students for their transitions to college.

Acknowledgments

The lead author wishes to thank the scholars associated with the SSRC Transitions to College Project, who provided thoughtful guidance and suggestions during the preparation of this article, with special thanks to Jennifer Holdaway, Margaret Terry Orr, and Luis Fraga for their insightful feedback and editing. Any limitations of this article are the responsibility of the authors.

Note

1. Serious debate exists among educators and advocates about whether appropriate measures are used for the reclassification of students; also, some argue that a disservice could result from the reclassification of EL students to enable them to access mainstream content courses without also providing them (and their teachers) with any additional language support as the content increases in complexity. Transparency and consistency in the reclassification process is also an equity concern in that simply pursuing high reclassification rates—often used as a measure of a district's commitment to the progress of ELs toward proficiency in English—may inaccurately indicate both student progress and school responsiveness in the absence of clearly delineated criteria and support mechanisms linked to sound instructional and assessment practices for ELs.

References

Abrego, L. (2008). Legitimacy, social identity, and the mobilization of law: The effects of Assembly Bill 540 on undocumented students in California. *Law and Society Inquiry, 33,* 709–734.

Albrecht, T. J. (2007). *Challenges and service needs of undocumented Mexican undergraduate students: Students' voices and administrators' perspectives.* Unpublished doctoral dissertation, University of Texas at Austin.

August, D., & Hakuta, K. (1997). *Improving schooling for language-minority children: A research agenda.* Washington, DC: National Academy Press.

Bloom, D., & Sommo, C. (June 2005). *Building learning communities: Early results from the opening doors demonstration at Kingsborough community college.* New York: MDRC.

Blumenthal, A. J. (2002). English as a second language at the community college: An exploration of context and concerns. *New Directions for Community Colleges, 117,* 45–53.

Brittain, C. (2002). *Transnational messages: Experiences of Chinese and Mexican immigrants in American schools.* New York: LFB Scholarly Publishing.

California Tomorrow. (2005). *California community college access & equity policy brief.* Oakland, CA: Author.

Callahan, R. M. (2005). Tracking and high school English learners: Limiting opportunity to learn. *American Educational Research Journal, 42,* 305–328.

Chávez, L. R. (1998). *Shadowed lives: Undocumented immigrants in American society* (2nd ed.) Fort Worth, TX: Harcourt Brace College Publishers.

Conger, D. (Fall 2005). Within-school segregation in an urban school district. *Educational Evaluation and Policy Analysis, 27,* 225–244.

Diaz-Strong, D., & Meiners, E. (2007). Residents, alien policies, and resistances: Experiences of undocumented Latina/o students in Chicago's colleges and universities. *InterActions: UCLA Journal of Education and Information Studies, 3,* 1–20.

Drachman, E. (2008). Access to higher education for undocumented students. *Peace Review: A Journal of Social Justice, 18,* 91–100.

Faltis, C. J., & Hudelson, S. J. (1998). *Bilingual education in elementary and secondary school communities: Toward understanding and caring.* Needham Heights, MA: Allyn and Bacon.

Faltis, C. J., & Wolfe, P. (Eds.). (1999). *So much to say: Adolescents, bilingualism, and ESL in the secondary schools.* New York: Teachers College Press.

Flores, S. M., & Chapa, J. (2009). Latino immigrant access to higher education in a bipolar context of reception. *Journal of Hispanic Higher Education, 8,* 90–109.

Frum, J. L. (2008). Postsecondary educational access for undocumented students: Opportunities and constraints. *American Federation of Teachers: American Academic, 3,* 81–107.

Fry, R. (2003). *Hispanic youth dropping out of U. S. schools: Measuring the challenge.* Washington, DC: Pew Hispanic Center.

Gándara, P., Maxwell-Jolly, J., & Driscoll, A. (2005). *Listening to teachers of English language learners: A survey of California teachers' challenges, experiences, and professional development needs.* Santa Cruz, CA: Joint Publication of the Center for the Future of Teaching and Learning, Policy Analysis for California Education (PACE), and University of California Language Minority Research Institute (UCLMRI).

Gándara, P., Rumberger, R. W., Maxwell-Jolly, J., & Callahan, R. (2003). English learners in California schools: Unequal resources, unequal outcomes. *Educational Policy Analysis Archives*, *11*(36), 1–54. Retrieved December 15, 2008, from http://epaa.asu.edu/epaa/v11n36

García, E. E., & Wiese, A. (2002). Language, public policy, and schooling: A focus on Chicano English language learners. In R. R. Valencia (Ed.), *Chicano school failure and success: Past, present, and future* (2nd ed., pp. 149–169). London: RoutledgeFalmer.

García, O., Kleifgen, J. A., & Falchi, L. (2008). *From English language learners to emergent bilinguals* (Equity Matters: Research Review No. 1). New York: Teachers College, Columbia University.

Gershberg, A. I, Danenberg, A., & Sánchez, P. (2004). *Beyond "bilingual" education: New immigrants and public school policies in California*. Washington, DC: Urban Institute Press.

Gibson, G. A., Gándara, P., & Koyama, J. P. (Eds.). (2004). *School connections: U.S. Mexican youth, peers, and school achievement*. New York: Teachers College Press.

Glick, J. E., & White, M. J. (2004). Post-secondary school participation of immigrant and native youth: The role of familial resources and educational expectations. *Social Science Research*, *33*, 272–299.

Gonzales, R. G. (2007). Wasted talent and broken dreams: The lost potential of undocumented students. *Immigration Policy in Focus*, *5*(13), 1–11.

Gonzales, S. A., & Rodriguez, J. L. (2007). The resource implications of NCLB for the recruitment, preparation, and retention of highly qualified teachers for English learners in California. In G. M. Rodriguez & A. R. Rolle (Eds.), *To what ends and by what means: The social justice implications of contemporary school finance theory and practice* (pp. 145–160). New York: Routledge.

González, N., Moll, L. C., & Amanti, C. (2005). *Funds of knowledge: Theorizing practices in households, communities, and classrooms*. Mahwah: Erlbaum.

Gray, M. J., Rolph, E., & Melamid, E. (1996). *Immigration and higher education: Institutional responses to changing demographics*. Santa Monica, CA: RAND Center for Research on Immigration Policy.

Hardway, C., & Fuligni, A. J. (2006). Dimensions of family connectedness among adolescents with Mexican, Chinese, and European backgrounds. *Developmental Psychology*, *42*, 1246–1258.

Higgs, E. (2005). Specialized high schools for immigrant students: A promising new idea. *Journal of Law & Education*, *34*(2).

Hoefer, M., Rytina, N., & Campbell, C. (2006). *Estimates of the unauthorized immigrant population residing in the United States: January 2005*. Washington, DC: Department of Homeland Security Office of Immigration Statistics.

Kim, D. H., & Schneider, B. (2005). Social capital in action: Alignment of parental support in adolescents' transitions to postsecondary education. *Social Forces*, *84*, 1181–1206.

Linquanti, R. (2001). *The redesignation dilemma: Challenges and choices in fostering meaningful accountability for English learners*. University of California Language Minority Research Institute. Retrieved September 29, 2007, from http:www.lmri.ucsb.edu/publications/

Lopez, J. K. (2007). *"We asked for workers and they sent us people": A critical race theory and Latino critical theory ethnography exploring college-ready undocumented high school immigrants in North Carolina.* Unpublished doctoral dissertation, University of North Carolina at Chapel Hill.

McNeil, L., & Valenzuela, A. (2001). The harmful impact of the TAAS system of testing in Texas: Beneath the accountability rhetoric. In G. Orfield & M. L. Kornhaber (Eds.), *Raising standards or raising barriers? Inequality and high-stakes testing in public education* (pp. 127–150). New York: Century Foundation Press.

Merino, B. (1999). Preparing secondary teachers to teach a second language: The case of the United States with a focus on California. In C. J. Faltis & P. Wolfe (Eds.), *So much to say: Adolescents, bilingualism, & ESL in the secondary schools* (pp. 225–254). New York: Teachers College Press.

Miksch, K. L. (2005). Legal issues in developmental education: Immigrant students and the DREAM Act. *Research and Teaching in Developmental Education, 22*(1), 59–65.

National Immigration Law Center. (2006, April). *DREAM Act: Basic information.* Retrieved September 8, 2006, from http://www.nilc.org

Natriello, G., & Pallas, A. M. (2001). The development and impact of high-stakes testing. In G. Orfield & M. L. Kornhaber (Eds.), *Raising standards or raising barriers? Inequality and high-stakes testing in public education* (pp. 19–38). New York: Century Foundation Press.

Nieto, S. (2000). *Affirming diversity: The sociopolitical context of multicultural education* (3rd ed.). White Plains, NY: Longman.

Olsen, L., & Jaramillo, A. (1999). *Turning the tides of exclusion: A guide for educators and advocates for immigrant students,* Oakland, CA: California Tomorrow.

Orfield, G., & Kornhaber, M. L. (Eds.). (2001). *Raising standards or raising barriers? Inequality and high-stakes testing in public education.* New York: Century Foundation Press.

Padilla, A. M., & Gonzales, R. (2001). Academic performance of immigrant and U. S.-born Mexican heritage students: Effects of schooling in Mexico and bilingual/English language instruction. *American Educational Research Journal, 38,* 727–742.

Passel, J. S. (2003). *Further demographic information relating to the DREAM Act.* Washington, DC: Urban Institute.

Passel, J. S. (2005). *Unauthorized migrants: Numbers and characteristics. Background briefing prepared for task force on immigration and America's future.* Washington, DC: Pew Hispanic Center.

Perry, A. M. (2004). *Philosophical arguments of membership: The case of undocumented immigrants and financial aid for postsecondary education.* Unpublished doctoral dissertation, University of Maryland, College Park.

Pew Hispanic Center. (2009, January). *Statistical profile of the foreign-born population in the United States, 2006.* Retrieved June 26, 2009, from http://pewhispanic.org/factsheets/factsheet.php?FactsheetID=36

Phillips, R. G. (1991). Model programs in minority access. *New Directions for Community Colleges, 74,* 23–30.

Portes, A., & Rumbaut, R. G. (2001). *Legacies: The story of the immigrant second generation.* Berkeley: University of California Press/Russell Sage Foundation.

Rangel, Y. T. (2001). *College immigrant students: How undocumented female Mexican immigrant students transition into higher education.* Unpublished doctoral dissertation, University of California, Los Angeles.

Rendón, L. I. (2002). Community college puente: A validating model of education. *Educational Policy, 16,* 642–667.

Rincón, A. (2005). *Paying for their status: Undocumented immigrant students and college access.* Unpublished doctoral dissertation, University of Texas at Austin.

Rodriguez, G. M. (2004). Vertical equity in school finance and the potential for increasing school responsiveness to student and staff needs. *Peabody Journal of Education, 79*(3), 7–30.

Rodriguez, G. M. (2007). Cycling on in cultural deficit thinking: California school finance and the possibilities of critical policy analysis. In G. M. Rodriguez & R. A. Rolle (Eds.), *To what ends and by what means? The social justice implications of contemporary school finance theory and policy* (pp. 107–143). New York: Routledge.

Ruiz-de-Velasco, J., & Fix, M. (2000). *Overlooked & underserved: Immigrant students in U. S. secondary schools.* Washington, DC: Urban Institute Press.

Rumberger, R. W., & Gándara, P. (2004). Seeking equity in the education of California's English language learners. *Teachers College Record, 106,* 2032–2056.

Rumberger, R. W., & Lim, S. A. (2008). *Why students drop out of school: A review of 25 years of research* (California Dropout Research Project, Report No. 15). Retrieved December 20, 2008, from http://www.lmri.ucsb.edu/dropouts/pubs_reports.htm

Rumberger, R. W., & Rodriguez, G. M. (2002). Chicano dropouts: An update of research and policy issues. In R. R. Valencia (Ed.), *Chicano school failure and success: Past, present, and future* (2nd ed., pp. 114–146). London: RoutledgeFalmer.

Schneider, B., Martinez, S., & Owens, A. (2006). Barriers to educational opportunities for Hispanics in the United States. In M. Tienda & F. Mitchell (Eds.), *Hispanics and the future of America* (pp. 179–227). Committee on Transforming Our Common Destiny, National Research Council. Washington, DC: National Academies Press.

Scrivener, S., Bloom, D., LeBlanc, A., Paxson, C., Rouse, C. E., & Sommo, C. (2008). *A good start: Two-year effects of a freshman learning community program at Kingsborough Community College.* New York: MDRC.

Shulock, N., & Moore, C. (2005). Diminished access to the baccalaureate for low-income and minority students in California: The impact of budget and capacity constraints on the transfer function. *Educational Policy, 19,* 418–442.

Seif, H. (2004). "Wise up!" Undocumented Latino youth, Mexican-American legislators, and the struggle for higher education access. *Latino Studies, 2,* 210–230.

S.I.N. Collective. (2007). Students informing now (S.I.N.) challenge the racial state in California without shame . . . SIN verguenza! *Educational Foundations, 21*(1–2), 71–90.

UCLA Center for Labor Research and Education. (2008a). *Underground undergrads: UCLA undocumented immigrant students speak out.* Student publication sponsored by the UCLA Center for Labor Research and Education, Los Angeles.

UCLA Center for Labor Research and Education. (2008b). *Undocumented students: Unfulfilled dreams.* Los Angeles: UCLA Center for Labor Research and Education.

University of California, Office of the President. (2008). *Annual report on AB 540 tuition exemptions, 2006–07 academic year*. UCOP Student Financial Aid Support.

USC Center for Higher Education Policy Analysis. (2006). *AB 540/undocumented student resource guide (cash for college edition)*. Retrieved from http://www.usc.edu/dept/chepa/pdf/AB_540_final.pdf

Valencia, R. R., & Solórzano, D. G. (1997). Contemporary deficit thinking. In R. R. Valencia (Ed.), *The evolution of deficit thinking: Educational thought and practice* (pp. 160–210). Stanford Series on Education and Public Policy. London: Falmer Press.

Valenzuela, A. (1999). *Subtractive schooling: U. S.-Mexican youth and the politics of caring*. Albany: State University of New York Press.

Yosso, T. J. (2005). Whose culture has capital? A critical race theory discussion of community cultural wealth. *Race, Ethnicity, and Education, 8*, 69–91.

Yosso, T. J. (2006). *Critical race counterstories along the Chicana/Chicano educational pipeline*. New York: Routledge.

"Someday This Pain Will Be Useful to You": Self-Disclosure and Lesbian and Gay Identity in the ESL Writing Classroom

Martha Clark Cummings

Newly returned to Brooklyn, New York, after four years of teaching in Japan, Martha Clark Cummings and her ESL students grapple with writing, language, and identity as they read Someday This Pain Will Be Useful to You, *Peter Cameron's young adult novel about James, a wealthy New York teenager who "question[s] his sexual orientation." Cummings particularly and sensitively deals with the question of whether to come to her students as a lesbian, especially after her experiences of living closeted in Japan. As Cummings considers this issue throughout her teaching narrative, she also provides a researched discussion on self-disclosure. At the same time, Cummings's students struggle with the cultural and socioeconomic disconnects between their identities and that of the fictional protagonist James, who considers attending Brown University and whose mother owns a standard poodle. Although the students live in the same city just across the river from James, they do not share James's cultural references, an issue that creates provocative occasions for writing and classroom discussion. Initially, Cummings anticipates a "'golden' moment" (p. 348) for disclosing her lesbian identity to students. As she contemplates the student-centered pedagogy of the ESL course and the educational needs of her students, she arrives at fascinating conclusions.*

"Every encounter with a new classful of students, to say nothing of a new boss, social worker, loan officer, landlord, doctor, erects a new closet whose fraught and characteristic laws of optics and physics exact from at least gay people new surveys, new calculations, new draughts and requisitions

of secrecy or disclosure. Even an out gay person deals daily with interlocutors about whom she doesn't know whether they know or not; it is equally difficult to guess for any given interlocutor whether, if they did know, the knowledge would seem very important."
　　　　　　　　　—Eve Sedgwick, *The Epistemology of the Closet*

"The important question, then, is not whether sociosexual aspects of cultural practices ought to be addressed but how this might be done."
　　　　　　　—Cynthia Nelson, *Sexual Identities in English Language Education*

Not too long ago, I returned to New York City from four years in Japan, expecting to feel liberated, let out the closet, free again to do as I pleased in the ESL classroom. In Japan, when I informed the director of my program of my sexual orientation, she suggested that I keep it "a secret forever." I grew to understand her perspective over the years. In the small city where I worked, such a revelation would have brought the local television, radio, and newspaper reporters to the campus, and I would quickly have become the most famous foreigner in town. And not in a good way. Being a lesbian in Japan is associated with pornography. In addition, as Jean Valentine explains:

[C]onceptualizing self in terms of sexuality is considered alien in Japan, as this makes doing into being, practice into essence, in that what you do defines what you are. In Japan, what you are, your self, tends to be defined through interaction, where you belong with others, your socially recognized networks of relationships. (107)

When my partner and I told our Japanese colleagues that we had left New York together in 1992, moving to California, then Wyoming, then, in 2002, to Japan, only one person remarked, "You must be very good friends." The rest commented on the fact that Japanese people did not usually move that much.

Back in New York, my partner and I went to City Hall in Brooklyn to become Domestic Partners, to claim our rights, and I began to think about what rights I had in the ESL classroom and what I might do with them. I felt fortunate to be starting a new teaching position at a large, urban community college, in a program that describes its overall educational philosophy as "based on the principles of whole language, which assumes that learning is a social activity," a program that "rel[ies] heavily on . . . three learning approaches: cooperative learning, the language experience approach, and fluency first" (Babbitt and Mlynarczyk 40–41). My interpretation of this was that I would have considerable autonomy in the classroom concerning what I might share with students, how I might creatively construct the basis for meaning-making in the classroom.

As part of fluency first (MacGowan-Gilhooly), teachers are required to have students read a full length work of fiction. I have since learned that choosing an appropriate text for these students is particularly challenging. I was therefore delighted when, prior to my third semester, when I was to teach a class that included five "multiple repeaters" of the course—that is, students who had taken and failed the course more than once—Peter Cameron published his very accessible and compelling young adult novel, *Someday This Pain Will Be Useful to You*. I have been a fan of Peter Cameron's work since he first started publishing short stories in *The New Yorker* in 1983. He is an author I trust and respect. In this particular novel, an 18-year-old young man who characterizes himself as "disturbed" considers a variety of issues, including his highly dysfunctional family, who live in New York City; whether or not he should go to college as planned; why his peers seem so distasteful to him; his love for his grandmother; and the correct use of the English language. He is also questioning his sexual orientation. In choosing this text, I was taking a step toward my further uncloseting. Or so I thought.

A Context for Teaching and Disclosure

It seems to me that over the last forty years, gay and lesbian academics have come full circle. We started out strictly closeted and thereby authoritative, that is, not problematizing identity and thereby not problematizing our classroom authority in the classroom. Then we came out and allowed ourselves to be vulnerable. Today some of us are postmodernly performing our position moment by moment and thereby remaining ambiguous. Some queer theorists even advocate intentionally playing the role of the authority again.

I began teaching ESL in 1973, in the era of Lesbian Separatism (Levy), as well as the beginning of the recognition of "homophobia" (Weinberg). NCTE and other organizations writing resolutions opposing discrimination against lesbians and gays (Crew and Keener) soon followed. I continued teaching ESL through the AIDS crisis in the 1980s, when coming out, in the classroom and elsewhere, became a matter of life and death, and through the establishment of Act Up!, with their slogan of "Silence=Death." The mood of the era was summarized by writer and activist, Michelangelo Signorile:

> Everyone must come out of the closet, no matter how difficult, no matter how painful.
>
> We must all tell our parents.
>
> We must all tell our families.
>
> We must all tell our friends.
>
> We must all tell our coworkers.
>
> These people vote. If they don't know that we're queer—if they think that only the most horrible people are queer—they will vote against us. (364)

Advocating that teachers present themselves with a gay/lesbian identity in the composition classroom, Harriet Malinowitz reminds us of the old adage, "If you're not part of the solution, you're part of the problem" (264). In her discussion of the place of sexuality in the composition class, she states, "What all of my students ... [had] in common was the awareness that they lived in a homophobic world, and that homophobia affected them in some way" (22). In addition, she suggests, nondisclosure directly impacts the dynamics by which the construction of meaning may operate. "Because lesbians and gay men must constantly assess the consequences of being out and negotiate the terms of disclosure, often necessitating elaborate monitoring of what is said and even thought ('internalized homophobia'), a particular complication is woven into their processes of construing and constructing knowledge" (24). The dilemma that arises is a composition class that advocates self-disclosure and exploration of personal themes for some but not all of its participants. The antidote, according to Malinowitz, is to treat sexual identity as another "negotiation of meaning" in the composition classroom. This includes a gay or lesbian teacher coming out in the classroom in order to further empower her gay or lesbian students.

In the field of TESOL, Cynthia Nelson describes the changes that took place in the 1990s in terms of "the groundswell of discussions that language teachers began to have in professional forums" at the time. She recounts, "teachers began to advocate for, and exchange practical advice about, such things as considering the educational needs of learners who themselves identify as lesbian, bisexual, gay, or transgender; including gay themes in curricula and teaching resources; addressing heterosexist discrimination and homophobic attitudes among teachers, students, and administrators; and creating open working environments so that no teachers have to hide their sexual identities" (14).

Gay, bisexual, transgendered, and lesbian teachers started groups of political and social support as well. Nelson's groundbreaking presentation, "We Are Your Colleagues" with Jim Ward and Lisa Carscadden at the 1991 TESOL convention in Vancouver was followed by a surge of activism that culminated in the formation of a GBTL task force whose mandate was to make recommendations to TESOL's executive board regarding the inclusion of GBTL people and issues at every level of the organization (Cummings and Nelson). In this context of change and possibility toward greater inclusion of gay identity issues in the classroom, I explored what it meant for me to bring my authentic self to teaching.

According to Paula Cooper and Cheri Simonds, the act of coming out is an act of self-disclosure, and "[a] major characteristic of effective self-disclosure is appropriateness. To be effective communicators we consider the timing of our disclosure" (34). No longer dealing with a formal and implicit protocol of secrecy, I considered that appropriateness might thereby help me decide whether or not to come out to my students. However, the more I considered coming out to my students, the more hesitant I became. Mary Elliot extends the point: "Self-disclosure implies the personal, the unacceptable or difficult, and the uncomfortable; self-disclosure of sexual orientation surely packages all three. Self-disclosure in the congruent or 'golden' moment rather than the incongruent moment can mitigate fear by removing much of the artificiality and sense of 'wrongness' from the disclosing moment, a sense that can be confused with the value of the disclosed content itself" (704). What this meant to me was that I would not start the course by announcing that I was a lesbian and had chosen a novel with a protagonist who seemed to be questioning his sexual orientation because it was a topic I couldn't get enough of. Instead, I would wait until the students recognized the issue as an important one in the novel and possibly in their own lives. I would wait, then, for the "golden" moment before disclosing my sexual identity to my students.

I decided this despite what I knew from the literature on disclosure in the English language classroom, namely that the matter is not that simple. As Judith Butler states, self-disclosure may conceal more than it reveals:

> In the act which would disclose the true and full content of that "I," a certain radical *concealment* is thereby produced. For it is always finally unclear what is meant by invoking the lesbian-signifier, since its signification is always to some degree out of one's control, but also because its *specificity* can only be demarcated by exclusions that return to disrupt its claim to coherence. . . . If I claim to be a lesbian, I "come out" only to produce a new and different "closet." The "you" to whom I come out now has access to a different region of opacity. (18)

As Mary Bryson and Suzanne de Castell observe of their experience teaching a lesbian studies course: "We found that we could not . . . represent ourselves 'as lesbian' within institutional contexts (such as our respective faculties of education) without instantiating profoundly unproductive essentialist notions of fixed, stable, and marginal 'lesbian identities'" (297). In other words, if I come out as a lesbian in my classroom, I am not only giving up heterosexual privilege and authority, but I am inviting my students to apply to me all of the labels and stereotypes they have in their minds about what a lesbian is, what a lesbian looks like, what a lesbian does, and finally, to attribute anything I do that offends or frightens them to the fact of my being a lesbian. When one of my students who feels wronged says to me, "You're only doing this to me because I'm a man," I assume he means because I am a lesbian. The space in which I can maneuver may grow smaller, not bigger, when I come out.

Disclosure as a Critique of Culture, or Coming Out Is Not Like It Used to Be

Ultimately, Elliot reminds us that the act itself involves crossing an "abyss" (704), which includes the experience of "dread, panic, confusion, and uncertainty of the actual moment of disclosure" (694), and yet revealing [one's sexual identity as a] "public 'identity,' because it is predicated upon private taboo sexual practices, can never achieve full status as an identity in the heterosexist mind. Coming out will almost always, therefore, feel more like the confession of a secret than we who live within the consciousness of a complex gay and lesbian culture would wish" (704).

In the one other ESL classroom in which I had come out, back in the early 1990s, the students, once they had recovered from their initial surprise and the fact that they did not have the language to adequately express the feelings they were having about my revelation, responded by telling me their secrets. They seemed to think I was inviting them to share a secret, too. And they did. A Japanese woman wrote an essay about her attraction to African American men, and a Chinese woman confessed that the only reason she was in New York was that she had had an affair with a married surgeon at the hospital in China where she had been a doctor. Somehow, if I did come out to my ESL students again, I had to do it in a way that would allow them to see that I was not confessing a dirty secret, but naming my place in a homophobic culture that was oppressing all of us.

Sarah Benesch, for me, represents the embodiment of a critical approach to teaching ESL composition that includes sociocultural critique. Describing her teaching of a lesson about the death of Matthew Shepard, she writes: "I focus on one assumption that emerged and was treated dialogically: that heterosexual men are justified in responding to the presence of homosexual men with anger or violence to assert a traditional notion of masculinity" (577). And by the end of the class discussion, her students realize that their violent reaction is based on fear. Nelson, too, suggests that "exploring, rather than shunning, homophobic attitudes . . . can lead to insights . . . about the ways in which language and culture operate" (86). Her suggestion makes a great deal of sense to me. As a sociolinguist, the exploration of language and culture through expressions of homophobia seems particularly enticing.

In order to engage in this kind of discourse, Karen Kopelson suggests that the instructor appear neutral. Such a stance is performative, "a deliberate, reflective, self-conscious masquerade that serves an overarching and more insurgent political agenda than does humanist individualism. It is never a stance that believes in or celebrates its own legitimacy but, rather, feigns itself, *perverts* itself, in the service of other—disturbing and disruptive—goals" (123). My problem with this approach is that my students know I have a passionate position on every issue that comes up in our discussions. How could I possibly be neutral? For example, much to my students' surprise I think watching television is such a waste of time that I don't have one. I care passionately about reading and writing and the movies, and I love to look at art. How could I be neutral about whether or not the protagonist of the novel we are reading is gay?

Other researchers suggest, dishearteningly, that it doesn't matter what we do, that no matter how diverse gay and lesbian people might be, in our homophobic culture, there is a lens through which gay and lesbian people are viewed that snaps into place at the first moment the word is mentioned and which cannot be altered. And yet, another approach, Queer Theory, suggests a difference could be made by moving the focus from "the repression or expression of a homosexual minority" toward developing "an analysis of the hetero/homosexual figure as a power/knowledge regime that shapes the ordering of desires, behaviors, and social institutions, and social relations—in a word, the constitution of the self and society" (Seidman 128). In other words, if an instructor were able to remain neutral, or at least ambiguous, she might be able to engage students in a discussion about why it seems so important for society to maintain the gay/straight binary and what, exactly, is at stake.

And so I viewed the option of neutrality as supportive of my decision to wait for a "golden moment" of self-disclosure, if one arose. Otherwise, would refrain from bringing up my own sexual identity in the conversation. I would try to do the right thing. In other words, I would help my students develop as writers and critical thinkers in the context of the novel we were discussing.

Reading and Writing about
Someday This Pain Will Be Useful to You

With the long, varied history of thought and action around disclosure of sexual orientation in the classroom in mind, I expected the discussion of this novel to be an emotionally fraught experience. It was a small class. Only fifteen had registered, and after the first three weeks, three had dropped out. We met for two 60-minute periods four days a week. The students also had tutoring for two periods on Fridays from a very experienced tutor.

Convenient for forming small groups that could speak English together, the twelve students included groups of four from each of three parts of the world. They were: Anastasia, a Ukrainian woman in her fifties with two grown children; Sophie, a Russian woman in her mid-thirties, the single mother of two young daughters; and a 19-year-old Romanian named Andre, whose stated goal after college was "to transfer to other college and keep performing myself." Rounding out the

Eastern European group was Nila, from Uzbekistan, the young mother of two children, who said, "I hope to get from this course more English, because when I came to United State I started learn English at the beginning, even I didn't knew what it means he or she."

There were four Chinese students under 25: Tang, from Mainland China, who, when asked on a first-day questionnaire what he hoped to do after graduation, wrote, "I have no idea but I am sure I have to work"; Stacy, also from Mainland China, whose best essay was about being her parents' second, hence "secret" child and growing up with her grandparents; Sunny, a Cantonese speaker; and Rebecca, from Macao, also a native speaker of Cantonese, who asked, "If I live here more than 5 years, My English will be better than now, wonna it?"

The other four students were Haitians: Henri, a man in his twenties who worked all night and had a very hard time staying awake in this 12:40–2:50 class on no sleep; Charles, a security guard at the Department of Homeland Security, who often told us "Never hesitate to call 911"; Monique, a troubled woman in her thirties who was unable to manage her life at home with two small children and a husband who was not anxious to help her become educated; and Paul, a 19-year-old who asked, "How hard I need to work to get an A+ in this class."

In teaching the course, I tried to follow the advice of *Changes*, a textbook I co-authored, wherein "the role of the instructor is often implied . . . setting up groups or pairs; answering questions about the activities, the readings, and the instructions for writing; structuring and facilitating class discussion and sharing, helping to make sense and order out of the sometimes conflicting and disordered group reports; adding the interpretations of the larger community" (Withrow, Brookes, and Cummings xiv–xv).

As for discussion of the novel, I kept to Kenneth Bruffee's notion of collaborative learning, and depended in large part on the students. In their groups, students decide what issues are important and relevant to them and write statements or questions about them that could be argued about. The students define the important issues as "sharable concern[s], . . . topic[s] that people talk, read, and write about. Issues grow out of concrete experience and connect several similar or related experiences" (31). Students then go on to write discussion questions about these issues. The concept of the discussion question is also derived from Bruffee's *generalization*, "an observation or judgment that says something about more than one person, object, or experience. It says something about many similar people, objects, or experiences" (32). Generalizations generated by these ESL students included: "Divorce hurts children as well as parents"; "Second and third marriages should be banned"; and "Rich people have more choices than poor people." The students decided together they could discuss or write essays about any of these issues.

What they noticed first was the vast social class difference between James, the 18-year-old protagonist of the novel, and themselves.

"This is a book about rich people," Paul, one of the young Haitian men, said after reading the first chapter. Others nodded in agreement. From the moment they opened the book and started reading, James' dysfunctional wealthy family was a source of constant fascination for them.

"How do you know?" I asked all of them, getting up to write their responses on the board.

They had not heard of Brown University, where James was supposed to go in September, but his sister attended Barnard, a famously expensive college. They knew because the family lived in Manhattan, in a neighborhood where the two teenage children could forget to lock the door, and not in Brooklyn, where we all lived, along with other recent immigrants and their teachers, bumped out of Manhattan by the soaring price of real estate. Moreover, the family had a dishwasher, they said. And they were offended by James' employment in his mother's art gallery. What bothered them about such employment? I asked, and they cited a passage in which James' mother explains, "You do not go there because you are needed. You go there because I pay you to go there so you will have a summer job and learn the value of the dollar and know what responsibility is all about" (8). As a group, these students were not in need of any lessons about the value of a dollar.

My students did not know what a standard poodle was, but they said that if this family had a big dog, they must have a big apartment to keep it in. The parents were divorced, also a luxury, and James' father lived in a building built by Donald Trump, on the Upper East Side, a notoriously rich neighborhood.

Washington Square Park and the dominant presence of New York University in Greenwich Village were also unfamiliar, but again, if this family lived in a neighborhood close to a park with a dog run, they were rich.

We came to their first serious issue in the novel, the fact that "Mr. Rogers," the mother's third husband had, as James describes it, "stolen [his] mother's ATM and credit cards, or at least 'borrowed' them while she lay dozing in her nuptial bed, and somehow used them to get $3,000, all of which he gambled away in the wee small hours of the morning" (15). We discussed this issue for some time. On the following day, I made it a freewriting topic, "What would you do if your loved one stole your credit card and spent $3,000?" Many of their responses were indignant.

"It's like I tell my children," Monique, a Haitian mother of two, said, reading aloud from her writing. "'Sorry' is not what I want to hear you say! Don't say 'sorry!' Don't do it! Then you don't have to say 'sorry!'" She became agitated enough that the rest of the class began to laugh nervously.

Tang, a heavyset Chinese boy, had a more magnanimous attitude. He wrote, "If my loved one stole my credit card and spent $3,000, I would be so disturbed, thinking why she wants to stole my card and spent that much money. I would ask her did something happened on her or any others. Why you can't talk to me or tell me need help."

The others were less generous. Mr. Rogers' stealing made the divorce justifiable, in many of their eyes.

The differences between James' family and their own was an issue that came up often in the freewriting these students did in class. Some of the answers were obvious. The parents were divorced. James and his sister treat each other badly. James could only have lunch with his father if he made an appointment.

As Charles, another Haitian student, described it in his freewriting, "I keep thinking about James family; it like a crasy family. The family is a rich family but money can not buy happiness. I was thinking of not having family relationship like this family and that's really holds my mind, a father told his son that; 'it's OK for me, if you gay.' That is really bad."

When he talked about it in class, after each group had asked some version of "Do you think James and his father have a disrespectful relationship? Why or why not?" Paul leaned forward, covering the left half of his face with one hand, and said, as if deeply ashamed, "When his father asked him if he was *gay*, that was *bad*."

"Bad in what sense?" I asked, wondering if this was my golden moment. My heart was pounding, my palms sweating.

"How could he ask him that?" Paul wanted to know.

"This is America. New York. Parents want to know exactly what's going on with their children. We talk about everything," I said.

"But . . ."

Paul could not express his indignation on behalf of the young protagonist in the novel. I waited for him to go on.

"The pasta . . ." Paul finally said, and at this point his classmates chimed in.

The scene was disturbing to all of us. First, at their lunch appointment, James' father told him never to get married. Then, after James ordered penne for lunch, his father said to him, "You should have ordered steak or something. . . . You should never order pasta as a main course. It's not manly."

A discussion of food in their cultures ensued. We talked about whether certain foods were eaten primarily by men and others by women. They giggled and explained to me that there were foods "that made you horny," that only men should eat. I could have circled back and asked, "What do you think provoked James' father to ask if he was gay?" But my students had not asked. The key issues in the book were theirs to choose. Whether or not James was gay was not one of them yet.

Later that day, in my teaching journal, I wrote:

> Is my coming out even relevant? How much do I, a 60-year-old lesbian,
> have in common with an 18 year-old gay boy who is just discovering his
> sexuality? Do I tell them I have been through a similar struggle? As an
> 18-year-old, alienated in the affluent suburbs of New York City, I fell in
> love with my best friend, we slept together, I discovered myself, she
> wanted to die, tried to kill herself, and was institutionalized? Wouldn't
> that be going too far? Where do I stop once I've started?

But I had let the moment pass. There would be another.

During the course of the semester, while reading and discussing
the book, other issues continued to preoccupy my students, always leading us away from the issue of the protagonist's sexual orientation. They
were alarmed that James was considering not going to college because
he thought it was a waste of time. They were confused by his dislike of
people his own age, puzzled by his sister's snide comments when James
visited his grandmother—in their cultures, loving your grandmother
and wanting to be with her was not only acceptable but the norm—and
baffled that James spent hours on the Internet looking at houses for
sale in Nebraska, Kansas, and Indiana.

It wasn't that they didn't write about James' struggle with his sexual orientation, particularly after reading Chapter 11, in which James
reads his co-worker, John's, profile online in "Gent4Gent" and imper-
sonates exactly the kind of person John is looking for. John invites
James, in the persona he has created, to a party at the Frick Museum.
The students puzzled over James' motivation in their reading journals.
Rebecca, a very serious young woman, from China, said:

> The meeting of John and James seem to be interesting. We learn that
> John is gay and James kind of loves him. They both work at the gallery
> why wouldn't James just tell John that he is interested in him. Maybe
> James is not completely gay or maybe he is turning into gay and don't
> know how to accept he is gay. He tell us that he does not care what people
> think of him but we are living in a society where there is a lot of interac-
> tion I think he must care about what other think of him. The thing that
> confuse me the most is the part where James meet John on the internet
> and did not let him know he real identity but yet James decided to go and
> meet John in person. Other than the name there is really no description
> or personally about John. I would like to know more about John. He seems
> like a real interesting character. James has mention several time that he
> wish to buy a house in the middle state and live there but he never men-
> tion about who he wish to live with. I was wondering why James did not
> include John in any plan if he love John.

When we talked about this scene in the novel, again it was not the
issue of sexual orientation that troubled the students, but the fact that
James had deceived a person he seemed to care for.

We talked about self-deception, an issue that comes up again and again in the novel. Their ideas and opinions about James and his family took shape, grew stronger, as they practiced expressing themselves in writing. Andre, from Romania, wrote, "He is not interested in nothing. Instade to go to college to have fun and learn he want to buy a house in Nebraska or Kansas and to stay on a porch and read books like an old men, I think he is the boring one."

Stacy, from China, pointed out the ways in which James' mother deceived herself by going to Las Vegas for her honeymoon, a place she had previously disdained: "Problem is not in the place. Is they both didn't have love. So whatever, where was the honey place?"

Paul wrote, "James deceive himself because he doesn't want nobody to know that is not happy even his self."

When we finished the book, students expressed surprise in their reading journals that James had known all along that he was gay. Paul said:

> I was surprised by the end of the chapter 14th when James said that he knew he was gay, and when he said that being gay was perfect. That's really surprised me. I thought he had a little problem with his father when his father asked him if he's gay, I don't know why because he knew he was gay, may because the way his father asked him. I would like to know how his mother and his sister will feel when they know that and what they will say about that. I remember his father told him he could help him if he gay I would like to know how?

During our discussion of the end of the novel, Charles suggested, quietly, that perhaps we had all had feelings like James did sometimes. Andre said it was all right for women, but for men it was sick. Here, finally, was a moment where I felt I must intervene.

"I think it's fine," I told him, "for men or for women. It may not be fine for you, personally, but it's fine." The students smiled at me benignly. Did they know? Should I tell them? Instead I told them something my dissertation advisor had said to me 20 years earlier.

"Do you know what a continuum is?" I asked, and Nila, the young woman from Uzbekistan, who seemed to have studied everything, said, "Yes. Connected. In chemistry. Like rainbow."

"Exactly," I said. "Maybe we are all somewhere on the continuum," I continued, drawing a semicircle on the board, "between 100% heterosexual and 100% homosexual," writing these words at opposite ends of my continuum. "Maybe that's OK."

"I am over there," Andre said, laughing, pointing to the 100% heterosexual.

"That's fine," I said. "But maybe we are not all over there with you. Not every minute of every day. And maybe that's OK."

No one said anything. But perhaps a point had been made, if briefly, about the fluidity and diversity of sexual identities. And as Malinowitz reminds us, "I believe that the long intermediate moment—which may, certainly, last forever—of being involved in the act or project of overcoming [one's internalized homophobia] is the real moment of pride" (267). Perhaps I had something to feel proud of.

For the final exam, I gave the students a choice of three questions that evolved from the work we had done together over the course of the semester (see Appendix). Ten of them chose Question One and two chose Question Two. No one chose to answer Question Three. Of the ones who chose to explain and illustrate why James was sad, Andre blamed James' family, as did Henri, "he don't enjoy it talking to his mom and his dad"; and Charles, "James . . . feels disconnected emotionally to his family where love, respect, and attention seems unexist." Rebecca suggested that "Deep inside of his heart he suffer because he can't act or live like others," but she did not elaborate. Paul explained that James' way of thinking made him sad. "James got fascinated from anything and this thing can make him sad. I remember one day, he was taking a walk with Miro (the dog), he saw a man and a woman were walking together. He thought that they were having fun, they seem they were in love. Just went to a restaurant or movie and he thought they will never have a wonderful time like that again and he's sad. James is the kind of man who got sad of his thought."

Nila, too, attributed James' unhappiness to his family life, noting that "They talked with the dog Miro then with each others."

Rebecca wrote about James' life, beginning by saying that she, like James, hadn't wanted to attend college and then describing how she was different from James. Only Stacy, a Chinese young woman who didn't say much in class, addressed the issue of James' being gay, writing:

> James was gay in the book. Although he in a free country, James was freedome to choose his lover sex, but his case is limited in people. I am regualar girl, I like guy, I can't accept a same sex be my boyfriend. I believe, my family member can not accept too. It's different like James. James' father agree his son was gay, he didn't reject his son was gay. One day, James told his father he was gay in their dinner. James father didn't angry with him and said: "well, women may make you think about get marry more time than a man." And James' father look like nothing. If I told my parents I be with a girl, they should be crazy. They can't accept their daughter be with same sex person. They will lock my at home, didn't let me outside, and bother me everyday until I changed. They would think this is not a normal thing, they can't cool down themselves and talk to me. But James father not, he felt nothing, James also. I think the reason is they both disappoint of women. Because James' father was a suffer marriage and James was a bad memory, So they disappoint the marriage and women. James saw his mother thinking about himself, it may make him be gay.

This essay made me smile, not only for the unusual language—"accept a same sex be my boyfriend"—but because she was addressing the issue I cared about in an open and honest manner, telling me what she really thought without worrying about my judgment of her ideas. What more could I ask?

Conclusion

Did reading the book have an impact on the sociosexual attitudes of these ESL students? Certainly. They also had a chance to express themselves and exchange ideas about other issues that were important to them: love, money, respect, family, and higher education. In addition, they saw an example of a gay young man who could not openly discuss his sexual orientation even though he was encouraged by everyone around him to do so. Through reading this novel, they experienced the ways in which homophobia affects everyone.

As for me—in future classes—I will continue to be alert to "golden" moments. Furthermore, I learned from this experience that being pedagogically prepared to deal with issues of sexual orientation and homophobia, through the creation of lessons that critically engage students might make the experience of teaching this particular novel more relaxing for me and more enlightening for my students. As Nelson points out about "[t]his gargantuan task" of disclosure, it is "nothing less than intimidating. After all, determining where to begin keeps many of us from ever getting started" (299).

I have, at least, begun. Whether or not I choose to keep my sexual identity "a secret forever" in the ESL classroom, I concur with Nelson that "The key issue is not so much whether teachers come out . . . in the classroom but the extent to which their own insights and quandaries about sexual-identity negotiations are informing their . . . teaching practices by shedding light on questions of identity and representation generally" (119). The continuing development of the perspectives I embrace for dealing with sexual orientation and homophobia, then, could very well lead to new understandings of identity, for me and my students.

Acknowledgments

I would like to thank my ESL students, who graciously gave me their permission to quote and describe them. I would also like to thank Sarah Benesch for saying "I think you should write about that" just when I needed to hear it; Cynthia D. Nelson for publishing her ground-breaking book just in time; Rebecca Mlynarczyk and two anonymous *JBW* reviewers for their helpful feedback on the first draft I submitted; Lisa Vice, my loved one of over twenty years, for her insightful responses to early drafts; and most of all, *JBW* Co-Editor Hope Parisi for her encouragement, support, insights, and trust in the process.

Works Cited

Babbitt, Marcia, and Rebecca Williams Mlynarczyk. "Keys to Successful Content-Based ESL Programs: Administrative Perspectives." *Content-Based College ESL Instruction.* Ed. Loretta Kasper. Mahwah: Erlbaum, 2000. 26–47. Print.

Benesch, Sarah. "Thinking Critically, Thinking Dialogically." *TESOL Quarterly* 33.3 (1999): 573–80. Print.

Bruffee, Kenneth. *A Short Course in Writing: Practical Rhetoric for Composition Courses, Writing Workshops, and Tutor Training Programs.* 2nd ed. New York: Little, Brown, 1982. Print.

Bryson, Mary, and Suzanne de Castell. "Queer Pedagogy: Praxis Makes Im/Perfect." *Canadian Journal of Education: Against the Grain: Narratives of Resistance* 18.3 (1993): 285–305. Print.

Butler, Judith. "Imitation and Gender Insubordination." *Inside / Out: Lesbian Theories, Gay Theories.* Ed. Diane Fuss. New York: Routledge, 1991. 13–31. Print.

Cameron, Peter. *Someday This Pain Will Be Useful to You.* New York: Farrar, Straus, 2007. Print.

Cooper, Paula J., and Cheri Simonds. *Communication for the Classroom Teacher.* 6th ed. Boston: Allyn & Bacon, 1999. Print.

Crew, Louie, and Keener, Karen. "Homophobia in the Academy: A Report of the Committee on Gay/Lesbian Concerns." *College English* 43.7 (1981): 682–89. Print.

Cummings, Martha Clark, and Cynthia Nelson. "Our Time Has Come: TESOL Forms Lesbian/Gay/Bisexual Task Force, Part 1." *TESOL Matters* 3.4. Print.

Elliot, Mary. "Coming Out in the Classroom: A Return to the Hard Place." *College English* 58.6 (1996): 693–708. Print.

Kopelson, Karen. "Rhetoric on the Edge of Cunning: Or, the Performance of Neutrality (Re)considered as a Composition Pedagogy for Student Resistance." *College Composition and Communication* 55.1 (2003): 115–46. Print.

Levy, Ariel. "Lesbian Nation: When Gay Women Took to the Road." *The New Yorker* 2 Mar. 2009. 30–37. Print.

MacGowan-Gilhooly, Adele. *Achieving Fluency in English: A Whole-Language Book.* Dubuque: Kendall Hunt, 1991. Print.

Malinowitz, Harriet. *Textual Orientations: Lesbian and Gay Students and the Making of Discourse Communities.* Portsmouth: Boynton/Cook, 1995. Print.

Nelson, Cynthia D. *Sexual Identities in English Language Education.* New York: Routledge, 2009. Print.

Sedgwick, Eve. *The Epistemology of the Closet.* Berkeley: U of California P, 1990. Print.

Seidman, Steven. "Deconstructing Queer Theory or the Under-Theorization of the Social and the Ethical." *Social Postmodernism: Beyond Identity Politics.* Ed. Linda Nicholson and Steven Seidman. Cambridge, UK: Cambridge UP, 1995. 116–41. Print.

Signorile, Michelangelo. *Queer in America.* Madison, WI: U of Wisconsin P, 1993. Print.

Valentine, Jean. "Pots and Pans: Identification of Queer Japanese in Terms of Discrimination." *Queerly Phrased: Language, Gender, and Sexuality.* Ed. A. Livia and K. Hall. New York: Oxford UP, 1997. 95–114. Print.

Weinberg, George. *Society and the Healthy Homosexual.* New York: St. Martin's, 1972. Print.

Withrow, Jean, Gay Brookes, and Martha Clark Cummings. *Changes: Readings for Writers.* 2nd ed. New York: Cambridge UP, 1999. Print.

Appendix

Final Writing Examination

Choose one question. Plan what you write. You may consult *Someday This Pain Will Be Useful to You* and a print dictionary. Be sure to refer to the book in your answer.

1) In Chapter 7, on page 87, Dr. Adler, James' psychiatrist, asks him, "How are you feeling today?" And when he answers, "I feel sad," she wants to know for how long. "Years," he says. Write an essay describing James' sadness. In your opinion, in what ways is he sad? Why is he sad? If you were his friend, what advice would you give him to help him cope with his sadness? Use examples from the novel to support your argument.

2) Compare your life with James' life. In what ways is your life similar to James' life? In what ways is it different from James' life? Use examples from the novel to support your argument.

3) James spends most of his time alone. At one point in the novel he says that there are only two people he likes, his grandmother, Nanette, and his co-worker at the gallery, John. Describe James' relationship with John. Why does James connect with John? Use examples from the novel to support your argument.

English May Be My Second Language, But I'm Not "ESL"

Christina Ortmeir-Hooper

Using three case studies and teacher-research based, Christina Ortmeir-Hooper explores immigrant students' experiences in first-year college writing courses. Ortmeir-Hooper is particularly concerned with the ways in which immigrant students create identity in mainstream English courses, as well as the responses of the students to the category of college ESL. Her data includes responses to an initial questionnaire about language background, samples of students' writing from their mainstream first-year writing courses, transcripts from audio-taped interviews, and classroom observations. Her analysis focuses on the students' choice of writing topics and revision decisions, especially in relation to topics centered on linguistic and cultural background, and immigrant status. Her results demonstrate the complexity, and even the disadvantages, of attempting to create narrow categories for immigrant students with second language backgrounds. One student relates his positive experiences as a second language writer, while two students resist the category. Ortmeir-Hooper, in addition to surveying the research on the issue of identity, recommends that we "move toward identifying these students who write in English as their second language as whole individuals with multiple, sometimes meshing and messy, facets and experiences, and not merely as singular products of their native culture and language" (p. 383).

Exploring the Dynamics of Generation 1.5

In recent years, there has been a great deal of interest in meeting the needs of ESL students in the composition classroom, particularly with the growing number of second language writers entering our colleges and universities. During the 1990s, much of the scholarship on second language writing focused on the experiences and instruction of international students studying at U.S. universities. International students were a steady presence at large research universities, where many second language writing specialists were conducting research, and international visa students were easily identified on campus, through international student groups, data on degree status and countries of origin that is required by the federal government, and TOEFL scores and applications.

Resident ESL students, however, have remained a more elusive group to study and more enigmatic to categorize.[1] In 1999, Linda Harklau, Kay Losey, and Meryl Siegal introduced their edited collection *Generation 1.5 Meets College Composition.* It was the first composition collection to use the term "Generation 1.5." referring to U.S. resident ESL students who had completed at least some of their secondary schooling in the United States. Census data from the U.S. Department of Education indicates that the number of English language learners (ELL), those students speaking a language other than English in the home, has increased to over 5.5 million students in U.S. public schools (U.S. Department of Education). Yet when these students graduate from high school, they often become anonymous on the college and university campus. Once they have gained acceptance into the university, their numbers are not tracked. As Harklau, Siegal, and Losey explain in their chapter, "U.S. colleges and universities collect virtually no information about U.S. residents' or citizens' native language status" (2). For many of these students, this is a welcome anonymity.

I would argue that the terms "ESL" and "ELL" and even "Generation 1.5" are fraught with all kinds of complications for resident students and for us as compositionists.[2] For students, these complications are emotional as well as tactical. Because what exactly does it mean for a student to be "ESL"? And when, if ever, does a student stop being an "ESL" student? If we take apart the terms "English as a Second Language" or "English Speaker of Other Languages" (ESOL), the terms seem purely descriptive in nature. But as Eli Hinkel, a second language specialist, noted in a discussion on the topic of labeling second language writers held on the SLW-CCCC listserv, the terms are far more nuanced, complicated, and significant for nonnative speakers. As Hinkel wrote:

> after 34 years in English-speaking countries, I am not an *English language learner*. I am a nonnative speaker [. . .] I speak *English as a second language*. I tell my students that it is possible to achieve more in a second language than many people can in their first. I think that students need to know that being a proficient nonnative can actually be a point of pride because it is a significant achievement. (Hinkel; my emphasis)

Hinkel's comments are indicative of the tricky space in which second language writers find themselves. The term "ESL" is not only a descriptor, it is also an institutional marker, pointing to a need for additional services and also to the status of someone still marked as a novice in the English language, an English language learner (ELL). For many U.S. resident second language writers, the question of when to or when not to be identified as ESL is a fluid one. And the complicated nature of what it means to be an ESL student is particularly difficult in the confines of the first-year composition classroom, where issues with writing and expectations may still be a challenge for these students. As composition instructors, we need to understand the fluidity of the ESL descriptor but also to understand what the experiences of these students are in the composition classroom.

In this essay, I examine the delicate nature of "ESL" identity for student writers. The essay begins by exploring the theoretical connections between identity and writing. I then present case studies of three first-year students and examine how they negotiate their identities as second language writers in mainstream composition classrooms. Finally, I discuss the implications of these findings for composition. In particular, I argue that these students' experiences raise compelling questions about our categories for second language writers, including the ever-growing use of the term "Generation 1.5," and our approaches toward these students in the composition classroom.

Connections between Identity and Writing

Robert Brooke, in his work on identity negotiation in writing workshops, has defined the social identity in two parts: the identity that is assigned to us by our environment and our social interaction and the identity that we assign ourselves. Yet those identity roles can be accepted or resisted by the individual; they are dynamic (Brooke 17). It is this process of compliance and resistance that often comes forth in the writing of college students. As Brooke explains, "Individual college students need to find their own way through the tangle of self-definition and social place which writing involves. [. . .] The problem facing young people is a problem of defining how 'I' will act in the society 'I' live in—

and secondarily, of defining whether or not some form of writing will aid in this process" (7).

Other compositionists have drawn upon the work of Erving Goffman and his theories on performance and social identity in order to explain the connections that can be made between student identity negotiation and their writing in the composition classroom. Drawing in part on Goffman, Roz Ivanič, in her analysis of adult student writers returning to higher education, explained that writing and identity have a two-fold relationship. First, writing is a key to developing a certain sense of identity. Second, writers often "perform" certain identities in their writing. Thomas Newkirk, in his work on the autobiographical writing of college students, noted that "all forms of 'self-expression,' all of our ways of 'being personal' are forms of performance. In Erving Goffman's terms, 'a presentation of self'" (3). The same can be said of immigrant ESL students. They are seeking to define and often "perform" themselves within the context of the university and their peers, while at the same time negotiating the complex realities of their unique linguistic and cultural experiences. Often, composition instructors only see a single aspect of that performance and are perplexed by the "backstage" realities that often influence these students' decisions in the composition classroom and on the written page.

The theoretical connections made by Brooke, Newkirk, and Ivanič provide the backdrop for reading the links between identity negotiation and writing in the experiences of the students that I discuss in this essay. The three U.S. resident second language writers in this study are often struggling between a classroom, home, and social identity. Some of them are eager to embrace "the anonymity" that writing superficially seems to offer; they see writing as a place that is "free from social, geographic, or national ties" (Ivanič and Camps 5). None of these students self-identify with an "ESL" label, despite the fact that English is, indeed, their second language. And all three students are eager to leave "ESL" labels and classrooms behind.

The "ESL" Label: A Deficit Model, or the Glass Half-Empty

As earlier studies of "Generation 1.5" students have noted, the "ESL" label is often problematic for students, not simply because of placement concerns, but also because the term is linked to a student's institutional experience with the term. In her study of "language minority students," Linda Lonon Blanton documented the problematic nature of the institutionalized "ESL" label. Blanton, in her critique of college preparatory courses and the kinds of instruction often in place in those courses, noted the range of secondary school experiences that "ESL" students may have had. Some may have spent years in mainstream classrooms, only to find themselves underprepared for the reading and writing demands of higher education. As Blanton explained, "When these students reach college, they may feel strongly that they shouldn't be placed differently from other U.S. high school graduates, and are offended when labeled *ESL*" (Blanton 123). As Harklau, Siegal, and Losey commented, even students who are still in need of some language instruction can view such support as "stigmatized and are insulted by designation as an 'ESL student'" (5).

The struggle between home and school identity may also lead to further complications about what it means to be an "English language learner." Yuet-Sim Chiang and Mary Schmida, in their work on language identity and ownership, studied American-born children of immigrant parents. They found that even though these students considered English their primary language, they "still struggle with trying to reconcile the home language and culture of their parents and families into their social identities." As Chiang and Schmida reported,

> What these students are experiencing seems to be serious disjunctures between the way they conceptualize their linguistic identities. That is, on the one hand, they are not fully comfortable speaking, reading, or writing their heritage language, whereas on the other hand, they are not fully integrated into the culture of mainstream, academic English by the virtue of the label, linguistic minority. (86)

Chiang and Schmida found that the label "linguistic minority" often hindered these students because they "are expected to stumble over the English language for it is not their native tongue" (93). Students then internalized these expectations and were led by them to "see themselves as incapable of owning the language" (93). The institutionalized labels that are placed on second language students clearly have a profound effect on how they define themselves in the college classroom and in their writing.

In Ilona Leki's four-year case study of Jan, an immigrant student from Poland, she found that similar issues of ownership, or lack thereof, played a role in how invested the student was in his education. Jan used what Leki called "smoke and mirrors to create a public image of himself to his teacher as a serious, hard-working student" (31). The reality, however, was that he felt divested of his educational experience. His goal was to "play the game" in order to get by. Jan saw his main objective as surviving the bureaucracy of the system and maintaining his G.P.A. Indeed, throughout his four years in college, Jan continually felt like an imposter, "stubbornly convinced that the whole educational enterprise was a game," a test of survival (32).

That "imposter" or outsider image is a strong one that perpetuates a deficit model of "ESL" that can discourage students from seeking academic assistance. This point is exemplified by Sue Starfield's study of discoursal identity in the essay writing of two black nonnative

English-speaking students at a South African university. Starfield found that "students' prior life histories, the socially structured opportunities, and the more or less privileged discourses they have had access to, affect their engagement in the essay-writing process" (130). Moreover, she learned that one of the students, Sipho, was having more difficulty in the university and in passing his classes because he did not readily identify as an ESL learner. As Starfield explained, "Although Sipho was very conscious of his poor English language skills, his shyness or perhaps a reluctance to adopt the institutionally available subject position of *disadvantaged second language speaker* and seek help with his essay writing compounded his lack of success" (131; author's emphasis).

It is this positioning, as a "disadvantaged second language speaker," regardless of English language proficiency, that is particularly salient when we consider the position of second language writers in composition classrooms, particularly those students that we are categorizing as Generation 1.5. Often, we fail to recognize that "ESL" refers to a great deal more than language proficiency or placement. As Harklau has noted,

> learning in a second language is not simply the accrual of technical linguistic abilities but rather is intimately related to identity—how one sees oneself and is seen by others as a student, as a writer, and as ethnolinguistic minority (e.g., Harklau 2000).[3] Therefore we need to understand how Generation 1.5 students' writing is interwoven with multiple, unstable, and ambivalent identities as immigrants, as young adults, as ethnolinguistic minorities, and often as people of color in the United States. ("From High School to College")

Harklau's comments are compelling. I would add that compositionists also need to find out and consider how those "ambivalent identities" play out within the composition classroom and in students' approaches to their writing. The case studies that follow begin to add some student perspectives to the complexity of those identity negotiations and what they mean for the student writer in the composition classroom.

Voices from the Composition Classroom

Methodology and Data Analysis

In this project, I bring together case study inquiry and teacher research. The project began as a case study inquiry into the experiences of immigrant ESL students in the mainstream first-year writing course. Specifically, I began with the following questions:

1. How do second language factors (culture, background, prior education, prior writing experiences, etc.) play a role in how immigrant

second language students construct and compose their identity
in a mainstream first-year writing course?

2. For immigrant students, what does it mean to be an "ESL" student in college? Do they identify with that categorization? Why
or why not?

The study was based at a midsize, land grant university in the Northeast. The university is not known for its diversity, although, like many
similar institutions, the demographics have started to shift in the last
few years. To select participants, I chose second language students who
were enrolled in sections of the mainstream first-year composition course.
Although the university does offer ESL sections of the course, students
self-select their placement.[4] To recruit participants, I informally surveyed fellow composition instructors, asking if they had any students in
their mainstream classes who spoke English as a second language and
had studied in U.S. high schools. One of my colleagues responded that
she had two such students in her course, and if they were willing to participate, she would be willing to let me observe her class and the students. I chose two students in a single course because it gave me more
control in terms of the variables, particularly the kinds of writing assignments, the teaching methods, and the course objectives. After learning about the project, the two students, Sergej and Misha, were eager to
participate and to share their experiences.[5] IRB approval required that
their responses and insights be kept private from the instructor until
the course had ended. Sergej and Misha were the only two nonnative
speakers of English in the class of twenty-four students; this was not
unusual for the university. The instructor was a graduate student in
the composition program with extensive experience in teaching composition and literature courses. Her course design emphasized student-driven activities and input, and it was influenced by process approaches
to writing along with discourse community theories. Assignments asked
students to explore their discourse communities, their literacy experiences, their perspective majors, and their own research interests.

The third participant was a student in my own first-year composition course in the semester that followed my research with Misha and
Sergej. At that point, I had considered the project complete, but when
Jane came into my course, the teacher-research aspect of this project
began to unfold. Jane's presence in my course complicated my understanding of Sergej and Misha's experiences. Although I have taught
ESL courses in the past, this particular class was a mainstream composition course with almost all native English speakers. When I told Jane
about the project, she was interested in participating, and we agreed
that I would not interview her until all coursework had been completed
and grades had been finalized. She was informed that her participation
in the study would not affect her grade.

The data for the study included the following:

- An initial questionnaire about the students' educational and linguistic background. (Appendix A)

- Writing samples from the students' first-year composition course, including personal narratives, literacy autobiographies, research-based essays, freewrites, reflective writing on their progress, and one-page reading responses.

- Transcribed audio-taped interviews with all three students. For Misha and Serge, I held three interviews throughout the semester. The first interview was based on the initial questionnaire; the second interview was based on writing samples from the midterm portfolio; then a final exit interview focused on their experiences in the composition course, their preparation for college writing at the secondary level, and certain traits in the writing samples. The questions for these interviews were generated for each individual based on prior interview material and the student's writing samples. For Jane, I held two interview sessions after the semester had ended, following the same protocol as was used with Sergej and Misha.

These three sets of data allowed me to triangulate my findings regarding the students' expression of their identity as second language writers and the complex nature of their experiences in a mainstream first-year writing course. In my analysis, I examined moments in the students' essays and classroom writing that spoke to their identities and their experiences as second language students. Specifically, I looked at what subject matter they chose to write about and how they framed themselves within that subject matter, particularly as it pertained to their cultural and linguistic backgrounds and their immigrant experiences. In looking through multiple drafts of certain essays, I paid attention to the students' decisions to revise, delete, or elaborate on subject matter that pertained to their identities as second language writers. I also studied their more reflective pieces of writing, such as their portfolio cover letters, to see how they interpreted the composition classroom and their place within it. My readings of the students' texts were informed and complicated by my interviews with the students and my observations in the classroom. In what follows, I share the insights, perspectives, and writings of Sergej, Misha, and Jane.

Sergej

Sergej came to the United States from Serbia in 1998 under refugee status. He and his family were sent to an urban city in northern New England with a 10 percent ESL student population. He could have come to the university a year earlier but opted to stay in high school one more year in order to improve his English. Although his home language was Serbo-Croatian, he had studied English since he was ten years old, but as he explained, "you don't have good teachers when you have war." He writes, reads, and speaks English extremely well, although there are still markers of his ESL background evident in his speech and writing. His parents had limited English proficiency, and although his mother was a professor of Russian and his father a lawyer in their homeland, both of Sergej's parents were working in less-skilled positions in the United States. In fact, they were unable to contribute to his college expenses, and Sergej depended on his part-time job, financial aid, and scholarships to remain in school. He wanted to finish college as quickly as possible and find a good job that would help him and his family be more financially secure.

When Sergej came to the university, he enrolled in the honors section of freshman composition and was not interested in an ESL section. In our first interview, I asked Sergej why he had not opted for the ESL section of the course. I share his response at length:

> *Sergej:* I'm not ESL.
>
> *Christina:* What do you mean?
>
> *S:* I don't take ESL classes. My senior year in high school I didn't take an ESL class. So I don't think that I qualify as an ESL student.
>
> *C:* Even though English is your second language?
>
> *S:* Ahh . . . I don't know. I guess I'm not taking the term right. I don't know what the term means. What is ESL student?
>
> *C:* Good question. From what you're saying, there is ESL as in "I need to take ESL classes."
>
> *S:* Yeah, that is the way I look at it.
>
> *C:* Ok, so it's like . . . "English is my second language but it doesn't mean anything. . . ."
>
> *S:* Yeah, it doesn't mean that I am ESL. ESL is more. I look at ESL as some kind of institution. It gonna help get your English to the higher levels.

Although he did not wish to be classified as an "ESL" student, he did identify himself as such to his composition instructor because he believed that it would give him "more privileges," and that, in general, teachers would be more forgiving of certain errors in his writing and his speech.

In reading through Sergej's work over the semester, the role of an outsider becomes apparent almost immediately. Although he writes about his personal experiences, his subject matter does not articulate any tangible sense of community or connection. In his writing, the pronoun "I" is often used to signal a sense of being outside the main community, and it is surrounded with descriptors such as "outsider," "not many friends," and "visitor." In most cases, these moments are followed by descriptions of nervousness, embarrassments, or silence," where I didn't know what to say." In one text, Sergej writes, "I am not a very social creature and I like it that way." He adds, "If I had more [friends/people in my life], I'd feel it would take away my freedom." His decision to cast himself as an outsider speaks to other moments in his life when Sergej has felt on the margins.

During the 1990s conflict in the Balkans, Sergej, as a Serbian, was forced to leave his home in Croatia as the conflict escalated. When he came to the United States, he was given no choice about where he and his family would live. When asked about his home address, Sergej responded with emphasis that he lived in "the projects," alluding to the fact that his family was receiving government assistance and had little choice in their housing decisions. When he came to the United States, Sergej and his family were placed in a city with a high Bosnian-Muslim refugee population, a population that was targeted and abused by many Serbian groups during the conflict. The tensions from the war have followed him, and he found that to be isolating, writing in one essay, "They [Bosnian students] may have had a problem with me, but I didn't really associate with any of them . . . I had a lot of free time in high school. I didn't have any friends to hang out with." Again, he reiterates that identity of himself as a nonmember on the margins. Sergej used the margin as a way of protection, so he could not be hurt or slandered by those around him. In our interview, he acknowledged the power of language in keeping him on the outside, asserting: "I am very direct as a person. But I am very careful too. I am careful when I say something that somebody else could use. I'm cautious. I've been misinterpreted so many times."

Although Sergej spoke in our interviews about his experiences in Croatia and the role that those experiences played in his attitude toward the composition course, it was striking that he rarely mentioned his cultural background or experiences in his writing. In fact in over thirty pages of writing, including one long and twelve short writing assignments, his homeland was mentioned in a total of fourteen sentences. In most cases, these events cast him in a subjugated role; he was being acted upon by others. The events of the war and the cultural background in general were things that he articulated as being placed upon him. This viewpoint became evident in the following excerpts from his essays and class assignments:

> I felt rather out of place when I came to the U.S. and all that propaganda against the country I still had connections with *made me* feel rather mad. I felt like retaliating for something when I was writing it. (My emphasis)

> *It [the war] changed my life upside down*, and instead of being an average student in Croatia who had everything going for him, I *ended up* in the United States having to pay for my own education." (My emphasis)

In these passages, the phrases "changed my life" and "I ended up" articulate his sense of powerlessness. These views were also apparent in other texts where he wrote about his parents and their decision to pack the car and leave his homeland, or about their expectations that he, as the only "good" English speaker, would translate and pose as them in legal or financial transactions. His loss of place and homeland was amplified by his loss of control, the sense that he no longer could act of his own accord but had to follow the directions and expectations of others.

His essays and in-class writing speak to this "lack of control," and that perception continued to dictate his current situation in school and in the United States. When I asked about the subject matter in the texts about his homeland or family, Sergej noted that these few writings made him feel "less indifferent" about his writing. They were the few pieces to which he felt some connection; however, he was adamant in his contention that no one cared to read about his personal experiences. In an interview, I asked him if writing about his homeland was too personal. He replied:

> *S:* I don't think it's personal. But I think nobody cares about it. So why write?
>
> *C:* Why do you think nobody cares about it?
>
> *S:* I don't know. What would somebody care? If somebody does care about it, I feel it's kinda [unintelligible]. Somebody kind of interested, but he is interested just to be nice about it. It doesn't really . . . give me a word here.
>
> *C:* You think people aren't interested in those experiences?
>
> *S:* I don't know. I . . . see . . . Take for example. I did write a few things about war. There is one freewrite.
>
> *C:* About traveling? Leaving Croatia?
>
> *S:* Yeah. And then I got comment "Thanks for sharing this." Right? I felt stupid. "Thanks for sharing this?" Thanks for sharing what?
>
> *C:* Was that difficult to write about?
>
> *S:* I just hate the thing that "Thank you for sharing this." Because like she . . . it seems to me that she is trying to be nice, to be concerned about it. But she doesn't really care. She is going to forget about it next year. I found it pointless. And I hate those comments. Sympathy and insincere.

His understanding (or misunderstanding) of the instructor's comment was indicative of the resentment that Sergej felt toward his instructor and the course throughout the semester. When Sergej spoke about the course, he was strident in his commentary. His difficulties with meeting the expectations of the instructor, particularly in terms of understanding the rhetorical situation of the classroom space, seemed to push him even further to the outside of a writing process in which he felt no investment. In the classroom, he did not often participate willingly in the community of writers that his instructor strove to create. He did not want to reflect upon his writing, he did not like to revise, and he found the assignments "pointless." At one point, he emailed his instructor to share his opinion of the "pointless assignments" she gave, and in a following class, he openly questioned her authority in the classroom. In our interviews, he was less confrontational and more confused. He just wanted to get through the course and move on. Even in the moments when he wanted to please his instructor, he wrote that he just "[couldn't] get it." As Sergej commented to his instructor in a midterm portfolio cover letter, "I thought I did fine but your comment say not so. Without you, I see nothing." As I read Sergej's comments, I am reminded of Newkirk's discussion on presentation and performance in writing. As Newkirk explained, "the sense we have of being a 'self' is rooted in a sense of competence primarily, but not exclusively, in social interaction. [. . .] We feel this competence under attack when our performance routines fail us, in a foreign or hostile setting when we have difficulty 'reading' the situation" (5). Sergej's estrangement from the course seems rooted in his difficulty in "reading" the classroom and the expectations of his teacher. The sense that his performance failed him became more apparent as the semester continued, and as a result, Sergej became increasingly indifferent to his writing.

The language and presentation of subjugation presented themselves again in his discussion of the course. In an interview I asked about his sense of ownership in his writing for the course, and Sergej commented, "She [the instructor] tells you what to write and you have to do it." His written responses for the class were filled with similar moments in which he talked about himself being placed in the object role by writing and the writing process, commenting that "[the writing] can never be perfect." And that "this process [of revision] proved me wrong. I realized that it is not possible to write something right in the first place." Indeed, Sergej seemed to equate revision with a sense of embarrassment and powerlessness. Even when he commented on the war and his childhood in our interviews, he brought himself back to the course and the revision process, saying:

> Sometimes I wish that I go back, think back; I really wish I had kept a journal of what I'd thought when I was in that situation. Like during the war. Chances are I'm never going to be in the war again. Then I really wish I had a journal. But then I was kid. Even if I had it, it would be kinda funny. And I hate going back to read my writing all over again. It kinda makes me embarrassed. 'Cause you look back at the ideas that you had before and you think, boy was I a kid back then. And then I know the same thing is going to happen two years from now. I'm gonna go back and see the way I thought now, and I'm gonna say, "Boy was I stupid." That's why I don't like going back. And when you revise that's what you do. I hate it.

His equating his experiences with the war and the process of revision are powerful. These moments speak to the difficult reality of students such as Sergej. Although his writing may not "read" as second language writing per se, in terms of expected errors, etc., elements of his past experiences were shaping his perceptions of writing practices and his expectations of the composition classroom.

Sergej was adamant that he hated the process of revision and writing put forth by his instructor, but he knew he must do well in order to maintain his scholarship and thereby guarantee his financial ability to stay in school. He felt caught between those two places. In his comments on writing the reflective assignments, he mentioned that he had to write them and that he strategically performed his "progress,"

> ['c]ause she's my teacher. I need an A in that class . . . Because when I write that . . . you can't say . . . "I am indifferent to every piece of writing that I do here." Completely indifferent to it. But I can't say that in the cover letter. So I have to lie.

Part of Sergej's resistance was cultural. He believed in an academic tradition that was more of straight transmission of knowledge. In our discussions, he often referred to universities in his home country, noting the differences in expectations and examinations. He reported to me that based on his knowledge of the Yugoslavian universities, collected from stories told by his parents and relatives, schools and universities there emphasized a more authoritative, impersonal approach. A system that, according to Sergej, was mimicked at the lower grade levels as well, and it was a system in which he excelled. Clearly, he found these academic traditions to be more rigorous than the ones he was finding in his composition classroom, where there was open discussion, a high level of student involvement, and an emphasis on writing over oral examinations. Sergej was clearly at odds with the academic traditions of the composition classroom. But he was also at a loss as to how to perform in this new setting. He saw himself as a competent student, even a competent writer, in his home language, yet in this U.S. university setting, his performances as a student and as a writer were failing him. It was "a foreign or hostile setting" in his mind (Newkirk 5). He was uncomfortable with the teacher's role and unable to define his rhetorical position in the classroom. At one time, he took the teacher's style as an opening to question her authority at every turn, a move that was seen by the teacher as disrespectful. And, at another point, he would read her every suggestion as an authoritative order, positioning his teacher as a difficult, unforgiving taskmaster. He moved back and forth between these two vantage points, struggling to determine what was expected of him. In the end, he constructed a classroom where there was no flexibility and little room for negotiation. But my own observations found a composition classroom that provided many opportunities for student voices, student-led writing prompts and activities, open discussions, and peer workshops. The teacher often asked for anonymous feedback on assignments and projects, for example, so that she could adjust the curriculum to meet student needs.

In Sergej's final portfolio, he tried to hide his hostility. When he approached his reflective cover letters and writing assignments, he made a point of performing his "conversion," as in the following examples from his cover letters:

> I was taught in my college composition course that I am to state everything that I am going to write about in my introductory paragraph. I don't like that, and if I don't like it, I can't be good at it. . . . So for my next essay, I will try to learn to like the theses statement.

> The only thing I didn't like were the cover letters, but I can understand a need for them.

Although Sergej's "conversion" performance did not tend to boost his own certainty, there can be no doubt that he was intending to build some solidarity with his instructor, despite his true ambivalence.

In the end, when I asked Sergej if it might have made a difference had he been in an ESL section of first-year composition, he was adamant that he did not belong there. (In truth, I agree with him.) Aside from a few missing definite articles, he insisted that his writing did not reveal his linguistic and cultural background. He did not classify himself as an international student and did not wish to be segregated from his "American" peers.[6] He did not seek any special services on campus and did not associate with any of the ethnic or international groups on campus. When we first spoke, Sergej had been unaware that a section of freshman composition was available for ESL learners. After learning about the ESL section of first-year composition, Sergej indicated that he would never have signed up anyway. He stated, "I don't really care. But I wouldn't. Because if you want to learn more . . . better English, you going to learn it from Americans, not the ESL students."

Misha

Misha, also a first-year student at the time of this study, was a computer science major. He immigrated to the United States in 1994 when he was ten, in comparison to Sergej, who arrived when he was seventeen. Various family members came with Misha, including a younger sibling, grandparents, and his mother. However, his father remained in Russia for reasons that Misha was unwilling to discuss. Misha attended fifth grade, junior high, and high school in another large New England city with a diverse population, though Misha noted that he was "the only Russian student. Everyone else spoke Spanish. Even the teachers." Throughout junior high, Misha took ESL courses and enrolled as an

ESL student so that he could attend "the better" junior high school in the city. When he reached high school, he says he was no longer an "ESL student," and he enrolled in mainstream English courses. Although Misha found the freshman composition course challenging, he had great success. His instructor was impressed with him as a student, both in terms of his effort and his writing.

In comparison to Sergej, Misha showcased his Russian background throughout most of his writing in the course. Of the four major assignments, Misha wrote one essay, his favorite piece of the semester, exclusively on his experience of coming to America. In addition, the opening to his research essay on the origins of beer included an extensive flashback in which he discussed the subject with his father while still a child in Russia. Furthermore, his final portfolio includes eight sample freewrites, three of which focus exclusively on his bicultural/bilingual experiences, and a reader response about education and literacy in his family. As Misha writes in an early draft of his literacy narrative:

> I have become literate in life and grew up much faster due to one of the sharpest turns my life has ever made — my immigration to American from Russia. Not only did this experience taught me the language and culture of a completely different society but it also gave me a dyadic personality of which I am very proud. . . . I have become an entirely different person.

Unlike Sergej, Misha was not forced out of his country by war. He left Russia partly because of religious discrimination and partly due to the promise of economic opportunities in the United States. Misha wrote that he had some initial fears about being "harassed here because I [was] a Jew," but those concerns never manifested in the eight years he has lived in the United States. Instead, his immigrant narrative and experiences have become something of value to him. His writing throughout the semester reveals a desire to remain connected to his Russian heritage, and my guess is that such a connection is particularly important, in light of the fact that he is trying to remain connected to his father, who remains in Russia. There are moments where his sense of loss leaks onto the page. In one instance, writing about his "dyadic personality," he tells his readers, "Just imagine tearing your whole existing life into bits and pieces, and selling off 50% of it, packing 20% of it, and leaving behind the remaining 30%. . . . It's like a giant part of me just ripped away, you know?"

But in the end, Misha remained optimistic. He writes, "I try to preserve my Russian heritage and at the same time keep my American heritage. . . . I have come a long way in terms of adjusting to this society . . . [understanding] how things work here." When he wrote about his place in U.S. culture, he was positive, noting in the final sentences of his literacy narrative that "this experience [of immigrating to the United States] have made me more literate in life itself and will make the future a richer place." In some ways, I am unsure how to read this conversion, this immigrant narrative. Is this part of Misha's performance? There is a part of me that remains skeptical. There seems to be a definite awareness of audience here, an American audience that wants to welcome this kind of affirmative immigrant story.[7] It meshes well with our optimistic "melting pot" vision of America. But in my conversations with Misha, he seemed to buy into this narrative as well, noting that this was a narrative in which he continued to feel pride and ownership.

Misha was confident of his abilities as a writer, and he showed great respect to his instructor and her knowledge on the subject of writing, even though he did not always agree with her. In fact, in an analysis of written interview transcripts and writing samples, Misha did not exhibit any indication of the level of disengagement or subjugation that Sergej manifested in his writing and behavior throughout the term. He noted that his friend Sergej just didn't understand how things "worked here," and that Sergej seemed to question the instructor's authority in ways that threatened his grade. Misha, on the other hand, saw the composition course as a necessary part of his college career. He welcomed the chance to write and relished the opportunities to explore his personal experiences and his cultural history. In fact, he described his literacy autobiography as "the best thing I ever put together." As Misha explained in our interview:

> I wrote the literacy essay almost like a memoir. It was really big. I had to narrow it down and stuff. But it was really cool I thought. I'd like to write like a bigger memoir, make a humongous thing out of it, write my whole story about how I came here.

That is not to say that he didn't disagree with his instructor, but he knew that he had to meet certain expectations in order to get the grade. And Misha was eager to get a good grade (like many students) and was willing to adapt some of his ideas of writing to achieve that end; however, he never resented the instructor's authority. Instead he continued to view his writing, his personal experience, as something over which, in the end, he maintained control. Misha exhibited this ownership in a conversation on his literacy narrative, explaining:

> She [the instructor] crossed out some stuff that I wanted to include in there. But you know, you do what she says; it's all for the grade. Now I'll go back, and I'll change some things to the way it was before. Change some stuff around the way I liked it.

His sense of ownership and control was in stark contrast to Sergej's experiences. While Sergej focused on his writing as strictly a requirement for the course, Misha saw value in writing that had merit beyond the classroom. Misha saw the instructor's authority and her feedback as constructive, but not overwhelmingly constrictive or silencing. In some ways, it strikes me that Sergej gave almost too much authority to his instructor. Misha, on the other hand, seemed more aware of the rhetorical situation and demonstrated a savviness that served him well. He saw some of his revisions as part of a larger rhetorical strategy. In the end, Misha seemed to be more comfortable in his environment, more at ease in the classroom, and more confident with his writing.

As I write about these two students, I am concerned that I am creating a simple linear model—in which recent immigrants, perhaps refugees, are placed on one end and immigrant students who have lived here longer are placed on the other end. So to undermine that tendency, I would like to share one final case as a way to complicate the picture and also to turn the researcher lens on myself.

Jane

As I completed my case studies of Sergej and Misha, I was also teaching my own section of first-year composition. Like every semester, I began the class by handing out brief surveys with questions requesting such information as students' nickname, phone number, high school, major, favorite music, favorite book, and so on. In addition, I asked students if English was their second language. As I read over the slips of paper that evening, I was not surprised to find that every student had answered "no" to the ESL question, given the university's demographics.

So when Jane handed in a draft of her first essay, a literacy narrative, I was surprised to read about her elementary school experiences in Hong Kong. I later learned that she had come to the United States in 1994, the same year as Misha. Jane's family spoke Mandarin Chinese at home, and she had taken ESL courses for over five years. Later, she would explain to me, "I consider English to be my first language now, because I don't think in Chinese at all. I consider it my first language because I think it, I write it."

But Jane also made choices to obscure her cultural background as well. When our class made maps of our various discourse communities, Jane drew a tree with three branches. For two of the branches, she labeled extensively her high school and college communities, the language and phrases that were used in those communities, and the people that were part of those communities. On the third branch, she wrote out her family name—no other details or descriptors. When we shared our maps in class, Jane barely mentioned this final branch and gave no other details. Like Sergej, she was guarded and cautious about her cultural background. In class, I respected her silence on the matter, but I was curious to know why. I had tried to create a classroom community where cultural and linguistic diversity were valued. My syllabus included a diverse array of authors, many of whom are nonnative English writers, and I openly shared my own bilingual/bicultural upbringing when we talk about language and communities. When I mentioned this research project to her, she agreed to participate without reservation. We agreed that I would make copies of her writing and keep some observational notes, and we would talk after the semester had ended.

As the semester continued, her writing continued to show evidence of caution and camouflage. As I read through her drafts of the literacy autobiography, I was puzzled by the choices she made. She wrote about composing her college application essay, and a line in her initial draft caught my attention:

> I wanted to talk about my experience with learning a new language and culture, but I didn't want them to know that English was my second language. I want to get into college for me as a regular student.

Jane deleted this section from the final draft of her literacy autobiography. In her subsequent personal experience essay, Jane wrote about the death of her grandmother. Again there was evidence that she wanted to conceal her cultural and linguistic background. The narrative failed to establish a setting for the events. In discussions with her readers in peer workshops, Jane revealed that the events occurred during one of her final trips to Hong Kong from Taiwan. In conference, she explained to me that she was hesitant about sharing the setting with her audience, although she would not elaborate on that decision.

When I spoke with Jane at the end of the semester about these choices, our conversation revealed a great deal about the identity negotiation in which she was engaging within the context of the course:

> *Christina:* So do you consider yourself to be an ESL student?
>
> *Jane:* Not anymore. (*Laughs*)
>
> *C:* What do you think an ESL student is?
>
> *J:* Umm . . .
>
> *C:* What stage is it? I mean, if you're not anymore, but you were? What's the difference?
>
> *J:* It is just . . . It is hard for me to think of little words in Chinese. I am so used to speaking in English. I think that's the difference. Some people I know still think in their native language and still have to translate it into English. I don't think I have to do that.

In our discussions, Jane revealed that she hadn't enjoyed her experiences in ESL classes during junior high and high school. She often felt singled out by ESL teachers, and she hated the label of "ESL." Jane further explained this in an interview:

You feel like you are behind everyone else. That you are not maybe as intelligent. Which is not true at all. But you feel very behind. I feel like the
ESL program is very isolating. They have their own little room that you
have to go to. At that age (junior high), it can really hurt a teen . . . an
adolescent's self-esteem.

She seemed to carry this feeling of isolation with her; making decisions
(consciously or unconsciously) to cover her cultural and linguistic background in order to blend with her peers. When I asked her why she
didn't elaborate on her family or cultural background during our discussion on discourse communities, she was somewhat defiant:

C: You didn't talk much about your family?

J: I included my family.

C: Yes . . . but it was a branch with your family name, nothing else, and
you didn't discuss it at all. Was that a conscious decision?

J: I don't really think about that. (*Laughs*) Maybe I just felt more comfortable not talking about it.

C: Do you feel uncomfortable talking about it?

J: No . . . It's not something I like to talk about with strangers. People I
don't know very well. It is not something I just bring up.

C: Why?

J: It is kinda like the whole issue with homosexuality. You don't say "hi,
my name is. . . . And I'm a homosexual." I don't think it is very necessary for me to mention.

I am struck by her fears of being "outed" as an immigrant — as a second
language speaker. She was very aware of the liability that was involved
with that label. She didn't want to be different. I am reminded of my
prior experiences teaching middle school ESL students and how diligently many of my former students worked to assimilate into American
culture, donning the latest Tommy Hilfiger fashion and mimicking the
English they heard on MTV. Anything to blend.

Jane told me that she was one of only ten ESL students in her high
school. It was a minority group that she resisted, and the role of "ESL
student" or "linguistic minority" is not one she wished to perform. Instead she reached out to join other more mainstream groups: cheerleading, the honor society, the newspaper, the prom committee. She did
not want to be defined against the backdrop of her linguistic profile. Yet
in her college essay she wrote about the American "society's ideal of
Beauty and how a young Asian girl just didn't fit the 5'8" blond hair
blue eyes look." In my interviews with her, Jane came across as a young
woman who wanted to challenge that ideal, but she was concerned about
being "too different." Part of her reluctance to embrace her cultural

heritage seemed to come from her sense that she was always singled out as the "different one," placed up on the auditorium stage during a school's diversity week, and consistently reminded that she was different when she so wanted to be the same. As Jane explained:

> I didn't like ESL . . . I didn't like how she [the ESL teacher] made it seem like it [ESL] was your only identity. Like my comparison with homosexuality. Like I think they try to make that [ESL identity] apparent to other people. And maybe some people don't feel like that's who they are as a whole person. Like it's a part of them, but it is not the most important.

Jane's experiences remind me that although we often have the best intentions to be inclusive and to value diversity, sometimes students feel pushed to define themselves in a singular way, cast in a role they do not want to play, and forced to choose one identity over another.

Complicating Our Definitions: A Discussion

Each of these students has complicated my own understanding of second language writers and made me question our current categories for second language learners. Sergej's experiences remind me how tacit culture is. Often, it is the unspoken element in the room, yet it dictates so much of how we "see" a situation and ourselves. Sergej, for his part, was unaware of how his perceptions of the composition classroom and of writing, in general, were driven by his cultural expectations and experiences. Jane's comparison of being "outed" as an ESL student still haunts me. Her indictment of ESL teachers and an ESL profession that singled her out and neglected to see the multiplicity of her identity is a powerful one. I feel implicated in her accusation — as an ESL teacher and a writing specialist. Jane makes me think about what it means to have an "ESL identity." She makes me question what I know about that identity and what it means for students like Jane when they approach their personal and academic writing.

Misha's experiences remind me that it is not all bad. He reminds me not to "throw the baby out with the bath water." This is not a call to end personal or reflective writing in the composition classroom. Nor should we reconsider our attempts at valuing diversity in that classroom. We should not return to monolingual assumptions about our students; nor should we retreat from writing opportunities that encourage all students to reflect upon their literacy experiences, their cultural and linguistic legacies. Misha reminds me that there are students out there who are eager to connect, to understand, and to write about their personal experiences with learning language and culture. Often these writing tasks are ways for students like Misha to write themselves into the classroom, to find their place among native-English peers. The value that Misha sees in writing about his homeland, his family, his second language experiences—the good, the bad, and the ugly—remind me of how powerful and personally rewarding such writing can be for students.

But we do need to proceed with prudence. "ESL," "bicultural," and "bilingual" backgrounds are not always seen as positive markers by students, no matter how we try to frame diversity as a positive attribute. I am aware that conducting a study of Sergej, Jane, and Misha has indeed reemphasized their difference. Although they were very willing to work with me and share their thoughts and writings, I cannot help but feel that I may have helped to recreate the wall that Sergej and Jane were desperate to pull down. In incorporating them into a study of ESL students, I have defined them within the very box that they want to avoid—a box that may no longer fit the diverse range of second language writers in our composition classrooms.

As Gwen Gray Schwartz has argued in her article "Coming to Terms: Generation 1.5 Students in Mainstream Composition": "Many mainstream instructors often assume that any student who is still in the process of learning English should be placed in an ESL class; understanding that there are gradations of 'ESL' is as important as educating mainstream instructors about the existence of Generation 1.5 students" (44). The institutional markers of ESL, ESOL, or ELL are often rejected by "Generation 1.5" students who wish to move beyond the status of English language learner and to leave those markers behind in mainstream classes, particularly upon arriving at large college campuses.

But what of the term "Generation 1.5"? Evidence from the recent meetings of the Conference on College Composition and Communication suggests that the term resonates among composition instructors. In fact, "ESL and Generation 1.5" was used as a heading for the Selected Topics guide in the CCCC 2005 and 2006 programs, and a number of sessions and workshops directly referenced "Generation 1.5" in their titles. At the annual Teachers of English to Speakers of Other Languages (TESOL) convention in 2005, there were thirty-one sessions that directly referenced "Generation 1.5." However, the term is beginning to be used in a way that encases all U.S. resident ESL students as if they were part of a singular category. Schwartz sought to qualify our discussion of Generation 1.5 students by introducing the concept of "cross-over students," as "college students who immigrated to the United States at some point in their formative years" and have crossed over into mainstream classes by the time they enter college (42). She noted, however, the multiplicity that these students may represent. As Schwartz has argued,

> The term "Generation 1.5" has been used to describe a broad range of students (e.g., those who left their home countries prior to any schooling, those who were born here but live in ethnic enclaves, and sometimes it is even used to describe second generation students), even though Rumbaut

and Ima originally defined the term to include only those students who were not born in the U.S. but who have received at least the latter years of their secondary schooling here in the States. The distinction is important because students who have received almost all or all of their schooling in the U.S. are bound to have different schooling needs and abilities than those who have straddled two countries' educational systems, sometimes becoming only partially literate in both languages. (43)

Students like Misha, Jane, and Sergej all fit the definition put forth by Rumbaut and Ima, yet their experiences vary greatly. Clearly, the term "Generation 1.5" has, itself, become problematic. As Harklau has noted, "Generation 1.5" is an "amorphous" term, and "we seem to be using it in many different ways." In fact, it is a term that has broadened with its popularity. On one hand, it has brought attention and interest to the issues of U.S. resident ESL students and their writing. But as Schwartz has also pointed out, "the term Generation 1.5 is overused, and its meaning has become diluted so that it no longer serves to be very useful in identifying, describing. and placing such students" (43). Harklau, in her own questioning of the term, has noted parallels to David Bartholomae's comments on the essentializing of the term "basic writer." Harklau explains,

> It occurs to me that like "basic writer," the term "Generation 1.5" unfortunately lends itself far too easily to essentializing. and to a discourse of "need"—a way to define multilingual students as in need of remediation. I see worrying trends towards colleges using the label Generation 1.5 to cordon off multilingual students and their language use rather than addressing what Smitherman has called "a broad-based challenge to address linguistic diversity throughout the body politic."[8]

I agree with Harklau's concerns. As the term "Generation 1.5" becomes more prolific, we need to reconsider our use of the term. As I have mentioned before, Sergej, Misha, and Jane all fit this definition—but all are highly English language proficient. In fact, each rightfully questions the identity marker of "ESL" (and also "ELL"). Are they still English language learners? If so, when do they ever graduate out of the category?

I would argue that the students in this study begin to challenge our assumptions of Generation 1.5, or perhaps they challenge us to qualify our use of the term. Even Sergej does not fit the typical picture of a refugee student struggling in the margins. None of these students do. Indeed, they all received top grades in their composition courses. Sergej has made the recommendation that other case studies be pursued because his experiences and his success should not become indicative of the norm. Indeed, Sergej's story was one of success in many ways. Despite his moments of alienation and disenfranchisement, he was eager to work hard and to finish his degree. In addition, he did well academically in his first year at college. Sergej was not indicative of those immigrant students who enter the college system "with limited proficiency in academic reading and writing, as well as limited content knowledge acquisition" (Bosher and Rowecamp 6). Yet despite his advantages, he still struggled with issues of identity and expectations. For his part, Sergej did not fully understand the rhetorical situation that he was expected to navigate in the classroom, and in that regard his experiences, his resistance, and his identity struggles were significant. If a student as successful as Sergej remained on the margins in his own mind, what is the fate of a student with less confidence and less academic prowess?

Implications for the Composition Classroom and Our Teaching

It is a complex route that students such as Sergej, Misha, and Jane navigate in their academic and personal lives. They wish to blend, yet they can easily become confused or resistant when their cultural expectations are challenged. Sometimes they view "outing" themselves as ESL students to be advantageous, and other times they may reject any special treatment altogether. They may want their pasts, their languages, and their differences to be acknowledged, discussed, and even celebrated, yet they may not wish to be forced into disclosure.

So given that, what strategies can we develop as composition teachers? It seems that, in some ways, we are trapped. The wide range of origins, immigration status, prior education, prior experience with ESL courses, feelings about home language and culture make these students difficult to box into a single definition. Furthermore, we do not want to "box" students into an ESL identity category of which they want no part. Yet at the same time, it helps us, as instructors, to be better aware of second language writers, for they often do come into composition classrooms with unique needs as writers. Literature on second language writers continues to help composition instructors to be more aware of the issues of pedagogy, placement, and assessment. The recent surge in interest in "Generation 1.5" and ESL writers is valuable for compositionists working with a more linguistically diverse population, and such an interest should be further encouraged so that every composition instructor is prepared to work with second language students. But at the same time, much of the second language writing literature requires us to be able to identify our students in the category of "ESL." When students reject the "ESL" label for any number of reasons, composition instructors can be left with the illusion of a monolingual classroom. It perpetuates a myth of monolingual space that is increasingly out of step with the reality of the first-year composition course. As Paul Kei Matsuda noted in "The Myth of Linguistic Homogeneity in U.S. College Composition," which appeared in the July 2006 special issue of *College English*[9]:

> The myth of linguistic homogeneity—the assumption that college students
> are by default native speakers of a privileged variety of English—is seri-
> ously out of sync with the sociolinguistic reality of today's U.S. higher
> education as well as the U.S. society at large. [. . .] We need to re-imagine
> the composition classroom as a multilingual space where the presence
> of language differences is the default. (641, 649)

This study of Sergej, Misha, and Jane highlights the multilingual nature
of the composition classroom in the 21st century—beyond the institutional labels and markers.

These student stories are not necessarily easily available to composition instructors. Students may be hesitant to talk about their pasts,
and teachers hesitant to ask. The key to this dilemma may be to establish a rapport with our students early on, both through writing and
conferencing. As composition teachers, of course, this is nothing new.
But often our knowledge of our students is reduced to a simple survey
of questions at the onset of the course with the question on "speaking
English as Second Language," embedded between "Favorite Book" and
"Intended Major." Students, like Misha, Sergej, and Jane, are less likely
to label themselves "ESL" and to examine their expectations within the
context of cultural and linguistic differences. Furthermore, they are
often hesitant to answer those questionnaires truthfully when they are
unsure what the "ESL" question implies (i.e., Will the instructor expect
less of them? Hold them to lower standards? Separate them from their
peers? Be on the lookout for markers of nonnative proficiency?).

When students do share their identities as second language writers, we need to consider what that means to the particular student. We
cannot assume that "ESL" is this monolithic, universal code word that
explains everything we need to know about a student. As teachers, we
can develop a greater sense of the world circumstances that often bring
these students into the United States and a greater understanding of
the communities that they are a part of before they arrive on our campuses. We need to consider that there are details that are layered
within those community experiences, within their experiences with the
institutional label of "ESL," and within their expectations of us as writing teachers. We need to be cautious that we do not force or perhaps
reinforce a label that the students are trying to leave behind; at the
same time, though, we need to continue to reaffirm the value of diversity and respect a student's right to create an identity that is not based
solely on cultural difference.

Composition, as a field, should continue to support initiatives, such
as the *CCCC Statement on Second Language Writing and Writers*, which
encourage writing program and university administrators to train composition instructors to work with a broad range of second language
students and to consider how such complicated issues of identity may
influence their classroom. Students like Sergej, Misha, and Jane may
be competent English writers. Indeed, their writing reflects only minor

difficulties with pronouns, missing articles, and the occasional questionable word choice or phrasing. For most composition instructors, these minor markers will not disrupt their reading of the student text or make them question the English writing competence of such students. However, as these three students' experiences show us, the writing is not the only factor that affects a student's performance and decisions in the composition classroom. It is important to understand that U.S. resident ESL students have a wide range of experiences, particularly in terms of when they arrived, the conditions under which they left their homelands, the conditions they met upon their arrival in the United States, and their educational experiences both here and in their homelands. Understanding that history, and their literacy histories in particular, may provide instructors with a better sense of U.S. resident second language students' rhetorical moves and strategies, as well as their attitudes and expectations of the composition classroom, particularly when their cultural and educational expectations may be at odds with the expectations of the teacher. We need to appreciate the fine lines and complexities that shape these students' lives and our interactions with them.

Finally, I propose that in our discussions of second language writers, we need to move away from a sense of singular identity to one of multiplicity. We must move toward identifying these students who write in English as their second language as whole individuals with multiple, sometimes meshing and messy, facets and experiences, and not merely as singular products of their native culture and language.

Acknowledgments

I wish to thank Michelle Cox, Jessica Enoch, Aya Matsuda, Paul Kei Matsuda, Michael Michaud, Thomas Newkirk, and Katherine Tirabassi for their generous insights and advice during the writing process. Special thanks as well to Deborah Holdstein and two anonymous reviewers for their thought-provoking comments and suggestions. Finally, I would like to thank Jane, Sergej, Misha, as well as their composition instructor, for sharing their classroom, writing, and personal experiences.

Notes

1. Joy Reid was one of the initial second language specialists to describe the differences between resident ESL students and international ESL students at the college level. She categorized resident ESL learners as "ear" learners of English and international ESL students as "eye" learners of English, based on their different educational experiences with the English language. Reid has noted that the "two groups of ESL students have learned English differently, and so their language problems have different sources and different solutions" (3).

2. In recent years, the U.S. Department of Education has limited its use of the term "ESL" in favor of the term "English language learner" (ELL) in its descriptions of second language students. This is particularly apparent in policies and literature that surround the No Child Left Behind Act. As a result, the term "ELL" has seen increased usage in discussions on second language students in K–12 settings and in some higher education settings.

3. Harklau is citing an earlier work of her own; Linda Harklau, "From the 'Good Kids' to the 'Worst': Representations of English Language Learners across Educational Settings," *TESOL Quarterly* 34.1 (2000): 35–67.

4. At the university, first-year composition is a single semester course, and special sections are offered for honors students and for second language students. The first-year composition courses are taught by a variety of full-time English faculty, lecturers, and graduate students in composition and literature. The ESL section of first-year composition is typically taught by graduate students in the linguistics program. I am aware that at many institutions, ESL writing courses are taught by ESL writing specialists, with a wide range of expertise in both composition and second language acquisition. In addition, many of these specialists are active participants in the growing field of second language writing. Although Misha, Sergej, and Jane all rejected the ESL section of the first-year composition, these ESL writing courses serve an important function for many second language writers in colleges and universities.

5. Pseudonyms have been used for all student participants.

6. In my conversations with the participants, "American" was often used as the term to describe their native-English speaking peers, regardless of citizenship or nationality.

7. I am aware that Misha could also see me as part of that idealized "American audience" as well. When I met with him and the other participants, I did share my own immigrant history and bicultural background. But in the end, I know that I represent the same kind of audience as Misha's teacher.

8. Harklau quotes a passage from Geneva Smitherman, "The Historical Struggle for Language Rights in CCCC," *Language Diversity in the Classroom: From Intention to Practice*, ed. Geneva Smitherman and Victor Villanueva (Carbondale, IL: Southern Illinois University Press, 2003), 7–39.

9. The July 2006 special issue of *College English*, edited by Min-Zhan Lu, Paul Kei Matsuda, and Bruce Horner, explores themes and issues relevant to my work here. As Horner explains in his introduction to the issue, "The essays gathered in this special issue of *College English* participate in an emerging movement within composition studies representing, and responding to, changes in, and changing perceptions of, language(s), English(es), students, and the relations of all these to one another" (Horner 569). The articles in the issue propose that students need to be able to work with "a variety of Englishes and languages" as readers and as writers (570). The articles in this issue raise provocative and compelling arguments about the state of composition and the place of multilingualism in the field's discussions. Horner writes that the essays constitute "a call for a radical shift from composition's tacit policy of monolingualism to an explicit policy that embraces multilingual, cross-language writing as the norm for our teaching and research" (570).

Works Cited

Bartholomae, David. "The Tidy House: Basic Writing in the American Curriculum." *Journal of Basic Writing* 12.1 (1993): 4–21. Print.

Blanton, Linda Lonon. "Classroom Instruction and Language Minority Students: On Teaching to 'Smarter' Readers and Writers." Harklau, Losey, and Siegal 119–42. Print.

Bosher, Susan, and Jenise Rowecamp. "Language Proficiency and Academic Success: The Refugee/Immigrant in Higher Education." Paper presented at the Univ. of Minnesota. Minneapolis. 1 Apr. 1992.

Brooke, Robert E. *Writing and Sense of Self: Identity Negotiation in Writing Workshops.* Urbana: NCTE, 1991. Print.

Chiang, Yuet-Sim D., and Mary Schmida. "Language Identity and Language Ownership: Linguistic Conflicts of First-Year University Writing Students." Harklau, Losey, and Siegal 81–96. Print.

Conference on College Composition and Communication. "CCCC Statement on Second Language Writers and Writing." *College Composition and Communication* 52 (2001): 669–74. Print.

Harklau, Linda. "From High School to College: English Language Learners and Shifting Literacy Demands." Keynote address presented at the 10th Biennial Composition Studies Conference. Univ. of New Hampshire, Durham. Oct. 2004.

Harklau, Linda, Kay M. Losey, and Meryl Siegal, eds. *Generation 1.5 Meets College Composition: Issues in the Teaching of Writing to U.S.-Educated Learners of ESL.* Mahwah: Erlbaum, 1999. Print.

Harklau, Linda, Meryl Siegal, and Kay M. Losey. "Linguistically Diverse Students and College Writing: What Is Equitable and Appropriate?" Harklau, Losey, and Siegal 81–96. Print.

Hinkel, Eli. "Re: ESL, ELL, or NNS." 11 June 2004. Web. Second Language Writing at CCCC. 11 June 2004. <SLW.CCCC@lists.unh.edu>.

Horner, Bruce. "Introduction: Cross-Language Relations in Composition." *Cross-Language Relations in Composition.* Spec. issue of *College English* 68 (2006): 569–73. Print.

Ivanič, Roz. *Writing and Identity: The Discoursal Construction of Identity in Academic Writing.* Philadelphia: John Benjamins, 1998. Print.

Ivanič, Roz, and David Camps. "I Am How I Sound: Voice as Self-representation in L2 Writing." *Journal of Second Language Writing* 10 (2001): 3–33. Print.

Leki, Ilona. "'Pretty Much I Screwed Up': Ill-Served Needs of a Permanent Resident." Harklau, Losey, and Siegal 17–43. Print.

Matsuda, Paul Kei. "The Myth of Linguistic Homogeneity in U.S. College Composition." *Cross-Language Relations in Composition.* Spec. issue of *College English* 68 (2006): 637–51. Print.

Newkirk, Thomas. *The Performance of Self in Student Writing.* Portsmouth, NH: Boynton/Cook, 1997. Print.

Reid, Joy. "'Eye' Learners and 'Ear' Learners: Identifying the Language Needs of International Students and U.S. Resident Writers." *Grammar in the Composition Classroom: Essays on Teaching ESL for College-Bound Students.* Ed. Patricia Byrd and Joy M. Reid. New York: Heinle and Heinle, 1998: 3–17. Print.

Rumbaut, Ruben G., and Kenji Ima. "The Adaptation of Southeast Asian Refugee Youth: A Comparative Study. Final Report to the Office of Resettlement." San Diego: San Diego State University, 1988. Print.

Schwartz, Gwen Gray. "Coming to Terms: Generation 1.5 Students in Mainstream Composition." *Reading Matrix* 4.3 (Nov. 2004): 40–57. Web. 24 Jul. 2005. <http://www.readingmatrix.com/articles/schwartz/article.pdf>.

Starfield, Sue. "'I'm a Second-Language English Speaker': Negotiating Writer Identity and Authority in Sociology One." *Journal of Language, Identity, and Education* 1 (2002): 121–40. Print.

United States Department of Education, Office of English Language Acquisition, Language Enhancement and Academic Achievement for Limited English Proficient Students (OELA). *English Language Learners and the U.S. Census, 1990–2000.* Washington, DC: 24 Oct. 2007. Web. <http://www.ncela.gwu.edu/policy/states/ellcensus90s.pdf>.

Appendix A

Initial Questionnaire

Please take a few moments to fill out the following questionnaire. This information will provide me with some necessary background for the research project. Thank you.

Name: _____

Age: _____   Sex: Male/Female   Major: _____

What year are you in at the university? (Please circle one.)

First-year   Sophomore   Junior   Senior

Have you attended any other universities or colleges in the past? _____ If yes, please name them.

_____

Current place of residency: _____

Please answer the following questions.

1. How many years have you studied English?

2. How many years have you lived in the United States?

3. What is your native country, and what is your native language?

4. How much schooling did you have in your native country?

5. Did you attend secondary school (middle/high school) in the United States?

6. If yes, where did you attend school?

7. What language(s) do you speak at home?

8. Do you continue to write in your native language? (If yes, describe what you write—i.e., letters, email, articles, poetry, etc.)

9. Have you taken any writing courses in your native country? (If yes, please describe the course briefly.)

10. What do you think is the most difficult part of composing a piece of writing in English?

11. When you compose a writing assignment for your first-year writing course, do you compose first in English or in your native language? Please explain.

12. Please explain the process that you used to write for this course (include brainstorming, revision, whom you spoke with about the writing, etc.)? How much did your writing change from the first class to now?

13. Do you think the expectations for writing in an American university differ from the expectations in your native country?

14. Are you aware that there is a first-year writing course offered solely for ESL students? _____ (If yes, was there a reason that you decided to take the mainstream course?)

15. Would you have preferred to be in a class with other international/second language students?

16. In your opinion, is it important for your instructor to know that English is your second language?

PART FOUR

Collaboration, Assessment, and Change

Before tutoring[,] writing was a solo experience. . . . Now my writing process always includes asking as many people as I can recruit to sit down with me, to ream my drafts, and to share their ideas with me. I can't imagine writing anything important without invoking the writer/tutor conversation.

—Former Peer Tutor Who Became a Technical Writer
in the Automotive Industry (p. 406 in this volume)

For the former peer tutor quoted above, writing remains a collaborative act.[1] Inspired by his work in the writing center, this tutor describes the importance of "invoking the writer/tutor conversation," as perhaps the most significant aspect of his writing process. He celebrates the ways in which the writing process can include intense and powerful conversations that move the writer from draft to revision to second draft to more conversation, the means through which writing can become a richly collaborative activity that begins outside the classroom through tutorials, moves to the classroom, and then back beyond college, where a newly learned skill is put into practice through the invocation of positive experience.

The articles in Part Four also present a shared conversation that moves through the permeable boundaries of our classrooms, past the wall of our institutions, and then back again to re-form and re-vision changing possibilities for basic writing amid the challenges of higher education. These articles examine the ways in which factors outside developmental writing courses shape the work of our students and ourselves inside our classrooms. Note that each article in Part Four (with the exception of Greg Glau's contribution) is written collaboratively, rather than in isolation. Such collaboration demonstrates a collectivity of purpose and mission, working together as writers and researchers. The authors of the articles in Part Four aim to document and re-form developmental writing education in concert with the changing priorities of postsecondary education in the twenty-first century.[1]

Chapter 11 focuses on writing centers, places in which peer and professional tutors offer perspectives on writing that enhance classroom instruction. Yet writing centers, like classrooms, are not utopian spaces that flourish on their own without careful reflection and action from administrators, tutors, and students. Chapter 11 offers a cross section of writing center practices that can allow students in our developmental classes to flourish. Brad Hughes, Paula Gillespie, and Harvey Kail report on results of a peer tutor alumni survey, noting that (as the opening quotation to this section reveals), that the survey respondents described their experiences as tutors to be generally positive, and often transformative in their attitudes toward writing, and in their interactions with coworkers and in personal relationships after college. Throughout this article, the emphasis on collaboration resonates not only in the responses of the alumni tutors, but also in the tone of the researchers and their enthusiasm for their work together. Indeed, this article received the 2010 award for article of the year from the International Writing Centers Association (IWCA).

The second selection presents IWCA's position statement on writing centers in two-year colleges. The statement was originally drafted by Jill Pennington and other members of IWCA, and first published in *Teaching English in the Two-Year College* with Clint Gardener (to learn more about IWCA, see http://writingcenters.org/). In the third selection, Anne Geller, Michele Eodice, Frankie Condon, Meg Carroll, and Elizabeth Boquet offer a compendium of antiracist practice for white writing center allies, including definitions, suggested actions, and a list of references. Throughout Chapter 11, the authors, working together, emphasize the collaborative work of administrators, tutors and students. Theirs is an active enterprise that encourages the processes and products of writing.

As the authors in Chapter 11 suggest, the best work that happens in writing centers can be described as a conversation between writer and tutor. The discussants learn from one another about how to work together, and how to grow together, from the exchange. In this way, writing centers present great promise as out-of-classroom spaces that provide students in basic writing new experiences as writers which they can bring with them when they return to the classroom.

Chapter 12 offers an introduction to the history of assessment and presents initiatives across the country based on the institutional work of outcomes assessment. George Otte and Rebecca Williams Mlynarczyk provide a thorough history of basic writing assessment and its challenges both inside and outside the classroom in an excerpt from their book, *Basic Writing*. Peter Adams, Sarah Gearhart, Robert Miller, and Anne Roberts report on an initiative to accelerate the basic writing program at Community College of Baltimore County, called ALP (Accelerated Learning Program). ALP aims to increase retention, and has been successful at moving students through their basic writing experience in less time, with less attrition, and with increased enrollment in subsequent courses. Likewise, Greg Glau documents the successful *Stretch Program* at Arizona State University, a yearlong college writing course that combines basic writing with first-year composition.

Note

1. Linda Bergmann offers a review of three books that "envision models of professional development as collaborative processes of education and reflection, not as episodes of training or developing skills" (524). As part of this review, Bergman discusses *The Everyday Writing Center: A Community of Practice* by Geller, Eodice, Condon, Carroll, and Boquet, which is excerpted in Chapter 11 of this volume.

Work Cited

Bergmann, Linda S. "Writing Centers and Cross-Curricular Literacy Programs as Models for Faculty Development." *Pedagogy* 8.3 (2008): 523–536. Print.

Writing Centers

What They Take with Them: Findings from the Peer Writing Tutor Alumni Research Project

Brad Hughes, Paula Gillespie, and Harvey Kail

Brad Hughes, Paula Gillespie, and Harvey Kail (from the University of Wisconsin–Madison; Marquette University; and the University of Maine, respectively) conducted a twenty-five-year survey—from 1982 to 2007— of alumni peer tutors from their institutions. They invited the alumni to respond to a series of open-ended questions, such as listing "the most significant abilities, values, or skills that you developed in your work as a peer writing tutor." In doing so, the researchers sought to understand the long-term impact of peer tutoring on the alumni tutors, rather than relying only on anecdotal evidence. The alumni provide positive and heartfelt comments that offer strong support for the enduring inspiration of writing center work in tutors' lives long after their college years have ended. "What They Take with Them" received the 2010 award for article of the year from the International Writing Centers Association.

> Any time I make an effort to understand another person's point of view, I reconnect to the values I learned in the process of becoming and serving as a peer tutor.
>
> —A former peer tutor, class of 1984

Within both the noisy and the quiet conversations in our writing centers, something extraordinary is happening. Undergraduate peer tutors are creating one of the most important experiences in their educational careers, a complex, multi-faceted experience whose influence persists not just years but decades after graduation. When undergraduate writing tutors and fellows participate in challenging and sustained staff education, and when they interact closely with other student writers and with other peer tutors through our writing centers and writing fellows programs, they develop in profound ways both intellectually and academically. This developmental experience, played out in their tutor education and in their work as peer tutors and fellows, helps to shape and sometimes transform them personally, educationally, and professionally.[1]

Through the Peer Writing Tutor Alumni Research Project (PWTARP), we have set out to explore and document what peer tutors take with them from their training and experience. We believe that by listening to what they have to tell us, we will better understand the powerful educational experiences of becoming a peer writing tutor in a college or university. Every writing center director has seen that student tutors learn as much about writing as do the students they tutor, if not more. We also know not only that tutors become better writers, but that they develop in a number of other highly consequential ways: as thinkers, as writers, and as developing professionals. As Kenneth Bruffee has argued since the 1970s, peer tutoring benefits the liberal education of peer tutors. We have received many eloquent testimonials to Bruffee's claim, as alumni send us, over the years and from far-flung locations, notes of gratitude for the lasting effects of our peer tutoring and writing fellows programs. The Peer Writing Tutor Alumni Research Project has made it possible for us to sample and analyze more systematically the reflections of 126 former tutors from our three institutions, Marquette University, the University of Maine, and the University of Wisconsin–Madison.[2] Collectively, the responses from these alumni total over 500 single-spaced pages.

The thick description that emerges from our research tells us in great detail about the value added of collaborative learning for the peer tutors themselves. Respondents assert that they developed

- a new relationship with writing,
- analytical power,
- a listening presence,
- skills, values, and abilities vital in their professions,
- skills, values, and abilities vital in families and in relationships,
- earned confidence in themselves,
- and a deeper understanding of and commitment to collaborative learning.

These categories which we use below to report the findings from the PWTARP are, like all classifications, admittedly imperfect: categories overlap in multiple ways, simple labels are reductive, and brief quotations from such rich data inevitably pale compared to the full source. We do, however, believe that these are powerful ways to conceptualize the influence that peer tutoring has on tutors themselves. Ultimately, in this article we theorize peer tutoring as a form of liberal education for peer tutors themselves. And we support this claim with empirical evidence that this is deep learning that endures years, even decades, after graduation. We open by defining liberal education, using Kenneth Bruffee's arguments about peer tutoring and liberal education and William Cronon's definition of the goals of a liberal education. We then describe our survey methods and our research participants. In the heart of the article, we develop and illustrate each of our major findings listed above, demonstrating the breadth and depth of what former tutors have taken with them. In our conclusion, we argue that this research has profound implications for writing centers themselves: systematic tutor alumni research allows writing centers to resituate themselves as central to the educational mission of our colleges and universities.

Collaborative Learning and Liberal Education

Kenneth Bruffee predicted it well. In his 1978 *Liberal Education* article on establishing peer tutoring programs, "The Brooklyn Plan: Attaining Intellectual Growth through Peer-Group Tutoring," Bruffee argues that the benefits for the tutors themselves go well beyond the gains in writing that one might anticipate from student tutors. Something more intense and intricate appears to be at work when students train and then engage repeatedly in tutoring writing. As Bruffee frames it, peer writing tutors form a "transitional community" in their tutor education, a temporary mutual aid group that fosters among them the kind of intellectual work that typifies knowledge-making communities in academe, in professions, and in civic life. Learning to learn collaboratively from and out of respect for each other, Bruffee argues, has a powerful impact on the peer tutors' own education:

> Experience with peer tutoring in the schools would lead us to expect some improvement in the tutors' own work through tutoring, especially if the tutors' academic record were poor to start with. But there is nothing in the literature on peer tutoring which would lead us to expect that average or somewhat above average undergraduates acting as tutors could develop rapidly through a process of peer influence a capacity [judgment] so essential to mature thought. (451)

When Bruffee argues that peer tutoring has something to do with the rapid development of "judgment" and "mature thought," he opens the door to a different conception of a liberal education from the popular notion that focuses on certain classic texts and authors to be seriously encountered and struggled with, from Aristotle to Darwin to Toni Morrison. Bruffee suggests that a liberal education equates not only to familiarity with this or that prized text but also to the development of certain skills, values, and abilities.

To help us understand and articulate further for ourselves the skills, values, and abilities of a liberal education, we turned to William Cronon's 1998 essay "'Only Connect' . . . : The Goals of a Liberal Education." To Cronon, liberal education does not consist of a required curriculum; it's not a list of courses to complete or facts to know. Instead, he focuses on the *goals* of a liberal education, on the "qualities of the human beings we would like that curriculum to produce" (75). And he urges us always to remember that the purpose of that curriculum "is to nurture human freedom and growth" (76). Cronon's goals provide a powerful theoretical framework for understanding the results of the Peer Writing Tutor Alumni Research Project. Underlying all of Cronon's goals is a deep concern for humanity—for connections among people—and an argument for the importance of communication within a liberal education. Among Cronon's goals: Liberally educated people "listen and they hear." "They read and they understand." "They can talk with anyone." "They can write clearly and persuasively and movingly." "They practice humility, tolerance, and self-criticism." "They nurture and empower the people around them" (76–78). As Cronon explains, liberally educated people

> follow E. M. Forster's injunction from *Howard's End*: "Only connect." More than anything else, being a liberally educated person means being able to see connections that allow one to make sense of the world and act within it in creative ways. . . . A liberal education is about gaining the power and the wisdom, the generosity and the freedom to connect. (78)

And Cronon emphasizes that being liberally educated is not a finished "state": it is a way of groping "toward wisdom," "a way of educating ourselves without any illusion that our educations will ever be complete" (79). Cronon's goals for a liberal education align powerfully with the results that Bruffee might well have predicted for our PWTARP: that the analysis and narratives offered by tutor alumni demonstrate, in multiple ways, the kinds of growth central to a liberal education.

Grounded in extensive praxis with the Brooklyn Plan, Bruffee theorizes that collaborative learning enhances the liberal education of peer tutors. Subsequent scholarship has either anecdotally supported Bruffee's claim or simply assumed it to be true. But we are now able to demonstrate empirically—and not merely characterize, as Boquet (474) describes what Bruffee does—that peer tutoring benefits peer tutors. As we share our findings from the PTWARP, we are also doing more than identifying skills, values, and abilities that tutors take from their experience and education. We are proposing a more comprehensive view of the value and influence of collaborative learning in writing centers, one that includes the impressive development of peer tutors themselves. This more comprehensive view of peer learning also allows writing centers, as we argue in our conclusion, to redefine their missions, recognizing themselves as unique spaces in the academy where peer tutors make dramatic leaps forward in their own liberal educations.

The Project

The PWTARP began with our desire to learn more systematically about our own tutor alumni, to probe beyond the anecdotal evidence we had from our informal exchanges with former tutors. Above all, we wanted to learn which abilities, values, and skills tutors developed from their education and experience as peer writing tutors and how, if at all, they had used those abilities, values, and skills in their lives beyond graduation. From early on we have also had another goal for this project. We have found it consistently illuminating and motivating to do this research across our three different universities and programs, including an undergraduate writing fellows program as well as peer-tutoring writing centers. Because of the strengths of this collaborative research, we wanted to encourage further research with tutor alumni and about tutor learning that went beyond our own three universities and any one time. So we created the Peer Writing Tutor Alumni Research Project (Kail, Gillespie, and Hughes), to encourage colleagues to do similar research. Through our web site we've shared our survey instrument for others to use and adapt, as well as advice for colleagues about getting started with this kind of research, obtaining approval for human subjects research, finding tutor alumni, choosing a sample, and maximizing the response rate.

The survey itself is deliberately open-ended and flexible because we wanted to give alumni room to respond in ways we could never anticipate, and because we want colleagues who participate in the PWTARP to replicate or adapt our survey design to their own institutions and to their own research goals. We tried to design open-ended questions that would elicit full responses, not too scripted, we hoped, by the questions.

We asked former tutors, for example, to list the "most significant abilities, values, or skills that you developed in your work as a peer writing tutor." Asking such open-ended questions invited some unexpected responses, and we got some. Would former tutors tell us that their writing had improved? In their professions, had they used abilities they developed from their tutoring? Had those skills carried over to their personal relationships? We also wanted to know whether tutoring experience gives alumni an edge in job interviews. At one of our conference presentations early in the process, an audience member asked us, "Isn't there anything negative about tutoring?" So we included that question on the survey: "Were there any downsides to your tutoring experience?" In addition, we chose to include a few quantifiable responses, in spite of our reservations about what numbers really mean in response to questions like these. So we attached Likert scales to some questions, especially to gauge the importance of the tutoring experience for our alumni. Although we've kept the core questions constant, we have all tweaked the survey slightly when we have sent it out, and we trust that others will do the same as they use it. For a current version of the PWTARP survey, see Appendix A below. For more information about our survey design, see Kail, Gillespie, and Hughes, "The Peer Writing Tutor Alumni Research Project: An Invitation to Research."

Anyone who looks at our research design and findings with an appropriately critical eye will naturally wonder whether our alumni's education and experience as peer tutors account for what they take with them or whether the peer tutoring and writing fellows programs at our universities simply do a good job of selecting student tutors. We have no doubt that the students entering these programs already have relatively strong writing and communication skills, and they do not enter this experience as blank slates with no values or abilities. Throughout our research, we have insisted on viewing writing fellows and peer tutors developmentally; our survey questions deliberately ask about developing—not about acquiring or about learning—skills, abilities, and values. In their responses to these questions, our tutor alumni, going back decades, are absolutely clear—in both quantitative and qualitative responses—that their education and experience as peer tutors played a crucial role in their developing much further and in sophisticated ways the skills, values, and abilities that they claim.

The PWTARP extends the work of various writing center scholars who have done research in two intersecting areas—tutor-alumni research and tutor-learning research. Some—perhaps even most—of the tutor-alumni research is, in fact, unpublished. We know, for example, of numerous writing center and writing fellows directors who have developed rich unpublished collections of surveys from tutor alumni, gathered over years and decades. These surveys serve an important function in local writing center assessment; surveying alumni also builds and maintains valuable connections with former tutors. In publications, several former tutors have offered insightful reflections about what they learned and how they grew intellectually and socially from their experience as tutors (Douglass; Kedia; McGlaun; Purdy). And since the 1980s, several writing center scholars have argued in print that tutoring prepares students for future careers, in teaching (Almasy and England; Clark; Cox; Denton; Hammerbacher, Phillips, and Tucker; Harris; Monroe; Neulieb; Zelnak et al.), as well as in many other fields

(Bell; Dinitz and Kiedaisch; Welsch; Whalen). Some of these arguments are theoretical, some based on anecdotal evidence, some based on research. As part of her important discussion of the multiple ways in which writing centers "enhance and advance a culture of academic seriousness," Molly Wingate examines what the writing center at Colorado College offers tutors: "skills for their professional lives," as well as "a community," "a locus where tutors learn about and practice teaching and where they can be with peers who are serious writers" (8, 10). In his book about secondary writing centers, Richard Kent mentions that students "who staffed The Writing Center gained confidence, perspective, and understanding as writers and people" (5). "These students grew to value the power of listening, the necessity of encouragement, and the respect of process" (6). In *The Longman Guide to Peer Tutoring*, Paula Gillespie and Neal Lerner welcome tutors to an "experience that can change your life, if you allow it to" (9). Drawing on written reflections that consultants complete at the end of each term and from survey research with consultant alumni at Wright State University, Nicole Macklin, Cynthia K. Marshall, and Joe Law not only explore tutor learning and career benefits of tutoring but also argue that such research should be part of any writing center assessment. Neal Lerner similarly recommends that writing center assessment include assessment of tutor learning (71). The most recent published research, based on our PWTARP model, is an ambitious study with responses from 135 former tutors at the University of Vermont, focusing primarily on career development (Dinitz and Kiedaisch).

Our Alumni Participants by the Numbers

Of the 148 surveys we systematically distributed to former tutors and writing fellows who had graduated as far back as 1982, 126 surveys were completed, yielding an extraordinary 85.1% response rate. The responses to the first section of our survey give us a demographic portrait of our former tutors and their lives beyond undergraduate studies and tutoring. Of the respondents, 58.7% were female; 41.3% male. All of the former tutors had completed a compulsory semester-long tutor-education course. Almost all had participated in regular staff meetings and ongoing education, about half had participated in social events for tutors and fellows, and 41.3% had presented at regional and national writing center and composition conferences. The number of semesters they were undergraduate writing tutors or fellows ranged from one to six; the average number of semesters tutoring for all alumni in this study was close to three (2.84). When asked about further education beyond their undergraduate degrees, 66.1% of those who responded to this question were pursuing or had completed advanced degrees in such varied fields as social work, composition and rhetoric, literary studies, law, journalism, education, divinity, history, psychology, microbiology, political science, counseling, creative writing, economics, music, professional writing, and medicine.

One of the important strengths of our study is that our respondents were not all recent graduates. Because the peer-tutoring program at the University of Maine has such a long tradition, stretching back to its beginning in 1981, the alumni respondents in our study ranged in age from 22 to 77, averaging 32.3 years old at the time they completed the survey. Of our respondents, 24% had graduated in the 1980s, 33.6% in the 1990s, and 42.4% between 2000 and 2007. Figure 1 shows the distribution of respondents across graduation years.

This variety in age and in stage of life gives us, in fact, even more confidence in the claims we make in this article—that the effects of having been educated and having worked as a peer tutor and writing fellow are deep, and that these effects endure for, in fact, decades after graduation. Students just a few years out of college might be expected to feel the effects of peer tutoring or fellowing in their further schooling or entry-level jobs. But it's powerful to hear former tutors twenty, or even thirty, years beyond their college experience tell us that they still feel the effects of a course they took and a job they held as undergraduates.

Reading the list of occupations pursued by these former tutors is fascinating for many reasons. First, it's a pleasure to learn what our former tutors have done after graduation. Second, it shows how many different kinds of occupations former tutors pursue. Finally, it demonstrates that the skills, abilities, and values tutors develop from tutor-

Figure 1. Graduation Years for Survey Respondents (n=126)

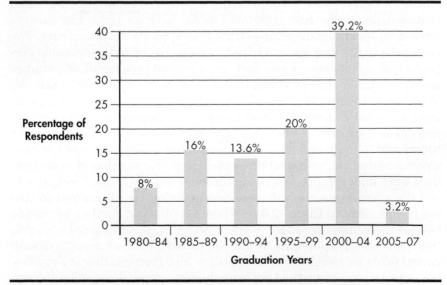

ing are widely applicable in varied careers, including ones far afield from teaching and writing. Of their careers, some of the most common were in teaching (at every level, from kindergarten to university level), sales, journalism, technical writing, writing in new media, editing, corporate communications, social work, counseling and psychology, management, law, and community, non-profit, and social-advocacy work. Other tutor alumni in this study included an aspiring actor, an assistant district attorney, a musician, the executive director of a national folk festival, a lobbyist, an anesthesiology technician, a mate on a yacht, a psychology researcher, a project manager for a remodeling firm, a mortgage administrator for a bank, a VISTA member, a Peace Corps volunteer, an office manager, an analyst for the US Defense Department, and a biotech patent agent.

One other number stands out from our research. In some ways, we hardly needed to ask a Likert-scale question to measure how important this experience had been for our former tutors and fellows: the response rate and the sheer volume and eloquence of what they wrote in response to the surveys answered that question. But with certain audiences and in certain rhetorical situations, there's nothing like a clear-cut, easily understood number. When we asked tutor alumni to rate how important their education and experience as tutors and fellows had been in their development as undergraduate students (Question 10), the response was stunning. On a scale of 1–5 (1 = unimportant; 5 = highly important), the mean was 4.48. For a summary of all of the Likert-scale responses, see Figure 2.

Figure 2. Mean Ratings for Likert-Scale Responses: Assessment of Peer-Tutoring Experience

QUESTION #	QUESTION	SCALE	n	MEAN
4	Would you rate the importance of your training and/or experience as a tutor in the *interviewing or hiring process for your first job?*	1 = not influential 5 = very influential	99	3.73
6	Would you rank the importance *for your occupation* of the skills, qualities, or values you developed as a tutor?	1 = unimportant 5 = highly important	102	4.39
7	To what extent has *your writing* been influenced by your training and/or work as a tutor?	1 = not influenced 5 = very influenced	103	4.32
10	Would you please rate the importance your writing center/ writing fellow training and experience as you developed as a university student?	1 = not important 5 = highly important	102	4.48

Our Findings

To analyze our findings, we used an organic, recursive process. Each of us independently read each response to the open-ended questions and developed detailed lists of themes that we saw. With some questions (the first, for example, in which we ask alumni to list skills, values, and abilities), it was a relatively straightforward task to group similar concepts and to identify the most frequent responses. Questions that asked for narratives, however, required more interpretation as we identified key concepts within a narrative (confidence and listening are good examples of what's illustrated in some of the narratives). We then compared our lists of themes and clustered these detailed themes into fewer more general ones; those most frequent themes formed the categories for the findings we report here. In developing these categories our aim was not only to convey the most common themes within the responses, but also to convey some of the richness of the data and to showcase some of the surprises. Reading, comparing, probing, debating the meaning of, and living with these responses over the several years of this research project—this kind of analysis was a joy for all of us. These everyday transformations of collaborative learning develop over time and with experience; they are described as enduring and profound.

In our analysis, seven key findings emerged, which we explain and illustrate, using the voices of tutor alumni, in the following sections of this article. From their education and experience as peer tutors, alumni developed a new relationship with writing; analytical power; a listening presence; skills, values, and abilities vital in their professions; skills, values, and abilities vital in families and in relationships; earned confidence in themselves; and a deeper understanding of and commitment to collaborative learning. To illustrate the richness of what tutors learned, we have organized these findings to move from those most closely related to writing to ones with far-reaching implications for intellectual, professional, social, and personal development and richer understandings of the collaborative nature of learning itself.

A New Relationship with Writing

It is a given, at least in the world of writing centers, that tutoring writing leads to improvement in the writing of the tutor as well as the writer. Our surveys more than confirm this commonsense notion of collaborative learning. Almost all of the former tutors report that the experience of training and working as a writing fellow or peer writing tutor helped them become markedly better writers: more organized, more concise, more focused, more persuasive, more fluent, more savvy. They clearly take with them from their undergraduate experience a satisfying sense of confidence in their writing, and they develop their careers, in part, on an instrumental and sophisticated literacy.

What interests us most in the survey results on writing is what they show us about the power of collaborative learning in writing centers and writing fellows programs to create educational change among the tutors themselves. For some former peer writing tutors, the changes in their own writing are explained in developmental terms—an intensification in specific ways of getting better at what they were already doing well to begin with: their writing has become more precise, more organized, more argumentative, etc. One former tutor (1995), now the editor for a small Maine town newspaper, expresses this paradigm clearly: "It wasn't so much a matter of learning any one skill or ability as finding a place that helped accelerate my growth in all areas of my writing."

The developmental model, however, does not entirely account for the changes that many former tutors experience. For them, becoming better writers involves something of a transformation as they entered into a new relationship with the writing process itself, and, most significantly, with other writers, as Bruffee predicted. By working in a reflective and respectful way with others, they experience their own writing process from an entirely new perspective. The surveys are filled with comments such as these: "It changed the way I approached writing completely," or "I began to think about writing differently through the writing center," or "It changed my whole view of writing."

Their attitude toward revision is emblematic of this new relationship with the writing process. Prior to their tutoring experience, they may have been exposed to the idea of revision, but they never saw it in action before in such exciting ways, both in their own writing and in the writing of those they worked with. Many tutors point out that their writing center experience enabled them to "depersonalize" a written piece, and "find out where and how it works or does not work." The ability to stand back from their own writing and see it "whole" suggests not simply the acquisition of a writing skill, but a new relationship between the self and language, as is suggested in this statement from a tutor who graduated in 1985:

> The peer tutoring experience can allow a certain detachment from one's own writing; that is, I can often remove myself from the fact that it's me writing and focus instead on the words and how they communicate ideas, the same way I would if I was reading and critiquing someone else's work.

The ability to "detach" or "remove oneself" from one's writing speaks eloquently to our sense that peer tutors become better writers not only because they "accelerate" the skills and abilities that they bring with them, but also because they come through their training and experience to a new and more mature understanding of the relationship between the writer's self and the writer's words.

Closely tied to this insider's view of the writing process and the ability to distinguish between one's words and oneself is the willingness tutors frequently cite in the surveys to open themselves to the kind of tutoring and critique that they formerly provided to student writers. The willingness to seek out and accept criticism is echoed throughout the surveys as one of the features of their writing that they carry with them beyond graduation, and is further evidence of their new relationship with writing. A technical writer for the automotive industry reflects that

> Before tutoring[,] writing was a solo experience. . . . Now my writing process always includes asking as many people as I can recruit to sit down with me, to ream my drafts, and to share their ideas with me. I can't imagine writing anything important without invoking the writer/tutor conversation.

This strongly suggests to us that learning to trust their language in the hands of others is one of the most important values that former tutors take with them, and is an outward reflection of an inner change, as one former tutor, now a college instructor herself, describes: "There was a shift inside myself—I was no longer a writer on the sidelines with some knowledge I could argue with myself about. Did I really know this? I was an articulate, confident participant in the process and interaction of ideas and writing."

Analytical Power

Former tutors and fellows tell us proudly that they become adept at problem solving through their training and work as tutors. In the tutoring situation the tutor must be able to solve many intricate and interconnected problems almost simultaneously. Thinking on one's feet, then, becomes essential to the successful tutorial, as tutor alumni frequently pointed out to us, and the basis for their creative problem solving rests on their becoming adept at analyzing—quickly—a piece of writing that is read aloud to them or that they read in preparation for a conference. What does the paper need? What does the writer need? What does the professor need? Perhaps there are fifty minutes to try to solve the multi-dimensional puzzle of tutoring writing. Perhaps there is half an hour. As we read and reread the surveys, we began to understand the tutorial situation as a kind of intellectual crucible through which the tutor must meld her rhetorical analysis of the student's text, the complex rhetorical situation created within the peer tutoring relationship, and the disciplinary and discourse expectations of the institution into a seamless whole of conversation. And, oh yes, the paper is due soon.

In many replies, analysis and self-confidence were paired. A few mentioned that their ability to analyze helped them read differently—permanently. Others framed analysis in terms of critical thinking. Some commented on developing a metalanguage that allowed them to talk with writers analytically. As one former tutor, now a management consultant, put it, "Most significant was a conceptual shift from encountering language in terms of what it says to dealing with it in terms of what it does. I can't emphasize the force of this movement between levels of abstraction enough; it changed how I read everything."

Tutors, through their analytical abilities, nurture and empower learning, deepen and enrich it in meaningful ways. This is a purposeful, active kind of analysis we see in few other college situations. And tutors continue to use these analytical and creative moves well into their lives as professionals, as liberally educated people, able to contribute to their worlds. An editor and author says, "I learned to read closely for unity and coherence as well as for purpose, genre, and audience in support of the revision process, whether my own or other writers'." In a similar vein, an executive director of a national folk festival explains:

> My time as a peer tutor honed my skills in being able to focus on the "heart" of a writing project, and to develop a writing strategy (mine and others') of targeting a project to its intended audience—considering what information it is fair to consider as "common knowledge" and what arguments need to be made above and beyond that shared information. . . . The majority of the marketing projects that I have developed have begun with an analysis of the audience for the message, and the core elements of that message. This strategy springs directly from the experiences that I had as a tutor, examining a lot of information (as in a disorganized paper), and guiding the writer to extract the crucial information.

A Listening Presence

Recognizing themselves as good communicators is almost universal among peer writing tutor alumni. Although the language that they use to describe their abilities to communicate varies from an emphasis on overall "inter-personal communication skills" and "collaborative style" to specific strengths in question asking and one-to-one conferencing, nearly all the respondents pride themselves on the ability to make meaningful contact with others in complex rhetorical situations. However, the single most frequently mentioned and specific communication skill that respondents across all three institutions and programs list and elaborate on is what they frequently refer to as "active listening." Nearly half of all the respondents single out a new appreciation for and facility with listening to others as a highly valued skill that they take with them across the border of graduation and into further studies and into careers, as well as into their family and social lives.

Listening clearly activates and reinforces other communicative abilities, alumni tell us. Being able to listen carefully is inextricable from a variety of other skills, abilities, and values that tutor alumni regard as significant. Tutor alumni tell us that listening translates into personal and professional choices—and actions. It is no coincidence, we believe, that Cronon lists listening first as a quality of a liberally educated person, and we agree. Because respect is stressed in our three programs, tutors can embody what Krista Ratcliffe calls rhetorical listening, a kind of listening by which people attempt not just to hear but to understand others. The listening that takes place in the writing center is close to Ratcliffe's goal of listening as understanding: "Standing under discourses means letting discourses wash over, through, and around us . . ." (28). The one-to-one conference that is at the center of most peer-tutoring practice proves to be a rich environment for cultivating the habit of active, rhetorical listening.

In the intimacy of the one-to-one setting, peer tutors must assume the responsibility for listening carefully to the writer. After all, the tutors are in charge of the session, and they feel obliged to provide what they refer to as a "sounding board" or "a fresh set of ears" or a "listening presence in the room," allowing the writer to work through the issues and complexities of the writing assignment at hand. As one respondent from Maine put it, students need to "talk it through . . . before they can write it out," and as one Marquette tutor put it, by demonstrating to the student writer that she was willing to listen, the writer "learns that I was willing to invest myself in the session." "Sit still, listen, and stay out of the way," as one former Marquette tutor put it, or, as one University of Wisconsin writing fellow phrased it, "I find that silence plays a big part in maintaining student ownership of the work at hand." Careful, purposeful listening in the tutorial is perhaps the most dramatic way that peer writing tutors demonstrate to writers and to themselves that they care about the student and about the student's writing, without appropriating the work of the writer. The tutor's listening empowers the student writer.

Listening also opens the door to many of the other skills and abilities that former tutors take with them. Many former peer writing tutors pair listening with effective question asking, which serves as a basic rhetorical move for building tutorial conversations. "Open-ended, patient questioning," one former Madison tutor wrote, leads to conversation, which becomes then a means of analysis. A Marquette tutor put this analytical aspect of listening nicely into perspective: "I like to listen to students both for what they were saying and for what they weren't." "My job, then," according to a UMaine tutor, was to "listen, empathize, and ask questions that will help the writer find her own solutions." All of this listening, question asking, followed by more listening calls for copious amounts of patience, and the patience necessary to listen well is a kind of side effect or prerequisite, perhaps, for developing the kind of active listening skills that the tutorial environment demands of peer writing tutors. "Patience, patience, patience" writes one former Marquette tutor in response to the question of what values, skills, or abilities he took with him.

While the tutor training class and the tutorial itself are training grounds for effective listening, it is obvious from our surveys that effective listening, in particular, and good communication skills overall play a vital role in the lives of peer tutors after they graduate. They acknowledge these skills as significant in the interviewing process for jobs, and once they have those jobs, the listening skills that they have developed serve them very well as they develop careers. As technical writers, they know how to listen effectively to engineers and software experts, and they know how to listen to bosses and co-workers, too. As one former UMaine tutor explained about his work as an editor for a daily newspaper, "Any time I make an effort to understand another person's point of view, I reconnect to the values I learned in the process of becoming and serving as a peer tutor."

One of the most surprising results of the surveys was this: learning to be an effective listener through peer tutoring has had a significant impact on former tutors' family and social lives as sons and daughters, parents, and friends. As one now-veteran mother noted, "You can't tell a toddler anything, but [you] can persuade her that you are listening to her perspective and offer alternatives that meet both your needs." Many former tutors report that their listening skills modeled on their tutoring experience have become an integral part of developing their relationship with partners and children. Not only does this "communication skill" lead to better conversation, better relationships, and better understanding among friends, it also, according to some former tutors, leads to a better understanding of self. As one former UMaine tutor wrote, "I realized through tutoring experience that I was one of those people who while conversing spent all the time internally phrasing their next point instead of listening to what the other person was saying." Another tutor wrote that listening made her "more human."

The significance of acquiring effective listening skills for former peer tutors cannot be overstated. It is for many a newfound strength from which they have built other important components of their character; from empathy to patience to self-understanding. As one former UMaine tutor put it, "I didn't so much learn to listen as I saw how important listening can be and how powerful it can be if you do it well. I guess listening could go down on the list as a value instead of a skill."

Skills, Values, and Abilities in Professions

Much of the academic work students do in college seems to bear little resemblance to the work they will be called upon to do in their careers after college. We have found, however, that the educational experience of training and working as a peer writing tutor or fellow has a direct and singular impact on the work that many if not most of those we surveyed engage in after graduation. As one former UMaine student put it, the correlation between peer tutoring and career relevance is "eerie." Our surveys clearly demonstrate that training and experience in tutoring writing have a lasting impact on most former students, beginning with the way they handle job interviews and continuing on to the types of career choices they make and their professional advancement.

For those who go into careers based on writing, such as technical writing, journalism, and editing, peer tutoring serves with the student's major as the foundation for entering the profession. As one former tutor, now a veteran editor for a daily newspaper, says, "in many ways, the extraordinary experience . . . of writing and talking about writing with other writers . . . never ended. . . . No workday goes by, quite frankly, without some echo of what I learned as a peer tutor." For many, the experience of being peer tutors "cemented" their desire to put writing at the center of their professional ambitions. In the surveys, they write eloquently of the "joy" of finding their way into the writing process by learning to help others find their way. They learn to accept criticism as an essential component of the writing process, and they take not only a willingness to be critiqued but also the desire for feedback from others into their working lives. Their familiarity with the give and take of peer review has stood them in good stead in newsrooms, editorial offices, and management meetings.

The influence of peer tutoring on those tutor alumni who become teachers is profound. For those who came into writing centers with their vocation as teachers already in mind, the experience of training and tutoring serves as an affirmation of their interests in and an apprenticeship to that first teaching job after college, a "first taste" as one tutor put it; collaborative learning continues to influence their teaching many years and teaching positions later. They bring with them from the writing center their practiced knowledge of writing processes, a respect for individual differences in writing styles among students, and the nuanced diplomatic and conversational skills necessary for the intimate instruction of the one-to-one conference, among other values and abilities. From their writing center and writing fellows experience, they also bring to their teaching a particular approach to teaching and learning: a deep respect for students and a collaborative ethic as well as a commitment to student-centered instruction. From a high school history teacher:

> I think my philosophy/approach to teaching is also informed by my experience as a [writing] fellow. My classes are highly interactive—usually discussion based—and reflect the writing fellows' philosophy that students should play a more active role in their own education. I do give a lot of responsibility to my students, as the WFP [Writing Fellows Program] does. And having gained more of a philosophical appreciation for the role of questioning, praise, and listening in the WFP, and especially [the seminar for Writing Fellows] . . . these have become staples of my teaching practice.

Many former peer tutors report also that their tutoring experience brought them to teaching as a profession in the first place. Phrases such as "revealed to me" or "gave me a first glimpse" or "made it possible for me to recognize myself as a teacher" or "made me conscious of my skills as a teacher" are common in the surveys of those who have gone into teaching as a direct result of their tutoring experiences. The writing center influence on undergraduate tutors who go on to become teachers at all levels of education is genuinely profound and, to us, deeply encouraging and satisfying.

While writing-based careers and teaching have both become important callings for former tutors, most go into occupations and professions that might not seem particularly connected to writing center work: sales, social work, acting, management, development work, legal work, medicine, etc. For many of these alumni, the writing center experience did not influence their choice of careers, but as many of them point out, "it made me so much better at what I do." For one thing, writing remains an important part of what many former peer tutors do, even if they do not have "writer" in their official titles. In addition, overall communication skills, particularly effective and active listening, are cited as essential to the development of careers in nearly all fields. Furthermore, survey respondents consistently identify the analytical and organizational skills they derived from the training and experience as foundational to their success. They frequently point out parallels in what they are now doing with what they learned as writing center tutors and writing fellows, such as the psychologist who talked in detail about the similarities between the analysis of prose and the analysis of personality or the web designer who argues that the structure of a good argumentative essay has served him well as he builds websites. Writing center training and tutoring provide students with a new kind of intellectual understanding of the structure "behind" things that they carry with them into a myriad of occupations and professions. Finally, the experience of writing center work becomes for many former tutors a model for work that is intellectually engaging, emotionally satisfying, and socially important. As one former tutor put it, his writing center training and experience "stand out as a kind of ideal for what I want to be doing."

Skills, Values, and Abilities in Families and in Relationships

By asking alumni whether the abilities, skills, and values that they developed from their peer tutoring experience have played a role in their social or family relationships, we hit another rich vein. We asked this question because we felt that the influence of peer tutoring extended beyond the professional, academic, and occupational realms of life, and because we're committed to exploring the breadth of the influence of this experience. Although roughly 15% of respondents said no or simply did not answer this question (more non-responses than was the case for any other question), the vast majority of tutor alumni responded with a definite yes. Many alumni explained that they have become valuable, trusted coaches for the writing that their children, partners, parents, roommates, and friends do, and some told, with joy, of the successes that friends and family have had with their writing. As several point out, giving feedback on or advice about writing to family, to loved ones, or to partners is tricky territory—that's where their diplomacy and tact and listening skills, often attributed to their tutor education and experience, have come in handy.

The influence on social and family relationships is, however, about much more than helping with writing. Our research participants have told us that the experience of writing tutoring and the values that underlie its practice are, in fact, preparation for developing strong, respectful, and collaborative relationships with family, partners, and friends. Over and over and with consistency, tutor alumni responses to this question reveal wisdom about connecting with others (a part of Cronon's exhortation to develop "the generosity and the freedom to connect" [78]), about developing and sustaining human relationships, and tutor alumni attribute these abilities and values directly to their tutoring education and experience. One respondent said, "The interpersonal and communication skills you gain through tutoring are invaluable in all aspects of life, whether you are tutoring someone on a five-page paper or trying to help your wife figure out how to baste a turkey. Tutoring is like communicating boot camp." They report that the non-judgmental listening and patience they learned as tutors are invaluable in communicating with their toddlers and teenage children as well as with adult partners. The active listening skills they developed as tutors help as they build relationships with others. They have learned to create a reciprocal dialogue, to have and to communicate respect for others' points of views and compassion for their situations: "To be a good friend, sister, daughter, etc., you have to treat others with respect and compassion." Some tutor alumni noted that the culture of self-reflection within tutor education and staff meetings leads to these powerful insights about family and social relationships: "I think having reflected critically on how we relate to students in conferences made me more aware of how I relate to friends and family."

Earned Confidence: Transcending Skills and Abilities

We found it striking that the word "confidence" itself or the concept came up in response to almost every question we asked. It's not a skill, not an ability—it's an attitude towards the self. It is a concept that neither Bruffee nor Cronon mentions specifically, but it reveals the kinds of attitudes that allow tutors to develop judgment within communities, as Bruffee advocates, and it allows the kinds of connections with others and the world that Cronon describes in a liberally educated individual. As confidence develops and grows, some tutors experience it and describe it as transformative.

Time and again, tutor and fellow alumni reported that their attitudes about themselves, their self-confidence, had developed significantly. By one count, the word "confidence" itself was used 177 times in the survey responses. And more than that, the answers projected attitudes of confidence; former tutors embodied it in their replies. This increased self-confidence underlies and is interconnected with all of the skills and abilities we discuss in this article.

Former tutors and fellows told us repeatedly that they had gained confidence in their ability to tutor. Once they got the full sense of tutoring's complexities, they report having felt intimidated initially, especially when they began to grasp that the work they would do with writers is high-stakes work. A tutor can influence how well a student does on a paper, can help students think more deeply and critically about subject matter, can help writers gain admission into law and medical schools, can get them that coveted interview with Teach for America, or can even give them a leg up on a Rhodes or a Truman Scholarship. But these former tutors and fellows go on to tell us that their confidence grows as they experiment and succeed with writers.

Once they acquire that tutoring confidence, they speak of those high-stakes sessions in upbeat, energetic ways. One tutor listed "courage under fire" as something she had gained. Another said,

> I felt *empowered and confident* as a peer tutor in writing because I possessed effective writing skills and could participate in an academic dialogue on writing and peer tutoring, but I felt *good* because I used this knowledge and skills to accomplish a meaningful end. That is, helping others to improve their writing abilities. (Emphasis hers)

Tutoring seems to have had a powerful effect on former tutors' confidence in job interviews. A former drama major working as a restaurant server said that if she could get the job interview, she'd have it nailed because of her confidence in her speaking skills. An environmental educator was told that his "conversation and questioning skills during interviews were strong qualities." An anesthesia technician attributed to tutoring his being "calm and relaxed" during his job interview. He commented that this calmness was also a function of maturity, but he went on to say that tutoring had contributed to his maturing process. He said, "Though I don't empirically know this for certain, I feel confident that my experience in the W[riting] F[ellows] program aided in my maturation as a whole person, since *articulating one's ideas* has so much to do with learning and growing" (emphasis his).

Most striking, perhaps, was the enthusiasm tutors expressed about their abilities to write. They claimed that tutoring made them feel "confident, comfortable, and skilled" at clear, concise writing. They gained respect on the job and were praised by their bosses for "having a flair with words." A few, including one technical writer, claimed to be able to write with "style and voice." A clinical social worker said, "I AM a writer. I feel confident calling myself a writer." This reflection from a graduate-school-bound Japan Exchange and Teaching Programme alumnus summed up the statements of many:

> I think that the practical experience gained sitting across from diverse individuals and in the span of an hour getting to know their positions, their plight, and to get a sense of what they need, has given me a definite edge when faced with a one-on-one situations, whether in interviews, or confronting the guy behind the counter at the rental car station.

A Deeper Understanding of and Commitment to Collaborative Learning

A number of our previous findings suggest that the source for the transformational experience that many tutors undergo can be found in the collaborative nature of their tutor education and their writing center experience. In their tutor education and their tutoring sessions, they learn to value other students as well as their professors as instrumental in their own learning. They discover a new relationship with writing in large measure because they invest themselves in the notion that feedback from peers will make a difference. They acquire active listening skills because they find that, by demonstrating their ability to listen, they generate mutual trust and gain the kind of authority that they need in order to lead in a collaborative situation.

Student tutors earn confidence as they prove to themselves that they can, in fact, help other students become better writers. It may seem paradoxical, but it's the experience of focusing on another's learning that seems to change peer tutors themselves. Key to this, we believe, is that peer tutors take on an agency that's often lacking in their own classroom learning and in peer-review activities. Peer tutors are entrusted, often for one of the first times in their many years as students, with responsibility for guiding someone else's development and even learning, and they face a wide variety of writers and challenging writing situations, situations involving real writing with real consequences, over sustained periods of time. Tutors take this responsibility seriously and it can have a profound influence on them. Because of the intense individual interaction at the heart of peer tutoring, which necessarily emphasizes identification with others—a quality that Cronon lists in his definition of a liberal education—tutors learn to see writing and learning from another writer's perspective and to focus on what helps and what hinders learning. Unlike new teachers in a classroom with twenty or thirty students, tutors and fellows focus intensively on a single student and engage in a sustained, individualized conversation with a succession of individual students. From these conversations, they see first hand the power of collaborative talk. They discover how crucial it is to learning for writers to know that someone cares about, listens to, respects, and empathizes with them. They find common ground with strangers, and they learn how crucial it is to tap into another student's interests. They learn to talk about ideas with other students, developing "the ability," explained a former Marquette tutor, "to draw people into conversations about their ideas." They learn to be comfortable operating with less than one hundred percent certainty: "I learned that I don't always have the answers, nor does any teacher or tutor." They develop a willingness to take chances, to do the kind of creative problem solving we've described. They learn to see multiple right answers. And they learn to respect approaches very different from their own and discover how their own preconceptions can get in the way.

Peer tutoring inevitably puts the issue of authority on the table, and tutors have to grapple with it. Are they peers or are they tutors? How can they be both at the same time? This struggle is, we believe, at the core of the movement from perceiving education only as a hierarchical relationship to one that is also collaborative. As a Wisconsin writing fellow put it, what finally matters most is "Establishing a relationship with a student based on mutual respect, not solely on my authority as a tutor." Mutual respect is the key to genuine collaborative learning, and respect for other students is explicitly referenced throughout the surveys: respect for the diversity of writing strategies, respect for differing ways of thinking about important issues in the disciplines, respect for different learning styles, respect for the mutual struggle to write and be heard in the academy. Tutors come to understand and believe in the power of learning collaboratively with peers, of sharing knowledge and responsibility for contributing to understanding or solving a problem or creating new knowledge—just as Bruffee predicted—because they experience it again and again, up close and personal, and because they themselves benefit. Survey respondents from all three universities explained that they came to view *tutoring as learning*, and that they saw learning as reciprocal; tutoring "taught me how to empower the students, which actually empowered me as a tutor." As a former writing fellow from the University of Wisconsin–Madison explained, "I came out of the program with a deeper appreciation of a collaborative learning style of instruction." Many alumni make it clear that this collaborative approach to learning and to interacting with others—and the values underlying these approaches—persists well beyond the work of being a peer tutor.

Resituating the Writing Center:
A Second Claim for Centrality

Although the analysis we've offered here only scratches the surface of what alumni have told us, we've found analyzing and debating the meaning of our findings wonderfully challenging and enriching. We weren't surprised that former tutors took important things with them from their education and experience as fellows and tutors and from being part of a community of peer tutors. But tutor alumni tell us that there are many nuanced and sophisticated ways in which they have developed from this experience. Alumni are not simply parroting back what they heard in a one-semester tutor-education course. In five hundred pages of responses, they have given us, in narrative and analysis, detailed evidence that this is learning that sticks. How many other undergraduate courses and experiences could, fifteen or twenty years later, offer such detailed evidence of learning and such detailed evidence of staying power and transferability?

Our findings, together with those from the other formal and informal studies we discuss in our literature review, illustrate just how powerful a learning experience peer tutoring can be for undergraduates and, more specifically, just how much deep experience with collaborative learning gives tutors a sense of themselves as active participants in higher education who can contribute to the goals of liberal education described by Bruffee and Cronon. Our study demonstrates that the influence of being a peer tutor is strong, and that its effects endure—two years and ten years and even twenty years beyond graduation. As one respondent explained, "Being a writing fellow was the absolute highlight of my undergraduate education—it was an experience that changed my life, and for which I will always be grateful." Our results show that the influence of being a tutor cuts across future fields of study and professions. And the influence holds across institutions and across kinds of writing center programs, including a writing fellows program.

We're delighted to see many other colleges and universities be inspired to do similar research, using and adapting the PWTARP model based on their particular interests and needs. In recent years, colleagues at Swarthmore College, the University of Vermont, the University of Kansas, Penn State, Salt Lake City Community College, Duke, George Mason, and many other schools have surveyed their tutor alumni using versions of the PWTARP survey. As we've argued here and elsewhere, we believe that such research is a crucial form of assessment for writing centers and writing fellows programs, and an exciting and manageable form of research for tutors and directors to undertake.

Ultimately, however, our research about tutor learning demonstrates something even more important—a crucial understanding that writing centers with peer tutoring or writing fellows programs are more than sites of service to their institutions, much more. Through the influence our centers have on their student staff in peer tutoring programs, writing centers can and should make a second claim (Gillespie, Hughes, and Kail 36–38) for the centrality of their programs: the education of undergraduate students as writers, readers, listeners, creative problem solvers, and liberally educated human beings. As we have demonstrated, the skills, values, and abilities undergraduate tutors gain through our programs push open the door for each of them to a newly developing sense of self, a self with confidence earned by systematically "gaining the power and the wisdom, the generosity and the freedom to connect" (Cronon 78). By doing this crucial kind of assessment of tutor learning that we argue for in our PWTARP, writing centers can resituate themselves in the contemporary academy. Through systematic sponsorship of collaborative learning, writing centers not only help student writers improve, but also play a transformational role in helping student tutors advance their own liberal educations. Alumni research helps us gain a more complete understanding of the value of writing centers and gives us the language we need to transform institutional awareness of our educational purpose and significance.

Appendix A

The Current Version of the PWTARP Survey

Demographic Information:

Today's date:

What is your age?

What is your gender?

When did you graduate?

What was (were) your major(s)?

Have you pursued any additional education after graduation? Please specify degree(s) and institution(s). If you are currently a graduate student, please specify institution and degree.

How many *semesters* or *terms* did you tutor in the Writing Center?

Did you take a credit-bearing tutor training course as an undergraduate?

Yes   No

Which other forms of tutor development did you participate in? (Please check all that apply.)

_____ none

_____ regular staff meetings

_____ regional or national conferences

_____ summer workshops

_____ social events

_____ other (please specify)

What occupation(s) have you pursued since graduation?

Reflections on Your Tutoring Experience:

1. What are the most significant abilities, values, or skills that you developed in your work as a peer writing tutor? Please list them.

2. Of the abilities, values, or skills that you listed above, would you illustrate those that strike you as most meaningful by sharing an episode or event that took place during your time as a tutor or a trainee?

3. Did those abilities, values, or skills that you developed as a peer tutor seem to be a factor in your choice of job or graduate work? Would you elaborate?

4. Did these qualities seem to play a role in your interviewing, in the hiring process, or in acceptance to graduate school? How do you come to that conclusion?

   Would you rate the importance of your training and/or experience as a tutor in the *interviewing or hiring process for your first job*?

5	4	3	2	1
Very influential				Not influential

5. Do any of the qualities you listed in question one play a role in your social or family relationships? Can you give an example?

6. In your occupations(s), have you used the qualities you developed as a writing tutor, if at all? Would you elaborate? Give an example?

   Would you rank the importance *for your occupation* of the skills, qualities, or values you developed as a tutor?

5	4	3	2	1
Highly important				Unimportant

7. To what extent do you think your own writing has been influenced by your experience as a writing tutor? Please explain.

   To what extent has *your writing* been influenced by your training and/or work as a tutor?

5	4	3	2	1
Very influenced				Not influenced

8. What have you learned from working with the writing of others? Please elaborate or provide an example.

9. Were there any downsides to your experience as a peer writing tutor? Please elaborate.

10. Would you please rate the importance of your writing center/writing fellow training and experience as you developed as a university student?

5	4	3	2	1
Highly important				Unimportant

    Please explain your rating.

Notes

1. We are deeply grateful to the tutor alumni at our universities, not only for teaching us so much over the decades but also for contributing so fully and generously to this research project. We also want to thank the reviewers and the editors of *The Writing Center Journal* for their insightful comments, which strengthened this article, and Elise Gold for her eagle-eyed editorial help.
2. We want to acknowledge wonderful colleagues who have also taught the tutor-education courses at our universities: Virginia Chappell at Marquette University; Mary Bartosenski at the University of Maine; and Emily B. Hall who has directed the Writing Fellows Program and taught the undergraduate course for Writing Fellows at the University of Wisconsin–Madison since 1999.

Works Cited

Almasy, Rudolph, and David England. "Future Teachers as Real Teachers: English Education Students in the Writing Laboratory." *English Education* 10.3 (1979): 155–62. Print.

Bell, Elizabeth. "The Peer Tutor as Principal Benefactor in the Writing Center, Or It's Not Just for English Teaching Any More." *Writing Lab Newsletter* 9.9 (1985): 10–13. Print.

Boquet, Elizabeth H. "'Our Little Secret': A History of Writing Centers, Pre- to Post-Open Admissions." *College Composition and Communication* 50.3 (1999): 463–82. Print.

Bruffee, Kenneth A. "The Brooklyn Plan: Attaining Intellectual Growth through Peer-Group Tutoring." *Liberal Education* 64 (1978): 447–68. Print.

Clark, Irene Lukus. "Preparing Future Composition Teachers in the Writing Center." *College Composition and Communication* 38.3 (1988): 347–50. Print.

Cox, Earnest. "Coming Home: A Writing Center Staffer's Personal and Professional Journey." *Writing Lab Newsletter* 29.4 (2004): 1–4. Print.

Cronon, William. "'Only Connect'... The Goals of a Liberal Education." *The American Scholar* 67.4 (1998): 73–80. Print.

Denton, Thomas. "Peer Tutors' Evaluations of the Tutor Training Course and the Tutoring Experience: A Questionnaire." *Writing Lab Newsletter* 18.3 (1993): 14–16. Print.

Dinitz, Sue, and Jean Kiedaisch. "Tutoring Writing as Career Development." *Writing Lab Newsletter* 34.3 (2009): 1–5. Print.

Douglas, Michele. "Justification for Writing Centers and Tutor Training." *Writing Lab Newsletter* 27.5 (2003): 14–15. Print.

Gillespie, Paula, Bradley Hughes, and Harvey Kail. "Nothing Marginal About This Writing Center Experience: Using Research About Peer Tutor Alumni to Educate Others." *Marginal Words, Marginal Work: Tutoring the Academy in the Work of Writing Centers*. Ed. William J. Macauley, Jr., and Nicholas Mauriello. Cresskill, NJ: Hampton P, 2007. 35–52. Print.

Gillespie, Paula, and Neal Lerner. *The Longman Guide to Peer Tutoring*. 2nd ed. New York: Longman, 2008. Print.

Hammerbacher, Maggie, Jodi Phillips, and Shannon Tucker. "The Road Less Traveled: English Education Majors Applying Practice and Pedagogy." *Writing Lab Newsletter* 30.8 (2006): 14–16, 9. Print.

Harris, Muriel. "'What Would You Like to Work on Today?' The Writing Center as a Site for Teacher Training." *Preparing College Teachers of Writing: Histories, Theories, Programs, Practices*. Ed. Betty P. Pytlik and Sarah Liggett. New York: Oxford UP, 2002. 194–207. Print.

Kail, Harvey, Paula Gillespie, and Bradley Hughes. *The Peer Writing Tutor Alumni Research Project*. n.d. Web. 16 Dec. 2009.

———. "The Peer Writing Tutor Alumni Research Project: An Invitation to Research." *Writing at the Center: Proceedings of the 2004 Thomas R. Watson Conference, Louisville, Kentucky, 7–9 October 2004*. Ed. Jo Ann Griffin, Carol Mattingly, and Michele Eodice. Emmitsburg, MD: IWCA Press, 2007. 291–312. CD-ROM.

Kedia, Soma. "Everything I Needed to Know about Life I Learned at the Writing Center." *Writing Lab Newsletter* 31.7 (2007): 13–15. Print.

Kent, Richard. *A Guide to Creating Student-Staffed Writing Centers: Grades 6–12*. New York: Peter Lang, 2006. Print.

Lerner, Neal. "Writing Center Assessment: Searching for the 'Proof' of Our Effectiveness." *The Center Will Hold: Critical Perspectives on Writing Center Scholarship*. Ed. Michael A. Pemberton and Joyce Kinkead. Logan: Utah State UP, 2003. 58–73. Print.

Macklin, N., C. K. Marshall, and Joe Law. "Expanding Writing Center Assessment: Including Tutor Learning." *Writing Lab Newsletter* 27.1 (2002): 12–15. Print.

McGlaun, Sandee K. "Life after Tutoring." *Southern Discourse* 6.2 (2003): 4–5. Print.

Monroe, Meghan. "Reflection: How the Writing Center Rekindled My Passion and Purpose to Teach." *Writing Lab Newsletter* 31.6 (2007): 14–15. Print.

Neulieb, Janice. "Training Potential English Teachers in the Writing Center." *Writing Lab Newsletter* 22.3 (1997): 2–3. Print.

Purdy, James P. "Taking It with You: Personal Reflections on Life 'After' the Writing Center." *The Dangling Modifier* 10.1 (2003): n. pag. Web. 11 Mar. 2009.

Ratcliffe, Krista. *Rhetorical Listening: Identification, Gender, Whiteness.* Carbondale: Southern Illinois UP, 2005. Print.

Stukenberg, Jill. "Tutors' Column: Never Say 'No.'" *Writing Lab Newsletter* 25.10 (2001): 8–9. Print.

Welsch, Kathleen. "Shaping Careers in the Writing Center." *Writing Lab Newsletter* 32.8 (2008): 1–8. Print.

Whalen, Lisa. "Putting Your Writing Center Experience to Work." *Writing Lab Newsletter* 29.9 (2005): 9–10. Print.

Wingate, Molly. "Writing Centers as Sites of Academic Culture." *Writing Center Journal* 21.2 (2001): 7–20. Print.

Zelnak, Bonnie, Irv Cockriel, Eric Crump, and Elaine Hocks. "Ideas in Practice: Preparing Composition Teachers in the Writing Center." *Journal of Developmental Education* 17.1 (1993): 28–34. Print.

Position Statement on Two-Year College Writing Centers

International Writing Centers Association

This position statement presents a list of guidelines and best practices for developing and sustaining writing centers in two-year colleges. Writing center directors asked for an IWCA professional statement to help represent writing center work to institutional administrators and other colleagues and stakeholders that make funding and programmatic decisions at two-year colleges. As such, the document focuses on autonomous spaces for writing centers, as is practicable for local needs, and also presents the significance of employing peer tutors, and training all tutors in rhetoric and composition pedagogy. First drafted by Jill Pennington, Clint Gardner, and others for the International Writing Centers Association (IWCA) Conference in 2003, this final statement was approved by the IWCA Executive Board on January 25, 2007.

- Since many writing centers in two-year colleges serve writers at all levels and in any area of the curriculum across the entire institution, writing centers should, as other institution-wide programs, be as self-determining as they wish within the institutional structure. If affiliating with other learning support services compromises any writing center's mission, the IWCA recommends the writing center pursue autonomy of space, support personnel, and budget. If writing centers find pedagogical benefits to affiliating with other learning services, the IWCA recommends they collaboratively pursue their missions.

- As appropriate to their instructional missions, writing centers should be provided a physical space and location conducive to the variety of services provided. Writing with technology should be encouraged and supported; but a campus writing center should not primarily be perceived as or operated as a computer lab.

- Writing centers should avoid operating as proofreading services; rather, they should address editing and revising through practices consistent with current writing center pedagogy.

- Writing center administrators should be tenure-stream or continuing contract salaried employees, depending on local context. It is preferable that they have faculty status with a minimum of 50% release from their teaching responsibilities per semester to oversee the writing center.

- The writing center should participate in college program review processes within its own institution.

- Those hired as writing center administrators should have a background in writing center work and/or supporting student writers outside the traditional classroom.

- Tutors within the writing center should reflect the demographic, ethnic, and disciplinary diversity of the student body to whatever extent possible.

- Although a variety of tutoring models might be appropriate given institutional context, a peer tutoring model is embraced by the International Writing Centers Association as an acceptable model for two-year college writing centers.

- Peer tutors should be selected to work in a writing center based on performance in courses that require writing and should be endorsed by instructors.

- All tutors hired to work in a writing center should be appropriately credentialed.

- Tutors should receive appropriate, comprehensive, ongoing training via methods suitable to local context (for example, a course, a practicum, or a paid training period).

- Tutor training should be based on writing center and rhetoric/composition pedagogy.

- Tutors should be compensated for their work at a rate that reflects the expertise necessary to perform their duties. This rate should be, whenever possible, higher than minimum wage for hourly work and should be based on ability, expertise, and length of service.

- Tutors should be evaluated by administrators and should receive feedback about the effectiveness of their work.

- Writing center staff should be compensated for professional development and ongoing training and expected to participate in such training whenever and however possible (for example, attendance to local, regional, and national conferences and support in submitting items for publication).

Anti-Racism Work (Appendix to Everyday Racism: Anti-Racism Work and Writing Center Practice)

Anne Ellen Geller, Michele Eodice, Frankie Condon, Meg Carroll, and Elizabeth H. Boquet

In the full chapter "Everyday Racism: Anti-Racism Work and Writing Center Practice," the authors describe scenes of systemic racism at the writing center, and argue for actions that promote racial justice. The authors address possibilities for systemic change, and also address their limitations, as white women, for claiming empathy with people of color. The appendix to the chapter provides practical resources for addressing these issues and includes definitions of racism; manifestations of racism; white antiracism work; cautionary notes about empathy, and a short list of readings. These resources are appropriate for tutor training, and for further research and action, especially in regard to identifying and taking action to undo systemic and institutionalized racism. In this regard, the appendix works well with articles in Part Three of this volume. Like this appendix, several of the articles in Part Three focus the responsibility on educators and students from majority or "mainstream" backgrounds to gain greater awareness of their own prejudices and fears of difference. Mainstream educators and students, as Geller, her colleagues, and many of the authors in Part Three emphasize, also need to educate themselves about the histories and experiences of students and faculty whose racial, linguistic, and cultural roots they do not share. Engaging in this often meticulous work holds the potential to move our world beyond mere tolerance for diversity, to a truly more inclusive and equitable society.

Anti-Racism Work

Definitions of Racism

The following definitions come from a worksheet titled "Understanding and Naming Racism" and were developed for an anti-racism training for teachers in the St. Cloud, Minnesota, school district. They are intended to give a sense of the complexity and ubiquity of modern racism, but also and more importantly perhaps, to provide language for naming those everyday experiences through which racism in individual and institutional forms circulates and reproduces.

DEFINITIONS

Racial Prejudice: Dislike, distrust, or fear of others based on perceived racial differences. Individual racial prejudice is learned and, at the early stages of anti-racist awareness, is often unconscious.

Racism: Racial prejudice in combination with community, institutional, and/or systemic power.

Institutional Racism: Visible and often invisible differential and unequal treatment of constituencies based on race. Inequalities with regard to access, power, and inclusion that are sanctioned by commission or omission by an institution.

Systemic Racism: The web of ideas, institutions, individual and collective practices that, taken together, ensure the perpetuation of social, political, and economic inequality along racial lines.

MANIFESTATIONS

Unconscious or *Unintentional Racism:* Learned and deeply internalized racism that we carry with us through our days. Some part of our work as anti-racists is interior work: becoming conscious of our prejudices and actively working to transform ourselves. For example: feeling nervous or uncomfortable when encountering an individual or group of people from another perceived racial group.

False Attribution: The tendency to explain the actions or inactions of individuals or groups from perceived races other than our own in negative terms (while excusing our own actions or inactions). For example: assuming that a child of color is struggling academically because her parents are uneducated or uncaring or conversely assuming that academic excellence among children of color is anomalous (abnormal or unusual).

Triangulation: Assuming racial prejudices are shared among whites. For example: expressing negative, derogatory or racist views to other whites and assuming that they will all agree.

Unsolicited Nominations: Expecting or asking people of color to speak, for their race.

Racialized Neglect: Providing unequal and inferior service, support, communication, and/or care to people of color. For example: calling on, praising, or offering academic enhancement opportunities to white children in a classroom with more frequency than children of color.

Racialized Gatekeeping: Actively or implicitly preventing or obstructing people of color from obtaining services, benefits, or privileges that are normally or regularly available to whites. For example: regular tracking of students of color into remedial courses or programs. Or making exceptions to regular practices or procedures for whites, but not for people of color.

Individual physical racial violence: Physical assault motivated by race.

Symbolic racial violence: Verbal assault motivated by race or racism communicated and reproduced through signs and symbols (for example: the association of black men with violence and hyper-sexuality through media representations in film, television, and print).

Group or community sanctioned violence: Physical and/or symbolic assault motivated by race and participated in or sanctioned by a group or community.

White Anti-Racism

Based on Eileen O'Brien's sociological study of white anti-racist activists, *Whites Confront Racism: Antiracists and Their Paths to Action* (Oxford: Rowman & Littlefield, 2001).

There are three main ways in which whites come to the work of anti-racism:

Activist Networks: Many whites are introduced to anti-racism through activist networks on a range of social and political issues.

Growing Empathy: Many whites come to anti-racism by developing empathy for people of color through a variety of "approximating experiences."

Turning Points: Many whites come to anti-racism through a turning point in their lives typically spawned by a dramatic or cathartic event.

Most white anti-racists will recognize some combination of the above factors that have drawn them to the movement.

O'Brien identifies three forms of "approximating experiences." These are experiences that enable whites to feel some understanding of what it must be like to experience racism as a person of color.

Overlapping Approximation: Drawing analogies between racism and some form of oppression that a white person might experience (i.e., sexism or sexual violence).

Borrowed Approximation: Witnessing racism as a close friend, lover, or family member of a person of color.

Global Approximation: Noticing contradictions between strongly held ideals or democratic principles and the fact of racism.

CAUTIONARY NOTES ABOUT EMPATHY

One of the mistakes that many white anti-racists make is to assume that empathy is enough. Several critical race scholars have noted that comparisons and analogies between racism and other forms of oppression tend to disguise the disproportionate suffering of people of color under racism.

Also, white anti-racists sometimes also make the mistake of assuming that because they feel empathy, they actually do comprehend the lived experiences of people of color and are therefore qualified to speak on their behalf.

Short List of Readings

Aptheker, Herbert. 1992. *Anti-Racism in U. S. History: The First Two Hundred Years.* Westport, CT and London: Greenwood Press.

Frankenberg, Ruth. 1993. *The Social Construction of Whiteness: White Women, Race Matters.* Minneapolis: University of Minnesota Press.

Frederickson, George M. 2002. *Racism: A Short History.* Princeton and Oxford: Princeton University Press.

Lipsitz, George. 1998. *The Possessive Investment in Whiteness: How White People Profit from Identity Politics.* Philadelphia: Temple University Press.

Omi, Michael and Howard Winant. 1994. *Racial Formation in the United States: From the 1960s to the 1990s.* New York: Routledge.

Rutstein, Nathan. 1993. *Healing Racism in America: A Prescription for the Disease.* Springfield MA: Whitcomb Publishing.

Sue, Derald Wing. 2003. *Overcoming Our Racism: The Journey to Liberation.* San Francisco: Jossey-Bass.

Thandeka. 1999. *Learning to be White: Money, Race, and God in America.* New York: Continuum.

Access, Placement, Assessment, and Retention: Models and Challenges

Assessment

George Otte and Rebecca Williams Mlynarczyk

In this excerpt from their book Basic Writing, *George Otte and Rebecca Williams Mlynarczyk take on the vexed history of assessment of students in basic writing, from the 1970s to the first decade of the twenty-first century. These years coincide with the early days of open admissions at City University of New York (CUNY), through the demise of basic writing course offerings at CUNY's senior college campuses. Along the way, Otte and Williams Mlynarczyk present the highlights of basic writing assessment research, from Ed White's "Mass Testing of Individual Writing: The California Model" (1978), to Marilyn Sternglass's* Time to Know Them: A Longitudinal Study of Writing at the College Level *(1997), to George Hillocks Jr.'s study of high school assessment,* The Testing Trap: How State Writing Assessments Control Learning *(2002). Otte and Mlynarczyk offer the sobering assertion that basic writing assessment is subject to the changes and whims of an ever-shifting political climate. "Then these vast, carefully calibrated assessments," they write, "would come to seem narrow gates made by the narrow-minded, determined to preserve their positions of privilege" (p. 429).*

Assessment

A s attention to error waned, attention to assessment waxed, ultimately building to a kind of hue and cry in the 1990s. But assessment was always an especially problematic research problem, and the 1970s is the place to start to understand why. Part of the problem from the first seemed to be the lack of a solid research base. In 1978, the *Journal of Basic Writing* devoted an entire issue to evaluation. It concluded with a selected and annotated bibliography by Richard Larson, who found quite a bit of advice on responding to student writing but only two works worth including that bore on "decisions made about where to place student papers, and students, on scales that permit assigning the student to a particular class" (92). These were Paul Diederich's *Measuring Growth in English* and Richard Braddock's "Evaluation of Writing Tests." Larson reminded readers of what was at stake, saying that he hoped his bibliography would help teachers and "may fortify them against capricious efforts to adopt judgmental techniques that have not themselves been fully investigated and evaluated" (93). It was the fitting endpiece to a collection that was bracing in its frankness about what was lacking in the knowledge of assessments and the application of that knowledge.

The first two pieces in the issue set the tone. Rexford Brown, the director of publications for the National Assessment of Educational Progress, held that the tests in use were clearly inadequate and uninformative: "Like holistic essay scoring, multiple choice testing of writing is seldom diagnostic in any useful way" (3). Brown did hold out hope of improvement (even if it had a "nowhere to go but up" flavor), but Joseph Williams took a bleaker view. Ascribing a general "inability to find simple and reliable measures" to "some questions that I don't think we have attended to as carefully as we might have," he quickly added, "I wish I could say that I think the questions will help simplify this matter of evaluation, but in fact their answers, such as they are, seem to complicate it" ("Re-Evaluating" 8). Ultimately, according to Williams, the real issue is not even the ability to devise a viable system of assessment. It's who is doing the assessing. He tried to imagine a system that would be consistent, reliable, and objective—one that would "rationalize and defend admissions procedures," even result in "the adoption of better teaching methods":

> But it is not at all clear that such a system would be more than a self-justifying instrument that had taken its values and hence its measures from those who have not demonstrated any special competence in distinguishing competent writing in any world except their—our—own. That is a harsh charge to make against a whole profession and by no means includes every member in it. But I think it is essentially true. (8)

To a remarkable extent, Williams effectively articulated the problems that would, over the next decades, damage and defeat assessment programs that fed and shaped basic writing. For all their attention to matters of validity and reliability, all that was needed to render them invalid was a shift in political climate, one that raised the "right to judge" issue. Then these vast, carefully calibrated assessments would come to seem narrow gates made by the narrow-minded, determined to preserve their positions of privilege.

Foundational Work in Mass Testing

Though such suspicions were always in the air, not least of all in the 1970s, there was, at that time, a much greater, more pervasive sense of urgency about all the work to be done—and with it the hope that this work would vanquish the problems besetting the workers in the field. Looked at from another perspective, the problem raised by Williams was a kind of opportunity; English professors were invited to determine the values and measures that would distinguish writing competence. No one seized the opportunity like Edward M. White, Director of the English Equivalency Examination and Coordinator of English Testing Programs for California State Universities and Colleges (CSUC). White was the architect of the largest assessment program to date, and his contribution to the 1978 "Evaluation" issue of *JBW*, "Mass Testing of Individual Writing: The California Model," laid the groundwork for much organized assessment thereafter. The CSUC English Equivalency Examination, as its name would suggest, was originally designed to determine which students could skip college instruction, earning credit in composition simply by scoring high enough on the equivalency exam. But the scales were also designed to register, in addition to proficiency, minimal competency (and even performances below that). A happy marriage of carefully designed prompts that students could choose from and normative scales of performance that readers could refer to and apply holistically, the CSUC Equivalency Examination made evaluation, not least of all the "mass testing" of White's title, seem sufficiently fair and doable.

White's own work on assessment was invaluable in California and beyond. He was an indefatigable writer and researcher, with a special gift for practical synthesis, and he was there with a ready answer to the burning question. As Richard Lloyd-Jones emphatically put it in his bibliographic essay "Tests of Writing Ability" (1987), "The question is not whether to test but what kind to use" (159). Lloyd-Jones was no less emphatic about where to look for the answer; he said of White's *Teaching and Assessing Writing* (1985), "For most readers his book makes earlier works unnecessary except for historical reasons . . ." (160).

A variant on the CSUC English Equivalency Examination with its choice of prompts and six-point holistic scale was the CUNY Writing Assessment Test, and the CUNY Instructional Resource Center (IRC) would publish a series of monographs on testing. Some of the researchers from the IRC (notably Karen Greenberg, Harvey Wiener, and Virginia Slaughter) would create the National Testing Network in Writing (NTNW) to disseminate research and best practices. The Network's first two conferences, in 1983 and 1984, resulted in an important collection, *Writing Assessment: Issues and Strategies* (Greenberg, Wiener, and Donovan).

Assessment had clearly given rise to a rich discussion, but its main points were fairly clear and straightforward; the way to assess writing was through actual writing samples, scored holistically (hence White's 1984 manifesto "Holisticism"). The foe was what Rexford Brown had identified as the inexpensive but suspect way: multiple-choice, machine-scored tests that are "cheaper and easier to score" but have "glaring weaknesses" ("What We Know" 3). By the mid-1980s, the need to base assessment on actual student writing had become a kind of orthodoxy. As expressed in the preface to *Writing Assessment: Issues and Strategies*, "Multiple-choice tests cannot measure the skills that most writing teachers identify as the domain of composition: inventing, revising, and editing ideas to fit purpose and audience within the context of suitable linguistic, syntactic, and grammatical forms" (xiv).

In 1987, Lloyd-Jones could say that holistically scored testing was "now the system most used for mass testing" (165). A part that might stand for the whole is the story Harvey Wiener recounts in "Evaluating Assessment Programs in Basic Skills" (1989). In 1983, he and other CUNY colleagues had conducted a national survey of assessment in 1,200 institutions of higher education, discovering that 97% of them did assess entering students. But a subsequent survey done under the auspices of the National Testing Network in Writing showed that, beyond that basic reality, generalizations were difficult to come by. A variety of assessments, many of them homegrown, were used with little regard for reliability or validity. In consequence, Wiener and his colleagues created the College Assessment Evaluation Program to facilitate effective assessment design and evaluation. Without declaring the problem solved, Wiener's story was a clear account of progress toward clearly seen goals.

Disillusionment with Holistic Assessment

For some time, however, the clarity about assessment had been illusory, persisting for so long because of enormous intellectual and institutional investment. The real research basis for holistic writing assessment, largely unexamined and simply adopted, stretched back decades. Even before Paul Diederich published the 1974 manual, *Measuring Growth in English*, he had done research on assessment for the College Entrance Examination Board, work distilled in a 1961 research bulletin coauthored with John French and Sydell Carlton, *Factors in Judgments of Writing Ability*. It was this work that led Martin Nystrand,

Stuart Greene, and Jeffrey Wiemelt to declare Diederich "the father of holistic essay evaluation" and to say his real coup was to decide to give all factors, from spelling to ideas, equal weight:

> This proposal was in effect a psychometric fiat; no validity studies were undertaken to determine appropriate weights. In 1961, then, Diederich could plausibly argue—and in so doing shape an entire generation of writing assessment—that writing could be effectively, reliably assessed by reading one sample on one topic in one genre per writer if—*mirabile dictu*—readers could only be made to agree. (276)

This is not the indictment of arbitrary judgment it might seem; on the contrary, Nystrand and his coauthors, in their "intellectual history" of composition, are stressing what the climate of the times could support—and very nearly dictate. Their point is that the same formalism that gave rise to New Criticism in literary studies supported this insistence on the stable, univocal text in assessment. Like New Criticism, assessment needed to insist on careful reading—without interference by interpretive questioning, worries about authorial intention, and contextual considerations. But this attempt to approach objectivity and stability in assessment was in fact the highly unstable product of its time. Literary studies, pushed by the need to find "original" readings of texts, broke from formalistic approaches much earlier. Assessment, whose twin lighthouses were reliability and validity, took longer to unravel its belief in the univocal text. But it really only took a few voices saying, so others could hear, that the emperor had no clothes.

One such voice came from Pat Belanoff, who labeled all the past certainties "The Myths of Assessment" in a 1991 *JBW* article by that name. According to Belanoff, assessment lacked a clear purpose and focus as well as a clear consensus and basis. Here's how she put the "four myths":

1. We know what we're testing for

2. We know what we're testing

3. Once we've agreed on criteria, we can agree on whether individual papers meet those criteria

4. And the strongest myth of all, that it's possible to have an absolute standard and apply it uniformly (55)

Pointedly recast, these were in fact the fundamental premises under which the great assessment enterprise had been operating.

Belanoff was not articulating a sudden and general change of heart (or mind), of course. This was also not a matter of postmodernism finally knocking on BW's door. There had been some rethinking even and especially within the assessment community. By coincidence, the lead piece for the same issue of *JBW* was the published version of the keynote for the 1989 National Testing Network in Writing conference. The speaker/author was Rexford Brown, the erstwhile director of publications for the National Assessment of Educational Progress who had led off the evaluation-themed issue of *JBW* in 1978. Now the director of communications for the Education Commission of the States, Brown had a different (though by no means uncritical) take on assessment. Perhaps thinking of the landscape he had surveyed over a decade earlier, he saw much accomplished: "You certainly see more and more people using writing samples, whether they score them holistically or analytically or through primary trait or error analysis" (11). But for Brown the use of writing samples was no longer the assessment grail. The big challenge, as he saw it now, was how to teach and test for something much more elusive than formal traits, something he was calling "thoughtfulness," which would become better known as critical thinking ("Schooling and Thoughtfulness" 3–15).

The changing views on assessment reflected more than just a change in the intellectual climate. The job of assessment research in the 1970s and 1980s had been to address an urgent need, to tell BW instructors and programs how to sort and place students. If anything, the job had been done too well. The burning need had been answered with what was feeling more and more like a calcifying imposition. Teachers for too long had felt that assessments were imposed on them, circumventing their own judgments (particularly when those assessments governed exit as well as placement). The blame could be (and was) placed on specific assessments, but in another sense no assessment could be good enough. The research question dosed for much of the 1980s—not how to assess but whether to assess at all, at least in externally imposed and institutionalized ways—was once again opened.

Not How to Test, But Whether

For researchers, the empirical basis for questioning the vast (if various) assessment industry was to be through one of that industry's tenets: accountability. If assessments were necessary for placement and BW programs were salutary, could those salutary effects be documented?

The 1990s, and particularly the fourth National Conference on Basic Writing in 1992, offered a negative answer. Suddenly the thought-leaders in the field like David Bartholomae were asking if BW placement ought to exist at all. There were even anecdotal accounts, like Peter Dow Adams's, that being placed in BW courses did more harm than good ("Basic Writing Reconsidered"). Assessment research in BW had to turn from the means to the ends, had to make a case for assessment. Edward White's "The Importance of Placement and Basic Studies: Helping Students Succeed Under the New Elitism" (1995) defended assessment by arguing that the attacks gave support to the "new elitists" on the right who saw remediation as beneath the task of higher education and an unwarranted drain on university budgets. "Nonetheless," White reasoned, "if faculty and administrators could be persuaded that the required course and placement testing do in fact help underprivileged students succeed, they would be less likely to join those seeking to limit opportunity for them" (78). To that end, White presented data from two statewide systems, and then, in his conclusion, conveyed his hope—but also his sense of the powerful forces aligned against it:

> Those of us concerned about preserving the hard-won higher education opportunities for the new students may not be able to stem the elitist tide, at least not immediately. But we can present the data and the arguments for basic writing programs and force those opposing them to confront the social biases they are endorsing. The argument that our programs do not work is baseless, as the California and New Jersey data show; given adequate support, we can help most low-scoring students succeed. (83)

Other, smaller scale studies, such as William Sweigart's account of pre- and post-testing (1996), showed in a more localized setting what White's review of whole state systems revealed: that, by and large (and in statistically significant ways), BW placement and instruction seemed to work. But BW placement was also being reworked with important consequences.

Alternatives to Established Assessments

Beginning in the 1990s, assessment research itself was reorganizing, becoming less unidirectional and univocal. Pat Belanoff of SUNY Stony Brook advocated portfolios. Eric Miraglia of Washington State proposed self-assessment. And Daniel Royer and Roger Gilles of Grand Valley State University favored self-directed placement (an idea that caught on widely enough to result in their edited collection titled *Directed Self-Placement: Principles and Practices* [2002]). Particularly important were mainstreaming experiments like those of Rhonda Grego and Nancy Thompson of the University of South Carolina and Mary Soliday and Barbara Gleason of CUNY's City College, since these helped to surface multifaceted longitudinal assessments, information-rich alternatives to the snapshot placements like the timed impromptu writing test. At about the same time, the 1993 CCCC Position Statement on Writing Assessment effectively indicted widespread practices like the timed writing sample without mandating specific alternatives. Research was opening new avenues that focused on tying assessment to the curriculum it potentially drove.

Not surprisingly, representatives of the established methods responded to the changing climate for research on assessment. In his "Apologia for the Timed Impromptu Essay Test," White argued that the lately maligned test was not only preferable to multiple-choice assessments but also more efficient and reliable than alternative forms like portfolio assessment. But the discourse had changed. White's arguments were about economy, efficiency, and efficacy. There was something utilitarian about his take—a kind of "greatest good for the greatest number" argument that worked best in large institutions that never could assess each student's individual situation. The case studies approach used by such scholars as Barbara Gleason in "When the Writing Test Fails: Assessing Assessment at an Urban College" (1997) or Deborah Mutnick in *Writing in an Alien World* (1996) functioned on a different principle—the belief that if assessments failed a single student unfairly, then that was one student too many—and the cost, at least for that student, was too great.

For the new research vanguard, there would also be ironic upsets. The mainstreaming experiment of Soliday and Gleason at CUNY's City College, the focus of so much attention for so long, is an illustrative example. A three-year, grant-funded project initiated in 1993, it established that BW students (or rather students who would ordinarily have had BW placement) could function and even flourish in "enriched" versions of regular writing courses (whose other students would also benefit from this enrichment). As documented in "From Remediation to Enrichment: Evaluating a Mainstreaming Project" (1997), the project used an impressive array of assessment tools: traditional assessments (as a kind of baseline), student self-assessments, cross-read portfolios, even a cadre of outside readers/consultants. But meeting its own goals was not enough to ensure the project's success. The students it was designed to serve were being denied access to City College by the time the project had run its course. In "Evaluating Writing Programs in Real Time: The Politics of Remediation" (2000), written as a retrospective and even a postmortem of the project in which she and Mary Soliday had invested so much, Barbara Gleason concluded, "The empirically verifiable account that we were striving for in this evaluation was fatally compromised by the socio-political forces that had gathered around the issue of remediation" (582). In *The Politics of Remediation* (2002), Soliday would add, "Empirical accounts remain central to arguing for the worth of programs, but evaluation is a political enterprise in many respects, which is merely to say that alone, data won't do the job of ideological justification" (142).

But Soliday would not stop there. Empirical accounts may not be enough, but she stressed that accounts focusing on case studies of individual students may have their own fatal flaw. If they show what often eludes the "big picture" perspective, then they can also elide the "big picture" itself. This is true whether the goal is to argue for reform in approaches to BW or to argue that attempts at remediation are doomed enterprises and wastes of money. It really does not matter if a critic of remediation is arguing that remediation is unfair or suggesting that it is impossible. The problem with focusing on BW students as special (and especially needy) cases is, as Soliday sees it, that they come to seem unusual and their problems intractable when the real issue is for institutions to ensure that such students are adequately supported: "By invoking the discourse of student need, critics of remediation often focus on students' agency, eluding or downplaying the roles that institutions do or could play in enhancing students' educational progress" (*Politics* 138).

With the help of hindsight, Soliday sees that it is the political context that matters most even and especially when it comes to matters of assessment and placement. More than this, she sees that both sides were focusing on student success or failure without taking the institutional context sufficiently into account. Yet as events unfolded, even that broader context proved too narrow a focus. By the time Soliday's book was published, students with remedial placement were no longer admitted to City College, her institution, and the assessment that determined their placement was no longer made by the CUNY WAT. The real assessment revolution had happened outside the academy altogether.

High Schools as Gatekeepers

From the early days of open admissions, basic writing students had been labeled as "underprepared" for college. But in the 1990s there was a growing conviction on the part of policy makers that students who were leaving high school without being ready for college simply shouldn't get a high school diploma. In 1998, the National Governors Association published, on the NGA website, an "Issues Brief" titled "High School Exit Exams: Setting High Expectations" (Otte, "High Schools as Crucibles" 109). That "Issues Brief" is no longer available, partly because this is no longer policy proposed but policy implemented. According to *State High School Exit Exams: A Challenging Year*,

> In 2006, 65% of the nation's public high school students and 76% of the nation's minority public high school students were enrolled in school in the 22 states with current exit exams. By 2012, an estimated 71% of public high school students and 81% of minority public high school students will be enrolled in school in the 25 states that expect to have exit exams in place. (Kober et al. 10)

As a consequence, BW students are disappearing from higher education because they are not completing secondary education. In *Time to Know Them: A Longitudinal Study of Writing and Learning at the College Level*, Marilyn Sternglass managed to combine statistics with case studies to show that BW students could succeed if given time — something she could show only by tracking them over longer periods and with more in-depth attention than ever before. Yet even as *Time to Know Them* received the Mina P. Shaughnessy Award of the Modern Language Association in 1998 and the Outstanding Book Award of the Conference on College Composition and Communication in 1999,

Sternglass's college and the focus of her study, City College of the City University of New York, was phasing out basic writing—or, more specifically, the students who would have taken it.

At this point, the most important work on assessment of BW students is quite possibly not about college assessments at all. *The Testing Trap: How State Writing Assessments Control Learning* (2002) by George Hillocks, Jr., is about the assessments going on in the high schools, where graduation is increasingly determined by state-mandated testing. Hillocks is careful and balanced in his conclusions and finds some practices much more estimable than others, but the overall picture he paints is effectively summed up by his title. However wise or unwise the states are in test design and administration, state-mandated assessments—created a world away and shaped by policy, expediency, and political decisions—now effectively control which students will eventually be admitted to college. The assessment and placement of BW students have never been further removed from those who design and teach in BW programs.

Thomas Hilgers, making a brief for the 1993 CCCC Position Statement on Assessment, wrote, "It is my belief that bad assessment is what gets most students labeled as 'basic writers'" (69). Many in the field agreed, and their research certainly challenged the assessments as well as the BW label. The students so labeled, however, may be a vanishing species now that state-mandated assessments at the pre-college level have become more like a wall than a gate.

Works Cited

Adams, Peter Dow. "Basic Writing Reconsidered." *Journal of Basic Writing* 12.1 (1993): 22–35. Print.

Belanoff, Pat. "The Myths of Assessment." *Journal of Basic Writing* 10.1 (1991): 54–66. Print.

Belanoff, Pat, and Peter Elbow. "Using Portfolios to Increase Collaboration and Communication in a Writing Program." *WPA: Writing Program Administration* 9.3 (1986): 27–40. Print.

Belanoff, Pat, and Marcia Dickson, eds. *Portfolios: Process and Product.* Portsmouth: Heinemann-Boynton/Cook, 1991. Print.

Brown, Rexford G. "Schooling and Thoughtfulness." *Journal of Basic Writing* 10.1 (1991): 3–15. Print.

———. "What We Know Now and How We Could Know More about Writing Ability in America." *Journal of Basic Writing* 1.4 (1978): 1–6. Print.

Conference on College Composition and Communication. "Writing Assessment: A Position Statement." 2006 (revised 2009). Web. 10 Feb. 2010.

Gleason, Barbara. "Evaluating Writing Programs in Real Time: The Politics of Remediation." *College Composition and Communication* 51.4 (2000): 560–88. Print.

———. "When the Writing Test Fails: Assessing Assessment at an Urban College." *Writing in Multicultural Settings.* Ed. Carol Severino, Juan C. Guerra, and Johnnella E. Butler. New York: MLA, 1997. 307–23. Print.

Greenberg, Karen L., Harvey S. Wiener, and Richard A. Donovan, eds. *Writing Assessment: Issues and Strategies*. New York: Longman, 1986. Print.

Grego, Rhonda, and Nancy Thompson. "Repositioning Remediation: Renegotiating Composition's Work in the Academy." *College Composition and Communication* 47.1 (1996): 62–84. Print.

Hilgers, Thomas. "Basic Writing Curricula and Good Assessment Practices." *Journal of Basic Writing* 14.2 (1995): 68–74. Print.

Hillocks, George, Jr. *The Testing Trap: How State Writing Assessments Control Learning*. New York: Teachers College P, 2002. Print.

Kober, Nancy, Dalia Zabala, Naomi Chudowsky, Victor Chudowsky, Keith Gayler, and Jennifer McMurrer. *State High School Exit Exams: A Challenging Year*. Washington, DC: Center on Education Policy, 2006. Web. 12 Feb. 2010.

Larson, Richard L. "Selected Bibliography of Writings on the Evaluation of Students' Achievements in Composition." *Journal of Basic Writing* 1.4 (1978): 91–100. Print.

Lloyd-Jones, Richard. "Tests of Writing Ability." *Teaching Composition: 12 Bibliographic Essays*. Ed. Gary Tate. Fort Worth: Texas Christian UP, 1987. 155–76. Print.

Mutnick, Deborah. *Writing in an Alien World: Basic Writing and the Struggle for Equality in Higher Education*. Portsmouth: Boynton/Cook, 1996. Print.

Miraglia, Eric. "A Self-Diagnostic Assessment in the Basic Writing Course." *Journal of Basic Writing* 14.2 (1995): 48–67. Print.

Nystrand, Martin, Stuart Greene, and Jeffrey Wiemelt. "Where Did Composition Studies Come From?" *Written Communication* 10.3 (1993): 267–333.

Otte, George. "High Schools as Crucibles of College Prep: What More Do We Need to Know?" *Journal of Basic Writing* 21.2 (2002): 106–20. Print.

Royer, Daniel J., and Roger Gilles. *Directed Self-Placement: Principles and Practices*. Cresskill: Hampton, 2002. Print.

Soliday, Mary. *The Politics of Remediation: Institutional and Student Needs in Higher Education*. Pittsburgh: U of Pittsburgh P, 2002. Print.

Soliday, Mary, and Barbara Gleason. "From Remediation to Enrichment: Evaluating a Mainstreaming Project." *Journal of Basic Writing* 16.1 (1997): 64–78. Print.

Sternglass, Marilyn S. *Time to Know Them: A Longitudinal Study of Writing and Learning at the College Level*. Mahwah: Erlbaum, 1997. Print.

Sweigart, William. "Assessing Achievement in a Developmental Writing Sequence." *Research and Teaching in Developmental Education* 12.2 (1996): 5–15. Print.

White, Edward M. "An Apologia for the Timed Impromptu Essay Test." *College Composition and Communication* 46.1 (1995): 30–45. Print.

———. "Holisticism." *College Composition and Communication* 35.4 (1984): 400–09. Print.

———. "The Importance of Placement and Basic Studies: Helping Students Succeed Under the New Elitism." *Journal of Basic Writing* 14.2 (1995): 75–84. Print.

———. "Mass Testing of Individual Writing: The California Model." *Journal of Basic Writing* 1.4 (1978): 18–38. Print.

Wiener, Harvey S. "Evaluating Assessment Programs in Basic Skills." *Journal of Developmental Education* 13.2 (1989): 24–26. Print.

Williams, Joseph. "Re-Evaluating Evaluation." *Journal of Basic Writing* 1.4 (1978): 7–17. Print.

The Accelerated Learning Program: Throwing Open the Gates

Peter Adams, Sarah Gearhart, Robert Miller, and Anne Roberts

Peter Adams, Sarah Gearhart, Robert Miller, and Anne Roberts discuss the creation of the Accelerated Learning Program (ALP) at the Community College of Baltimore County (CCBC). The program evolved from increasing concerns about attrition rates for students who did not complete either the basic writing or college composition sequences at CCBC. * *Because Adams believed that the lack of college credit for basic writing courses could be demoralizing, he worked with others at his institution to develop an accelerated model that would blend a limited number of students who tested into basic writing with students in the first course of the first-year composition sequence. Students who test into first-year composition serve as role models of good writing and behavior for those students who test into basic writing. The students in basic writing must take an additional noncredit, three-hour course as part of the ALP in order to enhance their performance in first-year composition. Follow-up studies are in progress to determine the reasons why the ALP course has successful retention rates for students in basic writing.*

Historical Context

I n 2001, Mary Soliday, then at CUNY's City College, observed that in the early days of open admissions at the City University of New York, two groups favored basic writing courses for quite different reasons. The first group saw such courses as paths to success, courses that would help students who were weak in writing to conform to the conventions of the academy. The second group supported basic writing for quite a different reason, seeing it as a gate to keep unqualified students out of college-level courses and, thereby, maintain standards in those courses ("Ideologies" 57–58). Bruce Horner and Min-Zhan Lu have referred to these odd bedfellows as "the binary of political activism and academic excellence" (*Representing* 14).

---

*The Gates Foundation and other stakeholders determine student success rates by measuring the amount of time a student takes from first enrollment as a first-year student to graduation. A four-to-six-year graduation rate, beginning and ending at the same postsecondary institution has been identified as "success." However, one recent study examines persistence across institutions (rather than at a single institution), and has suggested that the college dropout rate may not be as high as some stakeholders speculate. For more information, see Afet Dadashova, Don Hossler, and Doug Shapiro et al.'s *The Signature Report: National Postsecondary Enrollment Trends before, during, and after the Great Recession.* (Bloomington: Project on Academic Success, 2011). You can also visit the *National Student Clearinghouse Research Center* for more information: <http://research.studentclearinghouse.org>.

In the 1990s, at what was then Essex Community College and is now the Community College of Baltimore County (CCBC), Peter Adams, then coordinator of the writing program, worried about the program. He recognized that an effective basic writing program might serve as a gate for students until they were ready to succeed in first-year composition and a path to college success as soon as they were ready. But he wanted to make sure that these developmental courses were more path than gate, leading students to success rather than barring them from it.

In Adams's first attempt to evaluate the program, he used data he had been compiling on an Apple IIe computer for four years. He had entered the placement results and grades in every writing course for students assessed since Fall of 1988. Using the 863 students who took the upper-level developmental writing course, ENGL 052, in academic year 1988–1989 as the cohort he would study, Adams calculated the pass rate for ENGL 052 as well as the pass rate for students who passed that course and took first-year composition (ENGL 101) within four years. Charts 1 and 2 display these data.

The pass rate of 57% in the developmental course didn't look too bad, and the whopping 81% pass rate in ENGL 101 was even higher than the rate for students placed directly into the college-level course. At first glance, it appeared that our basic writing course was doing a good job. In fact, developmental programs in writing, reading, and math have often pointed to such data as evidence that traditional approaches are working. As reassuring as these data looked, however, Adams worried that somehow they didn't tell the whole story, and when he undertook a more detailed, longitudinal study, he learned that his worry was justified.

Chart 1. Success Rates for Students Who Took ENGL 052 in 1988–1989

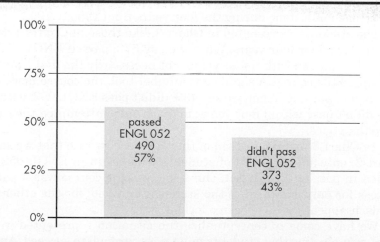

Chart 2. Success Rates for Students Who Took ENGL 101 after Passing ENGL 052 in 1988–1989

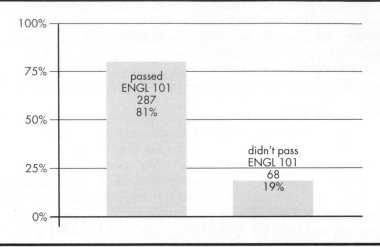

Looking at success rates for one course at a time masks the true picture. When Adams looked at the longitudinal experience of students who attempted ENGL 052 and ENGL 101, he discovered an alarming situation. Two-thirds of the students who attempted ENGL 052 never passed ENGL 101. The problem was not that basic writers were attempting first-year composition and failing; the problem was that they were giving up before they ever reached that course, a fact hidden when he had simply looked at the pass rates for the small number of students who did make it into regular composition.

Chart 3 presents the number and percentage of students who passed each milestone during the four years from 1988 to 1992.

The students represented in Chart 3, like those in Charts 1 and 2, were followed for four years. When we say 57% passed ENGL 052, we mean they passed within four years, not necessarily the first time they attempted the course. A significant number took the course more than once before passing. When we say 43% didn't pass ENGL 052, we mean they didn't pass within four years; many of them attempted the course more than once.

As Chart 3 reveals, instead of the 81% success rate that we saw in Chart 2, only about a third of students who began in ENGL 052 succeeded in passing ENGL 101. Our basic writing course was a path to success for only one-third of the students enrolled; for the other two-thirds, it appears to have been a locked gate.

We have come to conceptualize the situation represented in this chart as a pipeline that students must pass through to succeed. And we

Chart 3. Longitudinal Data on Students Who Took ENGL 052 in 1988–1989

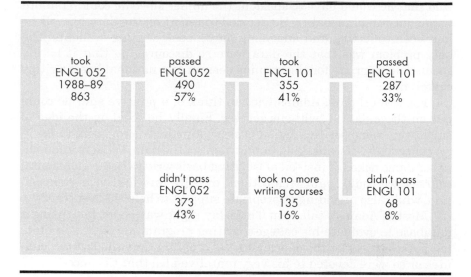

took ENGL 052 1988–89 863	passed ENGL 052 490 57%	took ENGL 101 355 41%	passed ENGL 101 287 33%
	didn't pass ENGL 052 373 43%	took no more writing courses 135 16%	didn't pass ENGL 101 68 8%

have concluded that the longer the pipeline, the more likely there will be "leakage" from it—in other words, the more likely students will drop out before passing first-year composition. Because the database we compiled in the early 1990s included data only for writing courses, we had no way of knowing whether these students dropped out of the college altogether, but we did know when they stopped taking writing courses. Further, since they could not achieve any degree or certificate at the college without passing ENGL 101, we knew that they didn't achieve any credential. Although our original intention in collecting these statistics was to help us enforce our placement system, we soon learned that it also helped us evaluate our writing program by allowing us to calculate the percentage of students who succeeded in passing each milestone in the program.

Then, in Fall of 1992, it became useful in another way. At that time, Peter Adams was chairing the Conference on Basic Writing (CBW), which led to his organizing the fourth national conference on basic writing, to be held at the University of Maryland in October of 1992. Things were moving along smoothly; David Bartholomae had agreed to give the keynote address, registrations were rolling in, and it looked like our carefully crafted budget was going to be adequate. And then, several weeks before the conference, Adams realized that he had a serious problem. Although the conference officially began on Friday morning, the organizers had planned an optional dinner on Thursday evening for those who arrived early . . . and more than a hundred people had signed up for that dinner. But we had not arranged nor budgeted for a dinner speaker.

Having already committed every cent in the budget, Adams realized that he would have to speak at the dinner since he couldn't afford to pay an outside speaker. He decided to report on the data his college had been collecting and analyzing on its basic writing students. The only problem was that the data were so discouraging that it hardly seemed appropriate for the opening session at a national basic writing conference.

For several days, Adams tried to think of a positive spin he could put on these data ... without success. Finally, he fixed on the idea of suggesting some positive action basic writing instructors could take in response to the discouraging implications of the data. What would happen, Adams asked, if instead of isolating basic writers in developmental courses, we could mainstream them directly into first-year composition, while also providing appropriate support to help them succeed?

Most of Adams's talk that Thursday night was about how using a database to evaluate his college's writing program had revealed quite low success rates for the developmental program; only the last ten minutes or so were devoted to his very tentative idea that the success rate for basic writers might improve if they were "mainstreamed" into first-year composition. The lengthy and heated discussion that followed this talk was completely focused on the "mainstreaming" idea. Finally, with most of the audience still suffering from jet lag, the conference participants more or less agreed to disagree, and adjourned for the evening.

Adams knew the title of David Bartholomae's keynote address scheduled for the next morning, "The Tidy House: Basic Writing in the American Curriculum," but he had no idea what Bartholomae was actually going to talk about. As he sat in the audience listening, an odd feeling crept over him. He heard Bartholomae suggest that

> ... in the name of sympathy and empowerment, we have once again produced the "other" who is the incomplete version of ourselves, confirming existing patterns of power and authority, reproducing the hierarchies we had meant to question and overthrow, way back then in the 1970s. ("Tidy House" 18)

David Bartholomae, starting from a very different place, was arriving at a conclusion similar to the one suggested by Adams the evening before. At that point, Bartholomae and Adams were probably the only two people in the room who didn't think this coincidence had been carefully planned. The fact that articles representing their two talks ended up next to each other in the Spring 1993 issue of the *Journal of Basic Writing* (Bartholomae, "Tidy House"; Adams, "Basic Writing Reconsidered") only heightened everyone's assumption that they had conspired to question the essential nature of basic writing at a conference on basic writing. They hadn't, as they both insist to this day, despite the fact that few have ever believed them.

In the years since that 1992 conference, a number of institutions have adopted various versions of the mainstreaming approach that was suggested at the conference. Arizona State University, with leadership from Greg Glau, developed the well-known "stretch" model, which allows developmental students to be mainstreamed directly into first-year composition, but into a version that is "stretched out" over two semesters ("*Stretch* at 10"). Quinnipiac University pioneered the "intensive" model, which has basic writers take a version of first-year composition that meets five hours a week instead of three (Segall 38–47). A few years later, Rhonda Grego and Nancy Thompson devised the "studio" approach at the University of South Carolina. In this model, students in first-year composition and sometimes other writing courses can also sign up for a one-hour-per-week studio section. There they meet with students from other classes to talk about "essays in progress" (6–14).

Many other schools developed variations on these approaches in the late 1990s and early 2000s. Our college was not one of these. Instead we endured a turbulent dozen or so years as three independent colleges were merged into one mega-college: the Community College of Baltimore County. In the process, fierce battles were fought, one chancellor received a vote of no confidence, tenure was abolished, and many faculty members devoted much of their energy to "aligning" the programs, courses, and policies of the three schools that had merged. By 2005, the worst of these struggles were over, and faculty were ready to return to more productive work. In the Fall of 2006, the English Department of the newly merged Community College of Baltimore County turned to the question of the low success rates in our basic writing courses.

In the meantime, many others were noticing the very low success rates for developmental programs nationwide. In a national study, Tom Bailey of the Community College Research Center at Columbia University, found similarly alarming leakage in all developmental courses, including reading and math:

> How many students complete the sequences of developmental courses to which they are referred? The first conclusion to note is that many simply never enroll in developmental classes in the first place. In the Achieving the Dream sample, 21 percent of all students referred to developmental math education and 33 percent of students referred to developmental reading do not enroll in any developmental course within three years.
>
> Of those students referred to remediation, how many actually complete their full developmental sequences? Within three years of their initial assessment, about 42 percent of those referred to developmental reading in the Achieving the Dream sample complete their full sequence, but this accounts for two-thirds of those who actually *enroll* in at least one developmental reading course. These numbers are worse for math — only 31 percent of those referred to developmental math complete their sequence. (4-5)

In "Outcomes of Remediation," Hunter Boylan and Patrick Saxon have observed that "[a]n unknown number but perhaps as many as 40% of those taking remedial courses do not complete the courses, and consequently, do not complete remediation within one year." Reviewing large-scale studies from Minnesota, Maryland, and Texas, Boylan and Saxon conclude that "[t]he results of all these studies were fairly consistent. In summary, about 80% of those who completed remediation with a C or better passed their first college-level course in English or mathematics." Just as we at Essex Community College discovered when we began to look at longitudinal data, success rates for individual courses conceal a serious problem, for "[i]t should be noted . . . that not all of those who pass remedial courses actually took college-level courses in comparable subject areas. An Illinois study, for instance, reported that only 64% of those who completed remedial English and reading in the Fall of 1996 actually completed their first college-level courses in those subjects within a year."

So the problem we had discovered on the local level in 1992 appears to mirror similar problems nationally: too many students simply leak out of the pipeline of the required writing sequence.

Development of the Accelerated Learning Program

At an English Department meeting in January of 2007, several CCBC faculty members proposed that we pilot some form of mainstreaming to see if we could improve the success rates of our basic writing students. After considering several different models, we settled on what we now call the Accelerated Learning Program (ALP) as having the greatest potential. While we were not among the pioneering schools that developed mainstreaming approaches in the 1990s, we have benefited greatly from those programs. ALP has borrowed the best features of existing mainstreaming approaches, added some features from studios and learning communities, and developed several new features of our own.

Of course, the program we eventually developed reflected the realities of our existing approach to teaching writing. The writing sequence at CCBC includes two levels of basic writing and two levels of college composition. To graduate, students must pass any required basic writing courses and then pass two semesters of college composition, both of which are writing courses. Only the higher-level college composition course satisfies the composition graduation requirement when students transfer to most four-year schools.

Here's how ALP works. The program is available, on a voluntary basis, to all students whose placement indicates they need our upper-level basic writing course. Placement is determined at CCBC by the Accuplacer exam. Students may retest once and may also appeal by a writing sample. In addition, all sections of writing courses require students to write a diagnostic essay the first week of classes; when this essay indicates students should be in a different level course, they are advised, but not required, to move to that course.

A developmental student who volunteers for ALP registers directly for a designated section of ENGL 101, where he or she joins seven other developmental students and twelve students whose placement is ENGL 101. Apart from the inclusion of the eight ALP students, this is a regular, three-credit section of ENGL 101, meeting three hours a week for one semester. We think the fact that the basic writers are in a class with twelve students who are stronger writers, and perhaps more accomplished students, is an important feature of ALP because these 101-level students frequently serve as role models for the basic writers.

Equally important, we avoid the sometimes stigmatizing and often demoralizing effects of segregating basic writers into sections designated as just for them by fully integrating them into a college-level course and then providing additional support in the form of a second course. The eight developmental students in every ALP section of ENGL 101 also take what we call a companion course with the same instructor who teaches them in ENGL 101. In Maryland, state regulations bar the awarding of credit toward graduation for "remedial" courses; since this companion course is currently conceived of as a basic writing course (remedial, by the state's terminology), students may not receive credit for it. The companion course meets for three hours a week for one semester. In this class, which meets immediately after the 101 section, the instructor provides additional support to help the students succeed in composition. The class may begin with questions that arose in the earlier class. Other typical activities include brainstorming for the next essay in 101, reviewing drafts of a paper, or discussing common problems in finding a topic to write about. Frequently, instructors ask students to write short papers that will serve as scaffolding for the next essay or work with them on grammar or punctuation problems common to the group.

Gaining Administrative Support

After the English Department agreed it wanted to pilot ALP, meetings were set up with the Dean of Developmental Education and the Vice President for Instruction. At first, the Vice President declared the college simply could not afford to fund classes with only eight students, but a last-minute compromise was suggested: faculty could teach the companion course that met three hours a week with only eight students for two credits of load instead of three. The Vice President agreed, reluctantly. But would the faculty?

As it turns out, they did. After all, the companion course would have only eight students, and, while it would meet three hours a week, it would not really require a separate preparation. It's more like a workshop for the ENGL 101 class. Most importantly, as faculty began teaching the course, they found that ALP was often the most rewarding teaching they had ever done. As Sandra Grady, one of the earliest ALP instructors declared at the end of the first semester, "That was the best teaching experience I've ever had," and Professor Grady has been teaching more than thirty years. All of us who have taught ALP courses have found having a class small enough so that we can get to know each student and pay attention to their individual needs provides a kind of satisfaction that is rarely possible with classes of twenty or more. Peter Adams, Robert Miller, and Anne Roberts, co-authors of this article, began teaching in that first semester, and Sarah Gearhart joined us in the second semester.

Results

As of the summer of 2009, the Community College of Baltimore County has offered thirty sections of ALP over two years to almost 240 students. The results, while preliminary, are extremely encouraging.

Chart 4 displays the results for a comparison group of students who took the *traditional* upper-level basic writing course in Fall of 2007. The data represent the results at the end of the Spring semester of 2009, so all of these students have had four semesters to pass their writing courses. Note that 21% of the original group have never passed ENGL 052. While it looks as though this group of students "failed" the course, in fact, many of them didn't actually "fail." For a variety of reasons, they simply gave up and stopped coming to class. Some became

Chart 4. Success Rates of Students Who Took Traditional ENGL 052 in Fall 2007

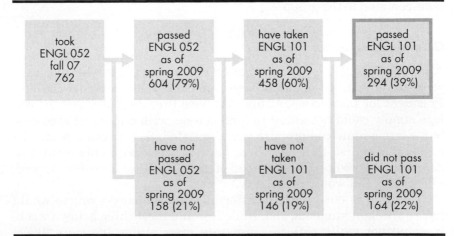

Chart 5. Success Rates of Students Who Took ALP 052 from Fall 2007 to Spring 2008

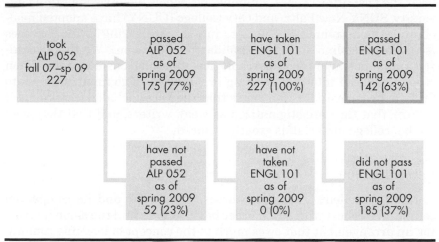

discouraged; others became overwhelmed. For some, events outside school demanded too much of them; for others, their personal lives required their attention. For these reasons, it would not be accurate to say that 21% failed. In addition, the 19% who passed ENGL 052 but didn't attempt ENGL 101 have clearly dropped out. This attrition rate of 40% is of great concern, as it was when we studied developmental students back in 1992.

Chart 5 presents the results for all the students who have taken ALP since the program began in Fall 2007, up to and including the Spring semester of 2009. While the first semester's cohort of 40 students has had four semesters to complete their writing courses, the remaining students have had fewer semesters. The most recent group, approximately 80 students who took ALP in Spring of 2009, has had only one semester. Despite this shorter time for most of the students, the ALP success rates are significantly higher and the drop-out rates significantly lower than for the comparison group. The boxes outlined in black in Charts 4 and 5 show the success rates for the two groups.

Why ALP Works

As we came to realize that ALP was producing striking improvement in student success, we began to speculate about why. What was it about ALP that we think are responsible for most of the gains in retention and success. Half of these are features we borrowed from earlier innovative programs.

Mainstreaming

Over the past fifteen years, a number of schools like Arizona State University, SUNY New Paltz, and City College (CUNY) have adopted models that mainstream basic writers into credit-bearing writing classes (see Glau; Rigolino and Freel; Soliday and Gleason). We think mainstreaming has a powerful psychological effect for basic writers. When students placed into basic writing are allowed to go immediately into first-year composition, their sense that they are excluded from the real college, that they are stigmatized as weak writers, and that they may not be "college material" is greatly reduced.

Cohort Learning

Each ALP student takes two courses, ENGL 101 and its companion course, in a cohort with seven other basic writers and the same instructor, an arrangement that owes much to the concept of learning communities. Vincent Tinto has argued that leaving college often "arises from isolation, specifically from the absence of sufficient contact between the individual [student] and other members of the social and academic communities of the college." He adds the observation that "membership in at least one supportive community, whatever its relationship to the center, may be sufficient to insure continued persistence" (55–61). As Faith Gabelnick and her co-authors have reported, learning communities, in which students take two or more courses with the same cohort of students, provide just such a community: "Learning community students value knowing other students in classes and realize an immediate sense of belonging" (67). Rebecca Mlynarczyk and Marcia Babbitt have observed similar results at Kingsborough Community College (71–89). In the ALP program, among the eight basic writers who spend six hours a week together in a cohort with the same instructor, we are finding similar increases in bonding and attachment to the college. The students begin to look out for each other in a variety of ways—calling to check on students who miss class, offering each other rides to campus, and, most importantly, helping each other to understand difficult concepts they encounter in their academic work.

Small Class Size

We have found the small class size of the companion course, only eight students, to be an essential feature of ALP. We arrived at the conclusion that the sections would have to be small by reading the work of Rhonda Grego and Nancy Thompson, who developed the concept of studios, "where a small group of students . . . meet frequently and regularly . . . to bring to the table the assignments they are working on for a writing course" (7). We knew we wanted the ALP students to comprise less than half the students in the 101 sections, where class size at our school is twenty, so we proposed a class size of eight for the companion course. We have concluded that many of the benefits of ALP derive from this small class size. Students are less prone to behavior problems when they are in a small group. The bonding mentioned earlier is more likely to occur. And the conversation can be focused on each individual's questions much more easily.

Contextual Learning

Both learning communities and studio courses credit some of their success to the fact that students are learning about writing in a meaningful context. Grego and Thompson point out that the conversations in studio sessions often explore the context for a writing assignment or for a teacher's comments on a student's essay (140–42). Similarly, learning communities, especially those that match a writing course with a "content course" such as history or psychology, tap into the advantages of contextual learning. The writing instruction seems more meaningful to the students because it is immediately applicable in the content course. In ALP, the ENGL 101 class provides a meaningful context for the work students do in the companion course. In more traditional basic writing classes, instructors frequently find themselves saying, "Now pay attention. This will be very helpful when you get to first-year composition." We don't have to say this in the ALP classes; our students are already in first-year composition. What we do in the companion course is immediately useful in the essays the students are writing in ENGL 101.

Acceleration

In the longitudinal studies we conducted, we discovered that many students never completed the sequence of required writing courses because they gave up at some point in the process. And the longer the course sequence, the more opportunities there are for such "giving up." Most startling to us was the nearly 20% of our students who actually passed the traditional basic writing course, but then gave up without ever even attempting ENGL 101. We have concluded that the longer the "pipeline" through which our basic writers must move before completing their writing sequence, the greater the chances they will give up and "leak" out of the pipeline. ALP shortens the pipeline for basic writers by allowing them to take their developmental writing and first-year composition courses in the same semester. This acceleration is one of the features we developed at the Community College of Baltimore County.

Heterogeneous Grouping

Another feature of ALP that was developed by CCBC is heterogeneous grouping. In most of the earlier mainstreaming models, basic writers were placed in first-year composition, but in sections populated only by other basic writers. Each group of eight ALP students takes ENGL 101 in a section with twelve 101-level writers who can serve as role models both for writing and for successful student behavior. We also find that the stigmatizing and demoralizing effects of placement in a course designed just for basic writers are greatly reduced by this feature.

Attention to Behavioral Issues

A third locally developed feature of ALP is our conscious and deliberate attention to behavioral issues. We believe that not understanding the kinds of behavior that lead to success in college is a major factor in some basic writers' lack of success. We work hard to help our students understand the type of behavior that will maximize their chances for success in college. For example, many of our basic writers have taken on more responsibilities than they can possibly fulfill. We ask students to create a time line that accounts for everything they must do in a given week, an exercise that sometimes leads them to make changes in their lives to increase their chances for success. Some students discover they need to cut back on their hours at work; others realize that they have registered for too many courses.

Behavioral problems often result from attitudinal problems. In class we talk about what we call the "high school attitude" toward education: the attitude that it isn't "cool" to appear interested in class, to be seen taking notes or raising one's hand to answer a question. Using humor and sometimes even a little mockery, we lead students to realize that the "high school attitude" toward "coolness" isn't "cool" in college.

And then there are the recurring problems with cell phones and Facebook, with arriving late or falling asleep, with not buying the required text or not completing the required assignment. ALP instructors are aware that these kinds of issues will need more conscious attention, and the small class size makes such attention possible.

Attention to Life Problems

A fourth feature of ALP we developed at CCBC is to encourage instructors to pay deliberate attention to problems in the students' lives outside of school. Many students who give up on our courses do so, not because of any difficulty with the material in the course but, primarily, because of circumstances in their lives outside of college. They are evicted from their apartment, their children become ill, their boss insists they work more hours, they find themselves in abusive relationships, or they experience some other overwhelming life problem. ALP faculty recognize the need to address these life issues. They find time to ask students how their lives are going. They frequently refer students to sources of outside support for such concerns as financial aid, health issues, family problems, and legal problems. When several students in the same class have a similar problem, instead of sending them to see an advisor, we have the advisor visit the class. We have assembled a roster of resource people who are willing to visit our classes and work with students on life problems.

Costs

Regardless of its success rates, ALP may appear to be prohibitively expensive, as our Vice President for Instruction had initially thought. But careful analysis reveals that ALP actually costs less per *successful student* than more traditional approaches.

To see how this could be the case, consider a hypothetical group of 1,000 students who show up in September needing developmental writing. Under the traditional model, we would need to run 50 sections of basic writing to accommodate them (our class size for writing courses is 20). Since the actual cost of these 50 sections would vary depending on the salary levels of the instructors, we'll make this calculation in terms of faculty credit hours (FCHs). Since faculty are compensated with 3 FCHs for teaching our upper-level basic writing course, the cost for those 1,000 students would be 150 FCHs.

Because only 60% of students taking our traditional upper-level basic writing course ever take ENGL 101, we would need to accommodate just 600 students in ENGL 101, which would require 30 sections. At 3 FCHs per section, the ENGL 101 costs for 1,000 students would be 90 FCHs, and the total for ENGL 052 and 101 would be 240 FCHs.

To accommodate those same 1,000 students in an ALP program would require 125 sections (class size for the ALP classes is 8). Because of the small class size and because the companion course is not really a separate preparation, faculty receive 2, not 3, FCHs for a section of the companion course. The 125 sections would, therefore, cost the college 250 FCHs.

Since all 1,000 students would take ENGL 101, we would need 50 sections to accommodate all 1,000 students. At 3 FCHs per section, the 101 portion of the ALP program would cost 150 FCHs, and so the total cost for the ALP model would be 400 FCHs.

Before deciding which model is more expensive, however, it is not enough to consider just the costs; it is also necessary to consider the outcomes. Under the traditional model, 39%, or 390 students, will pass ENGL 101. Under ALP, 63%, or 630 students, will pass ENGL 101. As a result, the cost *per successful student* for the traditional model (390 students divided by 240 FCHs) would be 1.625 FCHs. For the ALP model, the cost (630 students divided by 400 FCHs) would be 1.575 FCHs per successful student. ALP actually costs less per successful student than the traditional model.

In sum, for basic writers, ALP doubles the success rate, halves the attrition rate, does it in half the time (one semester instead of two), and costs slightly less per successful student. When these data are presented to administrators, the case for adopting the ALP model is compelling.

Plans for the Future

ALP has produced very promising results. For each of the past four semesters, it has resulted in success rates at least double those for our traditional basic writing course. Having achieved these preliminary successes, our plans for the future include continued and expanded study of the program, improvements in the program to make it even more effective, scaling up of ALP at CCBC to 40 sections per semester in Fall 2010 and to approximately 70 sections per semester in Fall 2011, and dissemination of ALP to other colleges.

First, we want to insure the validity of our preliminary data, which has indicated such dramatic improvement in success rates for ALP students over students in the traditional program. We are concerned about two possible threats to the validity of that data: the possibility that students who volunteer for ALP are not representative of developmental writing students at CCBC, and the possibility of instructor bias in grading the ALP students in ENGL 101.

To address the possibility that students who volunteer for ALP are not a representative sample, we have formed a partnership with the Community College Research Center at Columbia University. CCRC is conducting multivariate analyses of the effects of participating in ALP on student pass rates in English 101 as well as on other measures, including rates of persistence and passing college-level courses in subjects other than English. This study will make use of "matched pairs," selecting a student who has taken the traditional ENGL 052 to be matched with an ALP student on eleven variables: race, gender, age, financial aid status, full- or part-time status, prior college credits, grades in prior college courses, placement scores, program, high school attended, and high school diploma status.

We are also concerned about the possibility of unconscious instructor bias in favor of the ALP students. The English Department has developed rubrics that describe a passing essay for the basic writing course and for ENGL 101. However, considering the close relationships that naturally develop between ALP faculty and the eight ALP students with whom they meet for six hours a week, it is possible that occasionally instructors unconsciously pass an ALP student in ENGL 101 whose performance was slightly below passing level. To investigate this possible bias, we will be following the ALP students into ENGL

102, the next course in the writing sequence, comparing their performance there with that of students who took traditional ENGL 052.
ENGL 102 instructors will not have formed any kind of bond with the
students and, in fact, will not even know that they were in ALP.

Also, we will be conducting a blind, holistic scoring of essays from
ENGL 101 classes to compare the quality of the writing of ALP students who passed the course with the quality of the writing of 101-level
students. If we determine through this study that some ALP students
are being passed in ENGL 101 even though their performance is below
the passing level, we will investigate other ways of making the pass/
fail decision for these sections. We may, for example, decide to have final
portfolios graded by someone other than the student's own instructor.

In addition to investigating any threats to the validity of our data
on success rates of ALP students in ENGL 101, we will be investigating
whether higher percentages of ALP students, compared to students
who take the traditional basic writing course, continue to reach various
milestones such as accumulating 15, 30, and 45 credits, one-year persistence, completion of certificate and degree programs, and successful
transfer to four-year institutions.

Finally, we want to attempt to understand exactly what it is about
ALP that leads to its successes and which features contribute most
to the improved performance of ALP students. Using pre- and post-
semester surveys, focus groups, and faculty reports, we will attempt to
determine which of the eight features of ALP contribute most to student success.

We are fairly confident ALP works well in our context, so we look
forward to learning if it works as well in at other colleges. To this end,
we organized a conference on acceleration in June of 2009. Forty-one
faculty from twenty-one different schools attended. After a spirited
two-day conversation with lots of give and take and very good questions from participants, four schools agreed to pilot ALP on their campuses in the coming year: CUNY's Kingsborough Community College
(New York), El Paso Community College (Texas), Patrick Henry Community College (Virginia), and Gateway Technical and Community
College (Kentucky). We eagerly await their results. In addition, we are
hopeful that other schools will adopt the ALP model in coming years.
On June 23–25, 2010, we will be holding an expanded version of the
Conference on Acceleration at CCBC.

ALP has benefited greatly from the work our colleagues at other
institutions have done since that Conference on Basic Writing back in
1992. We have developed a model for developmental writing that shows
great promise, and we are certain that others will improve on our
model in coming years.

We are also convinced that this work is extremely important given
the present climate for higher education. The country has begun to pay
attention to basic writing and developmental education more broadly

in ways both negative and positive. There is a growing realization that the programs we began so hopefully during those early days of open admissions have not performed nearly as well as we had hoped. Some would conclude from these low success rates that our budgets should be reduced or even that our programs should be eliminated. Susanmarie Harrington and Linda Adler-Kassner observe that we are working in "an educational environment in which basic writing and remedial programs are under attack" (8). Mary Soliday points out that "Outside the academy, critics of remediation waved the red flag of declining standards and literacy crisis to justify the need to downsize, privatize, and effectively restratify higher education. By blaming remedial programs for a constellation of educational woes, from budget crisis to low retention rates and falling standards, the critics of remediation practiced an effective politics of agency." That is, they attributed the blame for these growing problems to the developmental students and "the 'expensive' programs designed to meet their 'special' needs" (*Politics of Remediation* 106). In 2005, Bridget Terry Long, writing in *National CrossTalk*, observed that "this debate about the merits of investing in remediation, which has an estimated annual cost in the billions, has intensified in recent years. There are many questions about whether remediation should be offered in colleges at all." Long goes on to take a close look at how we determine the success of "remedial" programs and to demonstrate that with appropriate measures—comparing students with similar economic and educational backgrounds—remedial programs do indeed seem to help students do better in college.

Despite the positive implications of more nuanced research such as that conducted by Long, the criticism of basic writing programs is not likely to diminish in the near future. And in the field of basic writing itself, the realization that many basic writing programs are falling short of the kind of results we had hoped for in the early days—a realization that first surfaced at the basic writing conference in Baltimore in 1992—is leading to the development of improved and innovative programs. In "Challenge and Opportunity: Rethinking the Role and Function of Developmental Education in the Community College," Tom Bailey notes that there has been "a dramatic expansion in experimentation with new approaches." Major funding agencies, both governmental and non-governmental, are beginning to see developmental education as an area of interest. However, if we are not able to improve our success rates, if we continue to serve as a gate, barring large numbers of students from receiving a college education, those who argue for a reduction or elimination of basic writing could prevail. That is why it is so important at this crucial time that we look for ways to make basic writing more effective. The very survival of our programs could be at stake. But there is an even more important reason for continuing to improve our effectiveness: the success of our programs is of life-changing importance to our students.

Works Cited

Adams, Peter. "Basic Writing Reconsidered." *Journal of Basic Writing* 12.1 (1993): 22–36. Print.

Bailey, Thomas. "Challenge and Opportunity: Rethinking the Role and Function of Developmental Education in the Community College." *New Directions for Community Colleges* (2009): 11–30. Web. 30 July 2009.

Bartholomae, David. "The Tidy House: Basic Writing in the American Curriculum." *Journal of Basic Writing* 12.1 (1993): 4–21. Print.

Boylan, Hunter R., and D. Patrick Saxon. "Outcomes of Remediation." League for Innovation. Web. 30 July 2009.

Gabelnick, Faith, Jean MacGregor, Roberta S. Matthews, and Barbara Leigh Smith. *Learning Communities: Creating, Connections Among Students, Faculty, and Disciplines.* New Directions for Teaching and Learning. San Francisco: Jossey-Bass, 1990. Print.

Glau, Greg. "*Stretch* at 10: A Progress Report on Arizona State University's *Stretch Program*." *Journal of Basic Writing* 26.2 (2007): 30–48. Print.

Grego, Rhonda, and Nancy Thompson. *Teaching/Writing in Third Spaces.* Carbondale: Southern Illinois UP, 2008. Print.

Harrington, Susanmarie, and Linda Adler-Kassner. "The Dilemma that Still Counts: Basic Writing at a Political Crossroads." *Journal of Basic Writing* 17.2 (1998): 3–24. Print.

Horner, Bruce, and Min-Zhan Lu. *Representing the "Other": Basic Writers and the Teaching of Basic Writing.* Urbana: NCTE, 1999. Print.

Long, Bridget Terry. "The Remediation Debate: Are We Serving the Needs of Underprepared College Students?" *National CrossTalk.* The National Center for Public Policy and Higher Education, Fall 2005. Web. 20 Dec. 2009.

Mlynarczyk, Rebecca Williams, and Marcia Babbitt. "The Power of Academic Learning Communities." *Journal of Basic Writing* 21.1 (2002): 71–89. Print.

Rigolino, Rachel, and Penny Freel. "Re-Modeling Basic Writing." *Journal of Basic Writing* 26.2 (2007): 49–72. Print.

Segall, Mary T. "Embracing a Porcupine: Redesigning a Writing Program." *Journal of Basic Writing* 14.2 (1995): 38–47. Print.

Soliday, Mary. "Ideologies of Access and the Politics of Agency." *Mainstreaming Basic Writers: Politics and Pedagogies of Access.* Ed. Gerry McNenny and Sallyanne Fitzgerald. Mahwah: Erlbaum, 2001. 55–72. Print.

———. *The Politics of Remediation: Institutional and Student Needs in Higher Education.* Pittsburgh: U of Pittsburgh P, 2002. Print.

Soliday, Mary, and Barbara Gleason. "From Remediation to Enrichment: Evaluating a Mainstreaming Project." *Journal of Basic Writing* 16.1 (1997): 64–78. Print.

Tinto, Vincent. *Leaving College: Understanding the Causes and Cures of Student Attrition.* Chicago: U of Chicago P, 1986. Print.

Stretch at 10: A Progress Report on Arizona State University's *Stretch Program*

Gregory R. Glau

Greg Glau recounts the high pass rate of Arizona State University's Stretch Program for students in basic writing over a ten period from 1994–1995 to 2004–2005. The Stretch Program, at its inception, offered a full year of English 101, a one-semester course stretched over two semesters for students who tested into basic writing. This program was created to address the problem of outsourcing basic writing to the nearby community college system, generally leaving students underprepared to succeed in university-level writing courses. Several different types of Stretch courses are offered to accommodate the diverse needs of specific student populations. With over ten years of results available for Stretch courses and "regular" one-semester 101 courses, Glau found that the pass rate for students enrolled in Stretch demonstrated a significant difference from the lower pass rate for the one-semester first-year composition course. The article ends with a postscript about the recent fate of Stretch given the variable conditions for basic writing at Arizona State University. If the future of the Stretch Program seemed vulnerable to changing times, this ten-year overview provides teachers, writing program administrators, and others seeking an exemplary model for success in basic writing.

In the fall of 1992, Arizona State University (ASU) had just completed several years during which its "basic writers" had been outsourced to a local community college.[1] There had been the usual conversations about whether or not "basic writers" belonged at the university, and that perhaps the local community college would serve them better. But what Director of Composition David Schwalm had originally feared had come to pass: once these students were told to take a community college "remedial" writing class (ENG 071), only a few of them ever returned to ASU to take other classes, and those who did were unprepared for the university-level work expected of them. The remedial classes (in which ASU controlled neither the curriculum nor the teachers nor the class size) simply did not serve these particular students well. In addition, students paid university tuition but received no college credit for these outsourced classes. Schwalm was determined to somehow bring these basic writing students back to ASU and to do so in a way that would help them succeed and be retained at the university (for more about the issues and problems involved, see Schwalm).

Working with John Ramage, then Director of ASU's Writing Across the Curriculum program, Schwalm and Ramage together determined that what ASU's basic writing students needed more than anything else was *more time*: more time to think, more time to write, more time to revise. And they wanted to ask ASU's basic writers to do what Andrea

Lunsford long ago suggested, to ". . . continually be engaged in writing in a full rhetorical context, solving problems and practicing conceptual skills in a carefully sequenced set of assignments" (288).

Schwalm and Ramage designed two pilot programs, both intended to give students more time, and both requiring students to use the same textbooks and to work with the same assignments as did the students in "traditional" ENG 101 classes. The following academic year (1993–1994) ASU piloted two versions of classes for students identified as basic writers. One was called *Jumbo*—a six-semester-hour basic writing class. The results for *Jumbo* were mixed, and student response to the approach and their subsequent writing performance did not seem to be at the same level produced by the other approach. That other approach was labeled *Stretch*, a two-semester sequence designed to "stretch" ENG 101 over two semesters. Unfortunately, both the *Jumbo* and the *Stretch* pilots were pretty small, but the consensus was that *Stretch* helped students more, and, unlike Jumbo, clearly the *Stretch* model was faithful to Ramage and Schwalm's original notion that ASU's basic writers needed more time. So, beginning in the fall of 1994, ASU's *Stretch Program* was initially launched, with 512 students enrolled.[2]

Both of these pilot programs attempted to do what David Bartholomae had suggested: to change the curriculum by first "chang[ing] the way the profession talked about the students who didn't fit" ("The Tidy House" 21). Schwalm and Ramage in effect were arguing that the students accepted into ASU but placed into a basic writing class did not give "evidence of arrested cognitive development, arrested language development, or unruly or unpredictable language use" (Bartholomae, "Error" 254). Rather, they saw ASU's basic writing students as capable, and able to *do* the university-level writing the Department of English required. But they also believed that this subset of students could use more time and more directed writing experience, so they would not only write more but also receive more feedback and revision suggestions on their writing. Also, they wanted ASU to move away from an outsourcing approach and toward a mode of *embracing* those basic writers, to move from a view that these students are defective to one that, as Mina Shaughnessy taught us, understands that "students write the way they do, not because they are slow or non-verbal, indifferent to or incapable of academic excellence, but because they are beginners and must, like all beginners, learn by making mistakes" (5).

Program Design[3]

Since ASU's computer system would not allow Schwalm and Ramage to name the two-class *Stretch* sequence something like ENG 101A and ENG 101B, they decided to have the first class carry the Writing Across the Curriculum label as WAC 101. So, even if the course was viewed as "remedial" (as so many basic writing programs are), this connection to

Table 1: Placement into ASU's Writing "Tracks"				
Stretch sequence	WAC 101	→	ENG 101	→	ENG 102
Traditional sequence	ENG 101	→	ENG 102		
Accelerated sequence	ENG 105				
ESL *Stretch* sequence	WAC 107	→	ENG 107	→	ENG 108
ESL traditional sequence	ENG 107	→	ENG 108		

the Writing Across the Curriculum program provided some political protection.[4] Because the WAC 101 classes were to be directly connected to specifically designated sections of ENG 101,the *Stretch* sequence was created to be *part* of first-year composition, rather than something *outside* and thus vulnerable to political attack.

Schwalm and Ramage wanted to give ASU's beginning writers more time to work on and revise and think about their writing, so instead of doing all the ENG 101 assignments in one semester, they wrote three papers each semester, each with multiple drafts, along with a portfolio analysis of their writing, which served as a final examination.[5] Just as it is important that *Stretch* students use the same textbooks that "traditional" ENG 101 students use, the direct connection between ENG 101 and *Stretch* assignments is critical.

To put this notion—that *Stretch* is a version of first-year composition—into a wider context, see Table 1 for the "tracks" students can take to fulfill their first-year writing requirement at ASU.

These several tracks are all seen (and represented to the administration and the public) as part and parcel of the same thing: the first-year writing requirement. What this new approach does is give our basic writing program protection from those who see such programs as remedial—if you want to attack *Stretch*, then you also have to attack the traditional version of ENG 101, as well as the accelerated version of first-year writing (ENG 105).

Contrast this model, where the basic writing program is part of the first-year writing program, uses the same books, asks students to construct the same assignments, etc., with one in which the basic writing program is seen as pre-English 101. That view makes it easier for BW programs to be attacked as "not belonging at the university" and as "high school courses." Not so with *Stretch*.

Since *Stretch* classes are college-level classes, *Stretch Program* students earn three hours of elective credit for the first part of the *Stretch* course sequence (WAC 101), credit that counts toward graduation at ASU, and then three hours of ENG 101 credit for their second semester's work (ENG 101). The list that follows gives a few more administrative details that will be useful to anyone contemplating a *Stretch* model for their own college or university:

- WAC 101/107 began as a pass/fail course, where the grades *Stretch* students earned for their papers and other work *accumulated* and counted as 50 percent of their ENG 101 grade. The original notion was that the pass/fail designation would take some of the pressure off of students during their first semester in college. However, students generally did not like the pass/fail aspect of WAC 101/107, as the class then did not help their GPA. So, in 2007, WAC 101/107 was changed to a graded class (largely because of those student concerns).

- ASU tries to keep the same teacher with the same group of students for both semesters. This doesn't always work out, of course, but it does most of the time, and *Stretch* students tell us that they very much like having the same classmates and the same teacher for two semesters. One thing we've noticed is that students who are together for two semesters generally build a useful "writing community." It takes some time for students to learn to trust each other in terms of peer feedback, and *Stretch* teachers almost always see, in that second semester, much improved peer review.

- Students place into all of ASU's writing classes based on their ACT or SAT scores.[6]

- ASU also offers sections of *Stretch Program* classes for international students, as these students especially benefit from more time to work on their writing.

- *Stretch* classes were initially capped at 22 students, as compared to 26 in traditional ENG 101 classrooms, so *Stretch* students would receive more personal attention. Beginning in the fall of 2004, all 100-level English classes were capped at 19.[7]

Long-Term Results

Not all of our data paints *Stretch* in a perfect light; frankly, there are areas we need to improve on. At the same time, however, most of the data indicates that the *Stretch* concept actually works and that thousands of students have benefited from the extra time and guided writing experience they receive with the WAC 101–ENG 101 *Stretch* sequence.

To track accurately what happens with *Stretch* students, we use a step model:[8]

A number of students register for WAC 101

A percentage of these students pass WAC 101

A percentage of these students register for ENG 101

A percentage of these students pass ENG 101

A percentage of these students register for ENG 102

A percentage of these students pass ENG 102

There are a number of ways to consider this data, and for our purposes here we will provide information on:

Student Profile

- *Stretch* student ACT/SAT scores compared to traditional ENG 101 students.

- Enrollment by students from historically under-represented groups (at ASU, we consider these to be students who self-identify as African American, Asian American, Hispanic, or Native American).[9]

Pass Rates

- For WAC 101 compared to pass rates for the previous community-college class (ENG 071).

- For *Stretch* ENG 101 students compared to pass rates for students taking traditional ENG 101.

- For *Stretch* students once they're done with *Stretch* and take ENG 102, compared to traditional ENG 102 students.

- For students from historically under-represented groups.

Continuation Rates

- Fall-spring retention (for *Stretch* students, that is from WAC 101 to ENG 101; for traditional students, it's from ENG 101 to ENG 102).

The step model, then, will examine:

A number of students register for WAC 101 [student profile]

A percentage of these students pass WAC 101 [pass rates]

A percentage of these students register for ENG 101 [continuation rate]

A percentage of these students pass ENG 101 [pass rates]

A percentage of these students register for ENG 102 [continuation rate]

A percentage of these students pass ENG 102 [pass rate]

We have—after a full ten years of *Stretch*'s existence and because ASU is such a large institution—some pretty large data sets. To provide a sense of the numbers we will detail below, here are a few statistics from those data sets:

- Number of WAC 101 students, fall semesters 1994 through 2004: 7,826

- Number of ENG 101 students, academic years 1994–95 through 2004–05: 45,668

- Number of WAC 101 students from under-represented groups, fall 1994 through fall 2004: 2,856

- Number of ENG 101 students from under-represented groups, academic years 1994–95 through 2004–05: 9,873

- Number of ENG 102 students, academic years 1994–95 through 2004–05: 53,516

- Number of ENG 102 students from under-represented groups, academic years 1994–95 through 2004–05: 10,531

Who Our Students Are

Arizona State University is a large, urban university with roughly 50,000 students on the Tempe campus. There are now versions of *Stretch* at the other three ASU campuses, but their data is so new that it is not included here.

As noted above, we place all of our students—roughly 9,000 in our first-year classes—into either *Stretch*, traditional ENG 101, or ENG 105 based on their standardized test scores. While from time to time we have conversations on whether we might somehow move to a form of directed self-placement (see Royer and Gillis, "Directed" and "Basic Writing"), we haven't yet figured out how to do this with so many new students each fall semester. To make matters worse, ASU (as of this writing) does not have mandatory orientation, so we wouldn't be able to provide placement information and advice to all incoming students. So for now we're continuing to place students based on their SAT verbal or ACT English scores (this appeals to the university administration since the students pay for this testing). At the same time, there do seem to be significant differences in the average scores of *Stretch* students, as compared to those placed into ENG 101. The following data is from fall semesters, as that's when most of our students start their classes here. For the 11 fall semesters (since *Stretch* was put into place: fall 1994–fall 2004):[10]

- 5,362 **WAC 101** students had an SAT verbal score, averaging **425**.

- 28,113 **ENG 101** students had an SAT verbal score, averaging **544**.

On average, then, the SAT verbal score for *Stretch* students is about 120 points *lower* than their counterparts who place in traditional ENG 101 classes. (There is roughly the same difference—120 points— between students placed into ENG 101 and those placed into ENG 105, our one-semester class that fulfills the composition requirement.) The same is true for ACT scores:

- 4,408 **WAC 101** students had an ACT English score, averaging **16**.

- 20,185 **ENG 101** students had an ACT English score, averaging **23**.

In addition, more *Stretch* students—by a large margin—are identified as belonging to an historically under-represented group (at ASU, we consider these to be students who self-identify as African American, Asian American, Hispanic, or Native American). Students from these populations—since the majority of them, historically, have not attended college—are sometimes seen as at-risk in terms of university success (and since twice as many place into our basic writing sequence of classes, they also are seen as at-risk based on their test scores):

- Over the 10 fall semesters (1994–2004), **36.49%** of the students registered in **WAC 101** were from these under-represented groups.

- Over the past 10 academic years (1995–96 through 2004–2005), **21.62%** of the students registered in traditional **ENG 101** were from these under-represented groups.

ASU has made great progress at including more students from underrepresented groups: in the fall of 1995, **18.7%** of our new students came from under-represented groups. By the fall of 2006, however, some **25.6%** came from those groups. At the same time, *Stretch*'s population was also changing: in the fall of 2006, **43.2%** of WAC 101 students came from those under-represented groups.

In effect, then, while traditional ENG 101 classes have about one student in five or so from one of these under-represented groups, *Stretch* classes have almost twice that number—almost two in five. This data reflects, of course, any cultural bias in standardized testing, in addition to how effectively (or ineffectively) a student's grammar-, middle-, and high-school education has prepared that student for the ACT or SAT. In Arizona such preparation is often worse than in other states, as our continually conservative state legislature constantly refuses—even under court order—to properly fund schools in poorer Arizona communities.

In any case, that's a snapshot of *Stretch* students: they're seen as the most at-risk because they have the worst test scores (by a significant degree), and more of them come from groups that historically have not attended universities.

How Our Students Perform

One way to measure how *Stretch* students perform is to consider how they do in comparison to other groups of students. You may recall that WAC 101 replaced the community college ENG 071 class. For the final five years (before we implemented *Stretch*) we asked our basic writing students to take **ENG 071**, the pass rate was **66.22%**. In comparison, students pass **WAC 101** at a **90.15%** rate. This pass rate—reflecting student success—is significant because when many students fail a class, they simply stop coming to school. So when ASU implemented *Stretch*, our retention rate immediately improved.

While our basic writing students clearly did better in WAC 101 than in the class they had been taking, ENG 071, how did they fare against their ENG 101 counterparts? To properly compare the two sets of students, we need to compare how both groups did when taking ENG 101 (this data covers academic years 1994–1995 through 2004–2005):

- The pass rate for ***Stretch* ENG 101** students averages **92.65%**.

- The pass rate for traditional **ENG 101** students averages **88.88%**.

Clearly, the WAC 101 semester, which gives these at-risk students more guided writing experience, helps them. *Stretch Program* students consistently pass ENG 101 at a higher rate than do their counterparts who take traditional ENG 101.[11] Incidentally, these pass rates hold true over time (see Figure 1).

How do *Stretch* students perform when they leave the program and take ENG 102? Again, *Stretch* students consistently pass ENG 102 at a higher rate than do their traditional ENG 101 counterparts (see Figure 2).

Figure 1. Comparative Year-to-Year Pass Rates

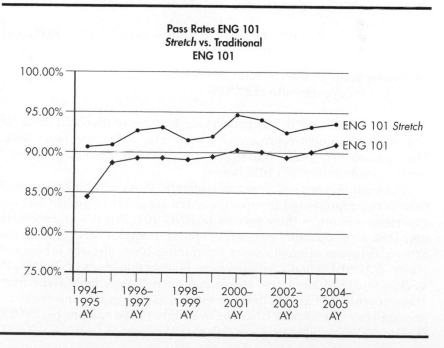

Figure 2. Comparative Pass Rates for *Stretch* ENG 101 and Traditional ENG 101

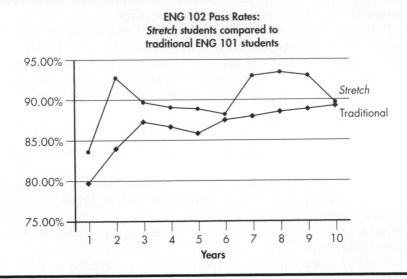

ENG 102 Pass Rates:
Stretch students compared to
traditional ENG 101 students

We see similar data sets—a higher pass rate—for students from historically under-represented groups. These students pass ENG 101 at a higher rate when they're in the *Stretch Program* (as above, this data covers academic years 1994–95 through 2004–05):

- Students from under-represented groups pass **Stretch ENG 101** at an average rate of **90.81%**.

- Students from under-represented groups pass traditional **ENG 101** at an average rate of **87.34%**.

As with students in our general student population, the data for students from under-represented groups also holds true over time. They consistently pass ENG 101 at a higher rate than do those students in traditional ENG 101 classes:

For both our general group of students, then, as well as students from under-represented groups, the extra semester of guided writing experience enhances their success in ENG 101. But it's important to note that we're *not quite* comparing apples to apples here. That is, the *Stretch Program* students we're examining have already taken and passed WAC 101, usually with the same teacher and group of students— so even with the lower test scores and even though more come from under-represented groups and are seen as at risk in the university . . . perhaps they *should* pass ENG 101 at a higher rate, since as part of the

Figure 3. Comparative Year-to-Year Pass Rates for Students from Under-Represented Groups in ENG 101

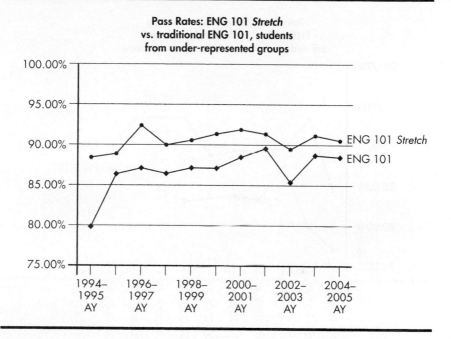

Pass Rates: ENG 101 *Stretch* vs. traditional ENG 101, students from under-represented groups

Stretch Program they have more time to spend on their writing, and are with the teacher for two semesters.

So how do *Stretch* students do when they move to the next semester and take ENG 102? Former *Stretch* students from under-represented groups—the ones with the worst test scores—appear to benefit from the extra semester of guided writing experience: they pass ENG 102 at a higher rate than do traditional ENG 102 students (this data covers academic years 1994–95 through 2004–05):

- **Stretch** students from under represented groups pass ENG 102 at an average rate of **88.65%**.

- Students from under represented groups taking **traditional** ENG 101 pass ENG 102 at an average rate of **84.17%**.

As with data for our general student population, these pass rates are as outlined in Figure 4. While recently the comparative pass rates have been getting closer, students who had the benefit of taking WAC 101 clearly benefit—in terms of passing—when they do take ENG 102.

It's important to note that *Stretch* doesn't seem to help one *group* of students as well as it helps others. That is, when we compare how, say,

Figure 4. Comparative Year-to-Year Pass Rates for Students from Under-Represented Groups in ENG 102

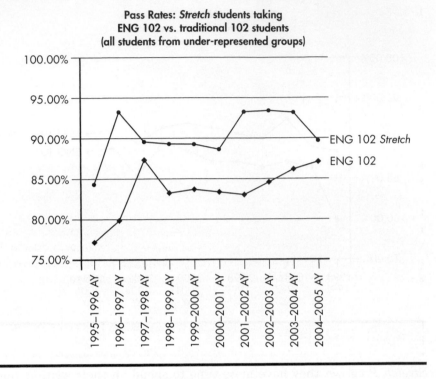

Asian American students succeed in ENG 101 as compared to WAC 101, we don't see much difference. While Asian American students pass ENG 101 at a 90.97% rate, their passing rate for WAC 101 is only slightly lower, 89.50%. But for our Native American students, the results are somewhat starker. Native American students pass ENG 101 at a rate of 86.22%; they pass WAC 101 at a rate of 81.68%. In effect, about five percent more of our Native American students fail WAC 101 than fail ENG 101.

The other two groups of students from under-represented groups (Hispanic and African American) pass both ENG 101 and WAC 101 within two percentage points of each other. The only big difference is the poor pass rate of Native American students in our WAC 101 classes, and at this point we do not have an answer as to why.

How *Stretch Program* Students Persist

Finally, how do *Stretch* students persist? One way to consider student persistence is to look at, for example, the percentage of students who pass ENG 101 in the fall semester and subsequently register for ENG 102 the following semester. Likewise, we can track *Stretch* students who took WAC 101 in the fall and then registered to take ENG 101 the following semester.[12] The cumulative percentages are:

- **90.90%** of *Stretch* students who pass WAC 101 in the fall take ENG 101 the next spring.

- **86.52%** of traditional students who pass ENG 101 in the fall take ENG 102 the next spring.

Figure 5 shows student continuation data from fall 1994–spring 1995 to the fall of 2004–spring 2005, demonstrating that during each fall-spring period, *Stretch* students continued to the next class at a somewhat higher rate than their traditional counterparts.

From a more qualitative point of view, *Stretch* students indicate that they feel the sequence improved their writing (about 90% say so). What they like most about the program is having more time to work on their writing, which validates Schwalm and Ramage's initial concept. Students also like being able to work with the same group of students and have the same teacher for both the WAC and ENG portions of the program.

Figure 5. Comparative Continuation Rates for *Stretch* and Traditional Students in ENG 101 & ENG 102

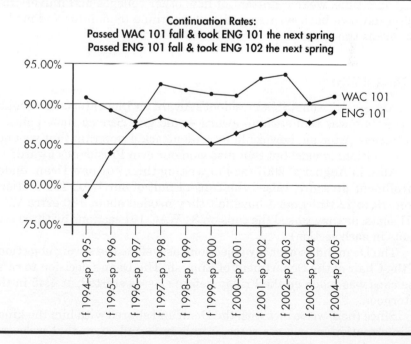

Continuation Rates:
Passed WAC 101 fall & took ENG 101 the next spring
Passed ENG 101 fall & took ENG 102 the next spring

Where Do We Go from Here?

The most recent modification to *Stretch*, as noted earlier, was to change the first class in the *Stretch* sequence from pass/fail to graded.

We continue to monitor the program, especially in light of the fall 2004 modification that dropped the cap on all 100-level English classes to 19 students. One area we're all concerned with is retention, usually measured by the number of first-time full-time freshmen who take classes one fall and then return the subsequent fall. As of this writing, we have two full years of data (2004–2005, and 2005–2006) and can say that "retention" rates for students taking WAC 101, ENG 101, ENG 102, and ENG 105 are all higher than they were when class sizes were larger. I'd hesitate to give all of the credit for student retention to the smaller class size, but it only makes sense that smaller classes help everything else the university is doing to aid retention.

We also have an eye on what our sister institution, the University of Arizona, is doing to help their basic writers. For the past two years the U of A has offered what they call ENG 101+, essentially a writing studio model in which students classified as basic writers are required to attend an additional one-hour session along with their writing class. These sessions are facilitated by the regular U of A writing teachers, and their preliminary results are very promising.

Is *Stretch* the correct model for every institution? Of course not: it works very well at ASU, and has for more than ten years now, and we expect it to continue to serve our basic writing student population. At the same time, we're cognizant of how other colleges and universities help their own basic writers and we'll continue to monitor and modify *Stretch* as time goes on.

A Postscript

In 2003, *Stretch* won ASU's President's Award for Innovation. My thought at the time was that such an award would give *Stretch* some political protection. After all, how could anyone attack a program that was not only a national model but that also won our own President's award?

Alas, in August of 2007 (as I'm writing this), our new Dean, under enrollment pressure, raised the caps of half of our WAC 101 sections from 19 to 22 (they must have felt they needed about 100 extra WAC 101 seats, as they raised the caps on 34 WAC 101 sections by three students in each section).

The Dean did so over my objections as well as the strong objections of the Chair of the Department of English. The Dean's decision to raise the caps was made on the Friday before classes started, at 4:45 in the afternoon.

Since then, we've met with the Dean and shared with him the kinds of information on success rates, ethnic mix, and so on that we've reported in this article. The Dean was apologetic; he seemed to understand the student population involved; he seemed to realize that, under enrollment pressure, he'd made an unfortunate decision; he spoke of more resources for us "now that I've seen this information." Time will tell, of course, so stay tuned, as what seemed to be a lemon on the Friday before classes began might yet turn into lemonade. At least with our basic writing program, there's never a dull moment!

Notes

1. For a discussion on the problematic terms "basic writer" and "basic writing," see Adler-Kassner; DeGenaro and White; Gray-Rosendale *Rethinking* and "Investigating"; Rosen-Knill and Lynch; Shaughnessy (40).
2. There are, of course, other approaches designed to help students identified as basic writers. See, for example, Crouch and McNenney; Fitzgerald "The Context" and "Basic Writing;" Gleason; Goen and Gillotte-Tropp; Grego and Thompson; Lalicker; Smoke; Soliday and Gleason; Winslow and Mische; Wiley.
3. For more details on the overall *Stretch Program* design, see Glau, "The *Stretch Program*," "Mainstream Plus," and "Bringing Them Home"; also see Lalicker.
4. For more on *why* basic writing programs often need "political protection," see Adler-Kassner and Harrington; Collins and Blum; Gilyard; Goto; Mutnick; Rodby and Fox; Soliday; Stevens.
5. When *Stretch* started, ENG 101 students wrote six papers, so it made logical sense for WAC 101 students to write three papers, followed by three more in their ENG 101 semester. Today (2007), traditional ENG 101 students write four papers over the course of a semester, so now *Stretch* students are both *stretched* (more time) and *expanded* (they write six vs. four papers in traditional ENG 101 classes) in terms of the work they do for their writing classes.
6. Students with an SAT verbal score of 530 or lower, or an ACT Enhanced English score of 18 or lower are placed into the *Stretch Program*. Students with a TOEFL score of 540 or less are placed in the ESL version of the *Stretch Program*. Students with a 620 or higher on the SAT verbal or 26 or higher on the SAT English can take our one-semester class, ENG 105. For a more comprehensive look at placement, see White.
7. As of this writing we have three full year's worth of data with these smaller class sizes. Since we dropped the class size to 19, pass rates are higher for WAC 101 and ENG 101 and 102 than they've historically averaged; DWE (drop-withdraw-failure) rates are lower, continuation from fall to spring is better, and student evaluation numbers are *all* better than they have been, historically, for all ranges of teachers (Professors, Lecturers, Instructors, Teaching Assistants, and Faculty Associates).
8. For a long-term look at basic writers using a longitudinal case study approach, see Sternglass.
9. Eleanor Agnew and Margaret McLaughlin provide a useful discussion that focuses on African American BW students; Laura Gray-Rosendale, Loyola K. Bird, and Judith F. Bullock provide a thoughtful discussion of

Native American student experience in BW and other classes. For a useful discussion of how we teachers represent race in our own research and writing, see Center.

10. Some students, of course, had both an ACT and SAT score, so there is some overlap in student populations for these score groups.

11. Students exit from the *Stretch Program* based on the teacher's judgment of progress, which is in turn based on the Writing Program's goals and objectives as articulated in our version of the WPA Outcomes Statement.

12. Of course, some students who pass WAC 101 or ENG 101 in the fall simply don't take an ENG class the following spring semester. Our thinking is that the small percentage of such students is probably about the same for both groups we're considering here, so the results, as shown, are probably pretty accurate.

Works Cited

Adler-Kassner, Linda. "Just Writing, Basically: Basic Writers on Basic Writing." *Journal of Basic Writing* 18.2 (1999): 69–90. Print.

Adler-Kassner, Linda, and Susanmarie Harrington. *Basic Writing as a Political Act: Public Conversations about Writing and Literacy.* Creskill, NJ: Hampton, 2002. Print.

Agnew, Eleanor, and Margaret McLaughlin. "Those Crazy Gates and How They Swing: Tracking the System That Tracks African-American Students." *Mainstreaming Basic Writers.* Ed. Gerri McNenny. Mahwah: Erlbaum, 2001. 85–100. Print.

Bartholomae, David. "The Study of Error." *College Composition and Communication* 31.3 (1980): 253–69. Print.

———. "The Tidy House: Basic Writing in the American Curriculum." *Journal of Basic Writing* 12.1 (1993): 4–21. Print.

Center, Carole. "Representing Race in Basic Writing Scholarship." *Journal of Basic Writing* 26.1 (2007): 20–42. Print.

Collins, Terrence, and Melissa Blum. "Meanness and Failure: Sanctioning Basic Writers." *Journal of Basic Writing* 19.1 (2000): 13–21. Print.

Crouch, Mary Kay, and Gerri McNenney. "Looking Back, Looking Forward: California Grapples with 'Remediation.'" *Journal of Basic Writing* 19.2 (2000): 44–71. Print.

DeGenaro, William, and Edward M. White. "Going Around in Circles: Methodological Issues in Basic Writing Research." *Journal of Basic Writing* 19.1 (2000): 22–35. Print.

Fitzgerald, Sallyanne H. "The Context Determines Our Choice: Curriculum, Students, and Faculty." *Mainstreaming Basic Writers.* Ed. Gerri McNenny. Mahwah: Erlbaum, 2001. 215–23. Print.

———. "Basic Writing in One California Community College." *BWe: Basic Writing e-Journal* 1.2 (1999): n. pag. Web. <http://www.asu.edu/clas/english/composition/cbw/bwe_fall_1999.htm>.

Gilyard, Keith. "Basic Writing, Cost Effectiveness, and Ideology." *Journal of Basic Writing* 19.1 (2000): 36–42. Print.

Glau, Gregory R. "Bringing Them Home: Three Perspectives of the *Stretch Program*—A New Model of University-Level Basic Writing Instruction." 1996

CCCC Conference. Milwaukee, March 1996. Published as ERIC document ED 403 558, 1997.

——. "Mainstream Plus: Basic Writing Programs that Work." 1998 CCCC Conference. Chicago, April 1998. Published as ERIC document ED 419 237, 1999.

——. "The *Stretch Program*: Arizona State University's New Model of University-level Basic Writing Instruction." WPA: Writing Program Administration 20.1–2 (1996): 79–91. Print.

Gleason, Barbara. "Returning Adults to the Mainstream: Toward a Curriculum of Diverse Student Writers." *Mainstreaming Basic Writers.* Ed. Gerri McNenny. Mahwah: Erlbaum, 2001. 121–43. Print.

Goen, Sugie, and Helen Gillotte-Tropp. "Integrating Reading and Writing: A Response to the Basic Writing 'Crisis.'" *Journal of Basic Writing* 22.2 (2003): 90–113. Print.

Goto, Stanford T. "Basic Writers and Policy Reform: Why We Keep Talking Past Each Other." *Journal of Basic Writing* 21.2 (2001): 1–20. Print.

Gray-Rosendale, Laura. "Investigating Our Discursive History: *JBW* and the Construction of the 'Basic Writer's' Identity." *Journal of Basic Writing* 18.2 (1999): 108–35. Print.

——. *Rethinking Basic Writing.* Mahwah: Erlbaum, 2000. Print.

Gray-Rosendale, Laura, Loyola K. Bird, and Judith F. Bullock. "Rethinking the Basic Writing Frontier: Native American Students' Challenge to Our Histories." *Journal of Basic Writing* 22.1 (2003): 71–106. Print.

Grego, Rhonda, and Nancy Thompson. "Repositioning Remediation: Renegotiating Composition's Work in the Academy." *College Composition and Communication* 47.1 (1996): 62–84. Print.

Lalicker, William B. "A Basic Introduction to Basic Writing Program Structures: A Baseline and Five Alternatives." *BWe: Basic Writing e-Journal* 1.2 (1999): n. pag. Web. <http://www.asu.edu/clas/english/composition/cbw/bwe_fall_1999.htm#bill>.

Lunsford, Andrea A. "The Content of Basic Writers' Essays." *College Composition and Communication* 31.3 (1980): 278–90. Print.

Mutnick, Deborah. "The Strategic Value of Basic Writing: An Analysis of the Current Moment." *Journal of Basic Writing* 19.1 (2000): 69–83. Print.

Rodby, Judith, and Tom Fox. "Basic Work and Material Acts: The Ironies, Discrepancies, and Disjunctures of Basic Writing and Mainstreaming." *Journal of Basic Writing* 19.1 (2000): 84–99. Print.

Rosen-Knill, Deborah, and Kim Lynch. "A Method for Describing Basic Writers and Their Writing: Lessons from a Case Study." *Journal of Basic Writing* 19.2 (2000): 93–117. Print.

Royer, Daniel J., and Roger Gilles. "Basic Writing and Directed Self-Placement." *BWe: Basic Writing e-Journal* 2.2 (2000): n. pag. Web. <http://www.asu.edu/clas/english/composition/cbw/summer_2000_V2N2.htm>.

——. *Directed Self-Placement: Principles and Practices.* Cresskill, NJ: Hampton, 2003. Print.

Schwalm, David E. "Teaching Basic Writing: The Community College on the University Campus." *WPA: Writing Program Administration* 13.1–2 (1989): 15–24. Print.

Shaughnessy, Mina P. *Errors and Expectations: A Guide for the Teacher of Basic Writing.* New York: Oxford UP, 1977. Print.

Sheridan-Rabideau, Mary P., and Gordon Brossell. "Finding Basic Writing's Place." *Journal of Basic Writing* 14.1 (1995): 21–26. Print.

Smoke, Trudy. "Mainstreaming Writing: What Does This Mean for ESL Students?" *Mainstreaming Basic Writers*. Ed. Gerri McNenny. Mahwah: Erlbaum, 2001. 193–214. Print.

Soliday, Mary. *The Politics of Remediation: Institutional and Student Needs in Higher Education.* Pittsburgh: U of Pittsburgh, P, 2002. Print.

Soliday, Mary and Barbara Gleason. "From Remediation to Enrichment: Evaluating a Mainstreaming Project." *Journal of Basic Writing* 16.1 (1997): 64–78. Print.

Sternglass, Marilyn S. *Time to Know Them.* Mahwah: Erlbaum, 1997. Print.

Stevens, Scott. "Nowhere to Go: Basic Writing and the Scapegoating of Civic Failure." *Journal of Basic Writing* 21.1 (2002): 3–15. Print.

White, Edward M. "Revisiting the Importance of Placement and Basic Studies: Evidence of Success." *Mainstreaming Basic Writers*. Ed. Gerri McNenny. Mahwah: Erlbaum, 2001. 19–28. Print.

Wiley, Mark. "Mainstreaming and Other Experiments in a Learning Community." *Mainstreaming Basic Writers*. Ed. Gerri McNenny. Mahwah: Erlbaum, 2001. 173–91. Print.

Winslow, Rosemary, and Monica Mische. "Rethinking At-Risk Students' Knowledge and Needs: Heroes' Decisions and Students' Quest for Identity and Meaning in a Content Composition Course." *Mainstreaming Basic Writers*. Ed. Gerri McNenny. Mahwah: Erlbaum, 2001. 145–71. Print.

Resources for Teaching and Research

Keeping Journals and Building a Course Archive

Keeping a classroom journal and building an archive of course materials can help us to follow the daily progress of our teaching. After the school term ends, these classroom journals and archives provide a significant record of classroom events that remain helpful in revising syllabi and assignments, writing annual reports, and writing journal articles and conference presentations.

Indeed, teachers' classroom journals and archives of course materials can serve as the starting point for research. After the end of a particularly long semester, I (Susan Naomi Bernstein) analyzed the classroom journal I kept in my daily planner and used my course materials archive (including video) to look for connecting themes and ideas ("Basic Writing: In Search of a New Map").

Marc Lamont Hill and his co-teacher kept journals along with their students in order to respond to daily writing questions connected to the course texts ("Wounded Healing: Forming a Storytelling Community in Hip-Hop Lit"). As Hill demonstrates, journaling with our students can become a significant means of communication for discussing difficult subjects. Indeed, in some cases instructors' journals may serve as models for students' responses.

As you read the essays in this edition of *Teaching Developmental Writing*, consider writing journal entries to record responses to the readings. Seeds of ideas from your journal can grow into classroom lessons or research or writing projects. Think about sharing the journal entries with other teachers, in a study group or online. This process can help to build solidarity with others, as we discover common questions and concerns, or convey our unique approaches to pedagogical issues.

Consider the following questions to prompt your journal writing:

- What activity did I find most interesting or engaging?

- What activity did I find most confusing or disengaging?

- What activity did the students seem to find most interesting or engaging?
- What activity did the students find most confusing or disengaging? Why do these activities stand out as engaging or disengaging?[1]

Consider collecting the following artifacts to further enhance your archive of the course:

- Copies of syllabi
- Assignment instructions
- Students' essays and other course documents for future reference

Consider building an archive of electronic materials for future reference:

- Take computer screen shots or photos of the board of items relevant to class discussion and writing assignments.
- With students' permission, take videos of class discussions or other special classroom events.
- If your class uses a course management system, Web site, social network, or other online venues, include materials from these virtual spaces as well.

Writing Conference Proposals and Articles

In 1977, Mina Shaughnessy suggested four questions that would address "some needed research" for basic writing. Although basic writing was not new to many colleges and universities, rhetoric and composition was at that time still a fledgling field, and open admissions was still a relatively recent concept at the senior colleges of the City University of New York (CUNY).[2] Some teachers at CUNY and at similar institutions expressed concern that they did not know how to teach students admitted under open admissions, students that generally had limited-to-nonexistent prior practice with writing for college. The teachers' writing experiences were generally more extensive and varied, and quite different from the experiences of the majority of students enrolled under open admissions. Because of this disparity in educational privilege and preparation for college, these teachers also believed that such students could not be taught.

Mina Shaughnessy responded to this perceived need with her book *Errors and Expectations: A Guide for the Teacher of Basic Writing* (1977), which was itself a research study based on thousands of placement essays written by students admitted under open admissions policies at

City College. In an article published in the same year, Shaughnessy presented four research questions that she believed would "generate specific research plans that would move us toward the [ambitious] pedagogy I speak of":

1. "What are the signs of growth in writing among adults whose development as writers has been delayed by inferior preparation but who are then exposed to intensive instruction in writing?"

2. "What sub-skills of writing, heretofore absorbed by students over time in a variety of situations, can be effectively developed through direct and systematic instruction at the freshman level?"

3. "What skills have we failed to take note of in our analysis of academic tasks?"

4. "What goes on and what ought go on in the composition classroom?"[3]

Our responses to these questions may well depend on our individual students, locations, departments, and working situations. At the same time, the generality implied in the questions can help us to forge connections across time and space. Because we are more than three decades beyond Shaughnessy's initial work with "adults whose development as writers has been delayed by inferior preparation," we can investigate whether prior research can inform current concerns or whether current concerns can shed new light on prior research. For example, we might ask: What are signs of growth in writing among adults whose previous experiences with writing have mostly concerned writing for standardized assessment tests? What skills in multimedia literacy can students learn to effectively develop through direct and systematic instruction in writing at the first-year level? What skills cannot be measured through placement and exit assessments? What goes on or ought to go on in the virtual or hybrid composition classroom?

The possibilities for questions reach as wide as the scope of our imaginations and our students' needs. Our questions may be inflected by our students' and our own differences from and similarities to each other, meeting or departing at intersections of race, class, gender, sexuality, ability, or language. Take notice of your questions, write them down, share them virtually or face-to-face with colleagues — and with students. From these moments, new scholarship is often born.

To move from writing teaching journal entries to writing conference proposals and articles based on your teaching, consider these practices:

Carefully reread your teaching journal and your archives of classroom materials. Make a list of analytic and persuasive topics based on themes and ideas you discover in your teaching journal and archives. As a writer with ADHD, my process for organizing my ideas into written form is often inductive rather than deductive. The excerpt from my teaching journal (next page) illustrates how I worked with induction as a starting point for writing the article "Basic Writing: In Search of a New Map." I have broken this process into steps that helped me to move from the journal toward a rough draft.

1. *Read the teaching journal and classroom archive to find a general subject for the article.* I knew that I wanted to write about new academic writers at the very beginning of their journeys through college. I also knew that the paradigm for basic writing was shifting from a student-centered culture to an assessment-centered culture, with the result that many courses for new writers had been eliminated from universities, and even from community colleges whose historic missions had included open enrollment. Related to this issue, I found that students admitted under open enrollment were actively intellectually engaged with course materials, contrary to media stereotypes of "remedial" courses.[4] Finally, I knew that I wanted to talk about what happened when our class read Dr. Martin Luther King Jr.'s 1967 speech "Beyond Vietnam: A Time to Break Silence."

2. *Narrow the general subject to three or four particular points.* Although I inductively understood why the ideas in my general subject were related, I knew that the reader might have some difficulty seeing these connections. Also I knew I would have difficulty trying to contain my divergent thoughts within the parameters and limitations of a journal article. I did substantial freewriting and several discovery drafts to try to narrow the article's focus. This writing and peer feedback — an invaluable resource — helped me to create a more cohesive plan for the subjects I wanted to address: (1) students' embodied engagement with King's "Beyond Vietnam: A Time to Break Silence," (2) students' resilience, and (3) a new map.

3. *Assign a code (a typeface, color, or symbol) to each point and re-read the journal and classroom archive.* Every time you find one of the three or four points in your journal and archives, apply your code to highlight where each point was mentioned, either implicitly or explicitly. The box on the following page shows the code I chose: **bold** for students' embodied engagement with King's "Beyond Vietnam: A Time to Break Silence"; *italics for students' resilience*, and <u>underlining</u> for the new map. Below, you will see how I marked an entry in my teaching journal using each of the typefaces. The entry I chose as an example was a breakdown of course activities for a day late in the semester. This entry included description of physical space, comments from students (assigned numbers as random placeholders not related to students' real names), and my editorial comments. I used entries like these to guide my research agenda for the article, and to write the classroom narrative.

JOURNAL ENTRY: BEGINNING BW.

—Arranged to attend writing lab hour with students.

—In lab, worked with students 1 on 1.

—Continued one-on-one in class—talked with all students—because of extended lab hour, had time to talk with everyone.

—*Lots of work trying to ~~get~~ organize and create a clear thesis statement.*

—**The social justice policy—great discussion about relationship to King:**

> **Student #1: because things are still the same, because they're still trying to keep us out—and high school ~~can't be~~ doesn't prepare us.**

> **Student #2: ~~We are~~ like King, we need to stand up for what we believe in.**

After class: Worked with Student #1 and Student #3 to write down their thinking.

Extended time gives us more time to focus on WRITING!

Think about why this writing matters. We often write because of others' demands—not unlike our students. Perhaps we write to complete a graduate course, or to work toward tenure and promotion. But what about the larger picture? Who is our wider audience? What is our deeper purpose? What important contributions can we make to the field of basic writing? How can our contributions make a difference in the lived experiences of students and teachers? These global questions motivate my writing as I begin each new project—and have guided me through writing blocks and frustrations since graduate school. The questions are challenging, and the responses are always changing. Nonetheless, when I consider the larger world, I find that my focus sharpens and that I can concentrate more on specific details and examples that are necessary for other readers to understand my perspective.

Create an argument by considering your audience and purpose. Ask yourself: Whom do I want to persuade? What action do I want readers to take as a result of reading my conference proposal or article? In the context of my argument, what angles do I need to consider? Remember that persuasive writing facilitates our practice with complex organizational skills. We learn from analyzing and synthesizing our own ideas. Indeed, as we write, we become better teachers of writing.

Consider what makes this research original. For instance, how would you describe your population of students? Are your students similar to or different from student populations included in previous studies? Is the location of your teaching unique? How would you describe the physical or geographic setting? What about the program(s) for which you teach? What special features do these program(s) have? What teaching experiences seem particularly significant? Were these experiences difficult, unusual, or transformative? Why do you think so? Such questions provide a starting point to contextualize your research with studies that other scholars have completed on similar topics.

Read the articles in this book that match your area(s) of interest to understand how research questions are framed. Use your teaching journal to outline the articles, or list the main points to study different models of organization and structure, and the different styles and approaches of each writer.

Pay careful attention to the bibliographies at the end of each article to find additional resources related to your subject area(s). *The Bedford Bibliography for Teachers of Basic Writing*, Third Edition <http://bcs.bedfordstmartins.com/basicbib3e/> includes an annotated bibliography of sources for basic writing scholarship, theory, and practice. Also see *CompPile* <http://comppile.org/> and *CompFAQS* <http://compfaqs.org/> for additional resources for composition and rhetoric, writing studies, and basic writing.

Teaching, Advocacy, and Action

As teachers and students working together we all have potential as writers, and all of us struggle with writing as well. We may have doubted our capacity to endure our struggles or our ability to achieve any measure of success (especially those measures of success required by the institution). At the same time, many of us, students and teachers both, also are engaged in surviving as writers within the limited time and space that we have to devote to writing within and beyond our institutional settings. Our own struggles may convince us that our experiences with survival are the same as our students. Yet when we claim that difference does not matter to us, we ignore the elephant in the living room.

We are not all developmental writers. As teachers, whatever our varied histories, we are not now labeled by postsecondary institutions as "developmental," "basic," or "remedial" writers. But our students, if they are enrolled in our developmental writing courses, *do* carry these labels and often the unfortunate stereotypes and consequences that accompany those labels. The reasons for these stereotypes and consequences often meet at intersections of race, class, gender, sexuality, ability, age, language of origin, or other categories that identify students as "different."

Even if we were developmental students a generation ago, or if we are recent immigrants, or if we teach part-time and support our families on low wages, we are in positions of authority over our students. We take attendance, grade students' writing, and increasingly prepare students for outside assessments that determine whether they fail or repeat the course, whether they can stay in school, or whether they will need to drop out or transfer to another institution.[5]

Additionally, our relationship to students may take on a different cast. We may be prone to imagining that our students do remain very different from us, their teachers. We may buy into current rhetoric that such students do not belong in college and that the students begin at such a low level that long-term progress may never be possible for them. We may construct assignments that do not challenge students to move beyond our perceived ability of their intellect. Because so much in a basic writing course hinges on measurable development in writing, we may become alarmed after a first reading of students' writing early in the semester. Our alarm may take shape as another unintended effect of categories of difference. Stereotypes of students in "remediation" may affect our judgment of students' potential abilities. The need to show that we have "college-ready" students may overcome the wish to teach the students we actually have in front of us. We may grow weary of the need to work with those students so that they learn to write not only beyond what they expect from themselves, but also beyond what we expect from them.

Yet students labeled "developmental" can be as capable as any other student of achieving long-term academic success. Many of the students enrolled in our courses attended schools that did not have the economic and material resources to offer adequate preparation for college writing. These students often need access to multiple and intensive experiences with writing.[6] Acceleration may work for some students, but other students often need more time. As some students learn over a longer period of time, perhaps a year or more, they grow and mature through the writing process. Developmental writing becomes a catalyst for some students to discover not only their potential as writers but also a passion for writing to persuade and communicate with readers beyond the classroom.

In this respect, we may claim a moment of solidarity with our students as we struggle with the writing process ourselves. We may need to revise not only at the word and sentence level, but also at the level of our critical thinking. We must learn (again and again) to move beneath and beyond the surface features of our texts to *transform* our writing. For many of us this process is deeply embodied—as students have often described. We sweat, we squirm, we walk away from our writing in deep frustration, we return with great hope. And sometimes we—

both teachers and students—choose not to return at all but to move on to projects that demand other talents and energies. Like that book manuscript we may have abandoned in order to fulfill obligations for teaching and service. Or that course we cannot complete because we must comply with the never-ending need to keep a roof over our heads and to feed our families.

As teachers of basic writing, we live in the throes of a major contradiction: While our programs and courses are downsized, outsourced, or eliminated altogether, we can see that the need for Basic Writing still exists. Our students, whoever they are, whatever their past experiences may have been, and in spite of or because of their similarities to or differences from us, are enrolled in basic writing. Our responsibility remains: We must provide spaces for them to learn to write, and we must resist the temptation to categorize their abilities or to prejudge their potentials. If we really believe that "everyone can write"[7] (Elbow), then we must extend this belief to our students and facilitate opportunities for students to learn to believe in themselves and their own possibilities for transformation.[8]

The questions regarding difference outlined in the following section are adapted from bell hooks's article in Chapter 7 and the Chapter 11 Geller et al. article and offer suggestions for building faculty awareness regarding race, writing, and difference. In particular, Geller proposes specific activities to directly address racial disparities and the discomforts of discussing raced in mixed communities. In Chapter 7, hooks addresses why faculty support groups around racial differences are necessary, and June Jordan and Gloria Anzaldúa, also in Chapter 7, address the intersections of race, class, linguistic differences, and schooling. While these questions are designed for professional development for teachers, the questions also may be appropriate for students enrolled in basic writing courses. Freewrite your responses to these questions, then consider sharing your responses with teachers or students either in traditional face-to-face settings for faculty and students, or on the Web.

Linguistic diversity. Anzaldúa suggests that there are many languages that Chicanos speak. She lists them as Standard English, working-class and slang English, Standard Spanish, Standard Mexican Spanish, North Mexican Spanish dialect, Chicano Spanish (Texas, New Mexico, Arizona, and California have regional variations), Tex-Mex, and Pachuco (called *caló*). Like Anzaldúa, list the languages you speak and write. Also discuss how language usage may change according to such variables as audience, purpose, and occasion. What are your attitudes toward these different languages? What does it mean to you to "speak American"? What might "speaking American" mean to our students, and to different groups of our students, including students who grew up in the United States but are undocumented, students who are legal U.S. residents but have spent considerable time in a country or region in which American English is not spoken, students who are first- or second-generation Americans, and students who are Native American and may or may not know the languages spoken by their predecessors?

"Diversity" and social justice. In *Teaching Developmental Writing: Background Readings*, the reader is often compelled to consider the difference between diversity (equitable representation of people of different races and cultural backgrounds) and social justice (equitable access to resources that prevent human suffering, and to offer equitable opportunities for all people to flourish and participate in a democracy). June Jordan's essay, first published in the mid-1980s, presents compelling insights into the intersections of teaching writing and issues of social justice, particularly around race. bell hooks's essay, about a decade later, addresses the inception of multicultural classrooms and curricula, and the resistance of some educators to these changes in the field.

In more recent essays, Mark Lamont Hill, Justin Hudson, Valerie Kinloch, Jane Maher, and Gloria Rodriguez and Lisceth Cruz, among others, point to racial inequities in public schooling. In these essays, the authors reiterate significant points about race, racial inequality, and educational inequity in U.S. schools. Like hooks, the authors argue for proactive change in our schools, and like Jordan, they understand these changes as a matter of social justice, changes that intersect not only with schooling but also with access to adequate housing and health care, sustainable employment, and fair treatment from law enforcement and the judicial system. Geller, Eodice, Condon, Carroll, and Boquet offer a list of helpful definitions for key concepts to understand systemic racism and critical race theory. Several of these essays present their most salient points through literacy autobiography and classroom narrative.

In your teaching journal, write a literacy autobiography or classroom narrative (or a combination of both). Make sure that your story includes your relationship to race and racism, or that it reflects on the relationship of your students to race and racism. If you feel your knowledge in this area is limited, see the bibliography offered in "Anti-Racism Work" (p. 426 in this volume). As bell hooks suggests, "When we, as educators allow our pedagogy to be radically changed by our recognition of a multicultural world, we can give students the education that they desire and deserve" (p. 276).

Values self-affirmation. In your journal, reflect on the following prompt with at least two–three pages of writing. The idea for this prompt is taken from "Recursive Processes in Self-Affirmation: Intervening to Close the Minority Achievement Gap" (Cohen, Garcia, Purdie-Vaughns,

Apfel, and Brzustoski). Their research investigated the connections between writing, values affirmation, and school success. Students considered "at risk" for school failure, these researchers concluded, were able to improve their learning and sustain their success by considering the relationship between their values and their persistence in school. Write in response to an adaptation of the prompt the researchers created, and share the prompt with your students.

Prompt
Which value or values from the list below would you count as most important to you? Would you include other values that are not on this list? Why is this value (or values) connected to your strengths as a writer? Why would this value (or values) remain important to you as you complete your academic work for the term?

Values List

- Being good at art

- Creativity

- Independence

- Living in the moment

- Membership in a social group (such as your community, racial group, or school club)

- Music

- Politics

- Relationships with friends or family

- Religious values

- Sense of humor[9]

Writing Studies: Creating Syllabi from *Teaching Developmental Writing*

In Chapter 3, Jonikka Charlton recounts her experiences teaching a basic writing class based on theories evolved from Downs and Wardle's approaches to writing studies, or "writing about writing." Downs and Wardle suggest that writing "shifts the central goal from teaching 'academic writing' to teaching realistic and useful conceptions of writing — perhaps the most significant of which would be that writing is neither basic nor universal but content- and context-contingent and irreducibly complex" (Downs and Wardle, 2007; cited in Carter, *BWe*, 2009–10). Charlton pushes this theory a step further by offering students in basic writing an approach to writing about writing based on their needs as beginning college writers. She writes:

> So, when students enter our classroom, the kind and amount of reading, thinking, and writing we ask them to do seems radically at odds with their past experiences, and many of them develop research questions designed to help them (1) make sense of their past experiences in high school, and (2) *understand how they can relate to their current and future learning experiences* [emphasis added]. (p. 109)

In creating syllabi using *Teaching Developmental Writing*, consider the following questions: Are certain essays or sections of the book particularly relevant to my program? What essays or sections of the book would be especially relevant for my students? Although this section focuses on basic writing courses from a writing studies perspective, also consider which selections from the book might be useful for graduate students new to composition and rhetoric and to teaching college basic writing?

What follows is a "writing about writing" syllabus for a basic writing course based on essays from *Teaching Developmental Writing*, and on Charlton's theory that students can use their course readings to "understand how they can relate to their current and future learning experiences," as well as being able to understand the larger social context in which their basic writing course work takes place. For example, a fifteen-week syllabus might look like this:

Week 1
Reading Assignments:
    Adrienne Rich, "Teaching Language in Open Admissions"
    Mike Rose, "Remediation at a Crossroads"

Week 2
Writing Assignment 1:
    Summary essay on readings from Week 1.

Week 3
Reading Assignments:
    Justin Hudson, "The Brick Tower"
    Jonikka Charlton, "Seeing Is Believing"

Week 4
Writing Assignment 2:
    Analysis essay on readings from Week 2.

Week 5
Reading Assignment:
    Jane Maher, "Raw Material"

Week 6
Writing Assignment 3:
> Synthesis essay: Find the common threads in the first five readings from this term.

Week 7
Reading Assignments:
> Gloria Anzaldúa, "How to Tame a Wild Tongue"
> June Jordan, "Nobody Mean More to Me Than You and the Future Life of Willie Jordan"

Week 8
Writing Assignment:
> Comparison Essay: Focus on the comparisons between Anzaldúa's and Jordan's approaches to language.

Week 9
Reading Assignments:
> Valerie Purdie-Vaughns, Geoffrey Cohen, et al., "Improving Minority Academic Performance"
> Anne Ellen Geller, et al., "Anti-Racism Work"

Week 10
Writing Assignment:
> Evaluation Classification Assignment: Classify the ways in which the writers in this section describe the intersections of race, education, and social justice.

Weeks 11–12
Research paper based on an intriguing question that you discover in the readings.

Weeks 13–14
Portfolio revision workshops.

Week 15
Portfolio due.
Note: For assignment suggestions, see "Common Writing Assignments" at the Purdue OWL, <http://owl.english.purdue.edu/owl/section/1/3/>. The suggestions offered at this link can be adapted for use in your own courses.

Additional Considerations

I try to imagine writing as a love affair waiting to happen—and one that unfolds through travel across time. So rather than focus too extensively on roadblocks or potholes, I instead offer the signposts I discover again and again with students as we travel down the feeder roads and the superhighways, the unpaved streets and treacherous mountain paths that bring us all, through our various meanderings, close to writing.

Reserve judgment. I reserve judgment, as I read the first paper, on infelicities of grammar and organization, or "deviation" from the standards, norms, or course outcomes. Instead I read mindfully and inquisitively, not as if I were the leader of an inquisition. That is, I read against the grain,[10] as students are often required to do. I read to find out what already is present in the texts—the strengths—and then address what's missing. In my comments for revision, I encourage students to take note of their strengths, to reconsider audience, and to aim to create the missing pieces from their compositions.

Recognize that grammar and style go hand in hand. I imagine that grammar and style are inseparable. I look at whole sentences, rather than isolated commas or mismatched verbs and subjects. I conceive of the verb as the center of the action. Is there actually a verb in the sentence? Is the verb strong? Is the verb a form of be (*is, are, was, were,* etc.)? This is the kernel around which the writer will grow the rest of the sentence. I encourage writers to experiment with verb choices, as well as with the sounds of verbs and their visual qualities—how the words appear on the page or screen.

Present the articles in *Teaching Developmental Writing* for language learning as part of the writing studies syllabus. In this way, students learn to analyze the concepts that I am trying to teach. How does Adrienne Rich use punctuation in "Teaching Language in Open Admissions"? How does Gloria Anzaldúa choose verbs in "How to Tame a Wild Tongue"? How do readers break down the meanings of these often difficult and—at the same time—very rich sentences? How would readers revise these sentences from twentieth-century into twenty-first-century language? Examining how and why language works can move us from reading for comprehension and information, to reading even more deeply to figure out the ways in which the structure of language creates meaning.[11]

Notes

1. Questions are adapted from Brookfield's article, "Understanding Classroom Dynamics: The Critical Incidents Questionnaire," which appeared in the first edition of *Teaching Developmental Writing.*
2. See Maher, Soliday, Gleason, and Horner and Lu, and Adrienne Rich's essay (p. 12) for additional histories and interpretations of that time and place. See Ritter, Otte and Williams Mlynarczyk (p. 427), and Greene and McAlexander for additional histories of the development at public and private institutions across the United States.

3. Deborah Sánchez and Eric Paulson have provided a beautifully up-to-date model for responding to Shaughnessy's question 4 in "Critical Language Awareness and Learners in Transitional College English" (p. 113). Their work points to several studies that critique current paradigms, as well as point to recent studies that adapt Shaughnessy's call for research through contemporary lenses. Also see Fleckenstein, Spinuzzi, Rickly, Papper, and Bazerman.
4. See Traub, for instance.
5. See as Mina Shaughnessy (1977), Marilyn Sternglass (1997), and Attewell and Lavin and their coresearchers (2007).
6. See Geller, Eodice, Condon, Carroll, and Boquet's "Cautionary Notes about Empathy" (p. 425).
7. See Elbow (2000).
8. Adapted from Bernstein, "Writing Challenges," (http://www.csupomona.edu/~crse/handouts/read_grain.html).
9. Adapted from Bernstein, "Many Roads to Writing."
10. Adapted from Bernstein, "Writing Beyond Stereotypes."
11. See Bartholomae and Petrosky, *Facts, Artifacts, and Counterfacts*. For textbooks by the same authors, see *Reading the Lives of Others*, and *Ways of Reading*. Also see Comfort.

Works Cited

Attewell, Paul, and David Lavin. *Passing the Torch: Does Higher Education for the Disadvantaged Pay Off Across the Generations?* New York: Russell Sage. 2007. Print.

Bartholomae, David, and Anthony Petrosky. *Facts, Artifacts, and Counterfacts: Theory and Method for a Reading and Writing Course.* Portsmouth: Boynton, 1986. Print.

———. *Reading the Lives of Others: A Sequence of for Writers.* Boston: Bedford, 1995. Print.

———. *Ways of Reading: An Anthology for Writers*, 9th ed. Boston: Bedford, 2011. Print.

———. *Ways of Reading: Words and Images.* Boston: Bedford, 2003. Print.

Bazerman, Charles. "Theories of the Middle Range in Historical Studies of Writing Practice." *Written Communication* 25.3 (2008): 299–318. Print.

Bernstein, Susan Naomi. "Many Roads." *Bedford Bits.* Bedford/St. Martin's, 11 July 2011. Web. 8 Mar. 2012. <http://blogs.bedfordstmartins.com/bits/>.

———. "Writing Beyond Stereotypes." *Bedford Bits.* Bedford/St. Martin's, 9 May 2011. Web. 8 Mar. 2012. <http://blogs.bedfordstmartins.com/bits/>.

———. "Writing Challenges: From Developmental to Transformational." *Bedford Bits.* Bedford/St. Martin's, 18 Jan. 2011. Web. 8 Mar. 2012. <http://blogs bedfordstmartins.com/bits/>.

Brookfield, Stephen. "Understanding Classroom Dynamics: The Critical Incidents Questionnaire." *Teaching Developmental Writing*. Ed. Susan Naomi Bernstein. New York: Bedford, 2001. 181–89. Print.

Cohen, Geoffrey L., Julio Garcia, Valerie Purdie-Vaughns, Nancy Apfel, and Patricia Brzustoski. "Recursive Processes in Self-Affirmation: Intervening to Close the Minority Achievement Gap." *Science* 17 (2009), 400–3. Print.

Comfort, Carol. *Breaking Boundaries.* New York: Prentice, 1999. Print.

Elbow, Peter. *Everyone Can Write: Essays Toward a Hopeful Theory of Writing and Teaching Writing*. New York: Oxford UP, 2000. Print.

Fleckenstein, Kristie S., Clay Spinuzzi, Rebecca J. Rickly, and Carole Clark Papper. "The Importance of Harmony: An Ecological Metaphor for Writing Research." *CCC* 60.1 (2008): 388–419. Print.

Greene, Nicole Pepinster and Patricia J. McAlexander, eds. *Basic Writing in America: The History of Nine College Programs*. Cresskill: Hampton UP, 2008. Print.

Ritter, Kelly. *Before Shaughnessy: Basic Writing at Yale and Harvard, 1920–1960*. Carbondale: Southern Illinois UP, 2009. Print.

Roozen, Kevin. "Journalism, Poetry, Stand-Up Comedy, and Academic Literacy: Mapping the Interplay of Curricular and Extracurricular Literate Activities." *Journal of Basic Writing* 27.1 (2008): 5–34. Print.

Shaughnessey, Mina. *Errors and Expectations: A Guide for the Teacher of Basic Writing*. New York: Oxford UP, 1977. Print.

Sternglass, Marilyn S. *Time to Know Them: A Longitudinal Study of Writing and Learning at the College Level*. Mahwah: Erlbaum, 1997. Print.

Traub, James. *City on a Hill: Testing the American Dream at City College*. Reading, MA: Addison-Wesley, 1994. Print.

About the Contributors

Peter Adams has taught developmental writing at Community College of Baltimore County for over thirty years. In addition to teaching, he currently acts as director of the Accelerated Learning Project, which has succeeded in doubling the success rates for developmental writing students at CCBC. His past professional responsibilities include acting as chair for the Council on Basic Writing for three years, serving on the editorial board of the *Journal of Basic Writing*, coordinating the CCBC writing program, and serving as a chair for the college's committee on general education and the CCBC English Department.

Gloria Anzaldúa was a prominent Chicana/tejana lesbian poet, essayist, teacher, and cultural theorist whose groundbreaking *Borderlands/La Frontera: The New Mestiza* (Aunt Lute Books, 1987) combines bilingual poetry, memoir, and historical analysis to illuminate the transcultural Mexican American "borderland" experience. Her subsequent works include *Making Face, Making Soul/Haciendo Caras: Creative and Cultural Perspectives by Feminists of Color* (ed., Aunt Lute Books, 1990) and *Interviews/Entrevistas* (Routledge, 2000). She was the recipient of an NEA Fiction Award, the Sappho Award of Distinction, and the American Studies Association Lifetime Achievement Award. Before her death in 2004, Anzaldúa wrote and taught in northern California.

Nancy Apfel is a research associate in the Child Study Center and Psychology Department at Yale University. She focuses on social psychology research in interventions to reduce the academic achievement gap between minority and white students.

Susan Naomi Bernstein has published this fourth edition of *Teaching Developmental Writing: Background Readings*, as well as three previous editions (2007, 2004, 2001), two shorter ancillary versions (2000, 1998), and the textbook *A Brief Guide to the Novel* (Longman, 2002). Her articles on basic writing have been published in the *Chronicle of Higher Education*, *Journal of Basic Writing*, *Modern Language Studies*, and elsewhere. "Beyond the Basics," her blog on writing processes, learning differences, and social justice, appears on Bedford/St. Martin's *Bedford Bits*. She is a past co-chair of the Council on Basic Writing and a past coeditor and current associate editor of *BWe: Basic*

Writing e-Journal. She taught her first basic writing course in 1987 and has worked with students for more than two decades in urban and rural settings in New York, Ohio, Texas, and Pennsylvania.

Elizabeth H. Boquet holds dual roles at Fairfield University as a professor of English and the first-ever dean of Academic Engagement. She is a coauthor (with Anne Ellen Geller, Michele Eodice, Frankie Condon, and Meg Carroll) of *The Everyday Writing Center: A Community of Practice* (Utah State UP, 2007), and the author of *Noise from the Writing Center* (Utah State UP, 2002), which posits the presence of "noise" and excess as an important distinction between the pedagogy of writing centers and that of the general academy.

Patrick L. Bruch is associate professor of writing studies in the Department of Writing Studies at the University of Minnesota–Twin Cities. He is coeditor of *The Hope and the Legacy: The Past, Present, and Future of "Students' Right to Their Own Language"* (Hampton, 2005), and has published articles on the social dynamics of teaching writing in books and journals, including *College Composition and Communication, Symploké, Journal of Developmental Education, Journal of College Reading and Learning, Journal of Advanced Composition*, and *Rhetoric Review*. He is also coeditor of the writing textbooks *Cities, Cultures, Conversations: Readings for Writers* (Allyn & Bacon, 1998) and *Reading City Life* (Pearson/Longman, 2005).

Meg Carroll, director of the Writing Center at Rhode Island College for twelve years, has also served on the board of the Northeast Writing Centers Association and acted as a representative for the International Writing Centers Association. She is a coauthor (with Anne Ellen Geller, Michele Eodice, Frankie Condon, and Elizabeth Boquet) of *The Everyday Writing Center: A Community of Practice* (Utah State UP, 2007).

Shannon Carter is an associate professor of English in the Department of Literature and Languages at Texas A&M Commerce, where she served for many years as director of the Writing Center and the Basic Writing Program and, more recently, director of first-year writing. Her primary teaching interests include writing (academic, civic, community, and multimedia), undergraduate research, and research methods and the digital humanities. Since 2007, she has led the Converging Literacies Center (CLiC), an interdisciplinary research center she established with Dr. Donna Dunbar-Odom to study and support the literate lives of local citizens and students. Author of *The Way Literacy Lives: Rhetorical Dexterity and the "Basic" Writer* (SUNY Press, 2008), her work has appeared in *College Composition and Communication, College English, Community Literacy Journal, Kairos, Computers and Writing Online*, the *Journal of Basic Writing*, and *BWe*. She is currently at work on her second book, *Writing for (a) Change: Literate Social Action in a Rural, University Town*. Grants supporting this and related work include a recent NEH Office of Digital Humanities

Start-Up Grant (Remixing Rural Texas), for which she serves as principle investigator.

Jonikka Charlton, an associate professor of English and coordinator of the First-Year Writing Program at the University of Texas–Pan American, specializes in rhetoric and composition, writing program administration, and teacher preparation both at the university level and in PK–12. She has published many articles, including recent entries in *WPA*, the *BWe*, and *Praxis*. Her article "The Illusion of Transparency at an HSI: A Pedagogical History of Becoming Public WPAs" (coauthored with Colin Charlton) was included in *Going Public: The WPA as Advocate for Engagement* (Utah State UP, 2010).

J. Elizabeth Clark is a professor of English and the codirector of composition at LaGuardia Community College. An active participant in the ePortfolio and Capstone projects at the college, she also regularly leads faculty professional development seminars through the Center for Teaching & Learning. She serves as co-chair for the Council on Basic Writing in addition to serving on the review board of the *International Journal of ePortfolio* and the editorial boards for *College Composition and Communication* and *BWe*. Her publications have appeared in *Radical Teacher* (where she served on the editorial board from 1998 to 2011), *Peer Review*, *Minnesota Review*, *Journal of Medical Humanities*, and *Women's Studies Quarterly*.

Geoffrey Cohen is the James G. March Professor of Organizational Studies in Education and Business at the Stanford University School of Education. A primary focus of his research addresses the effects of group identity on achievement with a focus on underperformance and racial and gender achievement gaps. Additional research programs address hiring discrimination, the psychology of closed-mindedness and intergroup conflict, and psychological processes underlying antisocial and health-risk behavior.

Frankie Condon is an associate professor in the English Department at the University of Nebraska–Lincoln, where her professional areas of specialty include composition and rhetoric, writing center theory and practice, and critical race theory. She is a representative for the International Writing Centers Association and a coauthor (with Anne Ellen Geller, Michele Eodice, Meg Carroll, and Elizabeth Boquet) of *The Everyday Writing Center: A Community of Practice* (Utah State UP, 2007).

Jonathan C. Cook teaches at the University of Colorado, Boulder. His primary research investigates the psychological, physiological, and interpersonal consequences that can arise when people are chronically exposed to the possibility of negative evaluation because of one or more of their important social identities.

Lisceth Cruz is currently a graduate student researcher in the School of Education at the University of California, Davis. Her research focuses on how educational issues affect disenfranchised, underserved, and vulnerable student populations. Cruz is also a program coordinator in the UC Davis Student Programs and Activities Center, dedicated to the recruitment and retention of Latino/a students in higher education.

Martha Clark Cummings has taught at the Monterey Institute of International Studies, the New School Online University, Hunter College, and the Center for Language Research at the University of Aizu in Aizu-Wakamatsu, Japan. Her research focuses on the differences between face-to-face and computer-mediated instruction and narrative inquiry in second language acquisition. As part of the U.S. Department of State English Language Specialist Program, she has trained English language teachers in Cyprus, Thailand, Tunisia, and Turkey. She is the coauthor of two ESL textbooks, *Changes: Readings for Writers* (St. Martin's, 1998) and *Inspired to Write* (Cambridge UP, 2004). Additionally, her writing has appeared in the *Journal of Basic Writing*, *The Language Teacher*, and *PacCall*, among others. Currently, Cummings teaches the MA in TESOL Program at Hunter College, an online MA TESOL Program at Anaheim University, and writing at Kingsborough Community College, and serves as chair of the TESOL Standing Committee on Diversity.

Lennard Davis grew up in a deaf family, which led him to study and write extensively about the idea of "normalcy" in culture. At the University of Illinois at Chicago, he is currently a professor and the department head in the English Department, a professor of disability and human development in the School of Applied Health Sciences, and a professor of medical education in the College of Medicine. He also is director of Project Biocultures, a think tank devoted to issues around the intersection of culture, medicine, disability, biotechnology, and the biosphere. His research on disability has been published widely in scholarly journals, and he is the author of *Enforcing Normalcy: Disability, Deafness, and the Body* (Verso, 1995), *Bending Over Backwards: Dismodernism, Disability, and Other Difficult Positions* (New York UP, 2002), and *Obsession: A History* (U of Chicago P, 2008).

Michele Eodice, a professor of writing, is director of the University of Oklahoma's writing center, associate provost for academic engagement, and executive director of learning, teaching, and writing. She is a leader for both the International Writing Centers Association Council of Writing Program Administrators (additionally serving as the association's president from 2007–2009) and the Conference on College Composition and Communication. She has published copious peer-reviewed articles and chapters on coauthorship, peer collaboration, writing center practices and community, and student research practices. She is also the associate editor of development for the *Writing Center Journal*.

Nancy Farnan is a professor at San Diego State University and the interim associate dean for Faculty Development, Research, and

Special Projects. She teaches credential and graduate courses in English education, reading/language arts, and middle-level education and specializes in teacher education, reading education, writing education, assessment, and secondary school reform initiatives in the linked learning field. She is the coauthor (with Leif Fearn) of *Writing Effectively: Helping Students Master the Conventions of Writing* (Allyn & Bacon, 1997) and *Interactions: Teaching and Writing in the Language Arts* (Houghton, 2000).

Leif Fearn, having served on the faculty at San Diego University in both teacher education and special education for forty-three years, currently teaches writing instruction, educational psychology, and social studies. In addition to being a published fiction writer, he has written on creative thinking and creative problem solving, writing instruction, grammar, spelling, gifted education, and Indian education. He is the coauthor (with Nancy Farnan) of *Writing Effectively: Helping Students Master the Conventions of Writing* (Allyn & Bacon, 1997) and *Interactions: Teaching and Writing in the Language Arts* (Houghton, 2000).

Julio Garcia has worked as a postbaccalaureate researcher in the Intergroup Relations and Diversity Lab at Columbia University.

Sarah Gearhart is an English instructor at the Community College of Baltimore County–Essex.

Anne Ellen Geller, an associate professor in the English Department and director of writing across the curriculum at St. John's University of Liberal Arts and Sciences, focuses her research on student and faculty writers, writing centers, writing across the curriculum, writing in the disciplines, writing program administration, and coauthorship. With Michele Eodice, Frankie Condon, Meg Carroll, and Elizabeth Boquet, she coauthored *The Everyday Writing Center: A Community of Practice* (Utah State UP, 2007) as well as many other chapters and articles. She was awarded a 2010–2011 CCCC Research Initiative Grant (with Michele Eodice and Neal Lerner) for a project entitled "Seniors Reflect on Their Meaningful Writing Experiences: A Cross-Institutional Study."

Paula Gillespie is the director of the Center for Excellence in Writing at Florida International University. Gillespie is a cofounder (with Brad Hughes and Harvey Kail) of the Peer Writing Tutor Alumni Research Project (PWTARP) as well as the Writing Center Summer Institute, a weeklong writing-intensive retreat for professionals. With Neal Lerner, she coauthored *The Longman Guide to Peer Tutoring*, 2nd ed. (2008), and she coedited *Writing Center Research: Extending the Conversation* (Routledge, 2002), which was selected by the International Writing Centers Association for best book of 2002. Most recently, she received the 2011 Ron Maxwell Award for Distinguished Leadership in Promoting the Collaborative Learning Practices of Peer Tutors in Writing.

Gregory R. Glau is an associate professor and the director of the University Writing Program at Northern Arizona University. He is the coeditor (with Linda Adler-Kassner and Chitralekha Duttagupta) of the *Bedford Bibliography for Teachers of Basic Writing*, 3rd ed. (Bedford, 2010), coauthor (with Craig Jacobsen) of *Scenarios for Writing* (Mayfield/McGraw-Hill, 2001), and coauthor (with Duane Roen and Barry Maid) of *The McGraw-Hill Guide: Writing for College, Writing for Life*, 2nd ed. (2010). He was a member of Arizona State University's *Stretch Program* when it received the President's Award for Innovation in 2003.

Allison Harl is an assistant professor of English at the School of Arts and Humanities at Ferrum College, where she teaches basic writing, composition, world literature, American frontier literature and film, and rhetoric. Her scholarly interests include reading and writing connections, literature and film of the American West, and composition and community partnerships.

Marc Lamont Hill is one of the leading hip-hop generation intellectuals in the country and has served as an associate professor of English education at Teachers College, Columbia University since 2009. He also holds an affiliated faculty appointment in African American studies at the Institute for Research in African American Studies at Columbia University. His award-winning work, which covers topics such as culture, politics, and education, has appeared in numerous journals, magazines, books, and anthologies. Dr. Hill has lectured widely and provides regular commentary for media outlets such as NPR, the *Washington Post*, *Essence Magazine*, and the *New York Times*. He is the host of the nationally syndicated television show *Our World With Black Enterprise* and also provides regular commentary for CNN, MSNBC, and Fox News Channel, where he was a political contributor and regular guest on The O'Reilly Factor. He is the author of *Beats, Rhymes, and Classroom Life: Hip-Hop Pedagogy and the Politics of Identity* (Teachers College Press, 2009) and *The Classroom and the Cell: Conversations on Black Life in America* (Third World Press, 2011).

bell hooks has held distinguished teaching positions at Yale, Oberlin College, and City College CUNY, and is currently Distinguished Professor in Residence in Appalachian Studies at Berea College. Born Gloria Jean Watkins in Hopkinsville, Kentucky, she chose the lowercase pen name bell hooks, based on the names of her mother and grandmother, to emphasize the importance of the substance of her writing as opposed to who she is. In her long and fruitful career as a teacher, author, and social activist, hooks has explored the interconnectivity of race, class, and gender and their role in producing and perpetuating systems of oppression and domination. She has published over thirty books, the first of which—the highly praised *Ain't I a Woman: Black Women and Feminism* (Pluto, 1981)—was ranked by *Publishers*

Weekly as one of the twenty most influential women's books of the last twenty years in 1992.

Justin Hudson was valedictorian of his class at Hunter High School, where he graduated in 2010. His graduation speech "The Brick Tower" was published in the *New York Times*. After graduating, Hudson matriculated to Columbia University.

Brad Hughes has been director of the Writing Center at the University of Wisconsin–Madison since 1984 and the director of writing across the curriculum since 1990. He has pioneered the use of electronic discussions in college courses, and he is a regular contributor to *Another Word*, the UW–Madison Writing Center blog. He is a cofounder (with Harvey Kail and Paula Gillespie) of the Peer Writing Tutor Alumni Research Project (PWTARP), and he has published numerous chapters, articles, and reviews about writing instruction and writing center administration. He also serves on the editorial board for the *Writing Center Journal*.

David A. Jolliffe is professor of English and of curriculum and instruction at the University of Arkansas, where he also holds the Brown Chair in English Literacy. He is the founder of the Arkansas Delta Oral History Project, through which mentors from the University of Arkansas collaborate with students from ten high schools in eastern Arkansas to uncover and record local histories. He is the coauthor of *Everyday Use: Rhetoric at Work in Reading and Writing*, 2nd ed. (Pearson/Longman, 2005) and *Academic Writing: Genres, Samples, and Resources* (Pearson/Longman, 2005), as well as the author of *Pre-AP Strategies in English: Rhetoric* (College Entrance Examination Board, 2004).

June Jordan was a celebrated poet, novelist, essayist, teacher, and political activist. The author of twenty-six books, Jordan is the most published African American writer in history. Before her death in June 2002, she was a professor of African American studies at the University of California, Berkeley, where she founded and directed Poetry for the People, a popular community outreach program that influenced local high schools, churches, and prisons by bringing poetry back from an elitist perspective to its roots in oral tradition. On the strength of her poetry and books such as *June Jordan's Poetry for the People: A Revolutionary Blueprint* (Routledge, 1995) and *Affirmative Acts: Political Essays* (Anchor, 1998), Jordan received numerous grants, fellowships, and awards. Her poems have appeared in more than thirty anthologies. Her memoir is *Soldier: A Poet's Childhood* (Basic Civitas Books, 2001). Other collections, *Directed by Desire: The Collected Poems of June Jordan* (Copper Canyon Press, 2007) and *Some of Us Did Not Die: New and Selected Essays of June Jordan* (Basic Civitas Books, 2003), were published posthumously.

Harvey Kail is an associate professor of English and the writing center coordinator at the University of Maine, where he teaches composition, composition pedagogy, analytical and persuasive writing, and foundations of literary analysis. He also has special interest in the global development of writing centers and collaborative learning. He is a cofounder (with Brad Hughes and Paula Gillespie) of the Peer Writing Tutor Alumni Research Project (PWTARP), and he received the Ron Maxwell Award in 2004 for his work with peer tutors. The College of Liberal Arts and Sciences at the University of Maine also named him as its outstanding teacher in 2008.

Valerie Kinloch is an associate professor in literacy studies (adolescent literacy and English education) in the College of Education and Human Ecology at Ohio State University. Her most recent work investigates democratic learning, literacy practices, and spatial affiliation in the education of diverse student populations, particularly in urban contexts. Her book on the life and literary contributions of poet June Jordan titled *June Jordan: Her Life and Letters*, was published in 2006. Kinloch's writings have appeared in *College Composition and Communication*, *English Education*, the *Journal of Advanced Composition*, *Developmental Education and Urban Literacy Monograph*, the *Encyclopedia of the Harlem Renaissance*, among others. Dr. Kinloch was awarded a Spencer Foundation Small Research Grant as well as a National Council of Teachers of English (NCTE) grant-in-aid to support her research on the writing, literacy, and activist practices of African American and Latino/a high school students in urban settings. Her most recent book *Harlem on Our Minds: Place, Race, and the Literacies of Urban Youth* (Teachers College Press, 2009) reflects this research and in particular, explores how community gentrification and politics of place affect lives and literacies of youth in historic Harlem. She is the recipient of the 2010 AERA Scholars of Color Early Career Award.

Marisa A. Klages is an assistant professor of English and codirector of composition at LaGuardia Community College. She also currently serves as the director of outcomes assessment for the College and as the project director for Global Skills for College Completion, a national grant funded by the Gates Foundation.

Jane Maher is a professor in the Basic Education Program at Nassau Community College, where she has taught basic writing since 1987. For the past ten years, she has also been the director of special programs in the college program at the Bedford Hills Correctional Facility for Women in Westchester, New York, sponsored by Marymount Manhattan College, where she developed and currently coordinates the Pre-College Program, in addition to teaching, tutoring, and mentoring. She is the author of five biographies, including two of extraordinary educators: *Mina Shaughnessy, Her Life and Work* (NCTE, 1997), which shows the way Shaughnessy's work and vision made it possible for open admissions' students to find a place in the academy; and *Seeing Language in Sign* (Gallaudet UP, 1996), which describes the way that William C. Stokoe began the linguistic revolution in American Sign Language that lead to the Deaf President Now protest.

Laura R. Micciche is the director of composition and an associate professor of rhetoric and composition at the University of Cincinnati. Her research interests include writing studies, pedagogy, rhetorical theory (contemporary, rhetoric of emotion, public rhetoric, feminist theory), writing program administration, and academic work practices. She is the author of *Doing Emotion: Rhetoric, Writing, Teaching* (Boynton/Cook, 2007), which explores emotion as something that people do rather than have, and the coeditor (with Dale Jacobs) of *A Way to Move: Rhetorics of Emotion and Composition Studies* (Boynton/Cook, 2003).

Robert Miller established himself as an experienced educator over his thirty-year teaching career at Arizona State University and City College of San Francisco, among other schools. Miller is currently an assistant professor of English at Community College of Baltimore County.

Rebecca Williams Mlynarczyk is a former coeditor for the *Journal of Basic Writing* and professor emerita of English at the Graduate Center at CUNY. Her research interests include basic and second language writing, student journal writing, ethnographic research methodology, and the scholarship of teaching and learning. She is the author of *Conversations of the Mind: The Uses of Journal Writing for Second-Language Learners* (Routledge, 1998), co-author (with Steven B. Haber) of *In Our Own Words: Student Writers at Work*, 3rd ed. (Cambridge UP, 2005), and coauthor (with George Otte) of *Basic Writing* (Parlor, 2010).

Christina Ortmeier-Hooper is an assistant professor at the University of New Hampshire, where she teaches first-year composition, ESL, advanced composition, technical writing, and teacher education courses. Her research interests include second language writing, teacher education, and immigrant literacy. She has coedited *Second Language Writing in the Composition Classroom: A Critical Sourcebook* (Bedford, 2011), *Reinventing Identities in Second Language Writing* (NCTE, 2010), and *Politics of Second Language Writing: In Search of the Promised Land* (Parlor, 2006). She has also published in *TESOL Journal* and has presented her work at CCCC, NCTE, and TESOL.

George Otte taught for many years as an English professor at Baruch College, where he was also director of writing programs. He served as coeditor for the *Journal of Basic Writing* (1996–2002), and he coauthored (with Rebecca Mlynarczyk) *Basic Writing* (Parlor, 2010). His current focus is online learning. He is now at CUNY Central, where he founded the CUNY Online Baccalaureate, CUNY's first entirely online degree, in 2006. He serves as the chief academic officer of the CUNY School of Professional Studies, which also offers an Online BS and an Online MS in business.

Eric J. Paulson is a professor in the department of curriculum and instruction at Texas State University–San Marcos. His research interests focus around college transitional readers' deliberate and non-deliberate responses to texts and conceptualizations of literacy processes, utilizing approaches applied within a social-constructivist framework that include eye movement research, miscue analysis, retrospective miscue analysis, reader stance, and metaphor analysis. He is the coauthor of *Scientific Realism in Studies of Reading* (Routledge, 2007) and *Insight from the Eyes: The Science of Effective Reading Instruction* (Heinemann, 2003), as well as coeditor of *College Reading Research and Practice* (International Reading Association, 2003).

Valerie Purdie-Vaughns is an assistant professor in the Psychology Department and has completed research with the Intergroup Relations and Diversity Lab at Columbia University.

Adrienne Rich was a prolific poet, theorist, and political activist whose influential writings spanned more than half a century. Her commitment to social justice and the women's movement took shape during the mid-1960s, when she taught in a remedial English program for New York City's recent immigrants and other students who were underrepresented in college admissions. Her numerous volumes of poetry and collections of essays explore themes of linguistic privilege, sexual identity, and patriarchal systems of oppression. Rich taught at Swarthmore College, Columbia University, Brandeis University, Rutgers University, Cornell University, San Jose State University, and Stanford University. She had been honored with the National Book Award, two Guggenheim Fellowships, the Book Critics Circle Award, and a MacArthur Fellowship, among other awards. Her most recent book is *Tonight No Poetry will Serve: Poems 2007–2010* (Norton, 2011). Adrienne Rich died in Santa Cruz, California on March 27, 2012.

Anne Roberts is an assistant professor at Community College of Baltimore County, where she teaches developmental English and composition. She has also taught classical languages at nearly every level from elementary school to college.

Gloria M. Rodriguez is an assistant professor in the School of Education at the University of California, Davis. Her research interests include school finance/resource allocation; educational leadership from a critical, social justice perspective; notions of educational investment that reflect efforts to build upon community strengths in order to address community needs within and beyond educational settings; and educational conditions and trajectories of Chicana/o-Latina/o communities and other communities of color, as well as low-income populations in America. Recently, she coedited (with A. R. Rolle) *To What Ends and by What Means? The Social Justice Implications of Contemporary School Finance Theory and Policy* (Routledge, 2007) and coauthored (with J. Fabionar) "The Impact of Poverty on Students and Schools: Exploring the Social Justice Leadership Implications" in *Leadership for Social Justice: Making Revolutions in Education*, 2nd ed. (Prentice Hall, 2009).

Mike Rose identifies literacy—its definitions and its acquisition— among his principal teaching and research interests. As a professor of social research methodology at the University of California, Los Angeles, Rose explores the cognitive, linguistic, and cultural factors that affect engagement with written language. He recounts his experiences in his autobiographical work *Lives on the Boundary* (Penguin, 1989) and has also written *Possible Lives: The Promise of Public Education in America* (Penguin, 1996). Rose recently published *Why School?: Reclaiming Education for All of Us* (New Press, 2009).

Deborah M. Sánchez is a reading instructor at North Carolina Central University and a doctoral student in literacy education at the University of Cincinnati. Her thesis is titled "Hip-Hop in the Literate Lives of Students in Beginning College English Courses." Her article "Hip-Hop and a Hybrid Text in a Postsecondary English Class" appears in the *Journal of Adolescent and Adult Literacy*.

Mina Shaughnessy began teaching composition at the City College of New York in 1967 and served as the director of the school's Basic Writing Program until her death in 1978. She founded the *Journal of Basic Writing*, and in her foundational work, *Errors and Expectations* (Oxford UP, 1979), examined the question of where it is "best to begin a course in basic writing." She is widely recognized as a leading figure in the field of basic writing and a strong advocate for open admissions. Many thinkers and teachers in the field of developmental writing trace their roots to Shaughnessy's early inquiries about writing pedagogy, which, above all, stressed respecting students and their strengths, rather than focusing exclusively on weaknesses or deficiencies.

Rachel Sumner is a research assistant at Columbia University.

Amy E. Winans is an associate professor of English and associate director of the Honors Program at Susquehanna University, where she teaches writing and thinking, literature studies, comparative literature, and literature and gender. She is a coeditor of the anthology *Early American Writings* (Oxford UP, 2001) and associate editor for the Pedagogy and Profession section of *Modern Language Studies*. Her articles have appeared in *College English*, *Pedagogy*, and elsewhere.